Storyteller

Storyteller

The Many Lives of Laurens van der Post

J. D. F. Jones

JOHN MURRAY
Albemarle Street, London

First published in 2001
by John Murray (Publishers) Ltd,
50 Albemarle Street, London W1S 4BD

The moral right of the author has been asserted

A catalogue record for this book is available from the British Library

ISBN 0-7195-5580-9

Typeset in 12.25/13.5 Monotype Garamond by
Servis Filmsetting Ltd, Manchester

Printed and bound in Great Britain by
Butler & Tanner Ltd
Frome and London

For Jules, again

Contents

Illustrations

The author and publishers would like to thank the following for permission to reproduce illustrations: Plates 1–9, 11–22, 24, 25, 27–29, 31–33, the Estate of Laurens van der Post; 10 and 23, the author; 26, Cobus Bodenstein; 30, PA Photos (photographer Ron Bell); 34, Times Newspapers Ltd (photograph Martin Beddall).

Every effort has been made to trace the copyright holders of illustrations but in the event of any omissions the author would be glad to hear from them.

Foreword

Sir Laurens van der Post did not want a biography in his lifetime and, apart from suffering a necessarily modest book by an American academic in 1969, he blocked various attempts to write one. His reasons may become apparent in the pages that follow. After his death a couple of days after his ninetieth birthday in December 1996, his surviving child, Lucia Crichton-Miller, with other members of his family and friends, decided after long debate that this authorised biography be permitted. I was given exclusive access to Laurens's archives and a guarantee of independence in whatever I chose to write.

I have referred to my subject as 'Laurens', since that is how he always preferred to be addressed. He had been christened in the Afrikaans and German style 'Lourens' – abbreviated by his family as 'Louwtjie' (pronounced low-key), or 'Louw' – but in his first passport he chose to become 'Laurens'. His wartime companions often called him 'Lawrie', or 'Van', which sounds to me an expression of affection. When he came to Britain he anglicised the pronunciation of his surname.

I have reserved for an appendix my acknowledgements and my thanks to the many people who have helped me. The exceptions I really have to make are my research assistants, Mark Ingle (in South Africa) and James Sanders and Louise Stein in Britain. In a just world their names would sit with mine on the masthead. This book is almost as much theirs as mine. Finally, Jules Cashford has forbidden me to describe what this book owes to her.

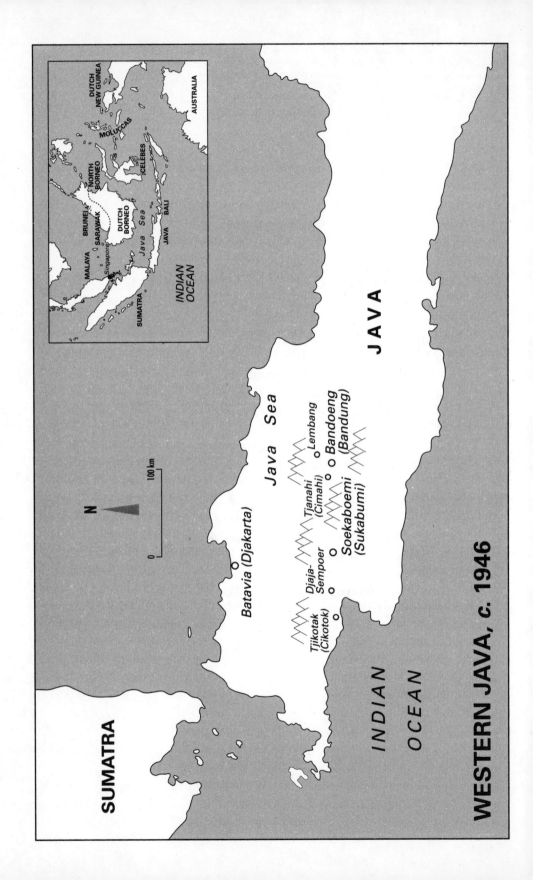

SUMATRA

Batavia (Djakarta)

Java Sea

JAVA

Lembang

Bandoeng (Bandung)

Tjimahi (Cimahi)

Djaja-Sempoer

Soekaboemi (Sukabumi)

Tjikotak (Cikotok)

INDIAN

OCEAN

N

100 km

0

WESTERN JAVA, c. 1946

DUTCH NEW GUINEA

MOLUCCAS

NORTH BORNEO

CELEBES

BRUNEI

SARAWAK

DUTCH BORNEO

MALAYA

Singapore

Java Sea

JAVA

BALI

SUMATRA

INDIAN OCEAN

AUSTRALIA

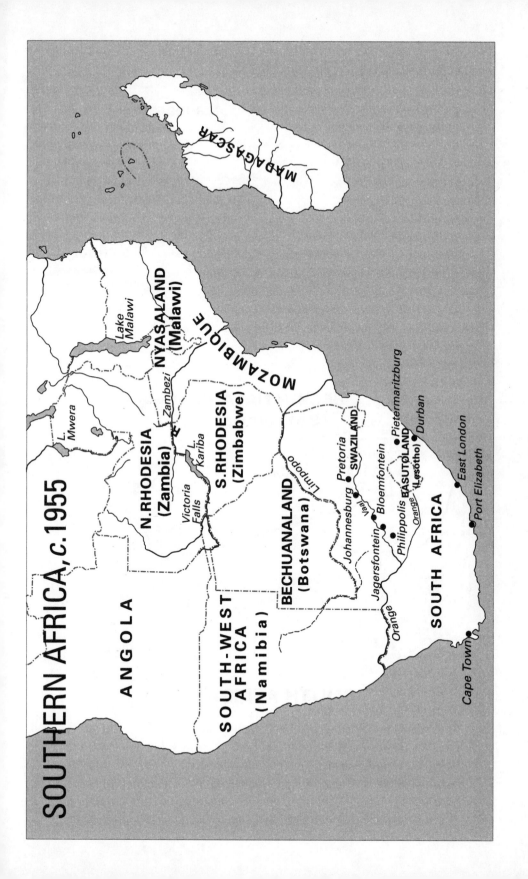

SOUTHERN AFRICA, c.1955

MADAGASCAR

ANGOLA

SOUTH-WEST
AFRICA
(Namibia)

N.RHODESIA
(Zambia)

NYASALAND
(Malawi)

Lake
Malawi

L.
Mwera

L.
Mwera

MOZAMBIQUE

S.RHODESIA
(Zimbabwe)

Zambezi

Victoria
Falls

L.
Kariba

BECHUANALAND
(Botswana)

Limpopo

Pretoria

Johannesburg

Vaal

SWAZILAND

Pietermaritzburg

Durban

Jagersfontein

Bloemfontein

Philippolis

Orange

BASUTOLAND
(Lesotho)

East London

Port Elizabeth

SOUTH AFRICA

Orange

Cape Town

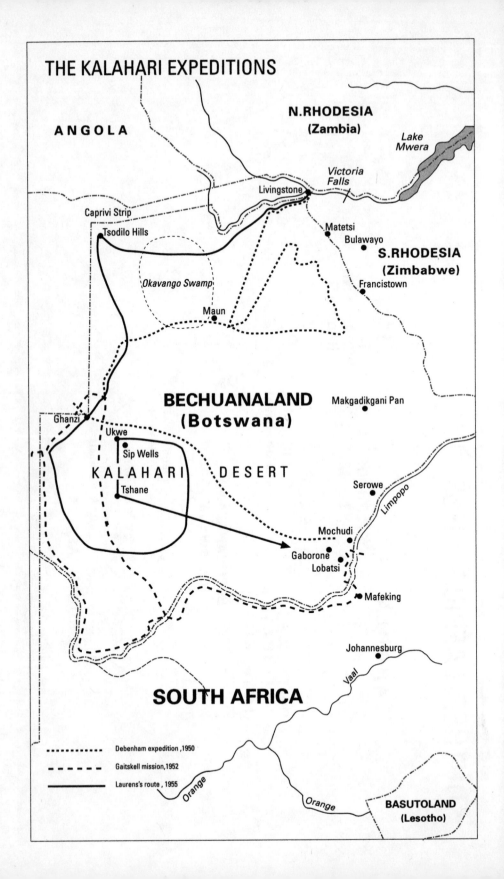

THE KALAHARI EXPEDITIONS

ANGOLA

N.RHODESIA (Zambia)

Lake Mwera

Caprivi Strip

Victoria Falls

Livingstone

Matetsi

Bulawayo

S.RHODESIA (Zimbabwe)

Tsodilo Hills

Okavango Swamp

Francistown

Maun

BECHUANALAND (Botswana)

Makgadikgani Pan

Ghanzi

Ukwe

Sip Wells

K A L A H A R I   D E S E R T

Serowe

Limpopo

Tshane

Mochudi

Gaborone

Lobatsi

Mafeking

SOUTH AFRICA

Johannesburg

Vaal

⋯⋯⋯ Debenham expedition ,1950

– – – Gaitskell mission,1952

——— Laurens's route , 1955

Orange

Orange

BASUTOLAND (Lesotho)

Laurens van der Post's 'Hottentot' Descent

Krotoa-Eva (1643–74) m. Pieter van Meerhoff (1637–67)

Petronella Meerhoff (d. 1713) m. Daniel Zaaiman (d. 1714)

Pieter Zaaiman (?–?) m. Anna-Maria Koopman (b. 1690)

Engela Catharina Zaaiman (b. 1721) m. Abraham Pelser (b. 1721)

Anna-Maria Jacoba Pelser (b. 1745) m. Johannes David Griesel (?–?)

Anna Dorothea Griesel (b. 1764) m. Jacob Johannes Kruger (b. 1756)

Anna Jacoba Kruger (b. 1783) m. Joachim Scholtz (b. 1783)

Sophia Jacomina Scholtz (1809–64) m. Andries Johannes Lubbe (1801–71)

Andries Petrus Lubbe (1830–1921) m. Elizabeth Louisa Liebenberg (1830–97)

Maria-Magdalena Lubbe ('Lammie') m. Christian Willem Hendrik van der Post
(1867–1954)   (1856–1914)

Laurens Jan van der Post (1906–96)

The van der Post Family

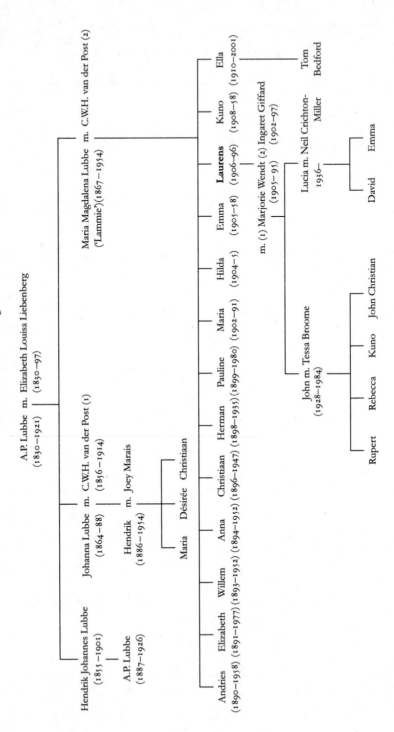

'Do you think it is right to rake up the past?'

'I don't feel that I know what you mean by raking it up. How can we get at it unless we dig a little? The present has such a rough way of treading it down.'

'Oh, I like the past, but I don't like critics,' my hostess declared with her hard complacency.

'Neither do I, but I like their discoveries.'

'Aren't they mostly lies?'

'The lies are what they sometimes discover,' I said, smiling at the quiet impertinence of this. 'They often lay bare the truth.'

Henry James, The Aspern Papers

Introduction

WHEN LAURENS WAS very old, his housekeeper Janet Campbell once
lost her temper with him and declared, 'You're just a farm boy from
the Karoo!' Sir Laurens was incensed.[1] But she had a point, and it raises
the question behind this book. How did an Afrikaner lad of no apparent
distinction, the near-youngest son of a large, respectable but not particularly notable Afrikaans-speaking family in the South African interior,
emerge to be an international figure, a best-selling writer, an adviser to a
British Prime Minister, counsellor to the future King of England and
godfather to his heir, recognised authority on both the Bushmen and the
great Swiss psychologist C. G. Jung, patron of the environmental movement, and an inspiration to countless men and women around the world?

An important part of the answer is that Laurens was an enchanter.
Imagine a gathering where the old man with bright blue eyes and wispy
hair hobbles to his chair, smiles benevolently at his audience, asks invariably whether everyone can hear him ('If not, make the sound of an elephant!'), pauses for a moment as though to gather his thoughts, and
starts to talk, without a note, without a hesitation or correction.[2]

Brilliant in the lecture halls, he was equally at ease in small 'fireside'
gatherings. In Britain, America, South Africa or wherever, he would
happily travel to however obscure a venue, where a dozen or so friends
of friends would gather around him. He would accept a cup of weak
coffee, settle in his chair, and then he would talk, quietly, almost without
verbal emphasis, his words carefully chosen, measured, poetic, evocative,
and every one of his audience felt that he was speaking for them alone.
Of course, he had done this many, many times, yet there was never a
sense of recital or repetition. He would go on for an hour, or two hours,
never for a moment losing the rapt attention of his audience. It was a
spellbinding gift. He was a magician, a storyteller of genius.

He told stories about the Bushmen of the Kalahari Desert, for
example, and everyone remembered that he had written books about his

explorations there. These stories he connected with the meaning in our lives today of the Bushman, the last primitive man, the 'Noble Savage' who has been significant for us since Rousseau. He related these stories, and their meaning, to the thinking of his own friend and mentor, Carl Gustav Jung, about whom he had written a popular and influential book. We were reminded that he had travelled extensively in Africa, not only in the Kalahari but in wartime Abyssinia and the mountains of Nyasaland (and we remembered the beguiling prose of *Venture to the Interior*, a book which had made him famous and which has been in print for fifty years). And he had turned his Bushman journeys into novels which are also still in print today, *A Story like the Wind* and *A Far-Off Place*.

Laurens would often be asked in these sessions about his years in the Japanese prisoner-of-war camps of Java, after enduring which he had risked his colleagues' sometimes angry disagreement by preaching for-giveness; his experiences there had produced other books, factual and fictional. What he declined to talk about was his private role behind the scenes of public life: in particular his sustained efforts to mediate in the affairs of Southern Africa, and his close relationship with Mrs Thatcher and with Prince Charles. It cannot be stressed too strongly that his per-sonal appearances at these storytelling sessions were mesmerising. We were all grateful to be enchanted.

Laurens lived a very full and very long life. He was born in what was then the Orange Free State in 1906 and died in a Chelsea penthouse in London two days after his ninetieth birthday. As a young man he went out in search of a wider world, which led him as a journalist to Durban, Japan, England. Thereafter he divided his life, and his loyalties, between Britain and South Africa. Success eluded him until the war. After surviv-ing the Japanese POW camps he set off on a sequence of expeditions to Africa, which gave him the material for a number of his most popular books and assured him lifelong success as a writer, eventually publishing twenty-four volumes, many of them international best-sellers.

But this was only one of his many lives. He became a mythologist of the Bushmen of the Kalahari Desert; he involved himself in the politics of Southern Africa over a span of fifty years, beginning as an enemy of apartheid and ending as a champion of the Zulus; he wrote travel books as well as novels, made television films and saw several of his books adapted for the cinema; an Afrikaner without a drop of British blood, he became a proud member of the English Establishment and an indefatigable traveller on the international lecture circuit; and in old age he used his fame and popularity to promote the causes which were dear to him, particularly the environment and Wilderness.

A curious feature of these many lives is that Laurens consistently pre-ferred to keep them separate – his many friends, as some of them realised, were kept in what they described as 'boxes' ('Wilderness', 'Jung', 'Zulus', 'Bushmen', etc.), and many people knew him only in one or two of these 'boxes'. It was possible to be a good friend of his in Aldeburgh and have no idea of why or whether he had just been to Balmoral with Prince Charles, to Jung's house outside Zurich, to the Umfolozi game reserve, or to preach a sermon in New York.

One of the tasks of a biography is to bring together these strands – these 'boxes', these lives – and show how they coincided and inter-related in Lauren's career in a way which he chose to camouflage and which was often therefore invisible. The occupants of each 'box' were offered their own 'story', whether in print or in person, and these stories, had they known it, were frequently contradictory. They were one aspect of Lauren's constant desire to keep control, whatever inventions or deceptions that might require. This makes his life richly complex, far more than has previously been understood.

Many of us love his books: they are inspirational, they lead us to aspire to a higher moral and spiritual life. But we discover after a while that we begin to ask questions. Can this all be – well – *true?* The closer we get to Laurens's detail, the more we become perplexed by the growing suspicion that Laurens wasn't all that he said he was. We return to his books, where his non-fiction tells us about his life – and wonder, did this *truly* happen?

In one sort of book (non-fiction) an author says, 'This actually hap-pened . . .', and under a literary, even a social convention, we accept it and follow that journey, trusting it is true to fact. It could be argued that the author enters into a specific contract of trust with his readers, inviting, even allowing, them to believe him. In another sort of book (fiction), we, as readers, inhabit a different part of our mind and relinquish ourselves to our, and the author's, imagination, realising that anything may happen and nothing has to be factually true. Many people cherish the memory of what Laurens told them about, say, the Bushman's myths and legends. Would it matter if his own experience of the Bushmen was largely an invention? Perhaps not initially, for all stories, if well told, persuade us of their truth, which is a truth of the imagination. Only later do we ask: was he really there? Did a real Bushman tell him this tale or did he pick it up from a book written fifty years before? Laurens's Bushman stories are 'true' as he tells them, but when investigated in the real world they are not always his own experience. That need not matter, except that he denied the distinction.

Here is the distinction. We may listen to 'stories', as we have done to

storytellers down the ages – Laurens inherited the tradition – and accept
that they need not be literally accurate. But it is another matter when the
storyteller tells us a story about himself. When we discover the storyteller's tales about himself to be inaccurate, embellished, exaggerated,
distorted, we protest that we would prefer to hear what actually happened. There comes a time when we have to ask whether many of
Laurens's stories in which he himself plays a 'real-life' part – and which
enchant us for that reason – are indeed true to the facts of an objective
reality beyond the tale. We read his own fascinating accounts of a South
African boy who came to England, fought in the war and emerged to literary fame. We want to believe those stories and assume that they are, literally, true in the sense that they did actually happen in the way he said
they did. But what if he is *still* conflating fact and fiction, as he allowed
himself licence to do in the lecture hall?

What if Klara, Laurens's Bushman nanny, never existed? What if he
did not come of an aristocratic, let alone a Huguenot, family? What if
he was not really familiar with Japan or the Japanese language; if his
war record was not quite as he described; if he had not been Lord
Mountbatten's personal representative? What if he had not played an
important role in the Rhodesian settlement in 1980? What if his private
life was not all one might expect of the spiritual adviser to the future
King? Questions such as these could fill a page, and they will be tackled
below, when the reader will have to become detective, like the biographer, to follow the trail.

As a detective, I have had to trace the origins and provenance of
Laurens's stories about his life. As this book will make clear, he was a
master fabricator. His stories, often a complex web of truth and lies, were
tailored for different audiences. His books, at least until the final years,
were carefully constructed and relatively watertight, his broadcasts and
newspaper interviews less so. His correspondence and private conversations (which occasionally surface in diaries and memoirs) often boasted
fantastic mutations of the actual truth. Over a period of fifty years from
1946 to 1996, Laurens created multiple versions of his stories – multiple
lives, multiple versions of himself. Maintaining these fabrications must
have required a skill sometimes bordering on genius. Certainly, tracking
and unravelling them has been a complex and at times frustrating task.
Sometimes I have had to concentrate on quite small-scale and detailed
exaggerations (and may seem nitpicking) but that is because they are significant links in the web. Preoccupation with the factual truth and structural detail of Laurens's stories proved the only way to understand the
reality of his life and his dream of something more.

It is important to emphasise that there is a pattern to Lauren's inventions. Some of us select, and thereby edit our life histories; there is nothing particularly unusual in that. Writers are perhaps especially prone to embellishment when they write about themselves: the autobiographies of many respected authors – particularly travel writers – would not survive close scrutiny. What was different about Laurens was that, first, his inventions were always designed to enhance his own distinction and position himself at the centre of events; and that, second, he invited respect as the embodiment of the values he brought to life in his books and his talks. Laurens's willingness to represent himself as 'someone other' provoked, indeed demanded, examination of who he really was.

Laurens's instinctive predilection for the truth of the imagination over literal facts and events would never be better seen than in his account of his experiences during the Second World War. This was the time when he found himself, so to speak, after years of confusion and failure. For that reason this biography will start not on 13 December 1906, when he was born, the eleventh of thirteen children, in an obscure South African village called Philippolis, but when he joined the British Army. He told stories about that, too . . .

PART ONE

'On doit des égards aux vivants, on doit aux morts que la vérité.' ['To the living, we owe respect; to the dead, we owe only the truth.']

Voltaire, *Première Lettre sur Oedipe*

I

'Laurens of Abyssinia'

L AURENS NEVER WROTE an autobiography in the conventional sense, yet all of his books, including his fictions, are studded with autobiographical elements. In *Yet Being Someone Other* (1982), for example, which follows most directly the story of his life and, as he invariably used to add, 'the story of our time', he records that in 1938 he sent his wife and two children back to South Africa because he was convinced of the inevitability of war and 'knew I would have to go to war when it came'.[1] In several books, he also claims that he already held a commission in the South African Army.

In his life of C. G. Jung, Laurens says that he volunteered for active service on 1 September 1939, and tells a charming anecdote of his application for a commission in 'a famous British regiment'. The Colonel enquires why this South African has picked this particular regiment. '"Well, it is quite simple, sir," I told him. "In 1848 we fought a battle against the British in South Africa and a platoon of the Regiment captured my grandfather, who was fighting against them . . . Then in the Anglo-Boer War in 1902, a company of the same battalion captured my father . . . so I thought it must be a pretty good regiment." At that he beamed, saying "Come on in. Come on in!"'

The trouble with these stories is that they simply are not true. Laurens's only military background was that he had been a member of his school's compulsory Cadet Corps.[2] He had not lived in South Africa since 1931, and there is no evidence that he had a commission in the South African army. In England the War Office records insist that he did not enlist in September 1939. He did indeed send his wife and two children to South Africa in 1938, to the distress of his nine-year-old son John, who had not been told that his father would be staying behind in England, and who only discovered it at the quayside. After the outbreak of war Laurens continued working as a Fleet Street journalist for the South African Argus Group, apparently in low spirits, hoping to get a job with the BBC, possibly as a war correspondent. Incidentally, his grandfather had not fought against the British in 1848 but was in fact on their side.[3]

In February 1940 Laurens was taken to hospital with some sort of infection. On 25 February his mother Lammie wrote to him (in Afrikaans): 'My dear old Louwkie, I am so upset to hear that you are ill ... It is a fiasco that I am not able to be with you ... I [shall try] to send you a couple of hundred pounds ... Louwkie, I understand your throat is a problem for you and you can only make it better if you move to a dryer climate. Louw, can't you leave and come and rest on the farm with me?' Lammie was preoccupied, as she usually was, with the need to sell the various van der Post family farms in the Orange Free State. She evidently had not been told of any determination on Laurens's part to join the British forces, and certainly she would not have wanted her son to be identified with the British Army. On 3 April she wrote again: 'Louw, you must come back home. I don't know why you are holding out against the country of your birth but even if you yourself do not feel like coming back then at least Lourens you must think of visiting poor little John ... Lourens, I beg you, in God's name be a man and do the right thing for your child ... If it has to do with some difficulty or other, take me into your confidence – a mother can always understand ... Your loving mother, M. M. van der Post.'[4]

In the end, Laurens went to war on 22 May 1940. He enlisted in Acton, West London, not in a distinguished regiment but in one of the less regarded units of the British Army, the Military Police. For some reason he faked his date of birth as 13/12/1900, adding six years to his age. (Did he calculate that a thirty-nine-year-old would come up for promotion sooner?) According to Defence Ministry records, he was soon transferred to an officer training course, the 168th Officers Cadet Training Unit at Aldershot. There is no evidence to confirm his claim in *Yet Being Someone Other* that he passed out first on his course and was declared 'exceptional in every way'. On 30 September he was commissioned 2nd Lieutenant and was transferred into the Intelligence Corps: presumably the authorities had noted his familiarity with several languages – Dutch, French, some German, leave aside the African dialects which he used to claim. He was posted to London as an Intelligence officer and appointed Acting Captain on 3 January 1941.[5]

Throughout the summer of 1940 he had spent weekends with his English lover, Ingaret Giffard, who was destined to become his second wife, at her family home in Camberley in Surrey, not far from Aldershot. He had met her in 1936 when both their marriages were under strain. Jimmy Young, Ingaret's husband, who was on friendly terms with

Laurens, was based in Portsmouth, where Ingaret would also visit him. She was assigned to a munitions factory and became famous there as the only female the workforce had ever encountered who did not know how to make a cup of tea. Ingaret accompanied Laurens to Victoria station to see him embark for an unknown destination.[6]

The Abyssinian campaign of 1940–41 is today one of the less remembered operations in the Second World War. It deserves a higher profile. At a moment when fortunes were low, a tiny number of British officers and NCOs, leading largely Indian and African troops and with South African support, took on up to 300,000 Italian troops, drove them to a speedy and humiliating surrender, and restored the Emperor Haile Selassie to the Abyssinian throne from which he had been exiled in 1936. It was the first Allied defeat of the Axis powers and, by regaining East Africa and control of the Red Sea and so the back door to Egypt, it was of considerable strategic importance. Laurens played a part in the early months of this campaign, in the invasion of the Abyssinian mountains from the deserts of the Sudan. He did not write about it for more than thirty years, and then in the unlikely context of his cookery book, *First Catch Your Eland*; he returned to the subject only briefly, repeating a small number of anecdotes in subsequent books.

The Italian colonisation in 1930 of the ancient and independent nation of Abyssinia had ignored the protests of the League of Nations and had been accompanied by terrible massacres of the local population. There was therefore widespread resentment of Italian rule, which British strategists realised could be harnessed if a guerrilla mission could be infiltrated into the appallingly difficult mountain territory which made up much of the country. The forces available to General Wavell were very limited because he had so many demands on his reserves – Cyrenaica in Libya, from where the Germans would soon threaten Cairo, and Greece, Crete, Iraq, Syria. But the security of the Red Sea as an Allied supply route was a fundamental priority if a Middle East front was to be held. Wavell started off in East Africa with just three battalions in the Sudan, together with 4,500 men of the local Sudan Defence Force, some obsolete aircraft and two more bomber squadrons whose role was to keep the Red Sea open. Haile Selassie, the Emperor of Abyssinia, who had been living in British exile in Bath, was secretly conveyed to Khartoum in July 1940. The plan was to enable him to be transferred back into his kingdom to the mountains of the Gojjam, between Lake Tana and Addis Ababa, where rebellion had been simmering and where he could become a rallying point for the 'Patriot' movement of his people.

The military strategy was to be a pincer movement. From the North, General Platt would re-conquer Eritrea and from there strike south to the Italian headquarters at Amba Alagi. From Kenya in the South, General Cunningham would reconquer Italian Somaliland, and, once across the River Juba, would race to seize Addis Ababa. While this was happening – and it happened with extraordinary success – the Emperor would be brought to his capital from the West, smuggled across the Sudan border and carried across the near-impassable terrain up into the mountains of Gojjam. He was indeed delivered back to his palace in Addis Ababa on 5 May 1941.[7] Laurens was involved in this latter operation and in the course of it became a loyal admirer of the Emperor, remaining in touch with him afterwards – he was a guest, for example, in 1966 at the Addis Ababa silver anniversary of the Return – until Haile Selassie was murdered after the Ethiopian revolution of 1975.[8]

'Mission 101', as the probe from the West was called, was launched in August 1940, when an ex-army coffee and dairy farmer in his late fifties who had lived in Abyssinia for years, Colonel Dan Sandford, crossed secretly into the Gojjam mountains with a couple of colleagues and established himself and a radio with a loyalist local chief. His job was to rally Haile Selassie's friends, to promise the Emperor's return, and to harass the Italians. In late November he was joined by Major Orde Wingate, who became the military commander of Mission 101 (Sandford was in charge of the politics). Wingate, one of the most brilliant, controversial and difficult of Britain's wartime leaders, who would find fame and death with his Chindits in Burma, was an expert in the new theories and skills of guerrilla warfare. Other officers with a special knowledge of Abyssinia, like Wilfred Thesiger, the Arabist and traveller, were sent across the border up to the Gojjam in late September.

It was clear that if the Gojjam rebellion was to be sustained, to join up eventually with the Allied invasion from the North and from the South, not only would a nucleus of expert officers and sergeants to lead the locals be needed, but also a feasible supply route for weapons, ammunition and the Maria Theresa silver dollars essential to win back the allegiance of the tribal chiefs. The approach would have to be made from Khartoum in the West, but there were no roads, only hundreds of miles of desert, dense tropical bush and then a sheer climb of 9,000 feet to the Abyssinian plateau. The solution would be camels – 15,000 of them, almost all of which would leave their bones on the mountains.[9]

At the time that Mission 101 was being set up (later to link up with the

Frontier and Ethiopian battalions and be christened 'Gideon Force' by the arch-Zionist Wingate), Laurens was a newly-commissioned Intelligence Corps officer in London. Someone in the War Office spotted that he was a South African and supposed that he would be familiar with Ethiopia, forgetting that 3,000 miles separated Ethiopia from the Union, and not knowing that Laurens had never been closer to Ethiopia than Nairobi for a couple of days in 1926. Moreover he must surely know about camels (Laurens later admitted that he had never seen a camel in his life). So in mid-November he was sent off from Liverpool via the Cape and north to Cairo.[10]

From Cairo he took train and barge up the Nile to Khartoum, and then travelled by truck to Roseires on the banks of the Blue Nile. Promoted to Acting Captain, on 13 February he set out on the trek from Umm-Idla, the nearest village to the Abyssinian frontier – he later gave the impression that he was in command of the operation, but was in fact one of half-a-dozen British officers and some invaluable sergeants from the Coldstream Guards. Each camel caravan, or *hamlia*, of about two hundred animals and their drivers was led by a British officer. One of these, who became a friend of Laurens, was a Life Guards captain, W. E. D. Allen, who published an early record of their adventures and deserves more than a footnote. Bill Allen was a maverick Etonian and Ulsterman, an authority on Georgia and the Ukraine, a Mosleyite MP and a passionate cavalryman. He was a career MI5 officer for years, though it is not clear whether he was infiltrated into the Mosleyites or had been suborned from them.[11] Nor do we know whether Laurens realised this.

Allen's principal role on this occasion was to straddle 'Prester John', the mule which was enlisted by Laurens to lead a reluctant camel train through unfamiliar bush, rivers and eventually mountain passes. They travelled in late evening and at night and lay up in the daytime, partly to escape the heat and partly to evade Italian aircraft. Laurens and Allen, according to both their versions, spent the nights debating Dostoyevsky and Saki and D. H. Lawrence. Allen was clearly charmed by Laurens: 'Rosy-cheeked, mild-voiced and rather plump, with wide blue eyes, he is a Boer with a love of England and a house in London,' Allen wrote in 1943. (Laurens afterwards detested this book because it described him as 'plump'.) Laurens, Allen went on, was a poet who had translated Baudelaire into Afrikaans and knew Japanese, had made a crossing of the Kalahari and was a practising Christian. He was also 'a consummate camel master and amateur vet'. Most of the above is inaccurate, and – unless Allen made it up, which seems unlikely – it is interesting that Laurens was claiming knowledge of the Kalahari many years before he

actually went there. 'Prester John', Allen wrote, with undisguised sentiment, 'carried me for six hundred miles [and] never stumbled once.'[12]

Laurens, it turned out, had rather mixed feelings about Bill Allen. In
a letter to Ingaret written two months later he complained that 'Allen . . .
was so oblivious of his [beautiful] surroundings that he could only talk
Dostoyevsky to me. These blasted intellectuals.' Allen, he said, was 'a
great, big, bearded, intellectual bore.' (Laurens always prided himself on
shaving every day wherever he was throughout the war. Apparently he
had promised Ingaret to do so.) In another letter to Ingaret, Laurens
described Allen as 'tall, good-looking, self-centred, lovable, mad, and
languid with Celtic twilight . . . He had been divorced three times and
was growing a beard. Once we crossed the border he rode a mule in grey
flannels and red mosquito boots, with a yellow and blue bandolier
around his waist, Arab headdress and a curved sword. He always got
lost . . .' When Allen found Laurens doctoring sick camels at night he
would say, 'Van, aren't you overdoing the St Francis business?', infuriating Laurens who knew that the health of the camels was critical
to their mission.[13]

Laurens, Allen on Prester John, and their men rode along the Dinder
valley shooting for the pot, Allen in front, Laurens at the rear: 'I seldom
met a man who worked so hard and knew so much,' Allen wrote. The
trek became a nightmare, littered with the stinking corpses of camels. It
was the worst possible terrain for them, and some units lost half their
animals. Laurens, to his gratification, lost none – perhaps two or three if
you watch the diaries closely – and Allen testified fulsomely to his skilful
care of the wretched beasts. Nine days out from Umm-Idla the party
approached the war zone. They were heading towards the escarpment,
passing through one of Africa's most remote regions. Of course, they
were not alone, as Laurens implied in his account: Allen mentioned that
five *hamlias* would sometimes meet up in the evening, to drink Chianti
and eat venison. On the last day of February they were ordered to halt
and make camp.

The Emperor caught up with them, to be greeted by a levée of his
chieftains ('above the munching of the animals and the rustle of the
camp there trickled the pagan music of the pipes. It was probably the
strangest scene since Bonnie Prince Charlie crossed the Tweed with his
Highlanders on the eve of the industrial revolution,' Allen wrote).
Laurens and Allen were presented to the Emperor, to drink whisky, eat
pistachio nuts and Turkish Delight, and converse in French. Many years
later Laurens recalled that occasion and described how in 1966 the
Emperor had reminded him of their first meeting.[14]

On 2 March they climbed the escarpment, some of the camels tumbling and breaking their necks. There was a chill in the air, and the Sudanese, as well as their camels, began to suffer. Laurens's own accounts of this journey, published thirty-five and forty years later, differ only in details from Bill Allen's contemporary version. Laurens states that the British officers first met the Emperor at Shaba, near Khartoum, immediately on their arrival. He says that he had the largest group of camels, a hundred and fifty-seven. He describes how the Italians dropped incendiaries on them which started dangerous bush fires. He tells of how, as fire advanced on them and the camels refused to cross a river to safety, he ordered the animals in Zulu (of which he might have had just a few words) and lo, they followed Prester John across the water just in time! And he describes what he remembered in old age as the crisis of the trek – how, when they reached the cliffs of the escarpment, the mule train which was supposed to take over from the camels was not there. So Laurens disobeyed his orders to return the camels and their drivers to Khartoum, and persuaded them to continue with him up into the cold and rain of the mountains – which the Sudanese agreed to do, he says, out of gratitude for British rule.[15]

A few weeks later Laurens was able to send his personal memories of that journey in a series of letters to Ingaret. 'I have done one of the longest and most continued treks of anybody in this war since I said goodbye to you at Victoria', he began. 'Very few DC's have been here and where I am going with my company tomorrow no-one has ever been.' On 1 May he wrote, 'We left the desert . . . behind us when we crossed the Blue Nile and came into a great white, wide country of dense acacia forest and deep, empty forlorn riverbeds. God, how white and yellow that country was, it shone and shimmered and glared with whiteness and it blazed and trumpeted with yellowness. The sky went black with heat and anger. Your shirt burnt the back of your neck, it was hell to handle a machine gun. Trees, trees everywhere and not a patch of shade. Oh! God, those phantom shadeless trees, miles and miles of them, sweet, have to be seen to be believed. They are there but they throw no shadows, they were like a sort of sun-weed, swinging and shimmering with a silly-symphony somnolence in that vast sea of the sun.' Then there were the birds – droves of doves and pigeons in millions, hawks and vultures, great carrion storks, buzzards 'so hungry that they one day pinched my bully-beef out of my dixie'; and at night under the Southern Cross and the stars, to remind him of his home, there were the cries of hyenas and a lion or two, 'and I would feel so good and confident and sure, everyone was tired and worn out, the camels tired and sore, but I would look at them and think, "This is the kind of thing I was born for".' They travelled like that for 200 miles. 'It was my private little Iliad.' While the Italian planes searched for them, they hid under the elephant grass. Laurens always loved his memories of those days: it was, he said, a 'Richard II country'.[16]

On 12 March 1941, at 7,000 feet, Laurens and his party moved into the parklands and alpine uplands of the heart of Abyssinia. The Italian air force bombed them as they headed for the fort at Burye, the temporary base of Gideon Force. The Italians were known to be planning to counter-attack, in a bid to capture the Emperor. Wingate was in his element, leading night-time sorties to strike at the Italians: his aim was to demoralise them and drive them beyond the Blue Nile canyon. The Sudanese were freezing cold, but they stood firm. In Allen's sentimental words, 'a sword of rare metal had been cast out of a dozen Englishmen and a few hundred Africans'.

This was the moment – in Burye, in the last week of March 1941 – when Laurens vanished from the scene ('malaria and dysentery had laid low the indefatigable Boer', writes the ineffable Allen), and he was evacuated by air to Khartoum. Laurens never mentioned this illness, or his forced retreat, in later books. Indeed, he gave the impression that he remained active in the field. He described in detail in *First Catch Your Eland* (1977) the hospitality he enjoyed in various households in the Gojjam. In the same book, he said he travelled thousands of miles through Ethiopia: 'I went out of it by way of Eritrea and came back to it through the formidable Tigre. I also went out through Harar down to the coast of the old British Somaliland . . . I have been down the escarpment at Mega and crossed the great lava deserts that separate Ethiopia from the Somali Republic and Kenya. I have followed the system of lakes that lie deep down in that great Rift . . .'[17]

None of this is recorded in any official document. After March, Laurens does not appear in the autobiographies of colleagues like his senior officer Hugh Boustead, a colonial officer from the Sudan, Wilfred Thesiger, who would become a famous Arabian explorer, or, for that matter, Bill Allen.[18] It is definite that he was in hospital and then convalescing in Khartoum in April–May 1941 so he cannot have been in Addis Ababa on 5 May, when Haile Selassie re-entered his capital exactly five years to the day after the Italians had taken it. The victorious procession was led by Wingate: his Gideon Force had triumphed, though this was not the end of the Allied Campaign. Many thousands of Italian troops elsewhere in the country had been forbidden by Mussolini to surrender and had to be mopped up, a process which took until the beginning of December.

Laurens's old friend and colleague Carel Birkby, a South African war correspondent at the time, claimed that Laurens was wounded by a mortar splinter. If so, Laurens never mentioned it afterwards. More interesting, his old editor and friend from Cape Town in 1930, Desmond Young, later described in his memoirs how he had bumped into Laurens in the Abyssinian bush. Desmond Young was head of public relations for the Indian Army at the time and was accompanying a famous *Life* magazine photographer, George Rodger (who later co-founded the Magnum picture agency). Rodger recorded in his own memoirs that some months after this brief encounter he came across Laurens in Jerusalem. Laurens told him how, immediately after they left him in the bush, he had been attacked by bandits and had spent the night holding them off with his tommy gun. Only later did Young remember that Laurens had been accompanied by at least a platoon of troops, and that he should not take at face value Laurens's brave tale of a single-handed battle through the night.[19]

The War Office records claim that Laurens left East Africa in early June 1941. This is perplexing because he would later make brief references in his books to the later stages of the Campaign. The best source ought to be Laurens himself through Ingaret, who on 2 November received a telegram saying, 'JUST OUT AGAIN HOPE WRITE REGULARLY NOW DEAREST LOVE' (i.e. out of Ethiopia). Before that she had not heard from him for more than four months.

This was followed shortly by a letter to Ingaret: 'I had a struggle to get away [from Abyssinia]. They tried hard to keep me in the Emperor's army – offered me a battalion – [but] I came away, and now, as I did last November, stand on the edge of new things . . . These last six months have been rather grim.' He wrote of operating in a country 'which throws up every conceivable enormity of nature as easily as an English meadow produces buttercups'. He said he had got back from hospital in time for the 'Amba Alagi show' (a 10,000-foot peak commanding the road from Asmara south to Addis Ababa, where after a critical battle the Italians had capitulated on 18 May).

He was then, he wrote to Ingaret, sent off to the lakes, the region south of Addis, 'to raise another army', where 'we did a lot of guerrilla fighting in incessant rain and mud in sodden, steaming bush . . . But I would not have missed it, dearest, and we finished our job'. He added that he must be the only member of the original band to have gone from the beginning, right through Abyssinia and finishing at Mombasa. Back in Cairo he found twenty-nine letters from Ingaret waiting for him. (He replied, 'I understand about you and J. I can't help feeling sad there isn't a more direct solution, but it is a very selfish envious sadness.')

A few days later he wrote again; now he was worrying about money, promising that he would sort out Ingaret's missing allowances with the Command Paymaster as soon as his malaria treatment was finished. (Presumably he was supposed to have arranged for Ingaret to receive a portion of his pay; he did not mention any allowances for his wife in Cape Town.) 'About ourselves I have not changed since Geneva and never shall.' He was, he said, back in his staff job but it was not his sort of thing and he wanted another command in the field. He and his companions were having problems sleeping on hotel beds: they found they all preferred to doss down on the floor . . .[20]

The extraordinary point, and a clue to his future life, was that *Laurens was making this up*. The inescapable truth is that he never went back to the Abyssinian fighting after his hospital episode in April and May. In *First Catch Your Eland* he described his extended Abyssinian adventures in romantic detail, but in *A Walk with a White Bushman* (1986) his guard slipped and he said he had had to leave the Emperor because he had been recalled 'immediately' and sent to North Africa. According to War Office records, he 'disembarked East Africa' in June, and was 'posted to the Middle East' in August. He was then engaged in training commando units. He was seen several times in the King David Hotel in Jerusalem in October, he was photographed by a Polish friend on a brief visit to Tobruk, and he and Wilfred Thesiger worked together in Palestine and shared a holiday in Petra in November. At one point he did a commando and explosives course in Latrun, outside Jerusalem, a setting which he would later use in *The Seed and the Sower* (1963).[21]

Moreover, it is possible – though it cannot be proved – that he paid a brief convalescent visit to South Africa in May or June, where an interview with the 'South African Who Built Up Patriot Army In Abyssinia', as the headline had it, appeared in the Natal *Daily News* on 5 July 1941. This article contains various fantasies – that when war broke out he spent three months in the Navy; that he had just come out of hospital after recovering from a mortar wound; that he built up a Patriot Army of 3,000 (no reference to his fellow officers); that he was mentioned in dispatches (he wasn't). Some of these stories also appeared in a book about the campaign published by his journalist friend Birkby. The clear implication of this newspaper report is that Laurens was being interviewed *in Durban*, where, readers were reminded, he had been on the staff until three years earlier (the true figure should be thirteen). *The Seed and the Sower* also carries a reference to a snatched journey to South Africa.[22]

None of this was known by Ingaret in London, who spent much of 1941 worrying about Laurens's fate in distant Abyssinia and copying out the more dramatic extracts from his batch of hospital letters from May to send to their friends and family. She heard nothing until November. Then, on 12 January 1942, he wrote to her that he was 'going farther away. I can't even give you an address . . . Hold me, dear, please, and if anything should happen to me now – and you may never even know how and when and why – know you did for me what you wanted to do, that I knew it and loved you.' He added that he had been an Acting Major since last May, though there is no record of any such promotion and his letters continued to be addressed to, and signed, 'Captain'. He begged Ingaret to believe that she would at last receive the money he had promised her, which suggests that she had been lending some to him.[23]

He was on the point of sailing for the Far East, and Ingaret would not hear from him again for more than three and a half years.

2

Special Mission 43

W HEN LAURENS EVENTUALLY wrote about the events of the early
months of 1942, in *Yet Being Someone Other*, published forty years
later, he saw that 'the random elements [in his life], above all the Japanese
factor, fell into their rightful place in the wider plan of my life . . . the
truth of my own past caught up with me as it did with Conrad's Tuan
Jim', at the headquarters he had set up on the 'Mountain of the Arrow',
Djaja-Sempoer, in western Java. 'Going down the mountain one
morning and walking along a spur towards the beautiful valley below', he
came to a small plateau which suddenly 'shook, bubbled and erupted
with Japanese, who charged on me with their bayonets fixed'. Laurens
was helpless and unarmed. 'But something else in me knew different. It
took over command and called out in a loud and clear voice as of a
stranger . . . "*Dozo chotto mate, Kudasai . . . Makatoni osore – irimasu-ga shib-
araku omachi Kudasai-ka?*"'

He later explained that these words came back to him from his
Japanese lessons in 1926, and that they were a highly polite way of saying,
'Would you please excuse me and be so good as to condescend and wait
an honourable moment?' The Japanese is indeed largely, if not wholly,
correct.

The Japanese soldiers, Laurens remembered, skidded to a halt. Their
officer approached and enquired whether this was truly Japanese, and
had Laurens perhaps really visited Japan? He then demanded, where
were Laurens's men? Laurens assured him that there was a plague of
typhus on the mountain, calculating that this would deter a search, and
asked if he might go to collect a badly-wounded companion. The
Japanese agreed, and Laurens dashed back into the jungle to alert his officers and men before returning to give himself up and lead the Japanese
away from his remaining companions. Laurens explains in *Yet Being
Someone Other* that this was an example of 'the other voice' in him taking
command, its authority saving his life, ensuring that 'the bluff had

worked and saved the bulk of my officers and men to carry on for months more'.[1]

This makes a splendid and memorable tale which redounds greatly to Laurens's courage, self-sacrifice and quick-thinking, and indeed to the acuity of his 'other', but it is also perplexing. After the war, when the history of the mysterious Special Mission 43 was first disinterred, questions arose. Why was Laurens wandering alone and unarmed on a mountain in Java, away from his base camp? How did the Japanese know where he was? Would a Japanese officer really have allowed a captured officer to go back into the mountains by himself to find a wounded soldier? Could Laurens have remembered, after fifteen years, an obscure Japanese courtesy? And what happened to the rest of his men?

The full, and truer, story, and the fate of Special Mission 43 under Laurens's command, is far more complicated, as it has subsequently been compiled from the memories, tapes, diaries and reports of the men involved at the time.[2] Laurens had been sent out East from Palestine, originally destined for Singapore, then for Malaya, possibly for Sumatra, but owing to the speed of the Japanese advance south through Southeast Asia he found himself instead in the Dutch East Indies. His fluent Dutch qualified him for a role in the Allied retreat in Java. On 15 February the Japanese had captured Singapore and 60,000 Allied prisoners in one of Britain's greatest military disasters. They were expected to land in East and West Java on 1 March. A certain Brigadier Field, an Intelligence officer in S. W. Pacific Command, preparing to flee to Ceylon, asked Laurens to stay behind in command of 'Special Mission 43'. Field's signal to the Director of Military Intelligence in the War Office, London, dated 24 February 1942, reads: 'Have organised escape party leader Captain van der Post with Lieut. Commander Cooper RNVR Lieut. Black Intelligence Corps Lieut. Lemaire General List. Now reconnoitring routes and hideouts. General plan to assemble parties in jungle country southwest coast of Java thence by motor boat to Sumatra thence by native craft to Colombo. Would emphasise this purely Military Organisation, no connection SOE, at special request of van der Post . . .'[3]*

Laurens's task in Java therefore was *not* to engage in guerrilla warfare against the Japanese but to try to gather the stragglers from the Allied forces, many of them in flight from Singapore, and somehow evacuate as many of them as possible. The chaotic situation was confirmed by

---

*Laurens's stipulation about the Special Operations Executive would have related to the fact that SOE men were considered spies, and subject to execution.[4]

Field Marshall Wavell himself, who wrote a scathing report of the evacuation from Singapore in February/March: 'The behaviour of our troops from senior officers to privates was in many cases deplorable.' He was particularly rude about the Australians.[5]

Laurens, with his two volunteer officers, Black and Cooper, gathered supplies, weapons, a radio and other recruits, in readiness for the retreat into the jungle. He had already made a quick reconnaissance on the south coast of Java to try to find a suitable beach or landing strip for evacuation. This plan was frustrated when the RAF Catalina aircraft on nearby Guinea were put out of action by Japanese bombing. Laurens afterwards said that he volunteered for Special Mission 43 on condition that he would remain in command of the Mission whatever the seniority of any officer who joined him. We do not have Field's response to that.

They withdrew inland to Soëkaboemi, a hill-town popular with the Dutch in a district called Bantam, and made contact with Blackforce, a largely Australian body which was fighting a rearguard action and was in disarray. On 6 March this group moved west to Tjikotak, rather closer to the coast, where Laurens first made contact with an important figure in this story, a Dutch mine manager called David Kriek, who commanded the local unit of the amateur Dutch Home Guard and promised assistance. Already by this stage there was little prospect of armed sorties against the Japanese invaders, and as early as 8 March the Dutch Governor-General announced the capitulation of all his own forces. Laurens, distressed by the spinelessness of the Dutch, as he later put it, dismissed any thought of surrender and moved his men again, up to Kriek's Tjirotan gold mine higher on the mountain. Another important character now made his appearance, though Laurens and Kriek would later disagree on the precise timing of his arrival. This was Paul Vogt, a Swiss geologist and sculptor who lived in the mountains, spoke the languages, and was known and trusted locally. He would become a friend of Laurens for the rest of their lives.[6]

In *The Admiral's Baby*, published in 1996, more than fifty years later, Laurens recalled his first sight of Vogt. He claimed that he met him in a bar in Tjikotak, in the darkness of (inevitably) a 'Conradian' night. A burly unkempt man suddenly emerged out of the jungle: he drank his beer then called Laurens outside. 'You do not know me and I do not know you. But I know somehow that your fate is joined with mine. If ever you need me, do not hesitate to send for me.'[7] Kriek and Vogt would both, many years later, deny this dramatic story. Kriek said that, when Laurens was deserted by his Dutch colleagues on their surrender, he recommended his geologist Vogt as a man who might be willing to help.

Vogt did indeed join Special Mission 43 a couple of days later, when Laurens commissioned him Captain in the British Army so that he would not be vulnerable to the Japanese as a Swiss neutral and civilian. Vogt was to be invaluable, together with his beautiful Javanese wife, whose influence in the villages secured a flow of food and information. Vogt would remain at liberty in the mountains with Cooper until early August, when the Japanese retaliated against the local villages, and the two men gave themselves up, only narrowly surviving.

The Allies surrendered formally on 12 March 1942, at which point Special Mission 43 had withdrawn deeper and higher up the mountain, at Tjitjatrap, where they were soon joined by remnants of Blackforce, giving the party a strongly Australian character. There followed a miserable and difficult month. Laurens's men were falling sick – several died of typhus, several committed suicide by cutting their wrists, and others later asked, and were permitted, to give themselves up. The Dutch doctor who was treating them with a fast-decreasing store of medicines decided to retreat. There was no question of armed resistance; in fact there is no record of a shot being fired. It rained constantly, so British officers would leave their weapons behind when they toured the four small camps which Laurens had set up on the mountainside of Djaja-Sempoer. He was wracked with recurrent attacks of the malaria which he had caught in South Africa many years before; both Kriek and Vogt afterwards said that he was frequently incoherent with fever. The Japanese confiscated the gold from the Tjirotan mine, but for the moment they left Kriek at liberty and he afterwards said that he kept in touch with Laurens, both personally and by messenger. Two Australian officers, Guild and Stewart, decided to make a bid for the coast, bravely refusing to let Vogt risk acting as their guide: they and their men were quickly murdered by local bandits. The Japanese had large forces in the area but did not seem too alarmed by the presence of a small number of British and Australian escapees in the high hills. They would deal with them in due course.[8]

These were the grim circumstances in which Laurens was captured on 20 April. He would later state that the date of his ambush was 'sometime towards June', but the detailed evidence of the Australian soldiers with him clearly rules that out, as do the dates of Laurens's subsequent incarcerations. In the special report which he wrote in 1947 he gave a June date, adding surprisingly that 'it is not necessary to go into details' of his capture. Those details would later become important. So, why, and in what circumstances, was he taken prisoner? Why did he fail to describe in his report the principal fact – the reason for his capture?

Laurens, Vogt and Cooper were based near the top of Djaja-Sempoer. There were three outposts lower down the mountain, and an early-warning trench system manned by Dutch territorials. An Australian Warrant Officer, 'Bluey' Phillips, in his later report on the episode, specifically said that on 9 April he, together with an English colonel and eighteen other ranks, was captured by the Japanese and taken off to Soekaboemi jail. Another Australian, Lieutenant R. W. Allen, in his postwar account, gave the later and more convincing date of 20 April, when in his report he subsequently stated that the 'Number One' camp lower down the mountain was surprised and the Japanese took approximately twenty prisoners including van der Post. He added a dramatic coda: 'On the morning of April 20 Lieutenant-Colonel van der Post had ordered me to send all available fit men from my post to his, and for me to remain with the sick.'

What was Laurens thinking of? Allen added: 'About 6pm the same day I met Private McCrae on the trail near our own hut . . . He informed me the Colonel and others had been captured by the Japanese, he had escaped and the patrol was on its way to my post.' Allen went to make contact with Cooper. Commander Cooper's version, in an interview forty years later, seems to confirm this: 'I was at our HQ on Djaja-Sempoer . . . when van der Post decided to set off down the north slope to visit Number One post, which was under the command of Warrant Officer 'Bluey' Phillips . . . Sometime after van der Post had left HQ I heard a commotion coming from the direction of Number One post which was approximately 15–20 minutes away. I heard a couple of shots and started to make my way down the northern slope to see what was going on. On the way I was confronted by Private McCrae who told me that whilst van der Post had been sitting down talking to Phillips, they had been surrounded by Japanese. Van der Post had gone to talk with them.'

A fourth witness and participant was another Australian, Sergeant Kevin Young, who was commanding one of the outlying posts and who was ordered by a runner to proceed with his section to van der Post's HQ. They never got there, because they were intercepted on the trail in early afternoon by Japanese soldiers and taken prisoner: 'We had the impression that the Japs knew where to find us . . . We talked about it a lot in the POW camp but we couldn't work out how it had happened. I've got a lot of suspicions . . .' Young and his men were taken back to a Japanese army truck on which Laurens, Phillips and a dozen men were already loaded.

A final source was Paul Vogt, who cannot have been a direct witness of the capture but who, interviewed years later, said he understood that the Japanese had sent a messenger to Laurens's camp with a white flag requesting a meeting. Laurens went to talk, and was promptly taken prisoner. What Vogt did not explain was why Laurens should have been accompanied by a dozen of his men, and how the Japanese thereafter knew where to find Young. In none of these versions of the events of 20 April was Laurens ever alone, as he said he was.[9]

Laurens's version, complete with Japanese courtesies, therefore begins to read rather strangely. His own official Army report on the fate of Special Mission 43, written in 1947 while he was still a serving officer in Java, would return to haunt him. In the six-page dictated document, finally dated February 1948 and entitled 'The Story of Number 43 Special Mission', Laurens protested his 'diffidence', explained that all documents had been lost, and made it clear that he would not have written it except for the need to regularise the position of 'Captain' Paul Vogt.

In this report, stamped 'Secret', Laurens explained how he had been instructed to recruit the members of his Mission; how he insisted that he must be in absolute command after the capitulation (a request which, he said, was referred to the Chiefs of Staff); how he was abandoned by his Dutch liaison officer; how he met up with Vogt; how a large number of his party, assumed to be close to a hundred-strong, were wounded or suffering from malaria or dysentery; how the Japanese steadily tightened their grip on the district, bombarding him with 'love letters' demanding that he come out and surrender; and how Captain Guild and Lieutenant Stewart were killed in their attempt to break through to the Sunda Strait. Curiously enough, Laurens then referred to his own capture 'sometime towards June' in a single paragraph without any detail – except for the statement that 'the party of Japanese and armed coolies that captured me were brought to the foot of the mountain by the Dutch mining director who had been my territorial sergeant in the mining village some months before . . .'[10]

This casual and potentially libellous sentence would plunge the elderly Laurens into a bitter row in 1979–80 and would seriously scar his reputation in Holland. What Laurens had never dreamed, when he dictated this rapid memorandum under orders, relying on his five-year old memory, was that under the 'Thirty-Year Rule' it would be released by the Defence Ministry for public scrutiny in 1978.

This is exactly what happened. It was picked up by the Dutch press and David Kriek immediately declared that he must be supposed to be the mining executive in question and that he had been defamed as a traitor by a man he had helped survive. He bombarded Laurens in 1979 with letters of protest, which made clear his indignation at what had been done to him by the man for whom he believed he had risked his life.[11] Laurens ignored three of these letters, until Kriek threatened legal action. In the meantime Laurens was furious that his memorandum had been released without warning: he lambasted civil servants with letters threatening to take the matter to 'the highest political levels'. The civil servants, to their credit, stood firm. Laurens was forced to respond to the injured Kriek, who had produced a 1947 letter in which Laurens, then still in Java, had commended him for his patriotic courage.[12]

Kriek refused to be ignored, accusing Laurens of 'nothing but mere shame' because in 1948 he had in fact written 'a novel' in place of an official report. Kriek promised to sue him 'for having intentionally injured my honour and good name'. Laurens was at last provoked to reply: he explained that he had not replied earlier because he was deeply involved in negotiations for peace in Rhodesia; he was protesting to the War Office for publishing a secret document; and no, he had not been referring to Kriek when he mentioned the 'mining director' who had betrayed them. He added a 'To Whom It May Concern' letter dated 1 January 1980 emphasising that Kriek's behaviour had all along been exemplary and expressing surprise that anyone might have thought that he had been referring to him.[13] This did not satisfy Kriek, who now wrote his own book, *43 Special Mission*, 'to rescue his honour'. It was published in Holland in 1985, and arrived in an English translation on the Internet only in 1998.

David Kriek is worth quoting at length to compare with Laurens's own version of his capture, which seems to involve no-one else in the drama but himself. Kriek took the reader through the whole story in minute and cumulatively persuasive detail. He recalled that he had first met the man who introduced himself as Lieutenant-Colonel van der Post on 6 March 1942. Nobody in Laurens's party was capable of operating or repairing their radio sets, which meant that after the British lost access to the Dutch radio relay station on the island, they were totally cut off from their headquarters in Ceylon and for the rest of their mission were unable either to relay intelligence or to arrange submarine pick-ups of their men (an important point which Laurens passed over in his own versions). He, Kriek, had arranged Laurens's introduction to Paul Vogt. He had looked after Captain Guild's Australians and then sent them on to join Laurens. He used to visit Laurens's mountain base. He remembered that Laurens and many of his men were ill. He and the British, he claimed, were betrayed to the Japanese by his mine colleague, an electrician called Van

Rijn. He himself was seized and interrogated by the Kempitei (the Japanese equivalent of the Gestapo). Released, he had nightly contact with a messenger from Vogt. He had continued to visit van der Post, disguising these trips as hunting expeditions. He did not know of the circumstances of Laurens's arrest. In September he heard of the end of Special Mission 43. Kriek was soon afterwards detained for three years in a Japanese camp. He added a quotation from a report allegedly written by Paul Vogt, to the effect that 'Kriek did everything to assist us, which was very important for Number 43 Special Mission'.

Shortly after the Japanese capitulation in August 1945, Kriek continued, 'I bumped into Colonel van der Post again . . . He greeted me in a friendly enough manner, but declined my offer of assistance . . . I left for Batavia at the beginning of September and van der Post arranged for lodgings for me in a hotel opposite his HQ, promising to meet me the next day. I waited for him in vain, and went back to join my wife and children a few days later.' Kriek said he also wrote a friendly letter in 1975, suggesting they meet when Laurens was next in Holland, but never received a reply.

Kriek quotes Vogt as saying that Laurens decided in the end to meet a Japanese delegation and make a 'mission-surrender' in which he would declare that the rest of his group consisted of typhoid patients. And Kriek – an old man by now – denounced him for abandoning the rest of his men to die a slow death on the mountain, while his own pockets, as he had said himself, were full of medicines. 'More than 70 [of Laurens' original party of 100] were left to die . . . Was van der Post an inspirational saviour of Dutch and Indonesians alike? Or was he a ruthless pursuer of individual survival?'[14]

Many of the questions that arise can never now be answered. Was Laurens alone when he wandered, unarmed, down the hillside on the morning of 20 April? And if not, why did he say that he was? Had he no suspicion that he was about to encounter a Japanese patrol? Why had he ordered those of his men who were healthy to join him in the valley? Had he perhaps taken the painful decision that Special Mission 43 was hopeless and that surrender was the best chance of saving his and some of his men's lives? If so – and it might have been a sensible, even brave decision – had he discussed this with his men, giving them the option of joining him or taking their chance in the jungle? Why was he carrying precious medicines, as he himself confirmed – could it be that he knew they would be needed when he and his men were in jail? After his capture, was it he who told the Japanese where to find Lieutenant Allen's group? Did he truly convince the Japanese that the rest of his men had typhoid (in which case why didn't they round them up, without fear of resistance)? How many men were 'left to die', as Kriek put it, on the mountain? And was it a Dutch technician – though surely not Kriek – who betrayed them?

In great old age, from his home in Ascona, Vogt has confirmed that Laurens's allegation against Kriek was unjustified. He emphasises that the breakdown of Special Mission 43's radio, and therefore of any contact with the outside world, was fundamental to its failure. He explains that Laurens had indeed 'left behind' sixty or seventy men on the mountain, but most of them, mainly Australians, were subsequently brought into the camps. Vogt was disabled as a result of his experiences: he was deafened by a blow on the ear from a sword, tortured under water, and afterwards diagnosed with various chronic ailments; he needed and earned the British pension which Laurens managed to secure for him in 1948.[15]

There is yet another mystery. Laurens presented himself in Java as a Lieutenant-Colonel. How and when did Acting-Captain Laurens van der Post become a Lieutenant-Colonel and continue in that rank for the rest of his days? The War Office has no record of any promotion in February 1942. There is no hint of a message that he had been promoted 'in the field' by, say, Brigadier Field when, in his 24 February signal to the War Office, he assigned 'Captain van der Post' to Special Mission 43 – Field would not have had the authority and, if he had tried, a signal would have been sent to Kandy and London. Nor did Field make any reference to a promotion when he sent Ingaret a considerate letter on 1 August, 1942 ('I cannot tell you what he is doing but think you can rest assured that he is *not* in Japanese hands, though you must not expect to hear from or about him for some time.' By this time Laurens was indeed a prisoner, though the War Office did not know it). The Army, for obvious reasons, is very strict about rank, and punctiliously records and gazettes all promotions.[16] Promotion in the field is surely a romantic achievement which Laurens would have described in his books, yet he is always silent about the circumstances of his elevation. The vexed question of his rank was to rumble on until 1948.

Somehow, in the days after Brigadier Field's escape to Ceylon and London, Laurens became not just full Captain or Major but Lieutenant-Colonel. Perhaps in this dire emergency, expecting imprisonment in a Japanese camp even if he survived their bayonets, he had the chutzpah to realise that the more senior his rank the better his prospects of survival.

The theory falls down, though, because everyone in Java, from the moment of Field's departure, saw him as a Lieutenant-Colonel, complete with insignia. Robin Black, for example, who went on after the war to an extremely distinguished career as Governor of both Singapore and Hong Kong, in old age remembered being recruited by 'the Colonel'. Throughout the days in the jungle, all the soldiers who later reported on their experiences without exception referred to him as 'the Lieutenant-Colonel'. There is no hint of a suggestion that his rank was dubious.[17] Admittedly, the situation was chaotic, all sorts of people were fleeing to Java and a great deal of illicit rank-changing went on as men from every background were rounded up into the camps. But this was something bold and different.

A second possibility is that Laurens did take on a phoney rank, and had to live with it for the rest of the war. Then why – come the Japanese surrender in 1945 – did he not go to the nearest General and say, 'This is what I had to do. Here are my pips. I am only a Captain after all!'? He did not, and it would land him in a bureaucratic minefield in 1945–47.

A third possibility is that Laurens was indeed promoted 'in the field', on or about 23 February, when he was given command of Special Mission 43. His team had been well chosen: Lieutenant-Commander Cooper was a navigation and wireless expert, Black was a high-flying Intelligence officer who had several Chinese languages, and a fourth member, Lieutenant Lemaire, spoke Malay. But why should an Acting Captain who did not have a particularly long or distinguished record have been chosen for command over the heads of Cooper and Black? Perhaps his fluent Dutch was a reason. It would have been necessary for him to have a rank senior to his colleagues – temporary promotion was not uncommon in the war, and after the operation the officer would invariably be bumped back to his original rank – but Laurens as a captain would anyhow have been senior to Black . . .[18]

One has to wonder whether Laurens, after insisting to Field that he be in command of the Mission however senior any stragglers who joined him, was indeed given a temporary rank and that the records of the promotion went missing. After which, of course, with the effective end of Special Mission 43 at his capture, he should have reverted to Acting-Captain. In the event, Laurens was trapped: he proceeded into captivity, where he discovered that he was expected to exercise the responsibilities of his temporary status. There is evidence that in the camps he was careful to stay in the background. Moreover, as the prison months dragged on, some of the officers who were close to him began to realise that there was something odd about his rank and his military history.

There is one last element, a theme which Laurens would take up on at least three occasions in his postwar books. He puts the argument best in his Preface to *The Diaries of 'Weary' Dunlop*, the Australian surgeon who was a fellow-prisoner in 1942. 'I remember quoting to him one of my favourite texts from the Bible of the Armed Forces [*The King's Regulations*] which I had used many times before during the War when, as the commander of small independent units behind enemy lines, I had to vary orders with which I had been issued at the outset from High Command at base. It was the clause – and I quote from memory – which implies something to the effect that when an officer carries out an order knowing that by carrying out that order he will defeat the purpose for which that order was issued, he shall be considered as not having carried out the order.' Laurens explains this again in *Yet Being Someone Other*, adding that 'This paradoxical pronouncement that I was to use again and again in my future career emancipated me immediately from a blind adherence to instructions'. Laurens repeats the same argument again in *The Admiral's Baby*.[19]

This argument, which cannot be found in *The King's Regulations*, is an interestingly obsessional point and it should be remembered in interpreting his insistence, when Brigadier Field gave him command of Special Mission 43, that he should not be outranked by any officer who might later join his group. Who was there, in the shambles of a retreating army, to remind him that, with or without a temporary elevation in the field, he was a comparatively humble Captain without even the prestige of a distinguished regiment to bolster his authority? The War Office records have nothing more to reveal. So far as they are concerned, Laurens would be a Captain for the duration of the war.[20] So far as Laurens was concerned, he chose to continue as a Lieutenant-Colonel, not just in the camps but also after the Japanese surrender in August 1945.

The Japanese records show that on capture he gave his rank as 'Acting Lieut.-Colonel' and that, again, he gave a date of birth six years older than his real age.[21] It is worth remembering in what follows that Laurens, thirty-five pretending to be forty-one, was significantly older than the majority of his fellow officers. This would help explain how he was seen as something of a father figure by those around him.

3

'The Desired Earth'

SOEKABOEMI JAIL WAS bad, as all the survivors agree. Laurens was delivered there, after a four-day journey, on or about 24 April 1942, together with his Special Mission 43 colleagues. There he met Wing-Commander Nichols, who was to be an important companion for the next three and a half years and a lifelong friend. They spent six weeks in Soekaboemi, a name which means 'the Desired Earth', where they were given to believe that they were under sentence of imminent death. The traumatic impact of this experience would remain with Laurens for many years.

He first wrote of Soekaboemi briefly in *Venture to the Interior* in 1952, and then more fully, forty years later, in *Yet Being Someone Other*. In these first days, 'the crisis of instant death and a final sentence of execution' was constantly repeated. Years later, Laurens would describe how one evening he was warned by a friendly jailor that he would be killed in the morning. He wrote about it again in several of his books.[1] In his old age he made the insensitive point that the future South African President Nelson Mandela might have spent twenty-seven years in jail but he never faced the promise of execution in the morning.[2]

The fullest description of his memory of these first days in Soekaboemi is found in an unpublished manuscript in Laurens's archives. It is called 'The Desired Earth', runs to only two chapters, was dictated some time in the early 1980s, and appears to be the opening of an autobiographical book which would tell the tale preceding *The Night of the New Moon* – that is to say it would describe the prison years, whereas *The Night of the New Moon* is about the closing days of the war. The extent of 'fictionalisation' in 'The Desired Earth' is impossible to assess, but it contains a fascinating clue to Laurens's future writing.

He describes how he is in his cell, watching two tiny lizards running across the wall. A kindly Japanese warder comes to warn him, in a shared smattering of Japanese and English, that he is to be executed in the morning – and that this time it will not be the mock-execution he has already suffered. Laurens recalls how he had witnessed an earlier execution, of an Ambonese, and how he afterwards felt that he had refused the condemned man's gaze of acknowledgement; 'the shameful truth was that in the moment when he needed it most, I had withdrawn my companionship and left him to his end, perhaps more alone than ever before.'

Remembering this, Laurens asks the guard whether 'it' is certain. Yes. So Laurens has to prepare himself. The guard then volunteers a secret – that he is a Christian: what can he do? Laurens asks him to be sure that he is present at his execution, so that he will not be alone like the Ambonese he had rejected. Laurens asks him to bring water, a razor, a comb. He looks out at the thunder and lightning of the regular Javanese evening storms and finds calm and relief in them. He worries only about the method of his death: he decides to plead for shooting, not hanging or beheading. He sleeps, and he dreams of the sheep leaving the kraals of the family farm of Wolwekop. The guard wakes him and helps him wash and shave. Then he produces a glass of water – the glass of purification for the long journey. The guard reminds him that he must pray, and joins him in that prayer.

They march to the office of the Kempitei: 'You have been found guilty of a spirit of wilfulness to the Imperial Japanese Army.' Laurens awaits his sentence.

'Do you know Colonel Nichols?'

Laurens, near-panicking as he fears still more interrogation, denies that he knows Nichols.

'Colonel Nichols is an Air Force Colonel. I shall now take you to Colonel Nichols and you can look forward to some very happy times with us. The Imperial Japanese Army in its mercy has decided to pardon your error.'

Not surprisingly, Laurens by this time is 'so unnerved, bewildered and shaken with the unexpected that I was shivering as if in an ague of malaria'. He has been within fifteen minutes of death.

'And it was at this moment of utter emptiness that I became aware of another presence and a voice, only audible to myself: a steady, warm, English voice, direct and without pure accent of any kind, saying in a matter-of-fact way: "I think we had better get into the truck immediately. I do not like the look in the eyes of the driver and those guards walking down on us".' Laurens follows his friend, the guard, to a lane and a truck: he would never see the guard again. He is in a state of shock, 'my senses reeling as if caught in some kind of hallucination or delirium and yet, through it all, there was a feeling of a steadying, military presence by me and climbing into the truck with me . . .'

Laurens continues: 'It was as if I had been overwhelmed and my personality taken over and acting under the orders of another. It was to take many months before this would grow into a definite physical shape, but it was so real to me in this sudden unreality of a reprieve into life that I already knew its name . . . This then was how John Lawrence joined me . . . who armed me for what was about to happen and in this profound sense made us not two but one . . .'

The manuscript returns to the frantic days in Soekaboemi immediately before the Japanese landing and the liaison with Blackforce, the news of this battle and the Allies' surrender. And a dream: a telephone call from 'a young girl whose face I had once seen as a boy . . . It was, I thought, the most beautiful face I had ever seen and it has remained so with me always since . . .' But the connection is broken, and the manuscript peters out. The Dante/Beatrice parallel – the man once glimpsing the face of the beloved – is noted. It is impossible to say why Laurens abandoned this book, or how he would have continued the story, whether of himself or of 'John Lawrence'. The fascination of the above passage, to readers of his postwar books, is that here we have the 'John Lawrence' who featured in various of his fictions, notably the three novellas brought together in *The Seed and the Sower*, which became the film *Merry Christmas Mr Lawrence*.[3]

In the years to come Laurens was often asked, 'Are *you*, Laurens Jan, the same person as John Lawrence?' This interaction of fact with fiction, reporting with imagination, would always be a feature, and a confusion, in Laurens's life. Here, in this abandoned brief manuscript we find Laurens coming as close as he ever would to an answer.

Laurens frequently wrote or spoke about the eve of his execution, and the tale is vivid, horrifying and also heroic. Of course, so many years later there can be no witnesses to the episode. There can be no independent confirmation of this simple fact; it is impossible to track down the Japanese officers or Korean prison guards who might have been privy to it. Perhaps – in the light of what this present book will reveal of Laurens's propensity throughout his life to fantasise – one might wonder whether he was truly on the brink of execution in Soekaboemi Jail. No other British officers were executed at the time. What was the particular offence which had singled out Laurens from his fellows? He had been wearing uniform when he was taken prisoner; he had not tried to escape; his Intelligence Corps background was not known to his captors; his crime of 'wilfulness', as the Japanese apparently put it, was shared by others. And why did Laurens not mention this traumatic episode until many years and many books afterwards, not even in *Venture to the Interior*, when he makes much of having to witness the execution of two other prisoners?

The mystery will probably never be solved. But Laurens, who had been reading Dostoyevsky – he and Bill Allen had been discussing him in Abyssinia – would have remembered how Dostoyevsky had been taken out one dawn to face a fake execution, an experience which he later retold in his novel *The Idiot*.[4] And of course the Japanese, in their first interrogation of the new prisoners, might well have used the threat of imminent death . . .

While we cannot confirm Laurens's early experiences in Soekaboemi, there are plenty of sources for the miseries that followed. He did indeed join Wing-Commander (not 'Colonel') W. T. H. Nichols, with a collection of British and Australian prisoners. These were soldiers and airmen who had been captured while trying to escape from the Allied collapse and capitulation, and who were therefore considered 'hard cases' by the Japanese, whose attitude to POWs was always sharpened by the belief that they had been disgraced by the fact of their surrender. There was also a misunderstanding by those few of the Allied officers, like Laurens, who believed that they knew Japan and understood that the Japanese would be exercising a civilised supervision, according to their traditional code; they had not heard of the atrocities which were even then being committed in captured Hong Kong, and which were a warning for the future.

Nichols had been an RAF officer since 1928. Born in 1910, he was younger than Laurens and only senior to a 'Lieutenant-Colonel' by virtue of his professional commission and longer experience. He had been taken prisoner when trying to lead a small Signals unit along the south coast of Java in a vain attempt to break out of the enemy circle, and he finished up in Soekaboemi as senior officer among about 200 Allied troops. His style was modest and low-key but he emerged as a brilliant and indeed heroic leader of men. Laurens, never over-disposed to praise others, always proclaimed his admiration of and friendship for Nichols. As he later wrote in an obituary (in *The Times*) in 1986: 'War inspires in the British people . . . all sorts of forms of courage . . . but I doubt if it inspires courage, moral and physical, of greater quality than that demanded of a prison commander, physically without power, cut off and apparently forgotten by his own kind, and in the cast-iron grip of a ruthless enemy, so unpredictable that every minute was a moment almost of life and death in balance.'[5]

So Laurens, consigned to Nichols, was fortunate. They were together to go through gruesome experiences at Soekaboemi, before they were transferred in June 1942 to the less-menacing environment of subsequent camps, and they would stay together until their liberation in August 1945.

Their worst moment was vividly remembered by Laurens in his first post-war book *Venture to the Interior*. Nichols and his officers are paraded to witness the killing of a Eurasian and an Ambonese: one of them is decapitated, the Eurasian is bayonetted – his 'skin at the first plunge snapped like a drum'. They die bravely. The twenty-five British and Commonwealth officers struggle to control themselves, while the Dutch and Ambonese around them are fainting.

'. . . said Nick, "I needn't remind you chaps who we are, and why we are here, stand fast!"' One of them, Ian Horobin, 'though still on his feet, was dead to this world, a condition that did all honour to him'. Laurens and Nichols put their arms around him, to hold him up, and it becomes a moment of extraordinary intimacy: 'All sense of isolation, all my restless, seeking self, my desperate twentieth-century awareness of isolation and doom vanished . . .' That night, Horobin takes the evening service, and for hours Laurens tells the men tales of the animals in Africa, realising then 'how deep, how life-giving and strengthening was this vision of Africa in my blood . . .'

There is a problem here. By 19 June Laurens and his fellow-prisoners had left Soekaboemi and cannot have witnessed an execution on that date and in that camp. Laurens has therefore got his dates wrong, deliberately or not, and perhaps for literary effect.

This episode had a dramatic impact on Laurens. The horror of the story would become a dominant image of his time in the camps.[6] But in fact it was an atypical occasion. Throughout the rest of Laurens's prison years, according to his friends, there were no other executions. There was plenty of 'bashing', as a fellow prisoner John Denman puts it, and of brutal violence, just as there were heavy punishments by sadistic warders, several of whom would in due course be hanged for war crimes. The danger to Laurens and his colleagues was not so much a threat of unpredictable murder as the certainty of progressive malnutrition, disease and starvation. Laurens was probably not exaggerating when he later wrote that if the war had not ended when it did – following the Hiroshima bomb in August 1945 – they would all have been dead within a few months.[7]

Other descriptions of Soekaboemi have survived. Ron Bryer, for example, who was later shipped to Nagasaki where he survived the dropping of the A-bomb, described in his autobiography many years later the ten-foot high walls of this top-security prison, with bamboo guard towers at each corner, commanded by Sergeant Saito, a sadist with an obsession for killing cats. He vividly recalled Laurens's arrival: 'It was late afternoon when the access door opened and unseen hands roughly thrust inside a solitary figure . . . The newcomer wore khaki drill shorts and a shirt without insignia of any kind. He had no hat, and a fairly recent head wound bled slowly at the receding hairline . . .' Bryer greeted him and 'sensed immediately an aura of authority surrounding him . . . the Colonel had arrived and soon became a mysterious man of standing in the camp.' It was the Colonel, says Bryer, who taught them Japanese numbers so that they could drill to the guards' satisfaction, it was the Colonel who persuaded the men to stop pilfering, after he had accepted a beating on their behalf.

'Except for the Colonel, our officers in another part of the building were rarely seen. In some mysterious way he kept an abiding faith with himself and men of lower rank grew to trust him implicitly.' At night Laurens made his rounds to each cell to check that all was well. 'There came a few words of hope and comfort in the soft voice. A goodnight . . . Some evenings he came, pale as a walking ghost, ill and shaking with the chronic malarial fever he fought alone.'

Ron Bryer paints a similar portrait of Laurens after they were moved to Bandoeng, with its better food, relaxed discipline, batmen for officers, a settled routine and not too much violence.

> The Colonel continued as a man apart. He still appeared at all hours among the lower ranks . . . Always he dressed plainly in khaki drill shirt and shorts, open sandals on bare feet, and wearing a nondescript brown hat of woven straw. Fluent in the French and Dutch languages as well as our own, he now offered tuition in Japanese to anyone interested . . . He was a great storyteller, coming in the evenings with tales which never failed to hold audiences enthralled . . . Tales of counter-espionage. Hidden cities of Africa. Big game hunting. All stories from the heart, but most especially of the lives and customs of the native African peoples he knew and loved so well.[8]

A similar picture can be found in the memories of Soekaboemi of an Australian, Frank Foster: 'Lt.-Colonel van der Post filled a noble role of succour to our struggling troops in the hills of Java . . . With a wide knowledge of medicine, together with an uncanny appreciation of the Eastern mind gained from travel in Japan, this Englishman was what

Diggers term "a gentleman to the finger-tips" . . . From then on we had a leader within the iron hand of harsh captors . . . There can be such a thing as prison bravery, and in this man we witnessed British fortitude at its best.' Foster gives a fascinating picture of life inside Soekaboemi under the Japanese sergeant-major he nicknamed 'Basher Bill': the smuggling of white Chinese bread, tins of cocoa and toothpaste into camp hidden under the official baskets of rations; the athletic competitions with prizes of bully-beef and butter; the working parties which gave the prisoners a glimpse of the outside world; and, of course, the daily abuse and violence.[9]

A veteran Australian soldier, Sergeant A. F. Field, managed to keep a diary which opens soon after Laurens's arrival there:

28 April 1942: Fever gone but palpably weak and exhausted . . . was given native delicacy of banana enclosed in a close resemblance to pudding by Col. van der Post, an English officer who is doing great work amongst us malaria patients . . .

10 May 1942: . . . in the evening attended a short service conducted by the Colonel and Flt-Lt. Horobin in the absence of a padre . . .

4 June: Another spasm of malaria . . . the Colonel gave me two slices of bread and margarine and Joost gave me half bread ration and a hunk of ginger cake . . .

Sergeant Field and his fellows spent days making a 'plaque' to present to him. The Australian records include another typical comment, from Sapper Dick Bailey: 'The Japs picked us up and took us to a place called Soekaboemi and put us in some sort of jail. Here we met Colonel van der Post, you probably know of him. He was like Jesus Christ to us with his help and encouragement.'[10]

They were all transferred in early June from Soekaboemi to Bandoeng, about sixty miles further inland to the East, and high on a plateau. 'Java Z', as the prisoners called it, was a much larger camp, able to handle about 9,000 prisoners, and was immensely more comfortable. Even Frank Foster, who never conceals his hatred of the Japanese, described life there as 'the happiest of our existence in the Far East . . . it was a bad day for us when we left it'. The blessing of Bandoeng, at least in 1942, was that the Japanese gave unusual leeway to their prisoners, allowing them more or less to run themselves. It was a former military barracks, with streets of brick houses, and there were plenty of outside working parties for the men when the locals could slip them food and cigarettes and the interned Dutch men might glimpse their wives and families. The other value of these working parties was that the men were paid – a small sum but enough to buy bread, sugar, fruit and even milk at the official camp canteen.[11]

Immediately on his arrival in Bandoeng on 14 June, after a brief period in nearby Tjimahi, Laurens – still without insignia – was accepted as 'the Colonel'. But here this would cause a complication. The Commanding Officer at Bandoeng at this time was one of the most remarkable figures of the war, the Australian surgeon, Lieutenant-Colonel 'Weary' Dunlop. He was a giant of a man, a boxer, an international rugby player, a brilliant doctor, a natural leader, but he was essentially a medical officer; the operating theatre was his priority, and he did not think it appropriate to continue in command when a party of British and Australians arrived in the camp, including two 'senior combatant officers', as he described Nichols and van der Post. (A Lieutenant-Colonel was the highest rank permitted by the Japanese in their local POW camps: more senior officers were transferred, often to Manchuria. Weary had been promoted Temporary Colonel when he took over the Bandoeng hospital in March, but he never 'put up' his rank because he wished to stay with his patients.)

In his *Diaries*, published in 1986, Weary wrote: 'Laurens van der Post is the most impressive character. South African in origin, he speaks English, French, Dutch, German, Russian and Malay, some Japanese and numerous African languages [Laurens had evidently been spinning his yarns] . . . He is an "intelligence wallah" and is not in his usual costume piece.' To Weary's astonishment, the newcomers hesitated to take over from him. Nichols, after a few days, accepted Weary's point, but Laurens persuaded him that the Australian should continue because, he argued, it was appropriate that the camps be led by a healer. Years later, Weary, who remained a friend of Laurens until his death, would admit his exasperation at Laurens's refusal to accept the responsibility of a Lieutenant-Colonel in the British Army, particularly when he was 'a natural leader and diplomat'. In his diary entry for 8 June Weary made the mysterious point that he had been asked to comply by Nichols and Laurens 'for confidential reasons advanced'. The three officers shared a concern about the morale of their fellow-prisoners: there were occasions when, to Laurens's horror on his arrival, morale was so low that the officers were jeered by the men. He set himself, without a formal role in the camp administration, to correct this.[12]

It would be a short-term compromise because in November, after five months, Weary was sent off with his men to the Burma Railway, where he became one of Australia's national heroes. Nichols took over command of the Bandoeng camp. But while Laurens was universally acknowledged to be his right-hand man behind the scenes, the reasons for his diffidence were never understood. Nichols, always loyal, would never after the war comment on whether he guessed, or had been party to the fact, that Laurens was not truly a Lieutenant-Colonel. Weary, similarly, would only afterwards comment that 'some mystery remains'.[13] Some other officers and men realised that Laurens was from the Intelligence Corps, and it was appreciated that the Japanese must not know this if he was to be protected from interrogation. They therefore thought they understood why Laurens kept himself in the background. Graeme Allen, a Royal Navy Lieutenant, remembers that Laurens 'was a bit of a mystery man . . . He spread the impression that his life in the army had been very "cloak and dagger", and that it was all so hush-hush that unfortunately he was unable to tell us anything about it. However, we did note that he never took part as a senior officer with direct responsibility for the officers and men.' Sid Scales, a New Zealander and a gifted painter, afterwards said of Laurens, 'There was a cloak-and-dagger atmosphere about him – a mystery man – there were some who thought he was a great bullshit artist.'[14]

A few of Laurens's closest colleagues realised that there was something odd about his position; he never spoke of his military background or of his regiment. John Denman, a dear friend for many years to come, later admitted that he 'guessed' the rank was phoney. Their suspicions were confirmed when, the Japanese reversing their prohibition on badges of rank or regiment, Laurens became very vague about his military background and suggested merely that the camp craftsmen make him a springbok, which, he suggested, referred to his unpronounceable South African regiment.[15]

One wonders whether the joys of Bandoeng look so rosy in hindsight because these men were later to proceed to deprivation and horror, and some to their deaths. John Denman talks of 'Java Z' as 'the Ritz of the POW Camps'. Laurens wrote of these first Bandoeng months as 'the golden age of our captivity'.[16] Weary Dunlop afterwards remembered that when he arrived in Bandoeng he 'could scarcely believe their luck'. He soon took a more realistic view: 'Actually the camp is one great racket, supplies (which obviously come from N[ippon]) sources, such as flour, being retailed back to our troops . . . Van der Post . . . manages the D[utch] with the greatest of ease and gets all sorts of things out of them.'

Weary's *Diaries* are an extraordinary document, complementing Laurens's own journal of life at that time, with the difference that the medical officer's detail is more clinical and precise. Thus, he tells us of the prisoners' precise rations; the number of detainees in June 1942 (1,360 Dutch, 846 English and Australians, 365 Ambonese, 761 Menadones, etc.); the arrangements for camp administration; new arrivals (2,000 on 17 June); the departure of most of the Dutch on 19 June; the changeover of Japanese warders, with pungent comments on their characters; his own reluctance to impose necessary punishments on his men; the officers' easy-going life of gardening, reading, bridge and making jam. Colonel van der Post in particular turned out to be an excellent marmalade cook . . .

Weary worries about the condition of Gunner Billy Griffiths, where his role was an example not just of his heroic stature but of what the violence of the camps could lead to. Griffiths, a youngster from Lancashire, had been ordered by the Japanese to clear some mines and one of them had exploded. He had lost both eyes and both hands and, in the Tjimahi hospital, appealed to be put out of his misery. Even the Matron suggested to Weary that this would be a mercy, but Weary, with the endorsement of John Denman, in the next bed, refused and operated. A Japanese officer arrived, noted the English prisoner's condition, and prepared to have him bayonetted. Weary placed himself between them and made it clear, as Denman watched, that they would have to kill him first. Billy Griffiths survived and led an exemplary life, for many years a leading member of St Dunstan's Society for the Blind. Laurens got to know him a couple of months later, and he, Denman, Griffiths and Weary remained in touch for all the many years ahead. (Weary and his fellow Australians, 1,000 men and 54 officers, were taken away to Burma on 6 November. He carried with him, at appalling risk, his private radio, which he passed off as 'medical supplies' as he strode past the guards. Laurens gave him a farewell supper party.)[17]*

It was evident to the more conscientious officers that disintegration of discipline among their men posed a great danger. Part of the problem, no doubt, was the low self-esteem of men who had been defeated with almost derisory ease, particularly of those who had surrendered without putting up a fight. They were a motley collection of nationalities, services, regiments, and the Dutch were particularly confused and distressed. By contrast, there was a noticeable *esprit de corps* among the unit

---

*On the Burma Railway, Weary, who was a surgeon of genius, carried out major operations using scalpels made of sharpened bamboo.[18]

which arrived in June from Soekaboemi under Nichols – men who had together come through a grim ordeal. One prisoner, Harold Goulding, later recalled Laurens's advice to him: "'Accept", he said, "that you are here for life, and from now on, what happens here is the only reality. Stop looking out through the barbed wire. Turn your back on it, and concentrate on what is happening in the here and now. Make that your life . . ." This was magnificent advice . . . and made the adaptation to POW life much easier.'[19]

Another problem was the universal affliction of all prisoners, military or civilian – acute boredom combined with constant insecurity: how to fill their time and employ their (fading) energy. The officers had to tackle this. Sport was always important and there was a great deal of soccer, volleyball and athletics and a little hockey, boxing and cricket, so long as these activities did not consume too much precious energy. Bridge was a passionate (and sedentary) pastime.[20] But these Java camps have been remembered for a separate distinction. Laurens was a driving force in developing an ambitious education project, in which literally hundreds of men took part, ranging from illiterate Australian troopers to graduate students. This was the aspect of the camp which Laurens described most often in the postwar years, and he was justifiably proud of it as 'Senior Education Officer' – although the 'prison university' was not in fact Laurens's original brainchild: Weary Dunlop had set up an education programme at the Landsop camp in April, and this was its extension. Laurens afterwards gave particular credit for the overall organisation to Gunner Penry Rees, a Cardiff graduate whose special subject was French and who would later make a career as a headmaster in South Wales. Rees remembers thinking that Laurens enjoyed the role of number two behind the scenes. He also remembers what a caring and considerate officer he was to the men.

Laurens himself taught Afrikaans and very basic Japanese, Captain Rae-Smith took Classics and Mass Observation, Major Denman gave classes in Architecture and Art, Squadron Leader Alex Jardine taught Navigation, Flying Officer Ed Stearn specialised in English Law, Don Gregory, who was a fellow of New College, Oxford, lectured on Ancient History to degree level, and Major Pat Lancaster of the King's Hussars taught men to read and write. For writing materials, the students used toilet paper, which the Japanese supplied in abundance because of their fear of infection, and which the POWs were forbidden by their officers to use for its designed purpose. By September 1942 more than 1,200 'students' were attacking thirty different subjects each week, ranging from book-keeping to *The Odyssey*. As Laurens later commented, the

Australians in particular 'identified themselves . . . with the kind of expeditionary force they encountered in the pages of Homer.'[21]

Again, in these early days at Java-Z, Laurens and Nichols also set up a camp newspaper called 'Mark Time', a lively publication produced by some of the prisoners with journalistic experience which flourished for nine months or so. Duplicated on paper secretly obtained by Laurens, it contained as much news, gathered from the secret radios, as could be safely recycled; cheerful contributions, poems, stories, memoirs, profiles, sports reports, morale-stiffening editorials, cartoons, drawings and a column by Laurens under the pseudonym 'The Walrus'. Evidently this was also the period when Laurens discovered his gift as a storyteller in front of an audience: *Flamingo Feather*, for example, was apparently conceived as a serialised tale of African adventure with which Laurens entertained his men in the long depressing evenings of captivity.[22] There may be a clue here to his future career, as he found that in camp his stories worked well (like telling a tale to put a child to sleep, when the storyteller is permitted any and everything, however fanciful). Maybe he never entirely made the necessary transfer into the peacetime world when literal truthfulness once again becomes a moral imperative.

Church services were important to some, including Laurens, though he admitted that he had no particular creed or sect. A succession of padres in the camp, Anglican and Roman Catholic, had help from Ian Horobin, a close friend of Laurens and one of the most interesting of the prisoners. He was a Tory MP (as he would continue to be after the war) and a devout man who took many of the services. Laurens used to say that Horobin had saved his life at Soekaboemi when, under torture, he had refused to tell the Japanese the details of Laurens's mission; Laurens would repay the debt fifteen years later. Horobin ran a camp 'Cabinet' which debated political issues.[23]

Then there was Entertainment. The POWs renovated a sizeable hut in the compound, dubbed 'Radio City', to contain a stage, a proscenium and an orchestra pit. The prisoners included professional actors, designers and artists, and when the Japanese gave them the English literature library from the local Dutch school, a range of plays was mounted, from *The Importance of Being Earnest* to Somerset Maugham's *The Circle* and a Noel Coward revue; there were also cabaret shows of varying degrees of bawdiness, sometimes combined with wrestling displays. The Japanese officers were always invited and relations were for once cordial (except once when a drunken Japanese sergeant became enraged with Ian Horobin's portrayal of Lady Bracknell because he assumed that a real woman had been smuggled into the camp). Afterwards, the prisoners would entertain their hosts to dinner. Weary records in July 1942 'a wonderful show of food: fried rice and *nasi goreng* with eggs and spices . . . balls of rice cake . . . 4 bottles of port (2 Portuguese, 2 Aust.), 2 bottles of beer. Also some excellent Mandarin oranges . . . terrific intaking of breath, succulent noises and belches . . . songs sung included opera, "O Sole Mio" (castrato), Nipponese songs and English and Australian songs. And the "Internationale".'[24]

There was of course a harsher side to all this, as Billy Griffiths's fate shows. Some prisoners were required to labour at turning sisal into string and rope, using ancient hand-powered spinning jennies under the supervision of 'Mad Harry', one of the most sadistic guards.[25] The maintenance and healthy functioning of the camp latrines was a constant obsession of the officers, for obvious reasons. Burial parties were punctiliously observed by the Japanese.

From the beginning, Laurens was operating as Nichols's number two in Java Z and, even more discreetly, employing his Intelligence Corps background and responsibility to organise a supply of information into the camp, using prisoners in work parties to bring back news at great risk. He was also nominated by the Japanese to set up and run the camp 'farm' on the shaky premise that he had been a farmer in England and South Africa. It was an important task: the prisoners were confronting severe malnutrition, exacerbated by being unused to rice as a staple diet and lacking funds to buy enough eggs, bread, cheese, butter, fruit, milk and meat from the nearby town. As a result many rapidly began to suffer from 'burning feet', pellagra, beri beri, ulcers, optical neuritis and other tropical diseases. Dunlop warned Laurens that the POWs' diet must be improved if they were to survive. Weary arranged for '*katjang idjoe*', the local bean-sprout, a valuable source of Vitamins C and B1, to be served regularly, and tried to add one duck egg each every week.

Laurens's first idea was to rear pigs – and the Japanese enthusiastically agreed, providing him with half-a-dozen superior animals. It was the beginning of a nightmare. Sties had to be built from precious bedboards and an eccentric Japanese-Korean guard nicknamed 'Donald Duck' was assigned to supervise the operation (he became very attached to Laurens and took up much of his time discussing Shakespeare, Dostoyevsky, Greta Garbo, Einstein and Marlene Dietrich, which Laurens had to tolerate for the sake of the project). But when the Japanese delivered another 250 deeply inferior pigs, for which they had no intention of providing enough food, disaster followed. 'I was told that the only reason why the pigs did not prosper was because my spirit was bad and that unless things improved I would be held responsible and severely punished for "my wilfulness".'

The Japanese were distracted by a delivery of hens and ducks, a thousand of each: the ducks had to be marched out to the paddy-fields every morning under armed escort. They too were doomed: 'the same food troubles that were slowly killing us, and exterminating our pigs, hit them cruelly and hard,' Laurens recalled. In fact the importing of pig swill into the camp helped the prisoners' diet, because locals would hide morsels of meat and food in the buckets.

Next came fish ponds and rabbits. The latter became a great success with the men, who refused to eat them and adopted their favourites as pets, a focus for affection which could not be otherwise expressed. When the camp was moved, Laurens remembered, the Japanese promised to send the rabbits after them, provided they were properly addressed: 'We wrote the name, numbers and ranks of their owners with indelible pencil on their ears. I shall always remember my last glimpse of four hundred odd rabbits, sitting upright in a full, equatorial sun, so strong that their ears had become translucent and one could read plainly in them legends in purple script such as "1238547 Gunner Martin". But we never saw the rabbits again, and many a soldier and sailor was quite heart-broken.'

Laurens's only success was his vegetable gardens. He and his eighty full-time assistants grew a whole range of plants which flourished in Java's extraordinarily beneficent climate and soil. The Japanese only interfered to insist that he also grew egg-plant – a vegetable which they believed (and Laurens witnessed, to his surprise) responded to the light of the full moon, which he considered appropriate for what he saw as a 'moon-haunted' people.[26]

They had the occasional bonus, apart from a scrawny chicken or a genetically-deformed piglet. Nichols recalled how a working party once caught a giant Java lizard, fully 12 feet long: 'They marched into camp, some 600-strong . . . in impeccable Japanese ceremonial drill order, with the great creature paddling along behind the leading Company, secured by ropes. The Japanese Adjutant took their salute with grave approval . . . This made a useful extra 150 lbs. or so of fresh meat for us.'

Nevertheless it was clear that the prisoners were being slowly starved to death on one of the most prodigiously fertile islands in the world. They were saved by their ability to buy, or trade, in the early days, for modest local supplies from the other side of the perimeter; by the skills of their few doctors and minimal medicines; by their senior officers' determination to secure high-protein supplies of eggs, liver, beans, soya, fruit – and by their organic home-grown vegetables! John Denman recalls the Dutch dentist filling his teeth with cement using a drill made from an old bicycle. Teeth smashed by 'bashings' were replaced in aluminium; spectacle lenses (similarly broken) were made from glass bottles.[27]

Inevitably there were deaths. John Rae-Smith, an Oxford don of great charm and intelligence, much loved by Laurens and his colleagues, died of TB due to the appalling conditions when he was transferred from the plateau of Bandoeng down to the coastal humidity of Batavia – and also because he insisted on giving away to his men his food and money allotted by doctors and fellow-officers. But the scale of casualties did not approach that of Burma or Haruko. Denman, who has survived to old age, says, 'We had the cushiest time of all the POWs of the Japanese.' Nichols proudly boasted that nearly all his men survived – though many were severely damaged.[28]

The Dutch internees had money, at least at first, and guards could be bribed to allow food to be brought in. Laurens also found to his surprise that he could borrow money from wealthy Chinese businessmen: in particular a Mr Tan, who was inside the camp, made a substantial loan on the basis of a 'chitty' signed by Laurens guaranteeing repayment by the British Government after the war. In 1948 Laurens took satisfaction in 'ensuring that, despite much hesitation by London accountants, Mr Tan was repaid in full'. (The British Treasury repaid Mr Tan £4,500, not the half-million pounds which Laurens later said that he had borrowed from Tan.)[29]

Money in the early months had been the cause of a serious dispute inside the camp. In October 1942 it was announced that prisoner-officers, though not the men, would be paid at the rate of their Japanese opposite numbers, with a deduction for food, accommodation, etc.! Denman, Nichols and Laurens were determined that most of this money should be withheld to be used for the troops on the basis of individual need – for instance, to buy an egg for a sick man. Laurens initially argued that all income should be shared out equally between all prisoners but that any scheme should be voluntary. To Weary's and Laurens's disgust, many officers refused to agree to their private money being shared around rather than being used to assure them a supply of smuggled whisky. Weary threatened to resign his command, and then became irritated with Laurens for declining at the last minute to support his proposal. Eventually a voluntary scheme was forced through, as in other POW camps. In reality the Japanese 'pay' came in the form of local prison 'scrip', worthless for most purposes and usually late in arriving.[30]

4

Prisoner of War

THE NATURE AND flavour of life in the camp are best conveyed through an extraordinary document, a daily journal which Laurens kept from 14 December 1942 until 26 November 1943. The battered exercise book, containing 140 closely-written pages, details, with occasional euphemisms or coded phrases, the daily routine of the prisoners' lives. Laurens wrote it in secrecy: its discovery by the Japanese would have brought severe punishment, which is perhaps why after eleven months he decided that it was too dangerous to continue. He buried it in the compound, and although he set his own Japanese prisoners to dig for it after the Allied victory, it could not be found. Some years later, it was dug up by a Javanese peasant who took it to a local official who must have read the final sentence: 'My address is 13 Cadogan Street, London SW3'. The result was that one day Laurens, now a successful and well-known writer, received in the post the diary which he had never expected to see again.

The importance of this journal, apart from the fascinating minutiae of the POW world, is that here Laurens is writing *on the night* of his experiences, rather than doctoring or revising them after the passage of years. Here he had no occasion to gloss, or embellish, or fictionalise his personal experiences. A totally authentic document, it deserves to be quoted at length.

Laurens starts on 14 December 1942, six months after he had arrived in Java. For the first page, he writes in Afrikaans – 'Yesterday was my birthday . . .' – but three days later switches into English, the language he maintains until the end. This is interesting because one would have thought that, if discovered, he would have been more secure from interrogation if he had continued in a language which the Japanese could not translate. He afterwards said that he decided the Japanese would have been even more enraged if they had discovered a document which they could not read, but a likelier explanation is that Laurens, after more than ten years as an adopted Englishman, was now so much more at ease in English that, under the stress and secrecy of a night-time record, he found it easier to stay with his new language.

17 December: The camp giggle is interesting: a sort of helpless, eye-watering chuckle with an air of – well, here I am properly caught, what a fool I have been . . . it is astonishing how many people have been affected by it . . . It is involuntary and, I am sure, a more pleasant manifestation of hysteria . . . people suddenly stop half-way through a sentence, completely forgetting what they have been saying. They will get up to do something and sit down again helplessly . . . It happens to all of us a hundred times a day.

18 December: Altered pig-sties again for gentlemen who show such fine concern for welfare of our porkers.

19 December: . . . idea [of] Christmas uptaken vigorously by hosts . . .

20 December: . . . Must try and do more. Not happy yet about self. Went to church . . . [A] time-wasting meeting. They [British Officers] discussed whether red-haired women sweated more than others . . . Hate myself; very restless, very bad. . . .

21 December: We all think Dutch little insane on question of rumours. They really believe any rumour better than none . . . [a] deliberate evasion of reality, probability . . . Dutch officers . . . think rumours do good . . .

23 December: . . . address instructors. Arrange killing our four male pigs . . . menu for Xmas dinner: sardine fritters, duck soup, roast duck, cheese, coffee . . . Ducks in batches 500 now marched under guard to paddyfield alternate days wonder how one 500 distinguished from other.

24 December: . . . our home-made hooch made us feel quite drunk. How I hate that feeling.

25 December: Xmas church service by H[Horobin]. Very good. Excellent dinner. My conscience (belated) worries me: I feel bitter over things done and very much of an exile in my mind and heart and goodness. John [his son] always with me. I have done so little for him: I will try and make up to him and Ingaret.

27 December: Church. Sermon by Horobin. How very good he is, much better than our two departed padres . . . I do believe profoundly Christ but not as Horobin or church does . . . How it rains –

28 December: Gave H's [Horobin's] cabinet outline of African problems. They decided form Imperial Federal Parliament.

30 December: . . . spent night facing up problems of stay here, we may be here many years . . . Always afraid letting game down. My poor Ingaret, John, M and Mother: I am so miserable about them. Last night I dreamt went to see Ingaret and told she had left day before married. Thought in the night would write story of 'Flamingo Feather' for camp.

3 January: . . . tattooing – . . . all convicts look to it after a year, essentially narcissistic step; a psychological disease, indulgence of which bitterly regretted by doers afterwards . . . personally think . . . not unnatural . . . professional sailors, soldiers do it but as additional sort of uniform.

5 January: . . . Have had little happiness really, but entirely own fault. Terrible entanglement of myself . . . Rae Smith bad haemorrhage . . .

6 January: Our fellows in barracks discussed among themselves, 'What better?': 'Here another 6 months with certainty of release' or 'Three weeks W. Desert fighting with chance of being killed.' Desert won.

16 January: . . . [Horobin] is banker, politician, economist, mathematician, poet, musician, theologian . . . His knowledge, really great, enormous, pity he tries to make it more. The snag is: he has not got a spark of humour, animal feeling . . . My friend Star of the Field [pseudonym for one of the most sadistic guards] has been pursuing his celestial duties in our camp with customary inconsequence. He has been slapping heartily for internal reasons of his own.

17 January: . . . Star of the Field was shining very brightly . . . There is in many ways reign terror.

18 January: . . . ditty about me last night . . . 'Pity for Colonel van der Post / who has more jobs to do than most / He never chides or disagrees / But sometimes smiles in High Chinese . . .'

19 January: . . . sad morning: one of those things happened today which circumstances our life here make impossible to describe, a fact which has discouraged me from keeping diary in the past, because one cannot adequately write of the life that really matters. Enough to say that the authorities 'severely but justly' punished Pilot Officer Miller for having been the subject of a typist's error in their index . . . he is now in hospital with, among other things, a haemorrhaged eye . . . Nick [Nichols] protested. Poor Nick, he has a hell of a job and does it superbly.

This journal really deserves to be published in full. It is a remarkable record of the misery and suffering of a prisoner-of-war, a farewell testament on behalf of a band of men who, in their hearts, did not expect to survive. Again and again Laurens is tormented – as, he knows, are his comrades – by guilty thoughts of his family.

It ends in November 1943:

3 November: Soon I will have to close this and bury it. It has been a hopeless sort of job, this: you can't write frankly, you have not time and whatever you write anyway is going to get you in trouble. But in case anything happens to us ... I wrote this hoping that someone some day might find it and reading between the lines get an idea of how we lived. I think we have nothing to be ashamed of: on the contrary, we have lived as though release was certain and not far away, all the time believing the contrary; we have been cheerful, feeling always the contrary; we have helped one another gladly; we have been patient and uncomplaining, and endured not without dignity petty insults, humiliations and constant threats, and to the end felt more than ever the good, thank God, that was our cause ... Please give my love to my Mother, Ingaret, and John van der Post whom I love dearly and thought of without break ... and to Marjorie and Lucia. There is much that I could have explained if only I could see them, but they must just believe that I have done nothing they need be ashamed of ... I have done my best ...

8 November: ... it is one of the hardest things in this prison life: the strain caused by being continually in the power of people who are only half-sane and live in a twilight of reason and humanity.

And finally:

26 November 1943: This is my last entry because the signs are such that I cannot afford to ignore them any longer. I believe that we may be moved at any moment to Batavia: and from Batavia heaven knows where ... I wish this could have been a franker document. I don't think anyone could picture from it how humiliating our treatment has been, how in a land of plenty, if it had not been for our own efforts, we would long since all have been dead of malnutrition ... we are lucky to be alive still ... My love to my family and Ingaret should anything happen to me. May God Bless them all and do not let Europe forget this was a good war for a good cause. Our imprisonment has taught us all the more how good it is. My address is –[1]

Laurens was in fact fortunate, in comparison with so many thousands of his colleagues. His journal dates from the first years of his captivity. After November 1943, when he buried it, there would be nearly two years more to survive. But unlike many of his companions he (with Nichols and Denman among a few others) would remain in Java and not be sent to the mortal hell of Haruko or the Burma Railway.

The prisoners' isolation was almost, but not entirely, complete. Laurens, in his role as an Intelligence Corps officer, managed to set up contacts outside the camps, principally with Chinese merchants, who provided a flow of information about what was happening on the island. He had a much greater problem obtaining Japanese military information until, as he describes in *The Night of the New Moon*, a Korean Christian called Kim made contact in late 1944 and sent warnings of the dangers that the prisoners faced as the Japanese armies retreated. It was Kim who in June 1945 alerted Laurens to the Japanese plan to concentrate all the Java POWs in Bandoeng where they could be liquidated when the Allied invasion began.

The other source of information, vital to prison morale, was a small number of secret radios, totally forbidden by the Japanese, and whose discovery would have brought execution. One was hidden in a chair and escaped detection even when a guard sat down on it. Another was hidden inside a pair of wooden clogs. Another radio was broken up into the smallest parts, and Denman remembers Laurens, with immense coolness, juggling the parts from one pocket to another while he and his colleagues were searched. Only the senior officers were privy to the news of the Pacific and European war fronts, for fear of jeopardising the secrecy of the radios.[2]

The most dramatic radio story came towards the end, when the prisoners desperately needed to know what was happening in the outside world, because they realised that their lives were in extreme danger. The radio used by Laurens's group broke down at the critical period. A valve needed to be replaced, which was of course impossible. Then a Scottish pilot officer, Don Donaldson, who was responsible for the smuggling of food into the camp, came up with an idea. The Japanese Lieutenant who was nominally in command of the camp (though his sadistic NCOs were the effective authority) had a luxurious radiogram. Donaldson coolly broke into the Lieutenant's rooms one night, swapped the radiogram's valves for valves from the broken radio, and escaped undetected. The radio wizard, a New Zealander, Bill Phillips – later a distinguished economist – managed to get the radio working again after three nights fiddling in the dark inside his mosquito net.[3]

In summarising the story of these terrible years there is an inescapable impression of days, weeks, months, slipping into an indistinguishable and eventually irrecoverable sequence of detail, characterised above all by their ignorance of what the future would bring. Some officers resorted to bridge and idleness, while others, led by Nichols, maintained an unending and exhausting campaign to keep up 'standards', to rally morale, to maintain a firm and dignified relationship with their Japanese overlords. There was an inner group of officers around Laurens to whom he would always be loyal and grateful. Nichols he acknowledged as the central hero. Of Laurens himself, Denman – an architect and a Major in the Guards – said many years later, 'Some people say that Laurens was a hypocrite and a liar. To me he was a saint . . .'[4]

Many of these men did not believe in their heart of hearts that they would come through. The British officers around Laurens were greatly exasperated by what they considered the facile optimism of their Dutch counterparts who, they felt, seized on rumours, and spread them around, that liberation was imminent. Perhaps the Dutch thought that such optimism was good for morale. Laurens and his friends hesitated to debate even among themselves when the war might end, whether they would survive. They all wrote letters home: none arrived, and they received none from their families. The Japanese at one point sanctioned an official postcard in which the prisoners might declare their good health and the excellent conditions; a few of these arrived in Europe more than twelve months later. In one Australian camp the Japanese allowed the broadcast of twenty-five names a day, which gave comfort to some relatives. The British Intelligence services tried to relay all possible details gathered from escapees and other informants. Laurens, his friends remembered, kept writing letters to Ingaret – 'my sister', as he always described her. She never received them. He used to be very vague when his companions asked him about his wife and children, just as he was always mysteriously discreet about his military background.[5]

Violence was constant and increased over the years, though conditions in these Java camps never remotely approached the atrocities of, for instance, the Burma Railway. Laurens and his friends always agreed that they had been very lucky, but Laurens's emergence after the war as a 'typical' POW, and also his public plea for forgiveness of the Japanese, infuriated prisoners elsewhere who had gone through an unimaginably more terrible ordeal. Some of them never forgave Laurens for taking this position. Others defended him while confessing that they could not share his view. Fifty years later, for example, Captain George Cooper, who could never bring himself to 'forgive' the Japanese for what they had done to him and his colleagues in the Java prisons, described Laurens as 'the nearest man I ever met in my lifetime to Christ'.[6]

Officers like Nichols and Laurens who went to protest against injustices such as 'bashing' – which often meant ferocious assaults by Japanese, and in particular Korean, guards – were respected by their men because they often returned showing evidence of a beating. The most vivid example, described by Laurens years later, took place in the closing months of the war when a particularly sadistic guard called Gunzo Mori – who with his Korean sidekick Kasayama would later be hanged for his many atrocities – summoned a parade of officers and proceeded to beat them up in turn. Laurens remembered that he had been increasingly conscious of mounting pressure among the Japanese as defeat approached. A senior RAF officer, MacGuire, was smashed to the ground with a huge chair, as Laurens, to his alarm, saw that a machine gun was being mounted on the gates. As Laurens's turn came, he approached Mori feeling, he said, 'as if I had become another person. . .' He took his beating, and then, 'as if I heard from deep within myself very clearly a voice of command from this other self, ordering me as with the authority of life itself: "Turn about! Go back and present yourself to Mori for another beating."'

So Laurens – he later wrote – turned around and before the next officer could take his place, offered himself for a second beating. The tactic was brilliant as well as brave. The demented Mori, seeing before him the very figure he had just dealt with, was jerked out of his passion: 'He stood there glaring at me, a strange inner bewilderment at this unexpected turn of events showing in the sombre glow of his dark eyes.' He gave up in disgust and walked off.[7]

Is this story fact or fiction? The Imperial War Museum has letters from men who were in the camp stating that it is both incredible and untrue. Flying Officer Ed Stearn, for example, in an unpublished memoir, insists that he was present at the beating of the senior officers and that Laurens's 'romantic' story of having offered himself for a second punishment 'simply did not happen'. But John Denman, more than fifty years later, insisted that the event did take place, and he was next to him. Alex Jardine was there and remembers that it was possible – but he had been clubbed senseless. Other letters written over the years to Laurens agree that this is exactly what happened, and comment on Laurens's quick initiative. Laurens would later use a similar, even more heroic episode in his novella from the camps, *The Seed and the Sower*, which became the film *Merry Christmas Mr Lawrence*.[8]

As one day blurred into the next, in a climate without seasons in which the clouds built up every afternoon and then released their cooling showers, the years divide into the periods spent in successive camps. For some months in 1943 the prisoners were taken down to the coast to the so-called Cycle Camp in Batavia; there they were saved from despatch to Japan or Burma (where many of their predecessors had already been consigned) by the shortage of Japanese shipping, which had suffered heavy losses at Allied hands. Then they were taken back to Java Z and again, in late 1944, down to Cycle Camp, where Laurens and Denman celebrated Laurens's birthday with an avocado pear.

In June 1945, as the Japanese faced defeat, Laurens and most of his colleagues were moved up-country again, back to Tjimahi and almost at once to Landsopvoedingsgesticht (understandably known as 'Landsop'), where conditions were much worse. 'The congestion was so great that even the Japanese had to acknowledge that life would be impossible unless our new prison were treated like the hold of some kind of ship,' Laurens remembered. 'They provided us with rough timber, so that in every room we could build layers of wooden bunks on which we slept in narrow tiers from floor to ceiling. But perhaps the fact which illustrates best the density of our concentration is that the men stood in queues twenty-four hours a day all the time we were in this prison for their turn at the latrines, and we had to have on duty constantly a chain of officers and men passing buckets of water filled from an open irrigation ditch, which fortunately ran through the middle of our new camp . . .' Landsop, which stood under a beautiful volcano whose name translates as 'the ship turned upside down', had been a sort of Dutch Borstal, built to house a few hundred boys. As Nichols afterwards recorded, in his precise way, between May and August 1945 it held 782 officers and 2,145 other ranks.

This was the camp where the prisoners knew they would be killed if the Japanese embraced a suicidal defeat. Landsop was intended as a Death Camp.[9]

To the prisoners of war throughout Asia these last weeks were the most dangerous. Through their hidden radios, Laurens and his senior officers monitored the American advance from island to island. They were all too aware that in defeat the Japanese might exterminate their prisoners, and they planned for the worst. They realised that, jammed helplessly into Landsop, they could be mowed down by the machine guns mounted on the surrounding parapets. A small group of elite teams was organised in great secrecy: the purpose was to select men who, in the mayhem, would attempt – with their colleagues' suicidal support – to break out of the camp so as to carry word of their fate to the Allied forces. These men were chosen for their physical stamina: most prisoners were deep into the lethargy and disease of malnutrition. An alternative version has it that a very small number of prisoners were selected to break out – all non-Europeans, who would have the best chance of survival. Laurens was proved right: the Japanese High Command, it was afterwards confirmed, had indeed planned to massacre the POWs. It required the personal intervention of the Emperor and of his brother to assert authority over the Generals.

It may also have required the A-bombs over Hiroshima and Nagasaki. In *The Night of the New Moon*, which opens with Laurens debating in a New York radio programme with a bereaved Japanese professor the justification of the bomb, Laurens describes his continuing fear that General Terauchi would defy his Emperor, fight to the end and kill all the prisoners in 'a spirit of revenge for what they would instinctively regard as a blasphemous outrage on their sacred land . . .' It was afterwards discovered that in Borneo hundreds of prisoners had indeed been murdered during death marches.[10]

The Bomb was dropped on Hiroshima on 6 August 1945. The war ended on 15 August.

5

Java

SUDDENLY, IT WAS over. Laurens described in *The Night of the New Moon*
how, on 21 August, he was summoned by the Japanese commander
of the camp, who offered him a glass of wine – refused by Laurens, who
was swaying with exhaustion and famine – and who declared, 'I drink
sincerely to your victory . . . We Japanese have decided to switch, and
when we Japanese switch, we switch sincerely.'

Reading more closely, and referring to Laurens's own final version of
these events in *The Admiral's Baby*, it is clear that the Japanese officer must
already have acknowledged surrender to Nichols, not just because the
Japanese had a punctilious regard for military convention which would
have required them to surrender to the commanding officer, but also
because Laurens was informed that the 'senior RAF officers' had already
been told to arrange the immediate embarkation of their men. Laurens
must have discussed this with Nichols earlier in the day, though he never
mentions it, and agreed that he would, as the Japanese requested, remain
behind when the rest of the POWs left.[1] The evacuation of the camp
was carried through with remarkable speed: as John Denman recalled,
they were all given about half-an-hour to get ready, were marched off to
a waiting wood-burning train, and were sent back to Cycle Camp in
Batavia, where they had to wait for another six weeks or so before transport was available to take them home. Denman recalled that in the rush
they had not realised that Laurens was left behind. Only later did they
understand, when he visited them in Batavia (and when Denman had the
occasion to phone him to warn him of a serious riot in the town), that
he had chosen not to go home, like everyone else.[2]

From August 1945 Java saw one of the most difficult, and today least
remembered, operations in the immediate months following Allied
victory. The British Occupation of the Netherlands East Indies, from 29

September 1945 to 30 November 1946, occupies only a brief reference in most war histories; it cost hundreds of British and Indian casualties, and in the end it failed, in that it merely delayed the civil war between the nationalists and the Dutch colonial empire. After a bloody, if brief, struggle, the Dutch gave up and the Netherlands East Indies became independent Indonesia.

Java, with a population of about sixty million, was the most important constituent in the Netherlands East Indies (other islands may have been larger, but their populations were smaller). In 1942 the Japanese had recalled from exile two of the leaders of the Indonesian nationalist movement – Sukarno and Hatta – and allowed them to form an anti-colonial, anti-Dutch, essentially collaborationist organisation. As the Japanese found themselves on the defensive, they encouraged this brand of nationalism. When they surrendered, Lord Mountbatten, Supreme Commander in South Asia, had told the Japanese that they were responsible for the maintenance of order and the protection of the enormous number of detainees – a task which they obeyed, to a certain degree, as Laurens personally observed.[3]

Why did Laurens stay behind in Java, and remain there for twenty months when he would surely have shared the anxiety of all his fellow prisoners to leave Asia, to go home, to be quit of these horrors after more than three years of misery and captivity?

In *The Night of the New Moon*, and then in *The Admiral's Baby*, published twenty-five and fifty-one years later respectively, he explained that he had first thought that it was his duty to remain. The Japanese admitted to him that they doubted their ability to protect the prisoners of war and the internees, as they had been ordered to do. It was almost a cry from the heart for help, and Laurens, though his physical condition was poor, immediately agreed. That was certainly noble of him, and his language qualifications were unique: he spoke English and Dutch, some Japanese and a little Malay. As an Afrikaner, he could claim a fellow-feeling for the Dutch colonists. He had come through the war without hating the Japanese, he had an instinctive sympathy for the cause of the Indonesian nationalists. He loved being at the centre of affairs – being needed and *effective* after the years of prison inactivity. He said he felt he had somehow failed to play a proper soldier's role in the war.

In his book, he describes with relish being saluted by the Japanese warders and stretching out to sleep on the Japanese commanding officer's couch. 'You will have to learn,' he told the Japanese General, according to *Yet Being Someone Other*, 'as I have had to in all these years in your power, how there is a way of losing that can become a way of winning.' At which the Japanese hissed with emotion, bowed, and responded, 'That is a very Japanese thought!' From that moment on, Laurens had the full co-operation of the Japanese. For the next three weeks, he played a central role in attempting to keep the fragile peace as the Allies, preoccupied with a hundred more urgent problems, worked out what to do with the Dutch East Indies (which had been declared Mountbatten's responsibility); though desperately short of resources, the Supremo sent off HMS *Cumberland* to assert authority.[4]

But why did he stay so long (as Nichols and other POW friends kept asking him in their letters)? He was not unaware of the limits of what he, as one man, could achieve in keeping the Dutch and Indonesians from each others' throats. He despaired early on of his power to persuade the Dutch to acknowledge that their empire was ended, that they could not return to the colonial supremacy they had enjoyed for centuries.[5] And yet he stayed until June 1947.

Though he spoke of duty, and perhaps was aware that this was a way to distinguish himself, there must have been other thoughts in Laurens's mind. He had one obvious reason not to go home on the troop ship with the others. When they were greeted at Southampton or Liverpool the question would inevitably be asked, *who* is this *Lieutenant-Colonel* van der Post? The question of Laurens's rank would hang over him for the rest of his time in the army. That was surely one reason to stay away until these things could be sorted out.

The second problem was Ingaret, awaiting him in London. Laurens had often talked about her in the camps to his friends, yet – extraordinarily – he always described her as his sister; he even sent Nichols and Denman to call on her in Cadogan Street in London after their return in 1945–46 as his sister, a deception which they fell for until, three years later, they were invited to the wedding! There can be no doubt that, after the diary was buried, and throughout the period when only two official postcards were allowed by the Japanese, both sent to Ingaret and arriving a year later, Ingaret remained lively in Laurens's emotions. After August 1945 she deluged him with passionate letters, but she was still tied to her husband Jimmy and these letters travelled a roller-coaster of conflict and confusion.[6]

There must have been another consideration in Laurens's mind. Should he attempt to go back to Ingaret from his position in the British Army? If not, what would he do? His prewar journalistic career had hardly been a success. He would be one of a large number of half-colonels. Did he want to stay with Ingaret or go home to South Africa? What should he do about his wife and two young children, whom he had not seen since 1938 and had apparently not contacted during those years? Even if the marriage had been dead to him ever since he had met Ingaret in 1936, he had responsibilities for his children and for someone who still believed herself to be his wife. He had ties with his extended family. What of a future career?

Fifty years later, he put it like this: 'When I had obeyed my instinct to go straight from prison back to military duty, there had also been a feeling of guilt that I was not rushing back to my home in England where I had been reported "Missing" and then "Believed Killed". I had not been home for more than five years, and had not seen my mother and my two children in Africa for ten years . . . And still I had put this strange prompting [i.e. to contribute to peace] before reunion with them all . . . All feelings of guilt totally vanished . . .'[7]

Of about 80,000 detainees in Java, the great majority were Dutch. The official record says that there were 6,078 POWs, of whom 1,243 were British, 376 Australians, 330 Indians and 61 Americans. Laurens's first task was to persuade the Dutch to stay inside the camps, where, ironically, they were protected by their former Japanese warders. The Indonesian nationalists, in these first weeks, exercised a *de facto* government. In the unlikely event of an armed arrival of Dutch metropolitan troops, the internees would have been doomed. In a real sense they were the hostages as Laurens and his newly-arrived British colleagues struggled to mediate.[8]

Laurens wrote three versions of his time in Java. The first was a confidential Political Survey for the Foreign Office, written to order in December 1946. It ran to an unprecedented 25,000 words, and is a remarkably vivid and personalised despatch considering its official status; it is also far more impressionistic and imprecise than is usual in such reports. A second version was his report to the Foreign Office in mid-1947, which concluded with a visibly desperate optimism for the future. His third description was written forty-five years later: *The Admiral's Baby* (published when he was eighty-nine), was to be his last full-length book and retells a fuller story, in much more detail and complete with Laurens's memories of his Indonesian friends, his Dutch critics and his British colleagues. He also prevailed on his publisher to include the full text of his Foreign Office report.[9] It does not make for the most gripping of his books, but it is evidently an old man's compulsion to set the record straight, insofar as he chooses to remember it. A temptation in 1996 to set himself at the centre of this long-forgotten drama – indeed, to draw himself as its hero – may be understandable, so long as the reader remembers a wider context.

As the years went by, Laurens became increasingly vague about his precise status in Java. He often described himself as 'Military Governor of Batavia', usually adding that he had been appointed by Lord Mountbatten himself: the implication, and sometimes the direct statement, was that he was reporting personally to Mountbatten. In a significant moment thirty years later, Laurens amended his *Who's Who* entry. In 1979, it read, among other things, '. . . commanded 43 Special Military Mission' and then, 'attached to British Mission, Batavia, until 1947 . . .', which is correct. In 1981, Laurens's entry (and entries are always submitted by the subject) now reads '. . . Lord Mountbatten's Military-Political Officer, attached to 15 Indian Army Corps, Java . . .'[10] Mountbatten had been assassinated by the IRA in 1979, and Laurens had immediately changed the reference, without fear of contradiction.

It is therefore necessary to get the record straight. As we have seen, Laurens was asked by the defeated Japanese on 21 August 1945, presumably with the concurrence of his own senior officer, to stay behind to liaise between the detainees, the defeated Japanese troops and the Indonesians, as part of an effort to keep the peace until Allied forces arrived. He had no official standing, even as he set up his Mess, greeted a small Allied reconnaissance team, and toured the camps in which many thousands were in dire need both of supplies and of protection from the locals. When Admiral Patterson arrived in HMS *Cumberland* with a cruiser squadron on 15 September, Laurens went out to meet him and quickly won his trust and friendship. He became Patterson's 'military adviser' under the (unquestioned) rank of Lieutenant-Colonel. In *The Admiral's Baby* he fleshed this out: 'Laurie, he said . . . From now on consider yourself for all practical purposes my Military Governor of Batavia.' This hardly seems an official appointment, even if it had been within Patterson's power to make it; after the arrival of General Christison, Laurens did indeed become 'GSO 1, Political' (General Staff Officer) to the General Officer Commanding Netherlands East Indies. He thereafter became Military Liaison Officer on the staff of the newly-arrived British Consul-General's Mission, headed by Gilbert MacKereth, and after the British troops left on 30 November 1946 he became Military Attaché to the British Consulate-General in Batavia.[11]

This detail needs to be noted since in *The Admiral's Baby* Laurens frequently quoted from his fan-mail. He showed to his friends, and included in the book, a farewell letter dated 10 January 1947 from Air Marshal Lawrie Pendred, Mountbatten's Director of Military Intelligence: 'Since December '45 . . . it has been your view of the situation which has pulled the big bells when peals were rung . . . You have done more in your quiet way to influence policy than anyone else . . . You taught me all I ever knew about the NEI [Netherlands East Indies] and I am very grateful . . . I'm sure you are looking forward to visiting your properties in England and the Union' (Laurens had no 'properties'). Similarly, he quoted a Dutch friend: 'It is extraordinary . . . how lucky the British have always been because, no matter where and in what situation they find themselves, life always throws up someone qualified to serve their unforeseen needs. Look, even here in all this mess . . . someone like yourself, who knows the Japanese, the Dutch and the Javanese, is there ready at hand for them to use.' Laurens could only agree. He was, in his own view, the only person who could talk to all sides. 'I had no honourable option but to serve on through another kind of war, far more distasteful than the one behind us.'[12]

There must have been hundreds of British officers who could be described as 'personal representatives' of Mountbatten, as Laurens often called himself. Nor is there much evidence of a closer relationship. Mountbatten visited once and Laurens introduced him to the Indonesian leaders; he reported most evenings by radio to Headquarters in Kandy, which passed on relevant information to Mountbatten and to London. His postwar contact with Mountbatten was very rare and he does not feature at all in Mountbatten's own archive.[13]

The official surrender documents were not signed in Tokyo until 2 September. General MacArthur had vetoed any re-occupation of Japanese-held territories before then, so these first few weeks of power vacuum, after Laurens's release, were extraordinarily dangerous, because the Dutch internees were yielding to a natural temptation to leave the camps and were being murdered by the Indonesian nationalists. With Major Alan Greenhalgh and Captain van Till, who had been parachuted in on 25 August to set up the RAPWI organisation (Relief of Allied POW and Civilian Internees), Laurens could do little but reconnoitre central Java and await the Allied arrival. The Japanese scrupulously obeyed their orders to protect their prisoners, although the Indonesians acquired plenty of arms from them. In the words of the official war history, 'It was now quite clear that the situation as described to Mountbatten when he was made responsible for the whole of the Netherlands East Indies had been a supreme example of wishful thinking. Instead of willing co-operation by the Indonesians, there was not only an open threat of war but also a considerable Indonesian force trained and equipped by the Japanese and ready to fight anyone attempting to restore Dutch domination.'[14]

At this point, Laurens – whose health, it must be remembered, was very frail and who had immediately come under great pressure – was for-tified by the arrival of Paul Vogt. 'I think recognition came to us both at once. In Dutch with a deep guttural Swiss accent my new visitor said "Thank God Colonel, it's you at last!" ' They embraced.

Vogt was well informed about the Javanese situation and immediately agreed, for the second time, to join Laurens. His first service was to intro-duce Laurens to Colonel Radu Abdul Kadir Widjojoatmodjo, an Indonesian senior officer in the Dutch army, previously a diplomat in the Middle East, who had spent the war years in exile. ''Dul' was to become one of Laurens's greatest allies and friends in Batavia. He and his wife Shri shared a house with Laurens for much of his time there, as Laurens and his colleagues struggled, and eventually failed, to hold the balance between their Dutch and Indonesian loyalties, a struggle which was per-sonified in the dilemmas of 'Dul and his wife. Another member of Laurens's team was his secretary, a young local Jewish/Eurasian woman called Sybil Bauer, an ex-internee: 'She was as efficient and loyal as she was good to look at, with fine-drawn features and eyes of an almost antique darkness, and an abiding expression of serenity which is almost impos-sible to define. In addition she spoke Javanese, Medoerese, Malay, English, and of course Dutch, all fluently and all indispensable for the work she had to do.'[15]

In *The Admiral's Baby*, Laurens described sentimentally how, when HMS *Cumberland* arrived at Batavia's harbour of Tandjongh Priok on 15 September, he dressed in the better of his two sets of prison clothes, with the badges of rank made for him by Australian POWs together with a hat badge – 'not that of my regiment, which had been too diffi-cult and convoluted for them, but was taken from what they remem-bered of the badges worn by South African officers with whom they had served in the Western Desert . . . the head of a springbok'. Laurens, Greenhalgh and van Till approached the warship cautiously, and Laurens remembered enough semaphore training to signal, he says, 'British offi-cers approaching'.

'Soon we were alongside and there was a ship's ladder ready with an Able-Seaman to help us up. The bosun, seeing my home-made badges of rank, immediately began to pipe me on board. It was one of the most won-derful sounds I have ever heard in my life. I was so deeply moved that I did not know quite how I was going to contain myself . . .' Laurens, scarcely three weeks out of prison, his scalp shaved, must have been a ragged and starved figure. It was here that he met Admiral Wilfred Patterson. Laurens wrote him a letter in January 1947: 'No-one can ever take your place in our gratitude and affection . . . I still feel that "the transition period", as is called that period of 15 to 30 September – was the period that set the tone for the future and prevented serious bloodshed in the NEI.'[16]

Patterson described these first emotional and precarious days in a round-robin letter to his family and friends dated 7 October of that year: 'I went ashore the first day in a large Packard, supplied by the Japanese, with a Captain in the Kempitei as my personal escort. It was amusing driving with my own flag on the car and all the Japanese presenting arms. I also took one man with a revolver with me as a matter of form . . . I went to the POW Camp where they put up a first-class parade, some 1,200 British and 750 Dutch. They looked frail but bearing and morale was magnificent. When they dismissed, I went into the naval messdecks and saw some 100 sailors . . . they hoisted a White Ensign as I went in and presented it to me afterwards. They had made it themselves from bits and pieces smuggled into the camp. Other days I visited the women internees camp and hospitals. They were frightful, but the spirit of the women was simply magnificent . . '. Colonel van der Post and Major Greenhalgh (who had parachuted in early in September) I co-opted as military staff. The former's ability to speak Malay, Japanese, Dutch and his intimate knowledge of the political situation in the island were invaluable.'

Patterson, who had been sending signals reporting on the situation, continued: 'I said I was holding an ugly illegitimate baby but an interesting child. I hoped they would soon send a competent Nanny and in the meantime I was fairly happy we could keep rocking the cradle until the Army arrived . . .'[17] And in Laurens's later account: 'I remember the wording exactly to this day: "Most Immediate. En Clair. CS5 to SACSEA: We can continue to rock the baby to sleep only if you people outside the house would not make so much noise." I promised the Admiral that night that, if I lived, I would one day write a story about all that had happened and was happening to us in Indonesia, and call it "The Admiral's Baby".'[18]

The situation was desperately delicate as Patterson waited for Allied ground troops to arrive – 'bedlam' was how he described it. The first British officers turned up in the last days of August. Laurens's job was to persuade the Indonesian leaders to control their followers at least until enough soldiers had arrived to provide security for the internment camps. The Seaforth Highlanders were the first troops to arrive, and Patterson immediately sent them ashore with 400 sailors to try to guard the camps. (Patterson later recalled how he landed a *Cumberland* football team at this time: 'They found themselves being cheered all the way to the ground.' It was some time before they realised that their red-and-white shirts were the colours of the Indonesian nationalists.)

The Admiral was soon assisted by the arrival on 30 September of General Sir Philip Christison and Major-General D. C. Hawthorne, sent by General Sir William Slim to control army, air and naval forces. 'I am afraid', Patterson wrote, 'I have left General Christison with a baby that shows every sign of waking up and being cross.' But before the arrival of 'Christie', as he was known, the Admiral had been carrying through the necessary conclusion to the Japanese war. On 19 September he accepted the formal surrender of the local Japanese General on the quarterdeck of the *Cumberland* with Laurens at his side. He refused the Japanese request that they retain their Samurai swords. After Laurens's reconnaissance of the island and his assessment of the situation, with the help of Paul Vogt, 'Dul and Lt Jongejans, the principal interpreter in the prison camps, Christison authorised a dangerous face-to-face meeting between Laurens and members of the national leadership in Batavia, including Soetan Sjahrir and Amir Sjarifoeddin, who were to become the central Indonesian figures in the months ahead: they chose to speak English at this first meeting, not Dutch. Laurens always believed that it was from this moment that he became the subject of fast-growing Dutch suspicion. But the meeting encouraged him.[19]

Laurens was also encouraged by the visit of Lady Mountbatten, who had insisted on touring the liberated camps throughout her husband's command from Burma to Sumatra and Java. She was introduced to Laurens on the *Cumberland* and, in his own description, he explained the speed and inevitability of the nationalist eruption in South-east Asia: 'Not only did both Lady Mountbatten and the Admiral ask me questions, they clearly intimated that they wanted more. By now, too, a number of officers on deck had, at a sign from Flags, drawn in around us to listen and I felt myself compelled to talk about the Dutch spirit of empire, and how it had never been a true expression of the people of Holland at their best.'

Laurens was gratified again the next day when the Japanese interpreter, Taji, came to say goodbye. He confessed that his mother had been English and a Christian. Taji reminded Laurens how he had told the Japanese General that there was a way of losing which becomes a way of winning. The General, he said, 'was thunderstruck to see [Laurens] sitting beside the Admiral on the day of the surrender. He felt you must hate them for not seeing that you were a General yourself, and that you were entitled to special treatment and should have been sent to join the

other Generals in Manchuria.' Laurens replied (he said), 'Taji, tell the
General that I was just a soldier and no more.'

Laurens quickly formed a passionate respect and admiration for
General Christison, as Commander of AFNEI (Allied Forces in the
Netherlands East Indies). 'Christie', a Scottish baronet, had trained as a
doctor, served in the First World War, then fought in Burma in the
Second with 15 Indian Army Corps. He had been sent to Java by
Mountbatten to be 'a soldier-statesman' with a warning that he would be
required to 'carry the can' if things went wrong. When he took over from
Admiral Patterson the two men agreed that Laurens must be used to
clarify matters and so must fly to Kandy in Ceylon to brief Mountbatten.
(Laurens kept in respectful touch with Christie after the war. As late as
November 1980, after Mountbatten's death, he wrote to him to say that
the Supremo's memory had 'diminished alarmingly' in his later years, and
made the wildly inventive statement that, when Mountbatten became
Viceroy of India, he – Laurens – had 'quite a lot to do as a go-between
with Nehru'.)[20]

This trip to Kandy, unexpectedly, took Laurens to London for a few
weeks. The session with Mountbatten in October 1945, the most important of the few which the two men would ever hold, is described at length
by Laurens in *The Admiral's Baby*. His mission was to convey to
Mountbatten that Britain should not accept the Dutch version of the situation in Java. Mountbatten took the point and sent him to Europe to
report to the War Cabinet, in particular to the Prime Minister, Clement
Attlee, and, more surprisingly, to Sir Stafford Cripps, who would shortly
become Chancellor of the Exchequer. (Laurens afterwards told a story
of how, in his innocence, he had discovered on the trip that he had no
cash to pay for a NAAFI meal; rescued by a stranger, he later repaid the
favour by taking the man to lunch at Claridges. This is suspiciously reminiscent of an episode in the film *Lawrence of Arabia* – Laurens always
enjoyed journalists' later parallels between T. E. Lawrence and 'Laurens
of Abyssinia'.)[21]

Not the least important result of his trip to Kandy was that it began
the regularisation of Laurens's dubious status. Laurens went straight
from Mountbatten to General Sir William Slim, one of the greatest of
Britain's wartime leaders. The detail of their conversation is not known,
but the immediate result was that Laurens was transferred into the
Indian Army and given a regular commission: Defence Ministry records
have it that Laurens became a real if Temporary Lt.-Col. with effect from
1 December 1945, attached to 15 Indian Army Corps whose nickname
was 'the flying hockeysticks', taken from the three interlocking 'V's on

their insignia: for the rest of his life Laurens would proudly sport the 'hockeysticks' on his ancient bush shirts.[22] In all the mystery of Laurens's military career, it seems probable that General Slim was the senior figure to whom he first came clean about his problem, and who began to sort it out – though there would be more difficulties ahead.

Laurens arrived at Lyneham in Hampshire in late September 1945. He was taken straight to the War Cabinet office. In *The Admiral's Baby* he recalled how Ingaret's mother 'nearly fainted with shock' on hearing his voice on the telephone because she believed he was dead. This cannot be true because Ingaret had known for some time that he had survived the war, contrary to earlier reports that he was missing, believed dead.

He was seen first by Cripps and then by the Prime Minister. His appreciation of the political and military situation in Java must have been impressive because Attlee sent him immediately to The Hague, where he met the Dutch Cabinet.* Laurens was still suffering from the effects of malnutrition, and the long session with the ministers was an ordeal. He was appalled to find how ignorant the metropolitan Dutch were of the reality on the ground in Asia. We have to rely on Laurens's assessment of the importance of this mission; Mr Attlee's archive, which is voluminous on the subject of the Dutch East Indies, contains no mention of Laurens or any contribution by him.[24]

Laurens spent a week in Holland, where he made a broadcast at the request of the national radio system, as he also did for the BBC in London. He tried to emphasise to the Dutch, 'speaking as one who had been born in a British colony and in the context of empire, that I believed there came a moment when colonial subjects, no matter how beneficial their subjection, found that colonialism was not good enough for them. It could seem unfair, it could seem all sorts of other things, but there was an imponderable longing for their own identity which was unrecognised in the assumptions and hypotheses on which colonialism was based.' On 1 November, Laurens broadcast anonymously for the BBC, speaking as 'a British officer who has spent the last three and a half years in Java'. He described how the 'nationalist' minority of the population was very small but nevertheless included the educated specialists who had it in their power to control all essential services. The immediate problem, he

---

*He mentions in passing that he was last there in December 1939 on 'a short mission to the Netherlands on behalf of our Foreign Office': it is not known why, or whether, an obscure South African journalist would have been employed in this way, although his passport does show a mysterious Foreign Office visa to travel to Holland in *October* 1939, i.e. after the war had started.[23]

argued, was not so much the nationalist movement as 'hunger, fear, ignorance, exhaustion and spiritual derangement', all the result of the years of Japanese occupation and terror. Referring to the recent assassination in Sourabaya in the East of a Brigadier Mallaby, he blamed this on the Japanese success in sowing anti-European hatred, 'a tragic and abnormal psychology, created by yellow Fascism in an atmosphere of organised lying and intimidation'. Laurens urged on his BBC listeners, 'a very light, deft, firm and sensitive touch to manage the startled and wounded steed' (this was at least a change of metaphor from the Admiral's baby). He ended – over-optimistically, it turned out – with the argument that Java was on the first steps to normalcy.[25]

After a meeting with the Foreign Secretary, Ernest Bevin (who professed admiration for the Boers), Laurens flew back to Java. He had of course been with Ingaret in Cadogan Street, and they may have hoped to use this unexpected interlude to agree their plans for their future, but nothing between them was to be so easy. On 8 November 1945 Laurens wrote to Ingaret from Ceylon to describe his journey – 'I felt quite sick with longing for you' – and to tell her how he had taken the opportunity of a stopover in Malta to meet her husband Jimmy Young. 'He is a very dear person and I thought how right you – and to a great extent I – have always been in our feeling for him.' Jimmy had driven his car next to the plane when it had taxied and 'looked very wistful and rather sad and I suddenly wondered if these past terrible five years had not left all of us rather empty . . .'

He wrote again two days later: 'I think, beneath all preoccupation with the immediate, unceasingly of Ingaret, and [of] Ingaret and me. It is a reassuring, not a disturbing thinking . . . if your own inner-self allows it freely without fear or compromise, let us try to be together from next time onwards for always.' Back in Java, on 20 November, he wrote again, 'I cannot promise you perfection but I am prepared to accept without qualification your problem as part of the problem of my own life.' On 4 December he wrote again, passionately, but warned her that he could not see an early return because the situation was deteriorating ('enough damage was done by my being away'): he hoped to send 'Dul to London to report and asked Ingaret and Jimmy to put him up. He and his fellow-officers were reading Rilke in a translation sent to him by Ingaret.

She had apparently (in a letter now lost) described Jimmy's homecoming. Laurens replied, 'that was a very sad [letter] and I do feel for you and understand and send you all my love. But I do not think that in the nature of things it could be otherwise; that for this tangled fate [which] we have wished, and perhaps secretly willed for ourselves, it is right and proper to demand the utmost sadness from us. Jimmy is such a dear and decent person that your problem can never be anything but difficult and so sad and God knows it is a dearness and decency that cuts across the problem even from my remote end . . . [This problem] would have existed for the two of you even if I had never been there. Sooner or later you or Jimmy will have had a demand from your own inner dignity, a summoning for explanation and justification . . . My work is terrific and I feel very sad about life here. The misery is endless . . . I am glad I came back to it and I am also sorry and damn angry I left you.'[26]

It seems evident that Ingaret was in love with Laurens yet still felt affection for Jimmy. Perhaps she was not certain in her mind that she could rely on Laurens. As for Laurens, he may have been in love with Ingaret, but he was not in a hurry to resume his life in Europe.

6

The Colonel

LAURENS HAD INDEED returned to a fast-deteriorating situation. The Dutch authorities, notwithstanding Laurens's visit to The Hague and his broadcast, were increasingly disposed to reassert their colonial authority, and were bitterly furious with the British (and particularly with Christison and Laurens) for frustrating them. The nationalists effectively controlled large parts of Java and Sumatra. A serious episode at Sourabaya in early November, when Brigadier Mallaby was killed and heavy fighting ensued, with 400 Allied casualties and 6,000 Indonesians killed, finally convinced Mountbatten that the British could not attempt to restore Dutch rule by force.[1] The film actor turned best-selling author, Dirk Bogarde, wrote vividly about a thinly-disguised Java during this period in his novel *A Gentle Occupation* (1980). The Dutch-speaking Bogarde was also in the Intelligence Corps in Java after the war, though he never met Laurens. His novel refers to various episodes, such as the murder of Mallaby, the massacre of passengers on a crashed Dakota, and the provocative extension of the British military enclave in Batavia. It was a dangerous place, even inside the British compound – Laurens mentioned to Ingaret that he had been walking in his own garden in early morning when two bullets whistled past his head: 'In my job, the war is certainly not over.'[2]

The atmosphere of these times is glimpsed in the diary kept by Lt.-Col. Bryan Hunt, a senior Intelligence Corps officer (who incidentally notes on 18 November 1945 that 'L van der Post (ex-internment) has been made a half-colonel for political int. He knows Japan well and speaks Malay'). In a typical entry, for 17 March 1946, Hunt writes: 'Gen. Hawthorne says we can't leave with a clear conscience until the Dutch RAPWI are secured. The Dutch Army is in no state to fight a war; no HQ nor services organisation. Bandung more noisy with mortar bombs flopping about, but not near our mess. We really shall have to take over the whole town (we occupy only the north part) . . . R. Signals had a party to which I was invited with G1 (Bobby), Pip Bogaerde (ADC) etc., then played tennis at GOC's house, followed by awful film and dancing. His parties are awful, so formal . . . That woman of his (M) hangs around, whereas she should be in jail . . . It creates such a bad feeling among the Dutch. H. has interesting sex habits.' (This was precisely the background to Bogarde/Bogaerde's novel.)[3]

There was in effect a private war raging between the Dutch (and their supporters) and the Indonesians. The British had to commit more and more troops in a hopeless attempt to maintain law and order; Christison warned Mountbatten that his men in Sourabaya were virtually besieged. The only encouraging development was that, following the mutual shock inspired by the bloodshed there, the Indonesians formed a new Cabinet led by Sjahrir, whom Laurens always greatly respected, and also containing Sukarno and Mohammed Hatta, which could no longer be dismissed by the Dutch as being pro-Japanese. The Dutch indicated they were willing to talk, but it soon emerged that extremists on both sides were beyond the moderates' control. Sjahrir was nearly assassinated and Sukarno and Hatta retreated to safety. Co-ordination between the Dutch authorities in Batavia and in The Hague seemed non-existent. Laurens could only persevere with his mediation, increasingly trusted by the moderate Indonesian nationalists and increasingly distrusted by the Dutch of nearly all complexions: the fact that he spoke Dutch and was of largely Dutch descent can hardly have helped. In his official Report he allowed himself to refer to 'the unscrupulous, ungrateful and scurrilous campaign conducted by the Dutch' against the British exercise in December to enlarge the Batavia enclave, disarm civilians and attempt to impose a tolerable degree of order. Meanwhile the overriding concern was to complete the safe evacuation of the remaining internees.[4]

Laurens, after his return from London and in the throes of a correspondence with Ingaret which required him to think hard about the future, remembered that he had a family in South Africa. Astonishingly from the time of his release in mid-August until December he had not found time to write to his mother, and the evidence lies in his letter to Lammie dated 13 December 1945:

My Dearest Mother

I am writing this from Padang in Sumatra . . . This is the first letter I have written to you since my release. I have often wanted to but my work did not give me the time or freedom of mind to write you the letter I wanted to write. But today is my birthday and I can't think of a better day for thanking you for all you have been to me and the unselfish love you have given all of us.

I think you are the greatest person I have ever known and though my fate and character keep my life far from you, you are always very close to me. I never regretted my life in prison, thanks to your example of facing adversity and sorrow without ever flinching. I have not in the war done anything you need be ashamed of and in prison I worked hard to help others . . . Of course, when I came out, I longed to come home as I do every day, but I felt my duty was here. I am one of the few, perhaps the only one, who can help. I am so much part of the misery, the very great and tragic misery, that has been inflicted on these millions of people, that I have to stay and see it through . . . It has been a strange war but only people who have seen what the Japanese are really like as conquerors can appreciate what the world has been saved from . . .

Always
Laurens[5]

We have no means of knowing whether Laurens had written even at this time to his wife Marjorie or to his two children.

The British troops departed at the end of November 1946, and their exasperation is summed up in Laurens's description of the Seaforth Highlanders, who had been the first to arrive fourteen months before, chanting 'Merdeka!' – 'Independence!' – as they marched to the port. General Christison was replaced in due course by General Mansergh, of whom Laurens would later write in blistering terms, so much so that the Imperial War Museum contains indignant rebuttals by Mansergh's admirers. Laurens later consoled himself by quoting in response the alleged words of a certain Brigadier Campbell: 'It may surprise you, but I believe the General was impossibly jealous of you. Your role gave you something that the army could not deal with in terms of rank . . . He just could not accept that people could rate you more highly than himself.'[6] In Mansergh's and Campbell's conflicting opinions of Laurens, we can only speculate which was the more perceptive.

Life was made tolerable for Laurens by the arrival of Gilbert MacKereth early in 1946. MacKereth and his wife Muriel became dear and lifelong friends. He had had a successful record in the First World War and moved through the consular branch of the Foreign Office, including a spell in Abyssinia, an experience which he shared with Laurens.*

---

*By a strange coincidence, before the war he had been cured of a sight disorder by the pioneer psychologist Hugh Crichton-Miller, who was the grandfather of Laurens's eventual son-in-law.

The MacKereths were Laurens's neighbours, joining a small group of friends which included Laurens's secretary Sybil Bauer, 'Dul and Shri, and Colin MacLaren, the Consul/Information at First Secretary rank, who worked closely with Laurens. They were all under great pressure. ''Dul and I changed roles,' Laurens claimed afterwards.

''Dul, who was supposed to be my liaison with . . . the Dutch, more and more depended on me for his contacts with the Indonesians. It was sad to see how this noble and great hearted Indonesian, with his own vision of a raceless and classless Indonesia, gradually became so suspect to his own countrymen that they ceased seeing him of their own accord and instead made me the intermediary.' (We might wonder about this, since 'Dul was dead when Laurens wrote it.) At the same time, Laurens noted, his own Dutch friends dropped away from him.

Sir Archibald Clark Kerr had been sent out as British Ambassador. He and MacKereth put together, in March 1946, an agreement between the Indonesians and the Dutch, but it was not ratified in The Hague and Sjahrir's position was consequently weakened. Sukarno now emerged from the shadows, even as Laurens continued to have faith in Sjahrir, with whom he felt an indefinable affinity. In October 1946 both the Foreign Office and The Hague decided to attempt another conference between the Dutch and the Indonesians, as a last chance to recover the initiative after the failure of Clark Kerr's agreement. Lord Killearn, who had been British Ambassador in Cairo during the war, came out from London and over four weeks mediated the Linggadjati Agreement which was to precede the withdrawal of the British forces on 30 November. It would have been an appropriate moment for Laurens to leave, but he chose to stay on as Military Attaché. At this point MacKereth asked Laurens to write the Official Report on the British Occupation. It took him three weeks: a copy of this document sat, unopened, or so Laurens says, in Laurens's Aldeburgh house until he came upon it in the 1980s.[7]

The pressure of separation was beginning to tell on both Ingaret and Laurens throughout 1946. Vilified by the Dutch and increasingly distrusted even by those in the British military who disliked his sympathy for the nationalists, Laurens was heavily dependent on his small circle of friends: Muriel MacKereth, he later wrote, 'gave me a kind of care and affection that I had been denied for so long . . . Without her I do not think that I could have taken the increasing rejection, and ultimately hatred, that was hurled at me by the Dutch.' From Sybil, he had the loyalty, and perhaps more, which he also needed – letters from his colleagues who had returned home often contained jesting references to Sybil. He played tennis with Gilbert MacKereth, who was a former Oxford Blue. At one point, he later recalled, he was so weary that he began to drink heavily, as in prewar days, until he recognised the danger: 'Such a feeling of horror went through me that from that moment on I have avoided spirits like the plague . . .'[8]

It is hardly surprising that he and Ingaret felt the strain. In March 1946, she told him ecstatically that her divorce from Jimmy was in process, and that under a new law she would be free in September. He wrote back to her with his plans to go back to South Africa 'to tidy up that side of my life' – but warned her that she must not hope for his return to England before June. Ingaret replied on 9 April, 'I have worked very hard in order to understand how to love you, Laurens, very hard indeed. I was just an ordinary, plain, little married woman who never conceived that I should not live happily ever after in my marriage. But when I didn't, and you came along, and strange new things happened . . . I was really unprepared.' She had by now discovered that Laurens had throughout the war been describing her as his sister: 'Darling, never call me your sister again, will you? I have got quite an obsession about it . . . I do long and long for your return.'

Laurens replied on 26 May: 'You ask and I say yes, for ever and always . . . I sleep alone . . . and I think indefinitely of a girl whom I used to call my sister. She is still called so because of a hangover from the past . . .' Warning that he could not see a date for his return, he went on, 'As far as I am concerned, Batavia is most moral. All my love, and when you are ready, I am, but I am not coming back to London unless it is to 13 Cadogan Street with you, and certainly not to hide out in a Swiss hotel.'

The letters went to and fro throughout 1946, most of them from Ingaret. She was becoming more desperate and lonely: Jimmy had moved out; she was trying to write plays, she worried about a new lodger in Cadogan Street, she suggested that it would be all right if Laurens returned to the house; she wondered whether to rent a flat in the south of France and she added, unconvincingly, 'I do not regret this parting between us. It has had an invaluable contribution to make.'

Ever since Laurens's quick visit to London in autumn 1945, Ingaret had been totally committed to him. She sent him dozens of almost incoherently passionate letters, many of which he ignored. She often said that she understood that neither of them was quite 'ready' and sometimes, nearly in despair, told Laurens that she almost wanted to go back to her husband Jimmy. She could not understand why Laurens was delaying his return so long, nor why he wrote so rarely, whether to her or to his family. 'Perhaps, my darling, there is never going to be room in your life for me.'

Laurens wrote from hospital, where he had dengue fever, 'I am incapable of writing duty letters to you.' He added that he was to become Military Attaché and that he might be going on a mission to Australia. 'I have thought it over a lot and the best thing of all is for me to keep out of England and the worse thing of all for us would be a game of hide and seek on the Continent. You will have to, I am afraid, work this out alone – I will confuse both you and Jimmy, as I did in the past, if I came near you. So I do not propose coming back to England for a long time – i.e. not until you sound the all-clear . . .' He and Ingaret then started to reproach each other about other lovers. But Laurens added, 'All I want is that when this phase of my life has come to its logical end, to go away with you somewhere into the most profound silence, and find out with you what we must. *Voilà tout –*'.

Evidently still preoccupied with Java, he said he did not have time to write as often as she did. He was still not offering her the precise commitment she was pleading for; as a married man in name he was unable to marry Ingaret even when, or if, he freed himself of his war.[9] In September 1946 Laurens went to Australia, and was away from Java for three weeks. He never said afterwards why such a trip was professionally necessary, and the best explanation may be the most frivolous, as remembered many years later by his colleagues. The Australian Navy was in port and apparently it was decided that 'Lawrie' was looking tired and in need of a holiday. He was lured on board to a cocktail party, diverted to the Captain's quarters, and when he looked through the porthole he saw to his horror that the ship was moving. 'Where are we going?' he is supposed to have asked: 'Australia!' replied his captors. He had been shanghaied, and it would be three weeks before he got back to Java, full of enthusiasm about Australia in his letters to Ingaret. There was no suggestion that the visit to Australia was part of an official mission.

But the letters are still tense. 'I will try to write more often. You are quite rightly irritated with me . . .' He was still trying to explain why he had told the POWs that Ingaret was his sister. He defended himself by lashing out about an alleged Belgian lover – and asked why she had not congratulated him on his OBE, which he had just been awarded for his 'War Services': the citation did not clarify whether this referred to the POW camps or to his subsequent role in Java. For the first time he talked of returning home next April by way of South Africa and rejected his old friend Enslin du Plessis's apparent argument that he should have come back already: 'You want more time on your own, dear: and anyway what does Enslin expect me to do when I get back, join the *Argus*? Bah!'[10]

On 21 December Laurens was once again apologising for his failure to write, explaining that he was overworked, protesting that he had not had a cigarette or a glass of beer for six months, worrying about Ingaret's sad letters. One of Ingaret's surviving letters casts an interesting light on the mystery of Laurens's true rank and also on his domestic arrangements: 'When I got your bank's monthly account, there was no pay for last month. Perhaps you gave other instructions when you took back those little pay dockets that I gave you. Till now they have been paying you as a Captain as usual. Now they have not paid you at all.'

She had to wait for another nine months to see him again, and she never knew how nearly she lost him at the end.

In April 1947 she sent him details of her generous divorce settlement. She said that she had dinner with Jimmy after he had married his new wife Molly. 'I remember how you never wrote to your own family. And how their letters remained unopened for days. I expect mine go through the same fate . . . Perhaps to ask for a letter after six years of silence is too much . . . I love you so much but it only makes me sad.'[11]

Laurens may have had his own way of coping with the bachelor life. Bill Drower, who was a colleague in the Batavia consulate in 1946–47, remembered how Laurens's secretary Sybil, whom everyone liked, came to him one day in tears and said, 'Laurens has done me wrong, he's made me promises and promises, I'm in terrible trouble, I don't know if I'm going to have a baby . . .'[12]

Laurens left Java at the end of May 1947, nearly two years after the war had ended. After completing his mammoth report for MacKereth, he travelled inland with Sjahrir and his Consulate colleague Colin MacLaren, and was charmed by a meeting with Sukarno, who arranged for him and MacLaren to visit the ancient Buddhist site at Boroboedor. It turned out to be a deeply regenerative experience for him, reminding him, he later said, that the Indonesian values were superior to those of Dutch materialism. Laurens recognised that the secret of Sukarno's authority, and his potential supremacy, lay in his extraordinary gift of rhetoric: he also guessed that the Indonesian leadership would remain united.[13]

Remembering this tour fifty years later, Colin MacLaren, the First Secretary, who worked daily with Laurens in Batavia during 1946–47, emphasised how Laurens had established excellent contacts with the Indonesian nationalist leaders. Hatta, they felt, was the brightest, Sukarno was handsome and charismatic but not so intelligent. There was no special relationship between Mountbatten and Laurens, said

MacLaren, who liked Laurens but reckoned he had 'a Jesus Christ complex', somehow believing that he had a special role to play in this impossible situation; he afterwards thought that in *The Admiral's Baby* Laurens had put himself disproportionately at the centre of events. Another of the Batavia diplomatic team, Lanham Tichener, was more sceptical. On 16 December 1947 he wrote to MacLaren from London: 'I still have very mixed views about [Laurens] – I think he's a mixture of saintliness and a fake . . . the two qualities are often to be found in the same body . . .' By contrast, the same month MacKereth wrote to MacLaren to tell him that they had successfully lobbied the Foreign Office to adjust Laurens's OBE to the much more prestigious CBE (Commander of the British Empire): 'No man deserved it more . . . He is a lovable creature and I long to see him at peace with himself . . .'[14]

Early in 1947 MacKereth had warned Laurens that he and Muriel were being recalled at the end of British occupation: he suggested that it was time for Laurens, too, to leave. The two men knew that, with the Linggadjati Agreement still not ratified, time was running out for a peaceful resolution. Laurens exerted himself to write to everyone he knew in positions of influence to alert them of the dangers ahead – to start 'a kind of whispering campaign' – but his morale was not helped when the Foreign Office sent out an official to 'screen' him.[15]

What Laurens's colleagues and friends may not have realised was that the question-mark over his true status had been raised again, this time by the army bureaucrats. It started on 20 March 1946 with a note about him from an illegible Colonel at headquarters: 'The above officer has received no Army pay since his release from POW camp in August 45' (one wonders how on earth Laurens had been able to survive on zero income). Alarm bells sounded. The Officers Accounts Branch of India Command in Meerut replied on 10 April, requiring details to confirm Laurens's posting to Christison's staff and the date and purpose of his trip to London and The Hague. On 3 May the GOC AFNEI was writing (copy to the War Office London), 'It has come to notice that the present position of No. 148089 Lt.-Col. van der Post, IC, GSOI (POLINT) at this HQ, is irregular.' After he had reported to Admiral Patterson, 'Lt.-Col. van der Post's existence was subsequently brought to the notice of both the Supreme Allied Command and Gen. Sir William Slim, then C. in C. ALFSEA. It is understood that on the orders of the latter, Lt.-Col. van der Post was posted to this HQ in his present capacity. The authority for this, however, is not known, and no posting order can be traced. Similarly, no casualty for this officer's promotion to Lt.-Col. appears to have been published, and BAPO Meerut states that his office has no record of Lt.-Col. van der Post . . . It can thus be seen that considerable regularisation is necessary.' The General asked that, apart from sorting out urgently all allowances and pay due, 'the War Office be asked to clarify the position regarding rank held by Van der Post during his captivity'. This was followed by a flurry of signals between the various Army bureaucrats.

In other words, the Army in 1946 spotted that there was something odd about Laurens and his rank. The simplest explanation for this latest embarrassment for Laurens (for such it must have been – he would have been dreading this since 1942) was that General Slim had fixed his Indian Army Commission and rank as Temporary Lt.-Col. in 15 Indian Army Corps in October 1945 in Kandy, but had failed or forgotten to send through the necessary 'casualties', in the Army's curious phrase. The problem with this is that the only source for Slim's intention is Laurens himself, writing many years later.[16] The Army today remains adamant that it has no 'chitty' in confirmation of Laurens's promotion. It is also strange that Laurens seems to have waited for many months before the problem of his pay was noticed by his Adjutant – especially at a time when Ingaret was worrying him about money.

But it was the same Brigadier Field who had sent Laurens off with Special Mission 43 in February 1942, who re-emerged in 1948, and took a hand in bringing the mystery to a conclusion. In a letter from Nanking, where he was Military Attaché, dated 12 March 1948, he replied to what appears to have been an appeal from Laurens for help to sort out Paul Vogt's position as well as his own. 'I can assure you that I did everything, within the limits of my English and my powers of recollection, to put right the difficulties which you describe to me. I must admit that the legalistic attitude which someone is adopting never occurred to me or anyone else in Java at the time' – which suggests that Field may indeed have promoted Laurens 'in the field'. The first objection to this is that in his letter to Ingaret in August 1942 Field had made no reference to it, and the second is that Laurens never claimed in the years ahead that he had been granted the honour, sung throughout the ages, of promotion on the field of battle, which would be uncharacteristic.[17]

During that same month, March 1948, the War Office dug up another possible irregularity: the Army Council started to investigate the status of Special Mission 43 in 1942. Nichols, now promoted as a Group-Captain in Essex, was asked, no doubt to his astonishment, whether he knew of 'details of its formation, command arrangements, role and any orders given to the Mission to surrender or to continue fighting after the [Dutch] capitulation . . . The Council is particularly anxious to know whether No. 43 Special Mission existed as a properly organised force with orders to fight on in Java after the Dutch surrender.' Air Vice Marshal Sir Paul Maltby chipped in with the unhelpful though no doubt accurate recollection that Allied HQ at the time 'had no knowledge of van der Post's function other than as an escape organisation, that we had no W/T [radio] link with him, that the instructions to continue fighting were not sent by us to him . . .' On 8 April 1948 Nichols simply said he didn't know what they were talking about, and the inquiry was dropped.

Instead, the line was drawn when Laurens was told by another illegible official on 12 June 1948 that the *bona fides* of Special Mission 43 had been at last agreed: Captain Vogt's status was confirmed and a pension would be paid; and the War Office have 'all your queries well in hand and they told me a day or so ago that the question of your rank of Lt.-Colonel from 23 Feb. 1942 has been approved.'[18]

So, at long last, Laurens was a Lieutenant-Colonel, backdated to the day he took command of Special Mission 43. What had happened behind the scenes? It may be guessed that there had been much confusion as the Indian Army, following India's independence in August 1947, had reassigned its British officers in various directions. The relevant records are missing. Someone must surely have pulled strings, called for the papers, done the deal. Ironically, or perhaps by no coincidence, Laurens had officially left the Army on 20 March 1948, a few days after Brigadier Field's letter.

Back in Java, the Linggadjati Agreement failed. Under its terms, brokered by Britain, the Indonesian authority over Java and Sumatra was recognised while the Dutch and the Indonesians agreed to a federal United States of Indonesia. Technically, it was eventually ratified in March 1947, but there was ever less hope of its being implemented. The Dutch, as Laurens and his friends had been warning for many months, were in no mind to cede their authority in the East Indies, as Britain was doing in India and Burma. Laurens, with the departure of the MacKereths and what he observed as the growing despair of 'Dul and Shri, felt increasingly abandoned. He was convinced that the Dutch were going to present the Indonesians with an unacceptable ultimatum which would precipitate civil war. He was right. On 27 May the Dutch did just that, in contravention of Linggadjati, and on 20 July launched a military strike. Western conciliation failed, and the UN Security Council was unable to arrange a cease-fire; Britain reluctantly imposed an arms embargo. Before this, Laurens had been given permission to leave. As he afterwards described it, Sjahrir and the Indonesian leadership garlanded him with presents and kind words, unlike the Dutch. They had appointed 'Dul Acting-Governor-General – a stooge status, as a distressed Laurens saw it. He left at the end of May 1947 and took Sybil with him for a holiday in Singapore.

Sjahrir was outmanoeuvred and was sent off to the United Nations. Amir Sjarifuddin became Prime Minister in July 1947, as the Dutch launched a military offensive. The UN called for a ceasefire which, under American and British pressure, the Dutch felt obliged to accept. Sukarno replaced Sjarifuddin with Hatta. Throughout 1948 the situation was chaotic and explosive, with civil war threatening. A Communist insurrection was defeated, and the Government thereby assured itself of American support. The Dutch attempted a second 'police action', capturing Sukarno and his Cabinet. There was civil war, and Sjarifuddin was executed – Laurens afterwards claimed that he died with Laurens's gift of a New Testament in his pocket. The Dutch were eventually compelled, largely by the Americans, to relinquish their claim to sovereignty in December 1949.[19] Laurens's earlier assessment of the situation in Indonesia had been proved correct, although he had long since vanished from the scene.

Sir Gilbert MacKereth, as he became, had incurred the displeasure of London for his advocacy of Indonesian nationalism and was in effect exiled, being sent as Ambassador to Colombia; he retired in 1953. General Sir Philip Christison became GOC Northern Command in 1946 and retired in 1949. Admiral Sir Wilfred Patterson became Admiral Commanding Reserves in 1947 and also retired in 1949. Field Marshal Sir William Slim became Chief of the Imperial General Staff 1948-52 and Governor-General of Australia 1953-60. Lord Louis Mountbatten successively became the last Viceroy to India, the Fourth Sea Lord, and Chief of the Defence Staff (1959-65); he was assassinated in Ireland by the IRA in 1979. Clark-Kerr became Lord Inverchapel and served as Ambassador in Washington. 'Dul was forced to move to Europe, where Shri died young.

Sybil and Laurens never met again, though she sometimes sent him a cheerful postcard.[20] Laurens never returned to Java.

PART TWO

'I have remembered more than I have seen . . .'

Benjamin Disraeli

7

'My Mother's Country'

THERE ARE FANTASIES, mysteries, evasions in Laurens's life from the very beginning. It might be suggested that he inherited a family disposition to embroider; certainly he inherited a family 'myth' of its origins. He probably never challenged the stories he absorbed from his mother. In this he was not untypical of a wider Afrikaner society, which was always fearful of what it might discover if it searched too far back. There might, for example, be a non-European bloodline which threatened disgrace in the apartheid years. The Free State is a remote and isolated part of the world. Then again, Laurens, eleventh of a family of thirteen living siblings, plus an older step-brother, may have felt underacknowledged. His father died when he was only seven. The defence against a fear of inadequacy can sometimes be invention and fantasy.

Laurens's books, always autobiographical whether fiction or non-fiction, make much of his mixed descent, from a mother of whom he wrote 'Africa is my mother's country', and a father who was 'of Europe'. From this Laurens claimed a middle ground which he was later to occupy so profitably. As he ventured into the interior of Africa in a 1949 Comet, he wrote, 'Somehow my life must find a way out between my father's exile and my mother's home.'[1] He had understood the tensions which would occupy his long and famous life.

His real family background he never knew. He wrote of a paternal background from the minor aristocracy of Holland; of an Afrikaner mother whose origins went back to the very beginnings of white settlement in South Africa; he suggested, more and more strongly as the years went by, that he had a large strain of French-Huguenot blood; he wrote of his father as a senior statesman and barrister, who fought the British in the Anglo-Boer War and was exiled for it; his first memories, he said, were of a Bushman nurse called Klara; his maternal grandfather occupied a majestic farm on the edge of the Karoo and had fought the British in 1848.

A great deal of this is at best exaggeration. His father, who arrived in South Africa in 1859 at the age of three, came from a Dutch family of no discernible distinction, and he had so little sense of exile that he never bothered to go 'home', even on holiday, although he could have afforded to do so and to take his large family with him. Laurens's grandfather, who had moved into town from the farm before he was born, never fought against the British – on the contrary, he appears secretly to have harboured pro-British sympathies, as in the Boer War, when the immediate family was identified with the Boer cause. And there is no evidence for Laurens's stories that he had a Bushman nanny who would influence the future course of his life.[2]

In Laurens's portrait of his parents, developed in many books and interviews, he relied on hearsay, anecdote, and family legend mediated by his mother. He was concerned to show that he had a special and distinguished background, and writes of his father and mother in respectful and romantic terms; yet, strangely, he fails to capture essential truths about two fascinating characters.

His mother's African background was more complex than Laurens ever dreamed. She may not have known it either, since the thread of family memories would have been broken when her own mother had been orphaned as a child in the Liebenberg Massacre. Myths took the place of facts, but today it is possible to trace back to the beginning the forerunners of the Lubbe family into which Maria-Magdalena, always known as Lammie, was born. Out of a bewildering mass of detail, three basic points emerge.

The first is that Lammie was born of an absolutely typical Afrikaner genetic cocktail of Dutch, German, French, Scandinavian and 'other' genes, in that order. Laurens must have been about twenty per cent German in origin compared with seven per cent French; he had no British blood, though he would choose to become an honorary and nationalised Briton. Second, Laurens had only a small infusion of French-Huguenot blood on his mother's side. Many of the half-million Protestant Huguenots who had fled from persecution in Catholic France before and after the Revocation of the Treaty of Nantes in 1685, had moved to Holland or England, from where a small number, usually the lower classes, had emigrated to South Africa. There they often flourished, becoming a superior element in the new 'Afrikaner' society, perhaps because they arrived in family units, unlike many of the Dutch and German immigrants. Their names have survived: Du Plessis, Du

Toit, Le Grange, Labuschagne, and others, though soon pronounced in a most un-French manner. As he grew older, Laurens increasingly insisted that his bloodline was not German and Dutch (as it was), but French and Huguenot. His grandmother, he wrote in *Venture to the Interior*, 'was not Dutch, but came of a French family'. In fact even the little Huguenot blood Laurens could claim was not entirely respectable. He never knew, for instance, of his ancestor Maria-Magdalena Mouton, or her aunt, Maria, who in 1714 disgraced the family by taking a slave lover with whom she killed her husband. In the style of the day, the slave was put to death by impalement, in a manner too gruesome to describe, and Maria was tortured by branding irons and then strangled.[3]

Although his grandmother's splendid name – Elizabeth Wilhelmina Paulina Dediée Zaalberg – may have suggested to Laurens an aristocratic as well as a French root, all these names carry a family reference, and there is definitely no reason to believe that the name 'Dediée' proves a French background. In his old age Laurens would declare that the Afrikaners were all descendants of the Huguenots – which is both nonsense, because the Huguenot immigrants had been so few, but at the same time true, because few Afrikaners today do not contain a smidgeon of Huguenot blood in their veins.[4]

Third, and most dramatically, Laurens could if he had wished have traced his ancestry directly back to a Hottentot 'Princess' – and beyond her, to her mother, who was probably Bushman* – giving a particular *frisson* to his future obsession with the Bushmen, and to a late book of interviews whose title calls him a 'White Bushman'.

During the earliest days of the Dutch presence at the Cape of Good Hope, Jan van Riebeeck had arrived in 1652 to set up a supply station for the Dutch vessels sailing to the East Indies; from this modest beginning proceeded the establishment of the white population of South Africa. Relations with the nearest indigenous 'Hottentots', locally known as 'Strandlopers' because they lived next to the beach, were difficult, and van Riebeeck took into his household the daughter of a local 'Hottentot' chief, niece of the senior chief, attractive and so pale-skinned that she was said to have a Bushman mother. Krotoa, renamed Eva, learned

---

*For non-South African readers, it may be explained, in broadest summary, that the Bushman and the 'Hottentot' were both the 'original' peoples of South Africa; they must always be distinguished, on grounds of language group, physique, and hunter or herder culture. After the arrival of the black Bantu speakers and the Europeans, the Bushmen managed to survive longer because they retreated into less accessible regions. Today, terms such as 'Hottentot' are widely considered offensive.[5]

Dutch and became a valued interpreter for the Governor. Van Riebeeck needed to develop trading relations with the 'Strandlopers'. The European tradition was to use marriage as a diplomatic tool, and he therefore arranged for Eva to marry the junior surgeon in his party, a certain Pieter van Meerhoff, in a ceremony which may be described as South Africa's first 'state wedding', and indeed the country's first sanctioned multi-racial marriage. Van Meerhoff, from Denmark, was one of South Africa's earliest explorers, opening up routes into Namaqualand. There were three children, but thereafter the story takes a darker turn. Van Meerhoff was sent to Madagascar in 1667 on an expedition, probably to hunt for slaves, only to be killed there. Eva became notorious in Cape Town as an alcoholic prostitute, and was exiled to Robben Island, whose prison, three hundred years later, was to house Nelson Mandela. She died in 1674 and was buried in a common grave above which now stands Cape Town's 'Groote Kerk', the mother church of white Afrikanerdom. Perhaps she may be seen, romantically and unhistorically, as the South African Pocahontas.

Eva was one of Laurens's ancestors. There is nothing particularly unusual in a mixed-race background, though Laurens certainly never knew of his rather surprising connection. Afrikaners have never denied their responsibility for the Coloured population of South Africa which today totals several million. But there is a certain fascination in discovering that Laurens and his family are descended from the woman who is today often spoken of as 'the Mother of the Nation'.[6]

Apart from the Lubbes, Laurens's seventeenth and eighteenth century ancestors were modest immigrants of German or Dutch origin. There is a distinction between the 'Voortrekkers', who have been greatly glamorised in South African history, and the 'Trekboers'. The Voortrekkers were Afrikaners determined to travel north beyond the authority of British rule and establish for themselves a kind of independence. The Trekboers had the simpler, apolitical intention of crossing the Orange River in search of better farming country, and once they had found it they were content to settle. They might have no animus against the British, and indeed were often appreciative of British administration.

The Liebenberg families who made up their 1836 Expedition were pre-eminently Voortrekkers. They travelled north as far as present-day Parys, near the Vaal River, where – historians disagree on the detail – they might have made their nightly *laager* over-confidently. They were attacked by the Matabele, a northern branch of the Zulus, at dawn and were wiped out, except for a few children who had been sent off to the river with their nursemaid because they were disturbing their parents. The maid hid with them and they were eventually found by scouts from another group of Trekkers. The records differ, but it appears that four small children survived the massacre, one of whom was Elizabeth Louisa Liebenberg; she later married Andries Petrus Lubbe, who, according to family legend, was a boy in the party of Trekboers which rescued them – this cannot be true because he was far too young. The Liebenberg Massacre has always been remembered in Afrikaner history, perhaps because of rumours that white children had been abducted by the natives, always a situation to provoke horror in settler societies, in America as in South Africa. Laurens often wrote and spoke about this Massacre, though in *Venture to the Interior* he mistakenly located it in Louis Trichardt, hundreds of miles to the north.[7]

A. P. Lubbe came of largely German stock and settled in the Fauresmith district of the Orange Free State, sixty miles north of the Orange River. Laurens's mother would later describe how A. P. Lubbe went farming at Driekoppenspan, on the main road to the Kimberley diamond fields, a fortunate location which enabled the Lubbes to develop a profitable business breeding horses and supplying them for transport. He bought his farm from a local Griqua* called Jacob Jaars by the simple tactic of allowing Jaars to buy top hats, mirrors, liquor and eau-de-cologne on Lubbe's account from the local shop-keeper. 'Oupa' Lubbe and his farms played an important role in Laurens's childhood. In her memoirs Lammie – Lubbe's daughter and Laurens's mother – does not attempt to deny that the first farm 'was paid for with brandy'. Jacob Jaars descended into poverty in old age, and Lammie remembered how he used to call at what had been his own farm, apparently in good humour, for a regular shot of brandy. Another farm was bought from the Griquas in the same manner. It was not uncommon for the Afrikaner Trekkers to acquire their land in this way.

Lammie, in an unpublished memoir which she worked on for many years, but of which only fragments have survived, writes of her child-hood in Driekoppenspan as the happiest days of her life. 'Father was a wonderfully good-hearted man – kindly towards poor children or orphans and people in need. But he had a quick temper and something

---

*A group of half-castes who had been moved to the north bank of the Orange River as a buffer between the black tribes and the white settlers. The British later moved most of them again, with the agreement of their leader Adam Kok, many miles east to Kokstad, though some of them stayed in and around Philippolis.[8]

inexplicable made him very impatient when it was time to be off by cart, and then the horses felt it . . .' He was greatly soothed by music, and Lammie would play the harmonium or the piano for him: a Boer farmer who owned both these instruments must have been doing well. Lubbe later dedicated Driekoppenspan to horses and bought the 3,000-morgen (about 6,000-acre) sheep farm of Boesmansfontein, ten miles outside Philippolis, to which he moved his family. He bought Boesmansfontein not from the Griquas for brandy and top hats, as the family used to say, but from the London Missionary Society, which had at one stage thought of moving the Griquas to that site. Lammie, born in February 1867, had mixed feelings about the move, but enjoyed 'an orchard with a huge mulberry tree that gave me enormous pleasure. The branches were high and wide – lovely to sit on and the tree bore wonderful big mulberries that I would gorge myself upon to my heart's content.' (That mulberry tree should be remembered.)[9]

The more important base for Laurens's family, Fauresmith, was founded in the late 1840s and one of the founding fathers was A. P. Lubbe's own father, Andries Johannes Lubbe. Curiously, Laurens never mentioned that his great-grandfather was a prominent and long-remembered leader of the Trekboers. The explanation may be that Lammie, like the rest of her family, never showed much interest in Andries Johannes or the Fauresmith branch – another indication that Laurens depended heavily on his mother for the family history.

Fauresmith is today a small town south of Bloemfontein and Kimberley, but when the first Free State Volksraad (the Orange Free State Parliament) met in 1854 to settle on a capital, Fauresmith only just lost out to Bloemfontein, and it then gained in importance when the major diamond field of Jagersfontein was discovered a few miles away. The van der Posts acquired many acres of farmland not because they were particularly keen on farming but because they had hopes of finding diamonds.[10]

This was a period of confusing frontier history. The Voortrekkers were aiming ever northwards, while the Trekboers were happy to settle down. There is a problem with Laurens's version of his grandfather's political affiliation, which might cast light on Laurens's own future career. Laurens several times claimed, following the family mythology, that the very young A. P. Lubbe had fought against the British in the Battle of Boomplaas, a skirmish between Sir Harry Smith's forces and some republican Boers in 1848. Lammie, in her handwritten manuscript, corrects this to say that her father was 'present' at Boomplaas. Almost certainly, Lubbe belonged to the *pro*-British party of Boers, some of whom were present at Boomplaas though only in moral support in the rear, and was secretly hostile to the Boer 'rebels', led by Andries Pretorius, on this occasion firmly despatched by Sir Harry Smith with a loss of only two officers and twenty men among the British, and an estimated forty Boers.[11]

This is the first hint of Laurens's grandfather's pro-British sympathies, which would be sustained though concealed throughout his long lifetime. Fifty years later he and his family, including Lammie, would find themselves on opposite sides and the van der Post family would represent a classic example of the way Afrikaner families were divided by the Anglo-Boer War. None of this was later acknowledged by Laurens, but as a young boy he was close to his grandfather and he might have imbibed from him his first sympathies for England, the Crown and the Empire, in opposition to the views of the rest of his family.

After the acquisition of Boesmansfontein A. P. Lubbe prospered and acquired other farms which he would eventually parcel out among his children. His first wife, Elizabeth Louisa, died in 1897, and under their joint Will these farms were divided among his family; Lammie inherited Wolwekop, a 3,000-morgen grazing farm which had been part of Boesmansfontein.[12] Lubbe kept a farm called Langkuil, a town house in Philippolis, and carried on in Boesmansfontein as though it was still his and not by rights the property of his son Hendrik. He had given up his parliamentary seat by 1891.

The European Father

IN THE MEANTIME, a young Dutch teacher called Christiaan Willem Hendrik van der Post had arrived in the district as a lowly tutor on various farm schools, and among his pupils in 1878 were A. P. Lubbe's two daughters, Johanna and Maria-Magdalena, always known as Lammie, who was then eleven. Laurens's story that his father was paid £1 a month is absurd, since that was the going rate at the time for a black house servant. 'CWH', or 'Van', as he would be known, moved briefly to teach at Grey College in Bloemfontein in 1879 at £200 a year, and then for two years became headmaster in the local school at Fauresmith. In 1885 he married Johanna, sometimes called Anna. She gave birth to a son, Hendrik (Henk), a year later, but seems never to have recovered her health. She was ill for three years and, nursed by her sister, she died on 29 October 1888, aged twenty-six. The next year CWH married that sister, 'Lammie', who would give him thirteen more children.[1]

C.W.H. van der Post had arrived in Cape Town from Leiden, Holland, on 13 March 1859 at the age of three. His father was Hendrik Pieter van der Post, and the records describe his profession under the category of 'Street Seller/Retailer/Merchant/Middleman', and the reason for his emigration as 'deterioration of business'. This tallies with the family legend that Henrik Pieter had been compelled to leave Holland because of bankruptcy brought on by his honourable guarantee of the debts of a friend. Many Europeans who came to South Africa in this period would today be called economic migrants, but the van der Posts used to speak of themselves as coming of aristocratic stock who had fallen on hard times. Laurens was so convinced of this that his lifelong friend, William Plomer, would describe him without hesitation as 'one of the sons of an impoverished nobleman'.[2]

The Dutch genealogical records contradict this romantic tale. They reveal that, for at least two hundred years before the journey to South Africa, the van der Posts had been what may be described as lower-middle-class residents of Leiden, no doubt respectable, working as junior clerks in the municipality or as sextons, teachers, wool-carders. There still is a family legend that the original name was 'van der Does', whose representative, a simple soldier, so conducted himself in the defence of the *Noord-pos* (North Post) of Leiden in 1574, during the Dutch war of liberation, that Prince William of Orange granted him, at his request, the right to change his name to 'van der Post'. This story can only be apocryphal. There was in fact a famous Johan van der Does, a great humanist and scholar, a leader of the Dutch revolt against the Spanish, and a commander at Leiden – so why would the soldier want to change his name? The family has always believed that the 'van der Does' name was dropped when CWH's parents arrived in South Africa because the words can be mistaken for an obscenity in Afrikaans. At a family reunion in 1994, the tale, and the obscenity, were cheerfully repeated by CWH's last surviving daughter, Ella.[3] Further evidence of the van der Posts' aristocratic status is attached to a family crest, which still hangs on various family walls and boasts the inscription 'Postis Inornatus et Stabilis', presumably a reference to the heroic episode in Leiden in 1574. This becomes less convincing when it is realised that 40,000 Dutch families had crests, of whom only 400 could be described as aristocracy.

Hendrik Pieter arrived in South Africa with his wife, Elizabeth Dediée, and two young children. He did not prosper. He found work as a bank teller in Montagu in the Cape Colony, and went bankrupt again. His son CWH was almost entirely self-educated, and would become one of Afrikanerdom's early intellectuals, a successful law agent, an active politician, an author and translator, a fluent linguist and a stout advocate of the emerging Afrikaans language, not to speak of playing a principled role in the Anglo-Boer War, for which he suffered six years' exile to the Cape.

After his early years as a schoolteacher, CWH switched to the law, which brought him a successful and lucrative career. He was never a barrister or an advocate, as Laurens and the family believed, but a law agent. This required no great qualification, and was much less prestigious, but an accredited law agent could turn his hand to many things, from financial advice and share-dealing to conveyancing and auctioneering, from drawing up wills to debt collection. CWH was clearly very successful, building up a chain, based in Fauresmith, of four main branches and several subsidiaries in the south of the Orange Free State between 1885 and the outbreak of war in 1899. CWH's brother Willem managed to become a full attorney despite being blinded as a young man when, according to the family story, he and his friends got involved in a racial incident in the local black township.

CWH never extended his practice into the legal capital Bloemfontein. Fauresmith and Philippolis can easily sound remote and rural *dorps*, but this was an area of feverish diamond speculation, fuelled by the presence of the immensely rich Jagersfontein mine, and CWH and Willem did good business for that reason. CWH's closest friend, W. H. Beddy, was chairman of the diamond company, and CWH at one stage even offered to mortgage his wife's Wolwekop farm to enable another friend, manager at the nearby Koffiefontein mine, to buy dynamite and thereby ensure the continued running of the mine, at the outbreak of the Anglo-Boer War.[4]

Assertive, heavily-bearded, a self-made intellectual whose private passion was literature, this was the man whom Lammie married in 1889. More mysteries here suggest a family drama. On 7 October 1889, CWH wrote to his brother-in-law, Lourens Hermanus Fourie (after whom Laurens would one day be named), sending a message by hand of a clerk. He explains that he has been trying to send a message to Lammie, who is not at home in Boesmansfontein but is apparently at a place called Koksfontein. The clerk finds that her parents have just been there to fetch her back. CWH's associate, Gerrit Sem, subsequently informed him that, according to a certain Hendrik Strauss, 'It's going badly there [i.e. at Boesmansfontein]. The old man is perpetually enraged, and the treatment that the young lady is getting there is positively brutal [*gruwe-lyk* – a strong word suggesting violence]. I saw her, after the letter arrived there, in a very bad way indeed, and my feeling is that if Hendrik Strauss can say this then the situation must be grave indeed.'

What was going on? Had Lammie, aged twenty-two, tried to run away from home? Was her father assaulting her? Because he did not want her to marry CWH? Or because *she* did not want to marry CWH? At this time she seems to have been in love with a neighbour, four years younger than herself, called Thomas Visser, and although Visser would eventually become a successful doctor and politician, A. P. Lubbe may not have favoured the match, whereas he had presumably been happy to have CWH as the husband of his elder daughter Johanna. The truth will never be known, but perhaps the clues lie in the family relationships described in Laurens's second novel, *The Face Beside the Fire*, when Laurens would have been privy to Lammie's memoir. The episode is noteworthy because it is a harbinger of later strains and divisions in the family, in which the patriarchal A. P. Lubbe would be at odds with his daughter, his son-in-law, his own son, and much of the family.[5]

Some confirmation of a family crisis can be found in the singular circumstances attending the wedding of CWH and Lammie on 14 November 1889. The ceremony took place not in the Dutch Reformed Church in Philippolis, as might have been expected, but in the home of CWH's partner Gerrit Sem in Philippolis. It was on a Monday. The officiating minister was not Colin Fraser, the well-known Philippolis dominee, but a minister who rode over from Fauresmith. Lammie is described as being 'of Philippolis', not Boesmansfontein, which might suggest that she had left home.[6]

The honeymoon was in East London, and the first son of CWH's second marriage, Andries, was born in September 1890. There followed Elizabeth (known as Bets), Willem, Anna, Christiaan (Pooi) , Herman, Pauline, Hilda, who died in her second year, Maria (Marie), Emma, Lourens (Louwtjie), Kuno, and Ella.

CWH's legal practice prospered and, as was common in those days, being a big fish in a small pond, he went into politics. He became a member of the Volksraad in 1887 and was active there until October 1899, at the outbreak of the Anglo-Boer War. Unlike some of his colleagues, he rejected his right to exemption from military service and went off to join the war. Laurens's later claims that his father had been 'a kind of Prime Minister' of the Orange Free State are an exaggeration. He was briefly Chairman of the Volksraad in Bloemfontein from April 1896 to April 1897, but he was ill for much of that period and was eclipsed by his rivals. In 1897 he was not re-elected either to the Chair or to the Vice-Chairmanship. He was active in committees and delegations, a substantial political figure in that small world, but it was never on the cards that he would run for President, as Laurens later suggested. Laurens said, perhaps correctly, that his Dutch birth was held against him. CWH used to say that he was 'Dutch by birth, Afrikaans by adoption'. When Laurens afterwards wrote that his father had died 'of exile', he was romanticising, but it is probably fair to say that CWH was always an outsider, in the sense that he was conscious of his intellectual and cultural isolation in the *platteland* society in which he had chosen to lead his life.[7]

He would have had other networks to support him. There is no evidence to prove it, but it is likely that CWH was a Freemason. In those days Masonry was all-pervasive among the Free State 'Hollanders'. Many leading figures made no secret of their allegiance to this ostensibly secret society: Presidents Brand, Reitz and Pretorius of the Orange Free State, for instance, were Freemasons, as was General Louis Botha, the Transvaal Prime Minister, and CWH's partner Sem had been Master of the Lodge in Philippolis. That may help explain why CWH and Sem did not play the senior roles that might have been expected of them in the Dutch Reformed Church congregation in Philippolis. The web of Masonic connections may also explain some of the strange aspects of the wedding. No doubt CWH would have described himself as a Christian, but – like his son – he does not appear to have been devout; many years later Laurens told a friend that he could not remember his father ever attending church, though this was the unreliable recollection of a small child. In this CWH differed from Lammie, whose passionate religious sentiments would eventually take her out of the Dutch Reformed Church to the Seventh Day Adventists.[8] CWH's adventures in the forthcoming Anglo-Boer War strongly suggest Masonic links.

It is often said that the war of 1899–1902 became inevitable after the failure of the Jameson Raid of 1895, when the mining magnate Cecil Rhodes, with the connivance of the British Colonial Secretary, Joseph Chamberlain, tried to overthrow President Paul Kruger in his Transvaal Republic. The raid had brought the two Boer republics, the Transvaal and the Orange Free State, closer together. Chamberlain, increasingly determined to achieve, by force if necessary, his aim of a closer consolidation of South Africa, sent Sir Alfred Milner as his High Commissioner, his pro-consul, to Cape Town, and they persuaded the British Cabinet, vulnerable to the jingoism of the day, that war was necessary and inevitable. The British had a great shock. The Boers seized the initiative from the start, thanks to their superior mobility and marksmanship, but were eventually pushed back by the enormous numbers of troops which London was compelled to dispatch. Resisting an early surrender, many Boer commandos took up guerrilla warfare which persisted until the Vereeniging peace treaty of May 1902. By this time many thousands of Boer women and children had been sent into 'refugee camps', later to be termed 'concentration camps', where 20,000 would die – an atrocity which has never been forgotten by Afrikaners.[9] CWH played a significant and fascinating role in this war.

As war became inevitable, the ambivalence of the Trekboers' allegiances came to the fore again. Many of the settlers in the Free State, and particularly in the southern districts adjoining the Orange River, were not so enthusiastic for an encounter with the British. It is easy to assume that the Orange Free State was Afrikaner, but Bloemfontein, the capital, and some of the *dorps*, were substantially English in culture and language. So, when hostilities broke out in October 1899, the response of the Fauresmith and Philippolis districts was by no means unanimously pro-

Boer. There were divisions within families and the van der Posts were no exception. CWH, with Lammie's passionate support, was immediately committed to the cause against the British. He resigned his position as Dutch Consul, which exempted him from fighting, and, at the age of forty-three, went off to the war.

His worst experience was the minor battle of Blaauwdrai, when he was present at the death of his brother-in-law, Lourens Hermanus Fourie, said to have been the first Free Stater to die on Free State soil. He was devastated. Lourens Fourie was killed on 13 December 1899, and when CWH's eleventh child by Lammie was born on that same date in 1906 he was named Lourens, surely *in memoriam*. When the boy grew up he would change his name from the Germanic 'Lourens' to the relatively French 'Laurens', though his immediate family never accepted the change and always called him 'Lourens'.

CWH does not appear to have had much experience of the front line except for the shoot-out at Blaauwdraai when he had to command the Boer retreat. He was after all in his mid-forties and his skills were better employed in administration, tactical planning, dispersing the quarter-million pounds contributed by the Transvaal to the Free State, requisition of supplies and horses, and raising men for a commando when, at least in this part of the Free State, there was a widespread reluctance to fight. The critical battle of Magersfontein took place on 11 December. As the British advanced on Bloemfontein in overwhelming numbers, CWH, with a price of £500 on his head, slipped back through their lines after the capture of Fauresmith in March 1900 to join up with the main Boer forces.[10] By the end of March it looked as if the British had won and most Boers in the southern part of the Free State were, quite sensibly, prepared to give up. The Boers' traditional concept of a commando was that they set off for at best a couple of months and then returned to their farms. British rule in the past had not been too painful: what was the point of fighting a fruitless war?

But CWH, who had abandoned a profitable business and who could have claimed immunity both as a politician and as a consul, refused to give in. He spent the next months in the mountains on the run, sleeping out in the South African winter and certainly damaging his health. In September 1900, according to Lammie's memoir, President Kruger sent his best scout to accompany CWH through the lines to the Transvaal and install him as Commandant in Barberton, and also as Government Commissioner responsible for the women and children in the Eastern Transvaal. As General French advanced on the defence-less town, CWH went out to meet him, to prevent casualties and to surrender the town. He now knew that the game was up, and decided there was no point in further Boer resistance. CWH, who considered himself a gentleman, was disconcerted to be greeted by General French (who probably didn't agree) with a shout of 'Damn you!' Exasperated, CWH, who had been trying to save lives, replied, 'Damn yourself!', at which French threw him into gaol. He was rescued, according to Lammie's later account, by several English officers who had been courteously treated by CWH when prisoners, and who successfully urged French to treat him more civilly.

He then became involved in a mysterious relationship with Field Marshal Lord Roberts, the English Commander-in-Chief. Roberts was very senior in the Masonic hierarchy, as was his successor, Kitchener. As already noted, CWH was probably a Mason too. Unknown to anyone in his family, including his wife, the two men seem to have reached an understanding, with far-reaching consequences for CWH, as we shall see.[11]

CWH himself never knew of another, more disturbing aspect of this family-at-war. A. P. Lubbe, his father-in-law, out on the farm at Boesmansfontein, had been doing well, almost certainly selling horses to the British Army while managing to conceal his pro-British sentiments from his passionately pro-Boer children. They did not dream that he was also supplying the British with information. His postwar claim for compensation for damage and loss reveals not only that he disowned his son Hendrik for his Boer sympathies but that in the early months of the war he had been feeding a British Intelligence officer, Colonel Byng, with information on Boer commando movements.

On 23 June and then on 20 July 1903 Lubbe wrote to the British authorities pleading for compensation for damage to his farms: 'I am an old man of 73 years. I was never on Commando and never had anything to do with the War . . . I was always bitterly against the War . . . I had only one son, a married man of 47 years of age . . . I had absolutely nothing to do with him or his family . . . I have tried to persuade him (when he came on my farm with a patrol) to surrender, failing that I told him never to put his feet on my farm again.' Lubbe added that he had 'assisted the [British] columns with valuable and reliable information from time to time.'[12]

CWH, out on commando, had been sending his father-in-law friendly letters with details of Boer operations and plans. In all innocence he tells A. P. Lubbe on 30 January 1900 of the strength of his commando, its exact location and its plans to sabotage the railway line on the western front. On 6 February he writes again to tell him of Hendrik's military movements. It can never have entered his head that his father-in-law was not to be trusted. Hendrik, Lubbe's eldest son – Lammie's brother – would be shot and killed in an engagement with the British at Heen-en-Weer outside Fauresmith on 21 August 1901. Hendrik's own son Andries, aged only fifteen, witnessed his father's death, hit by an accidental bullet from his own men. The young Andries was traumatised and, inheriting Boesmansfontein from his dead father, eventually hanged himself on the farm in 1926 from a pear tree next to the Bushman springs, because he had made a cousin pregnant and, wrongly believing that this was a capital offence, decided to anticipate the verdict. The cemetery at Boesmansfontein, which still exists today, records the family tragedy.

Lubbe's second wife died in the Springfontein concentration camp after virtually the entire population of Philippolis had been moved there by the British. But Boesmansfontein, unlike many other farms, was left unscathed – her husband's reward for his services.[13]

When CWH went off to war, Lammie was left in Fauresmith with eight children. Her memoir, written years later in near-illegible Afrikaans (some of which has been lost by the family), casts fresh light on the experiences of Afrikaner women and children during the Anglo-Boer War. There was never any doubting Lammie's political persuasion, unlike her father's. In Fauresmith, the town was being looted by the British troops: this was where CWH's collection of 'old glass and porcelain, paintings, horns, native weapons and other items' was lost, presumably including his collection of Bushman artefacts. 'The English troops stormed the house, broke the windows, kicked open the doors and then set about demolishing the place. Our beautiful Scheedt Meyer piano was dragged outside into the back yard and its keys methodically broken. Every cupboard, table and chair was smashed, in our living room was a wonderful carpet made specially in Holland . . . this too was ruined . . . a most marvellous collection of beautiful paintings and animal horns . . . pulled off the wall and burned right there.' The family silver, china and glass, hidden with a neighbour for safe keeping, were discovered and destroyed.

The family were to be taken away to one of the 'concentration camps'. Lammie had been in danger because, when CWH had taken to the hills, he had left ammunition and a sabre (picked up at Magersfontein) in a croquet box which he had buried in the garden. The British heard of this from a disloyal servant. Lammie was tipped off that they were coming in the morning, and knew that if they found the weapons they would burn down the house. At dead of night she, the Dutch governess, Miss Voorders, and the two eldest boys retrieved the box and ordered a servant to dig over the entire garden to conceal what had happened. They then hid the bullets and the sword in a feather mattress: 'but no matter how carefully we did this, there were little white feathers everywhere in the room and down the passage . . .'

Captain Hammond, who sounds a decent man, arrived in the morning and demanded the sabre. Because Lammie felt she could not tell a lie, she said she would give it to him in two hours' time; surprisingly, he agreed. He returned with a warrant to search the house, but his men did not find the lumps in the mattress. The resourceful governess then threw the rest of the ammunition down the drain. 'The situation in Fauresmith became worse and worse!' Lammie's memoir continues. 'Our servants were all taken away. Miss Voorders and I had to do everything. Andries and Henk had to look after the cows and milking. Both were just children.' They had only the rarest message from CWH.

The van der Post family was after all spared the camps. They were taken by wagon from the devastated home in Fauresmith to nearby Edenburg, where CWH's local manager, Johnny Hugo, told them that CWH had managed to 'secure a permit' to bring them to him, on parole at Laingsburg in the Cape. Lammie and the children had not seen CWH for fourteen months. A few weeks later they were allowed to move to the more congenial town of Stellenbosch, where three more children would be born. After the Vereeniging peace agreement CWH repeatedly petitioned to be permitted to return to the Free State, but he was refused because he would not sign an Oath of Allegiance. However, according to Lammie's later memoirs, 'Father [CWH] later signed a sort of declaration – after we had lived in Stellenbosch for five years'.[14]

It is clear from these handwritten reminiscences, which she began to write in the early 1930s and which she used to send to Laurens in London, that Lammie never understood, and probably never wondered, why CWH, and she, had been spared imprisonment although he was a committed and determined 'rebel'. Many of his fellows were sent off to prison as far away as Ceylon, whereas he had been awarded 'parole' and allowed to retreat to not-unpleasant exile in Stellenbosch, and his wife and children had been spared the mortal danger of the concentration camps.

The explanation can be found in the meticulous records of the British Army. Lord Roberts had annexed the Free State on 24 May 1900, and the Transvaal on 1 September, a few days before CWH was captured.

Confiscation of rebel property seemed on the cards. CWH therefore, for whatever reason, decided to cooperate – or, to use a more emotive word, to collaborate. And in return for that he kept his properties, escaped jail or exile, and recovered his family.

What exactly did CWH do? According to a military memo dated 23 January 1901, referring to his application to move from Laingsburg to Stellenbosch, 'He has since figured in some of the intelligence reports as having been talking freely'. The records also contain an undated memorandum by a British officer, 'I know the man [CWH] and do not think you would find him any trouble to you.' According to an affidavit by CWH, Lord Roberts had initially told him that, as a 'rebel', his property would be confiscated, 'against which I protested, as the fact that I had fought for my country, to which alone I owed allegiance, could never place me in the position of a "rebel"' – at which, he says, the English Commander-in-Chief assured him that there would be no confiscation after all, and indeed that his property would be protected while he was away from his home. In another undated memorandum CWH, recalling his meeting with Lord Roberts, makes it clear that in return for past behaviour Roberts decided to allow him to go on parole to the Cape, but as he was about to leave recalled him to discuss 'several matters'. CWH continues, 'The result of my conversation with His Excellency was that I undertook . . .'

Astonishingly, the next page is missing from the Pretoria archive – the only missing page in the file: removed when and by whom?[15] Or simply an archival error? But the gist is clear, and a brief 'outline for a memoir' which CWH later drew up confirms his involvement in some sort of peace mediation, because he records a 'discussion with Lord Roberts' followed by a journey to Heilbron (on the border of the Transvaal and the Free State) and a letter to General de Wet, before he proceeds to the Cape. This is confirmed by another undated note about CWH in the military file concerning his later claim for compensation: 'Was peace delegate to Steyn and de Wet. Failed in his mission and allowed to proceed to Cape Colony on parole.'[16]

We can be pretty certain that Lammie never knew any of this, although she can hardly have believed that her husband was, in the eloquent Afrikaans word, 'a *bittereinder*' (those who fought to the bitter end). In an early stab at a memoir, posted to Laurens in 1931, she writes: 'It is certain that if all the Boers had done their duty . . . England would not have won. There were however many "traitors", many *hands-uppers* [those who surrendered] . . . The *hands-uppers*, Lourens, drew eternal revulsion and scorn upon themselves and they felt it for years. They were considered to be scum and never did one *hands-upper* even stand a chance to be chosen to fill any trustworthy position in public life.'[17]

CWH played a brave role in the Anglo-Boer War. In the end he realised that the Boers had lost. But one wonders whether his subsequent career – affluent, secure in his properties, home at last from exile, refusing the Oath of Allegiance to the English King, somehow disillusioned and clearly weary – might not be explained by those weeks in the Transvaal in 1900 when two Masons met and found that they could do business together.

This was the family into which Lourens Jan van der Post was born, on 13 December 1906.

9

A Free State Boyhood

L AURENS WAS BORN some months after the family first arrived from the Cape in Philippolis, and some weeks after they moved into what is today 7 Colin Fraser Street, their home for the next generation. In Stellenbosch, in exile in the Cape colony, CWH had busied himself with running his small brickworks and with his writing – he was already the author of two successful novels: *Piet Uijs* and *Ignaas Prinsloo*, which Laurens afterwards described, rather inaccurately, as the first 'Afrikaans novels'. He had seriously considered emigrating to Argentina. Now he decided to base himself not in Fauresmith, which had suffered badly in the war, and where his house had been ransacked, but in the smaller *dorp* of Philippolis, nearly forty miles down the road. From now on his health was never good.[1]

Philippolis was, and still is, a pleasant, small, sleepy place, its one main street dominated by the Dutch Reformed Church, its houses attractive and modest in what has become known as the 'Karoo' style of vernacular architecture. The Karoo, a vast expanse of South Africa's shrub semi-desert, does not really start until thirty miles south of Philippolis, and the Kalahari Desert does not start for more than three hundred miles to the North-West. From Bloemfontein to Philippolis there is rolling veld, dry yellow grass in which coarse green pastures respond to the rainy season. It is a haunting landscape of low *kopjies* (small hills), freckled with dark green bush on their slopes, extending to lavender and purple mountains on the distant horizon. The sky is clear and blue. At night there is an intensity of stars, as Laurens so often described. There is no hint today of any free-ranging game. The land seems scarcely populated, with an occasional sudden glimpse of a sort of oasis, a homestead with water and a deep green enclosure of trees, tall poplars and willows, orchards, though seldom any lawns. There is no sign in the district of the wild freesias that Laurens often mentioned.

Wolwekop, the 3,000-morgen farm inherited by Lammie after her mother's death, and eventually inherited by Laurens – its name means Hyena Hill – stands below an attractive group of low hills looking out over a flat expanse of veld, with more *kopjies* on the horizon. The adjoining farm of Boesmansfontein, the main base of Laurens's grandfather A. P. Lubbe for many years, lies in a similar landscape, with *kopjies* behind the farmhouse, but is rather less striking. The key feature of Boesmansfontein – which means 'Spring of the Bushman' – was, and is, its perpetual gush of water, never running dry, out of a rock surrounded by giant pepper trees. The village of Philippolis is set in a hollow and is one of South Africa's historically most interesting *dorps*, because in the middle of the nineteenth century it was the capital of Griqualand, having been chosen by the Reverend John Philip as a missionary base for the Griquas.[2]

The van der Post house, one block distant from the single dusty main street, was a spacious, rambling, single-storey building, built in the 1870s. CWH made various improvements and extensions over the years, and added the next-door property to make room for his large family. Some of the servants would have lodged in an adjoining barn and stable block, but most of them probably lived in the Philippolis 'location', the black township. The house was cool and spacious (cold in winter), though with only one storey, so the children had to double-up. Philippolis had a brisk social and cultural life (though somewhat subdued after the war) with drama, literary and debating societies, plenty of balls and parties, cricket, croquet and tennis clubs and a circulating library, in addition to the church and the Masonic Lodge; CWH and Lammie played a full role in the community.

This was of course a rigidly segregated society. CWH and Lammie were educated and intelligent people, with advanced views about such causes as the education of women, but it should not be assumed that they were more liberal than the rest of their society in their attitude toward race relations. There is a telling illustration in Lammie's memoirs of the war years, when 'a kaffir constable' told her to go indoors because of the military curfew: 'He *took hold of my arm* in order to push me inside. At that moment I was blind with indignation. I pulled loose and said, "Kaffir, get off my *stoep*" [verandah]. He wanted to push me in again, when the Captain grabbed him and kicked him off the *stoep* and told him he would break his neck if he came here again. The Captain then said to me, "I can't stand this, that the Kaffirs should lord it over you Dutch women."'[3]

The family would have spoken Afrikaans at home, but because education was mainly in English the children all grew up bilingual; Laurens does not seem to have picked up Sesotho, as many farm children did, and his father's interest in Bushman antiquities did not extend to the black tribal cultures. CWH spoke excellent English, and Laurens would often remember the size and range of his personal library in various languages. One of CWH's hobbies was to translate Tennyson or Wordsworth into Afrikaans. When Laurens wrote that his father was 'of Europe', he was accurately describing CWH's sense of belonging to a cosmopolitan, European culture. His letters show how he often felt intellectually isolated in Philippolis: he cherished his closer, educated friends, and appears to have had a warm, sometimes light-hearted relationship with his older children, though to the youngsters like Laurens he may well have seemed formidable.

Contrary to Laurens's later memories, there is no evidence that the family went on holiday to the coast, let alone to Cape Town, which would have been a major journey. They might visit their extended family in the district, or the children might go to stay with their older brother Henk in Jagersfontein, but CWH travelled infrequently after the war. Sometimes they would take a cart, or a barouche, and drive the eleven miles to the banks of the Orange River – also known as the Great River, or the Black River – where, after the dusty road, they would swim in the broad, swift-flowing opal-green water, the banks lined with a thin ribbon of dense vegetation.[4]

In *Yet Being Someone Other* (1982), Laurens remembers how he had been taken by his father to Cape Town in 1912, where, he said, CWH was to attend a conference of national statesmen. He recalls (though he was not yet six) his first sight of the sea, and then of the great harbour. He remembers, 'fixed like a fly in amber', how his father had recalled for him his own profound emotions on first landing at the Cape (when CWH had been three). 'That night there was a great storm. Such sleep as I had was troubled perhaps by the first inkling that life was not made with the clear-cut simplicity for which one longed, but that the reality might be profoundly ambivalent and the manifest appearance only skin deep.' Similarly, Laurens claimed to remember accompanying his father to Cape Town in 1909, when he would have been two years old, to a National Convention of the country's leaders. In fact CWH wasn't there in 1909 and they did not go to Cape Town in 1912. Both episodes are warnings that Laurens's stories from his childhood cannot be taken literally.

Laurens always wrote of Philippolis as though it were isolated in the African interior, one thousand and one miles – he said – from the ocean.[5] In fact it was on the main road between Cape Town and Johannesburg and only a couple of miles from the country's principal railway line. It is about three hundred and fifty miles from the sea, at East London, and communications were good.

Of the various farms owned by the family, Boesmansfontein and the adjoining Wolwekop were an easy journey from Philippolis by horse or trap. Laurens in his books would run together Boesmansfontein, Wolwekop and the Philippolis town house in a deliberate confusion. In fact the two farmhouses were modest – Wolwekop particularly so, since it was used mainly as a grazing station – whereas the Philippolis town house was spacious and comfortable though certainly not grand. The town house's glory was its large and beautiful garden (it is still there), which Laurens frequently described, crowded with fruit trees of every variety – apricots, quinces, grapes, pomegranates, pears, peaches, cherries – running down to the *spruit*, the village stream, and a tennis court where Laurens would later play with his first girl friend, Tibby Steytler. What Laurens never mentioned is that on the other side of the *spruit* is the Location, so that when as a child he slept out on the *stoep* he was more likely to hear the hubbub of the local African population than the sounds of the bush; he was always tempted to romanticise his African background for the European reader.[6] In one respect Laurens did not need to exaggerate: the weather in the Free State is ferociously African – blazing hot in summer, far below freezing in the winter nights.

His father had quickly resumed his legal practice, now in partnership with Gerrit Sem, who had managed to keep going through the war years. He had sold the Fauresmith practice in 1902. Both CWH and Sem were active in local politics, with CWH a particularly effective Mayor of Philippolis pressing through a variety of reforms and improvements, sometimes alternating with Sem. CWH was a dominant figure, even as his health began to crumble. He was increasingly disillusioned with national affairs, though he resumed his Volksraad membership from 1907 to 1910. After the 1910 creation of the Union of South Africa he withdrew from politics, having 'an ingrained aversion to hypocrisy'. He wrote to a friend in January 1911: 'I am well out of it. I have had more than enough of representing an illiterate, ignorant, prejudiced and partly untruthful majority.'[7]

Laurens's later written descriptions of this period are highly imaginative. For instance, he says that his Philippolis household frequently entertained the South African political leaders of the day, including the country's most famous statesman, General Smuts: the household affairs, minutely recorded in the archives, show no such visits. He describes how he accompanied his father in 1913, a year before CWH's death, to one of the family farms on the edge of the Kalahari. His father, he claimed, did him the favour of taking a six-year-old boy because he was so adept at opening and closing the many farm gates on the roads. There is even a family photograph of the white-bearded patriarch in his spider, the two-horse cart in which they travelled. Yet there is no evidence in CWH's detailed letter-books and files, that he went on so long and so difficult a journey in 1913. In fact, for much of that year he was bed-ridden, his days seemingly numbered, and he had no great need to make a last journey to inspect the beacons of an unfenced and undeveloped expanse of scrub-bush. Had he needed to go to Vryburg and beyond, rather than make the long, slow and exhausting journey hundreds of miles by carriage he could have taken the train, which had been extended into the Northern Cape.

More likely there was just a small boy, eleventh in a family of thirteen, perhaps feeling under-regarded, however loving and supportive the family, trying to put himself forward in the affections of a powerful, dis-tracted, ailing father. Many years later Laurens would remember his father's enormous beard, his quick temper, and how he smelled of drink. And, to the family's indignation, Laurens wrote in *Venture to the Interior* of being woken one night and being taken to plead with his enraged father to put down his sword and not go off to kill someone. The family would afterwards protest that this story was untrue, while not denying that CWH had a powerful temper and that at one point there was a huge row in the Philippolis Town Council.[8]

Laurens also wrote, in many of his books, of his first memories – of the apricot skin, the blue glass beads and the stories – of his Bushman nurse Klara. Curiously, she changes in the course of the books. In *Venture to the Interior*, she is not mentioned; in *The Face Beside the Fire* (autobio-graphical fiction) there is a duplicitous 'Hottentot' nurse called Klara; in *The Lost World of the Kalahari* Klara's mother is said to have been Bushman; in *The Voice of the Thunder* and in *A Walk with a White Bushman* Klara is a full Bushman. In *A Story like the Wind* she is called Kora.[9]

In fact there is no proof in support of Laurens's memory of a Bushman nurse. His last surviving sister, Ella, suggested that there may have been a Griqua girl at one point. The older sisters, we know, were given responsibility for the babies, and a few months after Laurens's birth Lammie hired a young girl, a poor (white) relation, presumably to help in the nursery. But of Klara there is neither record nor memory; Lammie's memoir never hints at a Bushwoman.[10] The same applies to two elderly Bushmen whom Laurens recalls as part of the establishment on his grandfather's farm; again, there is neither record nor memory. Interestingly, only after the great success in the 1950s of Laurens's books about the Bushmen was his nursemaid, previously unmentioned, developed as a character, first Coloured, then Bushman.

Laurens writes in various books of Boesmansfontein, where his grandfather, the patriarch, held sway over the dining table and the evening prayers, yet he never mentions that A. P. Lubbe in fact moved out of Boesmansfontein just before Laurens was born, in 1906, and moved into his town house in Philippolis, just across the road from CWH and family. No doubt Laurens saw a lot of his grandfather as a child, but not the way he claims in his descriptions of the black servants coming into the farmhouse for evening prayers – an unlikely event in the Free State in those segregated days. The description of delicious meals being brought from the kitchen by the Coloured cook into the large dining room squares not with Boesmansfontein but with the layout of the Philippolis house, even as it is today.[11]

Does Laurens confuse the three houses because he was always being taken to and fro? It is more probable that CWH, Lammie and children would have regularly driven out to Wolwekop – which belonged to Lammie – and would have called at Boesmansfontein on the way. Laurens's memories of counting the sheep into the kraal, of watching for lynxes on the hill, would have come from his weekends, or his school holidays, out at Wolwekop. He was brought up in a village, not on a farm. He was not a farmer, nor a member of a primarily farming family. His memories of the Boesmansfontein farmhouse are exaggerated: the homestead was pulled down before the Second World War, but the foundations remain and show that its total dimensions were eight by sixteen yards, without any sign of a verandah. It was a typically modest structure for the region, and not to be compared with the more impressive town house in Philippolis.

Laurens was surrounded by a host of siblings. Later he would hint that his brother Herman had been Lammie's favourite child. Lammie, preoccupied with a large family and household and active in the local community, may have seemed distant. CWH, ageing, sickly, formidable, intellectual, semi-retired, building himself an extension to accommodate his study and a billiard room, presumably as a refuge from the family next door, may not have been enough of the warm and concerned father whom Laurens craved.[12]

During these boyhood years, Laurens became a precocious reader, which stimulated a vivid imagination. He read not only the child's versions of Homer, Shakespeare and Malory, which his father gave him, but also the popular history books of 'D'Arbez', pseudonym for the Dutch teacher, J. F. van Oordt, who had preceded CWH in the Fauresmith school. D'Arbez was a successful and prolific children's author, who wrote in Afrikaans and who sought to give Afrikaner youth a version of their history of which they could be proud. D'Arbez was undoubtedly a formative influence on the young Laurens: the books of his maturity betray D'Arbez in his romantic historical understanding, his anecdotes can often be traced back to D'Arbez's books and he would have been influenced for the rest of his life by the lurid illustrations which adorned D'Arbez's texts. Above all, it seems to have been from D'Arbez that he derived his colourful though inaccurate idea that decent Afrikanerdom had the French Huguenots to thank for its decency as well as a measure of shame concerning his Dutch and German origins.[13]

The van der Posts lived well. The invoices confirm regular shipments of all sorts of luxuries, from caviar to cheese (which came directly not from Holland, as Laurens wrote, but from Port Elizabeth). There were plenty of servants, of course. CWH was always busy, manoeuvring the syndicates which were buying up farmland in the hope of diamonds, and dominating the affairs of small-town Philippolis. He was capable of many acts of charity – for instance, he was instrumental in sending Petronella van Heerden to Holland to train as South Africa's first Afrikaans woman medical doctor; she afterwards remembered him in a wheelchair on his *stoep*, promising to help. Lammie, whose last two children were born in 1908 and 1910, was active in town affairs. She was also very busy in Afrikaner women's politics, nationally as well as locally, holding various positions in the Orange Women's Association, the OVV.

The family imperative was education. So long as CWH was alive, all of the children were sent to university. Andries, the eldest, after a first degree at Stellenbosch, went to Holland and then Cornell, and several of the others went to Holland or England. With CWH's death in 1914, the situation changed, and Laurens was the first of the sons who did not get a university education; he always claimed that that was his own decision.

Laurens remembered his father's large library. He also remembered reading 'the classics', sitting high in the large mulberry tree – which would have been difficult, because there was no large mulberry tree in Philippolis, let alone one which could house twenty children, as he described later. He borrowed that from his mother's memories of her own childhood in Boesmansfontein. He invented a drought in 1911 when they had to carry water to the prostrate sheep, digging up tubers in the veld to take the place of sandwiches for his school lunch, and so on.[14] Of course, most childhood memories exaggerate, but there is a pattern and a relentless inflation to Laurens's claims which is unusual.

More important, he would reminisce in old age of how, as a small boy, he used to go out to Wolwekop at weekends with his eldest brother Andries, who needed to inspect the farm. One day Andries had an epileptic fit, and the young Laurens only just managed to halt the horses. Andries, said Laurens, demanded his young brother keep his illness secret, and so always took Laurens, not his other brothers, to the farm to open gates. Laurens, bored, took to reading his father's books and thus, he claimed, became so expert in the classics that he lost any interest in going on to university. In consequence, he said, he became a journalist, went to Japan, learned Japanese, and this saved his life in the war. The story is ingenious but unconvincing. Andries's health was no secret in the family, and there was no need to restrict knowledge of it to Laurens.[15]

After 1910, when CWH had quit politics, he aged rapidly. His health had always been frail and he was frequently confined to bed, suffering from bronchitis which he dated from the wartime months on commando; his sight was so poor that he often had to dictate letters to his daughters, and he was sometimes to be seen in a wheelchair. Anecdotal evidence, and heavy brandy bills, indicate that he was a drinker.

He died on 20 August, 1914, at only fifty-eight, though this would not have been considered a premature death at the time. Lammie, who would survive him by forty years, decided that she had inherited a major financial crisis, a story which has been echoed by the family ever since. It isn't true.

Family legend has it that, unbeknown to CWH, his partner Sem had invested the firm's funds heavily in an Australian speculation which collapsed, leaving the partners heavily in debt, at which point CWH died. Lammie, according to the story, heroically refused to go bankrupt, and spent the rest of her life repaying the debt, thereby accepting the impoverishment of herself and her children.

This heart-warming story is also fictitious. The Sworn Evaluator for CWH's Estate was Gerrit Sem, which surely disproves the story that Sem had been responsible for a financial disaster in Australia. The fact that Sem remained a close friend of the family for many years makes it unlikely that Lammie believed him to be the source of her problems. He is buried in Philippolis near to CWH's grave. Unlike the story spread by Lammie, the facts are that CWH, on his death, left an Estate worth £33,000, which would have made him a rich man in 1914. But £23,000 of this was tied up in land, comprising the Free State farms of Panfontein, Tafelbergsdam, Poortjesdam, Twijfelhoek and Wolwekop, various properties in Philippolis and Stellenbosch, and one-third of a syndicate of farms in British Bechuanaland, adjoining the Bechuanaland Protectorate, totalling 16,000 morgen, i.e. about 30,000 acres. There was a long list of 'moveables' including 1,512 Merino sheep, 27 oxen, two stallions, and a number of insurance policies. The legacies included £5,000 cash for Lammie, £1,669 for Hendrik, the Wolwekop farm under entail for Andries, and £303.17s 3½d for each of his children.[16]

One of the consequences of Lammie's complaint was that she denied, as long as she could, her children's inheritance of £303 each from their father. She delayed the settlement of his Estate for seventeen years, until in 1931 she secured signed 'receipts' for £303 from all the children – but even then their receipts were phoney; she hadn't actually paid out, though she was now at last able to wind up the Estate. She continued to hang on to their inheritance until in 1951 several of the children insisted on a promissory note, but only at Lammie's death in 1954 did they actually receive their father's inheritance, increased to £1,000 by a modest allowance for interest over all these years. In the meantime, in 1938, her son Herman had died in obscure circumstances, overwhelmed by debts of about £250.

Lammie's problem in 1914 was that she had lost the cash flow from CWH's firm. The obvious solution would have been to sell off some of the farms while maximising the rentals on the others. But she had a pathological objection to selling land, sharing CWH's obsession with the potential bonanza from any farm which might turn out to conceal diamonds or asbestos. CWH had bought the northern farms very cheap in the 1890s when British Bechuanaland was incorporated into the Cape Colony, and arguably he held on to them too long, borrowing injudiciously, because thereafter the World War, drought and disease drove the Vryburg district into a long depression. Lammie therefore set herself to cut back on all possible expenses – including her younger children's education – while pleading poverty to stall demands from creditors. She put off paying an inheritance tax demand for £55 on one of her farms for eight years until the Master of the High Court in Kimberley threatened her with imprisonment.[17]

The settling of the Estate was extremely complicated, and Lammie managed to draw it out for many years while she battled with the Master, resisting all his attempts to make her pay outstanding debts and duties. On 6 August 1917, for example, she wrote to him, 'I do not understand how you can say "that no determined effort is being made" to complete the liquidation of the Estate. I am busy with it, so to speak, "night and day". I think you have no idea of my *terrible difficulties* . . . Surely, Sir, you are there to *protect* orphans – you are a father yourself. Can you not see that if you force me to realise now you will cause great loss to my orphan children?' On 18 September she asked whether she might pay succession duties in instalments. In the same week she was arguing with the bank about an overdraft of £1,993. In December she borrowed £5,000 from the Church. In 1918 she was forced to agree to sell Panfontein and, in 1920, various portions of the other farms. She told the Master on 7 April 1919 that she had been left with debts of £11,000 and with eight children to educate (this figure of £11,000 is hard to understand). The Master was still getting nowhere. On 10 July 1921, she wrote, 'I have given the children the best advantages as to education. One son is studying medicine in London. One passed BA – is now teaching – one daughter is in last year BA, one passed Matric . . . owing to the scarcity of money and fall in produce prices both these girls had to study at home last year. There are still four smaller children in school.'

This correspondence went on for years, revealing the atmosphere in which Laurens grew to adulthood. Yet Lammie clung to the farms which CWH had accumulated. In December 1921 the Bechuanaland Syndicate, which was called 'CWH Selections', divided the farms, which totalled 55,000 morgen, by a drawing of lots, and Lammie thereby acquired sole ownership of Chippenham, Stilton, Armidale, Hatherley, Mahakane and Tlaping. The Master was by now threatening prosecution. 'I have been struggling on for the children's sake but really I feel as if I cannot go on any longer . . .' she wrote to him on 12 November 1922. 'I want the farms to help me through this difficult time . . . I really have not a penny to spare . . . confidentially I may tell you that my children and myself are practically living on bread and water.' She moved out of Philippolis in 1923 and went to stay with her various children, but the argument went on: 'I have held out *so long* only for the sake of the children, because there is just a chance to sell a farm for a fair price if I can hold out for some years still.'[18]

In the meantime, there had been what Laurens later referred to as the family's 'civil war'. Lammie had always been passionately pro-Boer and anti-English, though she spoke and wrote English as well as her husband and children. In 1914, with the 'Rebellion', passions ran high. That year some Afrikaners under the leadership of General de Wet took up arms against the Government decision to go to war against Germany and against the German presence in neighbouring South-west Africa; the uprising, which also sought the renewed independence of the two Boer republics, was put down. The van der Posts, like many Afrikaner families, were deeply divided. Most of the children seem to have supported the rebels; the eldest brothers, Henk and Andries, were on the Government's side. Lammie was passionately for General de Wet and travelled to Pretoria to support him at his trial. Andries wrote from California to his friend Jack Holloway on 12 July 1915, 'It is going to be a sad home-coming . . . Mother, brothers and sisters are in total disagreement about South African affairs . . . Henk and I are the two black sheep of the family.'[19]

Andries had taken it upon himself to step into his father's shoes as family patriarch. He was intelligent, earnest and well-educated, but did not have the charm or the good looks of most of his brothers and sisters: his niece (Tiny) remembered, many years later, that 'Poor Andries was not blessed with a pleasant personality – he was very dour and serious and had no sense of humour'. He also had a deformation of his back, a 'hump' which Laurens must have recalled in 1958 just after Andries's death, when he wrote *The Seed and the Sower*, in which one of the brothers is a hunchback. CWH's letters to Andries had always been affectionate and full of pride for his son's academic achievements, as when he sent him to study in Holland: 'Andries, my boy, you leave here pure and chaste. See to it that the day you return and you press your lips to those of your mother and your sisters that you are still chaste. If you are not, then rather never kiss your Mother and sisters again!' (Small wonder that Andries was shocked by the goings-on among the passengers on the ship to Europe.)[20]

Andries's letters to his best friend, Jack Holloway*, have survived, and cast light on the atmosphere in the van der Post family and also on the flavour of small-town South Africa in those days between the Anglo-Boer War and the First World War. Both of them were passionately interested in the development and emergence of the Afrikaans language. Andries was at heart a frustrated student of language and literature, although he specialised in agricultural science as a career. His letters often relay family news. His brother Willem is going to Stellenbosch University and Anna will also go to college. He sees himself as a Cincinnatus (the Roman who was called from the plough to become Tyrant and save his people – it was also one of his father's pen-names). Henk has met Joey Marais, whom he will marry. (There is a letter by CWH in which he describes how Laurens, aged five, intends to supplant his brother and marry Joey himself!) In March 1912 Andries and his half-

*Holloway would have a successful political career and later became South Africa's Ambassador in Washington and eventually Secretary for Finance in Pretoria. Andries became Trade Commissioner in London.

blind sister Bets are confirmed at the local church – Andries must have been rather old for Confirmation. On the eve of his departure to Europe, CWH reminds him of the family motto 'Postis Inornatus et Stabilis', and Andries goes to say goodbye to his eighty-three-year-old grandfather, A. P. Lubbe. Anna is having a secret romance. In February 1914 Andries leaves Europe precipitously for America, possibly because he thinks that war is coming. In October he is mourning the news of his father's death: 'It is difficult to believe that I will never see Papa again and that now nothing will come of all our schemes of working together . . . God's will be done! For me there will be enough to be done in South Africa; just think for example of my dear Mother and all my brothers and sisters . . .'[21]

Andries did not in fact go home for another twelve months, so his younger siblings' complaints about his brusque and authoritarian attempts to replace their father may have become exaggerated in their memory. But his letters to Holloway illustrate the impact of the political 'civil war' in the family, as well as Lammie's perception of financial disaster. Although Lammie's problem was one of cash-flow rather than actual poverty, she adamantly refused to sell assets, and cancelled the family policy that all the children, girls as well as boys, go to university. Kuno, Laurens's younger brother, could not complete his college education for lack of funds. Ella and Emma had to struggle and save for years to finish their training. Laurens always insisted that it was his choice not to go on to university, claiming that he defied his family on this, which may imply that Lammie might have found the funds if he had really wanted to go, but it must be wondered whether his mother's refusal to admit that she could afford it was at least a contributory factor.

Laurens's education, which started at the local Philippolis school, had earlier been interrupted for the same reason. In 1918 he went to Grey College in Bloemfontein, one of the country's leading schools (where his father had briefly taught). He would afterwards claim in his *curriculum vitae* that he had been at Grey from 1918 to 1924, but in fact after one year he was taken away and sent to the local school at nearby Frankfort, where he lodged with his sister Anna and her husband, the Plewmans; he remained close to the Plewman family all his life. In 1923 he returned to Grey for two years, boarding for the second year, and he afterwards recalled playing for the school's first rugby team and participating in a famous boycott of school meals, for which the boys were all beaten. *The Seed and the Sower* features a barely-disguised Grey College, and a savage initiation ceremony which was certainly based on fact. He did not mention that his leaving Matric grades were an undistinguished

B (Maths), B (Lower English), C (Higher Afrikaans), C (Physics), D (History) and E (German).[22]

After Laurens left home and moved to Durban, notwithstanding subsequent public and published protestations of devotion, he would never again be particularly close to his mother and, because he was usually abroad, he did not keep in regular contact with her as did most of her children. Interestingly, several of his novels contain portraits of mothers who are saintly, beautiful, cool, distant, undemonstrative.

No diamonds were ever found on the van der Post farms. After leaving Philippolis Lammie spent much of the next fifteen years moving between the homes of her grown-up daughters before her return to Wolwekop in the late 1930s, living there very modestly (it was and is a very modest house) with an English companion, Miss Bush, and supervising the sheep farm. Her father, A. P. Lubbe, had died in Philippolis in 1921. Boesmansfontein had been farmed by the grandson, Laurens's cousin, A. P. Lubbe Junior, who killed himself in 1926. The farm, by a nice twist, was eventually bought by the Jacobson family, who demolished the house which Laurens evoked in his books and built another some distance away. The original Jacobson had been a *smous*, a Jewish pedlar, an immigrant from Lithuania. In a story famous in both families, A. P. Lubbe had taken pity on him and had lent him either 100 or 130 gold sovereigns with which to bring his family out from Europe to join him. The Jacobsons eventually prospered, and today's small museum in Philippolis is a gift from the family to the community which took them in.[23]

The van der Post home in Philippolis was rented and its wagon house became a Jewish Synagogue and school. In 1939 the property was bought by a member of the pro-Nazi *Ossewabrandwag* organisation, who had great trouble scrubbing the Star of David off the wall. The house was sold again and then stood empty, deteriorating in the 1970s; it has since been restored and become a national monument, the 'Van der Post House'. CWH lies in the Philippolis cemetery.

The family scattered. Hendrik was a lawyer, and would be an MP and town mayor of Jagersfontein for years. Andries went to teach at an agricultural college in the Cape and then became a diplomat. Herman was a doctor who would die young in 1935. Willem was also a lawyer, who came back from the war in Italy, entered the mining industry in Jagersfontein, and eventually took over one of the family farms. Pooi was a lecturer in Afrikaans in Durban, and in the 1930s retrained in London as a doctor and anaesthetist. Kuno was a bank manager who became a professional soldier. The daughters were all well educated by the standards of the time, and some of them became teachers, but inevitably they took up domestic life after they married. Anna married Percival Plewman, who went on to a distinguished career in Public Administration. Pauline married a psychologist, Professor Schmidt. Emma married a dairy board executive. Bets, Marie and Ella all married teachers.[24]

Laurens went to be a journalist in Durban. He was just eighteen.

I O

Durban and Voorslag

LAURENS FREQUENTLY DESCRIBED, in later years, how he determined to become a writer, and therefore decided it would be sensible to start as a journalist. He wrote to various newspaper editors, and was rebuffed by the Afrikaans press because he did not have a degree. His brother Pooi, who was working as a lecturer in Durban, sent him an advertisement for a trainee reporter on the *Natal Advertiser*. Laurens travelled to Durban, which was largely English-speaking. He started in March 1925.[1]

Many years later Laurens invested his descriptions of this period with a good deal of imagination. However, it is not difficult to return to the *Advertiser* of 1924–28 to compare the detail of his actual journalism with the claims he would later make in his reminiscences. In the *Advertiser*'s files we can today locate many of the themes and stories which would be developed in Laurens's future career.

He started as a very junior reporter, probably not entirely fluent in English at this time, whereas his Afrikaans, he later explained, gave him opportunities for freelance translation work in Durban's business community. But he was not unique in speaking Afrikaans in Durban, as he suggested; his brother Pooi, for instance, was teaching Afrikaans in the local Polytechnic.

Nearly sixty years later he paid generous tribute to his first Editor, Harold Wodson. Laurens's claim that 'the whole of his staff' had been recruited in England is nonsense, but the newpaper's culture was indeed oriented to the Metropolis, so Laurens would have been an unusual choice to fill the vacancy. Laurens, who had both charm and intelligence, seems to have become Wodson's protégé. The *Advertiser* was not remotely a distinguished or respected paper at the time, struggling along on a circulation of 5,000 and therefore able to afford only a small staff of journalists who would have to turn their hand to anything; it would for this reason have been an excellent training ground for a tyro. He was sent to evening classes to learn shorthand and typing (he would never be skilled in either) and he did the usual round of court reporting and social coverage. But the *Advertiser* of the 1920s, reflecting its readership, was utterly provincial in its opinions and attitudes and, of course, racist – not just in its attitude to the blacks, but in its undisguised contempt for the Afrikaners, their language and history.[2] Here Laurens learned to juggle his Afrikaner background with his English aspirations. In years to come the *Advertiser* would change its name to become the *Daily News*, a much more substantial newspaper, and Laurens would rejoin it in 1948 as an Assistant Editor.

The young Laurens was delighted with Durban, and several of his later books evoked the city in detail. This was where he first met both Zulus and Indians. His report on the visit of the Prince of Wales in his newspaper cuttings book has the contemporary comment in his hand, 'I should be shot for having written this piece. It is unworthy of even the American *Ladies' Home Journal* . . . [I will] apologise to all those who had the bad luck to read it'. (This candid self-criticism would become, fifty years later in his autobiography, 'the editor and his staff congratulated me on what they said was the most memorable bit of reporting of the day. Privately I remained unconvinced. . .') He was soon appointed the Shipping Correspondent, which must confirm his editor's confidence in him, since Durban was one of the great harbours of the southern hemisphere.

It was not just his own modest and unsigned contributions to the paper which shaped the young reporter, but also his exposure to the topics which his Editor seemed to favour. Articles in the *Advertiser* about the Bushmen, their paintings and their history were so frequent that it seems likely Laurens was influenced by them: in February 1926, for example, there was a long series on the 'Denver African Expedition' to the Kalahari Desert. The paper gave detailed reports on the progress of the winter whaling fleet. Durban's harbour, its comings and goings, were reported every day. There were articles about romantic expeditions to the interior. The paper published hyperbolic features about Durban's leading families, such as the Campbells, whom Laurens would later know, and the Natal sugar barons, and in May 1926 there appeared a surprising international perspective, a new interest in the Far East, combining criticisms of Hong Kong set against a curious new admiration for Japan. In March 1925 the paper carried a gushing review of a lecture by the young local poet Roy Campbell. A number of articles by 'Mr. Junior Reporter' – probably Laurens – gave first impressions of Durban. Laurens was being taught to turn his hand to anything, from world peace, the modern novel, the 'poor whites', life on the *Veld* or the local dry-dock, to a Durban art exhibition and a gossip column called 'After Dinner Hour'.[3]

Sometimes, Laurens was allowed to go off on an assignment of his own choosing, though this did not guarantee that his articles would see the light of day. For instance, in mid-1926 he heard of a 'newly-arisen' Zulu Prophet called Isaiah Shembe* who had founded his own church, and he travelled into Zululand, north of Durban, to interview him, probably because his church had an annual festival every July.

Laurens was greatly impressed by this Old Testament figure and frequently quoted this experience many years hence, describing him as 'one of the most beautiful men in spirit, mind and body that I have ever met'. In 1960 he wrote an unpublished note describing the occasion. He remembered sitting in the shade to await the prophet and looking out over a classic African landscape: 'a long line of women were hoeing the magenta earth. They were naked to the waist and their strong bodies and full breasts were a legendary aubergine in the sun.' When Shembe arrived, 'I thought I had never seen a more beautiful person . . . On his head he wore the round ring which among the Zulus was the sign that the man was complete also with goodness and wisdom . . .' They talked for hours; one is reminded of Laurens's later recollection of his first meeting with Jung. Shembe described to the young white reporter how in August 1914 he had seen five great stars fall out of the night sky – a vision, he later understood, of the five great powers about to plunge into a terrible war in Europe. Shembe knew then that he had been called to prophecy: but *how*, when no-one spoke any more of Umkulunkulu, the great First Spirit. Years later, Laurens in his books often mentioned Shembe and Umkulunkulu, but on this first sighting they did not impress his sub-editors on the *Advertiser*. His piece was 'spiked', he ruefully recalled, as 'all my eye, Betsy Martin and mumbo-jumbo'.[5]

Laurens learned to concentrate on the more prosaic interests of the *Advertiser* reader. He begins to emerge, usually unsigned, on the 'Point and Shipping' page, which would describe the return of a whaler with two whales lashed to its sides, or the killing by the *Larsen* of an 88-foot blue whale, or the good fortune of *Sir Liege du Egeland* with six whales. Then, on 24 April 1926, there was a prominent feature article called 'Blue Water – a Landsman's Voyage on HMSAS *Protea*' by 'L'. This must be

*Shembe founded the Church of the Nazarene, which eventually became one of South Africa's most successful Zionist separatist churches among the black population; he was hardly 'newly arisen' since he had founded the church in 1911.[4]

Laurens, because he described the same *Protea* trip in *Yet Being Someone Other*. There is however a gulf between the experience and its recollection sixty years later. The later memory refers to a terrifying gale off Port St Johns, and gives a dramatic description of a thirty-six-hour struggle to keep the *Protea* afloat. When its officers were near despair and other ships in the vicinity destroyed, the *Edinburgh Castle* liner had bravely turned about to attempt a rescue. In Laurens's article at the time, 24 April 1926, his main theme is his seasickness; notwithstanding 'uncommonly fine weather' he spent the first twenty hours flat on his bunk counting rivets in the ceiling and trying to keep from vomiting. The *Protea* does indeed meet the *Kenilworth* [not *Edinburgh*] *Castle*, which is heading for home and prophesies fine weather. It is absolutely clear that this is the reporter's first sea voyage, and he doesn't enjoy it.[6] This was the period when Laurens did or did not venture out on Durban's fleet of small whaling ships, about which he would later write at length.

This admittedly negative rather than positive evidence deserves a digression in view of the light it may cast on Laurens's blurring of fact and fiction. First, there are the frayed and dusty copies, or rather the out-of-focus microfilms, of the *Natal Advertiser*. After his article about his painful experiences on the *Protea*, on 14 August 1926 the *Advertiser*, unusually, made a great fuss about a 'specially commissioned' article called 'There She Blows! – Out with the Whale Hunters off the Natal Coast'. This turned out to be a powerful, well-written piece in which the anonymous writer boards the *Egeland*, whose skipper is a Captain Kasperson, and they go out and catch a whale. The writer is evidently not new to this business – the captain knows him, the stoker is called 'Mlangeni, it is a pretty matter-of-fact experience, though very interesting for the innocent reader, and no-one mentions seasickness. The prose style is definitely not Laurens's.

But one might very plausibly guess that the author was Roy Campbell. The poet was out of work and short of money at the time; he was a close friend of Leif Egeland, son of the family which owned many of the Durban whaling ships. In his unreliable autobiography, *Light On A Dark Horse*, he reminiscences of how he had 'often been out on our tiny cockleshell whalers'; and Leif Egeland recalled sailing into violent storms on the family whalers when Campbell cheerfully smoked his pipe through weather which made even Egeland queasy.[7]

Turn now to Laurens's 1982 autobiography, *Yet Being Someone Other*. In a long description of life on the whalers, there are a score of references and images, small details, which echo the *Advertiser* article: the sleeping arrangements in the cabin, the alarm clock, the blow of the blue whale,

Durt Whaling season. May - Oct.
?

the boy in the crow's nest, 'Mlangeni the Zulu stoker, the commands in Norwegian, the ship drifting silent as it waits for the kill . . . Laurens then specifically claims to have spent three seasons on the whaling ships. This is impossible, not just because his Editor would not have allowed him so much time off, but also because the whaling season coincided with the local winter hockey season, when the young Laurens was utterly committed both to playing in, and to reporting on, the hockey fortunes of Natal. For instance, the major *Advertiser* article about whaling clearly refers to the end-season weeks of August 1926; in that period Laurens was playing hockey in Pretoria before he went off to Japan.

The conclusion must be, in the absence of other evidence, that Laurens never went whale hunting but took over the experiences of Campbell, from the newspaper article and also, when he got to know him, from night-time conversations on the beach at Sezela, and made them his own. He might also have benefited from the reminiscences of David Divine, another poet and a colleague on the *Advertiser*, who had often gone out with the whaling ships. None of this should detract from the imaginative achievement of his 1967 novel, *The Hunter and the Whale*, but it certainly raises questions about the autobiographical *Yet Being Someone Other*.[8]

We know where Laurens was every winter weekend from 1925 to 1927 because he was appearing either for the Durban team, the Nomads, or for Natal's provincial team, and he confirmed it by acting as 'Zero', the *Advertiser*'s Hockey Correspondent. Although it cannot be absolutely proved beyond doubt that Laurens was Zero, how otherwise would the *Advertiser* coincidentally acquire a hockey reporter, an excellent sports writer who travelled everywhere with the Durban or Natal teams? Hockey was in fact the field in which the young Laurens made his first real sustained impact on the *Advertiser*. It was an obscure minority game in South Africa in those days, and until Laurens's arrival in Durban it was ignored in the *Advertiser*. Suddenly it was given prominent coverage. 'Zero' did not hesitate to praise the midfield play of young van der Post, or his brother at the centre.

The *Advertiser*'s hockey coverage started in June 1925, and regular attention was no doubt essential if the interest of a rugby-mad white readership was to be sustained. Years later Laurens couldn't resist embellishing his sporting achievements when, in *Yet Being Someone Other*, he claimed that before he moved to Durban he had captained his school team for three years and played for his Province. Similarly, he was not the Natal captain in 1927, as he claimed, and he certainly did not captain South Africa, as he afterwards sometimes told people. Meanwhile the simple detail of the hockey coverage on the *Advertiser*'s sports page proves that Laurens cannot have been at sea.[9]

The hockey is also the certainty which casts doubt on the most famous of Laurens's memories of his youth. Laurens frequently described, over the rest of his life, what he called the 'parable of the cup of coffee': he even told it to a visiting ANC delegation in London sixty years later. In his favourite Pretoria café, he said, he had witnessed a pair of Japanese tourists being insulted as 'niggers' by the woman proprietor. He defended them, befriended them over the next fortnight, and 'some months' later was invited to Japan.

From 'Zero's' reports on the detail of the inter-provincial hockey tournament, we know that Laurens was indeed in Pretoria on the afternoon of 3 August 1926, where the final game, Natal v. The Cape Province, began at 4 pm. Natal won (it was their only victory that weekend). The game would have finished at 5.30, with winter-dusk coming on, and the team would have been on their bus by 6 pm if they were to drive to Johannesburg to catch the overnight train to Durban. That doesn't give time to eat waffles in a café which, anyway, in Pretoria wouldn't have been open on a public holiday. Furthermore, Laurens sailed for Japan scarcely four weeks after the hockey tournament in Pretoria.[10]

This story, which Laurens retold on innumerable occasions over the years, becomes yet more unconvincing when compared with William Plomer's *Autobiography*. Plomer quotes from a news item in the *Advertiser* of 13 January *1928* – eighteen months *after* the voyage – reporting an 'unfortunate incident' in a tea-shop the previous day when a respectable Japanese gentleman had been thrown out. This was followed a few days later by a letter in the paper from Captain Mori (whom Plomer and Laurens got to know on their voyage to Japan in 1926, and who must have been in port) deploring the incident, which was in turn followed by a letter regretting the insult to *Captain Mori* himself.[11] Clearly, this is uncannily close to Laurens's memory of an alleged incident in Pretoria in 1926, and becomes even more interesting when one remembers that Plomer was living in Japan in 1928, and so he can only have heard of this, and the newspaper exchange, from Mori, with whom he had become a good friend. Laurens, still in Durban in early 1928, would have been aware of the newspaper letters.

During that same month he had been swept up in the final dramas of the project which would be the lasting memory of his Durban years – a new literary magazine. *Voorslag*, which in Afrikaans means whiplash, or live-wire, was published in Natal in 1926 and 1927. It caused a stir at the time, and since then has been given considerable, perhaps excessive, prominence in the country's cultural history. The reason for this is that it was founded and edited – albeit for only three issues – by two of South Africa's finest writers of the century. Laurens in his later years tried to maintain that he had been a near-equal in an editorial triumvirate.

The poet Roy Campbell, born in 1901, was a son of the influential and respected Durban family of Dr Sam Campbell. Roy was a larger-than-life character, an exuberant rebel and romantic, who came early to his prime as a poet of great gifts. In 1924 his poem 'The Flaming Terrapin' was hailed in Britain and America as well as at home. Returning from a brief episode at Oxford, he determined to create a literary and also political periodical. He was enabled to do this through the patronage of Lewis Reynolds, the young son of a wealthy sugar family. Campbell and his wife and baby were invited by Reynolds to live on his estate in a simple beach cottage at Sezela, south of Durban.

In mid-1925 he was approached by an even younger local writer and poet, William Plomer, who was about to have his first novel, *Turbott Wolfe*, published in London by Virginia and Leonard Woolf and their Hogarth Press. Plomer had been born in South Africa, gone to Britain to be educated at Rugby, and came back again to help his parents in a trading store in the heart of Zululand. There he had written an extraordinary, indeed a revolutionary novel, which addressed the colour line and featured a multi-racial marriage; it caused a violent sensation in white South Africa. (Laurens would later claim, falsely, that he, Laurens, wrote the first novel about the colour line by a South African-born writer.)[12]

Plomer and Campbell, though temperamentally dissimilar in many ways, achieved an instant rapport in their rejection of Natal's provincial and philistine society. Campbell immediately urged Plomer to become his co-editor, and, after a cautious delay, Plomer agreed and moved to Sezela where he occupied his own rondavel. Plomer saw the role of *Voorslag* as being 'to sting with satire the mental hind-quarters, so to speak, of the bovine citizenry of the Union'. The two young men plunged into the planning and editing of their magazine, while not neglecting their own writing and reading. In fact most of the first issue was written by them, either under their own names (Campbell reviewed *Turbott Wolfe* and Eliot's *The Waste Land*, while Plomer started to serialise his new story, *Portraits in the Nude*, which satirised Afrikaner society), or under pseudonyms. They had the political wit also to publish an article by General Smuts, the statesman, currently out of office, on his favoured philosophy of Holism. The founder-editors could be happy with the reaction they had provoked, though they were soon to fall out with their more nervous backers.[13]

At this point they met Laurens, a nineteen-year-old cub reporter on the local *Advertiser*. Laurens afterwards said that he and his Editor, Harold Wodson, had fallen out over *Turbott Wolfe*, which Wodson lambasted as 'A Nasty Book On a Nasty Subject' in his headline, though he had the kindness to indulge Laurens's protests and then played a role in introducing Laurens to Dr Sam Campbell and to Roy. At about the same time Laurens met Plomer's mother and brother in the newspaper library, which led to an invitation to meet Plomer, and this in turn resulted in the suggestion that he help them as the 'Afrikaans Editor' of *Voorslag*.

Laurens was clearly dazzled by this meeting with two famous local authors, both already published to international acclaim. He used to visit them at weekends, taking the train on Saturday night and walking miles to their retreat on the edge of the Indian Ocean, and there they would work, and talk, and Roy would declaim his latest poem. Laurens's friendship with Plomer would last a lifetime. Roy would eventually drift into fascism and drink and be estranged from both of them. This enchanted period at Sezela lasted only four months, but it remained one of Laurens's dearest memories, so perhaps it is not surprising that in his old age he liked to claim that he had been their equal. The editors of a facsimile reissue of these first three numbers of *Voorslag*, reprinted in 1985, probably got it right in their Introduction: 'Van der Post . . . was at the time perhaps little more than an intelligently observant acolyte'. This same reprint insists that *Voorslag* was 'one of the striking events in South African literary history'.[14]

One reason why Campbell recruited Laurens was that he intended to turn *Voorslag* into a truly South African publication and therefore bilingual, and eventually trilingual, with Zulu contributions as well as English and Afrikaans. The first step was to find an Afrikaner, possibly a local journalist. Campbell himself spoke Zulu but not Afrikaans. The two senior editors' ignorance of Afrikaans literature led to an extraordinary situation which has not before been noticed, probably because so few subscribers and readers of *Voorslag* would have read Afrikaans fluently, or would have had reason to peruse the occasional Afrikaans article when they could instead enjoy Campbell's newest poem or get indignant with Plomer's novel-in-progress.

Laurens was expected to contribute an Afrikaans article to each issue, and for Number Two he was asked to write about the present state of Afrikaans culture. Here was a nineteen-year-old from the 'backveld', as his Editor described him, without a university background, who was required to write with authority about a subject which was the focus of intense political and academic debate at this time. He did not deny that he found it a heavy burden, but he eventually produced '*Kuns ontwikkeling in Afrikaans*' (which means the development of Afrikaans as a cultural language) for the July 1926 issue.

The article to which Laurens put his name is suffused with the higher academic controversies and jargon of the time, demonstrating an accomplishment, a polished if pedestrian style and a scholarly depth far beyond a teenaged school-leaver. It reeks of the lecture hall (and as such was no doubt a successful piece of commissioning, assuming that anyone read it – it has never received any attention in subsequent writing about *Voorslag*). It was probably written by one of Laurens's brothers – either Andries, who was intelligent and highly educated and obsessed with these matters, or more likely by Pooi, who was at that time lecturing on Afrikaans in Durban at the college founded by Dr Campbell, and about to publish an Afrikaans textbook.[15]

If Laurens's first substantial by-lined article was not his own, the second and last article he contributed to *Voorslag*, in Number Three, of August 1926, has a different problem. It was called '*Nimrods van die See*', and is an account of an expedition on board the little whaling ships which used Durban as their winter base. On closer reading it turns out to be a near-exact translation, into good Afrikaans, of 'There she blows', the article which had appeared a few days before in the *Advertiser*. That article, as we have seen, was written not by Laurens but probably by Roy Campbell.[16]

Did Campbell realise that he was re-running his own article? He might not have minded. His biographer describes him as 'a great myth-maker', a writer whose two autobiographies 'do not merely distort and conceal the truth; they substitute for it an elaborate and consistent un-truth, a realistic mask which has to be torn aside before an attempt to see Campbell as he was becomes possible'. Campbell cheerfully told the most outrageous and unbelievable tales: 'He gave himself a heroic role in all the stories, boasting in such a way that not even the most credulous reader would believe him.'[17] Laurens must have learned much in his apprentice days with *Voorslag*, and this may have been an abiding example.

By this time *Voorslag* in its first incarnation was near its end. Reynolds lost patience and tried to impose editorial control over Campbell, who resigned; Plomer and Laurens followed suit. The journal limped on for another eight anodyne, unmemorable issues. Laurens still had his newspaper job, and offered somehow to support and house the others, but there was no need. Campbell, now with two small children, made a sort of accommodation with his wealthy Durban family, then returned to Britain. For Plomer too it would be the end of his South African days. Laurens, as we shall see, was sent on a sea voyage to Japan, and managed to arrange for Plomer to accompany him. Laurens came home again from Japan; Plomer stayed.

A final reference, in a letter from Campbell to Plomer on 7 June 1927, when they were vaguely thinking of a successor to *Voorslag*, may help elucidate the relationship between Campbell, Plomer and the young Laurens. 'Perhaps the very reason I liked him,' Roy Campbell wrote, 'was that he accepted everything I told him without questioning it. We'll have him as a bottle-washer if we have him at all.' His wife Mary Campbell added: 'You say van der Post should be a bottle-washer – it is quite unnecessary that he should be anything.'[18] Of course, Laurens would have been distressed if he had known about their comments.

Laurens clung to his memories of those weekends in the sound of the ocean breakers, and of one particular evening, 14 August, as they completed the editing of the third and final number of *Voorslag* while Campbell, nursing his new child, walked the beach at night:

> It was a lovely early Spring night, cloudless, cool and clear, and to soothe the restless little Anna, Campbell suggested that we walk up and down on the beach. I remember even at one stage making little fires at the side of our walk to keep her amused. But the night was dominated for me by a full recital, from beginning to end, of Campbell's poem, 'Tristan da Cunha'. After weeks of struggle he had at last got it ended to his liking . . . As we walked up and down in the dark along the beach, Campbell at moments seemed to me to be in danger of dropping Anna, because he wanted so much to follow his habitual custom of waving his hands almost like a Zulu when he spoke . . . The sound of his voice was caught up in the sound of the great swell of the Indian Ocean breaking on the beach, sending its wash powerfully in our direction, so that the foam and the spray came out of the dark with a wonderful sort of unworldly glow . . . the sound was covered with such a sheen of quicksilver water that it became a mirror for the universe above, and we walked trampling the stars and the Milky Way under our feet . . . When at last Campbell came to the end of his long lyrical poem, I was really in tears . . . It was a moment in my life which has never dimmed.[19]

This was Laurens's recollection, at the age of eighty-nine, of an African evening seventy years before.

11

Japan, 1926

Laurens's visit to Japan in 1926 as a very young reporter for the Durban *Natal Advertiser*, was one of the seminal experiences of his life. He spent only a fortnight or so in Japan, the sea voyage on the *Canada Maru* taking another six weeks in either direction, yet for the rest of his life he would remember, and write about, the adventure. His companion on the outward journey from Durban was William Plomer, who stayed on in Japan for two and a half years and, after the war, resumed a close friendship with Laurens which lasted until his death in 1973. The Captain of the *Canada Maru* was Captain Katsue Mori, who would be immortalised by both Laurens and Plomer in their later books, and who, after an interval of many years, would become again a friend of both of them. This voyage changed the course of Plomer's life in an immediate way. The result for Laurens was delayed: he would, afterwards, insist that it had literally saved his life, because it gave him the smattering of Japanese which he used when ambushed in the mountains of Java in 1942; more convincingly, it furnished him with an instinctive sympathy for the Japanese which would be invaluable during his three-and-a-half years in a Japanese POW camp.

The circumstances of the invitation to travel to Japan are confusing, despite the fact that Laurens's own much-repeated version seems straightforward. Descriptions differ of these events of 1926: the authorised version, given in fullest detail in *Yet Being Someone Other* (1982); Laurens's own articles which appeared in the *Advertiser* between December 1926 and February 1927; William Plomer's autobiography; a revised edition of Plomer's autobiography in 1975; Laurens's lengthy introduction to a re-issue of Plomer's *Turbott Wolfe* (1965); and a later unpublished memorandum by Laurens. Even Captain Mori, in his nineties, added a note.

The authorised version, as recounted by Laurens nearly sixty years after the event, tells at great length of how, after the dramas at *Voorslag*, he and

Plomer set sail on an unremarkable Japanese cargo ship, the 5,000 ton *Canada Maru* – 'the ship of legend', as Laurens dubbed it. This was to be the stuff of high romance. Laurens was invited to meet the Captain and first encountered the smartly-uniformed quartermaster: 'He led us across the deck and, although I did not know it, across a far frontier in my own mind.'[1]

Laurens always explained that this invitation followed directly upon the 'coffee cups' racial incident in Pretoria. Whether it did or not, the context of Laurens's and Plomer's journey in 1926 is that Japan had set itself, after centuries of isolation, on a diplomatic and commercial initiative into Africa. Someone in South Africa was concerned to promote this new trading connection, and part of the strategy was to promote Japan's 'image' in the face of, at best, ignorance, and more likely, superstitious hostility. The *Advertiser*, situated in the target harbour of Durban, was the obvious medium, and Laurens was chosen for the assignment. He eventually responded with eight or nine long feature articles which were all uncritically enthusiastic about Japan, its civilisation, its energy, its charm, in contrast to China, Hong Kong, and so forth.

A journalist would immediately see that this journey was what is known in the trade as a 'freeby' – an all-expenses-paid jaunt in return for which the lucky reporter is expected to write articles which will be positive and helpful to the cause. A three-month trip from South Africa to Japan would have been a very substantial 'freeby' indeed, and it is inconceivable that this would have been negotiated on a personal basis between the ship's Captain and a junior reporter. The acceptance and the assignment would have to come from the Editor. And the *strategy* behind the invitation would certainly have come from an even higher authority. The teenaged Laurens would have been a pawn in a much larger game. There was probably a business background: Laurens was entertained by the Rotarians in Tokyo, and after his return he addressed the Durban Rotary Club. His Editor, Harold Wodson, was an active Rotarian.[2]

Captain Mori, then in his mid-thirties, must have been highly esteemed to be entrusted with Japan's diplomatic-commercial venture into Africa. After Laurens received the invitation, he hesitated, he says, because of his concern for the plight of the Campbell family and Plomer after *Voorslag* had folded. His friends protested, so he (or his Editor) accepted, having arranged with Mori that Plomer would travel with him, ostensibly representing the respectable Natal *Witness* paper of Pietermaritzburg. All this was fixed by Laurens, including persuasion of the *Witness*'s Editor Desmond Young, raising funds for Plomer's fare, and even dividing his wardrobe so that Plomer would be presentable. The *Canada Maru* set sail on 2 September 1926.

Laurens's description of the voyage, it should be remembered, was written long after Plomer's death, when he was still working out complex feelings about his old friend. Plomer, according to Laurens, was seriously seasick, whereas he, with 'my experience in whalers', was unaffected by the Indian Ocean swell. The young Laurens began to understand that he and his friend 'had been born totally different psychological types'. Plomer and Captain Mori instantly became great friends and settled down to translate *Turbott Wolfe*: Laurens admitted his jealousy of this intimacy, and his consequent sense of rejection, but tried to contain his feelings. He set himself to make friends with the other officers and to start learning Japanese. He and Plomer had plenty of time to read – Laurens for the first time tackled D. H. Lawrence and *The Plumed Serpent*, while Plomer returned to Shakespeare and English history. Then there were athletics in which, Laurens claimed, he was initiated into judo and was so thrown around by Mori that he began to suspect a Japanese hostility towards the West. He was then introduced to kendo, the Japanese version of stick-fighting.[3]

Their first landfall was Mombasa, the principal port of Kenya. 'It was my first encounter with tropical Africa, and the quick, electric-green of the thick surging grass, brush, flamboyants, jacarandas, acacias already crowded with sun-beetles and crickets to salute the day with platinum voices.' They were made aware of the conservative attitudes of the local whites: an important and radical book by Norman Leys had to be smuggled to them. The ship's carpenter died and was buried, in the teeth of local protest, in the Christian cemetery. Mori and the two young men went up-country briefly to Nairobi, and Laurens recalled the roaring of the lions which they heard (he said) from the train. Mori was snubbed by the Governor. He bought lion whiskers. Laurens had a headache and was cured by an aspirin, 'my first ever'. In their hotel, a white woman rode her horse into the dining room: 'Her face was unmistakably of England, and of the England of the post-War gentry who had suffered and proportionately lost more in four years of killing than any other section of the country. It was fine-boned and well-shaped but the skin was beginning to wrinkle through time and dehydration under the sun of Kenya.'

The sea journey resumed. Plomer was still seasick. There was a shipboard celebration of the full moon. Poems were composed, which Laurens was able to quote sixty years later. The young Laurens had much to meditate on: he was reminded of Joseph Conrad, who was for him one of Shakespeare's 'God's spies'; Laurens's own pilot in these China seas, he said, would be Conrad's *Lord Jim*. 'Accordingly, this moment in the *Canada Maru* was to live with me through the long, strange, dangerous and random years which were to follow, as one of personal revelation and intimation, no less intense for me than for Tuan Jim. It began with the lesson of learning how pursuit of my own craft and this experience of the sea, with the thrust of my own to the East, was also a search for my own truth.'

The ship passed Sumatra and Java, and arrived at Singapore, from where he and Plomer drove across the causeway into Malaya. Laurens, writing decades later, grants to himself and to Plomer various meditations, rather advanced for such young men, about the local psychological phenomenon of '*Mata-kelap*' (running amok). The *Canada Maru* then encountered a typhoon, which prostrated Plomer though not Laurens. The description of the storm, as of the journey, is long and dramatic, given considerable and Conradian dimensions: 'in the sense that all frontiers in reality are barriers, it still seems to me, as it did then, that being compelled to break through as we did was an assertion of universal design. The storm was part of the great law-abiding necessities which demand, for instance, that even the practised round of season cannot serve the change of one into another without storms to aid them . . .' Laurens remembers of his steward, 'The teeth of gold and the dentistry involved in their insertion became an image of the worth of the human round, and reassurance that the rule of experience scrupulously honoured as I had seen it observed all day, would assert itself over the abnormal in the storm and re-emerge, no matter what the odds against it, for the business of life as usual.'[4] The reader may ask, what does this *mean*?

Plomer recovers and they arrive in Japan. In *Yet Being Someone Other*, written nearly sixty years later, Laurens recalled these days in surprising and florid detail. The book devotes more than a hundred pages to this two-week visit. There is a witty and self-mocking description of the introduction of Plomer and himself to a communal hot bath: when they are given kimonos to wear, Plomer carries it off with conspicuous elegance – Laurens feels 'an intangible suggestion that a flowering dress was more welcome to his being than a man's tailored suit'. Laurens at this time did not understand that Plomer was homosexual.

This ignorance lay behind their subsequent experience of a night with geishas, arranged by Captain Mori, who intended it as the climax of their visit. Mori, who evidently favoured Plomer, allocated to him the senior and most beautiful geisha, Teruha. Laurens resented this: 'It was the first time I had been powerfully attracted by a woman of totally different race and alien culture.' But Teruha was destined for Plomer – which of course Plomer could not accept. 'Five years later I was to walk the streets of

London all night long with a near suicidal William: I learned only then that he was incapable of being physically attracted by any woman.'[5]

A photograph shows them all bedded down for the night on the same wide mattress – Laurens admitted to his innocence, Plomer was terrified, Mori must have been utterly bewildered. They had all consumed quantities of saki: 'I woke early, content at heart but in severe physical discomfort. I had an acute headache and was unbearably thirsty . . .' That is to say, he had a hangover! The beautiful geisha, Teruha, he later alleged, would one day become a Buddhist nun.

Their tour of Japan continued, with Plomer, to his embarrassment, being hailed in the local press as the heir of Shakespeare – an unreliable story which he had carelessly mentioned to Captain Mori. They were taken to Kobe, Nara, Kyoto, Ise, Tokyo and elsewhere, on what would become the usual tour for foreign visitors.[6] Laurens took ship again with Captain Mori, leaving Plomer behind and, via Hong Kong, China (though he spent no time ashore), Singapore, Ceylon, Zanzibar, Dar es Salaam and Mozambique, returned to South Africa and to the *Advertiser* in Durban.

Yet Being Someone Other is Laurens's late and considered version of the 1926 voyage to Japan. Plomer, in his own autobiography published originally in 1943, revised in 1945 and then again in 1975 (after he had resumed his friendship with Laurens), writes of Mori 'bearing us off to his far country very much as in the days of Captain Cook exploring navigators used sometimes to carry home for exhibition in Europe natives of the Pacific Islands'. Laurens and Plomer, according to Plomer, were very young but had the great gift that they had no racial prejudice. Plomer's description of the voyage is considerably briefer than Laurens's. He never mentions sea-sickness. He confirms the snubbing of Mori by the Governor, the purchase of lion whiskers and shipboard demonstrations of judo and kendo, though with never a suggestion that Laurens was dragged in. He mentions the lady-on-her-horse in the hotel (a stereotypical story of life in prewar Kenya). He notes that in the scenes of the war dance Mori betrayed 'a moment atavistic, a moment ominous'. He reports a typhoon off the coast of Formosa, after 'dreamy Indian Ocean days', and a ceremonial feast under the full moon. The fortnight in Japan he describes as strenuous, with visits to factories and hostels as well as temples and gardens. He admits that Mori had primed the most attractive and intelligent of the fully-fledged geishas to make up to him, perhaps because he wanted his new friend to fall for Japanese womanhood: 'Mori had chosen the bait he himself would have taken.' As he had planned, Plomer decided to stay on in Japan.[7]

The third version of this 1926 visit to Japan can be found in Laurens's own articles, nine of which were published at length in the *Advertiser*. They are described as 'his first contact with fresh civilisation, his impressions and thoughts'. The articles turn out to be pretty routine journalism unaided by the personal anecdote or insight which makes a good foreign correspondent. Laurens is given a prominent by-line; these articles would have been an important part of his journalistic maturity.

He starts with the two Japanese journalists, Messrs Shirakawa and Hisatomi, who had arrived in South Africa 'with a mission rather like that of an ambassador'. They had suffered racist rejection in Johannesburg and Pretoria – Laurens never suggests that he had been personally involved in any incident. 'Japan is doing its best to discover South Africa and it is time we sat up and returned the compliment. A well-established and permanent trade with Japan will benefit South Africa more than an unstable tourist traffic from the New World.' That is to be the theme of these articles, and America, China, Hong Kong, India, the West in general, are shown up negatively in comparison with Japan, which Laurens (who had never before been abroad) describes as 'the most interesting country in the world'.

A second article, on 31 December 1926, reports on Kenya. 'The Africa of tradition and romance does not exist . . . Kenya is profoundly disturbed . . .' 'The locals are inferior to our Zulus.' Mombasa is full of 'negative forces'. The author visits Nairobi but is not impressed. 'Not many months ago' a young lady had ridden into a top hotel, etc.; 'of course, one does not swallow these stories without salting them heavily . . .' There is no reference in the newspaper articles to Mori, to lion whiskers or to the carpenter's burial, and on the train journey they do not see or hear any lions in Tsavo.[8]

The 15 January 1927 article describes the sea journey from East Africa to Japan, which was given thirty pages in *Yet Being . . .*, as 'ennui and solitude'. The remaining articles described visits to Mogi, Kobe, Mount Mayesan, Nikko, etc. A couple of these articles are so different in style that one wonders whether Plomer helped out with the writing. Naturally, there is nothing about geisha nights, only a photograph and a caption about geishas, nor does the brief description of an exhibition of ju-jitsu on board suggest that the reporter was involved. Finally, perfunctorily, the reporter sails back home 'over a dark inhospitable sea'.[9]

Yet another gloss on this episode was drafted by Laurens in the last months of his life, in the summer of 1996, when he told his secretaries he wanted 'to set the record straight'. This is a strange and defensive document, unpublished, full of resentment at the dead Plomer's published version of the distant days of *Voorslag* and Japan (printed during the war, Laurens says darkly, when Plomer thought that he was dead). Laurens here repeats that he met the two Japanese visitors in Pretoria and bought them coffee: that 'some months' later 'they had carried such a good report of me back to Japan that Captain Mori had brought me an invitation to go to Japan at his company's and the Government's expense'.[10] Finally, there is Captain Mori's own reminiscence, published in his nineties in a *Festschrift* to Laurens called *The Rock Rabbit and the Rainbow*. He recalls a racial incident which two Japanese journalists suffered *in Durban*, in which the young Laurens had intervened. Out of gratitude, they asked Mori to invite him to the *Canada Maru* for supper, which led to Mori inviting Laurens and Plomer on his own initiative to come at once to Japan with him. They accepted, and 'a solid friendship flourished among the three of us'; he diplomatically forgets that he had no contact with Laurens for more than thirty years.[11]

Does the conflicting detail matter? Did Laurens meet the Japanese journalists in Pretoria or in Durban? Did the racial incident happen in 1926 or in 1928? Was Plomer seasick or did Laurens project his own sickness on to his friend? What happened to Captain Mori's translation of *Turbott Wolfe*? Did Laurens face Captain Mori over the ju-jitsu mat? Did they truly observe the Kenyan lady ride into the dining room? Did the beautiful geisha really become a nun? Questions such as these relate back to so many earlier episodes. Did Laurens ever go whaling? Did his brother write his first *Voorslag* article for him? Did he go alone to a Pretoria café on an August afternoon after his hockey team had won the final game in the provincial tournament, and yet – which he forgot to mention – had finished bottom but one in the competition? Or did he make it up?

In Laurens's life there is an unending confusion between the fact and the fiction which it is sometimes impossible to disentangle. From an early age Laurens slipped easily from literal truth to what he saw as imaginative truth. The important key is this: whenever he amended the literal truth, whether in his books or in his conversation, he invariably did it to *promote himself* – to position himself at the centre. We can see it again and again in his reminiscences of his youthful years in Durban, with their mix of fact and fantasy. It would become a defining characteristic of his life and of his writing, whether in the Ethiopian war, or in the Japanese camps, or in the Kalahari desert, or in postwar London, or in his relations with Jung, or in Southern African politics, or in the later years as guru and mystic: Laurens would always be the Hero of his tale.

I 2

The Reporter

L AURENS RETURNED TO Durban in early December 1926 after three
months' absence. Without Plomer, he had a better chance on the
long voyage of getting to know Captain Mori. He persevered with his
Japanese lessons with the Purser. In Durban, he later wrote, he was
struck down by a strange and critical fever and was only to see the *Canada
Maru* again as it departed the harbour. 'I saw Mori had lined up the whole
of the starboard rail with the noon-day watch, and all his officers, including my teacher, were in their best uniforms. As I waved, and the *Canada
Maru*'s siren pronounced its own deep-sea form of sayonara, they all, as
one, bowed formally and imperially to us. I stopped waving, came to
attention and tried to bow likewise. When I came out of my bow I could
hardly see the ship, my eyes were so blurred.'

He said he felt he owed it to his Editor and the paper to remain in
Durban at least another year, and stayed until February 1928.[1] After his
nine-part series on Japan had run its course, he is occasionally glimpsed
as a feature writer on the *Advertiser*. On 7 May 1927, for example, there
is an up-beat article describing 'How Durban Cares For Her Native
People', which praises the municipality's provision of hostels and beer
for migrant black workers and makes the unfortunate comment that 'the
problem is aggravated by the fact that the native is at a lower scale of
human evolution than the European'. 'Zero' resumes his hockey column
and 'congratulates Lawrie van der Post on being chosen skipper of the
team . . . He is in my opinion the outstanding player in Durban, a hard
worker who uses his head and possesses speed and stamina.' The paper's
hockey coverage is once again rather good.

In a July feature article, three young chaps go off on a joy ride into
Zululand in a car nicknamed 'Helen' (of Troy) – a kind of 'Three Men
in a Boat', in which they make fools of themselves in the bush and keep
their Zulu guide awake by throwing empty beerbottles at his head. It
reads like Laurens, and we know that his car was called 'Helen'.

More interesting, on 6 August 1927 the *Advertiser* ran a big feature called 'A Durban Whaler Amongst Ice of the Great White Barrier'. The hero is a Captain Thoresen (compare with Laurens's future books about a Captain Thor Larsen and a Captain Kasperson) who has survived terrible storms on a voyage to the Antarctic. The writer *imagines* that whaling must be a romantic business, but evidently he has no personal experience of the life. The journalist is not by-lined, but it reads as if it were by Laurens, and there are elements in the piece which recur in Laurens's later books.[2]

The Campbells had left for England, and Laurens, who had nothing more to do with *Voorslag*, may have been lonely. After the excitement of his Japan journey he was bored in Durban and with the *Advertiser*. What he never mentioned in his subsequent writing was that at some point early in 1927 he met Marjorie Wendt.

Theo Wendt, her father, had been founder and conductor of the Cape Town Orchestra, an important figure in the early musical history of the Cape and indeed of South Africa. He was a gifted musician who had struggled to bring classical and also contemporary music to this culturally isolated country. His regular orchestral tours of South Africa had done much to achieve this. But in 1924 his contract was not renewed and he eventually went to America, where he had a modestly successful career. In this same period he and his second wife, Maude, separated. His first wife Agnes, who had been a dancer and was the mother of their daughter Marjorie, had remarried and was living in England. Marjorie, born in 1905, was left adrift in South Africa.

Laurens met Marjorie in Durban when they were introduced by his newspaper colleague David Gamble. When he first met her she was being dragged along by a posse of dogs, which her absent step-mother had bought so that she could make a living by breeding from them. She was tiny, pretty and intelligent; she was a year the elder. They found that they had fallen in love and began to plan a life together in England, where Laurens intended to become a writer. There was never any question of his destination, although he had not a drop of English blood in his veins. He had been captured by English literature, and to a British colonial the only place to go was England, the centre of his cultural world. Marjorie was only too happy to accompany him, knowing that she could rejoin her mother, who lived in Dorset on the south coast. She went ahead in order to prepare her mother, who was said to be a difficult woman.

Laurens said that Harold Wodson, his Editor, wept when he told him that he was leaving.[3]

Laurens followed Marjorie to Britain in February 1928, arriving at Southampton on 5 March. He was just twenty-one. This was one of the rare periods when he kept a journal, which contains a memorable description of his first days in England. It is as jejune as most journals written at that age. On 15 February, on board ship, he wrote, 'I have never realised even in the first month of our love, how much I love her and how much she means to me. Today I am determined to begin my novel . . .'

Marjorie met him and warned him that her stepfather, a Mr Cochrane, was making trouble. Laurens wrote, 'His attitude is very stupid, for until we are married he has a far greater responsibility to Marjorie than I have to her. He is quite a good creature really but potentially a senile pervert. He treats Marjorie like a servant girl that has gone astray.' To avoid 'unpleasantness', Laurens and Marjorie decided to get married immediately, rather than to wait, as they had planned, for at least three months: 'Neither Marjorie nor I attach any importance to the ceremony. We will never feel more married than we do now. Going through with the ceremony is merely an act of grace on our part to please our families . . . Heaven knows what they would say if they knew we have lived together for practically a year. I am prouder of that year than anything I have yet done.'

Laurens and Marjorie went off to Bridport secretly and got married on 8 March. 'When we came back this morning and told her mother that we were married, she became very agitated. She has been treating us very coldly ever since. In fact the house has been unbearable . . . it is extraordinary that people should regard a mere matter of ceremony as of overwhelming importance . . . we are probably spending one of the strangest first wedding days that has ever been spent. We have no intention of honeymooning in this house and are leaving for London tomorrow.' Laurens added, 'I for one shall try never to practise any form of deception again because if any mischief has been done it has been the result of a deception.'

The detail of the next twelve months is not clear. Laurens visited Holland in May with a group of South African students, with whom he found himself out of sympathy: 'Nationalism means nothing to me, to them it is everything . . . they deny the right to compare cultures . . . they would be racially independent and yet refuse racial independence to the natives. This they justify on the grounds that their culture is superior to native culture. On this ground, however, they would have to concede to England the right of ruling us as English culture is obviously greater than our own.' He went on, 'Marjorie, poor child, is going to have a baby. It is unfortunate because we cannot afford it . . . God, it is depressing. I must work, work, and overcome this devastating feeling of despair in the pit of my stomach.'[4] Such was the conception of Laurens's only son John, who would be born on 24 December 1928.

On 7 July 1928, the journal continued, 'I have been trying all morning to start work on my novel.* Pierre de Villiers is carefully formed in my mind. I want him to be something more than alive, a symbol of eternal and apparently futile conflict . . .'

At some point, Marjorie and Laurens went to visit Roy Campbell, who was living in the Weald of Kent. His wife Mary was away.† They had not met since the closing weeks of *Voorslag*, when – as he reminded himself in this journal – Campbell had been 'like a highly-charged electrical battery'. Laurens was struck, and alarmed, by the change in his friend: 'He seemed to suffer from nervous exhaustion. The work he had done was good, although spiritually it had progressed little . . . He drank far too much at the time and talked to us, as it were, over an abyss where alcoholic fumes whirled round his feet. Several times too he told me the most outrageous lies out of sheer bravado. I have no moral objection to lies but they must be well done and contain imaginative qualities. Roy's were merely stupid.' Laurens remembered that Roy had had 'more influence on me than anyone I have known and I admire him almost as much as Plomer'. He noticed that when Mary Campbell returned Roy cheered up and became very much his old self again. Laurens did not know that

---

*Laurens must be dating the beginning of his first novel *In a Province*, in which the protagonist turned out to be called Johan van Bredepoel. The hero of a later novel, *Flamingo Feather*, was Pierre de Beauvilliers.[5]

†There may be a confusion here. Many years later Laurens told Roy Campbell's biographer that he had written to Roy immediately on his arrival; a reply the next day gave him urgent and detailed instructions as to how to find him, near Sevenoaks. Laurens later wrote that he was horrified to find Roy in a terrible state. It was freezing cold and several times in the night Laurens woke to find that Roy had covered him with his own single blanket. Roy agreed to come up to London with Laurens to meet his South African friend, Enslin du Plessis. Laurens makes no mention of Marjorie on this first visit, which would have been in March 1928. The visit to Kent with Marjorie, recorded in the journal, is clearly dated 28 July, when it would not have been freezing cold – yet Campbell is said to have left for France on 28 April, where he was joined by Mary in May. It is hard to believe that Laurens's journal contained fictions: the timing of the Campbells' travels is therefore in question.[6]

the Campbells had gone through a devastating crisis in 1927 when Mary
fell in love with Vita Sackville-West, the poet and novelist and the wife
of Harold Nicolson, and had a passionate affair with her which almost
destroyed the marriage. She returned to Roy, but in the next few years he
was always terrified that she would leave him again.[7]

Laurens had a difficult time in England for the fifteen months he
stayed there. He later claimed he and Marjorie were so poor that at one
point they stole potatoes from their neighbours' garden; they were financially helped by her mother Agnes. But he began to make friends in literary circles, some of whom would remain close. His entry to these
circles seems to have been through Enslin du Plessis, an Afrikaner journalist and a serious amateur painter, who worked at the office of the
South African Argus group in Fleet Street. He had travelled to Europe
to enlist in the First World War, returned briefly to South Africa (where
he had first met Plomer), and was posted back to London where he
became a respected member of the 'London Group' of artists. He
became a good friend to the young Laurens, offering him paternal advice
and putting freelance journalism his way. He also introduced Laurens to
a young French businessman called René Janin, who in turn opened the
way to the fringes of the Bloomsbury group.

Janin became a particularly close friend of Laurens. He was homosexual and was evidently attracted to the handsome South African, which
eventually forced Laurens to restrain the friendship. Cosmopolitan,
polyglot and dilettante, he introduced Laurens to a range of friends who
would have been beyond the reach of a young Afrikaner with no connections in England. Virginia Woolf – to whom Laurens was introduced
by Janin – describes Janin in her diary as 'a thin-skinned Frog all gesture
and wrinkle; a coffee merchant ex-diplomat; despises Society'. In the
same circle Laurens met Arthur Waley, the Orientalist, who gave him a
decent meal once a week, or so Laurens afterwards said, and who years
later would be a link with C. G. Jung. It was Janin who, one day in 1929,
brought William Plomer to Laurens's attic Hampstead flat. They had not
seen each other for two and a half years.[8]

Plomer had just returned from Japan, where Laurens had left him
after the *Canada Maru* voyage in October 1926. The two had kept in
touch: for example on 25 February 1927 Plomer wrote from Tokyo to
thank him for an offer of financial help and to commiserate on the
news that Laurens had malaria.* 'I don't think you will be happy until

---

*This is striking confirmation that Laurens did not first catch the malaria which was to
plague him for years in Ethiopia in 1941.

you go to London,' wrote Plomer in 1927, 'you are a good creature . . .' Plomer, rapidly and with the help of his Hogarth Press publishers, the Woolfs, successfully infiltrated London's literary society, which he greatly enjoyed for the rest of his life. In turn, his own friends – Anthony Butts, Teddy Wolfe, Arthur Waley, Beryl de Zoete, the Sitwells, E. M. Forster, Lilian Bowes Lyon – became friends of Laurens, either now or a few years later. One of Laurens's particular friends in this circle was Keith Millar-Jones, a lawyer with whom he enjoyed London's social life when they could afford it. Plomer also made a point of keeping in touch with Marjorie and Laurens's son John, and reporting on them to Laurens when he left them behind to return to South Africa in June 1929. Laurens reciprocated by arranging for Plomer to write a fortnightly article for the *Cape Times*, the fee for which allowed Plomer to move into London. Laurens also commissioned poems from Roy Campbell.[9]

Laurens, with Enslin du Plessis's encouragement, was 'writing essays, special features, short stories that were invariably rejected with monotonous regularity', and above all trying to compose 'a . . . novel about the impact of the East India Company on South African life'. The most successful evidence of his journalism was an article for *The Realist* called 'South Africa in the Melting Pot', notable for its forceful account of Laurens's view of the racial situation in South Africa at that time. He analysed the consequences of the second electoral victory of General Hertzog and the National Party in 1929. 'The white South African has never consciously believed . . . that the native could ever become his equal. He has never intended that the native should ever reach a higher state of civilisation than that necessary to make him a good servant . . . now, all that General Hertzog's policy will achieve is to slam the door more firmly in the native's face, though it is to be judiciously opened whenever a white farmer or a cigar-chewing Witwatersrand capitalist needs unskilled labour . . . At the back of the white South African's attitude to the native is always fear of the bitterest kind . . . he has looked at the native so often along the barrel of his rifle that he never sees in him a potential co-operator but always a dangerous enemy that at the first opportunity may rise and take by arms what is now denied him.'

Laurens went on to explain how the 'white South African' policy was doomed: 'Every day the native is being grafted, drawn more and more into the organic structure of South African society. The process of levelling-up and inter-mixture must accelerate continually . . . the future civilisation of South Africa is, I believe, neither black nor white but brown.'

Laurens added, piquantly in view of his future development, that he did
not say this out of 'any sentimental feeling about noble savages'. This
article was powerful stuff, well-written, impeccably liberal, very advanced
for the time, probably in advance of his own earlier position, and pro-
vocatively controversial. Laurens was very proud of it and kept a cutting
all his life.[10]

Laurens never completed his novel, and the manuscript has vanished.
He was also writing an occasional theatre column for the Argus group,
and sometimes acting as Assistant Theatre Critic on the *Nation and
Athenaeum*. But he had to give up. Freelance journalism was too difficult
for a young South African with only a few years on a Durban provincial
paper in his *curriculum vitae*. Laurens had arrived in England at a difficult
moment, with the Depression gaining ground, unemployment growing
fast, and, in his later recollection, a sense that 'the world was walking in
its sleep towards unparalleled disaster'. Many of his friends took a
communist position. Laurens always refused, though he claimed to have
marched with the unemployed in Hyde Park.

He was thrown a lifeline by the dynamic and imaginative Desmond
Young, Editor of the Natal *Witness* in 1926 and a rare enthusiast for
Voorslag, who had given an accreditation to Plomer when he and Laurens
were offered their trip to Japan. Young had moved to the *Cape Times* in
1929 and, according to Laurens's account, cabled him, 'Have just taken
on Day editorship *Cape Times*. Please come and help me clear up mess in
this country.'[11]

Laurens agreed, and arrived in the Cape on 8 July 1929. Marjorie and
John only joined him five months later; even at this early stage Laurens
was apparently not a particularly devoted father or husband. In the
meantime Plomer was a regular correspondent, anxious to make his *Cape
Times* articles* a success, and making an evident effort to keep Laurens in
touch. 'The money is really important to me, and I regard the job as a
good discipline, exercise or training.' Marjorie 'was well but of course
misses you unspeakably . . . I read of your slum campaign in the *Cape
Times* the other day. You certainly seem to have worked wonders.' As
Marjorie was leaving for South Africa in December, 'I went yesterday to
say goodbye to Marjorie, whom I found with your mother-in-law . . .
Marjorie was simply rather overwhelmed with preparations for her
journey. As for your mother-in-law, I hope you will forgive me if I say

---

*Plomer's twenty articles in the *Cape Times*, which do not seem to have been studied by
his biographer, are polished and personalised despatches of London life. His articles
from Japan to the Natal *Witness* in 1926 have also been forgotten.[12]

she is not exactly my favourite woman, and if I advise you to have as little to do with her as possible . . . I think you have taken a very wise step [to go back to South Africa].'

As early as March 1930 there seems to have been talk of Laurens returning to England again and a suggestion that Plomer join the *Cape Times*: 'If it involved going back to Africa I would not consider it for a moment because I don't intend ever to return there,' replied Plomer. 'A young poet called Stephen Spender has been amusing us (Butts, René & I) very much lately . . . I am sorry to say a great gulf is now fixed between Roy [Campbell] and me . . . I don't share his taste for low life and he doesn't share mine for something a little more discriminating.' This break in an old friendship would become final in 1933 when Mary Campbell, to Plomer's alarm, made advances to him and Roy found out. Plomer was beginning to be concerned about Laurens for some reason: 'I am very worried about you and so is René. I am so afraid that something is going wrong in your life . . . I miss you always very much.'[13]

Laurens spent a little more than eighteen months in South Africa between 1929 and 1931. The Editor, B. K. Long, was a brilliant leader writer who left much of the running of the paper to his Day Editor, Desmond Young. Young put together an impressive team of young journalists, which included Leonard Barnes, who would one day write an important book, *Caliban in Africa*; David Gamble, poet and critic; Piet Meiring, later to change sides and become a senior apparatchik in the postwar age of apartheid; and the slightly younger T. C. Robertson, who became a special friend of Laurens.[14]

Laurens always looked back on his brief time on the *Cape Times* with a sentimental affection. In a memoir for the paper's centenary issue, he wrote, 'I think the *Cape Times* achieved a stature not equalled in the history of South African journalism, perhaps not surpassed even by any other newspaper in the world'! He would often reminisce about the highlights of his time there. How he wrote a major late-night leader on the news of the death of D. H. Lawrence and inserted it in the paper on his own initiative, to be praised the next morning by the Editor. Contrary to Laurens's recollection the leader was modest and down-page, in fact appeared on 5 March, three days after Lawrence's death, and picked up on a recent article in the paper by Plomer which had extolled Lawrence's genius. (Laurens would sometimes claim that he had met D. H. Lawrence in London's Cafe Royal in 1928–29. This is a classic Laurens fantasy, because D. H. Lawrence never visited England after 1927 and Laurens did not arrive in England until 1928).[15]*

Laurens would recall how he wrote a series of articles exposing the scandal of appalling housing conditions in the Cape Coloured quarter called District Six, which led to his accompanying Princess Alice, wife of the Governor-General, in a visit to the area; the articles juxtaposed photographs of blacks' shacks with the luxurious stables enjoyed by the horses of the wealthy whites. He recalled how he covered the heresy trial of a distinguished Dutch Reformed Church academic, Professor Johannes du Plessis, a *cause célèbre* at the time, for many months and in great detail (T. C. Robertson later explained that Laurens had no short-hand so he had to accompany him to do the transcripts while Laurens added the descriptive passages); how he exposed a notorious case of police assault on Coloureds in Paarl, in the winelands outside Cape Town, which brought a unanimous and unjust acquittal by the local white jury; how this provoked Laurens to write a blazing leader in the paper which was then hardened up by B. K. Long who, in his outrage, inserted the word 'deliberately'; how that caused a political row and led to a major libel action which the *Cape Times* lost, to its fury and its great expense, a drama which probably contributed to the eventual departure of Long, Laurens and Young after the paper had decided not to go to appeal.[17]

There were other assignments for Laurens which must have made them exciting days for a young reporter. 'TC' used to tell of how they had sailed to the Antarctic, but this turns out to be TC's fantasy. But Laurens was indeed sent north to Mochudi, to cover the enthronement of a new Paramount Chief. This was Laurens's first credible sighting of the outer fringes of the Kalahari, though his eye-witness account in the paper does not always tally either with the facts of the occasion or with his later book: for instance, he alternately says that the new Chief was ten years old or sixteen, whereas the correct age should be twenty-two. He almost certainly met the novelist E. M. Forster, who attended the British Association's annual conference in Cape Town in 1929 and was the guest of Dr Petronella van Heerden, CWH's protégé from Philippolis; Laurens afterwards had a slight acquaintance with Forster in England. One of the speakers at the Association was the Abbé Breuil, the leading paleontologist, whose interest in the Bushmen would have

---

*Duncan Fallowell has recalled how in August 1983 he attended a dinner party at which Laurens told the film director Nagisa Oshima of his memories of D. H. Lawrence – the north Midlands accent, his hypnotic eyes, and how Laurens said he had actually seen him strike his wife.[16]

been registered by Laurens when he interviewed him; it is noteworthy that after July the *Cape Times* carried frequent articles about the Bushmen and the latest Kalahari expeditions. Finally, Laurens resumed his old Durban task of hockey reporting, while at the same time he played for the local team of Fish Hoek, and also for the Western Province.[18]

Laurens always remembered his exhaustion at the daily pressure of the job. He started, in Desmond Young's phrase, as 'our storm-trooper Number One', or so he said. He was responsible for the paper's cultural coverage, until he was promoted as a leader writer and was succeeded as music and theatre writer by T. C. Robertson. TC afterwards admitted that he was tone-deaf, so he used to take a musical aunt to every concert who would tell him what to say, which he would embellish from his reading of George Bernard Shaw's musical criticism. Laurens and TC had become close. When Laurens resigned, in November 1930, he stayed on in South Africa, long after Marjorie and John had returned to England, for reasons which are not clear. He and TC went to the Robertson farm in the Transvaal, Blesbokvlakte, near Middelburg, where Laurens wrote, TC studied economics and chased the local girls, and they travelled the district in Laurens's small car 'Helen', looking for Bushman paintings. In the evenings, TC recalled, they would read Trollope aloud to each other, because Laurens was determined to master English in order to become a writer. TC added that Laurens's Afrikaans went downhill from this point.

In Cape Town they were members of a young and bohemian group of intellectuals and academics. There was a great deal of drinking. TC used to tell of how he had a friend, daughter of a rich family, who would hide bottles in the fountain at the bottom of her garden. Laurens and TC would drive there after work, fish out the drink, and go off to join their friends. There was a certain amount of 'womanising' in which TC, the bachelor, was the more active. TC's recollection that Laurens and Marjorie were not estranged but lived apart does not tally with an account by Horace Flather, one of Laurens's colleagues, in his memoirs of going off one evening with the two of them through the Gardens to find a restaurant, when they remembered that they had left behind the baby John in the soaking rain. However, Marjorie and John returned to England in September 1930. Laurens joined her months later in the spring of 1931.[19]

He spent several weeks of this period not only in the Transvaal but also in the house of a young artist friend, Mary Cloete, outside George, in the beautiful Wilderness district on the Garden Route east of Cape Town. The same Mary, now Royds, met Laurens again by chance fifty years later in London, and she later recalled how they would creep down the monkey paths to the sea and Laurens would tell her tales of how they must be the first whites ever to have come down this path. She remembered him as 'a very confused young man', though utterly charming and extremely good-looking. He wrote her poems from the hilltop, it became a 'deep, romantic friendship', and she made a portrait of him which one day would sit in Prince Charles's study. She knew he was a married man, but there was no sign of Marjorie. She recalls that he was intensely ambitious, and was intent on going back to Europe, to be a writer.[20]

Nadine Gordimer, the distinguished South African novelist, knows of another episode which may give a snapshot of Laurens in these Cape Town days. A young Johannesburg couple had decided to combine their honeymoon at the Cape with an important court case for the lawyer husband. At the opening session the wife noticed an intensely handsome young Reporter with clear blue eyes, and exchanged a word or two. She returned to her hotel room to rest, to be disturbed by a knock on the door – it was the same Reporter, who flung off his clothes. There was no discussion, and they embarked on a wild and passionate two-week affair. They planned a life together, they would run away to Europe, but first she had to go back to Johannesburg where, to her horror, she discovered that she was pregnant; she was convinced the child could only be the Reporter's 'because she and her husband had been taking every precaution'. But no need to panic, they were in love. She telephoned and told him the glad news. She did not hear from him again. When she contacted his newspaper, she was told that he had left the country.

She had an abortion, and would never have a child. Many, many years later Laurens – for it was he! – asked Nadine to invite the lady, who happened to be a neighbour, to join them at lunch in her Parktown home. It was clear, says Nadine, that they had not met for many years. The lady drove Laurens back to his hotel. She remembered the same profile, the same blue eyes, the same overpowering charm. He laid his elderly hand on hers: 'My dear,' he said, 'Not a day has passed in all these years when I have not thought of you . . .'[21]

13

England in the 1930s

LAURENS SAILED BACK to England in March 1931 on the *Gloucester Castle*. He wrote about this voyage in *Yet Being Someone Other*, describing how he had worked his passage as a 'trimmer', carrying coal to the stokers for eight hours a day in appalling heat. It had given him a sentimental memory of the British working man, his dignity, self-respect, lack of bitterness, his features 'fine-drawn and ennobled by the great though inscrutable and uncompromising artist that sheer necessity is in the lives of those who are ruled by it'.[1]

When he wrote (in Afrikaans) to T. C. Robertson on 7 June, immediately after his arrival in Dorset, he made no mention of this, merely saying that 'my journey to England was very unsatisfactory. I had to travel steerage . . . my fellow passengers were Rhodesian and Kenyan settlers which affected us because the boat was a model of the original ark . . . Thus far I don't find England appealing. The climate does not agree with me . . . Campbell, I understand is half-mad from drink and nerves . . . my plan is now to get to an island in the Mediterranean Sea near Toulon as quickly as possible and to go and live there . . . In these circumstances don't come over for at least a year . . .' Laurens was exaggerating. His personal journal of 1930/31 switches into Afrikaans – so that Marjorie could not understand? – to describe how he was indeed travelling 'steerage' when some of the stokers were taken ill and passengers were offered ten shillings a day to help stoke boilers. Laurens did this for five days and, by the time he came to write *Yet Being Someone Other*, had turned it into something more dramatic.

In the journal, Laurens's depression is evident.

December 1930 (undated): There is a chance I'll accept a position with *The Times*. I have no stomach for it – what do I have the stomach for? – But I'll have to go for it for all sorts of reasons. For the time being Marjorie and I are living in the most dire poverty that exists . . . We have just enough money not to appear down and out . . . I remain unhappy . . . So many artificial and external influences were thrust upon me from my infancy that my natural abilities manifested themselves all crooked and stunted . . . If I can just get my foot in the door at *The Times*.[2]

He was never to land a job at *The Times*, contrary to what he afterwards told members of his family, who were under the impression he was Diplomatic Correspondent; but he was undoubtedly helped, socially and perhaps financially, by some older friends, Reggie Harris, a senior *Times* leader-writer, and his wife Lucia, who was John's godmother, and after whom Laurens and Marjorie would name their daughter. Mrs Harris sometimes took in John or went to stay at the Gloucestershire farm which Laurens later owned, to help Marjorie. The Harrises kept up a contact with Laurens's son and family after the war.

After his arrival in Britain, Laurens appears to have gone through a crisis of confidence. His journal continues: 'René [Janin] especially, and W.P. [William Plomer] to some extent, have too high an opinion of me. I know full well what's wrong with me, but I lack the will-power, and the interest in life, to get myself straight. I become very dejected when I think of my future . . .'[3] Why, after the excitements of the *Cape Times*, this sense of failure? Had he perhaps been asked to leave after the disaster of the Paarl libel action? Or was it the *cafard* of a young man, insecure in his profession, separated by his own choice from his family and his culture, who was becoming painfully aware that he had taken up marriage and fatherhood too young?

T. C. Robertson did not accompany his friend to Europe because he guessed it would be hard to find a job in the recession and because he wanted to return to university to do a post-graduate degree. After this he became a crime reporter on the *Rand Daily Mail*, fought a couple of by-elections, and in the war was recruited by Smuts to run his anti-Nazi propaganda campaign. He spent the rest of his working life as a respected early environmentalist, an eccentric and inspirational character founding and running the South African Veld Trust. He lost touch with Laurens for many years, but resumed a close friendship later, when he was one of the few people Laurens permitted to contradict or debunk him.[4]

In September 1930, when Laurens must have told him of his plan to work his passage home, Plomer had replied from England, 'I was quite sure all the time that you were unhappy in that cursed country, and I hope and pray that after leaving it this time you may never set foot in it again . . . Nothing enrages me more than the thought of the best years of your youth being poured into a sink like Cape Town.' He worried about

Laurens's health, and Laurens's plan of working his passage: 'Is this voyage not a little "Campbellesque" as a gesture?' He would not have realised that Campbell had been writing frequently to Laurens in South Africa, telling him the gossip about their London friends and hinting at an approaching estrangement from Plomer: 'I do not get on with his "milieu" of broken-backed intellectuals and nancy-boys, and he does not get on with my friends who are mostly boxers, steeple-chasers and rather grim fellows like [T.S.] Eliot and [Wyndham] Lewis.'[5]

Roy Campbell was now living in Provence, in Martigues near the mouth of the Rhone. Plomer, hearing of Laurens's plans, warned him of Campbell's character: 'His is a violently warped nature . . . and I fear his possible influence on you'. He need not have worried because Laurens and Campbell do not seem to have met when Laurens, parking his family near Blandford in Dorset, took himself off to Porquerolles, in October 1931, in order to finish his novel and, he once said, to attempt a play. Porquerolles is a tiny Mediterranean island, part of the Hyères group, offshore from Toulon. It became a special place for Laurens, and many years later he agreed to make a BBC film about *The Tempest* only on condition that it could be filmed there.[6]

Laurens did indeed complete a draft of *In a Province* over the next six months, most of which he spent alone on the island. His absence from his family began to worry people: his mother wrote in April 1932 to say that she had heard nothing from Marjorie in reply to several letters. Laurens returned to Marjorie and John at the end of May 1932, and they moved to Lyndhurst, in Hampshire. Various of his correspondents were also concerned for his health, and they also felt that he was revising his manuscript too often. René Janin, for example, now in Costa Rica, wrote frequently to William Plomer deploring some '*lamentable histoire*' at Lyndhurst and urging that Laurens return to the South of France as soon as possible – which Laurens did on 23 December. Janin would spend the next years in Central America, but the closeness and complexity of his relationship with Laurens are illustrated by the fact that Laurens dedicated to him his first novel.[7]

Plomer's letters to his friend are a good source for the period. 'I greatly enjoyed my stay at Lyndhurst,' he wrote in an undated letter to Laurens, 'but there were certainly various clouds in the air . . . With such a fine book on the stocks and with such a fine son at your knee you have, it seems to me, much to be proud and glad of . . . I spent last evening with Forster and he would like very much to read your book in manuscript when it is ready, if you are willing.' On 3 January 1933 he reported that Chatto & Windus had turned the book down: 'I now suggest that I write to the woolves [Leonard and Virginia Woolf] with a personal recommendation.'[8]

18 July 1933 is the date of the first known letter from Lilian Bowes Lyon to Laurens. He had first heard her name in a letter from Plomer on 18 December 1929: 'I gave a party this week . . . [he lists the guests] – and another girl called Lilian Bowes Lyon.' Some time in 1932, Lilian wrote to Plomer, undated, 'I liked your friend Laurens van der Post so much. I think he is unusual. He has the *quality* that one looks for in people and so rarely finds.' Plomer sent Laurens the letter; she now became one of his closest friends. Nine years older than Laurens, who was now twenty-five, she was in love with him and Laurens reciprocated; though many years later he was greatly angered when Plomer's biographer referred to their relationship as 'an affair', the fact is inescapable that they were lovers for at least three years. She dedicated her poems to him; after her death in 1949 the novelist Rosamond Lehmann – a dear friend of both – wrote to Laurens on 27 August 1949, 'There was nobody she loved as she loved you – well, you don't need me to tell you that.'[9]

Lilian was a remarkable and gifted woman who had had the courage to remove herself, unlike her sisters, from the repressive dominance of her father, Francis Bowes Lyon. His mother was a daughter of the Earl of Strathmore, so she was therefore a cousin of Queen Elizabeth, consort of George VI and the future Queen Mother; when she chose to live in the East End during the war she is supposed to have been dubbed the 'Queen of the Slums'. She became a novelist under the pseudonym D. J. Cotman, then a poet, strongly influenced by the countryside and particularly by her native Northumberland. Plomer, Laurens recorded many years after his death, once confessed to Laurens that he was thinking of marriage and had decided to propose to her. Laurens, who was involved with her at the time and who also knew by now of Plomer's homosexuality, was thunderstruck. Plomer was gently rejected by Lilian.

Plomer, like all her friends, was constantly worrying about her health, which was poor and getting worse. 'Lilian has taken her bones to the north, poor dear. She fell downstairs when she was last here and she was so light she feels as if a parachute were attached to her . . .' Again, also undated, 'Lilian is now in a nursing home . . . her trouble is diabetes, which is, I believe, more serious when one is young than when old . . . She is now rather weak, and troubled with her heart, and terribly *bored*. So if you could write to her soon . . .'[10]

In March 1934 Laurens bought the 109-acre Colley Farm in Gloucestershire, just outside Tetbury, a pleasant honey-stone market town on the plateau of the Cotswolds. It would have been impossible for

Laurens to raise the funds and it must be assumed that Lilian either paid for it or guaranteed a loan. At the same time she bought a cottage called Little Field, half a mile from Colley. There is a family memory of Marjorie going up to the attic window to look down on Little Field to check whether Laurens's car was parked at the cottage.

The farming project could hardly have succeeded. England's farmers were struggling in the depths of recession. Laurens could not seriously claim to be equipped to run an English farm, as a village boy who had only visited the family farm in the Free State at weekends or on holidays; he had no experience of dairy farming or of Britain's agrarian system and climate. No doubt he thought he would have time to write, isolated in the countryside from his busy London social life, but he could not abandon London if only because he needed to scrape a living there, so he was constantly on the train from Tetbury to Paddington. His friends' reaction was summed up in a letter to Plomer from René Janin in Costa Rica on 21 January 1934: 'The news of the Lilian-Laurens farming project has stunned me . . . It seems to me foolhardy, above all because it is based on a loan. Has Laurens given up writing? . . . I find the idea remarkable and imprudent.' This letter, in French, seems to confirm that the farm was bought through Lilian. Laurens's friends evidently found it hard to take his farming ambitions seriously: William Plomer wrote to Enslin du Plessis [undated], 'I hear that Laurens is turning into a complete farmer. I don't envy him – I'd rather find milk on the doorstep than have to extract it from a cow.'[11]

In the meantime, Laurens had achieved the great breakthrough which had obsessed him for years: *In a Province* was accepted by the Hogarth Press, the prestigious small Bloomsbury publishing house which had been founded by Leonard and Virginia Woolf. Plomer and his other friends had been anxiously trying to place it for some time ('I also dropped in a discreet phrase about Forster's having read it') and at last, on 7 September 1933, Laurens had the briefest and most gratifying of letters from Leonard Woolf: 'I am afraid we have been rather a long time over your manuscript. I think that you have undoubtedly improved it. It is a very interesting book and we should like to publish it for you.' Laurens kept that letter for the rest of his life, and never forgot his gratitude to the Hogarth Press which, incorporated into Chatto & Windus, remained his publisher until 1995.[12]

In a Province takes its title, at Plomer's suggestion, from *Ecclesiastes*: 'If thou seest the oppression of the poor, and violent perverting of judgement and justice in a province, marvel not at the matter'. The central figure is the twenty-five-year-old Johan van Bredepoel, who is recovering from a serious illness which can no doubt acquire a symbolic South African meaning. He goes to convalesce in 'Paulstad', a country town on the borders of the black territory of 'Bambuland'. That is to say, van Bredepoel goes on a journey; he does not want to resume his old life; his illness has taken him into the interior.

He recalls his country childhood, which contains various images and events familiar to us from Laurens's upbringing in Philippolis. The story then moves to Cape Town and the life of a boarding house in the shadow of Table Mountain. Van Bredepoel meets and befriends an African servant, Kenon, who has also just arrived from the interior and who soon begins to lose his natural self-respect: he forgets the confidence of his tribal upbringing. This is an early example of a South African genre known by the critics as 'Jim goes to Jo'burg'. Its most famous example would be Alan Paton's *Cry the Beloved Country*, and indeed there are various respects in which Paton's international best-seller is arguably derivative of Laurens's earlier and less commercially successful example. It might also be suggested that this is a paternalistic tradition in white South African writing.

The lonely van Bredepoel is changed by the young African's tragedy. *In a Province*, which has been 'about' Cape Town in the 1920s – even including references to the financial plight of the city orchestra founded by Laurens's father-in-law – turns into a political novel. Van Bredepoel's widowed aunt tells him, 'We all made a terrible mistake coming to this country. It hasn't done us any good.' Five long years have passed, and during a racial incident van Bredepoel meets Burgess, a trade union orga-niser, a communist, a revolutionary. They become friends. Laurens is here introducing a theme, a debate, which would interest him for many years, and which he develops in van Bredepoel's arguments with Burgess: 'Man, after all, wasn't governed entirely by economic forces . . . he doubted ever if much change in the world was possible, unless accom-panied by a change of heart.' Burgess lectures him: 'Your pity is a sham . . . no pity is worth the name of pity unless it has the courage and the actions that pity demands.'[13]

By extreme coincidence, van Bredepoel, who is now thinking of buying a farm in the fictitious district of Bambuland, meets Kenon there. Burgess also arrives to set up a political rally. Van Bredepoel argues with his friend; if there is any possibility of bloodshed, he should not hold the meeting. Burgess replies that the 'interests of the whole are far more important than the interests of the units.' '"Yes", says van Bredepoel,

"But the trouble is that the people you are trying to help are the very people most likely to get hurt" . . .' (This would be a consistent argument of Laurens many years later when he involved himself in the South African debate.) Burgess replies, 'All your life you have been sitting on your little liberal fence with your fears on either side. I know that you hate as I do the misery which the system in this country produces, but you hate the thought of the temporary misery that must accompany any reform, just as much.' (In turn this is an acute reference to the conservatism of white South African liberalism.)

Van Bredepoel is caught up in a police trap and the rally becomes a Sharpeville-style massacre. Burgess is wounded and van Bredepoel, assuming a position endorsed and preached by Laurens in later years, insists that his friend accept responsibility: 'I quite see that our social system inflicts many injustices on people like Kenon, but I cannot see that it is entirely responsible for their reactions to those injustices . . . Your enemy and mine in this country is not the system but the heart of every white man. You can't legislate a man's heart away.' To which Burgess replies, 'So you would just let the white people in this country go on having too much, and the black people not enough . . .' Van Bredepoel can only reply that 'It's terribly wrong.' And later he thinks, 'I am going to begin by minding my own step . . . If the system perpetuates a colour-prejudice, we can counteract it by refusing to admit a colour-prejudice in our own lives . . . If we are too rich, we can counteract riches by leading a simple life and helping the poor . . . No, Burgess. I might have believed in your principles once; I don't believe in your methods.'

Van Bredepoel and Burgess escape from a lynch party of the enraged local whites. In the pursuit, van Bredepoel is shot, and dies. The novel ends in incoherent rhetoric: 'Johan, Kenon! Poor unhappy children of life, courage! People like Burgess still sow out of their love of the oppressed the seeds of a terrible hate.'[14]

In a Province is a compelling and fast-moving novel, complete with a memorable portrait of Cape Town and a cast of convincing characters, which brings to life the political debate that was to preoccupy South Africa for the next fifty years. It is indeed a *political* novel, and as such is very different from Plomer's *Turbott Wolfe*, to which it owed various debts. Laurens, via van Bredepoel, worked through to the political position which he would hold for the rest of his life. It was not a position which would be embraced by the Burgesses of South Africa over the years ahead, nor by many South Africans who were not remotely communist or revolutionary, as Burgess is declared to be. It may be noted that it is not the revolutionary Burgess but van Bredepoel who is killed (South African liberals have always been pessimistic), as is Kenon.

Laurens effectively used his journalistic experiences to give verisimilitude to his fiction. This was a period when the black Industrial and Commercial Union was active. The two riots in the book, in Port Benjamin and then Paulstad, are possibly based on two actual episodes at the time, one in Cape Town, the other in Durban, which the Government blamed on communist provocation. Laurens's Port Benjamin is sometimes a conflation of the two cities and he would obviously have been very conscious of these alarming disturbances. Burgess, his fictional white radical, can only be based upon William Ballinger, a trade union organiser from England, whom Laurens knew and whose articles he published in the *Cape Times*.[15]

This is a remarkably coherent and eloquent book for someone writing his first novel in his second language. There is the occasional clumsiness of phrasing or plotting, and Laurens sometimes wanders into pulpit oratory, but the prose is taut, sentences are short, the descriptions are rarely too ornate, and the dialogue is convincing. All these are qualities which Laurens risked losing in his postwar books. Indeed, it would be hard to predict that the author of *In a Province* would one day write, for instance, *A Story Like the Wind*. Laurens was transformed in many ways in the years before and after the war: his prose style was another example of this. But his, and van Bredepoel's, ideological position, did not shift.

14

A Lost Soul

IN A PROVINCE was published in 1934 in a modest edition of 1,250 copies. It was well received, though never a grand success. Herbert Read, the distinguished critic and art historian, described it in *The Spectator* as 'a novel with a purpose which is also a work of art ... a very remarkable achievement': it was the best novel he had read for months. 'In a world paralysed between the extremes of marxism and fascism ... this book puts forward a point of view that imposes the burden of revolution on the individual rather than the state'. The novelist Compton Mackenzie wrote in the *Daily Mail* that 'An individual novelist of much promise has appeared.'[1] The poet Stephen Spender, in a 1935 book called *The Destructive Element*, linked *In a Province* with Edward Upward and Franz Kafka, 'because it is a serious political novel which is a complete refutation of the revolutionary tactics of Communists'. It was, argued Spender, 'a book which has as its subject revolutionary politics, but which is not propagandist'.[2] *In a Province* was also published in America in early 1935 by Coward-McCann. It made no great impact but was greeted by the *New York Times* Book Review as 'a novel which manifests a deep power and frequently a lyrical beauty, and which, nevertheless, shows a remarkable understanding of the political equation between fascism and communism ...'[3]

Here was a book of which Laurens was right to be proud. A part of its fascination is that, in the central issues of the 1930s debate about communism – crudely, 'means' versus 'ends' – it employed the new and exotic location of South Africa. The fact that Laurens was evidently unable to follow up with a second book betrays his confusion and dislocation in the years that led up to the war. He afterwards said he had been working on a 'book of warning', arguing that Germany had been taken over by ancient mythological forces which would lead to war. It was provisionally entitled *The Rainbow Bridge*. The rainbow, he later explained, was the natural image of awareness and consciousness; the Gods of *Götterdämmerung* were destroyed by their hubris, arrogating to themselves the right to walk over, rather than under, it. Laurens used to say that the manuscript had been lost, together with all his papers, in the London Blitz while he was overseas. It is not clear whether some of his 1930s documents were in fact lost in the Blitz. A fair number of papers have survived; possibly at some date he 'weeded' his records to gloss over a difficult and unhappy decade. The theme of *The Rainbow Bridge* was developed later in *The Dark Eye in Africa*.[4] *In a Province*, soon forgotten at the time of its publication, was re-issued in 1953 after the success of *Venture to the Interior*, and remained in print for at least thirty years.[5]

Although Laurens was enormously gratified by the publication and reception of his first novel, it could not solve his financial needs, which is why he set out on the dangerous course of trying to combine farming in Gloucestershire with journalism in London, rushing to and fro by train every day. His journalism was undistinguished, as one of a small team in the London office of the South African Argus group, working with his old friend Enslin du Plessis. Of course, he must have had help to run a mixed farm, including dairy cows, on this daily routine. Each morning Marjorie drove John to Tetbury primary school, terrified because she had no driving licence. Their London friends visited them (and Lilian next door). Laurens afterwards claimed that he had won a prize in the local Agricultural Show for 'Best-Kept Small Farm': but there is no record of any such award in the Three Counties archives, nor that he used to go out with the super-fashionable Beaufort Hunt, as he claimed fifty years later.[6] In the end, he gave up – farming in the 1930s Depression was a desperate business – and sold out in September 1937. Lilian wrote to tell him to keep the money. 'Whatever you do about Colley, Colley is yours. You made it yours by love for it, and all the loving work you put into it.' Later, when Laurens was in South Africa attending the birth of his daughter Lucia, and realised that Lilian had made a loss in selling the Little Field cottage, she wrote, 'No, invest the money and don't touch it unless you have to.' In the same letter Lilian added that she had just paid John's school fees.[7] His affair with Lilian seems to have matured into a close friendship.

When in London he mixed socially on the edge of the Bloomsbury group. His friends included Plomer, du Plessis, Stephen Spender, E. M. Forster, Cecil Day Lewis, Anthony Butts, Rosamond Lehmann, Keith Millar-Jones, Reggie and Lucia Harris. Roy Campbell had departed for good to France, then Spain. Laurens met Maynard Keynes and the Woolfs, with whom he argued about Dickens. In 1933 he became a friend of Lincoln Kirstein, later the founder of the New York City Ballet. Kirstein, who was flamboyantly bisexual, described Laurens in his 1995 memoir: 'Laurens, for me, had an extraordinary animal fascination, almost like a domesticated springbok or okapi. Extremely sleek, fair-haired, almost always laughing or smiling at everything and everybody, he spoke hardly at all but gave off an aura of intense goodwill, generous sympathy, and delight at being alive . . . He was a living encyclopaedia of South African lore, and was able to describe weather, landscape, colour and temperature as if it were the rehearsal for a poetic narrative which he'd not yet committed to paper . . . He had, for me, the gift of a narrative bard . . . What was even more fascinating and provocative was that he seemed to have no particular personality of his own.'*

Laurens was also evidently taken with Kirstein. On 21 December 1933 he wrote to him, 'I think of you always and long to meet you again . . . Knowing you has done me so much good and with one exception you are the only person who can make me want to write to him after writing my own muck all day.' Many of Laurens's friends, particularly in the 1930s, were homosexual, and evidently he moved at ease in homosexual circles. He had the gift of charming both men and women. At his death he felt the need to leave a memorandum attesting that he himself had never been homosexual.

In that same letter to Kirstein he gave a picture of the poet W. B. Yeats, whom apparently he had just met: 'I have never seen anybody more spoilt and touchy of what he imagines to be his grandeur. He loves to preach at a room full of people . . . though good manners are not all-important, it says a lot for those of the English who were there that they listened to him politely, comparing their national character unfavourably with that of cannibals, Hindus and Japanese, and God knows what . . .'[9]

However, Laurens was only, in his own words, 'a small, tentative part of Bloomsbury': he was discomfited, even repelled, by the over-intellectual atmosphere, as he would try to explain years later when he described his rejection of the Modernist movement. He later said in

---

*Kirstein describes how he spent time 'almost every day' with Laurens when he was in London. On 8 August 1933, for example, he and Laurens dined 'with William Plomer, his friend Bernard, the guardsman, and Morgan Forster and his Bob Buckingham, a constable. Laurens arrived at the restaurant late with a bagful of bottles of South African wine.' After much drink, 'Laurens saw that I could hardly get to my room and manfully supported me . . . Reaching my bed, I fell flat on my face, and I suppose that Laurens composed himself on the straw-matted floor . . . I heard Laurens murmuring his "Zulu clicks", and told myself that I didn't absolutely have to go to Paris . . . Sleep dropped its curtain, muffling any reply, and I swallowed oblivion.'[8]

Venture to the Interior that he spent these years travelling constantly between Africa and Europe, seeking to discover his identity; in fact, except for one period in 1936 and early 1937, he travelled very little, after he had finished the book and come home from the south of France early in 1933. His marriage was in difficulty. He was drinking heavily. He seemed unable to build on *In a Province* and produce a second book.[10] In spring 1936 he must have come to some sort of crisis. Between 13 April and 24 July he made no fewer than five journeys to or from South Africa, alone, on a German passenger liner with a strong Nazi administration called the *Watussi*, during the busiest season for farming. He wrote of the *Watussi* later but he never really explained what he was doing.[11] Whatever had possessed him, on the third outward voyage, in July, he met Ingaret Giffard.

This meeting has been publicly treated three times. In romantic detail, it features in Ingaret's autobiography, *The Way Things Happen*, published in 1989, in which the relevant final chapters were in fact written by Laurens; second, it is the climax of Laurens's second novel, the strongly autobiographical *The Face Beside the Fire* (1953); third, Laurens refers to it very discreetly in his own *Yet Being Someone Other* (1982). That meeting was the beginning of an intense and anguished triangular relationship, between Laurens, Ingaret, and her husband, which would only be resolved eleven years later.

Ingaret Giffard was at that time an elegant, sophisticated yet insecure woman of thirty-two, product of a Devonshire family which liked to claim descent from William the Conqueror. Her cousin was the Earl of Halsbury; the family had produced several Lord Chancellors, and Ingaret was extremely proud of this although she belonged to a comparatively impoverished branch – even her friends would admit that she was something of a snob. She enjoyed, and suffered, an extraordinarily intense relationship with her neurotic mother, 'Chubbs', who needed psychological supervision for most of her life. Ingaret and Chubbs remained deeply dependent on each other until Chubbs died in 1973.

Ingaret had been married since 1931 to Jimmy Young, son of a wealthy City businessman. They had spent a difficult year in the Sudan immediately after their marriage. On their return Ingaret had attempted a career as a novelist, actress and then as a playwright. She published a novel called *Sigh No More, Ladies,* and reached what would be the height of her success with the West End production of her play *Because We Must,* a typical 1930s drawing-room comedy/drama complete with French windows and mannered upper-middle-class characters. It ran for eighteen performances in

February 1937 and is remembered for the second West End appearance of Vivien Leigh, who had rather better notices than the play itself. Ingaret would spend many years trying to write a second acceptable play. This background brought her theatrical friends, notably Athene Seyler and her partner Beau Hannen, with whom Ingaret toured as an actress in South Africa in 1930. When Laurens met her on the *Watussi*, Ingaret was living in Chelsea with Jimmy and frequently visited Half-Crown Cottage in Aldeburgh, which she had bought several years before with a gift from her mother-in-law.[12]

In his autobiographical description of this 1936 voyage on the *Watussi*, published forty-six years later in *Yet Being Someone Other*, Laurens merely wrote, 'Of course, there was much else of great personal significance to these voyages, not least the human relationships which were to transform my life and which continue to this day.' He chose not to mention that here he had met the person who would become his second wife. In his earlier novel, *The Face Beside the Fire*, however, he wrote more fully of a shipboard romance between his protagonist and the English woman whom he calls Alys Denysse, in scenes which, notwithstanding Laurens's denials, everyone who knew them concluded were based on his meeting with Ingaret. 'This is my first experience of the heraldry of love', declares David, the hero. 'Often they would make of the night a home for their dazzled senses and sit with the ship's pulse vibrant beneath them, and a gold, metallic, clanking and clanging starlight against the mast and funnels above, until the dawn rang out like a bang on a Buddhist gong in some far Eastern temple.' Alys's husband and father-in-law meet the ship. David will have to overcome his demons and go out to claim his true love.[13]

In Ingaret's memoir, *The Way Things Happen*, eventually published in 1989 after she had been overcome by dementia, the meeting with Laurens, more accurately, takes place during the *Watussi*'s outward voyage. They dance ('he was not a good dancer but it did not matter'). They play deck-tennis ('which he played extremely well'). Laurens makes a point of showing her snapshots of a young woman and two children: he is warning her that he is a married man (there is a mistake here – he had only one child at the time). They go to his cabin and embrace on the bunk: 'It had not been an erotic indulgence; it had not been an expression of physical attraction. It was a human experience; but it was also something beyond human understanding . . . I was no longer alone: in fact I could never be alone again.'[14]

Laurens and Ingaret evidently fell in love with each other during that journey in July 1936, but nothing was to be simple. To begin with, they were both married, and to complicate things further, Jimmy and Laurens discovered that they liked each other. Jimmy was a bit of a playboy, happy to divide his time between a daytime job in the City and London's night-clubs, and Ingaret sometimes thought she was devoted to him, despite her feeling for Laurens.[15] Moreover Laurens was neither able nor content to sit at her feet and await a sensible conclusion. In 1936 Marjorie was pregnant and went out to Durban to give birth to a daughter, Lucia. The detail is not clear but Laurens seems to have stayed out there, in South Africa, at the end of his fifth *Watussi* voyage – his new passport was issued in Durban on 3 March 1937, so he must have been in South Africa at the time. He then indulged in various wild escapades, at a time when, his books claim, he was observing the fast-growing German Fascism, and even reporting on Nazi rallies. For example, he rediscovered a passion for a beautiful, young and bisexual South African heiress of the Central News Agency family called Joan St Leger Lindbergh, and pursued her to his favourite island of Porquerolles. Laurens lost her to a woman, but not before he and Joan had vanished on a ten-day binge in Paris, emerging in a state of exhaustion and near destruction.[16]

Laurens was confronting disintegration. It was early 1938 and it was now that he sent Marjorie and the two children to South Africa, on the argument that war was coming and they would be safe there while he would go to be a soldier. They did not see him again for many years.[17]

Those of Laurens's and Ingaret's letters which have survived give glimpses of the next years. The first is dated 2 August 1936, from Laurens in Johannesburg to Ingaret in Simon's Town, where she was staying at the British Royal Naval base with her brother: 'My Dear Little Patience – I am a pig for not writing . . . I have been working and waiting for my mother . . . you have not comforted in vain and you have helped . . . but I am in a wasteland and not sure I can get out of it.' Another (undated): 'Ingaret – where have we met before? I mean, long before the *Watussi*. I woke up this morning overcome with a feeling that I had known you a long, long time ago . . .' And a third, also undated, from Laurens in Fleet Street: 'Please ask me always to do what is necessary, to make the right and only the right contributions to your life and through you to Jimmy. We are in such a long voyage together . . .'[18]

Laurens returned from South Africa in March 1937, soon after Ingaret and a newly-prospering Jimmy had bought a house in Cadogan Street in a fashionable district of Central London. Jimmy in old age remembered Ingaret telling him, 'I have met a South African man who is in desperate need of help.' To which Jimmy, the most generous of men, had replied, 'Then he must come and stay.' As Ingaret's romantic autobiography puts it, 'I picked up the receiver. It was Laurens – and he was in London! I nearly collapsed from sheer joyful surprise. "Laurens!" My heart was now beating far more strongly than was my head. "How long have you been here?" "I arrived early this morning . . . when can we meet?"'

The solution was that Laurens was given a room in Cadogan Street during the week and went down to farm and family at the weekend. But – Ingaret recalled – it was too difficult: 'As I lay beside Jimmy in our huge double bed the tears would sometimes roll down my cheeks . . . and I had to let them roll, for I feared that by sobbing I would have shaken the bed and woken Jimmy. The torment of unfulfilled unity had become almost unbearable.' So Laurens eventually took a room around the corner.[19]

Ingaret developed appendicitis and her recovery was strangely slow. Laurens visited her hospital bed every day. To escape from what she felt was an impossible situation she went off to Portugal, in October 1937, and stayed there for about six months. Laurens wrote to her (undated), 'When I think back of what you have been and done for me, how you accepted me so darkly and yet so surely, my own contribution seems so inadequate and unequal, and is particularly inadequate in this matter of presenting myself, perhaps, as a kind of choice . . . I can't believe the three of us will fail to find for you and us all the best . . . PS. I wonder if you know how much I miss you.' The letters of the next two years reveal the anguish and confusion of all three. On 5 August, Laurens wrote to Ingaret in Innsbruck, 'I love being in your house and it is good to have Jimmy back. I find him a considerate, helpful and stimulating person to be with and these last days I have really had some good laughs.' He went on: 'Last week I went to see John and the farm. I am afraid the farm is doomed. I have had such a good offer for it.' On 11 October 1937, just before she went to Portugal, he wrote her a love letter: 'I feel blank to the edge of despair at the thought of this desperation which you find, and I believe, is necessary . . . You indirectly helped me to do something I ought to have done, even if I had never met you at all . . . It is a scientific fact that I love you and – I feel shy saying this. . . .'

On 1 November, when he could write to her in the Algarve, Jimmy – apparently also in Portugal – is a factor again: 'I realised again how much at heart I want to be in your life – and for you to be in mine . . . I am so glad that you and Jimmy are somewhere alone. I have always felt somewhat protective about your relationship with Jimmy . . . We could help each other.' Then on 20 March 1938 Laurens wrote from Dublin (Ingaret has just returned to Cadogan Street from Portugal and Laurens is in low humour), 'Frankly, my relationship with you which had seemed and been so clear suddenly went dark. It was one of the most awful things that has ever happened to me . . . you have decided that your relationship with Jimmy must be given the fullest trial. For God's sake let there be an emotional simplification in your life to match the quality of your decision . . . It may sound extravagant or even melodramatic, but a reintegration of all the scattered parts of my experience and personality into one single unit has become a matter of life and death to me. At the moment I am in a worse state psychologically than I have ever been . . . the only way I can help you just now is to help at a distance . . . my conviction [is] that for some time to come we ought not to meet. Goethe said that only things tested in loneliness were worthwhile.'

They continue to torment themselves. On 7 June 1938, Laurens to Ingaret in Aldeburgh: 'My hand is trembling very much today . . . yes, you were wise to stay, incredibly beloved. . . . You have suddenly taken a seven-league stride inside yourself and I wished I could race you, but my seven-league boots are worn out and I must get a new pair . . . I felt intensely proud to be with you . . . On Sunday, it seemed to me that this instinct of yours was regaining the courage of its prime . . . I feel closer to you at this distance just now than I have sometimes with you in the same bed.'[20]

Ingaret's replies are not so frequent in the archives: 'You never burden me, dear one. My only burden is the fact that all cannot be shared. I love you. One day you will believe it.' In 1938 at the time of Munich, she is ecstatic: 'This cloud that has lifted off our heads . . . is unbelievable.' But Laurens has vanished (he had gone to Porquerolles): 'Darling, I do wish I knew where you are. I feel you must have left that island or something . . . I do so wish I could hear from you.' Ingaret did in fact hear from Laurens from Porquerolles, in a letter dated 13 October 1938. He asked her to sort out a money problem, complained about the *mistral*, and mentioned that he had passed though Martigues where his friend Roy Campbell was remembered not for his poetry but for 'his misdemeanours in the bullring'.

At this point in October or November 1938 (the letter is also undated), Ingaret comes up with a wild idea in the depressed aftermath of Munich ('everyone seems to feel we have let the Czechs down'). She had decided that the three of them, Laurens, Jimmy and herself, should retreat to Portugal in order to avoid a certain war: 'I refuse to accept it. Just as I refuse to accept gasmasks on my face.' To go to Portugal would not be 'an escape of fear: it would be a definite desire to create something'. She immediately added that she would do this only if both Laurens and

Jimmy agreed to come with her: 'If you are going to fight then I will stay here until you get killed along with everybody else – and I grow old alone.' But she returns to her plan. 'Everybody here with children that can, is leaving London.' They could count on £300 per year, and live off it. It seems that she and Laurens have quarrelled, and she is sorry. 'Whatever happens, I feel you are the only man I shall ever know; and Jimmy the only child I shall ever have. It's a superficial world that imposes labels upon us, the wrong labels too, such as "Husband" and "Lover" . . . But although the world calls J. my husband, he is nevertheless, psychologically, my child. Which explains a lot of things. Just as you, whatever else you may be, are psychologically my man.'[21]

Needless to say, the threesome never escaped to Portugal as Ingaret suggested. Laurens came back from Porquerolles and resumed his modest role in the South African Argus Group office. Ingaret – and perhaps Jimmy? – was lending him money. He was hoping for a BBC job. War was declared on 3 September 1939. He told Ingaret that he did not believe that the war would last for long. His state of mind can be seen in a letter he wrote to her on 13 October: 'Your instructions shall be obeyed and I shall hand over the money to Jimmy immediately . . . The impersonality of my life terrifies me . . . It is horrible not to care about oneself passionately and intensely, for it leads to not being able to care about life and those who live it. Ingaret, dearest, I used to be so different. I remember as a boy of 14 writing in my diary, "I shall live my life as if it belongs not only to me but to all those who might come to love me." And I did try, there was nothing mean or mangy or secretive or underhand about it. I will try to get back to it again.' He continued, 'You have given me the will to try . . . but please go on just a bit longer . . . They say the worst part of drowning is not the drowning but the coming to. I feel rather like that.'

Ingaret was now in Liverpool working as a Censor. Jimmy was about to depart with the Royal Navy Volunteer Reserve.[22]

And so, in late 1939, in love with Ingaret, out of love with Marjorie, Laurens found himself with no money, no family, no farm, no career, no new book, no certainty of Ingaret. He was close to becoming a lost soul.

PART THREE

'Charm is the ultimate weapon, the supreme seduction against which there are few defences. If you've got it, you need almost nothing else, neither looks, money nor pedigree.'

Laurie Lee

15

A New Life

To take up the tale after the conclusion, in Java 1947, of Part One: in the years after the Japanese surrender, Laurens, choosing to stay on in Asia, began to sort out his problems. In early middle age, he had to think through his personal life. Did he really want to marry Ingaret, who had been waiting for him so long? Would he turn his back on South Africa and his young family there? Was he tempted to try to remain in the Army, or become a diplomat, rather than renew his ambition to be a writer? And how to tackle the problem of his dubious rank? During his two years in Batavia he must have wrestled with questions such as these. What is unmistakable is that Laurens had been through a process of transformation. In 1947 he was a very different person from the man he had been in 1939.

In the 1930s, he had been insignificant; now he had the confidence which came of achievement, senior rank, respect, a reputation as a hero and leader of men. But as a corollary of this, in the second half of his life he was concerned, sometimes perhaps unconsciously, to excise – to 'dump' – his prewar years. In the immediate postwar period, he had surprisingly little to do with his mother and his brothers and sisters in South Africa. He kept up few of his prewar friendships. He set his marriage and his children behind him, and took another wife, a woman he had told his friends was his sister (an image, he apologised to Ingaret, which was 'a hangover from the past'). He proceeded to refashion his (and the van der Post) history in accordance with his new sense of an English distinction and security.[1] Later, he would exert himself to contradict and delete his friends' version of their youthful years together. In sum, in 1947, at the age of forty, he began his life again.

This transformation in the dramas of wartime is the key to Laurens's postwar personality. This sense of two Laurenses – pre- and post-war – chimes with the double image which he was about to present of himself in his books. In the prison camp, he wrote in 'The Desired Earth', he discovered a 'John Lawrence', colleague of Laurens Jan, and in the novellas which make up *The Seed and the Sower* John Lawrence would re-appear. In his novel *The Face Beside the Fire* there are 'twin' protagonists and friends. When Laurens was being beaten in the camp, he discovered in himself 'another person'. An Acting-Captain, he became a Lieutenant-Colonel. Eventually his autobiography would be called *Yet Being Someone Other*.[2] This duality, which would have fascinated his psychotherapist friends, characterised his postwar years of success and fame. His son had been christened 'Jan Laurens'.

Laurens visited South Africa briefly in 1947 at the end of his Java days; in *The Admiral's Baby* he describes how he flew from Singapore to Karachi on 6 June 1947 and then to Alexandria, en route for London. 'One of the strangest of all synchronicities' then occurred – he encountered a South African military aircraft on the airstrip, and was recognised by the crew. On the spur of the moment he accepted their invitation to join them on their flight to South Africa. He went home.

In a number of books over the years he wrote that on his arrival in the Transvaal he had an overwhelming need to immerse himself in the bush:

> Before I could face my own family and my mother whom I loved without reserve, I had to absent myself from all other human beings and in secret make my way, accompanied only by two haphazard helpers chosen from a group of unemployed among my black countrymen, far off into the bushveld and camped there on one of my favourite . . . rivers, the Pafuri, and live alone with nature and the animals for company . . . I remember the first evening in the wild, seeing the first kudu bull as I made camp . . . He threw that lovely head of his back, and I looked at him with a tremendous feeling of relief. I thought, 'My God, I'm back home!' . . . All the killing and death, dropped from me, and only then could I go home and greet my own Mother.[3]

He would tell this wonderful tale again and again over the years. The trouble is that it does not tally with other accounts. Judge Chris Plewman, one of his favourite nephews, remembers a different sequence. As a young man, Plewman in Johannesburg picked up Laurens, who had just arrived, and Laurens's nineteen-year-old son John, who had travelled up from Durban, and the three of them then drove north, up to the Limpopo and the Pafuri rivers. Plewman has no memory of a kudu bull (though there may have been one) and Laurens was not alone on that first trip into the bush. As so often in his life, Laurens wove a convincing story. The essence – that Laurens recovered his soul by retreating into the bush – is no doubt true. The detail, as so often, is embroidered and sometimes invented: visiting his stepbrother Henk in Jagersfontein, for example, he told him that Winston Churchill had offered him a senior post in the British Embassy in Washington (impossible since Churchill was now out of office).

His daughter Lucia, then ten years old, who had no previous memory of her father, would always recall the drama and excitement of his home-coming.[4] Laurens stayed in South Africa for about a month, then returned to England and to Ingaret. But on the way he must have enter-tained second thoughts. Returning by sea from Cape Town to England – before rejoining Ingaret who awaited him desperately, having seen him only once in seven years – he met the Kohler family on the Union Castle ship. Charles Kohler, one of South Africa's most prominent farmers and businessmen, was the founder of the country's great wine and spirits co-operative, the KWV.

Kohler's daughter, Jessie Kohler-Baker, was taking her two children to Europe. Fleur was seventeen, coming to London to study drama, and Bonny was nine. Laurens was utterly charming and attentive to them – the daughters afterwards agreed that their mother had quite fallen in love with this handsome and distinguished soldier. But Laurens was concen-trating on Fleur, with the result that by the end of the voyage a be-dazzled Fleur had become engaged to Laurens. (Bonny at that time couldn't stand him.) The only stipulation was that, since Fleur was so young, and because her grandfather disapproved, the engagement would be private and not announced for the time being.

The Kohler-Bakers must have known that Laurens was married (he told them he had come from Java to South Africa to arrange a divorce). They cannot have known that he was committed to Ingaret, who at that moment was planning to meet the boat at Southampton. Back in London, Ingaret and Jimmy even gave a party for Laurens to which the Kohler-Bakers were invited, both sides unaware of the deception. Laurens was intensely romantic to Fleur; he even gave her his OBE ribbons. She and Bonny afterwards suspected that Laurens had been seriously considering whether he might switch horses, so to speak, in mid-ocean, and become a wealthy Kohler son-in-law rather than marry Ingaret.

The three Kohler-Bakers had planned an extended holiday, and did indeed travel to France and Switzerland, but Laurens persuaded them to cut short their tour and return to South Africa because, he assured them, the international situation was extremely perilous. Even after their departure Laurens maintained the engagement for another six months or so, while living with Ingaret and sending Fleur love letters and poems. When, at last, he wrote to break off the engagement, saying that he was going to marry Ingaret, Fleur was devastated.[5]

Laurens stayed with Ingaret.

Ingaret's situation had been transformed when, in January 1947, she and Jimmy secured one of England's first 'quickie divorces' – but Laurens still needed his release from Marjorie, and he also needed to find a job. Technically, he was still in the Indian Army, but he had many months of leave due (he said sixteen), and he had decided to leave the Army although, he claimed, he was offered an enticing career. Later, he was sounded out as a potential Labour MP, which is amusing in the light of his future allegiances (Ingaret was a card-carrying Labour Party member during the war). During these months he must have succeeded in sorting out his status and rank, not to speak of his back pay and allowances, and his official 'release' from the Army in March 1948.[6]

In some respects Laurens's position when he returned to London in 1947 was not uncomfortable. He was living in 13 Cadogan Street, which Jimmy had given to Ingaret as part of the divorce settlement. Ingaret also had her own cottage in Aldeburgh, on the East Anglian coast, and she and Laurens were frequent visitors to her mother's home in Camberley in Surrey. But there were plenty of demobbed officers looking for work in Britain in 1947, and Laurens did not want just to resume his junior prewar career and company. He had to find some way of making a living while he addressed himself to his long ambition, to become a writer.

He visited Lilian, who was by now dying, in great pain and with great courage. Diabetes was destroying her circulation, and she endured a series of amputations on her legs. During the war she had moved from Kensington to the East End, to Stepney, to help the victims of the Blitz. She became a local heroine.* Her particular friend in these years was Plomer, who spent the war working at the Admiralty. Lilian published three volumes of poetry between 1941 and 1946, and in 1948 her *Collected Poems* appeared with an introduction by Cecil Day Lewis and a dedication which included both Plomer and Laurens. To Plomer, Lilian admitted

---

*There is a tale that, after a particularly heavy bombing raid, she telephoned her cousin, the Queen, to ask for surplus furniture from Windsor Castle: fifty years later the Queen Mother indicated, affectionately, that this was a myth.[7]

she had contemplated suicide ('I just want to tell you that your visit, and our friendship, yesterday afternoon, saved me from going off the rails').[8]

Plomer had also resumed his friendship with Laurens, and gave him a copy of his autobiography, *Double Lives*. Laurens wrote to congratulate him, but was privately furious. In a letter at the time he merely said that 'there are a few things I regret you do not mention . . .' By this he meant that he felt Plomer had understated his role in the *Voorslag* episode in 1926. Plomer's own affection for and generosity to Laurens is clear from his response to a story called 'A Bar of Shadow' which Laurens began to write in 1947, based on his own POW experiences. 'I read much between the lines and feel that I have had a glimpse of, so to speak, an iceberg with most of its bulk below the surface . . . You have, it seems to me, been wonderfully "liberated" in your inmost being, and I have an impression that your mind has been accordingly.'[9] Plomer's judgement, as so often, was correct. 'A Bar of Shadow' marked Laurens's return to writing after many years. It is a remarkably effective piece of autobiographical fiction, treating as it does the execution of 'Hara', a sadistic Japanese guard, and is Laurens's first published effort to convey the need for pity and forgiveness through his protagonist, 'John Lawrence'. 'A Bar of Shadow' appeared in *The Cornhill Magazine* in the Spring 1952 issue, and in 1963 was republished as one of three linked novellas in *The Seed and the Sower*.[10]

Laurens did decide to return to journalism, which meant, if he were to aim high, that he rejoin the Argus group back in South Africa. He was offered an Assistant Editorship of his old paper in Durban, now renamed the Natal *Daily News*, with the expectation, if the job was a success, of promotion within the group. That could lead to a significant role in South African affairs.[11] Laurens had gone out in February 1948 on the *Athlone Castle* and managed to see his friend John Blandy* in Madeira. He wanted to see whether he could live there contentedly and whether Ingaret would agree to live there too. He left her behind on the understanding that she would join him as soon as he had found suitable accommodation for her, and in the meantime she would try to find a passage on the heavily over-booked ships. She was desperate to rejoin Laurens, pouring out her heart in letters full of domestic details, and trying to pull strings to beat the eighteen-month waiting list for a ticket, while Laurens replied with descriptions of the boarding houses which might have a room for her.[12]

---

*Blandy, of the island's wine industry, had bumped into Laurens in the army recruitment queue in May 1940.[13]

In these two months Laurens, for the only time in his life, wrote a flood of letters to Ingaret, more than thirty in eight weeks. From the *Athlone Castle* on the voyage out he wrote on 22 February: 'You have been wonderful to me, for I have been very difficult and in the beginning only one quarter in the visible and tangible world, and I don't think I could ever have lifted myself again above my own surface to myself and you and ourselves if it had not been for your sweet and true love.' The voyage, he said, was boring: 'I have not been to a single dance or cinema show. My wine bill for the whole voyage has been £1.8s.4d.' Then, on 5 March, he sent a telegram (and a false alarm) from Cape Town, 'HAVE ARRANGED EVERYTHING WITH MARJORIE MUCH LOVE'. The severing of the marriage overshadowed the rest of the year. On 5 March, Laurens reported that Marjorie 'looked very thin and forlorn but had dressed very carefully and very well and it all made me feel particularly bloody . . . She reminded me of all the nights I had come home drunk and she had put up with it.' She reproached him for not being honest about Ingaret. Lucia, their young daughter, joined them: 'I left them both in tears on the railway station.' He wrote from Port Elizabeth on 7 March, 'This life out here makes me want to vomit . . .' And on 9 March, in Durban, 'Here I am, back where I started from.'[14]

Laurens had gone to live with Elaine, the widow of his brother Pooi. Between them Elaine and Pooi had carried most of the responsibility for bringing up Laurens's son John during the war, when Marjorie was struggling to cope with two children on her own. John had been sent to one of South Africa's top private schools, Michaelhouse, the fees paid by a group of uncles, aunts and family friends, together with whatever Marjorie could manage; he had for years made his home with Pooi and Elaine. Pooi, originally a lecturer in Afrikaans, who had then retrained in Guy's Hospital, London, in the 1930s and become an anaesthetist, had died six months before Laurens's return. John, now nineteen, was at university in Durban, reading mechanical engineering, funded by scholarships and again helped by his South African relations: his relationship with his father would always be cautious and rather distant, both now and later when he went to build a successful career in Britain. At this time Lucia was growing up in Cape Town with her mother, who was forced to take various modest jobs (Lucia had been consigned to a boarding nursery at the age of eighteen months). Laurens's main concern was to persuade a reluctant Marjorie, who apparently loved him all her life, to agree to a divorce. Majorie was hesitant, changing her mind, threatening to have nothing more to do with the children. 'I am afraid I shall have to learn how to feel about them,' she said. 'I really only begin and end with you.' He gloomily told Ingaret that he was expecting a newspaper head-line, 'Ex-Colonel Deserts Wife . . . but now that I have made up my mind I do not care.'

The strain of separation was evidently telling on both Laurens and Ingaret. Laurens raised the subject of his prewar drinking: 'I have no conscience about it – I drank only for one reason, because I could not at the time do without it. I would have died or killed myself without it. I was too tired and too dead to carry on – I was living with death all the time . . . If there was any reason to be grateful for my being alive today, you must be grateful to drink – it was the only thing that made me warm. But it is brought up as a criticism of me – Marjorie did in such a noble tone . . . I have died many times these last eighteen years and I don't ever intend dying again, for it may be that I am only alive for the first time now . . .' On 20 April he remembered the old days in the prison camp when 'Java closed in on me with your last word to me that Jimmy would still have to come first – I remember I used to feel it like the burn of a red-hot iron . . . I sit here at the end of a bloody day in a bloody place full of people I detest, with a lot of children around me and a son who never speaks . . .' But he thought he had found a nice hotel for her. And then, on 27 April 1948, he sent a telegram to London: 'ALL IS WELL AND TRULY WELL ALL MY LOVE AND COME SOON.'[15]

These were turbulent times in South Africa. When Laurens returned, General Smuts, whom he greatly admired and whom he claimed to have known from childhood, was Prime Minister, enjoying an easy majority in Parliament for his United Party; thanks to his wartime prestige, there were few expectations that he would be challenged, least of all by the National Party, which had opposed South Africa's participation in the war. True, there were signs of growing militancy among the unenfranchised blacks – there had been a major strike in the gold mines in 1946, and the Indian and Coloured minorities were moving closer to the blacks through the Congress movement – and the National Party leader, Dr Malan, was bringing the Afrikaners together. But white Natal, where Laurens was going, remained 'English', anti-Afrikaner, anti-Indian, and pro-Smuts and his United Party, and so Laurens's surprise and alarm may have been all the greater when, within a few months, the situation was transformed before his eyes. In the 26 May 1948 election Malan secured a stunning victory by campaigning for a secure future for 'White South Africa'. The National Party found itself with a parliamentary majority of seventy-nine to seventy-one. Even Smuts lost his seat, and the country entered the long period of apartheid which made South Africa a pariah in the world for more than forty years.

During these months Laurens came to the conclusion that he would never make his permanent home in South Africa. He would always emphasise that, if he had stayed, he would have felt obliged to become involved in politics and this would have defeated his ambition to be a writer. He was doing a professional job on the *Daily News*, got on adequately with his Editor and deputised for him when he was away, but his heart wasn't in it. He was quickly caught up in a variety of problems in the extended van der Post family for which also he had no patience. He had no time for his own writing, and many of his old Durban friends had vanished.[16] The shock of victory for the National Party and the humiliating defeat of his hero General Smuts must have contributed to his decision to leave: while he had inherited some racist instincts, he was fiercely opposed to apartheid, though one suspects that he did not necessarily reject the profoundly paternalistic customs and attitudes which were about to be institutionalised. As he familiarised himself with his old trade as a journalist and caught up with the changes in his country after many years of absence, he realised that apartheid was not going to be a brief aberration.

Among his other tasks, Laurens was a leader writer on the paper, and it is no surprise to find that the editorial line was consistently opposed to the National Party. These articles are unsigned, and it is not usually possible to identify Laurens's own work, but sometimes, in the features, his identity is clear. On 7 July 1948, for instance, 'John Lawrence' writes a rave review of a new volume of poems by a certain Lilian Bowes Lyon . . . Then on 28 October there are complaints that a best-selling author called Sep Smit is churning out books under the pseudonym of 'van der Post' which is a bit rough on real authors like Laurens van der Post and his father CWH van der Post. Meanwhile, Ingaret Giffard has become a prominent book reviewer.

More interesting, during these months the articles in the Natal *Daily News* seem to prefigure all the issues of Laurens's subsequent life – including Russia, sea-voyages, whales, Bushmen, the Kalahari, Central Africa, Prince Charles (his birth), nuclear and environmental concerns, Japan, Java and domestic South African politics.[17] Laurens's mind would have been a ferment of future possibilities.

Then there was Ingaret. She had eventually arrived in South Africa in June 1948 after a dramatic sea voyage during which she had been extremely ill, and had been nursed, coincidentally, by a fellow-passenger, the redoubtable Madeleine Masson, who had been privy to some of

Laurens's low-life adventures in the South of France in the 1930s. Ingaret, almost excessively proud of her family's ancient lineage, was not impressed by Durban society. She was of course in a delicate situation in that city's old-fashioned world; although Laurens had taken rooms for her next door to Elaine's house, in the fashionable district of Berea, it must have been clear that she and he were 'living in sin'. Her delight in being with him at last was marred by her impatience that his divorce was taking so long, apparently because the lawyers were having difficulty in sorting out a financial agreement. To make things worse, Ingaret always hated hot climates, and Durban is both hot and humid. She had nothing to do except write occasional book reviews for the Natal *Daily News* on a page edited by Laurens. There were serious Zulu/Indian riots in Durban at the time, and it seems that Ingaret was caught up in some episode. Even Laurens was alarmed by one encounter with a mob: a friend remembers his panicking and demanding a revolver. In later life Ingaret would rarely return to South Africa and Laurens's letters during his own frequent visits in the years ahead invariably promised her that she would find the weather intolerable.[18]

Laurens and Ingaret decided to return to Britain. He never referred to this year in South Africa in any of his books. In Europe Ingaret would now be able to resume her interest in a career in psychotherapy. The South African divorce proceedings continued in their absence. They had Ingaret's pleasant house in London, containing a flat which could be rented to help pay the bills. But Laurens would need a job so, before leaving Durban, he started writing to influential contacts in Britain. He had no leads for months, and Laurens and Ingaret left South Africa by sea on 18 February 1949. In London, Laurens looked around for freelance journalism.

He tried the BBC, deferentially, quoting his friendship with Plomer and a BBC producer, John Morris ('I think I could promise not to stamp on anyone's political corns, and I do really know my Africa well'), but nothing came of it.[19] He met up with old friends – Cecil Day Lewis, Plomer, Leonard Woolf. Lilian Bowes Lyon had written to him in early February to say how happy she was that he was coming back. In the New Year, knowing that she was dying, she had written a letter of farewell to Laurens, to be given him by their friend Keith Millar-Jones after her death. Laurens visited her in April, as she wrote in a remarkable letter to Plomer: 'One thing about Ingaret and all that. I don't think it can *alter* Laurens. He always gives me *nowadays* a sense of being safe "in himself", and if Ingaret is part of the plan – well, good luck to her, she probably is a "silver lining" . . . None of us have what is called a "good life" nowadays, but *should* I do some pre-deceasing will you, to please me, push in your oar (*if needed*) to prevent it rocking L.'s boat? I am pretty certain that your oar, as far as he is concerned, re. me, is strong and conclusive. Your voice *counts*.'[20]

Lilian died on 25 July 1949, while Laurens was returning from Nyasaland, the next key destination in his life. Rosamond Lehmann wrote, 'I was so sure she would wait to see you again before dying, but she didn't . . . it has been torturing me to think of her last days. She always hoped to "blow the horn", as she put it, at the end (Childe Roland and the Dark Tower) and I can't bear to think she was defeated after all, simply crushed out, alone and in despair. Now I know that she wrote to you a few hours before she died, it makes me feel a little better.' Laurens later recalled that he had felt impelled to send Lilian from the bush an urgent letter with some pressed flowers. On his return journey, he saw the news of her death: a last letter from Lilian told him she had received his Nyasaland despatch only hours before she died. In her Will, she left Laurens £3,000 (a substantial sum in those days – the equivalent in 2001 of £60,000: he was one of her two principal legatees), 'also my small Dutch painting which he liked and his gift to me of a mahogany box inlaid with a sea-shell.'[21]

Laurens transferred the £3,000 to Ingaret at once, so that he would not have to show the figure in any argument about his alimony settlement with Marjorie. He committed himself to paying Marjorie £480 a year. She had been living temporarily in England with Lucia, now thirteen. Ingaret told Laurens in a letter of 3 March 1950, after her marriage to Laurens, that 'Marjorie . . . has been perfectly angelic and we have become great friends'. She added, in the voice of someone who has decided to assert herself at last: 'You have earned £535 this year, and paid them £260. *This has got to end.* And I am the person to stop it. And stop it I bloody well will. As I told M., the money was given to me by you to make up for all I lost in marrying. It is entirely for me to decide.' (She was referring to her loss of access to Jimmy's wealth.)[22] Marjorie and Lucia went back to South Africa.

Before this, in May 1949, had come the breakthrough which, though he can hardly have guessed it, would transform Laurens's life. He had been in contact since September 1948 with the Colonial Development Corporation (CDC), a Government body which had been set up in 1947, in the Colonial Secretary's words, 'to initiate, finance and operate projects for agricultural or other development in the Colonial Empire . . . The UK and the world at large is in need of increased production of main colonial commodities.' It was acknowledged that in this immediate postwar period various commodities were in short supply and there were not enough dollars available to buy them from America. This was the background to Laurens's work, as a middle-ranking colonial civil servant, in Nyasaland and Bechuanaland (to become Malawi and Botswana respectively), though he never described himself in these terms. He was in fact a contracted Senior Assistant, Animal Products Division at the CDC, but he preferred to write, afterwards, that he was engaged, rather mysteriously, in 'work of national importance' for which he had volunteered following his wartime experiences.[23] The CDC wanted someone with experience of Africa to travel to Nyasaland, a long-overlooked British Protectorate in Central Africa, to survey and report on two remote mountain regions. Laurens met Lord Reith, the formidable former BBC Chairman who would soon chair the CDC, and agreed to go straight out.[24] The result would be a book, *Venture to the Interior*, which became an international best-seller and transformed him almost overnight into a famous writer, thinker, explorer, hero. Everything in Laurens's subsequent life followed from the two months of his Nyasaland mission of 1949.

He left London on 10 May 1949.

16

Venture

A S EARLY AS December 1947, Laurens had approached among
others Sir Stafford Cripps, Chancellor of the Exchequer, in his
search for a job. This may have led to his introduction to the CDC. The
following September, while still in Durban, he was told that a certain Dr
Fowler, the CDC's Divisional Manager for Animals and Animal
Products, would arrange to call on him. The result was that Laurens was
commissioned to carry out a survey, 'To assess the livestock capacities of
the uninhabited Nyika and Mlanje plateaux of Nyasaland'.[1] He had run
a small mixed farm in England and a pig project in the POW camp, and
came of farming stock in the Orange Free State, but he had no scientific,
botanical or economic qualifications.

Mount Mlanje, 10,000 feet high at the southern end of Nyasaland, is
the highest mountain in the country, picturesque, mysterious, reputedly
the site of some of Rider Haggard's more lurid tales. Often dangerously
shrouded in dense cloud as it towers over the nearby tea plantations, it is
famous for its cedar trees, but its slopes also harbour mahogany, yellow-
wood and a host of other forest species. It was not, even then, 'unknown'
or 'unexplored': colonial officers, prospectors, adventurers, botanists,
locals had been familiar with it for years.[2] The Nyika Plateau, 600 miles
to the north, at the opposite end of this long and narrow country, was
less known and less dramatic.

Laurens kept a journal and also a pocket diary of the trip, which he
would afterwards turn into *Venture to the Interior*. Their tone is, predict-
ably, altogether more brisk and factual than the elegant and ambitious
prose of the subsequent book; his journal gives the flavour of the
journey.

Laurens left London on 10 May, flying via the Sudan and Kenya to
arrive in Nyasaland on 14 May. The first part of his journey was quickly
achieved and he was equipped and ready to leave for Mlanje after just a
few days.

Thursday 19 May: Drizzling and the mountains covered in mist . . . we began climbing at 9.15. It is an easy climb. All the way we met porters going down with beams of cedar on their heads. They yodelled as they went. Why do mountains make people yodel? . . . Amazed at depth of soil on plateau, 4–6 feet in places . . . lovely smell cedar everywhere . . . France's wife and baby in lodge . . . caught three rainbow trout . . .

Friday 20 May: Reason said wait another day, give it more rest [Laurens has hurt his leg and is laid up for two days]; instinct said, 'go' . . . climbed steadily from 7.45am to 4.45pm with only 20 minutes halt to have an orange each and some dates, and my leg lasted out . . .

Sunday 22 May: Miss my love so much. Cannot think or see straight without her . . . collect grasses . . . lovely smell [of cedar] but my heart too far away to appreciate all this beauty . . . caught seven fair-sized trout. Come back in dark. Sky clear, stars very bright . . . tea and fire in cottage. So good.

The fuller journal (of which the above are only the briefest examples) is here suspended and the pocket diary takes over in extreme abbreviation:

Monday 23 May: Mrs France stayed behind, lent her shotgun. Lovely day. Climbed to 8,900 ft.

Tuesday 24 May: Walked 5½ hours steadily today to cave in Sombani Valley. 'Rock of God of Wonders' . . . great fires raging . . . not impressed grazing. Eating plum pudding in cave.

Thursday 26 May: Left Nayame at 7.45am. Sure Chiperone blowing up. Took short cut but lost way. Did not make camp Ruo Gorge until 5.15 in pouring rain. Dangerous trip. Porters exhausted . . .

Friday 27 May: Lost France at bottom of gorge. Terrible trip back over top to tell wife . . .[3]

Here, in his appalled pencil, is the tragedy which lies at the heart of *Venture to the Interior*. The young forester Fred France volunteered to swim across a gorge in flood and was swept away, his body never found. Laurens forced his drenched, freezing and demoralised porters back over the mountain, to break the news to France's young wife.

But he had to continue with his survey. He came off Mlanje almost at once, and after (he later claimed) taking care of 'Al' and her baby, he made a wearisome journey, delayed by rain, up to Nyika at the end of May.[4] After the tragedy the rest of the trip was an anti-climax.

To return to the journal:

Wednesday 8 June: Wrote to Ingaret and sent her a snapdragon . . . Peaches as driver . . . nearly upset jeep within first two miles swerving to avoid a dog. I told him never to do it again but to drive straight on whatever the dogs did. He thought it a great joke . . . The village . . . has been terrorised for six months now by a man-eating lion and leopard. Their favourite food is little herd-boys . . . In deep gorge nearly drove over tall, beautifully-made native woman lying stark naked in the road, mad or drunk . . . to bed at 9pm drums beating . . .[5]

These pages, and days, Laurens did not use in *Venture to the Interior*. In mid-July he was back in Blantyre, where he reported to the local CDC people and also to London. He went back to Mlanje very briefly on 18–19 July. His recommendations for Mlanje, though the official detail is lost, were that it be left to itself as a natural forest reserve. On Nyika he was ambivalent: 'plateau country in the best and grandest African manner . . . very like the high veld of the Transvaal and Free State and the loftier plains of Kenya'. It was being seriously damaged by burning, although uninhabited. It could only be developed as a mixed afforestation region and if it was linked into the main transport routes of central Africa – which, he argued, could be done.[6] Laurens left Nyasaland on 20 July, 1949.

His report soon vanished into the bureaucratic maze of Whitehall. Various CDC officers debated his findings; many of his arguments about matters of rainfall, labour, road access, were contested, and, more importantly, so was the case for an emphasis on forestry and soil conservation. Laurens wrote to Lord Reith, the CDC Chairman, on 28 October 1951, 'The problem . . . seems to me not whether afforestation of the Nyika is possible but whether it is desirable and in the best interest of Africa that it should be so. I believe in a country as desperately short of protein and dairy products as Central Africa, it would be wrong to afforest land that can be used for cattle and sheep raising and dairying . . .' He suggested a pilot scheme, and seems to have concluded that forest would be right for Mlanje, cattle for Nyika.* Not the least interesting aspect of this letter is that Laurens was writing from Zurich,

---

*The CDC Annual Report in 1952 stated that the Nyika Plateau was 'suitable for large-scale afforestation with conifers', and that there was a possibility of a paper-pulp project. Over the next five years various pilot schemes were set up, until in 1956 the experiment was abandoned. By then Laurens had moved on.[7]

where he explained to Lord Reith that he was hoping to meet Carl-Gustav Jung for the first time.[8]

On 14 October 1949, Laurens and Ingaret had married, and on his honeymoon in France he wrote up his Nyasaland adventure. He came back to Britain on 10 December and the next day wrote to Leonard Woolf at the Hogarth Press, 'I have had a two-months rest after my journey to Africa. Sometime I hope to let you have some wild gladioli seeds I picked on a 9,000 ft mountain top. Meanwhile I have written a book. It is about 70,000 words long. I finished it half an hour before my train left Paris, and am having it typed. I feel on the whole very happy about it. I think it is a true and original book. Nothing like it has ever been written as far as I know. Would you like to have it?'[9]

Woolf immediately asked to see it, but on 31 December Laurens wrote urgently, 'I have been ordered to take a government commission out to the Kalahari at a moment's notice and leave in three days time. It is all unexpected and I am most distressed because it means I cannot revise my book before I send it to you . . . If this book is what I think it is, I shall be able to break with this roving life, of which I am heartily sick . . .' Laurens added that Ingaret had just completed a novel on Africa which he wanted her to submit to Hogarth (which would eventually decline it). On 14 March 1950, while Laurens was away in the Kalahari, Hogarth accepted his manuscript.[10]

Venture to the Interior is above all a *memorable* book. Millions have read it; it has always been in print, in many languages, and few have forgotten or criticised it, or cast doubt on its detail, let alone on its prose or its theme. It is, though, rather an odd book in its construction. The heart of the story – the ascent of Mount Mlanje and the death of the young forestry officer – is sandwiched between a long section on the flight out, which is filled with autobiographical detail, and a curiously perfunctory description of the investigation of the Nyika Plateau, which in fact took up the greater part of Laurens's time in Nyasaland but which, fearing anticlimax perhaps, he did not describe fully. The book also includes an early published account of Laurens's experiences in the POW Camps.

Venture to the Interior marked the beginning of Laurens's reputation as an 'explorer', which he would build on in the subsequent ten years when he turned his attention to the Kalahari Desert. His publicity invariably described him as an explorer, and he was happy to accept the description, but in truth his career, however distinguished, could never class him with the Livingstones, Spekes, Burtons, Thesigers. His venture to

Nyasaland illustrates the point, and also helps explain the scepticism which his name sometimes occasions among 'old Africa hands'. Contrary to the impression Laurens gives, Mount Mlanje was not, as the CDC well knew, a particularly remote or inaccessible district; it was frequently visited by local expatriates and colonial officials. Similarly, the Nyika Plateau, though remote, was typical of a hundred other undeveloped locations in British Africa. The CDC knew what it wanted – a report focussing on the livestock potential and the best future for these areas. Laurens on his return filed a conventional report and then went to join Ingaret in France, where in forty-nine days he produced the first draft of something far more imaginative.

The brilliance, and the success, of the book are to be found in the double meaning both of the 'venture' and of the 'interior'. Hence the extremely long description of his journey from Heathrow to Blantyre. This is far from being as unnecessary as it sounds. It is a Conradian framing device – like Marlow in the familiar settings of the Thames and Brussels before and after his journey to the heart of darkness in the Congo – but it serves two further purposes: first, it introduces the ordinary readers via the tedious detail of a long plane trip with which they can identify, to an alien and exotic destination which becomes accessible when it is clear that the narrator is just like them. It is also a narrative device which establishes Laurens at the very centre of the story, so that everything will now be seen through his eyes. The precise, rather modest purpose of the 'venture' is never admitted: 'something more definite and up to date' about Mlanje and Nyika was required by Whitehall, vaguely related to Britain's failing self-sufficiency in food supplies, is all that Laurens explains.

In *Venture to the Interior* we find for the first time one of Laurens's constant themes: 'We live not only our own individual life but, whether we like it or not, also the life of our time.' This is the cue in his preface for the statement that he had 'spent one half of my life leaving Africa for Europe and the other half returning from Europe to Africa', which leads directly to another autobiographical theme, an unresolved conflict in himself between the legacies of his mother and of his father: 'on one side, under the heading "AFRICA" I would group unconscious, female, feminine, mother; and under "EUROPE" on the other: conscious, male, masculine, father.'[11]

There follows an elegant, entrancing and also largely inaccurate evocation of his parents' history. 'Africa is my mother's country . . . Somehow my life must find a way out between my father's exile and my mother's home . . . It presupposed . . . this among other journeys.' The reader has been skilfully positioned at a point of more than a technical departure: it is also a departure for the 'interior' of the Africa in one's self.

The elevated tone of the journey includes a certain amount of absurdity (for instance, 'no-one has ever stopped to inquire into the effect of the native on the European' – Laurens must have forgotten Conrad, and even his friend Plomer). On the other hand, he summons up the sheer *endlessness* of the African bush (what Hemingway described perfectly as 'a million miles of bloody Africa'), then exaggerates by describing how the pilot brings the plane down over the Serengeti to giraffe's eye level – there was always a superabundance of game in Laurens's books. He is tempted into wild images – for example, 'In Africa the vision of an English lawn flies over the exiled British imagination like colours nailed to the mast of an out-gunned sinking ship of the line.'[12]

He arrives at last in Blantyre, commercial capital of Nyasaland, 'an unusually happy part of Africa'. It was, he said, a small ugly town, drab and insignificant. Still the accessible and understandable detail is maintained before we climb the mountain. He buys supplies, almost as his reader might go to a supermarket. This page is surely riveting to all armchair travellers:

I bought some superb hunks of bacon; coils of beef and pork sausages; tins of bully-beef, still the greatest of travellers' standbys, sardines, beans and peas; a bag of potatoes, plenty of rusks and biscuits, sugar, tea, coffee, cocoa, powdered milk, some tins of butter, a tin of marmalade, some tins of green figs, and a tin of Cape gooseberry jam. I put in a few surprises for myself and Quillan, and, to make sure that they would be surprises, wrapped them in clean, but ugly, anonymous sacking. I put in two plum-puddings, a two-pound box of assorted chocolates, some dates stuffed with almonds, and 28 crisp Jonathans. I put in a bottle of whisky for my guests and a bottle of cognac for the cold. I bought a good, wide, but not too heavy frying pan, a water bottle, tin mugs and plates, knives, spoons and forks and a tin-opener, an electric torch, a couple of hurricane lamps, and a large coil of manilla rope. I had my own clasp knife and had borrowed a double-barrelled twelve-bore for which I now bought twenty-five rounds of buck-shot. I packed three warm rugs; a trenchcoat with extra-warm lining, a ground sheet, thick socks and stockings, a thick polo-sweater I had had for twenty years; a pair of hobnailed boots and a pair of stout climbing shoes that had been made in Australia some years before. I took also a prayer book, Shakespeare, *Modern Love* and, of course, my sealing-wax. I bought a small first-aid outfit, some M.&B. and Sulphaguanidine, some quinine for myself and paludrine for the bearers. I was sure the bearers would be full of malaria and that the cold mountain air might bring it on. I even remembered that while I was at

Mlanje the doctor had come in to report a fatal case of blackwater fever. I bought a couple of bottles of peroxide of hydrogen because nothing convinces an African more that one's medicine is doing his sores good than this harmless disinfectant fizzing on his skin. That is a long way to winning his battle. I also took a large bottle of castor oil which all Africans love. I went amply prepared.

The trip is beginning to sound exciting as Laurens conveys the sense of it. Yet there is an edge to these preparations and he already begins to create a sense of foreboding. His host 'Alan MacBean' advises him to make contact with the Provincial Forestry Officer, 'Peter Quillan', at Limbe. Quillan is 'a "bit of a fanatic about trees" . . . I had a feeling that I was being warned.' Then there's a lad called 'Vance'. (Laurens gave *noms de guerre* to his characters: 'Peter Quillan' was in reality Chief Forestry Officer for the Southern Province, R. M. Willan, and 'Michael Dowler' was G. Fowler, Veterinary Officer in the Northern Province. 'Vance' was Fred France.)[13]

Laurens has an attack of malaria, and notes that 'the future had begun to register a new design in my blood, and that the fever marked the beginning of its struggle for awareness'. He drives the forty-five miles to Mlanje and is warned that 'Vance is *dead keen* about trees' [my emphasis]. He is also warned of the Chiperone storms which come down over the mountain. 'It is a good thing that neither Quillan nor I knew what we were playing against.' Vance sends him a letter in 'impetuous' handwriting. An exchange between Quillan and Vance 'might be a kind of warning . . . I found myself wishing suddenly that I had not had to come, and my heart went heavy with foreboding'. When Laurens meets Vance's wife 'Val', he records her apprehensive reservations, '. . . a sickening sense of intrusion'. There's trouble ahead.

All this is happening in a forest of cedars – 'Mlanje cedars', extraordinary trees which technically are not cedars at all.

Their colour, like their scent, was unique. It was green, of course, but like no other green; there was a sheen of the olive green of cypress, and the substance of the green of the ilexes of Greece and the Caucasus; the texture of the conifers of Columbia and the vital electrical sparkle of African juniper. In the bark, in the veins and arteries of those trees, the sap, a thick, yellow, resinous sap of a specific gravity and density most unusual in conifers, ran strongly. If you laid your ear to a trunk, it was almost as if you could hear this vital, this dark, secret traffic drumming upwards, skywards, from the deep, ancient soil, the original earth perhaps of Africa, to the outermost, the smallest spike of a leaf, sparkling in the sun a hundred, even a hundred and twenty feet above. So full were the trees of this vital sap that it preserved them even in death; no insect, no worm, no ants would touch even the driest morsel of it. It was the only ant-resisting wood in the whole of Africa. But when one threw it on the fire, as I would soon see, it was so full of life, of stored-up energy from another world, that it literally exploded into flames. It consumed itself joyfully and gaily, crackling explosively in flame with none of that lugubrious reluctance to burn of some other woods.[14]

Vance is to accompany Laurens and Quillan on their circuit of the mountain. 'I was not happy . . . I did not and I do not trust Africa all that much and I said so.' The reader by this time has been persuaded to agree with the author, to nod his head sagely as though he, too, has experience of the African bush. When they leave the Vances' cottage, 'I said to myself: "Dear God, I do hope nothing is going to happen to make those children regret their inadequate goodbye."'

The message can hardly have been posted more clearly. The three men and their porters run into bad weather. The Chiperone is building up. Laurens has been warned that these storms can last for five days. At this point, he stifles his instinct and, against his own judgement, agrees with the others to take a short cut across the Great Ruo Gorge. It is the wrong decision, as Laurens afterwards understands. The tragedy strikes on the next day, 27 May. The rain is solid, the porters freezing, and Vance volunteers to swim the raging stream on a rope. The rope snaps. 'At that moment we knew that he was dead.'

Laurens and Quillan have no hope of finding the body. They try to rally the terrified porters. They dress them in all the spare clothes they have, including Laurens's precious bush shirts with his 15 Indian Army Corps – the 'fighting hockey sticks' – flashes. Laurens blames himself for the tragedy, not Quillan: 'It wasn't he who had lain awake at night half-stifled by a sense of death and listening to the dark drummer of Africa beating up the weather around Mlanje.' They cross the mountain, twenty miles of climbing, in deep exhaustion and despair. They at last arrive at the Vances' hut.

'I took Val by the arm and said, "Val dear! Hold on to me for a minute and please listen carefully to what I have to say. Dicky is dead . . ." She looked at me and it was as if I saw, far down in her eyes, all their days together go out, one by one, like a series of candles . . . I saw something rounded and whole suddenly become such sheer, utter, and black nothingness that my own pulse missed a beat at the horror of it. And then the tears welled up and spilt.' Laurens and Quillan stay with her that night, then go to fetch help from a local tea planter who, to Laurens's comfort, tells him that she had been expecting something of the sort to happen. Laurens, in his book, says that he helped Quillan arrange Val's affairs and booked her a flight to England; he wrote letters for her and then he prepared his official report on Mlanje: 'I recommended in my report that Mlanje should be left to itself, to its mists, to its weather, and to its cedars.'[15]

It is hardly surprising that after these events the rest of Laurens's journey, and of his book, is something of an anti-climax. While Laurens waits, delayed, to travel north to Nyika, he has to work through his sense of guilt for Vance's death. True, if he had not come out to Africa on this project, Vance would still be alive; he would also be alive if they had not taken the short cut. But Laurens has all along been uneasy about his trip, 'had always been in a divided state about Africa . . . supposing my own conflict about it had been resolved, could I have ever got entangled in a set of circumstances so disastrous as those on Mlanje! . . . I could not help feeling that if I had been an utterly whole person, that day in the gorge would never have existed.' Laurens convinces himself that the unpredictable in Vance and the unpredictable in the mountain met and became one.

When he eventually goes north, by road rather than the weather-grounded plane, Laurens finds 'Michael Dowler', who lives on the edge of the lake. Dowler earns an affectionate portrait in *Venture to the Interior*. A bachelor, he has four African servants: 'He gave these children of African nature the consideration and affection he would have liked to give his own dark, unfulfilled self, only centuries of so-called European civilised values prevented him from doing this. We all have a dark figure within ourselves, a Negro, a gipsy, an aboriginal with averted back, and, alas! the nearest many of us can get to making terms with him is to strike up these precarious friendships with him through the black people of Africa.'

Laurens is on his way to the Nyika Plateau in the company of Dowler and forty-five porters. He wakes one morning in a deep depression, 'against all reason, and against my will and the evidence of my senses'. Then he looks at his diary and sees that it is 19 June, the seventh anniversary of that day in the Soekaboemi Jail when he and Nichols were taken to witness an execution. There follows Laurens's first published description of his prison days, and it leads to an episode of high prose, concluding with a dream: 'I saw my father and mother standing together smiling in our garden at home . . . it was morning. The sun was shining. They were admiring a rose. The rose was white and the rose was on fire.' Readers may spot the references to Dante and to T. S. Eliot. They will almost certainly not have noticed that Nichols and Laurens were no longer in Soekaboemi Jail on 19 June 1942.[16]

As the story of the Nyika expedition continues, Laurens begins to drift into the paternalistic, mystical view of the tribal African which would later colour his attitude towards the affairs of the continent. Perhaps he was also yielding to his taste for rhetoric. The African 'belongs to the night. He is a child of darkness. He has a certain wisdom, he knows the secrets of the dark ... he does not really care for the day. He finds his way through it with reluctant, perfunctory feet. But when the sun is down a profound change comes over him. He lights his fire, he is at once happy and almost content, sings and drums until far in the morning. All would be well if there were not still this hunger. And what should he do about it? We could tell him – we who have too much of the light and not enough of the night and wisdom of the dark. We could, but we will not because we are split against ourselves, we are infinitely prejudiced against the night.'

Leaving aside the excessive generalisation, Laurens is developing a theme to which he would return both in *The Dark Eye in Africa* and in his Bushman books. He continues: 'The problem is ours; it is in us, in our split and divided hearts; it is white, it is bright with day. We hate the native in ourselves; we scorn and despise the night in which we have our being, the base degrees by which we ascend into the day.' And he concludes this apocalyptic passage, occasioned by witnessing a tribal dance in a remote corner of Africa, 'If we could but make friends with our inner selves, come to terms with our own darkness, then there would be no trouble from without. But before we can close our split natures we must forgive ourselves. We must, we must forgive our European selves for what we have done to the African within us.' Reading this one can easily understand why Laurens would respond with such passion to the rather similar position of Jung, whom he had just met for the first time and who had been saying these things for many years.

Here, in a simple and devastatingly effective book, Laurens signalled that he would one day assume the role of the seer, the prophet, the mystic and the guru. He finishes with a simple description of the view from the peak of the Nyika Plateau. 'There was no wind any more. There was no cloud or mist in the sky. I have never known such stillness. The only sound was the sound of one's blood murmuring like a far sea in one's ears: and that serene land and its beauty, and the level golden sunlight seemed to have established such a close, delicate, tender communion with us that the murmur in my ears seemed also like a sound from without; it was like a breathing of the grasses, a rustle of the last shower of daylight, or the swish of the silk of evening across the purple slopes.' In passages like these, Laurens makes his African experience memorable and relevant to all of us.

After this, Laurens omits any description of the following three weeks. He wanted to go home – to his new life. 'The truth was that Africa was with me whether I came back or not. For years it had stood apart from me: a dark, unanswered, implacable question in my life. It was that no longer.' Laurens had quit Africa in the 1920s and then the 1930s. He had resisted a return, both before and after the war. Now, in this important journey to Central Africa – in this venture to his interior – he could claim to have come to terms with his inheritance. For the rest of his life he would have no difficulty in reconciling his African and European personalities, moving easily and frequently between the two continents. His next step would be to come to terms with the 'primitive' Africa which he had begun to recognise in Nyasaland. The book ends with a telegram to Ingaret: 'ALL DONE AND HASTENING HOME.'[17]

There are a few footnotes to the Nyasaland venture. Forty years later, when Laurens broadcast a BBC talk on 'The Art of Travel', he received a furious letter from a Jennifer Carden, who turned out to be Fred France's daughter, the baby who had lost her father on Mlanje in 1949. Mrs Carden was astounded to hear Laurens tell his audience that she and her mother were both dead; it was she said, 'an outright lie'. She explained that after the death of her father, her mother, Alice or 'Al', had brought her back to England, failed to settle, returned to Africa and could not settle there either, eventually returning to England, where she became a teacher in Welwyn Garden City and died in 1978. 'On the radio, you sounded like a kind uncle who made sure we were "looked after". Not to my knowledge.' Laurens sent her a letter of apology which also managed to criticise her for 'the extraordinary tone of hostility in your letter. The mistake was regrettable but understandable after the long span of years.' He said that he remembered her mother coming to see him in Aldeburgh in 1950, when he offered to help her, but she was determined to return to Africa, after which he lost touch, and was later 'officially informed of her death'.[18]

The France family resented Laurens's use, as they saw it, of their tragedy for his self-promotion and profit, especially because he had made such a transparently thin change of their names and had not consulted them. They would also surely have been distressed by the subtle way in which Laurens manages somehow to make France responsible for the disaster. Al's sister Mary Hartshorne always remembered the distress Laurens's book had caused the family and their indignation at his claim that he kept an eye on them afterwards. All he did, they said, was to arrange their flight home. The final insult, as Mary remembered, was that Laurens claimed, in the postscript of a letter to her niece Jennifer, that out of his concern for the feelings of the France family he had turned down an approach by the French director Jean Renoir to make a film based on *Venture to the Interior* 'which would have made me a lot of money'. (There is no evidence whatsoever that Renoir ever had such a project in mind.)[19] This same predilection for the imaginative also caught up with him in his description of a Nairobi hotelier in early editions of *Venture to the Interior*: he was sued for libel and had to pay up, to his publishers' exasperation.[20]

Indeed, the book was widely resented in Nyasaland. The obvious point continued to be voiced for years, that Laurens had absurdly inflated the mystique of menace of Mlanje and the scale of his expedition. Locals used to claim that they could climb it in a couple of hours. He also came in for criticism for having written so frankly about local characters, easily identified behind their pseudonyms, who had helped him. Local resentment of Laurens was later summed up in a comment, for instance, by a colonial official, Patrick Mullins: 'Reaction had begun with the presumptuous title, with its overtone of pioneering and exploration, whereas the reality . . . was that forestry staff spent their working lives on the Plateau, while visits by people such as ourselves were by no means infrequent. Nor had those on the spot been too keen about van der Post's description of his part in the incident which had formed such a central feature of the book, in which a forestry officer had been drowned. Also lacking in appeal for Nyasalanders had been the book's habit of psychoanalysing publicly some of those he had met briefly and from whom he had accepted hospitality.'[21]

The CDC made no comment or objection and Laurens remained attached to their staff as a Senior Assistant. However, he was conscious of the delicacy of his reputation in the Protectorate and it must have been one reason why he was reluctant to return later.

Both Mlanje and Nyika are remarkably unchanged since Laurens's journey.* Cedar planks are still brought down Mlanje's steep slopes on the heads of labourers. Some pines have been planted, and there are basic forestry huts for the use of walkers and mountaineers, but there is still no motor road up to the plateau. The Nyika also survives largely

---

*The small tea estate to which Laurens and Quillan retreated after Fred France's death briefly became a small hotel (the first multiracial hotel in the Federation of Rhodesia and Nyasaland, claims Jimmy Skinner, who leased the place from the book's 'Mrs Carmichael' – in fact Mrs Pereira).[22]

unspoiled. The CDC sent another expedition two years after Laurens, and as a result set up a Development Syndicate with the aim of producing pulp and paper. The project did not work out and in 1965 the high plateau of the Nyika was declared a National Park and given a rough network of single-track roads and some chalets for visitors. It remains a magical and remote place. We may guess that Laurens would have been well content.[23]

Although *Venture to the Interior* was accepted by Leonard Woolf in March 1950, the book did not appear until 1952, which is a long delay even in the British publishing industry. The reason is that it required substantial revision and editing, much of which was done by Ingaret with a skill and dedication she was to apply to many of Laurens's books. Laurens also had to spend much of these next two years in Africa. In August, with Laurens absent and Ingaret sending in more corrections, Cecil Day Lewis minuted to Ian Parsons, Hogarth's Managing Director: 'Yes, we should certainly publish and it is a remarkable story. But I wish he had taken more time over the writing, which is apt to get confused, or woolly, or over-pitched when he has something of special significance to himself to say ...' Day Lewis added a long list of queries, misprints, mis-spellings and infelicities. There were already signs of an interest from American publishers, promoted by Plomer. In a delicate side-show, Woolf courteously turned down Ingaret's own book, a rejection accepted by Ingaret with equal courtesy. In April 1951 the New York publishing house William Morrow made a successful offer for the US rights. Morrow would remain Laurens's American publisher for the rest of his life.[24]

Even in proof, *Venture to the Interior* was already attracting attention. Daniel George, who ran the influential (and commercially important) Book Society, wrote to Parsons on 20 April 1951: 'Now there you really have got something. Aren't you all excited about it? ... I don't know how to say how impressed I am ... I shall be astounded if it isn't everywhere proclaimed a masterpiece.' Morrow suggested American publication in September 1951 and added, 'We count it a real spiritual adventure as well as an exciting narrative': the writer, Frances Phillips, became Laurens's American editor and a close and devoted friend and fan for many years. The Hogarth Press were telling people the book was 'the most individual and original piece of writing' they had discovered for many a long day. Not surprisingly in the light of Daniel George's letter, *Venture* became the Book Society Choice; that guaranteed at least 20,000 sales.[25]

Publication had to be delayed to fit in with the Book Society's schedules, and in consequence *Venture to the Interior* was published first in the USA, on 24 August 1951. It was a great critical success. The *New York Times* said it was the finest book about Africa since Baroness Blixen's classic *Out of Africa*. The *Chicago Sunday Tribune* hailed it as 'the best travel book published since the War'. In the *New York Times* review, 'Van der Post was 'a calm, confident, compassionate man with a faraway look in his eye and magic in his pen'. The *New Yorker* compared Laurens with St Exupery, T. E. Lawrence, Apsley Cherry-Garrard and other 'mystic adventurers', who, it noted perceptively, all shared 'an inherent, paradoxical conservatism'.[26]

At last the British edition was published, on 14 January 1952. The idea of an Introduction by Laurens's friend Stephen Spender was raised and dropped. There was debate about the jacket illustration – Laurens preferred 'a heraldic-looking zebra on a lion-coloured field of grass with purple irises between and a deep-blue sky –'.[27]

In Britain *Venture to the Interior* had the sort of critical reception authors and publishers dream of, vying with even the American notices. The *Daily Telegraph* wrote, 'When a man of action is also a natural mystic, and there is added a genuine, powerful talent for writing, the outcome is likely to be something of the order of *The Seven Pillars of Wisdom* – in other words, a masterpiece.' Peter Quennell in the *Daily Mail* declared, 'No other book that I have read gives so vivid an impression of the vastness, variety and magnificence of the African landscape.' The *Evening Standard* made it its 'Book of the Month'. *The Listener* hailed Laurens as 'a thinking man-of-action, unsurpassed in his generation'. V. S. Pritchett in the *New Statesman* was positive if guarded: 'One is a little haunted by the doubt as to whether he has "truthfully" given us the story and has not really described his own special sensibility to an intolerable personal pain.' Only *The Spectator*'s reviewer, the traveller Peter Fleming, was more cautious: he took exception to Laurens's description of the sequence following Vance's death – 'tasteless both in conception and in execution' – and issued a prescient warning against Laurens's inclination to use 'reconstructed conversation, a dangerous device even if you have a natural ear for dialogue'.

Elsewhere, the reviews were ecstatic, except in the (Communist) *Daily Worker*, to which Laurens wrote in protest, with a tirade about 'the tragic pathology of the Communist dementia, which renders Communists incapable of recognising love when they meet it, prevents them from ever experiencing it, and compels them to see in the world about them nothing but the hatred which impels them from within'. The paper, to its credit, printed his letter.[28]

The South African newspapers echoed the praise. 'One of the most significant books yet written about Africa', wrote the *Cape Argus*, 'the most thoughtful and penetrating writing about the real essence of Africa since Conrad's *Heart of Darkness*'. The Natal *Witness* agreed, praising Laurens for 'a mind full of wisdom and humanity and an awareness of forces in this universe beyond our understanding'.[29]

Not surprisingly after this, foreign rights were rapidly sold to France, Germany, Sweden, Italy, Norway, Denmark, Holland. In America there was a fourth reprint by January. In Britain sales nudged 70,000 in June. Film rights were mentioned. Penguin took the paperback in Europe, Vanguard in the US. Laurens received his first fan-mail.*

During all the excitement, as Laurens was also travelling to Central and Southern Africa, he was asked by a Hogarth publicist for his personal details. He offered:

> I did not really begin to speak a civilised language until I was seven and no English until I was ten or eleven. Have spent most of my adult life with one foot in Africa and one in England. Devoted much of my moneyed leisure to getting to know Africa: there was hardly a mile of it I haven't walked, or a corner of it I have not looked into ... Farmed also in England until outbreak of war when, although technically in the South African forces, joined up as a private in England. Served in early Commandos and Special Forces ... etc.[31]

His imagination was working overtime again. Not a single word of this was true.

---

*Laurens's friend Joyce Grenfell, the comedienne, wrote to him to report that the Queen Mother had told Sir Evelyn Baring that his book was the first thing that made her want to live after the King died.[30]

17

The Novelist

WHILE THE HOGARTH Press was preparing for publication, Laurens was still a near-unknown South African in need of work. He returned to freelance journalism, and between 1950 and 1952 produced a series of articles, mainly book reviews, for *The Countryman*, a respectable but minor quarterly. As early as Summer 1948 *The Countryman* had published his account of running the pig farm in the POW camp. He wrote reviews, mainly of batches of travel books – for example, in Spring 1951, commenting on Patrick Leigh Fermor's classic *The Traveller's Tree*, he recalled the author as a cadet with him at Aldershot, 'dodging drill in order to finish a sonnet he was writing for a Rumanian prince on, I think, a fish-pond in the Carpathians'. Ingaret also featured briefly as a book reviewer in *The Countryman*.[1]

In the Spring 1952 edition, Laurens first told of how as a young man he had visited the 'Barahetla' – more correctly the Bakhatla tribe – where an enlightened chief had been required to hand over to a younger successor; in this article the moral is delivered by a certain 'Hlangeni: 'We pushed the people too hard; too much progress too fast is no good.' It was a sentiment which would frequently be echoed by Laurens in the years ahead. In the Winter 1950 issue he had written for the first time of the Kalahari and the Bushmen. In this same period he published 'A Bar of Shadow' in *The Cornhill Magazine*.[2] But none of this can have produced much money, so an offer at short notice from the CDC was welcome. Would he go out to Bechuanaland, another British Protectorate in Central Africa, where a mission was being set up to investigate the potential for a cattle industry in the utterly undeveloped Kalahari Desert?

Like Nyabaland, the Kalahari had been frequently traversed by white men for many years: for instance, Laurens was far from the first

European (as he later claimed) to climb the Tsodilo Hills, near the western perimeter of the desert, because the Hills have been visited since at least 1895. The point of this 1950 expedition was a technical agricultural survey, and the leader was not Laurens, as he implied in later years, but an Australian, Frank Debenham, emeritus professor at Cambridge and an Australian who in his youth had accompanied Captain Scott's tragic expedition to the Antarctic. Laurens's role was as organiser of the trip, which was to travel not with porters, as in Nyasaland, but in sturdy Bedford trucks. Laurens played a similar role two and a half years later, when the Commonwealth Relations Office and the CDC asked him to join another Kalahari mission under the leadership of Arthur Gaitskell, the economist brother of the Labour Party leader. Again, his job was to organise things and, again, he arranged to be joined by two friends and the same African staff. Both missions produced technical reports which led in due course to the creation of the Bechuanaland (later Botswana) beef cattle industry. Laurens never explained in his books that he in fact made a total of seven journeys to Central Africa between 1950 and 1952 in connection with this cattle project, much of his time taken up with tedious discussion of rail tariffs and refrigeration and trade agreements with the neighbouring territories. After the main Debenham mission in January to April 1950, he returned, by himself, in June 1950, in August and September, from October to December 1950, from August to September 1951 and from May to June 1952. Some of these visits took him only to Southern Rhodesia and South Africa. The Gaitskell Commission in 1952 lasted from 25 October to 17 December. In 1955 he returned yet again, independently, to make a series of television films.[3]

This hard slog of business travel was bound to delay the development of Laurens's career as a writer, and his letters show his irritation. All the time he was preoccupied with journeys and meetings, he was also trying to write his next book, a novel he had promised to Leonard Woolf and to which he attached great importance – *The Face Beside the Fire*.[4]

Laurens's direct contact with the Hogarth Press (which a few years before had become a part of Chatto & Windus), now that Leonard Woolf had stepped back, was not so much Ian Parsons as the formidable Norah Smallwood, London's outstanding woman publisher in the generation before women broke the long tradition of 'gentleman' publishers. Chatto & Windus, which she joined as a secretary before the war, was a small and respected literary publishing house with an enviable list of writers. When the firm bought the Hogarth Press in 1945 it added the separate and equally distinguished list built up by Leonard and Virginia Woolf. Laurens was always treated as a Hogarth author, because his first novel had been published years before by the Woolfs, and his books were always issued under the Hogarth imprint.

During the war, when Chatto directors such as Ian Parsons were on active service, Norah took her chance and exerted herself to seize a hold on the firm, as director, partner and eventually chairman, which she maintained for more than thirty years. Widowed in the war, she devoted her life to her work. To many in the industry she seemed a fierce and intimidating figure, her age a mystery; others respected and even loved her. A colleague remembers her in the later years as 'a thin, elegant woman of medium height, with a cloud of snow-white hair, apple-red cheeks and dazzling ice-blue eyes. She could well have been beautiful as a girl, and was still extremely distinguished; the combination of large eyes, high-cheekbones and hollow cheeks gave her the frail, slightly skull-like look associated with pictures of Jean Rhys.'[5]

Norah Smallwood and Laurens adored each other and were dear friends over many years. Her gifts lay in administration rather than editing, and Laurens always said that he did not need an agent because he left everything to Norah. She was one of his great admirers and looked forward to every new book, which she would praise extravagantly to him while sometimes expressing private exasperation to her staff about the sloppy state of his manuscript or his failure to meet deadlines. For twenty-five years the files are crammed with their fond letters – 'Norah Darling . . .', 'Dearest Laurens . . .' In November 1984 Laurens would give the Address at Norah Smallwood's Memorial Service at St Martin-in-the-Fields in London, a stone's throw from her office in William IV Street. He said, 'Norah never became a male fellow-traveller . . . Although at times she had to act like a man, take decisions like a man, be tough and unyielding as a man, there was always an *a priori* feminine vision that saw behind the problems of writers, publishers, staff and all she had to deal with, an uncared-for something, a kind of neglected orphan aspect that the woman in her could comfort and restore to the productive day of an exacting world.'[6]

After the success of *Venture to the Interior*, his publishers naturally had high hopes of *The Face Beside the Fire*. When they saw it, they were appalled, politely though they tried to conceal it. Ian Parsons wrote to Frances Phillips in New York on 13 May 1952, 'It's a long book – about 160,000 words – and full of wonderful things, but our united feeling was that the beginning and middle (which are brilliant) were much better than the end, and that the latter could be substantially improved with re-writing.' This rather faint endorsement was reciprocated by Frances. Morrow decided to take it, despite their reservations, because they agreed with the Hogarth Press that in the long run Laurens would prove reward-ing. *Venture to the Interior* was selling steadily in America. William Morrow confessed they were 'skeptical' about how well this new book would do, and offered only a small advance, $1, 000. Frances Phillips wrote a candid note to Parsons at Hogarth describing how she had broken the news to Laurens and Ingaret that she did not think highly of its chances. Already Laurens's publishers were looking forward to his next novel, *Flamingo Feather*. The problem, as Parsons pointed out, was that Laurens had put so much into this new book that it was by no means sure that he would be willing or able to do more than tighten it a little. What he meant was that he was prepared to risk a turkey for the sake of keeping Laurens on board, and would wait for the next book. *The Face Beside the Fire* was pub-lished in April 1953. That year Hogarth softened the blow by re-issuing *In A Province*, to favourable notices which went some way to cancelling out the disastrous reception to *The Face Beside the Fire*.[7]

The Face Beside the Fire is Laurens's worst novel, but it was very important to him because it was so intensely autobiographical, and the heroine so manifestly modelled on Ingaret. It was his expression of his debt to her. The clear references to Ingaret are not the novel's only autobiographical aspects: we now know that some of Laurens's family, including his wife Marjorie, found it distressing. In a prose style which suggests it may have been begun, or drafted, before the war, it tells of two young South Africans who are mirrored friends – 'David Alexander' and 'Alexander David' (shades of 'Laurens Jan' and 'John Lawrence'). The narrator, Alexander, stays at home on his family farm to report the drama of David's confused but eventually fulfilled life in Europe. Much of the two boys' childhood background in the 1920s is reminiscent of Laurens's own youth in Philippolis. There is a 'Hottentot' nurse called Klara; a loving and beautiful but distracted mother, who married the father after the sudden death of his chosen wife, her sister; a distinguished father, prematurely retired from politics, who retreats into his library and into drink, and who beats his son savagely. That produces one of Laurens's earlier prose fancies: '. . . on the morning that Albert Michaeljohn raised his stick twenty-three times to beat David, by so doing he lengthened the axis of the earth which runs through him as, indeed, it runs through all of us. And by lengthening the axis he slowed down the motion of the earth and so produced such a realignment of cosmic forces that the ab-original darknesses had been encouraged dangerously to close in on the uttermost outpost of starlight.'

The boys sleep on the *stoep*: 'As I watched from childhood, night after night, the familiar lights go up in the sky, the glittering constellations move into their appointed places, the vast Babylonian cavalcade of the sky start out for the dawn of renewal with such irresistible confidence that the far-off thunder of their advance set every star-beam a-tremble in our midst, and as I saw at that selfsame instant, Africa hurl its immense land swiftly at the distant horizon to salute one brave battalion after another as they passed, and send its great peaks soaring swiftly upwards and spread out its own rivers and lakes to hold the sky jewelled and alive in their deepest depths, at that instant something of oneness of being, longing, and destination of this cosmic occasion unfalteringly has been communicated to me.'[8] His publishers should have been warned.

The father dies and the mother retreats on vacation to the Cape. The detail of these pages suggests much about the affairs of the van der Post family immediately after 1914. The mother discovers that the family has been left in unexpected poverty. David becomes a gifted painter. He rejects his mother's plan that he enter the Church and escapes to London, to Alexander's loss, with the striking line, 'I can think of no worse death than living an untruth truly, living the part as if it were the whole'.

David is at first a successful artist. He meets an older woman, Helen Moystouan-Roswell, and is persuaded to marry her, although he does not love her. (Are there elements of Lilian Bowes Lyon in this portrait?) The narrator, Alexander, observes from his distant farm that 'the good, true, and real in life not only has no use for secrecy but shuns it like the devil' – did Laurens once believe that? David and Helena are married for ten years. In his despair he is drinking heavily, becoming an outcast. He returns briefly to South Africa. Alexander addresses his friend: 'Who is the natural man in our unnatural society? The black man . . . surely you must see how truly and poignantly the image of a little black man, member of a natural, instinctive people expresses all that is natural and unfulfilled within us?'

David sails back to Europe. There is a storm. He meets a woman, Alys, on the ship, and the intensity of the description and detail of their meeting suggests that Laurens is writing of his experience with Ingaret on the *Watussi* in 1936. David confesses to her that he has felt 'unemployed' for ten years, and that his artistic talent has dried up: 'Life tastes like sawdust to me – I'd rather not live any longer . . . and as she spoke he knew it was no longer true. So long as someone cared for him as this woman seemed to care, then it could no longer be true.'[9]

Alys clings to her intuition. She tells David of the shell of her own marriage. They confess their new-found love, but she is reclaimed by her husband and father-in-law at Southampton. David goes through a private ordeal in which he discovers that his drinking was a substitute for the milk he could not get from Helena's breast – indeed, his marriage to her had been incestuous! In a dream he debates this with Alex, and re-imagines his boyhood, his mother, his father, his memory of Alex's sister, 'a face by the fire'. 'How clear it was to him now: whatever the parents left of themselves unlived, the children had to live for them before they were free to take up their own proper and special burden for which they were born.' (This is yet another example of Jung's ideas popularised by Laurens.)

David frees himself of Helena: he goes deep into his soul, in embarrassingly ecstatic prose: 'I was allowed to speak to [the first man] and I touched his skin riddled with snake bite, his shoulder pierced by mastodon's spike, his skull deep-scarred with sabre-tooth's claw . . . He looked me fearless in the eye and in a voice that boomed like a drum in his stomach said: "Brother, it was worth it" . . . I spoke to a Bushman half-eaten by a lion in the Kalahari, his only vessel a brittle ostrich egg with red and black triangles painted neatly on it, now broken and sand-scattered. He looked in my grey eyes with the brown eyes of a people at dusk, slanted to bridge a chasm behind the face of a dying member of a dying and vanishing race. He too, my dying nomad brother, said: "Add, add quick before I go, it was worth it. I spoke to an aborigine . . ."'

David recovers from his fever and his crisis and goes to claim Alys. He confronts her father, as Laurens soars again into the prose which would be his publishers' despair. 'Here they were man and woman with no archaic drag on eager future between them, but both synchronised and made immediate . . . No faster than time immediate demanded would flame of spirit burn humble and eager body, but sparingly, caringly asking life's mercy and trueness for every drop and calory of the rare, irreplaceable, honey-sweet golden wax consumed. Yes, with this woman by his side, he had a flaming rose, with golden petals unfolding to mark all four seasons, he had golden rose-light, a hallowed halo, a pentecostal circle of radiant essence of original flame, the farthermost corner of outmost season containing . . .'[10]

When *The Face Beside the Fire* was published, in Britain on 19 April 1953 and in America six weeks later, critics agreed with the publishers that the opening chapters were promising but the rest a steep decline 'into a morass of sentimentality and psycho-analytical mysticism', as *The Times Literary Supplement* put it. Jack Lambert of *The Sunday Times* wrote: 'ill-digested psychology gushes up; father-images and mother-images chase themselves across apocalyptic sunsets; and the hero's difficulties are resolved in a manner, and in language, of puzzling banality'. (Surprisingly after this, Lambert became a friend of Laurens.) Marghanita Laski in *The Spectator* described the book as 'pretentiously silly ... eventually [David] meets the Only Girl ... and after inward communings of an unendurably imbecile intensity, Finds his Soul'. The *Daily Express* said it was impossible to believe so inferior a book was by the same man who had written *Venture to the Interior*. The tone of these reviews was echoed throughout the provincial and Commonwealth press. It was the same story in America. Sales were modest and interest in foreign rights was minimal. Not surprisingly, and unlike his other books, *The Face Beside the Fire* was reprinted only once, in the Collected Edition.[11]

Laurens had three distractions from this bad news. First, sales of *Venture to the Interior* were still buoyant around the world. Second, early in 1953 he and Ingaret spent two months in France and Spain, a visit made memorable by their new friendship with Rosemary de Llorens, a trainee psychoanalyst whom they had met in Zurich. Wife of Professor Julio de Llorens, who became Laurens's Spanish translator, Rosemary was a noted equestrian and show-jumper, with whom Laurens encountered the horse whose story he would tell many years later in *About Blady*.[12] Third, in the mid-Fifties, Laurens was trying to extricate himself from the consequences of perhaps the only one of his betrayals he was not able to talk his way out of. He had seduced and made pregnant a fourteen-year-old South African girl who had been placed in his care.

The existence of this other child, if made public, would have destroyed him. In 1947, as had been described above, he won the friendship of the wealthy Kohler family, going so far as to become privately engaged to the elder daughter, Fleur, although he was living with Ingaret while not yet divorced from Marjorie. Somehow the Kohlers remained in touch with him.

In 1952 Laurens's confidence had been enormously boosted by the success of *Venture to the Interior*; it was, at last, the breakthrough he had dreamed of for so long. When, in April, after one of his visits in connection with the Kalahari project, he mentioned to the Kohler-Bakers that he was travelling back to England by sea, the mother, Jessie – who was herself in thrall to Laurens – asked him to chaperone Bonny, who was now fourteen, to London where she was to study ballet. The grandfather, Charles Kohler, had died on the same day as King George VI –

6 February 1952 – and Bonny and Fleur, who had been living together in Britain, had been called back for the funeral. Bonny would return to London alone. She afterwards realised that Laurens had targetted her: 'He chose me. He knew that my father was weak and would not intervene.' And her mother had every faith in Laurens.

The result was that Laurens seduced Bonny on the ship and continued to sleep with her for more than a year in London. She was supposed to stay with one of her mother's friends but Laurens installed her in a bed-sitter off Sloane Street, not far from the home he shared with Ingaret.

Nearly fifty years later Bonny, now a composed and elegant American, a successful businesswoman who lives outside New York, is remarkably candid about the episode. She was just a teenager, she says, her hormones were rampant, and she believed she was in love with this good-looking, famous, irresistibly charming older man. They danced every night. They dined at the Captain's Table. And when he forced himself on her in her cabin she fell for one of the oldest lines in the book. 'This is not Sex, this is Romance,' he said, and she believed him. But then, she was only fourteen, and she had been offered a dream by a master of fantasy.

He kept her in Chelsea for about a year, while she attended her dance and drama classes by day. She was introduced to his friends, and also to his son; he was intensely romantic, deluging her with gifts, flowers, poems. When he was abroad, he wrote to her all the time. She was obsessed with him. He told her that he had a bullet embedded in his spine – a war wound. When Ingaret was away, he took her to his house. She never met Ingaret.

One day, now fifteen, she told him that she had missed a period – she still didn't understand what that meant. She was utterly innocent, her mother had told her of birds and bees, but amazingly she had not grasped that love might lead to pregnancy. 'I can't handle this,' said Laurens. Two days later she was on the boat back to South Africa. She never heard from him again. Her mother and sister had no idea what had taken place on the ship or during her time in England, or why she returned so suddenly. Bonny now did some modelling at a department store and one day she fainted. Her mother, worried about her, took her to her doctor, who revealed that her daughter was pregnant.

Bonny locked herself away for four days, and then she claimed that she had been raped by Laurens. Her mother took legal advice and wrote to Laurens. Ingaret replied and suggested that Bonny come to Switzerland to give birth, and then she and Laurens would adopt the baby. Bonny's mother refused, and Cari was born – a discreet distance away, in Port Elizabeth – on 30 January, 1954. The grandmother pretended that she was the mother; Fleur says that neighbours suspected that Cari was *her* child. Cari was told that Bonny was her big sister, and would only hear the truth when she was ten.

The Kohler-Baker women – Jessie, two daughters and baby – returned to London six months later to confront Laurens. They did not meet him or Ingaret in person but they saw his solicitor. Laurens was told that he would be charged with statutory rape if he did not make a settlement. The result was a monthly payment of £15 (the Kohlers were not poor, and clearly they did not want a scandal) until Cari was eighteen, plus a lump sum which was apparently sufficient for Bonny's mother to buy several fur coats. Ingaret was said to be incandescent about the episode.

Bonny's career as a ballet dancer had been destroyed. Young and vulnerable, she had been entrusted by her family to Laurens's care; he was forty-six and had been appointed *in loco parentis*. For Laurens, in the mid-1950s, the story, if it came out, would have been the end of him; he had committed an offence which might have brought him a prison sentence, and he would not have been forgiven by his high-minded friends.

After Cari's birth, Bonny did some acting at the State Theatre in Pretoria, and then, determined to move to America, joined a Paris-based dance troupe which had an engagement in Las Vegas. From there she went on to Hollywood, where she landed a film contract (and played a nun in *The Sound of Music*), but the cinema did not work out for her and she eventually moved into the fashion industry, where she had a successful career. She married and divorced an American actor, and brought up Cari in California – until Cari, a young student, returned to South Africa on holiday where she met and married Mauritz Mostert and in due course had four sons. They have been estranged from Bonny for many years.

That might have been the end of it, until Cari, brought up without a father, confused about the identity of her mother, grew increasingly desperate to make Laurens recognise her as his child. In the years after her marriage, her husband says, she wrote Laurens at least fifty letters, begging him to acknowledge her, and never had an answer. As she says, 'What was I to tell my sons?' Twice she managed to accost Laurens. The first time, when she was barely twelve, Bonny took her to one of Laurens's public lectures in Los Angeles. He recognised them in the sparse audience, and afterwards they went up to introduce themselves. Laurens, deeply discomfited, burst into tears; later he sent Cari a cheap locket. Years later Cari took her boys, with her husband, to confront Laurens as he arrived in Johannesburg airport. Distressed again, he tried to brush past her, making some anodyne remark about her boys – that is to say, his grandsons.

Just a couple of days after Laurens's death, in December 1996, the London newspaper *The Mail on Sunday*, which had been sitting on the story for more than five years – Mauritz Mostert was the source, and the *Mail* paid £6,000 – exploded it over its front page: 'CHARLES'S GURU AND A SECRET DAUGHTER'. Bonny had long since been living in New York. The newspaper flew Fleur from Johannesburg to America to try to persuade her sister to give an interview, but Bonny refused. She says that she now thinks that Laurens was 'sick' and that 'he knew how to pick his victims'.[13]

18

Flamingo Feather

I N THE LATE summer of 1953, Laurens pressed on with a new novel, *Flamingo Feather*. His social life flourished: the names of Graham Greene, Marjorie Perham, Donald Tyerman, Clement Attlee, Rosamond Lehmann, Herbert Chitepo, David Stirling, Leonard Woolf, all appear in his diary. By the end of the year he could assure his publisher that *Flamingo Feather* was being typed. As usual with Laurens's manuscripts, it needed heavy revision, and the final version was not delivered until the following July, by which time he was already working on his next book, *The Dark Eye in Africa*. Throughout these years Ingaret was working away at her own novels and plays – never to be published or produced – and editing her husband's copy.[1]

During the editing of *Flamingo Feather*, the Hogarth Press was determined to keep Laurens in public view. As well as re-issuing *In A Province* in October 1953 they published, in 1954, *A Bar of Shadow*, the novella which had first appeared in *The Cornhill Magazine* in 1952. At this second publication, *A Bar of Shadow* was well received. *The Guardian* described it as 'something unique in English literature, the nearest parallel is Dostoyevsky . . . it opens the gates on a mysticism which some may think is elevating, others bewildering.' The *Daily Telegraph* said it was 'a tiny masterpiece'. Laurens's friend Jack Lambert, however, queried whether Laurens's prose was equal to his moral aspirations. *The Times Literary Supplement* detected 'a self-conscious aiming at profundity'. Elizabeth Bowen in *The Tatler* insisted that this slim volume was autobiography, and declared it was Laurens's best work.[2]

Laurens's books are extraordinary in their variety. After *The Face Beside the Fire* and the utterly dissimilar *A Bar of Shadow*, his next book was something quite different again – an African adventure novel. He had had the idea in his mind for years: in the POW camp he thought of it as

'Flamingo Feather'. His publishers waited anxiously for him and, of course, Ingaret, to complete their revision. Frances Phillips in New York wrote to Norah Smallwood that she was 'fairly panting to hear what you think. It is a suspenseful moment, when you think of *Venture to the Interior* and then *The Face Beside the Fire*.'[3]

When he read it Leonard Woolf wrote to Laurens on 24 February 1954, 'In many ways it's a magnificent book [but] there are a good many places . . . in which you allow your exuberance . . . to get out of hand and the English becomes rather purpley.' He enclosed a list of Cecil Day Lewis's suggested revisions. Ian Parsons followed with a plea that Laurens should not allow 'a straight adventure story' to be slowed down by too many descriptive passages or philosophical digressions. Even as early as this, foreign publishing houses, particularly in Scandinavia, were asking for sight of a manuscript. In Sweden, for example, Norstedt asked for *A Bar of Shadow* – 'infinitely superior, from a literary point of view, to *The Face Beside the Fire*' – so as to pave the way for *Flamingo Feather*. The Swedes were particularly keen after selling 30,000 copies of *Venture to the Interior*. William Morrow in New York snapped it up at once for a $2,000 advance.[4]

On 31 May, Norah Smallwood sent Laurens an agreed contract: no advance, but a substantially increased royalty starting at 15 per cent. Her enthusiasm was expressed in a letter of 1 June to the Swedes: 'The plot,' she said, 'compares on a lighter level most favourably with any Buchan adventure story, and my memory of these is that the narrative was exciting, incredible and inexplicable, but always acceptable –' (surely an acute choice of words) – 'it gives the serious reader a deep profoundity of thought, coupled with some superb descriptive writing . . . and at the same time it tells a rattling good story.' She had the honesty to add that she hoped the strategy of first publishing *A Bar of Shadow* 'does the trick and recovers some of the ground that may have been lost over *The Face Beside the Fire*'. She then asked for, and secured, higher royalties. She may have understood that, rather as *Venture to the Interior* echoes elements in *Heart of Darkness*, *Flamingo Feather* is Buchan and Haggard rolled into one. As early as June the South African publishers were counting on *Flamingo Feather* to be their biggest seller of the year.[5] The necessary heavy revision, together with hopes of a Book Society choice, forced Hogarth to delay publication, but *Reader's Digest* decided to take the book for condensation, which meant serious money.

Flamingo Feather was at last published in Britain on 14 March, to immediate acclaim and high advance sales; William Morrow in America had published a little earlier. The jacket illustration was by Kathleen Hale, creator of *Orlando, the Marmalade Cat.* Penguin immediately approached Hogarth for paperback rights, and would keep the book in print for more than forty years. London bookshop windows were adorned with assegais, Zulu shields, knobkerries and the occasional stuffed animal. Foreign rights were rapidly taken up by the French, Italians, Germans, Spanish, Dutch, Swedes, Danes, eventually the Japanese and of course the Americans. The Finns regretfully said no: their delicate relationship with the Soviet Union made it politically impossible for them to publish an apparently anti-Communist novel. More dramatically, Paramount arrived with an idea for a film, to be directed by Alfred Hitchcock – a proposal which would run and run.[6]

Flamingo Feather is a preposterous yarn of a Russian-directed black assault on white Southern Africa which is foiled by two brave and resourceful South African friends, Pierre de Beauvilliers, from his idyllic wine farm in the Cape, and John Sandysse, from captivity in Soviet Asia. The story is very much in the tradition of *Prester John* and also of *King Solomon's Mines.* The possibility of a black army massing unnoticed just beyond South Africa's frontiers, supplied through a secret and unknown harbour on the Mozambique coast, cannot survive a moment's reflection, and could not even at the height of the Cold War. And yet the book has charm, pace, drama, colour, romance, character, conviction. It is outrageous fun from the very opening scene, when Pierre surprises intruders: '"Stop that and stand, Fingani dogs", I shouted at them in their own tongue.'

Few South African writers would have attempted, even in the 1950s, to get away with an adventure which so unashamedly portrayed the African as a tribal primitive, whether loyal or villainous. These Africans behave as Laurens, and many white South Africans, would like them to behave: the dying man smiles as he sees Pierre: '"It is you, Bwana: it is you I see: *Ekenonya! Ekenonya!*"' This is apparently 'an expression of the most profound gratitude of which the Amangtakwena are capable', spoken by a character – sadly dead! – whom many Afrikaners once upon a time would have recognised as 'a good kaffir'.

The story is inspired by a famous and tragic episode in South African history when in 1856 a young Xhosa girl dreamed a dream which forecast the expulsion of the white man into the sea if the Xhosas killed all their cattle. They did so, and countless thousands perished of starvation, while the white man remained and the cattle were not resurrected, as the dream had promised. Laurens attributes to Pierre a reminiscence identical with his own report of his youthful encounter in 1926 with the Zulu prophet Shembe, who had told him, 'Our dreams have been taken from us . . . the white people have taken them from us and now do all the dreaming.' There are other autobiographical elements: Pierre's father had exiled himself after the defeat of the Free State Commandos in the Boer War; the famous father died young; Pierre had grown up in the Interior; he had fought in the Second World War and been captured by the Japanese. But Laurens adds to this Pierre's close friend John Sandysse, with whose teenage sister Joan he had fallen in love before the war. Pierre and John were in a POW jail near Harbin in Manchuria. John escaped – on the night of the new moon – and vanished.[7]

The opening scene is set in July 1948. Pierre, a Huguenot South African, as his surname conveys, a wine farmer as well as an anthropologist of the Amangtakwena (a fictional branch of the Xhosas or Zulus), arrives too late to save a young Takwena aristocrat who has been attacked on his doorstep. He finds a spear, a seaman's cap, a pink flamingo feather, and a letter, or rather an envelope addressed to him, in the handwriting of John Sandysse. This is a powerful and speedy opening. The feather is the traditional tribal signal that a great dream has been dreamed and that a man from every Takwena group in the country must travel home to be told of its meaning. Pierre sends one of his Takwena servants to 'Fort Herald', and from there a thousand miles beyond. In the meantime, Pierre has noticed the involvement of an ominous import/export firm of Lindelbaum & Co. He investigates, and finds that a mysterious shipping line with Russian connections is operating out of Port Natal (Durban). He will try and track down his friend but he remembers a favourite maxim, 'Never to allow my thoughts to run ahead of the spoor'. The hunter has found his prey.

The trail leads to the Great Flamingo Water in Mozambique, undiscovered and unmapped even in this postwar age, and Pierre is joined by his uncle Oom Pieter, a character like John Buchan's Pieter Pienaar ('Yes, we must go on to fight the good fight to the end of our days, for though this Africa of ours, *ouboet*, is truly God's country, the devil is largely in possession of it'). They go down through the bush into 'the Dead Land' in an extraordinarily vivid and successful chapter which represents a descent into the Underworld, a necessary part of their quest (the detail is reminiscent of John Buchan's *The Courts of the Morning*). There is much description of wildlife in mythical quantities. The sheer physical detail of these pages adds weight and even conviction to a sometimes ridiculous plot – a trick employed by many thriller writers. Pierre and Oom Pieter arrive at the undiscovered harbour, and the flamingos whose 'ardent congregation' Laurens evokes in a purple passage. They find cargo ships, and a large military camp, guarded by white men 'with set square–jawed faces and Tartar eyes'. Pierre finds his friend John – in command of this Soviet-backed camp.[8]

John has allowed himself, for the best of reasons, to be enrolled in a great Soviet conspiracy to take over Africa. A Takwena army is to liberate southern Africa. This is just one part of the Soviet offensive – for example, cigarette lighters are to be filled with nerve gas for black servants to distribute to their South African white employers! (The American publishers asked to delete this, perhaps fearing that it would give readers ideas.) Pierre sets himself to return to what appears to be Swaziland, to raise the alarm, and struggles to get his warning acknowledged: 'The biggest disaster Africa has ever seen is bearing down on you.' Oom Pieter is killed, nobly. Pierre confronts the tribal gathering which is waiting to hear the Dream (again *Prester John* is visible). The Dream, however, is revealed to be invalid, betrayed, and the great crowd laments 'with anguish . . . how good it would have been, how wonderful a day if only there had been another true great dream to proclaim'. In a scene worthy of Rider Haggard, the defeated conspirators bravely march over the precipice to their death.

John and Pierre talk. John will destroy the military base but then return to Russia, to secure the life of the prisoner friend with whom he had escaped. The Takwena army will be disbanded. Pierre travels to central and southern Africa arguing against the 'determined policy of negation in the Dark Continent' – a specific reference to Laurens's work in the 1950s for the Capricorn Society, of which we shall hear more. He notes the irony, that only in South Africa was his argument accepted, but in quite the wrong way – they attributed unrest in Africa entirely to Communism, which is not what Pierre/Laurens intended. Exhausted, heartbroken, Pierre returns to the Cape where he finds John's sister Joan waiting for him: '"Oh Pierre, my darling Pierre, what have they done to you all these years?"'[9] Happy ending, at least for Pierre. And, as it turned out, for his creator.

Flamingo Feather is hardly Proust, or even Olive Schreiner, but it does work. *The Spectator* described it as a most exciting and charming novel in the style of Buchan and Haggard, reviving a tradition which many thought had died out. *The Times Literary Supplement* made the same references to Haggard and Buchan, adding that the book had 'more psychological and emotional undertones than those of his predecessors'. For

The Sunday Times it was 'a noble entertainment'. The *Daily Express* thought that Laurens 'knows his Africa as you and I know the Mile End Road'. The *Encounter* reviewer said, 'It is doubtful if any writer has depicted the climate, the veld, the forests, the Dead Land of the tsetse fly and sleeping sickness, the character of the Zulu, above all the birds, beasts and flowers of South Africa, as they are painted in these pages . . .' The *Daily Worker*, Laurens's old enemy, declared that 'the details of this plot are childish, and much of the book is curiously adolescent'. *Time and Tide* thought it could become 'one of those secondary classics like *King Solomon's Mines* and *Greenmantle*'.[10] Comparisons with Buchan and Haggard were strikingly frequent: Laurens had become a very canny imitator, while rarely praised for his own originality, except in the case of his later, more 'mystical' books, which, of course, were heavily indebted to Jung.

Interestingly, it was the South African newspapers which objected. The *Pretoria News* observed, 'He may indeed have known such an Africa as he portrays here, but it had most certainly vanished long before 1948.' The Johannesburg *Star* declared that the book recalled 'Chums', with fantasy which clearly surpassed any MGM Technicolor dreams as the hero penetrated the strange Duk-aduk-Duk forest, which it helpfully identified as the Dukaduka forest near St Lucia in Natal. The *Cape Times*, Laurens's old paper, was more forgiving, though it thought that he lacked the facility of Haggard and Buchan.[11]

In America the reviews were gratifying. The *New York Times* said that 'this gorgeously romantic and engrossing story is not literature with a capital L. But it is a grand adventure tale herewith urged upon everyone who ever delighted in the romances of Rider Haggard and cherished the Richard Hannay stories of John Buchan.' For the *New York Times* Book Review, it was 'that rarest of birds, a true African novel of adventure, and a scintillating one at that'.[12] Not surprisingly, *Flamingo Feather* sold well in the US.

By this time, Laurens was already planning a return to Africa. During the previous five years he had been frequently involved in the economic development of Bechuanaland. Now he had decided to attempt an ambitious and dangerously extravagant private project: an expedition to make a television film, and write a book, about his search for the Bushmen of the Kalahari Desert.

19

The Kalahari

THESE WERE THE days before the discovery of diamonds turned Botswana into one of Africa's most prosperous countries. The then Protectorate of Bechuanaland, while enormous, was largely made up of Kalahari Desert and Okavango Swamp, and the population was minuscule. The British colonial authority had done next to nothing to explore or promote the territory's economic growth. Its only significant commercial activity was cattle rearing.

The CDC, with support from local colonial officials, resolved on a major investment in Bechuanaland's cattle, which at the time were exported live and by rail either to Northern Rhodesia's Copperbelt, the Congo and Southern Rhodesia, or to Johannesburg. The centre of the new industry would be at Lobatsi, on the railway line near the Rhodesian border, where a large abattoir might be installed with a monopoly of all beef exports, handling 70,000 head a year; there would be 'holding grounds' for the abattoir and a massive 11,000-square-mile ranching and farming scheme in the Crown Lands in the North. All of this would turn out to be both controversial and flawed.[1]*

Frank Debenham was to head what was officially described as 'an independent mission to investigate the possibilities for cattle raising in the Chobe Crown Lands' (i.e. in the northern Protectorate). His two fellow members were Brian Curry, an experienced cattle farmer from Kenya, and Jack Games of the Southern Rhodesia Cold Storage

---

*In the words of the industry's historian, the CDC's 'early operations were nothing short of disastrous. The northern state lands operation, started in 1950, with heavy outlays on machinery and fencing, had lost so heavily by 1954 through crop failures, stock diseases, predators, floods and bad management that it was cut down to a fraction of the original size . . . thereafter it continued to die a slow death . . . it was abandoned in 1963 . . . the Lobatse abattoir itself . . . was delayed two years (to September 1954) owing to delays in delivery of machinery, condemnation of the new building and ensuing litigation . . .'[2]

Commission. Laurens himself was sent by the CDC 'to take charge of all the other arrangements for the wellbeing of the mission'.[3]

Debenham later wrote a book about his mission, *Kalahari Sand*, but the first published account was Laurens's in *The Countryman*. There he explained that the Kalahari was a desert only in the sense that it had no surface water: 'for the rest, it was a vast wilderness with a rich, original and intense vegetable, insect, animal and human life of its own . . . There was, it is true, sand everywhere in endless quantities, but no desert. The Kalahari sand was watered and fertile; it grew a dense grass cover in some places, and in others immense stretches of thick bush and dark forest. There was game everywhere: giraffes . . . and vast herds of elands . . . kudus and gemsbuck stared in unbelieving surprise, having never, I am sure, seen truck or man before. There were snakes as I had never imagined them, sometimes hanging down from the topmost branches of trees and pecking viciously at the heads of my bearers as they sat on top of the truck . . .' (This last image is derided by other travellers to the region.)[4]

Debenham's book is exceedingly warm about Laurens. 'Van', he says generously, was the mission's real head as far as organisation and planning were concerned: 'Van [was] certainly one of those people who never let grass grow under their feet . . . He looked all Nordic, yet he could summon at will the fire of the Latin races, the philosophy of the East and the endurance of the Boers of the Great Trek.'[5] Debenham had had good reason to be grateful when Laurens nursed him through a dangerous attack of dysentery.

The Professor's account, recollected in tranquillity, is a charming description by an innocent of an adventurous journey in one of Africa's most remote regions. Laurens's own pocket diary* gives a more candid version of their difficult and exhausting journey. After meeting Debenham in Salisbury on 6 January 1950 to discuss plans, he departs on his own urgent travels, to Bulawayo, Mafeking, Gaberone, Johannesburg, Lobatsi, Francistown, Maun, Livingstone, all to set up and double-check arrangements for vehicles, food, servants, communications, medicine, fuel, for a potentially dangerous expedition expected to take six to eight weeks. In the middle of this he went off into the Kalahari on a personal three-day reconnaissance to make sure that the midsummer conditions would not be unendurable. The other Mission members joined him at

---

*The pocket diaries also contain details of his daily expenses – throughout his life Laurens recorded meticulously his expenditure on meals, taxis, hotels, porterage and so forth.

the famous Victoria Falls Hotel, he cabled London that all was ready, and they set out into Bechuanaland on 2 February 1950. Laurens's pocket diary continues:

3 February: Woken in night by thunder: had to pitch tents quickly. Called camp at 4.45; away by 7.15. Noticed Professor not well . . . temperature 102.5, fear bac. dys.

4 February: Professor very sick in the night. Up with him several times . . . lion came fifty yards within perimeter camp – spoor passed only five yards from Prof.'s lavatory –

5 February: Prof. better but will take days to cure him . . . I have to be up at 4.30am every day to get camp moving. They all sleep like death.

6 February: Puncture delay. Shot eland for food . . . if I don't get them through quickly the rains will get us and that will mean weeks delay. I know I am pushing everyone to the utmost but it is necessary.

8 February: [We] did 44 miles heavy going but superb country . . . entered most beautiful pan [dry lake] ever seen . . . full of game. Lovely dairy country.

9 February: . . . Went out at 5 to collect plant specimens . . . Again many lion about. Stampeded buffalo almost into our camp.

12 February: Heat terrific. Had to stop every mile for engines to cool down and refill tanks. Water consumption 8 gallons a mile.

14 February: . . . Prof. ill again. I have to watch him like a hawk. Great source worry but he is a perfect dear . . . all very tired –

16 February: Much roaring and grunting of lion about. Natives frightened and quiet. Two more sick.

18 February: Arrived Maun to re-fuel, re-equip and rest. Sent Professor and Curry who very tired, to hotel. [I] stayed in camp to keep show together.

They left Maun again, heading west and then south, on 25 February, guided by Johnnie Marnewick, a local farmer who spoke good Bushman and would become an important figure in Laurens's later travels. The party now totalled nine Europeans and fifteen Africans.

4 March: Took Professor to pan; thinks water too chancy. Went over to lion's pan alone, rest too tired, and was charged and shot large black-maned lion.

8 March: Made early start but just about leave camp when police boy came to summons one of our Native bearers on charge of rape of native woman. 10.30 before I could sort it out: meant we travelled in heat of day and made slow progress; much trouble over-heating.

10 March: Much Bushman spoor . . . lovely grass-covered *laagte* [valley], full game.

11 March: Camp visited by wild family bushmen – gave bushmen lot plenty tobacco and all empty bottles and shot two springbok for them.

12 March: Most reliable [Bedford] truck broke down . . . nearly all our vehicles done now. Hopeless situation. Decided abandon further sorties . . .

13 March: They forget I have already made them look at far more country than they ever intended or were asked to see. Still, we have another 500 miles of desert to cross. Everyone so depressed –

14 March: . . . Very impressed most of country. Very dry but its standing up well. Found small family of wild bushmen in veld, very thirsty, very hungry: gave them water, tobacco, and then took them eight miles in trucks to pan. They had to be loaded in trucks like bags of potatoes because [they] did not know how to get on having never seen any – and shot two buck for them.

16 March: Disturbed night. At 1.30am Marnewick had a mamba entangled in his mosquito net and woke us up with his yell. Then dogs opened up on leopard . . . contacted several groups wild bushmen – pitched camp in ter-rific thunderstorm – sitting down in tents when two little bushmen walked into our midst – gave them tobacco, fed them and gave them dry place by fire to sleep.

17 March: Shot 3 hartebeest for bushmen and our boys. Bumped into lion, he looked as if he would charge but made off just as I was to shoot – killed eight-foot yellow cobra which just missed my knee –

They were now homeward bound. On 22 March they were approach-ing Lobatsi ('I am sad to leave this land of my childhood [as we know, this area had nothing to do with Laurens's childhood] but glad I have done with the Commission and everyone else. Have had no rest and no privacy from people with whom I have nothing in common'). In Lobatsi, there were wives, a dinner party, and the first mail for four weeks. They were all exhausted but Laurens made them drag themselves up to Matetsi, in the far North, for a quick inspection of promising cattle country; they escaped from Matetsi in the nick of time, leaving before dawn before the heavy rains moved in.[6]

A year later, in a BBC radio broadcast, Laurens explained, and rather glamorised, the difficulties the Debenham Mission had faced. It had been the wrong time of year – in the Chobe Crown Lands in the North it was time for the rains to break and the mission might get bogged down; in the Kalahari sands immediately south it was dangerously hot for European strangers. He remembered 'a hastily organised expedition in which I had taken part years before to the Great Mhkari-kari Salt Lake of the northern Kalahari. That expedition had nearly ended disastrously.' (This expedition is a mystery, and almost certainly a fantasy.) Hence his decision to go ahead of the others and test the conditions. His broadcast described how he had taken the risk and had set off into the Chobe bush. 'For three weeks we travelled up and down these silent and uninhabited woods, glades, savannahs and bush-ringed prairies of this fantastic land. The going was unbelievably difficult even though our trucks were plated in front like armoured cars to help us crash through the bush. There were of course no roads, so we had to force our way through dense bush and bristling brush-wood. We were proud if in one day . . . we had covered twenty miles . . . Wherever there was an open view there was a vision of bucking, leaping game. At dawn our camp would be ringed with lion and leopard spoor. Enormous elephant trails ran everywhere and the black soil in the savannahs was rugged with the tracks of ponderous buffalo. We were seldom out of sight of arched giraffe heads looking at us over flat acacia tree-tops with coy and maidenly curiosity.'[7]

In fact, conditions cannot have been too awful. Laurens kept a record of his daily radio-telephone messages to headquarters. One of the last, on 12 March, asks them to fly in not only the usual list of spare parts for the trucks, but 'any mail . . . as well as six dozen eggs, 6lbs bacon, 20lbs potatoes, some onions and one bag oranges . . .' If they were explorers, they were never out of touch with civilisation.[8]

This was the first and longest of Laurens's Bechuanaland journeys concerning the cattle project. Debenham's recommendations were quickly accepted in London, and the 'Bechuanaland Ranching Project' was approved in mid-May: Laurens was therefore sent out to Salisbury at once to finalise the technical details. He travelled to the region six more times, most of them on visits lasting about a month. The CDC officials responded to him appreciatively: 'I must say that Laurens is a marvellous chap. He has really put the accelerator down and got things moving in a remarkable way,' wrote the regional representative in Swaziland.[9]

The project did not go smoothly, however, and eventually, after Laurens's time, the northern part of it failed. Serious mistakes were made in the appointment of senior staff, which took up a lot of Laurens's energy. Word leaked out of the CDC plans with the result that speculators bought up land which the CDC then had to buy back at a premium. But Laurens continued optimistic. He wrote from Maun to Lord Reith, the CDC Chairman, on 21 May 1952, 'Neither Curry nor I have seen better cattle country in Southern Africa. Your cattle look superb, and the greatest proof of all: the calves born on CDC land are twice the animals their mothers were.'[10]

In the early 1950s, Laurens was totally committed to the ambitious expansion of cattle raising in the Kalahari. He mentioned the Bushmen in his official papers only in terms of recommending their potential value as herdsmen. It does not seem to have occurred to him that large-scale ranching, whether by the CDC or by the Tswana landowning class which would one day govern independent Botswana, would inevitably be detrimental to Bushmen's traditional way of life. Nor does he appear to have worried too much about the impact on the Protectorate's glorious wildlife of the fencing, culling and disease-control which would accompany a cattle industry. In a committee meeting on 25 May 1952 the ranch manager explained how he would be starting a mass slaughter of the local wildebeest, and this was agreed by all: the minutes add, 'Colonel van der Post mentioned the advisability of keeping this matter out of the press.'[11]

In October 1952, just after his return from a Scandinavian tour promoting *Venture to the Interior*, during which he met Karen Blixen, author of *Out of Africa*, Laurens was asked by the British Government to go back to the Kalahari yet again, with a Mission to look into cattle ranching in Western Bechuanaland. The Chairman would be Arthur Gaitskell, who masterminded the giant Gezira cotton scheme in the Sudan. Brian Curry had agreed to return from Kenya, and the other members would be an Arizona cattle expert, Professor C. V. Pickrell, and two highly respected local leaders, Chief Bathoen of the Bangwaketse tribe and Tshekedi Khama of the Bamangwato, father of the future Botswana President Seretse Khama. They were clearly appointed in order to ensure domestic agreement for the eventual proposals. Laurens was organiser once again.

The tone of Laurens's negotiations with Whitehall is noticeably more confident than it had been when he joined Professor Debenham. He now saw himself as an authority on the area. The Commonwealth Relations Office (CRO) was deferential: it would be such a pity if Laurens could not accept. He hesitated when first approached because he was, he said, 'deep in an exacting programme of truly important work for a year to eighteen months' (presumably on his next book). 'I would ask you to let me be in charge of the ship . . .' He would not go if this was not agreed (recalling his insistence in Java in 1942 that he be guaranteed command of Special Mission 43). He refused payment other than expenses, explaining, 'the finest water-diviner I ever knew would never accept anything but expenses for his work because, he said, "if I took money, the gift would go".* I feel about Africa like that. Besides, we all owe Britain more than we can ever repay.' Laurens added various suggestions for members of the Mission and warned that they must not have a woman because Brian Curry could not stand them. Could the CDC be persuaded to release for the expedition his friends John Marnewick and Cyril Challis?[12]

The mission left London on 25 October 1952 and, from Mafeking, entered the Kalahari from the South, in contrast with the Debenham Mission. To Laurens's delight, he was able to introduce his colleagues to the Kalahari under the worst possible conditions, approaching high summer and in a drought. If they could see the worst, they would better appreciate the potential. The trip lasted five weeks, and this time too the distances covered by truck were very large. Once again, the Mission members were positive about the area's potential; it was good ranching country, they said, compared with Texas and Queensland. Not surprisingly, in view of their Chairman's background, they urged a partnership scheme on the Gezira model, starting with a pilot farm.[13]

Laurens afterwards described the Mission in another BBC broadcast. In particular he spoke of the two Tswana members as a complementary pair. Bathoen he recalled as 'a man of steady, sober judgements and full of common sense', a musician, a pianist, a church organist. Tshekedi was a brilliant, forceful character with a quick first-rate mind. In this same broadcast Laurens talked of the Mission's experience of the coming of the rains: 'One day late in December, we camped down for the night and when I told . . . the others that we were camping in the place where we had camped six weeks before they would not believe me. The trees above our heads were green and covered with blossom, the grass was green and

---

*This is puzzling because Laurens was a contracted civil servant at the time.

from three to four feet high . . . As I shaved in the golden dawn light, the
noise of the wakening camp was almost drowned for me in the song of
birds and the singing of turtle doves. Even I . . . had hardly expected so
miraculous a rebirth.' The project, he said, could add 30–40,000 tonnes
of meat a year to Africa's inadequate food supplies. It could all be done
as an African/European partnership for less than the cost of one naval
destroyer.[14]

The moment of Laurens's conversion – when he understood that his
true concern for the Kalahari would be the protection of the Bushmen,
not the promotion of the cattle industry – is not clear. But it was during
these years, working as a civil servant on contract to Whitehall while
awaiting the success of *Venture to the Interior*, that Laurens 'discovered' the
Bushmen. He would, in a very real sense, live off them for the rest of his
life.

20

Bushmen

IN THE EARLY 1950s there was next to no international interest in the Bushmen. Their elimination in South Africa during the previous century had been largely forgotten. The British Colonial administration of Bechuanaland had no particular interest in what was assumed to be a remaining and elusive fragment of a declining people. There had been a couple of spasms of interest in America and Europe a century earlier, when individual Bushmen were exhibited in travelling circuses, or 'freak shows', and in 1925–26 the 'Denver African Expedition' dabbled in the area and returned with some photographs which purported to show 'Bushmen'.[1] But scholarly interest was near-absent until the Marshall family arrived from California.

Lawrence Marshall had made a fortune after co-founding Raytheon, the radar and technology corporation. Visiting Cape Town in 1949 to sell a radar system, he heard of an expedition to search for the 'Lost City of the Kalahari' – a fable current since the 1880s* – and decided to join it with his son John. Raytheon had designed the trigger of the Hiroshima bomb. Marshall, horrified by the consequence, decided to retire, and set off with his family in search of a Bushman society which, it was believed, did not make war. The Marshalls conducted seven expeditions to the Kalahari in the 1950s. They were amateurs, but they produced two influential results: a best-selling book (*The Harmless People*, by Elizabeth Marshall Thomas, in 1959), and a film, *The Hunters*, by the son, John. Marshall's wife, Lorna, also published a number of ethnographic papers. The Marshalls' work did much to establish an international image of the Bushmen as an ancient people, unspoiled, living in harmony with their environment. John Marshall later volunteered that that image was, sadly, false.

---

*The 'Lost City' was first reported by the explorer G. A. Farini in the 1880s; the ruins have never subsequently been discovered.[2]

Laurens's new interest in the Bushmen overlapped with the Marshalls'. His message was similar, but his influence throughout the world was vastly greater. The professionals who brought up the rear only slowly forced a more realistic understanding of a people who were perhaps not so primally innocent as had been portrayed.[3]

The Bushmen, more correctly called the San-speakers, were an aboriginal people squeezed between the expansion of the black Bantu tribes arriving from the North and the European settlers coming up from the South. Both blacks and whites behaved ruthlessly towards the Bushmen, so that they were exterminated in their traditional areas, and survived only in the remoter desert areas of Bechuanaland and South-west Africa. At one time they gathered near Laurens's home town of Philippolis, just north of the Orange River, but were in effect driven out by the Hottentot/Coloured Griquas (the words are used here in their original sense). Farther north, they were persecuted by both the Tswanas and by those Hereros who had been driven from Southwest Africa by the German colonisers. The Bushmen were despised by both black and white as a primitive and scarcely human people.

It has always been difficult to gauge their numbers, not just because their lifestyle does not lend itself to census, but because over the years there has been much adulteration of 'pure' Bushman stock. A distinction also should be drawn between what lawyers saw as the 'tame' Bushmen – those who had accepted contact with farmers and were in some sense 'settled', however miserably – and 'wild' Bushmen who continued as hunter-gatherers. These latter were the people in whom Laurens, and later anthropologists, were interested. In the mid-1950s, there may perhaps have been about 50,000 still at large in Southern Africa as a whole, in comparison with 40–50,000 more settled 'Bushmen' in general in Bechuanaland.* Since Laurens's days researchers have argued that most Bushmen have for centuries moved between pastoralism, which usually means working for Tswana or Herero cattle owners, and hunting and foraging in accordance with their stereotype.

In the romantic perspective which Laurens did so much to echo and establish, the Bushmen men were hunters and the women gathered tubers and fruit and leaves from the Kalahari bush. As hunters and trackers the men were extraordinarily skilled, with their poisonous arrows and great stamina. They lived in extremely simple conditions in small family groups, with no formal land ownership system but recognising the territory of

---

*This figure, larger than some estimates, was calculated by Professor Phillip Tobias at the time.[4]

other groups. Physically, the 'wild' Bushman was very short, about 5 ft high, fine-boned with tight-curled hair and a wrinkled, loose, apricot-coloured skin. All Bushmen were supposed to demonstrate steatopygia (the ability to store food in their buttocks) and the males ithyphallism (a permanent semi-erection). Both of these are a prurient exaggeration on the part of European observers; Laurens shared this and made coy references to the women's *tableau égyptien* (an alleged formation of the labia). Although entirely illiterate, and described usually by Europeans as 'child-like', the Bushmen had a sophisticated and ancient mythical cosmology, passed on verbally from one generation to the next.[5]

Europeans of the nineteenth century, even as they exterminated the Bushmen, respected their courage and resistance. Laurens sometimes said that his grandfather had led the Boer commando which was the last to wipe them out and that he personally killed the last Bushman painter. This cannot be true – his grandfather would have been a child in 1836 at the time of the last major operation against the Bushmen in his part of Griqualand.

Laurens was aware of the presence of the Marshalls in the territory when he arrived – he envied their comfortable travel arrangements – but was unaware of the imminent arrival of the academic anthropologists and ethnographers, for whom he had all too little sympathy, a reaction which was in due course heartily reciprocated. But there was an earlier link. Laurens's father had had an unusual amateur interest in the Bushmen, encouraged perhaps by the fact that his wife's family farms had Bushman connections. The name Boesmansfontein, Bushman's Spring, makes the point, as Laurens would frequently explain. CWH collected Bushman artefacts, and even exhibited them at the International Kimberley Fair of 1894. His original collection at Fauresmith was destroyed by British troops during the Anglo-Boer War, but his young son would have been aware of his interest.[6]

We can never now know the truth of Laurens's later statement that shortly after his father's death he wrote in his first diary, 'I have decided today that when I am grown-up I'm going into the Kalahari Desert to seek out the Bushman.' (That childhood diary of Laurens's has not survived.)[7] But in Conrad's *Heart of Darkness*, a book Laurens knew well, the narrator Marlow remembers looking as a child at the map of Africa and deciding, 'When I grow up I will go there'.

Other emotional connections with the Bushmen have been mentioned already. Were there truly two old Bushmen on Laurens's grandfather's farm? Which farm? Where would they have come from? When would they have been abducted, since the Bushman raids had ended years before? How would they have been kept on during the war when the family servants were taken away? Why is the nursemaid Klara not mentioned in the earlier books and articles and the television film? And why does she transmute in successive books from 'Coloured' to 'Griqua' to 'half-Bushman', until her triumphant emergence, at precisely the moment when Laurens was producing his best-selling books about the Kalahari? *The Lost World of the Kalahari* (1958) is dedicated to 'The memory of Klara who had a Bushman mother and nursed me from birth'. In *The Heart of the Hunter* (1961) he wrote, 'the first thing I remember in life is the light of a high-veld sunset aflame in the necklace of large glass beads round Klara's yellow throat'. (Laurens's home was nowhere near the High Veld.)

There is little evidence that after his adolescence Laurens gave much thought to the Bushmen for thirty years. His friend from the *Cape Times*, T. C. Robertson, afterwards recalled their expeditions in search of Bushman paintings in the Cape and the Transvaal in the early 1930s, but this is not the same thing as showing interest in the contemporary situation of the Bushmen.[8]

Yet at some point in the early 1950s there was, to use a phrase of Evelyn Waugh, 'a twitch upon the thread'. Laurens describes the moment in *The Lost World of the Kalahari*. He has been writing of his rare random encounters with tiny groups of Bushmen during his cattle-research travels. He then admits that, back in London, his imagination became troubled by these memories, and particularly the memory of a set of tiny footprints which he had come across in the sand of a Kalahari pan: 'It was almost as if those footprints were the spoor of my own lost self vanishing in the violet light of a desert of my own mind . . . Then one morning I awoke to find that, in sleep, my mind had been decided for me. I will go and find the Bushman.'[9]

The force of his new conviction is shown by the fact that Laurens, although well advanced in negotiations with the BBC over another project, abruptly dropped it and started to talk urgently to them about a TV series about the Bushmen, to be funded, organised, written and fronted by himself. For whatever reason of timing, he would now fulfil that childhood pledge. He would go to find the Bushmen.[10]

This decision is one of various examples in Laurens's life of his extraordinary gift for anticipating, and then responding to, the new concerns of a new generation. When he wrote *Venture to the Interior* his readers, weary of wartime drabness and insularity, were receptive to a tale of romantic and exalting adventure in an exotic location. Later he would understand the new interest in the life of C. G. Jung. Later still, he was in the vanguard of the Green movement, the concern for 'Wilderness' and the environmental crusade. He had an uncanny instinct. But his advocacy of the cause of the Bushmen was a master stroke, echoing as it did the generation's nostalgia for a simpler, perhaps more innocent, society. Following the Marshalls, Laurens used his gifts as a storyteller to popularise the Bushmen around the world. In so doing he made their sad story his own, just as he used their traditional stories which had been painstakingly collected by a German scholar eighty years before. In a word, he colonised them.

After *The Lost World of the Kalahari* in 1958, and its successor *The Heart of the Hunter* in 1961, in due course he followed up the theme with two thick novels, *A Story Like the Wind* and *A Far-Off Place*, in 1972 and 1974. Finally he published a purportedly true story, *The Mantis Carol*, in 1975. Four of these books were enormously successful and remained in print for many years. They all issued from the private expedition he made to the Kalahari in 1955, which produced first and foremost a six-part BBC series called *Lost World of Kalahari*.[11]

Laurens's relationship with the BBC, which became an important part of his later career, had had an awkward start. Before the war, when he needed all the freelance work he could find, he managed only a couple of broadcasts. In November 1945 Laurens broadcast a British officer's description of the situation in Java. When he returned in 1949 from Durban he made contact again with the BBC, using William Plomer's name as introduction, but because of his frequent absences in Africa nothing came of it, until on 12 August 1951 he was given fifteen minutes on the Home Service to describe his recent visit to the Hunter's Road, an historic but now overgrown highway leading from southern Africa northwards into the heart of the continent. Here, suddenly, Laurens found his distinctive broadcasting voice: the lions grunt over their kill, the elephant are tearing at trees, the nightjar calls, the baboon moans, a bush-buck barks, a hyena whines, a jackal wails, not to mention thunder and lightning – no wonder Laurens cannot sleep. Later he broadcast similarly personal and lively descriptions of the two missions in Bechuanaland.[12] As his literary reputation grew, the BBC became increasingly interested. He started to appear on the French-language service, he cultivated the friendship of Talks Department producers, using his charm to great effect, and in August 1954 he broadcast a long talk on the Third Programme about the Afrikaans language which caused offence back home in South Africa.[13]

In 1954 he put up an ambitious and expensive proposal that the BBC send him to the Far East to prepare a series of programmes on the subject of nationalism from Pakistan to Korea, Borneo to Japan, Indo-China to Burma. BBC managers were attracted to the idea but nervous: would Laurens stick to observation and interview rather than generalisation and personal opinion? 'As an observer of politics or economics, I think he scarcely begins . . .' cautioned Donald Boyd, Chief Assistant, Talks. He sounded out John Morris, Controller of the Third Programme, who was a friend of Laurens: 'He is politically a child and, when it comes to dealing with human beings, inclined to become entirely emotional and, often I fear, sentimental,' replied that friend, acutely enough: 'You would not really get your money's worth.' Nevertheless, the BBC was near to agreement.

It was this proposal Laurens mysteriously abandoned, citing his mother's illness: 'It is quite clear now that my mother cannot possibly recover. None of us knows when her moment will come . . . my mother's death will mean a great many new and protracted family responsibilities for me. I do not think I shall be through with them for another year or eighteen months at least.' Lammie did indeed die, on 29 September, but Laurens was not an executor of the Will and it is hard to see why he expected to be so preoccupied with her affairs.[14] In fact, over the next eighteen months his energies were taken up by his even more time-consuming project, involving another branch of the BBC – the filming, for TV, of his search for the Bushmen of the Kalahari. He was to discover that he was venturing into a medium in which he had no experience and in which the financial cost of failure would be alarming.

He proposed that he make a film not merely of anthropological interest but 'a story of true adventure' in the 'vast, practically unexplored scene of this part of Southern Africa'. A contract was arranged with untypical speed, and Laurens made grand plans to go out to South Africa with Ingaret in May 1955, to write some articles, visit his family, and spend three months researching Bushman history and art while making the host of arrangements which would be necessary for a desert journey of twelve weeks. He would have to buy food and equipment, organise fuel and supply points, fix permits and get letters of introduction, and enlist his companions. Brian Curry again agreed to come down from Kenya to shoot for the pot (he would be called 'Wyndham Vyan' in *The Lost World of the Kalahari* – he insisted on anonymity). John Marnewick (who became 'Ben Hatherall') would be guide and interpreter. In London Laurens succeeded in persuading the Rover Company to lend him several long-wheel-based Land Rovers on the promise that there would be plenty of indirect publicity, and that he would shoot a private film for their promotional use. On the same basis he got a new tent from British Nylon. To guarantee this publicity, and also to secure an extra income, he arranged exclusive coverage of the expedition with *The Times* and, for Switzerland, the *Neuer Zuercher Zeitung*. Laurens intended to do some more general journalism on the trip. He wrote to Piet Meiring, an old colleague on the *Cape Times* and now Director of Information in Pretoria, to ask him to arrange interviews with 'the more important people' in South Africa such as Hans Strydom, then Prime Minister, 'with whom he wanted to talk quietly and at length', and Doctor Verwoerd, who would shortly succeed him. ('I myself am not at all interested in politics and have no political axe to grind.')[15] Nothing seems to have come of this approach.

The most important planning element was to find a professional cameraman who would be acceptable to the BBC, and here Laurens made a big mistake. Near the end of 1954 he had been introduced by a friend, a wealthy South African widow called Clara Urquhart, to her Italian boyfriend Enrico Pratt (who would feature in Laurens's book as 'Eugene Spode'). They met again in London and Laurens liked him though, as he wrote later, 'it is true that he struck me as a profoundly unhappy person and perhaps I should have been warned by that.'

Mrs Urquhart was persuasive; it is possible that she was helping to fund the expedition, or at least Pratt's role in it. (She was a committed liberal, had worked with Dr Schweitzer, was a supporter of the ANC, and she later bought a London house for its exiled president Oliver Tambo.) Laurens and Pratt talked over an agreement, which with hindsight was not precise enough. Laurens would later turn his relationship with Pratt/Spode into the central theme of the first half of his book. Laurens allowed him to nominate his own assistant, who turned out to be not a South African cameraman, as he had asked, but a Cambridge post-graduate mathematician, born in South Africa but with no experience of film. In the book he is called Simon Stonehouse; his real name was David Morrison.[16] He was to be another disaster.

During his preparations in Britain, Laurens asked the Dominions Office if he might call on the Secretary of State to talk about the Kalahari. He seems to have wanted to find out the latest status of the Gaitskell Mission's recommendations, only a few of which had been implemented. The Secretary of State was unable to see him, and Laurens may not have realised that he was setting off alarm bells in Whitehall. Two dangers were aroused in the cautious minds of Dominions Office officials and both of them had comical aspects. First, Laurens told them he was taking Enrico Pratt as his indispensable cameraman. Second, he explained that he was thinking of Swaziland as the setting for Alfred Hitchcock's proposed film of *Flamingo Feather*. 'Secret' telegrams flew between the Dominions Office and the High Commission in Cape Town.

Since none of the officials had read *Flamingo Feather*, their fear at first was that the Paramount Chief of Swaziland 'might well have strong feelings about the making of any film that portrayed his people as a crowd of savage "fuzzy wuzzies"', however his country was disguised. When he started to read the book, Mr J. C. Martin's opinion did not change and he wrote to his opposite number in Cape Town, 'It does not strike me as the sort of story one would wish to have associated with any of the Territories in however remote a way . . . van der Post's hero traces the preparations for a Communist-inspired African rebellion to his fictitious territory. The simple tribesmen, having become the dupes of some very wicked Russians, are about to launch a Unionwide revolution when the hero, a full-blooded Afrikaner from the Western Cape, arrives on the scene. That is as far as I have got . . .'

The reservations about Pratt were more serious. Laurens had not known that Pratt was considered, by both the South African authorities and the local British diplomats, to be an 'active Communist'. He would therefore not be allowed to re-enter South Africa or Swaziland. Laurens, by this time in Southern Africa, protested furiously to the High Commission. He pointed out that Pratt spoke only Italian and bad French so he could hardly do any harm in Bechuanaland, especially in the desert. In any case, Pratt was definitely not a Communist, said Laurens, but was being victimised by the South African Police because he consorted with Mrs Urquhart and 'in particular, because he played the violin at a concert for natives in Johannesburg some years ago'. Laurens made the valid point that it was wrong for the British Territories to follow the South African lead in such matters.

The diplomats were in a quandary. They felt they could not, as they put it, 'allow an alien Communist to enter a primitive colonial society under conditions where no adequate supervision is possible. Moreover, we cannot ignore the possible reaction in the Union of South Africa'. However, Mrs Urquhart – also said to be a Communist although she was a wealthy sugar farmer – was a different matter, since she was a South African citizen and, it was said, a friend of Adlai Stevenson. The story is worth telling as an example of the manner in which British policy, particularly in the area of security, was always in danger of undue deference to the apartheid Government, even in the High Commission Territories where Pretoria had no authority at all. In the end, common sense prevailed. It was decided that Pratt was unlikely to be a danger and he got his temporary entry permit.[17]

Laurens and Ingaret arrived in South Africa in mid-June. There had been talk of Graham Greene, the novelist, joining them there but nothing came of it. Any general articles which Laurens wrote at the time have not survived, and he was probably concentrating on preparations for the expedition. He must have been acutely aware of the growing cost of the project. The BBC was paying him £4,500 for the world rights to six Kalahari films, and supplying 60,000 feet of film. *The Times* had agreed on 50 guineas per article, the *Neue Zuercher Zeitung* £120 for four articles, and *Holiday* magazine, which would soon become one of Laurens's most lucrative freelance outlets, offered $1,500, with separate payment for Pratt's pictures. Laurens and Ingaret visited Laurens's family, spent a week in Durban, motored through Zululand, Swaziland and Southern Rhodesia, and arrived at the Victoria Falls, where Ingaret fell ill and, out of some intuition, before she went home made Laurens promise to buy a special gun, a .375 Magnum Express. The Land Rovers arrived late from Britain, thanks to a strike, but there would only be a short delay; Laurens had to buy a fourth vehicle, such was the volume of supplies and film. The party was accompanied by a Land Rover mechanic and also, in due course, by five servants. Laurens was back in his old stamping ground, meeting old friends from his CDC days.[18] Then things went wrong.

The story can now be traced from the book that followed, *The Lost World of the Kalahari*. Laurens's construction of his account of the journey is similar to *Venture to the Interior*, and similarly odd. Like the earlier book, it starts with an extremely detailed description of the preparation, into which he mixes many details of his own family history and his earlier connections with the Bushmen, stirred in with an introductory version of Bushman history. There then follows a minutely-detailed account of his difficulties with Pratt/Spode. This should surely be an irritation to the reader who is looking for Bushmen – but Laurens had learned his skills with *Venture to the Interior* and knew he had to combine the prosaic with the exotic.

Does the reader become impatient with the squabbles with Pratt? Did he weary of the interminable plane journey at the opening of *Venture to the Interior*? Laurens's instinct told him to anchor his exotic journeys, almost unreal in their remoteness from his readers, in humdrum daily life. We have all been stuck next to bores on a plane journey. We have all been exasperated by neurotic colleagues, whereas a Bushman fire dance is hard to imagine. Pratt/Spode is frightened of the animals in the bush around their camp. Morrison/Stonehouse is a vegetarian in a situation where Laurens has to shoot for the pot. By the time the two leave, in distress or high dudgeon – halfway through the book – we are ready to go to the Okavango Swamp to search for the River Bushmen, to what Laurens called the 'Slippery Hills' with the prophet and healer Samutchoso, and we can almost understand why Laurens has to write a letter of apology to the Spirits and bury it in a lime-juice bottle. And in the end we arrive at the discovery of a living, functioning, dancing-singing community of 'wild' Bushmen.

They started out, Laurens reports, by crossing the Zambesi into the far North of Bechuanaland, following the tracks of the Debenham Mission of 1950. The first goal was to see if any of the River Bushmen were left in the Okavango Swamp. Laurens quickly discovered that the waters were unusually high that year and his passage blocked. He circled around the marshes on a long detour and took to the precarious dug-outs called *makorros*. Morrison/Stonehouse was already collapsing, and had to be evacuated. There is more to this story. Professor Phillip Tobias, one of South Africa's most distinguished scientists, was a friend of Morrison and his Natal family, and was in contact with him in the period after his retreat from the Kalahari. Morrison, Tobias remembers, was a brilliant and sensitive young mathematician, simply unable to cope with what he said was constant bullying by an autocratic Laurens. At one point, he said, he was ordered to lay his sleeping bag in the middle of an elephant trail. By the time he escaped from this, for him traumatic expedition, he was shattered. Over the next twelve months he was treated for schizophrenia, and a year later he killed himself. Laurens never mentions this. Did he not care? Might it have reflected badly on him? Here was a man who died, too young, like France in Nyasaland. Pratt/Spode was, in Laurens's account, also impossible, and was not doing his job as cameraman. Afterwards Pratt would talk of how impossible Laurens had been, how authoritarian, how obsessive, how eager to exaggerate the modest dramas of life in the bush. All accounts of the contretemps should be read with caution.[19]

Laurens and his party failed to find more than a couple of the River Bushmen, who appeared to have been defeated by the tsetse fly, but they did meet a man called Samutchoso, who offered to join them and, in due course, with his son, Samutchau, led them to the Tsodilo Hills, otherwise dubbed the Slippery Hills: 'I had no idea what forces were set in motion when I agreed without hesitation that he could come,' Laurens wrote.

With his new gun Laurens was shooting brilliantly, he says, and he allowed himself a purple passage as he encountered that most dangerous of animals, the buffalo: 'At that precise moment the copses all around us burst apart and buffalo, who had been within, sleeping, came hurtling through their crackling sides, with arched necks, thundering hooves, and flying tails, all with the ease and speed of massed acrobats breaking hoops of paper to tumble into the arena for the finale of some great circus.' A great bull buffalo advanced on him but he refused to shoot, for this was the buffalo of his dreams . . . He thought, heroically, 'Only one thing saved me. I was not afraid. Because of that I belonged to them and the overall purpose of the day.' Samutchoso understood. Overhead there was an aircraft carrying African labourers to the South African gold mines and, in Laurens's fancy, they were singing, for reassurance, 'Abide with me' . . .

Pratt rarely used his camera, according to Laurens, and retreated into silence. He insisted that he return to Europe, that he could not continue this brutal life any longer. Laurens had to confront the crisis: Pratt would go, to be flown out on a Chamber of Mines plane, but he must find another cameraman if the expedition was to be saved. He travelled urgently, and with much good luck, to Johannesburg and fortunately found Pratt's replacement, Duncan Abraham. He had lost only one week. They then travelled west and south, as Samutchoso led them to the Slippery Hills. But by accident they broke Samutchoso's condition that there should be no killing on the way.* The spirits were indignant. Laurens had found wonderful rock paintings, but his cameras and recording equipment mysteriously broke down and refused to be mended. The party was attacked by bees. Laurens, with Samutchoso's encouragement, wrote his letter of apology to the Spirits, 'We beg most humbly the pardon of the great spirits of these Slippery Hills for any disrespect we may have shown them unintentionally and for any disturbance we may have caused in their ancient resting place.' They all signed it ('some of whom thought it was going a bit too far'). Samutchoso said that they were forgiven.[20]

Laurens described, in his book, in his BBC films, and many times afterwards, how he had 'discovered' the Tsodilo Hills and their magnificent Bushman paintings with the help of Samutchoso and his young nephew or son, Samutchau. In fact the existence of the Tsodilo Hills and their paintings had been known to Europeans since at least the beginning of the century. Worse, but never mentioned by Laurens, was that in

---

*Laurens forgot to warn his white companions, who were shooting for the pot.

1951 a French team, the 'Panhard-Capricorn Expedition', led by François Balsan, had explored the Kalahari on a route remarkably similar to that of Laurens in 1955. Balsan wrote a book about it, translated into English as *Capricorn Road* in 1954. Laurens can hardly have been unaware of either the French expedition or the book.

Balsan described how he journeyed to the Tsodilo Hills where he 'discovered' the Bushmen rock paintings. He made contact with Andrew Wright and his daughter, who lived near the Hills and had located the paintings for them. Balsan then hired a guide, 'Kehore Hilli', who led him to the Hills with the help of an elderly relative. The extraordinary fact is that Balsan's photographs closely match Laurens's film and show that 'Hilli' may well have been Samutchau. But Balsan's account differs markedly from that of Laurens. 'Hilli' assures the Frenchman that he does not believe in the 'Spirits' of the Hills; there is certainly no prohibition on hunting during the trip to the Hills; and Laurens's pool of everlasting water on the summit is dried up (as it would be when Laurens went back in 1981), though Laurens's film in 1955 does show water. What we must probably accept is that Laurens, ignoring the reports of four years before, picked up the same two guides and dramatised a tale of what he described as a unique and historic climb to the summit of the Tsodilo Hills, where some of the finest examples of Bushman rock paintings are still to be found.[21]*

Now they were joined by a 'tame' Bushman from the Ghanzi farming district, called Dabe, who would act as their interpreter, and they pressed on urgently into the heart of the desert, where Marnewick/Ben remembered that, as a young boy with his father many years before, he had stumbled on a Bushman community on a track leading off the Gemsbok Pan. 'Ben's' memory was correct and he led them to a depression in the sand, where Dabe spotted something. '"There's a wild man down there!"' He cried out what Laurens always insisted was the Bushman greeting: '"Good day! I have been dead but now that you have come, I live again."' Laurens comments, 'We had made contact at last!'

They had found Nxou, who introduced them to his small Bushman

---

*It happens that the Professor Tobias mentioned above, then a young scientist at the University of the Witwatersrand, was a member of the Balsan expedition. In old age he confirmed the accuracy of Balsan's account – he remembers both 'Hilli' and his elderly relative, their guide – but since he could not bring himself to read *The Lost World of the Kalahari* (and Laurens's films did not arrive in South Africa for many years) he cannot confirm that Hilli *is* Samutchau. Thirty years later Samutchau was still guiding visitors to the Tsodilo Hills.[22]

settlement. There were, they reckoned, about thirty people. Laurens and his team named the place 'Sip-wells', because Nxou showed them how to suck water out of the sand in the classic and life-preserving Bushman way. Laurens is never precise about the location, but it was probably very near Ukwe. They stayed with them – camping a mile away, not living with them – for how long? Laurens was vague about this, and the point became important as his books about the Bushmen grew so influential. 'None of us doubted that we had struck a pure Bushman community living their Stone Age life,' he wrote, and he proceeded, in the final thirty pages of the book, to describe their life: their hunting, their games, their stories, their dances, their music.

It is fair to ask how well he really got to know them. How well did he communicate with them, through Dabe, the interpreter? *How long* was he with them? From the inadequate diaries we have, it cannot have been longer than a fortnight. On this flimsy foundation, and an inevitably distant acquaintance with no more than thirty Bushmen, Laurens would go on to build a substantial reputation. Laurens's book ends with a vivid and famous description of the hunting and killing of an eland, the great Bushman triumph, and their celebrations in the orgasmic Fire Dance. And at last, the next morning, they agreed to tell him their most profound mythical stories.[23]

But did they?

The Bushman Tales

THE SIX HALF-HOUR television programmes, *Lost World of Kalahari*, were shown in summer 1956 and were an enormous success. Today Laurens's film seems endearingly old-fashioned. A few years later a narrator would deliver his commentary to camera from the location, wearing safari kit or whatever. Here, Laurens lectures from a small studio, immaculate in double-breasted suit and pocket handkerchief. He has a map on the wall, with a stick to point at it, and turns on a bulky tape-recorder on the table when he wants to play a recording of a Bushman song. He even uses a piece of chalk to demonstrate his routes. His pieces to camera are much longer than would later be acceptable. There is a certain amount of TV trickery: some Kalahari wildlife shots were taken on the slopes of Table Mountain in Cape Town, and Dabe appears earlier in the story than was strictly true; it also looks as if two separate Bushman dances have been intercut into the same sequence, in which Johnnie Marnewick's farmhouse can be glimpsed in the background, suggesting that the dance may not have been as spontaneous or remote as it is described. Curiously, the film mentions and shows rather more Bushman groups than figure in the book: some of the 'wild' Bushmen we see are almost certainly not wild at all, and perhaps not even Bushmen. The most striking difference from the book is that Pratt/Spode is never seen or mentioned.

Into the film come flights of fancy about Laurens's childhood. There is, as in the books, a reluctance to clarify how long he actually spent with his Bushmen, though it helps to see on film Laurens bedding down for the night next to the fire and not, as he used to claim, tempting danger by sleeping alone in the bush.

Much of the film footage is fascinating. The search for the River Bushmen in the 'makorros', which float scarcely an inch above water; the pursuit and killing of an eland; the first clamber on to the Tsodilo Hills and the discovery of the paintings, dogged by a malfunctioning camera; the Eland and Fire Dances; the courtship ritual with its tiny cupid's bow and arrow. It is not at all surprising that Laurens's film had such a great impact, and was reshown many times all over the world. The BBC considered it a *tour de force*, 'one of the most successful film series we have ever undertaken'. Laurens was deluged with fan-mail which included many letters from former POWs who had been in jail with him. Nearly twenty-five years later a well-known British journalist, Christopher Booker – admittedly a friend of Laurens – nominated it as 'the most significant television series ever made'.[1]

As soon as the BBC film was finished, Laurens went off to Aldeburgh to write the first of the two books which came out of his Bushman expedition. He promised New York a manuscript of *The Dreamer that Remains* by the end of the year, but as always he fell behind and did not finish the first draft until October 1957. Ingaret was heavily involved in editing this manuscript and a final version was not ready until early 1958. His publishers forgave him. Norah Smallwood read it ravenously and wrote, 'It's so good, Laurens, and I am thrilled with it. And I do congratulate you on so many things about it and above all, for its warmth and humanity, and for your vivid painterly descriptions.' She wrote privately to Leonard Woolf to query the title and to raise the question of whether Pratt/Spode had been libelled. Woolf became very nervous about it; he was right and the underwriters refused to give coverage. William Morrow cabled to Norah Smallwood, 'A most inspiring reading experience; a perfectly magnificent book; as full of excitement as it is of thought and spirit'. They immediately asked about the successor volume – and they too were worried about libel. William Morrow, too, did not like the title, and suggested 'The Vanished People'; it would of course become *The Lost World of the Kalahari*. *Reader's Digest* and the book clubs were clamouring for sight of the manuscript. London and New York thereafter mainly argued about the distinction between Laurens's South African buffalo and the American bison – and over royalties.[2]

Getting the book to press presented the usual emergencies. Laurens was also distracted, during the summer of 1958, by family tragedy. His eldest brother Andries had died, and his youngest brother Kuno, whom he loved, now followed. As Laurens wrote to Norah, 'Of seven brothers I am now the only one left.'

He and Norah were both worried that Pratt might sue: though as Laurens wrote to Norah, the only reputation Pratt stood to lose was that of 'a somewhat gifted gigolo' who had lived off a rich woman for the past nine years.[3]

Pratt's solicitor sent a demand for £121. 1s. 1d. expenses and a promise of further action, upon which Laurens delivered a counterthreat of a claim for damages. He asked Clara to produce the 'blackmailing' letter which Pratt had written to him after he escaped to Bulawayo, and which Laurens in Muhembu had rashly posted on to her. No, replied Clara, rather cool by now, she had never received any such letter from Muhembu. Pratt was at this time regaling London dinner parties with tales of Laurens's authoritarian behaviour on the expedition, 'dispensing biscuits and lavatory paper with a lordly manner, patronising everyone', as the writer Anthony Sampson remembers him saying.

Tempers cooled a little after Ingaret intervened, but Pratt's lawyers pressed on. Laurens had sought to direct the filming operation, Pratt claimed, in minute detail and had tried to treat him as a mere cameraman; he had had to give up not out of 'cowardice' but because of a back ailment. Anyhow, there was no point in going to court since Pratt had no assets. Laurens believed that slipped discs were notoriously 'the most vulnerable thing used by contemporary neurotics to justify their failure to face up to reality'. Still, he agreed that he, too, had lost his hunger for a court action. Interestingly, the BBC film sequences in the swamp, when Pratt was still behind the camera, do not betray any glaring inadequacies, though Laurens had said that Pratt rarely deigned to lift a camera.[4]

The second round in this contest was more serious. The Hogarth Press lawyers advised that Laurens might have to 'justify the libel', which in British courts was always a dangerous business, and suggested that the publisher obtain an indemnity from the author, meaning that Laurens would carry the penalty and the costs if Pratt/Spode sued and won. Laurens's solicitors responded by suggesting a shared indemnity, and Laurens pointed out that Pratt, whom he described as Clara's gigolo, was a non-resident, which would be a disadvantage if he wanted to sue. Johnnie Marnewick and Brian Curry were asked to be ready to give evidence. Hogarth and Norah Smallwood stood strong behind Laurens, who made the canny point that Mrs Urquhart would be unlikely to support Pratt in an action because she would not want her relationship with him to be publicised – and Laurens correctly said that he only mentioned her in the book as 'my friend', never mentioning her sex. Norah Smallwood concluded that they should be prepared to fight any action on the argument that what Laurens wrote had been the truth. To cheer them up, sales orders were flowing into London, as were enquiries about foreign rights. Odhams had immediately taken *Lost World* for its book club and Penguin wanted the paperback.

Eventually, wiser counsels prevailed. Leonard Woolf suggested some

cuts in the manuscript. Norah Smallwood, dubbing Pratt 'the abomina-
ble Spodeman', urged Laurens to agree. He did so in the end, adding,
'Only of one thing I am certain; what is left is one of the mildest under-
statements ever uttered about an impossible character in the English
language.'

In the end, *The Lost World of the Kalahari* was published in the United
States on 29 October 1958 and in London on 10 November, to publicity which came easily after the success of the television series. Total
British Empire sales climbed to 225,000 over the next four years. (To
compare, *Venture to the Interior* had by now notched up more than 400,000
sales, as had *Flamingo Feather* – astonishing figures, even when including
paperback and book clubs.)[5]

Most reviewers in Britain linked the book to the television series;
some regretted the absence of photographs, which would eventually be
redressed by a 'coffee-table' edition in 1988. Cyril Connolly gave *Lost
World* the lead review in *The Sunday Times* and was kind, noting that the
whole book 'brightened' in its final chapters. But in the weekly journals
Laurens had a mixed reception. *The Economist* was irritated by the length
of the row with Spode, which it declared was annoying and irrelevant to
the matter in hand – the finding of the Bushmen, which was 'enthrall-
ingly handled and beautifully done'. In *The Times Literary Supplement*
Laurens took a drubbing: he was 'ridden with mystical fancies, with
theories of fate and destiny, with high-falutin' analogies, with symbolism
and Meanings and ornate significant metaphors': the book was a heavy
doughnut, with excellent jam in the middle but an awful lot of dough.
Doris Lessing, in the *New Statesman*, wrote that white African writers
used the continent as a peg to hang their egos on – and they included
Laurens and herself. And in *The Spectator* another expatriate South
African novelist, Dan Jacobson, was almost savage: 'I do not know what
Colonel van der Post is talking about in much of this book . . .': his quest
was, for Jacobson, 'a subject of the profoundest obscurity'; some of the
travel passages were exhilarating, but then Laurens 'plunges once again
into an obscurity that is as intense as it is portentous'.[6]

The American reviews were less grudging. 'A noble book, one which
will I am certain will become a landmark in the literature of African
travel,' the *New York Times* Book Review said. Rumer Godden in the *New
York Herald Tribune* swooned over the book's 'quality of magic . . . he can
give [his travels] a feeling of enchantment so that its happenings, though
in no wise exaggerated, are touched with a wisdom and vision larger than
themselves.'[7]

*

The Lost World of the Kalahari was the first of Laurens's books to attract serious critical attention from the academic world. Anthropologists would chew over it for years, but the literary critics were interested too. D. W. Lloyd, in the *English Academic Review*, for instance, pointed out that the book is a 'quest romance' in the earlier colonial tradition of the previous century. The traveller leaves his metropolitan home, describes his arrangements, travels to the wild interior, experiences trials and adventures, and as a result ultimately achieves a new sense of his mature being (a process which Jung called individuation). In this literary tradition the natives used to be seen as inferior people – stupid, lazy and brutal: the Bushmen had often been portrayed as the most inferior on the colonial scale of civilisation. But Laurens, Lloyd argued, transformed the colonial narrative because he *reversed* this thinking. For Laurens, the native might indeed be a child, but Laurens chose to value his simplicity and insisted, following in Rousseau's footsteps, that he has everything to teach the traveller.[8]

Seen from this perspective, the success of *Lost World* makes sense. Laurens indulges Pratt/Spode because they both share the same sentiment about Africa, but Spode has an 'inner weakness' and cannot stay the course, so the photographer is dismissed. To pay for his own weakness, Laurens must, in Bunyan-esque terms, pass through the Slough of Despond (the Okavango Swamp where his fellow hunters fall sick and the River Bushmen are nowhere to be found). When he encounters the buffalo, he breaks the colonial hunter's code, defying his companions: he refuses to shoot – and survives. Then they approach the Hills and break a taboo, for which they pay a price, even as they enter a primordial realm. The Spirits have found Laurens wanting, and at this stage they forbid him the prize. He expresses contrition, and is after all allowed to proceed on the quest, now accepting the African sense of a divine presence in the cosmos. Overcoming the last barriers, he is granted meaningful participation in Bushman life. He reverses the traditional, colonial view of the Bushmen's 'primitive values', and is rewarded when at last they tell him their most sacred myths. They dance, and the first rains begin to fall.

Of the very end of the expedition, when he leaves, he writes:

> That night too we heard our last lion. He was just at the right distance from us to make the sound of his roar perfect. I have always been grateful that I was born into a world and shall die in one where the lion, however diminished in number, is still roaring. Heard in his and my native setting, it is for me the most beautiful sound in the world. It is to silence what the shooting star is to the dark of the night.

The presence of the Marshall family in the early 1950s was not only known by Laurens (and the fact that they were known to be filming the Bushmen probably stimulated his decision to make his own film) but was widely discussed in academic circles. The Marshalls' work, followed by Laurens's popular success, seems to have been the catalyst for a near-explosion of professional interest in the Kalahari. In the 1950s no fewer than seven expeditions went in search of the Bushmen.[9]

The result of this is what has come to be known as 'the Kalahari Debate'. Very broadly, the traditionalists see the Bushmen as hunter/gatherers, isolated for many years; the revisionists (of whom Professor Ed Wilmsen is the leading example) argue that they were always part of a wider world, an underclass who had moved to and fro between hunting and herding and were very much in touch with the economic realities of the wider regions. Much of this debate, which became rather technical, passed Laurens by, but his books remained, to the academics' irritation, in everyone's minds. He was bound to be seen as an arch-traditionalist, with his emphasis on the primitive and unspoilt nature of what he insisted on describing as a Stone Age people, where even the 'tame' members (domesticated and in touch with Europeans) continued close ties with the 'wild' (the fast-vanishing Bushmen still living in desert isolation).

Laurens wrote of a society which he insisted was still, in the 1950s, profoundly at one with nature. He did not deny that they were in danger, but he campaigned to stave off further encroachment on what he saw as their freedom. There was of course a contrary argument: that these people should not be denied the benefits – education, health care, food, freedom from early death – which are supposed to flow from the modern state. The danger, as was only slowly understood in the 1960s, was that they might fall between the two worlds: they would lose their primitive freedom and yet be stranded on the margin of modern society, trapped by poverty, illiteracy, alcohol and dispossession. That danger was steadily realised, as Laurens observed with sadness when he returned to the desert for the last time in 1987.[10]

In the very period when Laurens's books and television programmes were making an immense impact all around the world (BBC ratings for his *Lost World* series were said to be second only to the Coronation), and while he became increasingly in demand as lecturer, broadcaster and visionary, academics were becoming exasperated with the lack of precision and the inaccuracies of his work. He openly declared that he was not a scholar, but he did after all present himself as an authority on Bushman folklore and culture. He never claimed to speak the languages, but he had been content to rely on a single interpreter in a land where at least a dozen

Bushman dialects were often mutually unintelligible. He failed to explain that the Tswana and the Sotho are two separate peoples who merely share the basics of two different languages: to describe the Bechuanaland leaders as Sotho, as he did, is a solecism, odder still because Laurens had been brought up not so far away. He never 'lived' with Bushmen: indeed he met very few and only briefly. He apparently thought – erroneously – that the Bushmen of his own Cape Province had been driven out and had moved to the Kalahari. His understanding of the Bushman beliefs and myths he gleaned in the Kalahari was always confused with the rather different culture of the Northern Cape, which had died out many years earlier. Similarly, he transposed the customs of Free State Bushmen into the Kalahari: for example, Heitsie Eibib is not a divinity known in the North, as Laurens seemed to think (it is a 'Hottentot' figure); nor is there a custom of placing a stone on roadside cairns, nor do the Kalahari Bushmen 'pray' to any divinity, nor – the most dramatic challenge to Laurens's thesis – does the god Mantis feature in Kalahari cosmology.

In his books he yielded to the temptation to enhance his own role as an explorer of virgin territories, whether out of ignorance or self-promotion. Repeated references to his journeys where no white man had ever been are invariably an exaggeration or an absurdity. Professionals, preparing to devote years rather than days to their Bushman studies, soon realised that Laurens was generalising about a far more diverse and complex society than he ever guessed. He talked and wrote of 'the Bushmen'. Successors agreed that there was nothing so simple. To the new professionals, a sequence of fleeting visits into the desert, a slight familiarity with rock paintings and a brief camp-site a mile away from one Bushman clan, was not an adequate foundation for five books, a television series and a lifetime of lecturing.[11]

It was Laurens, on the other hand, who was principally responsible for bringing the Bushmen to the attention of a wider world. Academics could hardly have been asked to turn a blind eye to what they saw as Laurens's amateur approach to their subject, but they may not have understood that the general public, watching yet another re-showing of Laurens's television series, or listening to the lectures which he gave around the world for forty years, especially in America, did not know and did not care. What the professionals did not appreciate was that Laurens was fostering the myth of the Bushman. His was a romantic and no doubt inaccurate portrait of this dying social group, but he believed he had something important to say about them – or the idea of them – to the world outside. The myth also served his own career very well.

*

After *The Lost World of the Kalahari*, Laurens wrote a sequel, *The Heart of the Hunter*, in which he continued the story of his expedition and then described and discussed the folktales and myths which his Bushmen friends had told him during those few crowded days near the Ukwe Pan. The tensions of the earlier volume have lifted and it is a happier tale as the party journeys home. Dabe, the 'tame' interpreter, becomes a central alienated figure. The book contains the beautiful memory of a young Bushwoman, surprised by Laurens at night, holding her baby to the sky: ' "What's she doing?" I whispered to Dabe . . . "She's asking the stars to take the little heart of her child and to give him something of the heart of a star in return." "But why the stars?" . . . "Because, Moren," he said in a matter-of-fact tone, "The stars there have heart in plenty and are great hunters. She is asking them to take from her little child his little heart and to give him the heart of a hunter." '

Laurens, who at the time of the CDC cattle project believed that the Bushmen should be integrated into modern society, now changed sides. He went to talk to a colonial officer. 'Stop immediately, I begged him, all further encroachment in the parts of the Kalahari where the Bushman still had a way of life of his own. The pressure to open up the great Crown Lands of the Kalahari to European settlement was certain to increase. I myself had abetted it unwittingly by surveys for economic development in Bechuanaland, which today I regretted . . . Let the Bushman have a corner entirely his own in the Africa that had once been his.'

Laurens went home to make his film, grateful that the British were planning to appoint an officer with responsibility for the Bushmen and their needs. He now understood that old and new, primitive and civilised, had come together in his life. If he honoured these things in himself, he might be able to help others to rediscover the same things. 'So I collected all I could discover of what has been written about the Bushman . . . His tragedy was the only one I know of in Africa for which white and black shared an equal guilt . . . I was compelled towards the Bushman like someone who walks in his sleep, obedient to a dream of finding in the dark what the day has denied him.'

His expedition safely ended, Laurens raised one of the most delicate aspects of his future role as the teller and interpreter of Bushman tales: his dependence on Wilhelm and Dorothea Bleek, Lucy Lloyd and George Stow, whose researches had started nearly one hundred years before. The second half of *The Heart of the Hunter* is a gathering of Bushman myths and stories. Laurens specifically says that he pooled all he learned in the past with what he himself brought back from the

desert.[12] The awkward question concerns what precisely he brought
back from his brief journey in the desert. How little was it in comparison with what he had inherited from the past?

Dr W. H. I. Bleek was not, as Laurens described him in *The Lost World
of the Kalahari*, 'an old German professor' in Cape Town, but a distinguished philologist in charge of the Library of the Governor, Sir George
Grey. He died in his late forties of lung disease in 1875, but his sister-in-
law, Lucy Lloyd, and his daughter Dorothea continued his researches for
many years. Their work is a monument of South African scholarship,
and it was matched by the pioneering investigations of a struggling geologist and ethnologist, George Stow, whose seminal book *The Native
Races of South Africa* was published posthumously in 1905 after Lucy
Lloyd had bought the manuscript from his widow. Stow lived in
Bloemfontein in 1879 when Laurens's father was teaching at Grey
College. In that small community they must have met, especially since
CWH's headmaster was a friend of Stow, who would lecture frequently.
This is probably where CWH's interest in the Bushmen began. All these
years later, Laurens owed – and acknowledged, up to a point – a great
debt to Stow and to the Bleeks.

Dr Bleek's interest in the Bushmen dated from 1857, and in 1870 he
set aside his massive work on a dictionary of Bantu languages when he
discovered that among the convicts working on the new breakwater on
Cape Town harbour were a number of Bushman prisoners. He persuaded the authorities to allow him to take two of them to a hut at the
bottom of his garden, in the Mowbray suburb, where they were encouraged to enjoy a degree of freedom and an evident friendship, while Bleek
and his sister-in-law struggled to master their ferociously difficult language. Other Bushmen followed, and the Bleeks kept in touch with them
when they returned home to the northern Cape. Bleek collected an
extraordinary archive, only a fraction of which has been published. The
most important of these narrators of Bushman myths and tales was
Xhabbo, whose name means 'Dream': his portrait is the frontispiece in
Bleek's main volume, *Specimens of Bushman Folklore*, out of print for many
years and only now re-issued in Switzerland in 2001. Xhabbo was con-
victed after hunting a springbok on the land of one of the farmers who
had dispossessed his people.[13]

The extent of Laurens's debt is hard to assess. He wrote, in *The Heart
of the Hunter*, that 'I have only used the stories I myself collected in so far
as they add to the light and substance of the theme I found there'. What
this probably means is that the great majority of the Bushman stories
which Laurens tells in *The Heart of the Hunter*, and which he would repeat

on countless occasions around the world in the years ahead, are in fact drawn from Bleek. It does not necessarily mean that Laurens was merely quoting from Bleek's text, or that he was not told the same stories by his own Bushman contacts in 1955, one hundred years after Bleek had first started to gather them. Perhaps these same stories had been handed down in Homeric fashion through several generations, so that Laurens was told, in the Kalahari in December 1955, what a Bushman convict had told the German linguist in Cape Town in 1870. There is certainly no reason why Laurens should *not* have recycled these wonderful stories of the Mantis, the Porcupine, the Rainbow and so on, to a twentieth-century audience. With his great gift for telling a story, he could enthral an audience of any size. In this ancient Homeric tradition, he would have been passing on, to the next generation, a collection of profound and mythical tales, adorning them on the way with his own embellishments and interpretation. But the original 'Homer' was Dr Bleek – or Xhabbo.

One might wonder, though, as Laurens did not, whether a story told by a Cape Bushman in 1870 really would have been retold by a Kalahari Bushman a century later, since other cultural traits were definitely not transferred. When a couple of academic specialists took a copy of Bleek to the Western Kalahari in the 1980s to read them to the local clans, they were greeted with bewilderment.[14] Had the stories died out? Or did these people come from a different society or language group? In which case is it likely that Laurens's own Kalahari contacts in 1955 would have told him stories identical with those in Bleek from 1870?

In fact, most of the Bushman stories Laurens recounts in *The Heart of the Hunter,* and which he would retell so often in the years ahead, can actually be found either in Bleek's *Specimens of Bushman Folklore* (1911), or his '*Short Account*' (1875), or Lloyd's *Account of Further Bushmen Material* (1889) or Dorothea Bleek's *Mantis and his Friends* (1923), just as much of Laurens's history comes from Stow. Laurens does not deny the debt – he acknowledges the Bleeks in his introduction to *The Heart of the Hunter* – but he is never specific about how large it is. He volunteers that his mother read Bleek's books to him when he was a child, and describes them as 'a sort of stone age bible to me'.[15] His own book turned out to be a sort of Apocrypha.

Midway through *The Heart of the Hunter,* with the journey ended and the Bushman stories yet to begin, Laurens offers an explanation of what he is up to. 'There was a great lost world to be rediscovered and rebuilt, not in the Kalahari but in the wasteland of our spirit where we had driven the first things of life, as we had driven the little bushman into the desert of southern Africa. There was indeed a cruelly denied and neglected first child of life, a Bushman in each of us.' Laurens would always afterwards emphasise that, when he gave talks about the Bushman, people would often tell him that they had splendid dreams. 'I realised that earliest and latest, old and new, primitive and civilised, had met in my life in a way which was perhaps unique.' Laurens was always concerned to emphasise the uniqueness of his experiences. 'If I succeeded in rediscovering my own first experience of the first things of Africa, if I honoured them in myself, I might help others to rediscover and honour the same things in themselves.' Never mind that he had no training or expertise, he would write of 'the peril of man when divorced from the first things in themselves'.[16]

This high-minded posture was bound to be a red rag to the academic anthropologists, ethnographers and sociologists who were beginning to arrive in the desert. One of them later wrote that Laurens's books and films 'project a false picture of the peoples who do live in the communities they purport to depict. Van der Post used a small number of impoverished Khoisan-speaking peoples, seen by him as "true natural man", for his own didactic purpose in an attempt to thwart the destruction of what little, as he thought, remained natural in modern humankind. This mocks their actual conditions of life.'[17] But Laurens and the academics were operating in different worlds and speaking in different tongues.

In the long and fascinating description of Bushman myths which occupies the second half of *The Heart of the Hunter*, there is, as has been mentioned, a very considerable duplication of Bleek's researches. Even Laurens's earlier first-hand description of the young mother presenting her child to the stars is near-identical with a Bleek story called 'What the stars say'. Laurens's Bushmen explain, just as Bleek's did, how they feel an intuitive 'tapping', a sort of extra-sensory perception, and how they hear the *sound* of the stars. Laurens has told, just like Bleek, of the dead hartebeest who magically re-assembles himself, and the stories of the striped mouse, the war with the baboons, and the hyenas who take perspiration from their armpits to bewitch the lynx. Laurens hears a version of Bleek's wonderful tale of the origins of death (the moon gives a message to the hare in the Hottentot version, which the hare gets wrong, so the moon strikes him – hence the hare-lip). Bleek and Laurens both have the girl who throws ashes into the sky and creates the Milky Way. When a star falls down, reports Bleek, 'our heart falls over . . . for the stars know the time at which we die . . .': Laurens's Bushmen seemed to have the same understanding of shooting stars. Laurens, following Bleek, has the equally spellbinding story of the lion who licks the tears of the young man. The Praying Mantis, the insect which is the favourite hero of Bleek's Bushman folklore, is still, according to Laurens's report in the 1950s, their trickster quasi-deity, and many of their stories still revolve around Mantis's family and adventures. The snag is that today's anthropologists and linguists insist that the Mantis plays no role whatsoever in the cosmology of the Kalahari; these, like Bleek, are scholars who have spent years pursuing these things, compared with Laurens's week or two, so their argument must be taken seriously.[18]

A story is the wind, says Bleek's Xhabbo – and one day Laurens, in a novel, would also call his own character Xhabbo, and repeat the sentiment. It may be noted that Laurens's version, in *The Heart of the Hunter*, is an inaccurate transcription of Bleek's own text; Xhabbo actually says: 'I sit . . . watching for a story, which I want to hear . . . I must wait . . . while I listen along the road . . . that I may listening turn backwards (with my ears) to my feets' heels on which I went; while I feel that a story is the wind. It is wont to float along to another place . . .' Laurens, in *The Heart of the Hunter*, substantially changed for his own ends this meditation of Xhabbo, who is in fact simply describing how he wants to go back to his home and his family; the revised version becomes, in Laurens's explanation, 'one of the most haunting utterances from the past of my country'. That may be so, and it may not matter particularly, but this is entertainment rather than scholarship. Years later Laurens would set a pair of novels in the Kalahari, *A Story Like the Wind*, and *The Far-off Place*, each headed with an even less accurate extract from this same quotation. '"The story is like the wind", a Bushman called Xhabbo said, "it comes from a far-off place and we feel it . . ."' There is a not-dissimilar misreporting in his description of the star which the Bushmen said had married the lynx, 'dawn's heart', as the Morning Star, Venus: Bleek specifically identifies it with Jupiter, but Laurens in this way asserts his own authority over the story, with his preference for the feminine Venus.[19]

There are, in Laurens's book, some interesting additions to the Bleek canon. He often recalled, for example, how Nxou, the young hunter in *The Lost World*, explained his reluctance to define his theology by saying, 'It is very difficult, for always there is a dream dreaming us.' There is nothing quite like this in Bleek, and some readers have been sceptical of Laurens's version, arguing that there is no 'dreamscape' inhabited by today's Bushmen as there is with the Australian Aborigines. This quotation, which came through a single interpreter, was very important for Laurens. It echoed the line from the anthropologist Lévi-Bruhl which he had used several years before as the preface to *Flamingo Feather*: 'The dream is the true God of primitive man.' (The plot of that novel centered upon the dreaming of a dream.) It may well be a Bushman concept, but it is widely shared by other cultures as well, ranging from the Chinese through Shakespeare to Calderon and elsewhere.[20]

Laurens himself believed that the most interesting myth he extracted from his Bushmen, which does not appear anywhere in Bleek, was their own version of the universal Promethean tale of the coming of fire and, therefore, of civilisation: it was stolen by Mantis from under the wing of an ostrich – which turns out to explain why the ostrich never flew again. At this point Laurens digresses into the wonderful African story of the hunter who spends his life pursuing the great bird of Truth; at the very end of his days, exhausted on a mountain peak, a single white feather falls into his hand, and he dies content. In *The Heart of the Hunter* Laurens attributes this story to 'a Hottentot servant on the Mountain of the Wolves when I was a boy'. He used to tell it on innumerable occasions in his lectures, attributing it to various sources. Occasionally he admitted that it is also told at length in Olive Schreiner's masterpiece, *The Story of an African Farm*, from which he argued that, since she spent her childhood in Philippolis (she didn't) her version somehow links with his own 'Hottentot'. It was never a 'Bushman' story, and may indeed have come from Schreiner's imagination, though the novelist Doris Lessing has traced the story back to the 'Conference of the Birds', a twelfth-century Sufi poem by the Persian Farid ud-Din Attar.[21]

However, *The Heart of the Hunter* is not supposed to be an anthology of Bushman myths. That could have been done by anyone with a copy of Bleek. The point of the book, and no doubt the reason for its great success, is that Laurens set himself to *interpret* these ancient tales, in accordance with his understanding of Jung. His competence as a scholar is therefore irrelevant to his higher purpose. Anthropologists would have located these stories against a social or cultural background, but Laurens was not interested in doing that. It does not really matter that his knowledge of Bushman history was erratic and often wrong, that he did not speak the languages, and that he had not spent his life baking in the desert, choking on sand and tormented by flies. It may not matter that we doubt whether he really gathered many stories on his brief visit, or that we realise that he relied so heavily on Bleek and, as the years went by, gave the Bleeks less and less acknowledgement. But we should also remember that he was constantly in debt to Jung for his interpretation of what were in effect myths and fairy tales.

His interpretations of these Bushman stories were often very imaginative. Take Porcupine, for example, the daughter of the god-insect Mantis: 'I soon realised how fitted she was in that world of first things to be the supreme expression of Mantis's intuitive soul. In Africa the porcupine is an animal that emerges only at night. Unlike the hyena she is a creative aspect of darkness: she does not go about to kill or injure any living thing . . . [her eyes] give her the power to see in the dark, as the soul gives men vision in its own dark night . . . All I have learnt about Porcupine convinced me that she is akin to Ariadne whose thread brought man, after his encounter with the beast, safely out of the labyrinthine depth of himself . . .' That is not something which would be written by a philologist or an ethnographer. Or take Bleek's story of Mantis's war with the baboons who have killed his son and are playing with his eyeball. Mantis manages to recover the eyeball and escapes with it in his bag of hartebeest skin: 'Mantis recognises that the over-intellectualised, over-critical argument is killing both the new vision and himself: the only solution is to withdraw from the argument, protecting the new vision by the natural, instinctive attitude which the bag . . . represents. His way leads to a place of water, grass, reeds, and green, growing things, an ever-recurring image of the source of first spirit.' Mantis puts the eyeball into the water and it grows again into his child, made new.[22] Not every reader will respond to this sort of approach, but no matter, this is no mere anthology.

In this light, Laurens's thesis about the Bushmen is a Golden Age fable: 'In our era of vast numbers and unreal collective abstractions, the story of this first individual and his imagination is more important than ever, if only because it establishes that at the very beginning of things man was an individual, a hunter before a herdsman, the single Adam made in the image of the first spirit before the making of the many . . . He lived, then, this first individual, in a state of extraordinary intimacy with nature . . . there was about his life none of this cold, inhuman feeling that the existence of numbers inflicts upon the heart of the individual in our days . . . Armed only with his native wit and his bow and arrow, wherever he went he belonged, feeling kinship with everyone and everything he met on the way, from birth to death.'

Laurens has here become the preacher, a part he was to continue to play for the rest of his life. He had a trick of pinning his sermons to claims of personal experience, whether in a prisoner-of-war camp or in the depths of the desert and the bush. 'Through the despised spirit of this vanished Africa,' he writes at the end of his Kalahari journey, 'I was brought to a new understanding, both of basic truths and of the civilised processes of life . . . All this became for me, on my long journey home by sea, an image of what is wanted in the spirit of man today . . . It is our own shy intuitions of renewal, which walk in our spiritual night as Porcupine walked by the light of the Moon, that needs helping on the way. It is as if I hear the wind bringing up behind me the voice of Mantis, the infinite in the small, calling from the Stone Age to an age of men with hearts of stone, commanding us with the authentic voice of eternal renewal: "You must henceforth be the moon. You must shine at night".'

That last sentence is a direct and unacknowledged quotation from *The Mantis and his Friends: Bushman Folklore*, edited by Dorothea F. Bleek, and published in Cape Town in 1923.[23]

Laurens's success with the television series and his new books had turned him into a national figure. From this position, he sought to develop a political influence in his adopted country, operating, as he would do for the rest of his life, behind the scenes. In the years ahead he would take pleasure in starting what he called a 'whispering campaign', and the aftermath of his Bushman programmes is the first example. Lord Ogmore quickly put down a question in Parliament, no doubt inspired by Laurens. The eventual result, largely a consequence of Laurens's television film and books, would be a 'Bushmen Survey' in Bechuanaland and, in 1958, the creation of a Central Kalahari Game Reserve, a name which was not intended as an insult to the humanity of the Bushmen, but which allowed implementation without bringing in new legislation. This process was delayed by academic infighting, with various professors in the London School of Economics blocking government funding. This led to an argument between the LSE and the University of the Witwatersrand in South Africa, which was of course much better placed to study the Bushmen. The row exasperated the civil servants, and in the end George Silberbauer from Johannesburg carried out the Survey with the help of Dabe, Laurens's Bushman interpreter. It was not published until 1965, by which time Laurens was no longer operating in this theatre.[24]

On 27 September 1960, the Resident Commissioner in Mafeking, Britain's senior civil servant responsible for Bechuanaland, gave vent to his exasperation with the British academics who, he suggested, seemed to be suggesting not only that they should have special status and facilities in his territory but that they should virtually take over the matter of the Bushmen. Thanks to his own administration, he said, the Bushmen had survived in Bechuanaland in greater numbers than in any other territory in the region. He poured scorn on the manoeuvres of the LSE to set up a 'Co-ordinating Committee for Bushman Studies' in London without bothering to involve any of the governments concerned ('what exactly a couple of United Kingdom academic experts ... can do to add

to the practical care of the Bushmen is difficult to envisage'). He was evidently irritated that the Anti-Slavery Society was now taking an interest
in his Bushmen and that there had been a successful campaign to stop
their recruitment to work in South Africa's gold mines.[25] In this murky
world, Laurens's politicking to improve the conditions of the Bushmen
ran – to use an appropriate metaphor – into the sand. He would not
have been particularly gratified to know that his own work, with that
of the Marshalls, had by then inspired a new influx of anthropologists
to the Kalahari. He had for some time now become more concerned
with the affairs, and the message, of the Capricorn Society.

PART FOUR

'He talked of yea-saying and lived the nay . . . Hence his life
does not convince us of his teaching . . .'

C. G. Jung on Nietzsche

22

The Establishment Man

IN THE MID-1950s, as he approached fifty, Laurens was an established figure, indeed an Establishment figure, an internationally successful author, a television personality, a frequent broadcaster, a prosperous and confident adoptive Englishman moving in elevated circles in London and preparing to launch himself into America. He was making more than enough money to sustain this lifestyle. When he was not travelling abroad – as he frequently was – his London diary was filled with social engagements with such people as Leonard Woolf, David Stirling, Donald Tyerman of *The Economist*, the novelist Graham Greene, the psychotherapist Alan McGlashan, as well as Ingaret's actress friends, Athene Seyler with her partner 'Beau' Hannen, Laurens's publisher Norah Smallwood, the writer Rosamond Lehmann, the Africa expert Margery Perham, J. B. Priestley and his wife Jacquetta Hawkes, and others like them. He had very few academic friends, and does not seem to have mixed much with the many South Africans living in London from the late 1950s.

He and Ingaret tried to spend as much of the summer as possible in her small Aldeburgh house, Half-Crown Cottage, where Laurens could write undisturbed, walk on the marshes and play tennis with Benjamin Britten, Peter Pears, and Mary and Stephen Potter. They went to France and Spain in the winter of 1953, to Spain again the next year, and on a number of publicity visits to the continent. A couple of months on the ski-slopes of Switzerland had become a regular part of their winter routine. In the late 1950s, he and Ingaret bought an apartment on the sea-front in Ospedaletti, near San Remo on the Italian Riviera. They sold it in 1969.[1]

Aldeburgh, by origin a fishing village on the east coast of Suffolk, was for more than thirty years Laurens's retreat and summer home. It had been discovered by Ingaret in the early 1930s when, convalescing from an accident, she bought Half-Crown Cottage. She and, in due course,

Laurens were enchanted by the peace and remoteness of this rather inaccessible corner of East Anglia and would spend every summer there. The winters, though, were too bleak and bracing for them and the cottage would be closed, or sometimes rented.

Although Aldeburgh has today become fashionable, its essential character has not been lost. Its single main street, set back one block from the sea, today contains some smart and expensive small shops, a couple of good restaurants, an excellent bookshop and, still, the surviving bakery, ironmonger and so on. But the main feature is the Front, a long row of pretty, sometimes eccentric, little houses, pastel-painted, often either occupied by retired people or the weekend homes of London's intelligentsia. These look out over the shingle beach and the grey North Sea. The fishing boats still go out from this shore, as in Britten's *Peter Grimes*; there is a lifeboat station, and still, in the middle of the pebbles, the Coastguard Tower in which Laurens rented the tiny middle floor from Geoffrey Castle and his novelist wife Margery Sharpe for an annual rental of One Pound and One Flamingo Feather. There he would sit every morning, gazing out to sea, while, to the sound of waves on the shingle, he dictated his next chapter to his assistant, who for years was Katherine Littman. Later he became the owner of the Tower for a while.

Half-Crown Cottage, set behind the seafront, is an attractive small house but standing directly on the street with no sea view or garden. Laurens and Ingaret eventually decided to move, and in 1970 Laurens's son John and his young family bought it from them after Laurens had found Turnstones, a short distance towards the river, a house with both a direct sea view and a small garden, although it is an undistinguished building. Laurens continued to use the Tower for his morning writing session, before his afternoon walk across the marshes. Ingaret did her editing, played bridge and tennis, and they both went up to London quite often by train from Saxmundham – in those days the railway served boiled eggs for breakfast in the buffet car – so that Laurens could meet his publishers and his friends.

They had quickly become members of an Aldeburgh 'set'. This was inspired and led by Benjamin Britten and Peter Pears, who lived in Cragg House, on the seafront. Britten and Pears had founded the Aldeburgh Festival after the war, and it soon became an internationally-famous summer musical event, responsible for much of Aldeburgh's later fame. Their particular friends included Stephen Potter, author of the 'Gamesmanship' books, and his wife, the painter Mary Potter, who had bought Red House, a little out of town, in 1951. They all had a passion for tennis, and Laurens and Ingaret soon became regular contestants on the

Red House court, with Laurens partnering Mary against Ben and Ingaret (who were both quite good). The Potters' marriage broke up in 1954–55, and in 1958 Mary 'swapped' houses with Ben and Peter, who had found that, as Ben's fame grew, Cragg House was too public. Mary moved into Cragg House, where Laurens would sometimes stay when he needed to come up to Aldeburgh in the winter, and Ben and Peter moved out to the Red House, though they eventually built a studio there for Mary.[2]

Other friends from London were also loosely attached to this Aldeburgh group before Ben died in 1976: Joyce Grenfell, who was devoted to the town, Rosamond Lehmann and Kenneth Clark, for example. Laurens also introduced his friend William Plomer to Ben. This meeting led to their collaboration on *Gloriana*, an opera written for the Queen's Coronation and initally a critical disaster, and what Plomer described as the three 'choperas' – his Church-operas *Curlew River*, *The Burning Fiery Furnace* and *The Prodigal Son*.[3]

There were also wider and long-lasting friendships, none more so than with Robin and Lilias Sheepshanks, ten miles outside Aldeburgh in Eyke. The original introduction seems to have been made through Britten, and the Sheepshanks and the van der Posts became dear friends. They knew Laurens well, they were aware of his faults, and they loved him.

It was the Sheepshanks who introduced Laurens to the most famous friendship of his life.[4]

Before Laurens's mother, Lammie, died on 29 September 1954 at the age of eighty-seven, her life had become steadily more eccentric, and Laurens's affectionate references to her in his books gave only a sanitised version of her later years. She was an extraordinary and formidable figure, not at all the elegant and feminine old lady whom Laurens eulogised. Leaving the Philippolis house in 1923, she had parked herself with various of her by then adult daughters before returning to her Wolwekop in 1938, and in 1940 urging Laurens to give up his hesitant idea of enlisting in the British Army and to come home to run the farm. Various of her grandchildren used to visit her on holiday at Wolwekop; one year several of them caught polio, including John, but her granddaughter Margaret, 'Tiny', had it worst and was disabled.

Lammie then, in her seventies, set off north for Twyfelhoek, one of the remaining family farms, where, as Laurens correctly described, she determined to rescue and develop a farm in a semi-desert region. He did not add that she was accompanied by two Italian POWs, or that the warmth of her relationship with one of them, Giovanni, scandalised her children. 'Tiny' van der Post and Chris Schmidt, her grandchildren, both have memories of violent family rows in which their parents furiously remonstrated with their grandmother about her lifestyle which was bringing shame on the family. The sons, appalled, used their influence in government to have Giovanni sent back to Italy. They never knew that their mother accompanied him all the way to Lourenço Marques to say goodbye. Some of them suspected, years later, that Lammie's fortune had declined because she had bought Giovanni an olive farm in Sicily.

Not content with this, Lammie in her eighties moved deeper into the fringes of the Kalahari, to another van der Post farm, Stilton. There, as Laurens described in *Venture to the Interior*, she spent three years drilling for water and living in a tent. Laurens's claim that she struck water at 157 feet must be discounted – it is much too deep for the Kalahari water table – but he did mention that she was aided by a German surveyor, a certain Muller. There is a lively family story that her friendship with Muller also, in due course, scandalised her sons, one of whom, Willem, was sent in 1950 to remonstrate. This confrontation, it is said, resulted in a physical encounter and a broken leg for Willem, who got no sympathy from his mother. It may, of course, be another family legend.[5]

In the end Lammie was forced to retire from the desert and went to live with her daughters once more, with Emma in Bloemfontein and with Marie on a farm near Harrismith. For more than twenty years she had been writing her memoirs, and the disappearance of all but a score of pages is a minor loss to South Africa's history, because she had a ringside seat at many of the century's events and, from the pages that have survived, she wrote vividly and accurately. She certainly sent sections of her manuscript to Laurens in London, even before the war.

Controversial to the end, Lammie converted from the Dutch Reformed Church to become a Seventh Day Adventist, and chose to be buried not in Philippolis at the side of her husband, who had been awaiting her for forty years, but in the Bloemfontein cemetery where she lies close to Herman, the favourite son who had died in 1935 mysteriously, owing money at a time when her own larger debt to him was still outstanding.

Laurens, whom she had chided over the years but seen only occasionally, visited her on her deathbed in September 1954. Norah Smallwood in a letter said, 'She recognised him when he arrived but was more or less unconscious by the time he left.' According to family memory, however, she saw a man in a waistcoat standing by the hospital door and demanded of the nurses, 'Who is he? Tell him to go away!' In fact Lammie died in the care of her daughters, on Emma's farm.[6]

Laurens was not close to his family. He had transferred his life to England and, while he remained always homesick for his native land, which he would visit frequently, he did not take many pains to keep in touch with his siblings or his nephews and nieces. Often his letters to his sisters admit that he has recently been in South Africa, but he regrets he did not have time to visit or even to telephone them. When they came to London, they found they were not particularly welcome. Tiny van der Post, who had a wonderful voice, won a bursary to train in London at the Royal College of Music. Laurens tried to discourage her from coming and, when she arrived, had no contact throughout the year but for a single supper. He did however arrange for her to sing for his friends, Britten and Pears. They told her that she would have a fine career if she did one final year at the College. She explained that her bursary had expired and that she would have no option but to return home, yet Laurens, who was then prospering, made no offer of help, and Tiny had to give up her solo aspirations; eventually she became a Reader of Music in Bloemfontein. Laurens had always considered himself short of money but even when he became well off he did not find it easy to be financially generous.

When the family did meet, there was affection and reminiscence. There was also political disagreement, though this affected the brothers rather than the sisters. Laurens, from his base in London, had taken a strong and widely reported position critical of apartheid. Most of his family were probably not supporters of the National Party government which had introduced it, but they thought his ideas were too radical. Several of the next generation recall witnessing, as children, passionate arguments in which Laurens was berated by their parents for promoting too rapid a move towards dismantling racial barriers. Laurens, from the mid-1950s, was famous in South Africa, and it is probably true that his reputation could have damaged the Army career, for example, of his favourite younger brother Kuno, though Kuno's future would anyhow have been jeopardised because he had volunteered to fight in North Africa during the war, a bad mark after the Nationalists came to power in 1948.[7]

Laurens never liked Andries, his eldest full brother. A scrawled paragraph by Laurens in his 1950 notebook runs: 'My elder brother – am not on speaking terms with him – he opposed my marriage to Ingaret – he has always repressed me and I hate him – my mother's boy too – our trade commissioner and in love with his own daughter – deformed, crooked, virtuous fellow.' But Laurens was central to Andries's domestic drama. It had seemed, to the family at home, that Andries and his wife Anna Coetzee were unable to have children. On that, of course, rested the eldest-son succession of the van der Post family, and also the inheritance of Lammie's family farm of Wolwekop. To their surprise, in the mid-1930s, Andries writing from Europe told them of the arrival of a daughter, Mignonne. There were suspicions, because Anna was apparently not pregnant when encountered slightly earlier in Paris by a member of the family; and Lammie demanded of Andries that he swear on the Bible that Mignonne was his own child – which he did.

Andries died in 1958, having been South Africa's Trade Commissioner in London from 1941 to 1950, and Mignonne, by then in her mid-twenties, was set to inherit. But the family's suspicions had persisted and at some stage – the sequence is not clear – Laurens, encouraged by the family, commissioned in London a private investigation into Mignonne's true origins. It was discovered that she had indeed been adopted, was therefore not in the 'blood line' and so, according to CWH's will, could not inherit. She was told by her mother that she was not, as she had always thought, a van der Post; that she was not an Afrikaner but a French Jew who had been taken into Andries's care in 1933; and that she would not inherit Wolwekop. Since all the older brothers had by this time died, the inheritor was – Laurens!

Mignonne, who married a university don and lives in Port Elizabeth, admits her distress, remembers her love for her adoptive parents, and says that for her parents' sake she tried to keep a civil relationship with her Uncle Laurens. But she declined to attend the family reunion in 1994 because, she then explained, she no longer felt that she was truly a van der Post.[8]

Laurens had little to do with his brothers and it was with his sisters, Emma, Marie and Ella, that he kept up an irregular relationship in the second half of his life. As the kid brother, however famous, they refused to take him too seriously, and he would be teased and challenged, in Afrikaans and English, on his rare visits. Ingaret was never a part of this circle. She did not like South Africa, never got on with the Afrikaner family, and only visited the country twice after her brief stay in 1948. Laurens's son John had been a favourite of his aunts and uncles until he left for Britain in 1952 at the age of twenty-three, whereas his daughter Lucia, living with her mother in Cape Town, was inevitably slightly out of touch, although she was welcomed to Durban by Elaine, Pooi's widow, when she went to school there between 1950 and 1953, staying with friends of the family. Both John and Lucia would make successful careers in Britain, independently of their father.

Laurens's son John was a handsome and gifted engineer. He came to England as a graduate apprentice at Rolls Royce, lost a year when he collapsed with a tropical lung disease (during which time he also wrote an unpublished novel and ran a coffee bar), and then went to the Atomic Energy Authority at Aldermaston, to the Gas Council and eventually to a senior job in the water industry. He chose to associate himself with Britain and only returned to South Africa on a few occasions. He was closer to his mother than to his father; indeed, in his younger years he seems to have felt abandoned by his father. When he arrived in London he was not invited to stay in Cadogan Street because Ingaret did not think there was room. Instead he lodged in Chelsea where he became a lifelong friend of a sculptor, Sean Crampton, one of whose students was Frances Baruch who was to become Laurens's last close companion. John married Tessa Broome, the adopted daughter of a ship-owning family. Based outside London, they had very little contact with his father and step-mother, wishing to live their own lives. Laurens for his part made little effort to keep in touch with them. After John fell ill, Laurens arranged for him to see his psychotherapist friend Alan McGlashan, which he did for some years. John died of cancer in March 1984, aged fifty-five, by which time he and his father had become much closer.[9]

The relationship between John and Laurens which, after he came back from the war, was always complicated and difficult, would distress Laurens in his later years. There is no doubting that Laurens loved his son, and was devastated by his early death, but John could never forget that Laurens had in effect sent him away from a happy early family child-hood and despatched him to South Africa, where he was brought up, however lovingly, by relations rather than his own parents; in a sense John, growing up in Durban, lost not only a father but also a mother, mainly because Laurens had failed to arrange sufficient financial support for the mother to look after their son. After John came to London, at the start of a distinguished career, he never really got on with Ingaret, although she would have wished otherwise. During John's final illness Laurens returned every week from Switzerland to be with his son.

Laurens was closer to the family of his daughter, Lucia. She remembers close and happy times with him when she came to England, and had the impression that he was trying to make up to her for the years when he had not been around. She married a barrister, Neil Crichton-Miller, and made a successful career as a journalist, notably as the women's page editor of the *Financial Times* for more than twenty-five years. As her family grew and she was busy with her career, Laurens's and Lucia's lives became less interwoven. Lucia and her family certainly benefitted on occasion from Ingaret's generous and thoughtful help, but it cannot truthfully be said that Laurens was particularly close to his children or grandchildren, at least until his last years. His grandsons David and Rupert remember that he did not seem involved with their interests as they grew up. David was an exceptional young tennis player; John's daughter Becky became a professional musician; Laurens never attended any of their appearances. In later years, however, Lucia and her husband Neil became fundamentals in the support system for the ailing Ingaret and the ageing Laurens.

Lucia is eloquent: 'John and I both sensed that we had to make lives of our own outside his sphere of influence if we were to survive as our own people. In a funny kind of way, I think this hurt him. John on his deathbed said to me that he really hadn't wanted to be an engineer, and when I asked what would you like to have been, he said, "Well, really a writer or film-maker, but with the shadow of Laurens over me, how could I?"' She goes on, 'I think another reason for family difficulties is that in some ways John and I were a permanent reminder of things he didn't feel good about. He knew he hadn't been much of a father, that in some way he'd let us down, and he felt uneasy and guilty about it . . . He didn't like it that John and I were not prepared to pretend that things had been other than they were – he would have liked to wipe the slate clean, but of course you can't do that. He couldn't stand the fact that we knew he wasn't perfect (we didn't mind – we loved him all the same) . . . He couldn't bear criticism – which I now understand as a form of insecurity . . . I believe Laurens loved John as deeply as almost anybody in his life, but somehow couldn't bridge the sense of failure, or cope with John's feeling of anger and sadness at what had been lost.'[10]

By the late Fifties Laurens, the eleventh child, had become the last surviving son of CWH and therefore the head of the family. This would haul him back into the family affairs which he had in effect escaped from in 1928, embroiling him in lengthy legal complications concerning the van der Post inheritance and in particular Wolwekop. CWH had made it clear that he wished Wolwekop never to be sold; Laurens decided to disregard that request.

Marjorie did not remarry. She continued to live quietly and in genteel poverty in Cape Town, where she had to take modest jobs. She published a readable and interesting biography of her musician father, Theo Wendt. She never complained about Laurens's treatment of her, and she occasionally visited London, where she and Laurens would meet, as they always did on his visits to the Cape; an attempt by her son John to persuade her to live in Britain failed when she found that she was too lonely in London and missed Cape Town and Table Mountain. Laurens had covenanted to pay her £480 a year after their divorce in 1949, and her two children helped support her in later years.

23

Capricorn

DAVID STIRLING WAS a well-born Scottish Catholic who, as a young Commando Lieutenant in 1941, had invented and set up the Special Air Service (the SAS) in the Western Desert. Never in any sense a liberal, he had become fascinated after the war by the challenging business potential of Africa, and he moved to what was then Southern Rhodesia in March 1946. He created the Capricorn Africa Society during the two years 1949–1951. Ultimately there were branches in London, Salisbury, Nairobi and Tanganyika.[1]

Years later, Laurens used to describe himself as the co-founder, with Stirling, of the Capricorn Africa Society.[2] This is untrue and conceals his real and positive contribution to the Society's development. In the beginning Stirling, who was at heart a Tory with a characteristic contempt for the 'socialists' who had come to power in London, was preaching a policy for the economic and political development of British Africa which, with the goal of 'the United States of Capricorn Africa'* on a Dominion model, was cautious and paternalistic. His first collaborator was a Rhodesian journalist, farmer and ex-policeman, N. H. Wilson, and in April 1950 they published a pamphlet, 'A Native Policy for Africa', which argued that a prosperous East and Central Africa would be a bulwark against Communism. They proposed massive white immigration, with land set aside for the blacks to develop at their own pace ('the black alone of all the great divisions of mankind has never produced a civilisation of its own'). They added that it would be necessary to guard against white exploitation of black, and stressed their rejection of the apartheid ideology to the south. But 'it is too early, probably by fifty or a hundred years, even to talk of setting up purely Native States as part of the eventual Capricorn African political federation, union or confederation.'

---

*The name refers to the region north of the Tropic of Capricorn, thus excluding South Africa.

Stirling and Wilson fell out, and Wilson left Capricorn. In April 1951 the inaugural meeting of the Society was held in Salisbury. The historian of Capricorn, Richard Hughes – who was an active member in Kenya – has made the sensible point that, from the Society's base in Rhodesia, the African Nationalist rumblings in British West Africa at that time must have seemed too far away to be relevant to Capricorn's elite gradualists on the other side of the continent.

However, 1952 brought the first glimmer of a slightly more enlightened thinking. 'The paramountcy of any race . . . is utterly rejected,' Stirling wrote, even while he and his members were strongly endorsing the campaign for a Central African Federation (of Southern Rhodesia, Northern Rhodesia, and Nyasaland) – a policy which would soon do much to alienate black potential members. At the same time, Stirling's draft of his planned 'Salisbury Declaration' spoke of the British settler as 'a worthy vehicle for the responsibility of administration in the six territories'. Stirling used his London contacts to lobby for British Government support which, not surprisingly, was not forthcoming. Eventually, in December 1952, 'the Salisbury Declaration' was published as the definitive statement of Capricorn's principles. Thanks to Stirling's fame and energy, they were widely distributed and often praised (in the *Daily Express* Max Aitken said that they were the most impressive event to emerge from Africa in the century).[3] The Capricorn policy, it now emerged, was one of partnership between the races with the whites in control, as they would be responsible for the economic development of the continent and for helping Africans to achieve Western standards.

It is hardly surprising that most white liberals, whether in Africa or Britain, and the great majority of politically aware blacks, never had any patience with Capricorn; it seems extraordinary that such essentially conservative ideas were being freshly developed so late by thoughtful and concerned whites, who never dreamed that a mere ten years later five of the six territories would have achieved black majority rule. In South Africa, the National Party Government was pressing on with the implementation of its apartheid policies of separate development which were intended to maintain white supremacy indefinitely. Capricorn always made it clear that it did not wish to interfere south of the Limpopo. North of that river, we can now see that Capricorn was from its beginnings a lost cause.

Laurens, far from being a co-founder of Capricorn, did not even meet Stirling until late 1952. In Stirling's own words, 'Laurens van der Post, who knew the country and the people better than all of us put together, was an inspiration, but he came later . . . It was reading his book *Venture to the Interior*, which first drew my attention to him . . . I vowed that I would meet him . . . I told him . . . that I thought his help was crucial to us . . .'[4] The two of them, aware of their heroic reputations, were attracted to each other and would be friends until Stirling's death in 1990. Laurens rapidly became a prominent member, a public spokesman and propagandist, although he was not particularly involved in the day-to-day running of the organisation.

It would be hard to pin down his precise influence, but Capricorn's policies now became distinctly more liberal, more 'multi-racial', while he was involved. Stirling became less concerned with the economic imperatives and ditched his enthusiasm for the Central African Federation. He wrote in September 1953: 'The Capricorn Africa Society . . . operates on a scale at least as wide geographically as that of the Pan-African racialism and . . . has an even stronger emotional appeal to the African'; and in February 1954, 'Surely the time has come to overhaul human relationships in Africa'. One hears the voice of Laurens in this.

At the Colonial Office in Whitehall they decided that Stirling had his head in the clouds.[5] But he continued to battle away. In Southern Rhodesia a small number of distinguished and well-educated Africans became members; in Kenya, with the Mau Mau rebellion at its height, Capricorn was unable to target the Kikuyu because political activity was forbidden: this factor would later damage the Society's prospects in the Colony. In Tanganyika, there would always be the problem that, under its United Nations trust status, Britain was required to bring forward African independence; there was, though, influential Capricorn support among the rich white farmers of the Ol Molog district, on the slopes of Mount Kilimanjaro. The racist instincts of the white Copperbelt miners would make Northern Rhodesia hostile territory, redeemed by only a few, more enlightened Europeans. Nyasaland was a non-settler backwater and would hardly feature large, which could also be said of its fellow protectorate, Uganda. The focus of Capricorn's efforts was therefore Southern Rhodesia, where the substantial white minority was bound to be influenced by the proximity of neighbouring South Africa, now engaged in the full implementation of apartheid.

This was the background to Laurens's engagement with Capricorn's affairs in the mid-1950s. There is no doubt that he responded to the high-minded but essentially cautious Capricorn vision of the future. He was an enemy both of apartheid and of African nationalism, and he enjoyed meeting the new African intellectuals, men like Herbert Chitepo (later to be killed), Lawrence Vambe, Chad Chipunza and Nathan Shamuyarira.

He would also have enjoyed his new white friends, both in Africa and England: Capricorn may never have had many members, but those it had often came from the Establishments in the different countries, with links to aristocracy and even royalty. It probably became a disadvantage to Capricorn that it was evidently rather posh.

Laurens made true and lifelong friendships in Capricorn, with people like Jeannine Scott (later Bartosik), who ran the London headquarters, and in Kenya with Dr Michael Wood, who founded the Flying Doctor service, and his wife Sue. It was during this period that Laurens visited the Congo with the Woods, travelling with them in their single-engine plane from Nairobi. The object was to visit Dr Schweitzer at his Lambarene hospital, where Michael Wood was appalled at the conditions he found, but Laurens stayed behind in Kinshasa. He had had a terrifying trip because the Woods seemed to be lost over the rain forest, as night came on and their fuel threatened to run out.[6]

Laurens's own views may have been consolidating at this time. In April 1952, for instance, soon after the publication of *Venture to the Interior*, he had addressed a London meeting at the prestigious Royal African Society in which he described what he saw as the lessons of European postwar experience in Asia and projected them on to Africa. It was a legend, he declared, that the white man was exploiting the black and that 'my black countrymen are hungry as a starving man is hungry for food for a social and political system such as ours, and that his great and crying needs are political . . . My black countrymen north of the Limpopo are not fundamentally interested in political representation on our model. They need medicines and doctors more than political slogans and trade unions . . . The black man needs a long sustained period of growth, of mental stability and security, of training and preparation . . . political peace and quiet and instinctive reassurance that what is good in his own traditions and wise and proved in his own customs will be declared valid and not blindly and wilfully pushed aside . . . Given this, a hundred years or more can peacefully and fruitfully go by before he will need many of the things which are now being wilfully thrust upon him . . .'[7] In 1952, '*a hundred years or more*'? This is the first sign that for the rest of the century Laurens would be a paternalist, out of touch with the overwhelmingly popular sentiment of his continent.

The long-planned Capricorn Convention eventually took place in a deserted hotel at Salima on the western shore of Lake Nyasa in June 1956. There, 200 'Africans' – white, black and Asian – gathered to debate the detail of the Capricorn programme. They also lived, ate and drank together. Simple as it seems, it was a breakthrough for many of them, for whom Salima remained an inspiring memory. A curious aspect is that Laurens, billed as a keynote speaker, did not turn up.

The choice of Salima had itself been odd. Africans in Nyasaland had been more hostile than most to Capricorn, which was always dogged by its original support for the Central African Federation. Though Salima was isolated – thought to be an advantage – it had an airstrip. The advance party, led by Susan Wood, Jeannine Scott and Peter Mackay, the ex-Guards officer who ran the Salisbury office, succeeded by frantic efforts in preparing the camp in time for the delegates, and the Convention was a success, not least because it won substantial international press coverage. Laurens's speech was read for him: 'Here, for the first time,' it said, 'we have a movement dedicated to a concept which is concerned no longer with these crippling and paralytic preoccupations with race, but is concerned only with the maintenance and advance of fundamental human values . . . We are both seed and natural seedbed for the new non-racial African world to come.' After two and a half days the delegates signed a Capricorn Contract, and also a Loyal Address to the Queen.[8]

Laurens was by this time well known, indeed famous, and his absence from Salima was a disappointment. David Stirling was not amused. Laurens made excuses: that he had a prior commitment, that he had recently devoted three precious weeks to the Society's business, and, years later, and in contradiction of this, that he was responding to Stirling's request that he stay in London to represent Capricorn there. None of these pass muster. The real reason why he did not go to Salima was that he did not care to venture again into Nyasaland, where his name was still mud because his *Venture to the Interior*, published four years before, had caused upset and anger, as he had recently learned.[9]

It had been impressed on him on the strenuous speaking tour he had made a few months earlier, in April 1956, when he did go to Nyasaland, as well as to Kenya and the two Rhodesias, sometimes addressing up to five meetings a day, urging them that the solutions to their problems must come from them, not from London. The various races must sit down side by side and plan 'a fundamental concept of living . . . in which there is no discrimination against people on the basis of race, colour or creed'. At a meeting in Umtali, for instance, he said, 'In Africa I cannot tell you how much later – how terribly much later – it is than we think'; so, 'if we are interested in preserving the civilised values, we must get the African to defend and uphold them as we do.'

That brief visit to Nyasaland had provoked irritation in the Letters columns of the local paper: 'There must be a great number of problems in van der Post's own country that he could give his ability and attention to, and leave us to find our own solution to ours,' wrote 'Haywire' to the *Nyasaland Times*.

The tour as a whole, on part of which he was accompanied by David Stirling, was however a success in that he attracted considerable local press coverage and, according to Peter Mackay, new memberships and donations. Laurens was always in his element crisscrossing Africa like this: he missed his plane from Nairobi to Ndola after talking late into the night about Mau Mau with his host, the Governor, Sir Evelyn Baring, and promptly chartered his own light aircraft, passing through the edge of a cyclone to arrive on the Copperbelt seven hours later with thirty minutes to spare before his first public meeting.[10]

A more central figure in Capricorn was an elderly Methodist minister, a former missionary called Dr Joe Oldham. He ran a YMCA Conference Centre at Dunford in Sussex, where Jeannine Scott first introduced him to Stirling. The two men, unalike in so many ways, instantly became allies; the cleric's influence on Stirling was probably greater, and more sustained, than that of Laurens. Oldham's book, *New Hope in Africa*, was the best exposition of Capricorn thinking, and engaged the attention, if not the support, of influential Africanists in Britain such as Margery Perham and Phillip Mason.

Capricorn at this time operated out of Jeannine Scott's flat in London. The society's great enemy was the Africa Bureau, also based in London, which worked for the cause of African independence – 'we cordially hated each other', Jeannine Bartosik remembers.[11] It led to a brief passage of arms with Canon John Collins (who ran the Defence and Aid Fund from St Paul's Cathedral). Laurens wrote to him in April 1957 to protest that he had heard that Collins was saying that Capricorn was opposed to the advancement of indigenous Africans. Collins replied that he admired the Christian integrity of Capricorn but believed that it was still too paternalistic and its refusal to operate in the political arena was a mistake: 'In my opinion any society which doesn't realistically take account of and give adequate scope to the indigenous and existing African Nationalist movement is in the long run likely to fail ... I am prepared ... to be shown that I am wrong.'[12] Canon Collins would soon be proved right.

Laurens was elusive because he was so busy and was away so often: Stirling used to urge him to call in at the Capricorn office and do his 'prep'. He did, however, use his travels in America to promote the Capricorn cause, for example with his Quaker friends and with the Carnegie Endowment, but America never took to Capricorn. In fact

Capricorn, by 1956, was fast being overtaken by events. The 'winds of change', as Harold Macmillan put it (a phrase which, absurdly, Laurens claimed was invented in his drawing-room), were sweeping down through Africa, and only Rhodesia, South Africa and the Portuguese colonies would defy them. The black membership of Capricorn, always puny despite what Laurens said, fell away rapidly as it became apparent that Britain was prepared to negotiate independence for most of the East and Central African territories. Historians of the period unanimously ascribe the failure of Capricorn and other inter-racial societies to their powerlessness.[13] The result was the disillusionment of the small number of black members, and this multi-racial phase quickly ended.

David Stirling became exhausted, sometimes appearing on the verge of a breakdown. Perhaps he knew that he had been defeated; he resigned the presidency and withdrew to London, to the gambling world of his right-wing Mayfair friends, and then to the Middle East, where he ran a private army in the Yemen Civil War and became an arms dealer to Saudi Arabia. He also set up Watchguard, a shadowy organisation which offered protection to heads of state friendly to Britain. He survived a bad car crash in Scotland in the early 1970s and then got even deeper into right-wing extra-parliamentary politics. His friendship with Laurens survived: after his death in 1990, Laurens described his life as 'noble, complex and significant'.[14]

The death of Capricorn as a political movement was signalled by a devastating confidential report written in September 1960 by Jonathan Lewis, its Executive Officer in London, after a tour of the region. Lewis, a former Colonial Officer, candidly declared that 'the Society can no longer be regarded as a serious force – or indeed as a force at all'. The leadership was divided and African support was minimal. There were 124 paid-up members in Kenya, of whom only four were African. In Central Africa there were 122 members, 49 of them African. 'The Society appears to suffer universally the handicap of a bad name.' Laurens responded furiously, describing Lewis's report as trivial, petty and negative. The people who had given Lewis these ideas, he added, were 'merely projecting their own inadequacy and sense of guilt on to the Society'. He was unable to attend the forthcoming Council meeting, but 'I know . . . that the Society has not ceased to be a multi-racial group although its African membership has, to a certain extent, gone under cover and disappeared from obvious view.' In a letter in December 1960 he admitted that it 'may not be as multi-racial as it used to be, but the purpose of the Society remains as multi-racial as ever'. He believed the Capricorn idea was needed more than ever in Africa, and he objected to the proposal that its funds be diverted into 'various benevolent and do-good activities'.[15]

Not for the first or the last time, Laurens's political judgement was wrong. Capricorn disappeared from any role for which David Stirling had created it. Its direct offspring was the Zebra Trust, under the patronage of Princess Margaret, which over the last forty years has successfully run a group of hostels for Commonwealth students in London. Laurens continued to associate himself with the movement, but his heart was no longer in it. Years later, after the South African majority-rule elections of 1994, he assured Susan Wood that Capricorn had helped 'to push the history of South Africa also in the right direction'.[16] This was surely wishful thinking.

The Dark Eye in Africa (1955), a book for which he cared deeply and of which he was proud, is today hard reading. It is, unpromisingly, the text of a talk which Laurens gave to the Psychological Club of Zurich on 3 March 1954, two years after he had first addressed it in the earliest period of his infatuation with Jung. The book contains this paper, a mere forty pages, with 'The Discussion', a transcript twice that length of the questions which were put up by the high-powered audiences, both then and later, together with Laurens's lengthy responses.

It hardly sounds an episode which would have justified more than a pamphlet. But to Laurens *The Dark Eye in Africa* was the culmination of certain ideas which he had been meditating since the 1930s when he attempted, unsuccessfully, to write 'A Book of Warning', as he used to put it, and which he tentatively called 'The Rainbow Bridge'. (That manuscript has not survived.)[17] To deliver this paper in Zurich must have signalled for Laurens the achievement of an international intellectual respectability. Judging by his habitual dismissal of academics, one might surmise that he had always suffered from an intellectual inferiority complex, having had no university education and knowing that he was no scholar. Here in Zurich, before some of the finest intellects in Europe, he was accepted, and was encouraged to expand his own views about what was one of the central issues of the age. His argument must be considered in association with his support at the time for the Capricorn movement. The book's dedication is, 'To David Stirling, for practising what he preaches in Africa, and to those of all races and colours who are trying to make Capricorn a true instrument of re-integration in Africa'.

The argument of this curious little book illustrates the ideology which

Laurens would embrace for the rest of his life. It is often interesting, even stimulating, but is also full of generalisation and platitude frequently derivative of Jung, without acknowledgement. Laurens presents himself to his sophisticated European audience as an African: 'I feel myself to have become a kind of improvised footbridge across the widening chasm between Europe and Africa.' He would approach the problem of Africa 'through the being of man' (whatever that means). There must be a change of heart in the white man. He appeals to his fellow-Afrikaners to cease their 'dishonourable and evil' treatment of South Africa's black and Coloured peoples; it is later than they think. He addresses the distinction between 'primitive' and 'civilised' peoples. Laurens, as a result of his recent meetings with the Bushmen, now believed 'that it is not we who are filled with spirit or soul but rather the dark and despised people about us': they were 'at one with' life. 'Whatever happens to them their lives are never lonely for lack of spirit nor do they find life wanting in meaning. To this day you have only to hear the Bushmen, Bantu, Hottentot or Negro laugh to realise how true that still is.' The African had responded to the arrival of the European by turning back to his neglected spirits, and that situation continued, as could presently be seen with the Mau Mau revolt in Kenya. 'The conflict in Africa is at heart a battle about being and non-being; about having a soul of one's own or not having a soul at all.'

Laurens extends Jung's idea of 'the shadow' into his argument. 'Whether we know it or not we all have within us a natural instinctive man, a dark brother to whom we are irrevocably joined as to our own shadow . . . The white man in Africa sees reflected in the natural dark man around him that dark aspect of himself which he has rejected.' It is this 'insidious civil war raging in the innermost being of modern man, which prevents the white man from ever seeing the black man as he really is.' Similarly, the black man has his own shadow, the unlived darker brother within. The debt to Jung is obvious.

Laurens brings in Germany: 'German mythology is the only mythology in which the forces of evil are finally triumphant.' He adds a reference to the Grail myth in which two knights, white and black, fight and discover at the end that they are brothers (but he misses the point – in von Eschenbach's story Parzival and Feirfiz are reconciled and they survive). What he is more importantly saying is that the contemporary struggle in Africa is so tragic because 'the black natural man in Africa attracts the European no matter how much he consciously rejects him'. Laurens illustrates this, effectively, by mentioning that he, like so many white South Africans, enjoyed their first and closest relationships as children with blacks (by which he means their servants). Unrest in Africa, Laurens boldly suggests, is 'an extension of our own individual unrest'.[18]

He then, in an elegant paragraph which has been picked up and quoted elsewhere, suggests that 'I walked Africa . . . because only thus was I able to walk among the mysteries and uncomprehended complexities of my own heart and mind. I discovered that I travelled in Africa in this way because it brought me to unknown places in my own uncomprehended spirit which I could not have reached in any other manner.' Africa, Laurens concluded, was the mirror of our age.

He appended to the lecture text a much longer verbatim record of the questions that were put to him at this and subsequent gatherings. The questions were sometimes intelligent and probing: Laurens's replies, as reported here, were sometimes brusque, even dismissive. He was pressed, for example, to be more precise about his incomprehensible exposition of the meaning of 'Time'. He was confronted by missionary widows who challenged him on his apparently tolerant attitude to Mau Mau and ritual murder in Kenya at the time, which Laurens insisted on seeing as 'signs of how deeply our failure to integrate the displaced African into our own way of life has penetrated'. He was criticised for ignoring the economic factor. He expanded on the dangerous subject of the African as 'primitive man' : 'anyone who would entice him further along this new road, therefore, arouses the fiercest resistance and provokes in him the greatest conflict and fear'. In this sort of context it is easy to understand why Laurens never won the admiration of more than a few black Africans.

Laurens admitted that his comments on the unconscious of primitive African man were a generalisation, but did not 'know of any better way of describing the difference which undoubtedly exists between indigenous and European societies in Africa'. He returned to Wagner, 'perhaps the greatest tribal music ever written. I have heard the same rhythms on the drums of Africa and encountered the same compulsions', and this leads him into the Afrikaners and their 'fanatical myth of a God-chosen people' which explained their sympathy for Nazi Germany. 'There is the same transformation of racial prejudice into legal imperatives; the same mounting hatred of the white-skinned Aryan for the dark non-Aryan breeds; the same absence of self-criticism and the same insensitiveness and intolerance to the criticism of others; the same conviction of unique national rightness and the same capacity for feeling misunderstood; the same exaltation of the state at the expense of the individual; and the same assertion of a *droit collectif* over the principle of the rule of law and the concern for the individual that goes with it.' This was published in 1955, comparatively early in the age of apartheid. No wonder his publisher did not expect a warm reception for the book in South Africa.[19]

Yet Laurens afterwards reverts to a sentimental view of the first Afrikaners in the seventeenth century. They were probably as brutal a bunch of European expatriates as any, but Laurens, who took pride in his descent, writes of them as 'the forefront of that movement to free the individual from totalitarianism of the spirit'. He refuses to answer directly a question about whether he would be happy if his son married a black woman (he was always sceptical about mixed marriage). He lashes out at the Dutch Reformed Church: 'The South African people carrying their Churches with them have receded to a point in their spirit where a racial myth, a racial dream of history, is their real god. That explains the ease with which Afrikaner priests go from the pulpit into politics . . . I call the process a betrayal of the religious urge which originally brought us to Africa.'

Laurens would never make a more devastating attack on his own people, yet he immediately followed it with the argument which would encapsulate his political position over the next forty years: 'The worst thing that anyone can do in these circumstances is to add to the race or individual's sense of ostracism . . . The European in Africa cannot be punished or hated into being a better person . . . Refuse to work off on Africa the moral ardour which you need for your own lives in Europe. Prevent yourselves from projecting this deep conflict which rages also in the spirit of the modern man in Europe on to us in Africa.'[20] Laurens here spells out the position he would hold after the failure of Capricorn. He detested, and publicly reviled, apartheid. But he would never agree that the outside world should take action.

Laurens delivered the manuscript of *The Dark Eye in Africa*, which had really been a matter of collating and revising the verbatim records of the question-and-answer sessions from the several occasions when he delivered the original lecture, at the end of 1954. William Morrow took the initiative, deciding to publish in the autumn of 1955, for an advance of $750. This was far too fast for the convenience of the Hogarth Press, but Norah Smallwood decided she could not be left behind and the book was rushed into print more quickly than usual. The problem, as ever, was that Laurens was so often out of the country, including a few days in late March interviewing Jung in Ascona. *Flamingo Feather* was selling well at the time, and both Hogarth and Morrow were nervous about how so different a book would fare: 'This is a book that the American public may or may not read!' Thayer Hobson of William Morrow wrote to Norah Smallwood, who replied, 'We none of us know what sort of passage it will have here, but it will certainly have a sticky one in South Africa.' Both firms published *The Dark Eye in Africa* in mid-October. It was declined by most of Laurens's usual foreign language publishers.[21]

It is a comment on Laurens's fame at this time that *The Dark Eye in Africa*, a peculiar and serious book, was very widely reviewed. In Britain the response was mixed but generally favourable. To the *Daily Telegraph*, it was 'brilliantly exasperating . . . He has become a angry seer . . . fascinating, inspiring, moving . . .' Laurens, said the *Evening Standard*, was 'the most remarkable man writing – and thinking – about Africa today'. *The Spectator* decided that in Laurens's 'peculiar Jungian-Blakian-Lawrencian kind of world, richly furnished with dark Gods, ancestral myths, unconscious truths and mysterious journeys', there was much that was profoundly true and admirably said. *Time and Tide* thought that Laurens would have done better to sit down to write 'a proper book' rather than publish his lecture. *The Times* said that it would have preferred him to make his points in fictional dress, and Geoffrey Gorer in *The Observer* that Laurens's prose was so tangled that he couldn't be sure he understood what he was getting at.[22]

It was chiefly the weeklies which demurred. *The Times Literary Supplement* pointed out that Laurens's argument owed much to Jung; he had failed to express it 'in that clear concise language essential to the proper presentation of such cloudy themes . . . Does not the woolliness of writing reflect a certain woolliness of mind?' Kingsley Martin in the *New Statesman* took a similar line: 'Mr van der Post's mysticism is sometimes merely a failure to think through a genuinely important idea . . . It is not Jung's fault that Mr van der Post sometimes talks sheer rubbish'! *The Economist* concluded that this book had not enhanced Laurens's reputation. In America the reviews were less divided. The *Saturday Review* gave Laurens the cover picture. The *New York Herald Tribune* declared, 'The publishers call this "one of the ten most important books we have ever published". It is.' The *New Yorker* acknowledged 'an important book . . . courageous, honest, wise, and often quite beautiful.'[23]

24

Against Apartheid

DURING THESE YEARS, and after the failure of Capricorn, Laurens was inevitably recruited into the struggle against apartheid. After taking South Africa out of the Commonwealth, the ideologue Dr Hendrik Verwoerd had been assassinated in 1966, to be succeeded as Prime Minister by the hard-line Police Minister, John Vorster. Laurens opposed apartheid: his only reservation was that he preferred not to speak out publicly against his native land from abroad. For many years he carried two passports, British and South African. When in South Africa he was happy to lash out at the Government in his many interviews and speeches. There would always be a contradiction in Laurens's political position, one which he shared with many white South Africans. Like van Bredepoel, the hero of *In a Province* in 1934, he bled for the miseries imposed upon the blacks under what he knew to be a monstrous system, but he could never bring himself to take his feelings to a bolder, logical conclusion. He was condemned to remain a paternalist, and at heart a conservative, and his critics would argue that this meant he was a racist. This is unfair. He always believed in a multi-racial, federal South Africa. But in the last ten years of his life he reacted with fear and horror to the imminent prospect of one-man-one-vote, because he believed this would result in the domination of minority groups by the ANC.

In Britain, these were years when the meaning of apartheid for the South African blacks was beginning to be understood, so that South Africa rapidly became a pariah state, as it would remain for a generation. The most effective expositions of the evil nature of the regime, heightened by news of the Sharpeville Massacre in 1960, were two books: *Cry the Beloved Country*, Alan Paton's novel first published in 1948, and *Naught For Your Comfort* by the turbulent priest, Father Trevor Huddleston, an account of his Sophiatown ministry, which had appeared to great acclaim in 1956.[1] Laurens knew Alan Paton and they corresponded and co-operated over twenty years. Arguably, Paton's novel was influenced by

Laurens's *In a Province* of 1934. Of course, *In a Province* had only a modest *succès d'estime* while *Cry the Beloved Country* was a phenomenal worldwide best-seller, and this may help explain a certain coolness in Laurens's private attitude toward Paton. Paton also chose to stay in South Africa and fight apartheid as a leader of the Liberal Party, although he had plenty of opportunity to follow Laurens into exile. Laurens's decision to live abroad was frequently held against him by white South Africans.

But on the surface at least they were friends and colleagues, two of a sextet of internationally acknowledged South African-bred writers: the others were William Plomer, who had by now shed all South African connections; Uys Krige, the Afrikaans poet; Jack Cope; and Roy Campbell, who had taken off for the Mediterranean years before. There is a photograph of four of them taken when they met in London in 1955 and signed a joint letter of protest to the Pretoria Government.

Laurens had met but did not really know Father Huddleston: he wrote to a Durban friend in May 1956 that he liked him very much but suspected that 'something of the devil' had got into him in the process of fighting the devil. 'Nonetheless I feel more than ever that we must none of us "cease from mortal strife" and never for a minute give in to these terrible people who are in charge of our country today.'[2] The tone of this letter might come as a surprise to readers who are more aware of Laurens's later political stance, when he railed against South African sanctions, supported Zulu tribalism and publicly criticised Nelson Mandela. In fact during the 1950s he not only associated himself actively with the anti-apartheid movement but offered himself to be used as a 'cover' for the dispatch of money into South Africa to support the victims (including Mandela) of government.

His principal contacts were Alan Paton, in Natal, and Canon John Collins, running the Defence and Aid Fund from his base at St Paul's Cathedral in London. From early 1957 Laurens was in close touch with Canon Collins and liaising with Paton. Apart from sending personal cheques for the support and legal costs of the defendants in the Treason Trials, and also to help Paton fund various Liberal Party causes, he helped Collins to 'launder' Defence and Aid funds to Paton in South Africa in the 1960s by pretending that these were his private, and therefore legal, contributions.[3] In a 1969 letter to Collins, Laurens wrote, 'The fact is that Alan knows where the money comes from but both he and I are breaking the law and are compelled to give ourselves some legal cover. We can only do this by pretending that the money he receives is a gift from me out of my dollar earnings in the US, [but] instead of having my dollar earnings sent to me from America I send a portion of them to South

Africa to pay into my account the equivalent of the sum of money you [i.e. the Defence and Aid Fund] give me in London.' In this letter he said that the South African Secret Police knew that he was paying money to Paton but could not prove that it was illegal.[4]

The Liberal Party felt compelled to disband in 1970 but the connection between Laurens, Paton and Collins remained. It was not always easy. John Collins was a loose cannon. In 1965 he addressed the UN General Assembly and, according to press reports, spoke of how the Defence and Aid Fund was trying to 'assist the underground movement' in South Africa. Both Paton – who was seriously endangered – and Laurens were appalled by this idiotic gaffe. They discussed, by letter, whether they could repudiate him. In a letter dated 19 August 1965 Paton said, 'I must say that John's speech would have terrified us, except that we have got beyond the reach of terror.' This was not the only occasion when Collins's enthusiasm, from the safety of St Paul's Cathedral, ran away with him. The extent of Laurens's contributions is not clear. They began in 1957 with a donation to help the accused at the 'Treason Trial' and continued throughout the 1960s and 1970s (for instance, in 1965 Paton asked him for Rand 4,000 to help the Liberal Party, in 1969 Laurens was promising to send Rand 2,000 from his American royalties 'for your various charities', and he was still sending what Paton acknowledged as 'a generous gift' until 1980).[5]

Paton and Laurens were polite to each other but they were never close; indeed, one suspects a mutual dislike. Their views were poles apart. In 1970, for example, Laurens frequently makes the point that international indignation about South Africa is a way of evading facing up to problems at home ('There is much that is wrong in England today'). He went on, 'I spent three weeks on the Tibet frontier not long ago [the usual exaggeration – it was a brief visit in 1966] . . . and I can assure you that nothing we do in South Africa is comparable to what the Chinese are doing in Tibet . . . The world is applying a degree of censure to us in South Africa which it is not applying either to itself or to any other country in the world . . . I wish we could be left alone so that the real solution of our problems could come out of ourselves and our own efforts.' Paton replied that South Africa and Tibet could not be compared – consider for one thing the unique links between Britain and South Africa: 'I hope you have recovered your true philosophical self.'[6]

They agreed not to argue, and the flow of letters, and donations from Laurens, continued. It was a nervous correspondence: Laurens was increasingly paranoid, in the 1960s and 1970s, about what he suspected was surveillance by the South African Special Branch. His main concern was that his mail to South Africa was being intercepted. 'The scale of loss of letters is inexplicable except on more sinister grounds,' he wrote to Paton. He was worried, he said, because these lost letters included cheques not only to Paton but also to his sisters. Many of Laurens's letters in these years explained, with apologies, that an earlier letter had mysteriously vanished, for which he blamed the South African Security Police or 'sabotage' by sorters in the London Post Office. It is now known that the Bureau for State Security (BOSS) was indeed keeping an eye on Laurens, and it is certain that they kept a file on him, though it is hard to believe that they had the resources to monitor all of his mail out of London, and in any case they would probably have tracked rather than stolen the mail; nonetheless it is a tangled world, and we know that the South Africans had placed agents in London sorting offices. A more likely explanation is that Laurens simply did not get around to writing, or sending, a promised cheque. Certainly his sisters got used to promises of money which was slow to arrive.

As the years passed, Laurens must have drifted lower in BOSS's priority lists: they can hardly have identified him as Enemy Number One. In 1977 he offered Paton the use of his Aldeburgh house if he wanted peace and quiet to write his autobiography. They had earlier agreed that Paton was giving up his commission to write the biography of Laurens's old friend, the poet Roy Campbell, because he could not stomach Campbell's near-fascist views: 'I could not bring myself to admire him,' wrote Paton. Instead he worked on his autobiography, something which Laurens explained he would never feel able to attempt for himself. He died in April 1988.[7] Paton did not know that Laurens had been telling their friends how relieved he was that Paton had given up the Campbell biography: 'He has clearly passed mastering the facts of [Campbell's] life and totally incapable of understanding so complex a phenomenon,' he wrote to a friend on 9 December 1975. He then threw in the sort of behind-the-back remark which was common between these South African authors, outwardly such friends: 'The more I think of Alan's effort the more dismayed I am. He was, of course, drinking like a fish himself – you realise of course that Campbell attracts him so because he is an image of Alan's secret, unrealised self.'[8]

Laurens's other writer-friend in South Africa, apart from Uys Krige, was Jack Cope, poet, critic, editor of the Liberal magazine *Contact*, and lover of Ingrid Jonker, the young Afrikaans poet who drowned herself, in eighteen inches of sea-water, on 19 July 1965. Laurens knew Ingrid and would always say that she was South Africa's finest poet. He and Cope, with Plomer's support, went to great pains, first to distract her from taking her own life, and afterwards to translate and ensure an English-language publication of the collected works of a woman who would become a cult figure, rather like Sylvia Plath, after her death at the age of only thirty-two. This was the translation used by Nelson Mandela when he quoted one of her poems at the opening of the first majority-rule parliament in May 1994: 'The child is not dead/the child lifts his fists against his mother/who shouts Afrika . . .' Jonker wrote the poem after an anti-pass protest march in 1960.[9]

Ingrid Jonker had come to Europe, in the same ship as Laurens, in 1964. She suffered from depression, and had had a difficult relationship with the novelist André Brink. Years after her death it was discovered that her archive, deposited by Jack Cope and others at Rhodes University, had been opened and some of it had vanished; immediately after her death other letters – from Cope, Brink and Laurens – also disappeared. Laurens once described Ingrid Jonker as 'fundamentally profoundly innocent, and totally without any immunities in this sophisticated and materialist world of ours'. Laurens added, 'She was an extremely lovely and physically attractive person and most of the men she met fell for her and thought of nothing else but going to bed with her. They succeeded in seducing a soul that was always full of love and eager to give with all of herself, as she did in poetry.' He added, 'In her last letter to me she wrote, "I can't tell you how often I think I could come back to your world in London, where they make lost women like myself feel like ladies. I still see the figure of William Plomer coming all smiling with flowers to greet me at The Ivy. Oh God, if I could only be back with you people again."'[10]*

In July 1964, after her visit to London in April, Laurens warned Plomer that Ingrid was not replying to his letters. They were both appalled when, a year later, they heard that she had killed herself. 'Her suicide to me is almost like the suicide of Afrikanerdom,' Laurens wrote to Plomer. 'She was rejected by her father, her people, and her lover, even Uys [Krige], so self-absorbed in his own emotions . . . I was so horrified . . . by the dangers of her child-like vulnerability that I wrote to Jack Cope and begged him to come over and fetch her back from Europe and offered to pay his fare! . . . But once Jack had her he just gave her cold pieces of his cold mind in return. He was the only person . . . who could have saved her. Perhaps he tried, I do not know and I may be unfair.' Laurens volunteered that perhaps he too should have done more – he had sent her £100 in response to her request when she was forced to work in a factory, 'but it was not money she needed . . . she needed, as

---

*This letter has not survived. This is Laurens's memory of it.

we all do and some of us thank God get, a loving and understanding human heart to take her in.'

He told Plomer that he had heard that the exiled black writer Nat Nakasa had also killed himself, in New York: 'You, William, who are our only living poet of Africa: could you not write about them, joined in death as they should be in life?' Plomer responded to this suggestion and wrote one of his finest poems, 'The Taste of Fruit', which was published in *The Times Literary Supplement* on 16 September 1965.[11]

Laurens and Plomer met frequently, and corresponded even more often until Plomer's death in 1973. Plomer had spent the war years at the Admiralty in a desk job in Naval Intelligence; he had been recruited by his friend Ian Fleming, who would later write the James Bond books which Plomer recommended to Cape, where he was reader. After a period of promiscuity – and at least one narrow escape from prosecution in 1943 when he seems to have been rescued by Fleming – he came to terms with his homosexuality and settled down with Charles Erdmann, a German Jew, a pastry-cook and waiter, who also became a friend of Laurens and Ingaret. Plomer had set South Africa behind him and was persuaded to return only once, in 1956.

When Laurens made contact with him again after the war, Plomer had become very much a part of the London literary scene, and he introduced Laurens generously to his world. It was a long time since he and Laurens had walked for hours at night along the Embankment as he debated suicide as a solution to his sexuality. It was also a long time since he had proposed marriage to Lilian Bowes Lyon. Now he was a senior and respected figure, celebrated for his edition of the Rev Francis Kilvert's *Diaries of a Country Parson*.[12] He quickly became Laurens's confidant once again. Laurens told him of his plans and travels, sent him his manuscripts, visited him and Charles in Sussex, invited him to Aldeburgh, asked for news of René Janin. Through the prolific correspondence with Plomer one gets the best sense of Laurens's often frenetic movements over these years. His affection for Laurens was never in doubt. Who knows what he felt about Laurens's affair with his own greatly-loved Lilian Bowes Lyon? He had declined to write the introduction to her *Collected Poems*, leaving the task to Cecil Day Lewis. He had published his first autobiography, *Double Lives*, in 1943 when Laurens was at war. Laurens's response to that book, on 5 September 1947 – the first time he had been able to read it – was ambivalent; it was now that he wrote to Plomer to praise him, but to say: 'There are a few things I regret that you do not mention.. . .' These 'few things' were to fester.

Plomer continued to oversee Laurens's literary ambitions, and in return one senses that Laurens was dramatising his life almost on behalf of his friend. On 18 July 1949, for example, he wrote from Nyasaland to tell him of his journey: 'One morning in a light so clear that I could see the markings of an Eland and Roan at 1500 yards, I walked through about ten square miles of purple iris . . .' On 7 February 1951 he reported from Austria that two avalanches had missed his pub by yards and killed seven people: 'It had fallen so fast that we dug the children out with their eyes peacefully open.' In April 1951 Plomer wrote to say how enchanted he had been by *Venture to the Interior*, of which, again, he must have seen a proof – 'Dear Lorenzo, I am very proud of your friendship.'[13]

Plomer was quick to offer support when his friend had bad news, such as the savage reviews of *The Face Beside the Fire* ('My dearest old William, thank you so much for your words of comfort and encouragement . . .'), or the rejection of Ingaret's novel ('I owe you a great debt also for comforting Ingaret in perhaps the only moment of near-defeat she has ever known'). In his turn Laurens, commiserating with Plomer on the death of his father, would reminisce of how he met the parents in Durban before he met William. They tell each other of their respective books. They never forget each other's birthdays. Plomer always calls Laurens 'Lorenzo'; for Laurens, Plomer is 'my dearest old William' and they gossip constantly: 'I saw Leonard [Woolf] yesterday and for the first time had great difficulty in keeping my temper: never knew what a fundamentally coarse and lascivious creature he is. I found myself thinking suddenly, "My God, I do know why Virginia committed suicide"' – this from Laurens of the man who first published him!

As old friends, they also constantly hark back to the past. In mid-1956, Plomer was planning to visit South Africa for the first time in thirty years, to attend a writers' conference and to visit some of the scenes of his childhood. Plomer never went again, but Laurens was ecstatic: 'It is and can be perhaps the most important journey you've ever made' – and reminded him to travel, in Chekhov's phrase, into 'a valley of the shadows of the past'. In November 1957, Laurens told Plomer of the death of their old friend from the 1930s, the coffee merchant René Janin, who from his deathbed had sent the message that they were both very much in his mind. Laurens's respect for Plomer was always as large as his affection: 'You know, of course, you started the revolution in Africa in 1926 [with *Turbott Wolfe*] and if any good comes out of the white man in the end, you put the first seed in the ground.'[14]

25

Holidays

WHILE LAURENS WAS forced to take up freelance journalism to help pay the bills, he did not try to depend on the pittance paid for book reviews but ingeniously targetted American glossy magazines, which paid very well indeed and also funded the foreign travel. His principal outlet was *Holiday*, a glossy and successful up-market monthly edited in New York. He also flirted with *Life* and *Reader's Digest*.

Exactly how Laurens was introduced to *Holiday* is not clear, though at about this time he briefly acquired a New York agent who persuaded *Life* to offer $2,500 an article – an offer which Laurens used to secure a long-term and lucrative relationship with *Holiday*, its rival. He started with one 8,000-word piece on Africa which appeared in March 1954, and followed up with another on the Bushmen, published in October 1956: this was essentially a reworking of the material from his books and which he had acquired during his 1955 expedition.[1] As his international reputation grew, *Holiday* grew still keener. Ted Patrick, the founding Editor, and Harry Sions, a Senior Assistant Editor, quickly became friends. Sions put up all sorts of ideas for articles. The Alps? Snow? More on Africa? The world of the Pacific Ocean? – to be tackled at Laurens's leisure, all expenses paid. It was a dream assignment for any writer. In June and October 1957 Laurens was discussing the detail of a six- to eight-week tour of Africa. His journey to Africa in January–February 1958 was largely paid for by *Holiday*: it was an exhaustive trip – in two months he visited Kenya, Tanganyika, Northern Rhodesia, the Congo, Angola, Congo-Brazzaville, Nigeria, Ghana, Southern Rhodesia and South Africa, before sailing home via Italy. The subsequent article appeared in April 1959 and, years later, the trip contributed to his book on African cookery, *First Catch Your Eland*.

In March–April 1959 *Holiday* paid for him to visit New York for consultation, when he was able to make contact with Quaker friends, meet his publisher and address a Washington seminar. He travelled to Japan for

1. The van der Post family in 1909: (*back row from left*) Henk, Andries, Elisabeth, CWH, Willem; (*middle row*) Maria, Hermann, Lammie, Laurens, Anna; (*front row*) Emma, Pauline (holding Kuno), Pooi. Ella was born the following year

2. Laurens in Philippolis, aged about 13

3. The cub reporter, Durban, 1925

4. The *Voorslag* team at Sezela, 1926. *Left to right*: William Plomer, Roy Campbell, Laurens

5. Laurens and Plomer arrive in Japan, October 1926

6. The night with the geishas, October 1926. Laurens is partly concealed mid-left. Plomer, with spectacles, has Captain Mori on his left and has his right arm around Teruha

7. Marjorie Wendt, when Laurens met her in 1927

8. In Porquerolles, 1931

9. Laurens, Marjorie and John in London, 1929

10. Colley Farm, near Tetbury

11. Plomer, Lilian Bowes Lyon and (*right*) Marjorie (with John) at Colley, 1935

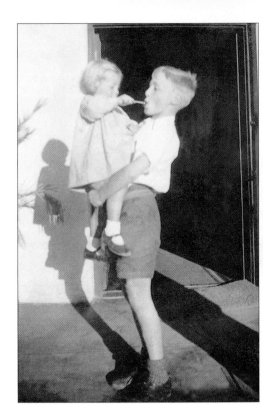

12. John and Lucia, South Africa, 1938

13. Jimmy Young and Ingaret Giffard, early in their marriage

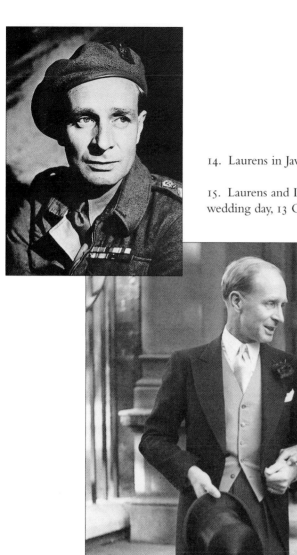

14. Laurens in Java, 1947

15. Laurens and Ingaret on their wedding day, 13 October 1949

16. With two particularly small Bushmen in the Kalahari

17. The Bushman 'Fire Dance', Kalahari, 1955

18. Laurens (and Samutchao) at the panel of Bushman paintings, Tsodilo Hills, 1955

19. A Kalahari breakfast on the 1955 expedition

20. Franz Taaibosch in Colorado with Joyce and Barbara Cook, 1938

25. Frances Baruch and Laurens in Africa

26. Cari Mostert

27. Meeting Captain Mori, 1960

28. At Balmoral with Prince Charles

29. In the Kalahari with Prince Charles

30. Godfather at the christening of Prince William, 1982

31. Introducing Chief Mangosuthu Buthelezi to Mrs Thatcher, late 1980s

32. Members of the original 'Company of Seven', (*from left*) Arman Simone, Bill Pilder, Laurens, Doug Greene and Bob Schwarz, plus Jim Morton, Dean of the Cathedral of St John the Divine in New York

33. Veterans of the Japanese POW camp at the launch of *The Admiral's Baby* in 1996. Laurens is in the centre, Billy Griffiths is on his right, and John Denman is on the extreme right of the photograph

34. Laurens's funeral, 20 December 1996. Centre (*from left*): Jane Bedford, Lucia and Neil Crichton-Miller. Tom Bedford is behind Lucia

Holiday, and as an extra bonus the magazine flew him to San Francisco in September 1961 to address a seminar which coincided with their Japan issue. He took the opportunity to spend five weeks in America, travelling and speaking in New York, Chicago, Denver, Salt Lake City and Los Angeles, concluding with an address on 20 October to the Analytical Psychology Club of New York in memory of Jung, who had died in June.[2]

During these years, Laurens produced several travel books from visits paid for by *Holiday*. His most productive assignment for *Holiday* was a two-month trip around the Soviet Union in April/June 1962. This produced a single enormous article, which took up almost the entire special Russian issue in October 1963. At 65,000 words it was an extraordinarily long piece for a glossy magazine, and demonstrates how considerable Laurens's reputation had become in America. More important, the same text, with many additions from the original manuscript, was recycled as a 130,000 word book, *Journey into Russia*, published in early 1964 in London and New York, though without the superb *Holiday* photographic portfolio of Burt Glinn, the brilliant photographer associated with the Magnum agency. It was a great success.[3]

Journey into Russia was extravagantly praised even by Sovietologists who might have been expected to be rude about a writer who cheerfully admitted that he knew little about the country, had never been there before and did not speak the language. This is the most interesting difference between *Journey into Russia* and Laurens's other travel books, whether of Africa or Japan, in which he makes it clear that he is the expert. There is a refreshing innocence, even a curious naivety, about this book, and it allows him to do what he does best – to write descriptions, of people and places, free of theorising and with less of the rhetoric and purple prose of so much of his writing.

His awareness of his lack of qualifications persuades him that he must leave Moscow as soon as possible and fan out across the immense territory. He therefore travels to Tashkent, Baku, Odessa and Kiev; takes the train east to Siberia, to Omsk, Novosibirsk and Irkutsk; endures the even longer train journey from Moscow to Khabarovsk, in the Far East; and finally moves north to Riga and Leningrad. Of course, there were many places he was not permitted to visit, and he was evidently under the firm control of Intourist, but he did benefit from travelling alone, and he would afterwards claim, characteristically, that he had undertaken 'perhaps the longest single journey through the Soviet Union . . . since the war by someone who is not a Communist'. This must help explain the interest which his book aroused in both Britain and America: he was manifestly not a fellow-traveller, nor was he an academic or a specialist.

Coming from South Africa gives him an unusual perspective. Again and again he compares the Russians with his own Africans. They are, he dares to say, relatively 'primitive' – a word which in Laurens's vocabulary is not at all pejorative, as he established in his Bushman books. 'I have always believed that the balance between primitive and civilised values has never yet been fairly struck in any society . . . I would suggest that the primitive is a condition of life wherein the instinctive, subjective, and collective values tend to predominate; the civilised condition of life is where the rational, objective and individual take command. Throughout history the two have been at one another's throats because it appears that the value of one depends on the rejection of the other.' (This stems from Jung, who wrote in many places that both these necessities, nature and culture, exist in us: and in any contest between them we want culture to win, but we do not want nature to lose.)[4]

Sometimes this combination of the specific and the general is unexpected and stimulating: 'One of the paradoxes that gave me much trouble on my journey was the contrast between the delicacy, tenderness and sensitivity that I was aware of in conversation with the Russians I came to know best; and the total absence of these qualities in the world they were making for themselves.' Or again, 'Outwardly life in Russia is ugly to a degree that might prove unendurable were it not for the immense compensations in the character of the people I got to know.' Laurens admits that his happiest times were, initially, in the Mediterranean atmosphere of Georgia, and then in Central Siberia, where he felt at home in 'a pioneering community that had many affinities with the world in which I had grown up in Africa' (but where he was startled to discover his hosts in Bratsk did not seem to know that until recently they had been surrounded by labour camps).

Journey into Russia is a long book which reads easily. There are few of the autobiographical inventions with which he liked to enliven his books. Here he claims only to have visited China in 1926, to speak a smattering of Chinese, to have spent a 'period' in Berlin in 1961, and to have visited Japan three times, none of which is true. Of course, because he was travelling alone and his is the only record, it is impossible to know to what extent he embroidered his adventures or enlarged on his actual encounters, but that is true of every travel book.[5]

The reviews were gratifying. 'Such an exercise in the exploration of thought and feeling . . . what a good book!' declared *The Times*. *The Times Literary Supplement* protested about 'misrenderings of literally almost every other Russian word in the book', and suggested that Laurens saw 'too many shadows of his own natives on the Russian landscape', but commended his detachment which had produced this 'excellent impression'. Peter Fleming in *The Sunday Times* pronounced that no foreigner had given a fuller or more percipient account of post-Stalin Russia, though added that there were passages of 'pure tosh'. The distinguished veteran Sir Robert Bruce Lockhart in the *Glasgow Herald* said that it was 'the best descriptive book on Communist Russia [that] I have come across by any author, Russian or non-Russian'. Only the left-wing Labour MP, Ian Mikardo, in *Tribune*, described Laurens as 'perversely myopic', yet even he encouraged people to read it.[6]

In America the doyen of Soviet commentators, Harrison Salisbury, hailed the book as 'pure joy – the observations and reflections of a mature, thoughtful man'; as a word picture this was 'the finest we have yet had of contemporary Russia'. *Newsweek* agreed that this was 'a work of extraordinary descriptions, deep sensitivity and thoughtfulness'. To the *New York Times* it was 'one of the best written and most provocative travel books of recent years'.[7]

After this reception, not surprisingly *Journey into Russia* was in the best-seller list for weeks. It became a Book Club Choice in Britain, Penguin immediately paid a £1,000 advance for paperback rights, and the *Sunday Telegraph* paid £3,000 for serial rights, which was good money at the time. William Morrow in New York took the initiative in launching a 'coffee-table' version for 1967, featuring sixty of Burt Glinn's photographs from *Holiday* and slashing Laurens's text back to a mere 30,000 words.[8]

'Laurens van der Post's knowledge of Japan spans his adult life: he speaks, reads and writes the language . . .' This is the editorial introduction of an article by Laurens in the Japanese special issue of *Holiday* in October 1961. It may be unfair to Laurens to blame him for his publisher's exaggeration, but in fact his 'knowledge of Japan' was based on a fortnight in 1926 and a little longer in 1960. His article starts with a recapitulation of his 1926 voyage in the *Canada Maru* and goes on to describe how he was enchanted by the country and by its people. He repeats the dubious detail of his capture in Java in 1942, with an additional reference to having been 'betrayed by a deserting Chinese servant'. He describes his May 1960 visit to Tokyo, 'boiling and bubbling with human beings'. Inevitably he resorts to generalisation about 'the Japanese', but admits the danger of drawing easy conclusions, resolving to leave the capital city and travel as much in the Japanese way as possible.[9]

Before he left Tokyo he went to visit Captain Katsue Mori, and this brief description conceals the most dramatic and moving part of his visit. Laurens had had no contact for thirty-four years with Captain Mori, his host and friend on his Japanese voyage in 1926. He did not even know whether the captain had survived the war, until he was given positive news from Peter Plomer, William's brother, in 1956. Laurens then wrote to him care of his shipping line, and enclosed a copy of *A Bar of Shadow*. Eight months later, in February 1957, he received through another intermediary a sticky response from Captain Mori: 'I am rather sorry to say, his first approach to me since thirty years ago was his book *A Bar of Shadow* . . . I was rather disappointed and disagreed with his opinion that such terrible and cruel man like Hara [the sadistic jailer in the book] was the innated nature of Japanese race.' Mori said he awaited Laurens's explanation.

Laurens, now that he had Mori's address, hastened to reply: 'I am sad that a gift which was sent to you with such patent good intentions should only have succeeded apparently in hurting you . . . I met and suffered under many Haras in the war but I never ceased remembering that there was such a person as "Mori San" and many others like him . . .' Mori seems to have relented, because Laurens tracked him down in Tokyo in 1960. He described in his article and in subsequent books how he visited the elderly Mori and his family to find that their house had just burned down. They nevertheless insisted on entertaining him in their one remaining room and sat down to a fourteen-course meal. The family then sang for him their version of 'Nearer my God to Thee' and Laurens in return told them a Bushman story about the Moon. The ancient friendship had been resumed. Laurens wrote triumphantly to Plomer, 'It is you Mori in particular thinks of as if you had only just parted. I was merely the instrument but you really gave his life a meaning it could not necessarily have had . . . When I sailed from Kobe a few days ago I could still see you waving goodbye when we left you behind in 1926.'

In his 14,000-word *Holiday* article and *A Portrait of Japan*, published seven years later, Laurens tells how he travels to Kyoto by the Tokaido road beside the sea, mostly in heavy rain. He stays in Japanese inns, which he describes at length, dwelling on 'Miss Waitress', the Bath, the Kimono, the discussion of a favourite *Haiku*, the Rice Mill, the Futon Bed. He visits various temples and gardens in Kyoto; he is entertained in a geisha party and his 'student companion' – presumably his interpreter, who must have been with him all the time – falls for one of the girls. Then to Nara, where the sun comes out at last, and Kyushu, with a brief and minor earthquake, and Hokkaido, and the article becomes little more than a very long travel piece by an accomplished and elegant writer after a visit of less than a month.[10]

During these years, the Hogarth Press and William Morrow busily exploited the material which Laurens had produced for *Holiday*. This made sense because Laurens invariably wrote far more than the magazine could carry. *Holiday* had the article and his American and British publishers had the original manuscript for recycling as a full-length book, and everyone was happy.

They could even issue a second, illustrated edition, using the stunning pictures which *Holiday* had commissioned from Burt Glinn. William Morrow took the lead with a photographic version of *Journey into Russia* – in America it was called *A View of all the Russias*. There were financial risks involved in committing themselves to 20,000-plus expensive copies of Glinn's lush colour pictures, but they pressed on, with Hogarth's support, and the result appeared successfully in autumn 1967. There was no need to compare it with the original article because it was twice the length and had many more illustrations. The same operation was performed on Laurens's article on Japan, published at 14,000 words as far back as October 1961. The original manuscript was more than double that length, and again Burt Glinn had photographs. Laurens wanted a bigger book, but Morrow and Hogarth persuaded him that the Russian format should be repeated, and the illustrated edition of *A Portrait of Japan* came out in 1968. These glossy versions sold well.[11]

Because these picture books were evidently spin-offs, critical attention was limited. The Russian book was well reviewed: even *Socialist Commentary* described it as an ideal gift for anyone who had been to, or intended visiting, Russia. The most interesting review of *A Portrait of Japan* was from William Plomer in the *New Statesman*, who must have decided that it was permissible to write about a book by his oldest friend. It was, he decided – perhaps there was an edge to this – 'a pleasant travelogue which keeps indicating that depths exist'.[12]

Not everything worked out. He wrote articles on 'The Snows of the World' and a 'Report on South Africa' which were spiked, in addition to a piece on Scotland. Plans for articles on 'The American Earth' and a major journey to China came to nothing. *Holiday* also turned down his offer to publish the introduction he had written to a new book on the Nile. Such are the tribulations of the freelance journalist. But the situation was complicated by a power struggle within *Holiday*, which Laurens's friends eventually lost. In October 1964 four of the top editors resigned in what seems to have been a succession battle following the death of Ted Patrick. The successors initially held on to Laurens – the magazine at the time was paying $15,000 for an assignment plus $15,000 expenses, which was serious money – and in particular wanted him to go to China, but eventually the Chinese refused him a visa, so he went off to India for the magazine instead. He thought he might also get a book out of it.[13]

This tour of India in 1966, on which he was granted all sorts of official facilities, lasted from 5 October to 17 December and ranged from Sikkim to Nepal, to Kashmir and Rajasthan, to Bombay and Benares. He suffered a recurrence of his chronic malaria and eventually abandoned his plan to write a book as being too overwhelming and difficult. Instead he produced three articles for *Holiday*, which were published over three years.[14]

After that, the new editors apparently felt they had no further need of him and he was evidently out of sympathy with them. In the light of his book sales by that time, it would hardly have worried him. *Holiday* struggled on until 1977, when it was merged with *Travel* magazine.

Despite parting from *Holiday*, Laurens continued his lucrative American journalism after 1968, though he developed an injury of his right hand and arm, probably after a tennis accident, and was warned that he must rest it and no longer write in longhand. From this year to the end of his life Laurens dictated all of his books and most of his letters. His literary style thereby changed significantly because (as many people discover) the rhythms of his dictated prose became longer, and often more complex, than his earlier handwritten work. The injury also, he afterwards explained, prompted him to stand back, to rest the arm, and to take a leisurely trip around Africa. He suggested to Time-Life a book on African food for their series on international cuisine. They flew him to New York in 1968, agreed a deal, all expenses paid, and Laurens then set off in November on a mad dash around West, East and Central Africa – there was nothing leisurely about it, whatever his subsequent description suggests. The readers of Time-Life, as they savoured Laurens's lyrical accounts of meals in these exotic places, could never have guessed at the author's professional dispatch, nor dreamed that so much of what he wrote was a spinning of words. For example, 'In my time, I have walked thousands of miles of Africa on my own feet – many more miles, I believe, than any European has ever done.'[15]

Laurens produced a manuscript very rapidly, dictated in his new style, but as usual over-long. Time-Life cut and edited it to bring it back to 40,000 words, excluding the recipes. The result in 1970 was *African Cooking*, sumptuously illustrated with mouth-watering dishes. The recipes appended to each regional chapter were also separately printed in another slim volume. It was an efficient freelance job, and nothing more was heard of it until in July 1973 Laurens suggested to the Hogarth Press that they might bring out a version of his full manuscript. Norah Smallwood at Hogarth hesitated for several years because the manuscript seemed neither fish nor fowl, neither cookery book nor travelogue. An anonymous Hogarth colleague was particularly hostile to the idea of running detailed recipes: 'One can hardly expect the female reader to spear an eland and roast its entrails over a fire of baobab twigs'; the reader also pointed out that the manuscript contained out-dated references to the Emperor Haile Selassie, since murdered, and recent events in Portugese Africa. But after careful editing, cutting it to a mere 80,000 words and killing all recipes, *First Catch Your Eland* was published at last in 1977. The title – a play on a famous line of Mrs Beeton – was dreamed up by Norah Smallwood, and detested by her staff. Laurens got a £3,000 advance. After he had persuaded Time-Life that publishing the original manuscript in full would turn it into a totally different book – 'a significant contribution towards the history of Africa' – they surrendered their rights for a token $50. William Morrow in New York took it a year later. Sales were never good.[16]

First Catch Your Eland is Laurens's most eccentric, least known, least important book, but it is not uninteresting. It opens with the now familiar evocation of his childhood and the rest of the family myth. Laurens proceeds with further fantasies: he had 'made the first systematic exploration of [the Kalahari] for the British Government after the War'; he had 'lived and hunted with [the Bushmen]'; he used to arrive at the Victoria Falls Hotel, 'not having had a bath for perhaps six months', where he would put on a dinner jacket [*sic*!] and order the best bottle of wine from the cellars. Forbidden to use his right arm, he was able 'to revisit the whole of Africa which I had explored over fifty years'; greatly depressed by what he found, he looked for the common element in Africa's warring and conflicting systems – food!

There are, though, two substantial elements in *First Catch Your Eland*. The first is a vivid and fascinating chapter about Ethiopia, describing that remote and ancient land through the eyes of an army officer in 1941. He skilfully incorporates the theme of 'food' into his personal narrative:

He came towards me on his horse, swathed from shoulder to stirrup in a white cloak, yellow with dust. His followers were armed with round metal shields studded with spikes. They waved swords and spears as they jogged behind him. Some had slim young pages to carry their swords; others carried flintlocks or guns and carbines of all sorts . . . This first meal . . . started with *tedj* [the local honey-alcohol], the main course was raw meat. I have never liked any uncooked meat or fish but out of politeness I have often been forced to eat both, as in Japan . . . the raw meat was passed, bleeding and still lukewarm from the living animal, from one guest to another. Each man would take the edge of the meat firmly between his teeth and then, slicing upwards with a sharp knife, would cut off a mouthful for himself – in the process narrowly missing taking the skin off his nose.

The section on West Africa conceals the fact that Laurens scarcely knew that part of the continent. He writes of eating coconuts in Dahomey, 'chicken yassa' in Senegal, 'joloff rice' in Sierra Leone. East Africa is similarly summarised, though Laurens knew Kenya rather better – he uses his fleeting visit in 1926, which in fact lasted only a few days: 'Karen Blixen and I often talked . . .' he adds, though he met the author of *Out of Africa* only once, in Scandinavia. Throughout *First Catch Your Eland* Laurens is intent on enchanting his innocent reader with the romance of his exotic adventures – for example, at Lake Rudolph 'some years ago', he met up with some nomads: 'I ate with them a soup of beans and lentils that may have been the very mess for which Esau, the hunter, sold his heritage to Jacob, the peasant. I drank camel's milk with them and ate the hump of a camel superbly roasted on a wooden fire.' The story reads very well.

He then moves to Portuguese Africa. Laurens had a soft spot for the undeveloped colonies of Angola and Mozambique and could sound reactionary when he touched on the nationalist revolutions which expelled the Portugese in the 1970s. These political changes, he promised his 1970s readers, were the result not of a true indigenous movement so much as the 'confused, muddled and unworthy scramble out of Africa by the British, French and Belgians'. Many observers of African affairs would not have agreed with him: Laurens's instincts were increasingly conservative, for all his public opposition to apartheid in his own homeland. He often exaggerated and distorted the real horrors of the Angolan civil war: he wrote, and spoke, of a massacre of 30,000 people by the black nationalist forces, and claimed that 4,000 Europeans were killed. Although 30,000 people may have lost their lives in total, the responsibility for the casualties should be shared between the insurgents and the Portuguese military and European deaths probably totalled fewer than four hundred.[17]

The second substantial section of *First Catch Your Eland* concerns South Africa, which occupies nearly half the book and is a paean of praise for his native land. We return again to the family home in the 'remote interior' and to reminiscences of childhood holidays in the Cape which were probably imaginary. He mentions that it was his brother Andries who introduced 'snoek', the notorious dried fish, to wartime Britain. He writes of bobotie, sosaties, bredie, pickled fish, koeksisters, tameletjies, king-klip, abalone, penguin eggs, moskonfyt, mealies, biltong, boere-biskuit, quince, mulberry, boerewors, melk-tert and a host of other examples of South Africa's remarkable and varied cuisines. In these pages the book comes to life. Laurens is writing, passionately, of the world which was his home. His exaggerations, his stories, his name-dropping, all fall away. It does not matter that he is romancing. He finishes with a memory of a Monday evening feast of marrow bones in his childhood home:

> The moment the soup was poured out and standing safely in the warm, the kitchen would break out into intense activity, for each marrow bone would be extracted and cracked so that the marrow would fall out, yellow, glistening and steaming into the buttered dish placed on the table to receive it. At the same time the cook would take out the fresh baked loaves of wholemeal bread. She would cut the crusts from either end of the warm loaves so that there were crusts enough for each plate of soup at the table. The crusts were quickly buttered, and the scent of bread provoked by the melting fresh butter as well as the smell of the marrow were among the most exciting I have encountered in any kitchen . . . As one drank one's soup one ate the warm fresh crust thick with marrow. I cannot recollect ever having experienced a more harmonious or perfect way of eating anywhere else in the world.

This is Laurens writing at his best. His prose is simple and direct and vivid. Inevitably, he exaggerates – the Philippolis gardens were 'immense' – and is inaccurate ('banhoek' is not the valley of exile, but 'banghoek', the valley of fear). The history is sometimes slapdash. But we can believe in the reality of the marrow, the warm crusts and the soup, in the years before the First World War in the Orange Free State.

It is perhaps surprising that a successful and high-minded writer should turn his hand to a sort of cookery book. Laurens was not himself a cook of any sophistication. He was always interested in food and cooking, but at his London dinner parties he employed a regular cook. Ingaret never went near the kitchen, having been brought up to assume that servants did these things. In South Africa, where the book's detail of the cookery is most convincing, Laurens called on the help of his sisters, and his diaries of the time are interleaved with their stained and scribbled Afrikaner recipes.[18] He never returned to the subject. *First*

Catch Your Eland, long-forgotten, occasionally glimpsed in second-hand bookshops, is best remembered as an example of his professional skill in locating and satisfying a literary market. It is also rather fun to read, even today.*

The critical response was, understandably, more muted than for Laurens's previous books. The novelist Angus Wilson in *The Observer* was kind, while astutely pointing out that Laurens's paternalistic love of African society blinded him to its enormities in a 'now lost (perhaps always mythical) Africa'. *The Guardian*, surprisingly, decided that it was a delightful and fascinating book although 'politically inadequate'. *Encounter* found it sentimental and picturesque. The Sunday *New York Times* Book Review was provoked to comment that Laurens's attack on Nehru for his takeover of Goa was hard to stomach 'from a white South African clubman'.

Some years later, Laurens ventured out on to a limb when he justified the killing of Africa's animals for the pot: 'This is the great difference between the human being who gets his food from an abattoir and the person who goes out and hunts it and tracks it down. In tracking it down and "living" with the animal, there is a relationship involved, and a value is at stake. The thing is never impersonal.'[20] This was an area where Laurens would have to clarify his thinking, because in his old age he would become a figurehead and an inspiration for the worldwide environmental and wilderness movements.

---

*In the POW camp, the prisoners used to fantasise about food. They would reminisce about it, draw pictures of it, and read recipes to each other. Sex, in comparison, was forgotten.[19]

26

Autobiography as Fiction

IN THE 1960s, Laurens returned to his memories of the Japanese war of twenty years before, and published two of his better books – *The Seed and the Sower* (1963) and *The Night of the New Moon* (1970), his memoir of the closing days of the war. He had written the first part of *The Seed and the Sower*, a long short story called 'A Bar of Shadow', in Zurich in 1949. It was taken by *The Cornhill Magazine*. After the success of *Venture to the Interior* and *Flamingo Feather*, the Hogarth Press re-issued it as a slim volume in 1954. The book was taken up by the French and, significantly, by the Japanese newspaper *Asahi Weekly* and then by *Chikuma Shobe* which printed 10,000 copies. In late 1957 Laurens came upon the idea of a three-part autobiographical-fiction, initially titled 'The Flower and the Seed'. This was eventually given the new title, *The Seed and the Sower*, when Laurens added two more related sections. Leonard Woolf himself wrote to congratulate Laurens but to warn him against the occasional purple passage which was out of harmony with the rest. Laurens and Ingaret made the necessary changes. At this period Laurens was not taking any advance from Hogarth but he was given the high royalty of 15 or 20 per cent. Offers for foreign rights were flowing in.[1]

The three linked stories, 'A Bar of Shadow', 'The Seed and the Sower' and 'The Sword and the Doll', are narrated over the twenty-four hours of a Christmas Eve and Christmas Day. A part of the fascination of these three haunting stories, all located in Java during the war, is that they merge the autobiographical memories of Laurens, presented in several books as fact, with fiction. How and where do we distinguish between the two in a volume which is here presented as fiction?

'A Bar of Shadow', the shortest at about 12,000 words, brings together at the end of 1949 the narrator (Laurens himself?) and 'John Lawrence' (who, in the unpublished 'The Desired Earth', was Laurens's *alter ego*). They reminisce about a sadistic Japanese sergeant called Hara, who had terrorised the camp 'in a peculiarly racial and demoniac way'. Hara is vividly described in terms which verge on the racist: he is a near-dwarf, his arms hang to his knees, his forehead is low and simian, he behaves with terrible brutality to his European prisoners, and he goes out of control at the time of the full moon: 'If ever there was a moon-swung, moon-haunted, moon-drawn soul, it was he.'

'John Lawrence' on Christmas Eve tells the tale of how seven years before he had been saved because the drunk and surely crazy Hara somehow realised that it was Christmas, and chose to grant him mercy with the words, 'Rorensu: Merry Kurisumasu!' – by which he meant 'Merry Christmas, Mr Lawrence'. After the war, Hara was tried and sentenced to death. John Lawrence visits him in prison and discovers that he feels pity, and forgiveness, for a man who has behaved honourably according to his code and who accepts that, with Japan's defeat, he would have to die. John Lawrence tries to console Hara with the thought that 'there is a way of winning by losing, a way of victory in defeat.' 'That, Rorensu-san,' replies Hara, 'is a very Japanese thought' (directly recalling Laurens's own memory of his conversation with a Japanese officer in August 1945). John Lawrence wishes, but fails, to embrace and forgive him. At the last moment he tries to return to the jail, but he is too late, Hara has been hanged.[2]

The 'Hara' figure reappears in the second novella, much longer at 50,000 words, titled 'The Seed and the Sower'. The original title on Laurens's manuscript, 'Judas Iscariot', is highly significant because it underlines the theme of betrayal, which seems often to be on Laurens's mind. The narrator and 'John Lawrence', spending the same Christmas together, reminisce about their South African colleague Jacques Cilliers. The narrator happens to have Cilliers's own narrative of his life story, written in a POW camp, buried, and recovered years after the war (as happened with Laurens's prison diary). Cilliers then tells how, brought up on a South African farm, he had 'betrayed' his young brother. Cilliers was handsome, successful, popular, athletic, destined to be a high-flying lawyer. His brother was the opposite in every way, gifted only as a farmer, a water diviner, with a beautiful voice; and he was a hunchback. Cilliers's guilt is that, as the affectionate elder son, he failed to protect his brother in a sequence of critical situations – at a school initiation, at a village encounter, in shooting a stunted and symbolic springbok. Cilliers finds that his successful adult life has become stale and empty. He goes off to the war, where he is a good and ruthless soldier. In Palestine he encounters a German monk, and begins to learn wisdom. In a malarial dream he sees Christ, and is inspired to fly back to South Africa to be reconciled with his betrayed brother, who is himself thereby enabled to resume his singing. Cilliers returns to war and is captured by the Japanese in circumstances almost identical with Laurens's own capture early in 1942. 'John Lawrence' as the narrator then resumes the tale.

Cilliers is under threat of of execution. He is protected, if only temporarily, by the Camp Commander, Yonoi, 'the most handsome Japanese we had ever seen', who seems fascinated by the good-looking if battered and malnourished Cilliers. Cilliers thereafter saves his colleagues from violence by publicly embracing Yonoi, to great scandal and humiliation. He is condemned to a lingering death, and in his last hours the disgraced Yonoi cuts a hair off his blond head which he will eventually place at the shrine of his ancestors.[3]

Many years later, this story was turned into the successful film, *Merry Christmas Mr Lawrence*, by the distinguished Japanese director, Nagisa Oshima, starring David Bowie and Tom Conti. To Laurens's distress, Oshima chose to emphasise a homosexual attraction between Yonoi and Cilliers. Yonoi was the second portrait in this book of the Japanese as sadists. It is hardly surprising that Captain Katsue Mori was initially infuriated by a book which teeters on the brink of generalising about a cruel and primitive national character, fervently though Laurens denied any such intention.

In the third section of 25,000 words, 'The Sword and the Doll', with Cilliers heroically dead, 'John Lawrence' tells his own tale of his experiences in Java as the Japanese invaded the island in early 1942. He describes a sequence of events very like Laurens's descriptions of his own experiences. As the Allies fall back before the unstoppable Japanese onslaught, 'John Lawrence' meets a young Dutch woman and spends a night with her. She vanishes and he does not even know her name, although he realises she might be bearing his child. After the war, he searches for her and fails to find her.

To those who knew of Laurens's own biography, this blurring of fact and fiction was likely to be uncomfortable; to those ignorant of Laurens's life, the fictional work was powerful stuff. His readers did not know of the unsettling dual personality of Laurens van der Post and 'John Lawrence'. The theme of a division between Laurens and 'John Lawrence' deserves the skills of a psychoanalyst. Here, in *The Seed*, are the two halves of the man, shown to be initially unable even to sustain a conversation with each other, who at the end, on Christmas Night, are embraced by the wife in 'the strange harmony at the heart of the storm'.[4]

The autobiographical references illustrate Laurens's lifelong preference for merging fiction with fact. The three novellas are ostensibly fiction but some obvious points may be noticed. The character of Hara was loosely based on a warder called Gunzo Mori. 'John Lawrence's' memory of his condemned cell in which he befriended two little lizards, and the imminence of execution, closely echo Laurens's description of his own situation in 1942. The suffering of the Allied prisoners taken by Hara to one of the outer islands, where only a few survived, refers to a murderous episode in Haruko, and Laurens's fictional and vengeful officer, Hicksley-Ellis, is surely based on one of his own colleagues.[5] The Japanese scorn that Allied soldiers had allowed themselves the shame of being captured certainly echoes Laurens's experience.

'A Bar of Shadow', written a dozen years before the other two, is strikingly brutal in its denunciation of the Japanese character: 'Collectively they were a sort of super-society of bees with the Emperor as a male queen-bee at the centre'. They were 'so committed, blindly and mindlessly entangled in their real and imagined past'; they 'could not respond to the desperate twentieth-century call for greater and more precise individual differentiation'; 'they were subject to cosmic rhythm and movement and ruled by cosmic forces beyond their control'; 'it was only at night that people so submerged in the raw elements of nature could discover sufficiently the night within themselves'. Hara is precisely described as 'the living myth, the expression in human form, the personification of the intense, inner vision which, far down in their unconscious, keeps the Japanese people together and shapes and compels their thinking and behaviour'.

The autobiographical sources of 'The Seed and the Sower' are also evident, and tantalising. Cilliers grows up in a village which sounds similar to Philippolis. He is very good-looking, as was Laurens. His relationship with his brother is problematic – as was Laurens's with some of his own brothers, while his *eldest* brother, Andries, had a hunchback. There was a traditional initiation ceremony in Laurens's own school, Grey College. The narrator's growing sense of unease and alienation, his 'distaste of life', would certainly chime with Laurens's own experience of the 1930s. The narrator follows in Laurens's own tracks to Palestine, to a monastery, to chronic malaria. And the Laurens figure would have been delighted to be granted forgiveness by the hunchback brother for betraying him and hailed for his bravery and nobility. Similarly, Cilliers's prison experiences repeat and also surpass Laurens's own: the buying of food from Chinese merchants, the 'total failure' of his mission on the jungle mountain, the retreat to Djaja-Sempoer, the surrender to save the village, the request to be shot rather than hanged, the thunderstorm on what he thinks to be his last night, the kindly guard helping him to wash, even the springbok cap-badge which the Australians give him to wear. This is the officer who will stand up to the Japanese Commander and save the lives of his colleagues and die bravely: it is the author's fantasy of himself as he would like to be seen, an elevation of Laurens's own less fatal experience in which he claimed he had offered himself for a second beating in order to defuse a dangerous situation.[6]

It is a novella which would easily lend itself to a longer analysis. In the two brothers we see the dual personality, Laurens Jan/John Lawrence, which hovers behind so much of Laurens's writing. One brother is crippled, stunted, a farmer, a water diviner, with a beautiful voice (the storyteller?). The other brother is the successful, handsome warrior and man of the world – and the 'Judas Iscariot', who is eventually forgiven so that the two aspects are in the end brought together and reconciled. We may go on to wonder whether in real life the 'hunchback brother' corrupted his gift of storytelling so as to keep the handsome, worldly brother in power.

This short novel sits easily with its predecessor, sharing some of the characters and the prison. The difference, since it was written twelve years after the first episode, by which time Laurens had become a successful author, is that the prose has become inflated: for example, 'Suffering is only a stroke of Time's implacable Excalibur dividing meaning from meaninglessness': 'his deep single-furrow plough turning over waves of Africa's scarlet earth like the prow of a Homeric black-ship. The swell of a wine-red morning at sea . . .': 'wind and spirit, earth and being, rain and doing, lightening and awareness imperative, thunder and the word, seed and sower, all are one . . .' Laurens's problem here emerged clearly: he had become too famous and successful an author for his editors to dare to strike out this sort of thing. Ingaret did her best, but she was too close to the writer.

'The Sword and the Doll' similarly tells the story of the Japanese invasion of 'Insulinda', the name which Laurens gives to Java, during which the narrator – again 'John Lawrence' – undergoes many experiences identical with those which Laurens suffered. The dialogue between the three adults has become extremely mannered and unbelievable. The profundities have now been brought to the forefront ('it was for me a sign of how greatly women long, in their deepest being, to help men to bring up into light of day what is uncertain, fearful and secret within them'). 'John Lawrence' is identified as the archetypal Soldier. The narrative eventually moves to John Lawrence's dispatch to Wavell's HQ and then to Laurens's own mountain, Djaja-Sempoer, 'The Ship Turned Upside-down'. Preparing to withdraw into the mountain, under orders to wage guerrilla war, John Lawrence arrives at a health resort, which sounds like Soekaboemi, and encounters various ineffectual and demoralised Dutch, as did Laurens before in real life he met Paul Vogt. An inadequate Australian unit is attempting to delay the Japanese advance (reminiscent of Blackforce) as John Lawrence gathers his men. He also meets a young Dutch woman, whom he describes in lyrical terms. The Japanese are on the way and the Dutch are hastily evacuated, except that the woman stays behind. She takes him to her room.

The unnerving part of this story is that everything appears to be based on the facts of 1942 and Laurens's own experience of them. Is it prurient to wonder whether the Dutch woman is, suddenly, an invention? But why choose 'John Lawrence' as the name of your fictional hero if you are not signalling: this is really Me?

The story ends on a down-beat. He has survived his subsequent imprisonment thanks to 'what that woman had given him out of her own prophetic intuition of life'. After the war he tries to find her and, perhaps, their child. He fails.[7] (Years later, two American producers tried to set up a film of 'The Sword and the Doll'. Their screenplay changed the ending: John Lawrence finds girl and baby, who all along have been in a nearby prison camp. The film was never made.)

With *The Night of the New Moon*, which was published in 1970, he reworked his experiences in Java twenty-five years earlier, as non-fiction. It is a slim, eloquent book, telling his story of the last months of the war and ending with the liberation of the POW camp in August 1945. *The Night of the New Moon* is dedicated to Wing-Commander Nichols, his senior officer in the camp, and Laurens's closest colleague. But once again, though in life he preferred to operate in Nichols's shadow, Laurens is at the heart of the tale.

The framing of *The Night of the New Moon* is an American radio interview in an unspecified year on 6 August. In the studio Laurens meets a Japanese doctor who had lost his family in the Hiroshima bombing. Laurens is inspired to try to explain to the doctor, on air, his own memory of that period, and his conviction that the dropping of the A-bomb saved hundreds of thousands of lives. He adds that 'the Japanese were themselves the puppets of immense impersonal forces to such an extent that they truly did not know what they were doing.' (In time of war it is so easy to make an enemy collective.)

This was Laurens's first detailed and full-length memoir of the POW camps, which even later he filled out in *Yet Being Someone Other*. It is noteworthy that he had not felt able to write a non-fictional description of these events for many years. His narrative is entirely egocentric, in the sense that we are offered only Laurens as observer, as expert, as authority, as hero ('I had also taken upon myself . . .'; 'my Chinese friends . . .'; 'my understanding of the Japanese national character'; 'one of my special duties'; 'my direction of the secret radio'; 'they sent me a message . . .'). One is aware of the contrast with Primo Levi's memoir of a German camp, *If This Is A Man*, in which we see *through* the narrator to the terrible things to which he bears witness.[8]

The detail refers to the last month of the war, when there was a lively danger that the Japanese would go down to defeat by liquidating all their prisoners in Asia, who were therefore concentrated in crammed conditions into a small number of prisons. They were now at their most perilous moment. 'I took Nichols apart and told him for the first time of the course of my years of lonely vigilance.' After days of terror, with machine guns trained down on the prison's crowded courtyard, Laurens says that he was suddenly sent for – it was 21 August 1945 – by the Japanese, who told him they had surrendered. He agreed to stay on in the camp in command of the essential liaison arrangements after his fellow prisoners were sent down to the coast. The moon, now 'full and overflowing', a symbol of renewal, of continuity, of restoration, was rising over the Bandoeng Plain.

The book ends with a brief summary of Laurens's own role in Java over the next two years – he would eventually write about that at length in *The Admiral's Baby*. He explains that he had not got round to this present book for all these years because he had been distracted by more urgent matters. He had refused to co-operate with the War Trials because 'forgiveness, my prison experience had taught me, was not mere religious sentimentality; it was as fundamental a law of the human spirit as the law of gravity . . . If one broke this law of forgiveness one inflicted a mortal wound on one's spirit.' He was writing this book twenty-five years later because he felt that the horror of Hiroshima and Nagasaki was being seen out of context. Laurens felt that he 'had been placed in a special position by life' to speak up and correct these misconceptions – once again claiming the first word and the last in an episode in which he was one of many.[9]

Laurens wrote twice about whaling in the South Atlantic. The first is a skilful and effective novel, *The Hunter and the Whale*, published in 1967. The second is a section of his autobiographical *Yet Being Someone Other*, which appeared fifteen years later in 1982. The two are very similar: the first person narrative of the novel, in which a teenage boy accompanies over four winters the Norwegian skipper Thor Larsen, is echoed in innumerable details in the ostensibly factual account of how Laurens, the young Durban reporter, went out to sea over three seasons with an identical Norwegian whaling captain, 'Thor Kaspersen'. In *Yet Being Someone Other* Laurens volunteers that *The Hunter and the Whale* was based on his own experiences and memories. But, as we have seen, there is no reason to believe that Laurens ever went out with the whalers, let alone for three or four seasons.

The Hunter and the Whale tells the story of a fourteen-year-old South African boy who, on his school vacation, goes out with a friend on one of the Norwegian-crewed small whaling fleet which operated out of Durban in the winter months. He quickly shows that he has superb eyesight and, more importantly, brings 'luck', so that the eccentric Captain Larsen makes him a favourite and encourages him to return every year, for four seasons, to occupy the crow's-nest as 'spotter' for the whale 'blows'. The school friend, Eric, suffers from seasickness, behaves badly, and quickly disappears from the story. On the boat the boy is befriended by the cook, the helmsman and the Zulu stoker 'Mlangeni, a romanticised figure, whose language the boy, of course, happens to speak. The boy is a young hero, a fine tennis player, a natural diplomat, an accomplished sailor although this is his first sight of the sea, and he possesses insights given to few of his age. He has also shot four elephant, which fascinates Captain Larsen – and so the theme emerges, the parallel between the hunting of the elephant and of the whale, 'the elephant of the sea'.[10]

The action is set in Durban in the mid-1920s, described in rich detail. The whalehunting is evoked brilliantly, and the boy's skill in the crow's-nest is convincing, even if his reflections are surprisingly mature. Yet he begins to wonder about the killing of these wonderful creatures, and to recognise some of his discomfort in the eyes of the crew. As the cook tells him, 'There had never been an animal so gentle, harmless or so deserving of man's respect if not love as the whale.' The answer he offers – an idea to which Laurens would often return – is that there was 'a dimension wherein the taking of life in order to live was understood and forgiven . . . Death in the service of life, dying to live, these were basic facts as good as they were true'. The dilemma is that there is no longer a need for the meat and oil of the whale.

The boy takes the point, and admits that he comes back to this life every year not just for the money but because the hunting grips him as much as the hunting in his own bushveld. He urges Captain Larsen to come to his home and shoot elephant, but the Captain is evasive, until one day an old white hunter arrives, complete with a comely daughter, having retired from his profession but fanatically determined to kill a whale. (This old white hunter, like the romantic Zulu, frequently appears in Laurens's books, and is sometimes traced back to an alleged childhood memory of the man who might have been the model for Buchan's Piet Pienaar or for Haggard's Allan Quatermain.) There is a sub-plot involving a Zulu insurrection in Durban, which echoes Laurens's lifelong apprehension of violent black rebellion against his own people ('I love and trust my aboriginal, my own native Africa, except when its spirit swarms'). Against this is set the boy's steadfast appreciation and defence of the individual Zulu stoker.

The hunter has killed 1,603 elephants, which greatly impresses Captain Larsen. In return for a chance to hunt a whale, he offers the Captain the prize of the greatest old elephant in the continent, now in his last days. He believes he has 'been hunting the wrong quarry. He should have been seeking not the greatest animal on earth but the greatest animal life had ever produced. And that, he knew, was the whale'. Hunter and Captain both derived their passion from their reading of Job: 'He was convinced it was God's will that before his end, he should also have the experience of what it meant to "draw Leviathan out with an hook"'. (There is an obvious comparison with *Moby Dick*, in which Captain Ahab takes himself and his crew to their deaths in his obsessional pursuit of the great white whale.)

The daughter tries to dissuade her father from his hunting bargain with the Captain. Meanwhile, riots break out in the city and thousands are killed. The ship sails out into a cyclone warning. There is a great storm, described with all of Laurens's power. A giant sperm whale rises, wrestling with a huge squid; the hunter fires a deathshot with the harpoon; he and the Captain are swept into the sea and vanish for ever in 'their predestined end'.[11] The boy understands that something of this same predestination had attended his meeting with the daughter, and the two of them exit together, for the interior.

The Hunter and the Whale was widely admired and sold well, though it was less successful outside Britain. In the happiest review the influential Raymond Mortimer in *The Sunday Times* declared that Laurens's noble imagination and view of life were Conradian; he assumed that Laurens must have spent time on a whaler and that the first two-thirds of the book were autobiographical. Mortimer pointed out that Laurens's two Nimrods might have been fascinating to him but he also knew they were monsters. The *Sunday Telegraph* said that Laurens was 'a romantic . . . epical and lyrical, he has a heroic view of life'. *The Observer* declined the parallel with Conrad but praised the evocation of natural life, on sea as well as on dry land. American critics were impressed, although the *New York Times* called it a tale of 'unbelievable solemnity' in which 'literary Calvinism overburdens his narrative' and spoke of 'the long, ponderous trek of his prose'.[12]

It must have been gratifying for Laurens to remember that Leonard Woolf himself had written to him on 1 January 1967 of his 'greatest admiration and enjoyment . . . How do you know so much about whaling and convey it to the reader with such brilliance and vividness? . . . It is, I repeat, superb.'

Giving the usual promotional interviews, Laurens told the BBC French Service that he had experienced whaling as a boy and that around this fragment of personal experience the oyster of a novel had slowly developed: the book was set, he declared, in 1926, 'the year in which the old Africa died . . . this is the year in which the primitive Africa and the pioneering Africa died simultaneously'. He suggested that his Hunter personified this. A real riot had in fact occurred at the time (he added that as Military Governor of Batavia he had had to deal with five riots a day!).[13]

no SM. Whaling in winter

In his autobiographical *Yet Being Someone Other*, Laurens returned to this alleged whaling experience and devoted fifty pages to his adventures with a Captain Thor Kaspersen, on a little whaling boat, the *Larsen II*. The details of these winter expeditions when his Durban Editor and the local whaling families, the Egelands and the Grindrods, allowed him to sail 'as often and for as long as I wanted', are extraordinarily similar to the earlier novel: the Captain drinks Schnapps and reads the Bible; the narrator (Laurens) confesses that he has shot an elephant (there is no evidence that he ever did so); the stoker is a Zulu called 'Mlangeni; the Captain admits to a sense of darkness after he has killed; Laurens discovers that he has a brilliant eye in the crow's-nest; they all eat bread-and-cheese sandwiches for breakfast; there is a big scene when the sardines arrive in shoals; the killer whales attack the blue whale; they sail for the edge of a cyclone; a comical duo at the Signal Station, 'Mr White and Mr Clark', crop up in both books; and so on. All of this is described as taking place over three seasons. There is no sign of the Hunter who took the Captain to a shared doom, but there is much about Captain Kaspersen's obsession with elephants, his dream of a singing whale and its meeting with an elephant. Laurens's growing unease about the killing of the whales is also there: 'What could this possibly have to do with the neces-

sities which were essential for the redemption of the act of killing?'
Laurens says he lost touch with Kaspersen, and after about six years
heard that he had died in the Antarctic. There may be an echo here in a
Cape Times news story on 28 November which reported that a whaling
Captain called Captain Evenson had been killed while shooting a
whale.[14]

Laurens, as we know, almost certainly never went whaling. To write a
vivid novel about whales and to use the first-person narrative convincingly, solely on the basis of other people's work, is a considerable
achievement. But *Yet Being Someone Other* purports to be the true story of
various chapters of Laurens's life. The book's recycling of much of the
detail in *The Hunter and the Whale* seems to confirm, to the innocent
reader, the autobiographical truth of the former, as a source for the
latter. It is much more likely that Laurens *reversed* this process: he
invented in the 1960s a fiction about whaling in the 1920s, and then,
fifteen years later, turned that fiction into autobiography.

27

Friendship

LAURENS, IN LATE middle age, was at the height of his fame. His books sold steadily in a number of languages, and particularly well in Britain, the Commonwealth and America. He was frequently interviewed or 'profiled'; he never turned down a journalist, and he would carefully prepare himself for their photographers. He broadcast steadily, and over these years made a number of television films. In 1969 he and Ingaret moved from Cadogan Street to a penthouse apartment on two floors in a Chelsea tower block with fine views looking out over the Thames. They had a seaside flat near the Franco-Italian border. Years later, they also acquired a second flat in the same Chelsea building several floors below, so that with three floors at his disposal Laurens was able to offer accommodation to visiting friends as well as to his resident housekeeper. They had also bought a little house in Clapham for the use of the housekeeper: Ingaret had a good eye for property; she bought it for £6,000 and sold it nine years later for £24,000 (the equivalent of £250,000 in 2000).[1]

Laurens continued to spend many weeks each year out of Britain, mostly in Africa or America; Ingaret rarely accompanied him, except on their regular and extended winter visits to ski in Switzerland or Austria. When he was away, she would see her patients and friends, swim, write, play bridge, and wait for Laurens's evening phone calls. She would also edit Laurens's manuscripts, which she did with a real skill – her editing talents were genuinely respected by the Hogarth Press and then by Chatto & Windus. Her importance in Laurens's career is clear if one compares the quality of his writing before and after her later illness. Laurens's manuscripts reveal how rigorously she trimmed his slapdash prose, corrected his grammar and spelling, and sometimes rephrased his over-ornate paragraphs.

There is something tragic in this. Ingaret had been the published writer and dramatist in the 1930s, and later diverted herself from her own writing (although she continued to work at her own unpublished plays and novels) to help his; she had been the introduction to Jung, and Laurens then took over as Jung's friend and biographer; she had provided the financial backing after the war which permitted Laurens to establish his own career; she had divorced her first husband to marry him and he later took up a public life with another woman. This may help to explain why he was so loyal to her when in old age she was overtaken by senile dementia.[2]

Ingaret's mother, Evelyn d'Oyly, 'Chubbs', died in 1973 after a wearying illness. Laurens was always fond of her, and Ingaret was intensely close to her. Laurens's two children, as we have seen, had made careers for themselves. There would be a total of six grandchildren, but Laurens was not an active grandfather. He became closer to some of them, particularly Lucia's daughter Emma, in his later years. John died and Laurens's relations with his sisters were irregular. The new element is that he became increasingly close to one of his nephews, Tom Bedford, the son of Ella, his widowed sister.

'Tommy' Bedford was a Rhodes Scholar, an architect and a rugby player. More than that, he had captained the Springboks national rugby team (his refusal to join the 'Broederbond' Afrikaner secret society is widely assumed to have denied him the regular role) and was a famous figure in South Africa. He was taken up by Laurens, who was very fond of him. To Tom, Laurens certainly became a surrogate father. Tom's South African marriage ended and he married one of Laurens's London secretaries, Jane Brewster, and moved to London, which brought him even closer to Laurens. Tommy Bedford and Jane were at Laurens's right hand throughout the last fifteen years of his life, and they filled not just an emotional role but a practical gap at a time when Laurens badly needed practical assistance. The three of them co-operated in many areas: the administration of the South African farm, preparations for various films, liaison with South African politicians and businessmen, development of the environmental and wilderness campaigns and Laurens's involvement in the politics of Natal.[3]

There were old and intimate friends, whose relationship had matured over the years, because Laurens and Ingaret were a sociable couple when they were in London. Laurens's publishers all became close friends – Norah Smallwood, Ian Parsons, John Charlton and many others, and also their American opposite numbers, as did his television collaborators. But this is to diminish the range of Laurens's social life: throughout his life Laurens was immensely and genuinely generous with his time. Even when he felt near-overwhelmed with writing commitments, he would always find time to meet a stranger, to make an introduction, to be interviewed by a visiting journalist, to speak to a society, however small, to write a foreword to someone's book.[4] This was a rare generosity, which must often have been exhausting, and it should not be forgotten when one reads of the vanity and dogmatism which undoubtedly grew upon him with age. His kindness, and his availability, were particularly valued by people who were lost or confused; he seemed able to provide them with a philosophy, to help them discover how they might lead their lives. They also loved him because they were susceptible to his most powerful weapon, which he deployed throughout his life: Laurens van der Post possessed an almost literally mesmerising charm. Very few people were immune to it. Those piercing blue eyes would transfix you, there could be no doubting his deepest interest in you, the tenor voice (its accent English-Establishment with an underlay of South African) would create immaculate cadences which made sense of your incoherence, and you were suddenly his to command. When you heard him weave his stories, you were easily enchanted. People so easily fell in love with Laurens, and he was not above using that.

Laurens himself evidently loved William Plomer, and they corresponded and met often during the 1960s. Ingaret joined them only occasionally. Their letters are a valuable source for Laurens's life and emotions (for instance, after a South African visit in mid-1961, 'I can hardly bear to speak about it . . . I doubt whether I'll ever go back and if I do I'll be in trouble, useless trouble').[5] To no-one else could he write so candidly.

In July 1962 another friend, the Conservative MP, Sir Ian Horobin, who had been in the POW camps with Laurens, was in trouble. Horobin had resumed a successful political career after the war, as well as continuing as warden of a boys' mission in the East End of London, which he had been since 1923. He was a devout Christian and a poet but also a homosexual in an age when homosexual activity was not tolerated. Charged with committing offences with boys and young men, he pleaded guilty, and told the judge of 'us poor devils who are born like this . . . It is natural for some people to love boys in this way'. Laurens was one of very few who bravely volunteered to give character evidence in court on Horobin's behalf. He explained that Horobin in Java had resisted torture and saved his life. (He would have privately remembered his exasperation in Java in 1946 when Horobin had the War Office send signals asking him to dig up the prison compound to try to find his buried poems.)

Horobin was jailed for four years, and disgraced; he had to withdraw his recent acceptance of a peerage. After serving his sentence he retreated to Tangier, from where he used to send Laurens his poems until his death in 1976. Laurens would later say that Horobin had been truly in love with the seventeen-year-old boy who had also been charged. (Horobin said in court that he had been 'virtually married' to him since he was thirteen.)[6] The homosexual Plomer responded sympathetically: 'It seems sadly primitive,' he wrote to Laurens, 'to have it unrecognised that our virtues are inseparable from what appear to be, in the eyes of the law, our vices ... Oh, what a sad world.' Laurens visited Horobin in prison, counselled him against suicide, and recruited Plomer's help in seeking a publisher for his rather undistinguished poems.[7] The episode was an example of one of Laurens's finer qualities – his loyalty to his friends.

Laurens felt able to pour out his own problems too: in November 1962 his brother-in-law's thrombosis, his son-in-law's serious illness with 'poor Lucia, who is about to have a child of course, almost demented ...' Plomer took a lively interest in all of Laurens's life, and in particular he warmly praised his successive books. He apparently helped John van der Post with a novel manuscript, while taking care not to raise hopes of its publication. He was also generously happy to pass on compliments to Laurens: for instance, a fulsome letter from the writer John Cowper Powys, which described Laurens as 'a great man, I can tell by looking straight into his eyes: for, like my old acquaintance Jehovah, I judge by the heart ... this chap is 2,000,000,000 times superior to that image of a conceited warrior Lawrence of Arabia'. Powys had apparently been delighted to hear that Laurens's brother Andries had coached King George VI in Afrikaans! Whenever Laurens was in South Africa he would send grapes and peaches to Plomer and his partner Charles, and they would respond in season with their own quince jelly.[8]

This was the period when Laurens was writing the introduction for a re-issue of Plomer's *Turbott Wolfe*. He took no less than twelve months to deliver a much longer piece than the publisher required, apologising to Plomer for this delay: 'I have never felt closer to Job than I have these last five months'. Plomer gallantly replied that he was fortunate not to have 'a conventional Introduction by someone else'; he himself was working on a libretto with Benjamin Britten for their *Curlew River* opera. When it was delivered at last, Leonard Woolf wrote privately to Plomer that it was very good but 'of inordinate length. It made me sardonically suggest that possibly the book ought to be called Preface by Laurens van der Post to a novel by William Plomer'.* Laurens refused to take a fee:

---

*In the 1965 re-issue of *Turbott Wolfe*, Laurens's introduction takes up forty-six pages out of a total two hundred.

as he put it rather sweetly to Plomer, 'I felt I had been paid in advance forty years ago'. The two of them sent inscribed copies to Captain Mori and to Enslin du Plessis.[9]

Lengthy as it is, Laurens's introduction is also very generous. He had presumably been asked to write it not only as an old friend and colleague of Plomer, who had first been published by the Hogarth Press, but because his name, as a best-selling author, would help promote a forty-year-old novel by a writer known and respected by a much smaller literary world. To compare the first impact of *Turbott Wolfe* in Natal with the shock and controversy of *Lady Chatterley's Lover* or *Lolita*, as he does, seems excessive, but he pins down the reason for its hysterical reception – the fact that young Plomer could not be dismissed in South Africa as a foreigner, or an ignoramus, or a propagandist, or an ideologue, or even a moralist. Laurens reaches back to a childhood memory of baboons which reacted to the sight of themselves in a mirror by smashing the mirror in fury. It was, he says, how white South Africa responded to *Turbott Wolfe*. 'For me in South Africa the day of reckoning started with *Turbott Wolfe*. It ended the age of European innocence in Africa.'[10] Laurens was paying his debt to Plomer, though this is not to suggest that he did not mean what he wrote. The missing element is that he did not admit his obvious debt to *Turbott Wolfe* for his own first novel, *In A Province*.

Laurens's intimacy with Plomer cannot be mistaken. He commissioned from the sculptor Frances Baruch a head of Plomer which he presented to the Johannesburg City Art Gallery. The two men exchanged bitchy remarks about their mutual friends notwithstanding their public loyalty to them. Jack Cope and Uys Krige were chided for their treatment of Ingrid Jonker and, a few years later, Laurens was describing them retrospectively as 'egotistical killers'. He was exasperated with both Stephen Spender and Cecil Day Lewis, reporting them as tired and old, and Plomer agreed, adding that he hoped that Day Lewis would be made Poet Laureate 'as a tonic' (he was, in 1968).

The two admitted to each other that they were getting on (Plomer was three years older than Laurens). They continued to share various political attitudes, though these had moved to the Right. Laurens was engaged in a public row in 1968 because he opposed the cultural boycott of South Africa (Plomer agreed with him), while at the same time being vilified in the Afrikaans press for funding subversion (he sued the *Dagbreek* newspaper for libel and won): 'You must be setting out central truths,' Plomer commented, and added a few weeks later, 'I feel more and more strongly, as you do, that to advocate cultural sanctions is the most retrograde and blind thing to do.' The mutual affection flourished to the end. 'Despite time and distance and wars and heaven knows how many other power-ful alliances of enemies of continuity [we] have never broken our long cord of friendship,' Laurens wrote in 1970. And again, 'It is above all your understanding, so steady and so whole even in my most difficult and provocative period before the War, and the knowledge that William was always there, that has helped me in no mean way, as D. H. Lawrence would have it, "to come through". Thank you, dear William, thank you.'[11]

Plomer had for several years suffered from heart problems. He died, unexpectedly, on 20 September 1973. Laurens's daughter Lucia recalls that it was the only time she ever saw her father weep. He gave an affect-ing address at the memorial service in London's St Martin-in-the-Fields on 7 November: 'He changed the imagination of a whole age in Africa,' Laurens said; he was the first person writing in English in South Africa to express 'anger in terms of love'. It was an elegant *envoi*.[12]

And yet, beneath their lifelong intimacy, was there not a strand of jeal-ousy? One suspects that Laurens envied his friend because he knew in his heart that Plomer was the better writer. The tone of some of Plomer's letters might suggest that he envied Laurens for – what? – his fame? The variety of his life? The range of his successes? His vigorous heterosexuality? The evidence for Laurens's underlying feeling does not fully emerge until long after Plomer's death.

As the years went by, and his memories of Plomer faded, Laurens in old age decided that he had not been assured his proper place in the story of *Voorslag*, whose brief appearance in 1926 had by now been elevated to a central role in the history of South African literature. In *Yet Being Someone Other*, he had published his own version of the 1926 journey to Japan, a version which did not entirely chime with Plomer's memoir of the same trip. A careful reading of *Yet Being Someone Other*, published in 1982, nine years after Plomer's death, shows that Laurens contradicted some of the detail in Plomer's autobiography, in a manner which subtly diminishes him. Laurens, we are reminded, had the idea that his friend accompany him to Japan and made it possible by arranging accreditation, but Plomer took the most luxurious cabin, next to the Captain, provok-ing Laurens's admitted jealousy when he secured Mori's prime attention as they worked on a Japanese translation of his novel. Plomer was 'basi-cally unmusical' until Laurens introduced him to Benjamin Britten many years later. He was a bad sailor, frequently incapacitated by seasickness; he slept late; he nearly fainted in the heat of a Kenya cemetery; the sea voyage had no special meaning for him as it did for Laurens; he could only make jokes about the Conradian dimension of the journey through the East Indies. When they arrived in Japan, Plomer was unable to

respond to the geishas at their special party, was terrified at the prospect
of a visit to a brothel, was in pain after climbing a hill, and almost fainted
again when Laurens's cigarette was slashed from his mouth by a sword-
wielding guard at a temple. When he left Plomer behind, Laurens writes
with a hint of condescension that, worried about his friend's future, he
gave him all his warm clothes and the rest of his money. He remembers
a premonition 'that I fought and would not accept for years, namely that
it was a double farewell: we were not only saying goodbye to each other,
but also to a William whom neither of us would ever see again, and
whom the England to which he was committing himself with such conscious determination would never know'.[13]

Again, in the last year of his life he decided to set the record straight,
as he told his secretaries, and dictated a 9,000-word memorandum on
'Campbell, Plomer, Paton and Myself'; it was never published. His
subject was 'a certain process of falsification of events', and the agent of
this falsification was William Plomer. He describes how Plomer, meeting
him on his own brief visit to London in September 1945, had given him
a copy of his autobiography, *Double Lives*. Laurens only read it two years
later, to discover that the section about himself and the circumstances
of the Japanese trip was 'totally untrue', and Plomer must have known
it. Perhaps, it occurred to Laurens, Plomer had thought he had been
killed in the war and could not contradict it; he then remembered that
prewar friends had warned him that William was profoundly jealous of
him. But at the time that had seemed preposterous. Laurens had seen no
point in talking this through with his friend, though his omission may
cast a degree of doubt on the professed affection of the following
twenty-five years. But he did not forget it: 'The shock is still there as
something I have never properly reckoned with, and perhaps should do
so now before it's too late . . .'

So why did Laurens accuse Plomer of 'a plausible lie'? It can only be
because, in *Double Lives*, Plomer described in his usual elegant style the
founding of *Voorslag* with Campbell and then added briefly, 'Among the
contributions to the second number of *Voorslag* was an essay in
Afrikaans by a Dutch friend I had made in Durban, Laurens van der
Post.' Campbell suggested that Plomer meet him, and he found 'a young
man of much charm and intelligence'. The only reason the older Laurens
could have objected to this was that, correctly, it did not set him at the
heart of the magazine.[14] The English-speaking Plomer seems never to
have suspected that Laurens's couple of Afrikaans contributions to
Voorslag were probably not his own.

*

In 1966, Laurens paid one of his frequent visits to the Jungians in Zurich, and met a thirty-year-old 'auditor' attending the lectures at the Institute, Frances Baruch. A gifted sculptor, born in Spain, living in London and of mainly German family background, she was to be his intimate companion until his death thirty years later. It is clear that Ingaret was never told, though some of her friends believed – correctly, we now know – that her intuition eventually led her to something of the truth. Frances, who could not train officially as an analyst because she did not have a degree, travelled frequently with Laurens, to India, South Africa, America and Europe, while Ingaret was left behind. Laurens was proud of her and, as the years went by, introduced her to his own friends. Out of loyalty to him, they were discreet, though everyone (except Ingaret) understood the situation. Most days, up to his last years, Laurens would visit Frances at her house in London's St John's Wood. Ingaret, as she subsided into dementia in the 1980s, used to make obscure gestures of hostility towards the sculpted head of her husband which had been made by this mysterious artist whom she never met.

Laurens's deception of Ingaret over the years had a routine. He frequently made the point to her that she ought not to accompany him on his travels because she disliked a hot climate. On 13 October 1966, for example, he wrote to her from Delhi: 'My Dearest Beloved Little Fellow ... I would not be alive physically or mentally if it were not for you ... I think it is a merciful disposition of providence you are not here: the temperature has not fallen below 92.' Laurens was in the company of Frances; it was their first long journey together. Or again, years later, on 31 August 1977 from Cape Town: 'I miss you terribly and I love you more than I can say', and a few days before, from the voyage out on the *Windsor Castle*, the last Union Castle sailing: 'The ship is full but I've seen no-one I like': he was travelling with Frances. Some of Laurens's friends are today willing to admit that, for all his apparently loving care of Ingaret when he was at home, he hurt her cruelly by his compulsive, unceasing absences abroad.[15]

Long before illness overtook her, and even before the arrival of Frances Baruch, Ingaret must surely have guessed that Laurens was, to use the cliché, a lady's man. His unbridled sexuality in the 1930s, temporarily frustrated in the prison camp, broke free again in the 1940s. After his Java secretary Sybil, and after his 'engagement' on the ship to Fleur Kohler-Baker, and even after his return to Ingaret in 1947, there were stories of his conquests: for example Group-Captain Nichols's daughter Vicky remembers how he was her godfather, how her mother's best friend, an actress, was her godmother, and how Laurens was discovered establishing an 'appropriate' relationship between godfather and god-mother. In South Africa he had a long-running reputation, some of which may have been rumour, but – as seen above in the episode of the fourteen-year-old Bonny – not without fuel to fan the flames.

With the arrival of Frances in his life, Laurens's career might have steadied: he was, after all, sixty years old. But he appears to have continued in some of his old ways. This is not the place to go into the details. Frances did not know, nor, of course, did Ingaret, whose effusive letters followed him around the world and who waited every evening for his phone call, unaware that he made a second phone call to Frances when she was not with him. Laurens, handsome and utterly charming, did not scruple to exploit the women around him. He may not have been the first to do that. However, it is one thing to have a long-term mistress, who may believe that she is the true love of your life, quite another to deceive her, as well as your wife, with other affairs.

Two examples may be enough: it is not necessary to name names. In his sixties, four years after meeting Frances, Laurens developed a long and intimate relationship with a young woman. They were often together in Aldeburgh – she would sometimes arrive at Saxmundham station at weekends just after Ingaret had departed to visit her mother in Camberley. They would also work together in London; the porter at the Chelsea block of flats became indignant when he found them together in a car in the basement – he thought it inappropriate behaviour for a man of Laurens's age and distinction. There were also foreign journeys where, literally, they shared a tent. Ingaret seems to have guessed something, and the young woman moved on, though she remained a devoted admirer.

Some years later, Laurens became fascinated by an even younger woman; he was evidently attracted to innocence and youth. With Ingaret, who was very fond of the girl, he took a great interest in planning her career; they decided that she should go to university and then train in Zurich as a psychotherapist. Without paying too much heed to her own wishes, they sent her back to the University of Cape Town, at their expense, and in her vacations they would fly her back to England or Switzerland, where she would look after Ingaret, whom she loved.

This had become a Svengali relationship. He told her that she was his muse. She afterwards realised that he often said that to women and, as she puts it, that Laurens had set an 'agenda' for her. He used to visit her in Cape Town. One day, in the Mount Nelson Hotel, he was resting on the bed and asked her to lie down beside him to comfort him, as she used to do for Ingaret. Innocently, she did so. Before she realised what had happened, he had seduced her. She was appalled. She could only think of Ingaret. 'I can love Ingaret better thanks to you,' she remembers him saying. She says she felt that she had been raped. He wanted to continue the affair, but she refused. He was seventy-eight.

She tried to maintain a relationship – she admired him greatly, and she and Ingaret loved each other – but had to discover that he had planned to use her, not just sexually but also to subordinate her life to looking after Ingaret. She could agree to neither.[16]

Before the war, contrary to his later memories, Laurens scarcely visited South Africa. Afterwards he went there repeatedly, as though he could not stay away. He took every excuse to film there, to give lectures, to accept honorary degrees (from Rhodes and the Free State, to go with his UK honours from the universities of St Andrew's and Surrey), and he was perfectly prepared to accept journalistic 'freebies' in return for newspaper articles so long as he could be accompanied by Frances and travel first class.[17] He also needed to sort out his family inheritance.

Lammie's death in 1954 had been followed by an imbroglio concerning the inheritance of the Wolwekop farm outside Philippolis. Andries, the immediate legatee, died in 1958 having failed, for no obvious reason, to take technical title. After his adopted daughter Mignonne had been disinherited, there followed a long period of legal confusion as Laurens spent many years trying to break the entail and to sell the place. Meanwhile he used the help of his South African family to try to supervise a farm which was severely run down – first Professor Schmidt, his sister Pauline's husband, then Stuart de Kok, his sister Marie's husband, and finally Ella's son, Tom Bedford. Laurens visited Wolwekop every year or two for sentimental reasons, and he listed it as one of his addresses in *Who's Who*, describing it to London friends as his South African estate, but there is no doubt that he always intended to sell it, once he could break the entail; he realised that he could not possibly run a 3,000-morgen sheep farm in the Orange Free State from a penthouse in Chelsea.[18]

Nor could he want to occupy the dilapidated Wolwekop farmhouse. On the other hand, there was the advantage that ownership of Wolwekop helped him to claim, for tax purposes, that he was 'domiciled' in South Africa, not Britain. Since the 1950s, as he explained to his accountant when in 1975 the Inland Revenue at last queried this: 'The position is that South Africa is my native country and that I possess a large farm and a most attractive home in the Orange Free State of the

Republic of South Africa; a farm which has some 7,000 sheep, and several hundred heads of cattle as well as other mixed farming aspects to it. I have visited the farm at least once a year and sometimes twice a year and regard it as my home to which I fully intend to return when I retire from my occupation as a writer . . . I have in fact only been technically resident in this country because I have written some of my books here.' The Inspector of Taxes accepted this highly fanciful argument, to Laurens's evident benefit. He had for some years been holding most of his money 'off-shore' to the tune of about £500,000.[19]

During the bewilderingly complex legal battle to do with breaking the entail, he frequently promised his surviving sisters that he had inherited the farm on their behalf and that he would share with them the revenue from the rental. In practice he sent them the occasional small cheque, in total about Rand 1,000 a year, at a time when the lease was bringing in Rand 5,000 rising to Rand 20,000, always protesting that his legal and tax bills were crippling. At last he sold Wolwekop in 1981–82, thanks largely to Tom Bedford's exertions, for approximately a gross Rand 550,000 (then worth about £300,000). From this he had to buy out the existing leasee and pay various substantial fees. Tom then persuaded the Reserve Bank, even at a time of strict exchange control, to allow Laurens to move the bulk of the balance to Switzerland. Laurens gave about Rand 20,000 to his sister Ella, about Rand 14,000 to his other sister Marie – they were the only siblings now left – and, in effect, five per cent to Tom in return for his help. To enable Laurens to sell the farm, his two children had to surrender their rights to inheritance, which they both did. John did so on condition that his mother benefit from the sale. He died, and Laurens never gave Marjorie the Cape Town flat he had held out to her.[20]

So in the end it had turned out to be a valuable legacy for Laurens. Today, neighbours reckon that Wolwekop, which has become an annexe to a group of neighbouring farms, would be worth around Rand 2–3 million (say, £250,000). These days, Lammie's farmhouse is even more primitive and run down. The landscape is still as beautiful as Laurens remembered.

PART FIVE

'Good or valuable writing is more than a technical skill; it depends on a certain moral wholeness in the writer.'

V. S. Naipaul, *Beyond Belief*

28

Xhabbo and Nonnie

L AURENS DID NOT return to the Kalahari Desert for twenty-one years after his 1955 expedition, but in 1970 he began to write a double-decker novel totalling nine hundred pages – *A Story Like The Wind*, which with its sequel, *A Far-Off Place*, took up much of his energy for four years. Building on the fame of his two non-fiction books about the Bushmen, they were also great popular, though not critical, successes. They tell of the ordeal of a Huguenot-Afrikaner, a boy in his early teens, François Joubert. His father, a radical Afrikaner educationalist with some of the character of Laurens's own father, dies young, as did CWH. His mother, oddly, is given the name of Lammie, Laurens's mother. The boy's mentor is an old white hunter-turned-conservationist, Mopani Theron. François saves from death a Bushman called Xhabbo, meaning 'dream' (the name of Dr Bleek's principal informant in the 1870s). François's beloved Bushman nanny is called Koba (not Klara or Kora this time).

He meets Luciana, a.k.a. Nonnie, whose name is evocative of Laurens's daughter Lucia and of Bonny, the young girl he seduced in 1952. There are clear echoes of *Flamingo Feather*, with a similar black liberation army intent on destroying the whites, though this time its villainous generals are Chinese, not Russians. The location again adjoins the Hunter's Road, the famous track leading from South Africa into the heart of the continent. Though the novel is set in the 1960s, there is no radio/telephone and no-one has a Land Rover; Mopani rides a Basuto pony; there is no sign of such basics as a generator, the Cape Coloured builders arrive by ox-wagon, and no-one considers taking a plane to travel to the Cape. In the world of *Prester John* this might make sense, yet it is clearly signalled as a contemporary drama and Laurens's conclusions and moral are intended to be contemporary.

The portrait of the Bushman couple is as romanticised. The subsidiary characters are shameless stereotypes. The dialogue is unbelievably arch, there is not a glimmer of understanding of how two fourteen-year-olds might actually talk to each other, and during twelve months in the bush and desert there is never a hint of a sexual current between these two epitomes of innocence, clearly though they are destined for each other.[1]

And yet somehow these two books work. They are not, as Laurens well understood, among the host of realist novels of mid-twentieth-century Africa. They do not attempt to tell of Africa as it was forty years ago, when nationalist guerrillas gathered to challenge white supremacy with Russian or Chinese support, they are a *fable*. Laurens explained this in a letter to an American friend: it is 'a modern parable . . . a world of nature and innocence, a garden at the beginning, violence and evil breaking into the garden and destroying it for ever and the agonising journey then of flesh and blood to deliver itself from evil and then recover and reintegrate the shattered fragments into a new and greater world. I think this story is immortal and is particularly active in one way and another in the mind of contemporary man, especially contemporary young people who long to reshape nature and life in this inborn sense of a "garden in the beginning" . . .'[2]

In *A Story Like The Wind* and *A Far-Off Place* Laurens is writing a tale of a boy and a girl in their passage to maturity. It is a classic quest tale. They suffer tragedy and bereavement. They pass through a sequence of dangerous adventures. They confront death. They are forced to kill. They suffer fear and exhaustion. They almost fail to complete their journey. They understand that they must put the past behind them. They are sustained by their growing love for each other and by their constant memory of their mentors, the wise old men and women who supervised their childhood. In addition, they have the crucially life-saving support of a dog, Hintza, an animal who, as in many myths, guards the threshold to the underworld and leads to transformation. And they are accompanied, supported, saved, by the Bushman couple, representing Primitive Man. Laurens used these novels to illustrate the thesis he had developed in *The Lost World of the Kalahari* and *The Heart of the Hunter*. As he put it, 'It was the terrible invasion of meaninglessness and a feeling of not belonging invading the awareness of man, that was the unique sickness of our day. And this sickness . . . was the result of the so-called civilised man parting company with the natural and instinctive man in himself . . . the journey within could not be resumed soon enough, the journey of what he called the exiled Jacob back to the Esau the hunter, whom he had betrayed and with whom he had to be reconciled before he could come home again to inherit his full self.'

Despite their absurdities, the two books have always been among his most popular. Eventually a commercial film was made called *A Far Off Place*, though the American studio played havoc with the story.

A Story Like The Wind is prefaced with a direct and unattributed extract from Dr Bleek. There follows a brief description of Laurens's own family background, and his explanation that he is writing this story in order to preserve 'something of what was wonderful and honourable about primitive life in Africa'.[3]

We start with no less than twenty-four pages about a dog. There can never have been a dog so clever, so brave, so wise, so strong, so devoted as the ridgeback Hintza, who is acquired, and trained to answer Bushman commands, by the thirteen-year-old François Joubert on a farm carved out of virgin bush on the 'remote frontier' of Southern Africa. François is brought up by loving if slightly distant parents in a multi-racial and multi-lingual paradise. He learns Bushman from his nurse Koba, who has a wrinkled magnolia skin and Mongolian features and, as always, wears a necklace of glass beads. His parents educate him at home in a school in which he is the single pupil – curiously, for a liberal household, they do not seem to have considered including the Matabele children who are François's playmates.

The detail of the description of life at Hunter's Drift is overwhelming and beautifully portrayed provided you are at ease with the high paternalism which characterises the relations between the white masters and their loyal and cheerful black retainers. The community of traditional Matabele, led by 'Bamuthi, is a throwback to the noble savage whom Laurens seems to have been seeking for years, and their eventual extermination in this plot may signal the moment at which Laurens for a while abandoned his faith in the Southern African 'tribal' black man in favour of the apricot Bushman. In old age he would resume an affection for what he saw as the noble Zulu.

The Bushman makes his entry when Hintza wakes François and summons him out into the night-time bush where they discover the injured Xhabbo, caught in a leopard trap. This is an astonishing find because the Bushmen were thought to have retreated long ago into the deep desert; equally astonishingly, the white boy happens to speak a fluent Bushman, a group of the world's most difficult languages. François rescues Xhabbo and installs him in a secret Bushman cave, to which he can bring supplies of medicine and food.

At this point François has begun to realise that his father is ill, as his parents go south for medical advice. François has to confront his loss, with the help of his 'uncle', the old hunter and game warden Mopani Theron, 'Bamuthi the Matabele headman, and the family cook Ousie Johanna. All of this is minutely described in a Fantasy Africa, a Garden of Eden from which readers may guess that François will soon be expelled. The wounded Bushman gives warning that evil is approaching. His intuition has told him, through the 'tapping' inside himself – a phenomenon which Laurens had described in his earlier books – which sent him messages from 'A Far-Off Place'. Xhabbo recovers from his wounds, and leaves, promising to return.[4]

François is diverted by a visit from Mopani, with whom he shoots a rogue elephant in a moment of initiation. He visits a witchdoctor in an innocent effort to save his father. He is then distracted by the arrival of Sir James Archibald Sinclair Monckton, owner of the adjoining property, together with his thirteen-year-old daughter Luciana, whose Portuguese mother was murdered by black nationalists in Angola three years before.

Luciana (of course) has 'one of the loveliest faces that he had ever seen'. He and Hintza dub her 'Nonnie', and she and her father are their guests at Hunter's Drift. Sir James, once a District Officer in this area, presses on to build 'a kind of fortress to defend a vanishing way of life against the impetuous future': a figure of caricature, he is clearly doomed. It dawns on François that his friend Xhabbo, 'a product of pure nature', and Nonnie, from a 'refined and sophisticated European culture', might both become significant in his life. Meanwhile he introduces Nonnie to the life of the bush. François is waiting for Xhabbo to return, and furnishes the cave with food supplies.

François's mother returns, his father now having died, and for fourteen months life carries on, though amid many ominous signs, including modern trucks on the Hunter's Road not to speak of a visit from the World Council of Churches! Sir James and Nonnie return, to general rejoicing, and Sir James takes a shine to Lammie. Then, with the call of the plover, and the bark of a jackal, Xhabbo is back. He has come to warn them that a mercenary army of thousands is fast approaching. François, Nonnie and Hintza race to the safety of the Bushman cave, and listen, helpless, as Hunter's Drift is captured and all its inhabitants massacred. They retreat into the ancient cave, 'the last temple left on earth': the boy, the girl, the Bushman couple and the dog – 'the dog that had been the first animal to become the friend of man; a man and a woman of the people who had been the first representative of man in Africa, and a boy and a girl who were of the people most recently come to the Dark Continent . . .'[5] The stars are tapping, telling Xhabbo of the way they must go.

A Far-Off Place takes up Laurens's story at this point. François's and

Nonnie's retreat to the cave – the temple, the womb – has an obvious symbolic meaning. They try to cope with the deaths of their parents and friends. François begins to realise how fortunate he is that, in this desperate situation, he has the support, the skills and the intuition of Xhabbo; Nonnie begins to learn from his woman Nuin-Tara her responsibility as a woman who will share her life with a man. They have confirmed the slaughter at Hunter's Drift, are being hotly pursued by the liberation army, and eventually make the unbelievable decision, based largely on Xhabbo's 'tapping', that they will not attempt to get through to the railway only nine miles away, or to Bulawayo, only fifty, but will flee westward, across a thousand miles of desert. François thereupon sleeps – literally, innocently – with Nonnie, 'overwhelmed by the many feelings released in him by so simple and natural an event'.

The journey is described with all the skills of a spellbinding storyteller who also knows the Kalahari very well. They are led by Xhabbo, who employs all the Bushman survival skills which Laurens had described in his earlier books. They manage to escape their pursuers – François shoots up an enemy helicopter – and set out on the impossible walk across the desert. François and Nonnie, observed by their sublime Bushman friends, grow ever closer, even as they exchange teenage banter. They succeed in crossing the first desert, then circle the dangerous populated area of the Okavango Swamp, and press on again, always westward. Nonnie and Xhabbo develop the symptoms of sleeping sickness. François, obsessed with the need to get through to the Atlantic coast in order to save their lives, breaks through the dunes at last, 335 days after they had set out. Below him is the Atlantic Ocean – and a fleet of warships. He has arrived at the beginning of a naval exercise of the Western Fleets, which immediately suspend their manoeuvres and take him on board, send doctors by helicopter to treat the sleeping sickness of Nonnie and Xhabbo, and turn François and Nonnie into international celebrities.

The two realise their lives have been saved first by the dog Hintza and second by the Bushman Xhabbo. François observes that it was strange that, in saving Xhabbo at the beginning, he was really saving himself as well as a Nonnie he did not know existed. The young white couple sadly say goodbye to their Bushman friends. Mopani preaches to them at length (and in Laurens's unmistakable voice) of their responsibilities in the region. François, Nonnie and Hintza are flown to Addis Ababa to be saluted by the Emperor Haile Selassie, after Hintza has peed on the Emperor's pet lions. The Emperor delivers an epilogue which echoes the plea of Laurens himself when he emerged from his Japanese prison camp: 'We knew out of our own suffering that life cannot begin for the better except by us all forgiving one another. For if one does not forgive, one does not understand; and if one does not understand, one is afraid; and if one is afraid, one hates; and if one hates, one cannot love. And no new beginning on earth is possible without love.'[6] Laurens would develop that theme in his future books.

Laurens first told Norah Smallwood at Hogarth that he was engaged in his Bushman novels in a letter dated 28 September 1970: he had, he said, an exciting new manuscript for her to read. As usual, another year would pass before he began to deliver, and Norah did not know until then that there would be two books under the overall title of *A Story Like The Wind*, in which Part One would be 'A Far-Off Place' and Part Two would be 'The Way of the Wind'. Laurens was rapidly becoming a more demanding and difficult author in his attention to detail of presentation, jacket illustration, marketing or publicity, though he never showed interest in the on-page editing of his manuscripts. The two linked novels became *A Story Like The Wind* and *A Far-Off Place*, and the title 'The Way of the Wind' was dropped. Norah Smallwood wisely required some substantial changes to the first volume, cutting back the detailed description of François's parents and insisting on an initial emphasis on the dog Hintza.[7]

The publication in Britain of *A Story Like The Wind* in 1972 was marred only by a furious row between Laurens and *The Times Literary Supplement*, which ran a hostile review a few days before publication day. Laurens became irate, and urged Hogarth to complain to the Publishers' Association. To their alarm, he tried to attack the *TLS* Editor for 'abusing editorial traditions', and to protest that his book seemed to have been reviewed by an anonymous anthropologist: 'I, Sir, grew up with Bushman survivors. I have been profoundly concerned with their spirit and culture as well as the desperate problem of their survival for some forty-five years, which your critic dismisses with such reprehensible superficiality and indifference'. He had tried to pass on his experience, 'because there seemed no-one else living at that moment either prepared or in a position to do so'. He was, he announced, currently preparing another expedition in the coming new year to the Kalahari to investigate and try to help.[8]

By November 1972 Laurens was promising to deliver *A Far-Off Place* early in 1973, and it was eventually published in Britain in September 1974. The Hogarth Press paid a £3,000 advance, and the Americans, William Morrow, took the book on condition they could make some cuts and, in particular, vet the dialogue: Norah Smallwood diplomatically decided to agree and not to tell Laurens about the deletions.

Though sales were good (Penguin kept its paperback edition in print for several decades), the reviews of both books were devastatingly bad. From then on, in 1974, Laurens lost the charmed critical reception which he had enjoyed for more than twenty years. He would afterwards say that the critics turned against him at this time when his friendship with Prince Charles became public knowledge and he had to carry a part of the Prince's 'shadow'.[9] But the widespread critical consensus was that he had lost touch with the language and attitudes of the generation.

Julian Symons in *The Sunday Times* was the only kind reviewer, offering comparison with *Kim* and *Kidnapped*, praising 'the old-fashioned nature of the story'; but even Symons described Laurens's 'message' as 'totally unacceptable, a myth about noble savages in tune with their surroundings that has no relation to the reality'. Various British reviewers called the book, in effect, a children's story, e.g. *The Observer*: 'Kids' stuff, in both good and bad senses: the political melodrama is reactionary wish-fulfilment, the absence of sexuality positively eerie.' Everyone pointed out that the dialogue was ridiculous. Jan Morris in *The Spectator* described it, almost with affection, as an anachronistic 'old man's book', and added acutely that Laurens was a mystic disguised as a novelist and a man of action who nevertheless 'seems dissatisfied with the role, and wishes always to translate his long ecstasy into something more positive, some plan of action, some practical purpose'.[10] In the *New Statesman* Victoria Glendinning nailed Laurens for his failings as novelist: he 'is loth to let facts speak for themselves. He interprets reactions, explains attitudes, enlarges on self-evident statements, and never uses one word where 127 will do. His characters make speeches.' To Auberon Waugh in the *Evening Standard*, *A Far-Off Place* was 'a load of rubbish', and he made fun of the sexual innocence of the teenage couple, ridiculed the plot and highlighted the African characters' habit of speaking in proverbs, 'like drunken fortune-tellers at a church fete'.* *The Listener* pointed out the 'wooden dialogue . . . straight out of the old world of Biggles and Bulldog Drummond'.

In the US it was much the same. Peter Driscoll, in the *Washington Post*, himself a South African and a successful thriller writer, concluded with

---

*It was some years later that *Private Eye* started to satirise Laurens's African nonsense-proverbs in its 'Dear Denis' series.

sympathy that the 'sage in Van der Post is constantly at war with the storyteller'. *Anti-Apartheid News* delivered the *coup de grâce*: it was, alas, not even the expected 'masterpiece of reaction', concluded the reviewer, who effectively mocked the plot and the characterisation – the Scotsman mercenary ('Guid God Mon'), a Frenchman ('I have a hunger formidable and a thirst sensational') and a Chinese boss who actually says 'velly funny'.[11]

These were the last conventional novels Laurens would write, perhaps not surprisingly in view of their reception. Yet both *A Story Like The Wind* and *A Far-Off Place* sold remarkably well. Why did the public buy two novels so conclusively panned by the critics? The answer must lie in Laurens's skilful juggling of fact and fiction. He wrote of a foreign landscape of which most readers knew nothing, and were therefore willing to accept. He gave authenticity to his tale by such tricks as quoting Dr Bleek's Xhabbo of one hundred years earlier, selective use of contemporary history (as in Angola), and an assured geography which readers would not question (for instance, the impossibility of two children walking across the Kalahari Desert).

No-one seems to have noticed that a successful film called *Walkabout*, directed by Nicolas Roeg and based on a novel by James Vance Marshall, had been released in 1970. It told of two young people, lost in the Australian outback, who were rescued by an Aborigine and led across the desert to safety.[12] It would be interesting to know whether Laurens had seen or heard of it.

29

A Mantis Carol

Laurens had by now returned to his third novel about the Bushmen, except that it was set not in the Kalahari but in New York, and he insisted that it was not fiction. It was called *A Mantis Carol* and is one of Laurens's most interesting, infuriating, least known books. He wrote it unusually fast and delivered a manuscript to his publisher in August 1974, explaining that he had not planned the book in advance and it was one of the most difficult things he had ever attempted. It may well have alarmed Norah Smallwood to be told that it was 'intended to be read not with people's minds but with their hearts and feelings as a kind of music', but the Hogarth Press agreed with his suggestion that it would be a good Christmas book; it therefore had to wait for publication until autumn 1975. Norah made various tactful suggestions for improving the manuscript – Ingaret does not seem to have been involved – most of which Laurens politely rejected.

Does *A Mantis Carol* belong on the fact or the fiction shelf? Laurens was at pains to emphasise in his Preamble that 'This is a true story which may well appear stranger than fiction', which he had told 'with due respect for its literal and statistical fact'. True, the characters, portrayed in most cases under their real names, are located in a particular month and a particular city in which Laurens, the narrator, plays – and speaks – the central part. But as so often with Laurens, his truth was only partial: he categorised his new book as a sort of memoir, but the deeper truth is that it was laced with fantasy.[1]

The book is short, scarcely 50,000 words, and the story is simple. In the mid-1950s, Laurens receives a letter from a New York Quaker and psychoanalyst called Martha Jaeger, who tells him of a dream of a Praying Mantis and asks him if he can explain its meaning. He interrupts his work in London, where he is writing *The Heart of the Hunter*, and travels to meet her in her Quaker society outside Philadelphia. There he is confronted by another woman, a sculptor, who tells him the story of

a Bushman, 'Hans' Taaibosch, who for many years before the war featured in a travelling American circus and who was welcomed into the
home of her friends, a lawyer and his family, where she met him. Laurens
is transfixed by this tale and, late into the night of 21 December – the
year must have been 1956 – explains in rhapsodic terms what he sees as
the 'meaning' of that Bushman's life.

Behind this episode is a fascinating story which Laurens does not
accurately explain. Franz Taaibosch – not Hans – was indeed a Bushman
who probably came from an Afrikaner farm in the northern Cape
Province of South Africa. He was abducted by a phoney 'Captain', Paddy
Hepston, to Europe where he performed in Music Halls as 'the Wild
Dancing Bushman'.* Part of his act was to sit in a cage, pretending to
rage as a 'wild savage'. The conditions under which he was made to
perform during the First World War attracted the attention of the Anti-
Slavery and Aborigines' Protection Society. The Captain, now calling
himself 'du Barry', and the 'wild Bushman', who became known as
'Klikko', turned up in Jamaica, where they were discovered by an
American lawyer called Frank Cook who worked for Barnum & Bailey,
the American circus company, and who apparently decided that he might
free the Bushman from the rascal Captain by bringing him on to the
American circus circuit. The Captain soon disappeared; Cook became
Taaibosch's legal guardian, and brought him into his own household,
where he stayed – apparently much loved – while continuing his performances in the summer months until his death in 1940.[3]

This is the point at which Laurens encountered the story. He describes
in *A Mantis Carol* how, when he was lecturing at the Quaker centre of
Pendle Hill in late 1956, his audience included 'an attractive woman
whom I took to be in her middle thirties'. She asked him about Hans (*sic*)
Taaibosch. Might he be one of the Bushmen of whom Laurens had been
speaking, she wondered, and later showed him a photograph of a
sculpted head which she had made. To her delight Laurens confirmed
that it was a head of 'the purest of pure Bushmen'.[4] (This is odd because
she must have known that he had for years been famous as the 'Wild
Dancing Bushman'.)

Laurens never clarifies this sculptor's identity or her relationship with
Taaibosch. The more important contacts, whom Laurens only discovered

---

*In the previous century various 'savages' had been brought from Southern Africa to
appear in freak-shows in America and Britain; the best-known example was the
'Hottentot Venus' who in the 1870s was put on exhibition with not-so-discreet emphasis on her unusual genitalia.[2]

after *A Mantis Carol* appeared in 1975, were Frank Cook's widow, Evelyn, and his daughter, Barbara de Romain, both of whom wrote to him, cheerfully enough, to explain how he had got things wrong. Mrs Cook wrote on 16 May 1978 to reproach him for 'so much mis-information in your book'. She and Laurens maintained an occasional, friendly correspondence until her death in great old age in January 1994.[5]

Laurens missed out on, and was unaware of, some of the more interesting aspects of Franz Taaibosch's extraordinary life. On 7 January 1990, many years after the book was published, the elderly Mrs Evelyn Cook – 'the old Circus Gal,' as she always signed herself – sent Laurens all sorts of fascinating information about her Bushman. Frances Sullivan, her stepdaughter, had taught Franz to speak English, and then her own small daughter, Barbara, became his great friend after they had all moved west to the Californian suburb of Glendale. In those days this district had a by-law whereby blacks had to leave the white areas by 6pm. Mrs Cook therefore kept Taaibosch secretly in the house, forbidding him to go out of doors, until he became friends with the neighbours. She remembered him asking her husband for $4 – $2 for beer, and $2 for the local whorehouse, where apparently the girls thought he was 'cute'.

After Mrs Cook's death, Barbara took over the correspondence. She later admitted her suspicion that Taaibosch had been 'exploited' by her own family even though they had cared for him and given him a comfortable home. She also explained that the sculptor who became a central figure in *A Mantis Carol* was Frances Patterson, 'a talented, sensitive and very fragile person' (reading between the lines of Laurens's book, this fragility is evident). Though Laurens went into rhapsodies on the theme of the Bushman's achievement of 'love', Barbara more convincingly wrote of 'the extraordinary warm human being he was [and] what can only be termed the tragedy which was his life'.[6] This reality must have impinged on Laurens's fantasy of a noble savage; he was not amused that his own version had been effectively challenged.

Rather than the 'true story', then, his imagination takes over very early with his description of a letter from a stranger, the analytical psychologist Martha Jaeger, who has had a recurrent dream image of a Praying Mantis. Laurens explains that she had read 'a book of mine on Africa' which talked of the Mantis as the God of the Bushmen (this is perplexing because Laurens's *The Lost World of the Kalahari* was not published until 1958, and he had not previously written of the Mantis). Laurens was struck by the coincidence of Jaeger's dream and his present investigation of the Bushmen, whose 'conscious mind corresponded in some sort to our dreaming selves'. Martha Jaeger then came to Ancona to attend the annual Jungian gathering, 'Eranos', in August 1956, at which Laurens gave a lecture; she met Laurens, and on her return sent him details of a new Mantis dream. She thereupon – explains Laurens in his book – wrote to invite him to visit New York, whereupon he dropped his work, where he was suffering from writer's block, and set off by sea for America.

This is a good example of his rewriting history. He had in fact for several years been committed to travelling to Canada in this same autumn of 1956, at the expenses-paid invitation of Ingaret's prewar friend and admirer, Karl Maurer, an expert on Rilke, who was a senior figure in the University of Manitoba in Winnipeg. Laurens had agreed to be Guest Speaker at the annual Arts Festival in November. He did not therefore selflessly lay aside his work to make a special visit to New York, he merely added it to his Canadian schedule. He sailed not to New York (as in the book) but directly to Montreal, on 14 November. He had a stormy crossing and arrived late without, he felt, having completed his preparations for his lecture. He gave talks in Montreal, Kingston and Toronto, arriving in Winnipeg to give his main address on 27 November. He did not, as stated in the book, then proceed to California and Texas, New Orleans and Washington, but returned directly to New York. He arrived there not on 13 December, as he says in the book, but on 5–6 December where he addressed the Analytical Psychology Club of New York, a long-scheduled commitment. He writes of his long affection for the Fall in New England, but does not mention that this was in fact his first visit to America.[7] (Nor does he mention another detail. When he arrived in Montreal he was accompanied by a young woman, in her mid-twenties. She checked into the local hospital for an abortion.)[8]

So Laurens, writing seventeen years later, innocently or deliberately adjusted the dates, which are confirmed in his passport and diary. Arriving in New York, battered and exhausted by the American winter, he was swept into the embrace of Martha Jaeger's Quaker community, a six-day experience which he never forgot. The relationship with Martha Jaeger, previously cool, even professional, warmed into a close friendship which lasted until her death ten years later. He addressed a series of meetings and, on the last night at Pendle Hill, he encountered the sculptor, who suggested she might drive him back to the Manhattan apartment provided by his publisher, so that she could ask him about her childhood friend, Franz Taaibosch.

The substance of *A Mantis Carol*, then, is the woman's account of the life of Taaibosch, followed by Laurens's response. In it she shows him photographs of the Bushman's life in America – playing golf in Miami in 1922, skiing in Vermont in 1924, smoking a cigar, on holiday in

Colorado in 1937. She explains, haltingly, her own relationship with Taaibosch and the Cooks and describes how she had loved him, just as he manifestly loved his American family. She even claims in Laurens's account that she had been with him at his death: 'Please dance for me, Dolly,' says the elderly Bushman. 'I have so often danced for you.'[9] She dances, and he dies.

They have arrived at his apartment, late at night, and it is now, he says, the turning of the year – the night of 21 December. Some readers detect an erotic note in this late-night encounter high over Manhattan. Laurens's prose now abandons restraint. 'Somewhere out there in an inconceivable dimension with no inhibitions of time or space, I was convinced that Hans Taaibosch, or, more precisely, the imperishable image made visible through him that once fashioned his unique child-man shape and fired it with clear, unembittered spirit, was once more, as he would have put it, on the spoor of whatever it was in the teeming unknown that could minister to his great hunger and so often made demonstrable in his dancing, and shared in so full a measure of his devout imagination, with the stars and all other systems wheeling in their several courses towards a single end.'

For the the remaining forty pages Laurens, the Seer, takes over from Franz Taaibosch, the humble Bushman exile. 'The great hunger, of course' – he tells her – 'is the hunger for love, and I am certain now that the point of Hans Taaibosch's apparently so irrelevant appearance in your world was to bear witness in his obscure way to the reality and power of love . . . He made the grade, as you would say here, from the Stone Age to the contemporary day without loss of dignity or clarity of spirit because for the first time in his own life – no, of anyone in the life of his race – he experienced love.' (Is Laurens saying that Bushmen do not love each other?) 'There was a Hans Taaibosch in all of us. We too had a cruelly deprived, imperilled natural self. In him and his almost exterminated race we could see how late the hour was and how urgent the need to succour a natural individual self, bring it across the great divide we had seen so abysmal in the spirit of man, and make it at one with the rest of us which, no matter how good the reasons advanced, had ruthlessly suppressed it.'[10]

One is tempted to ask, where does Laurens admit the Bushman in *himself*? He writes in generalisations, never rendering into individual practice the general thesis he lays forth or admitting his own 'deprived, imperilled, natural self'. How can we relate these high sentiments to Laurens's own life at the time?

A Mantis Carol, as we have heard, purports to be a true story with its climax on 21 December, and Frances Patterson and Martha Jaeger and Franz Taaibosch were certainly real people; in the book he flies home, his face pressed to the window, gazing at the stars and filled with the highest sentiments. In fact he had left New York on 15 December, in the *Queen Mary* sailing for Southampton. This is an important distortion: Laurens has shifted the dates so as to achieve his triumph in Manhattan at the very moment of the winter solstice, the cosmological turning of the year. In the book he goes back to the Kalahari and finds no trace or memory of Taaibosch: in reality he did not go back for twenty years. And in the subsequent correspondence between Laurens and Martha Jaeger there is never a reference to Taaibosch, to the Cooks or to Frances Patterson. He waited nearly twenty years to write this tale of his first visit to America, by which time Martha Jaeger and the sculptor Frances Patterson had both died. Franz Taaibosch, of course, had died in 1940. Only the Cook family remained to chide him.[11]

In a letter to Norah Smallwood dated 16 September 1974, Laurens asked her not to mention *A Mantis Carol* to Ingaret. Ingaret had always been Laurens's best editor, and the quality of the prose in this new book reveals that she did not play her usual role. Why not? Might she have been distressed by the intensity of Laurens's remembrance of two American women who had poured out their hearts to him, one of them a sculptor?

Once again, the facts, however fascinating, are less important to Laurens than the imaginative truth to which he converts them. What is presented as the story of a Bushman is really a story of the man who uniquely understands Bushmen and their meaning both for themselves and for contemporary life. Yet another act of colonisation.

A Mantis Carol did not achieve the large and sustained sales of *A Story Like The Wind* and *A Far-Off Place*. It was turned down by Laurens's usual publishers in France, Denmark and Norway. *Reader's Digest* confessed they couldn't make head or tail of it. Even Peter Calvocoressi, the head of Penguin, while agreeing to buy the paperback rights, described it as 'positively weird'. In New York, William Morrow's John Willey offered a $2,500 advance but admitted, 'I really found some of the sentences almost impenetrable'. Yet in Britain Hogarth quickly sold 8,000 copies, and as late as 1989 re-issued it as part of a Collected Edition. The BBC in March 1976 broadcast a half-hour extract.[12]

The reviews were cool, sparse and rather baffled. *The Sunday Times* concluded that it was 'a perfect Christmas fable, full of mystery but oddly satisfying.' *The Listener* decided that 'the book takes all sorts of risks, but the nobility of its concepts and the dignity of its expression carry it through.' The *Sunday Telegraph*, acknowledging it as both extraordinary and unclassifiable, added that it was 'a boiling-up of wisdom and daftness. Some passages are plain soppy or, worse, unreasoned'. In America the *Atlantic Monthly* decided that Laurens had swamped an attractive theme with turgid writing, but the *Christian Science Monitor* later printed three extracts.[13]

Years later, efforts were made to turn *A Mantis Carol* into a Hollywood film. Not surprisingly, they failed. A more important legacy of the book was that Laurens was invited to the Cathedral of St John the Divine in New York in December 1991 to deliver the sermon on the last Sunday in Advent. He told the story of Taaibosch, declaring that the cathedral was, in a sense, the Bushman's own church. This sermon was such a success that Laurens, becoming a great friend of the Dean, Jim Morton, returned to New York to give the Advent sermon in 1992, 1994 and 1995.[14]

30

Carl Gustav Jung

LAURENS FIRST MET Carl Gustav Jung in Zurich in October 1949. The introduction came through Ingaret. In the 1930s Ingaret's mother, Chubbs, had been distressed, suffering, it is now thought, from 'hysterical paralysis' or perhaps a 'wedding night trauma', and was treated by a greatly respected early Jungian, Dr Godwyn ('Peter') Baines, who had been a colleague of Jung in Zurich. At his suggestion Chubbs's second husband, Major John d'Oyly, wrote to Jung, who replied on 21 June 1934 offering to give her a single consultation before he could decide what might be done.

Whether or not Chubbs took up this offer is not known, but the Baines connection – he was a friend and near-neighbour – inspired Ingaret, who was extremely close to her mother, to interest herself in Jung and, under Dr Baines's influence, in due course to attach herself to a doctor and psychotherapist called Alan McGlashan. Encouraged by Baines and McGlashan, she decided to train as an analyst herself, and in 1949 she went to Zurich for about six months to attend lectures at the new C. G. Jung Institute. She was never fully qualified, in terms of the Institute's regulations, but she benefited from working under the supervision of Toni Wolff, Jung's colleague and intimate friend, who died in 1952.[1] McGlashan would soon become one of Laurens's closest friends.

Laurens, as he afterwards explained, had in earlier life been hostile to both Freud and Jung. His meeting with Jung, together with the influence and example of Ingaret, achieved a conversion, and for the rest of his life he was a passionate exponent of Jung's philosophy. As early as *Venture to the Interior* (1952), his books are permeated with Jung's thinking. 'I have known, perhaps, an unusual number of those the world considered great,' he began his 1976 biography, *Jung and the Story of Our Time*, 'but Carl Gustav Jung is almost the only one of whose greatness I am certain.' After the 1949 visit, he was asked to give a lecture at the Zurich Institute in October 1951, and he lectured there again in March 1954 when, he wrote to Donald Boyd at the BBC, his lecture was 'too much of a success'; it was attended by Jung himself, and Laurens and Ingaret spent much of the day with him. Jung then agreed to do a BBC interview with them both.[2]

In November 1951 Laurens wrote several relaxed and irreverent letters from Zurich to William Plomer: Zurich was wet and misty ('By Jung, it is dreary'), but the local Swiss were more sympathetic than he had expected, and he was revising his book, which must have been *The Face Beside the Fire*, writing reports of his Bechuanaland project, and attending a few lectures, 'including a protracted exegesis of the Holy Grail legend by Emma, the wife of Jung . . . a fascinating study by a remarkable and beautiful woman, and I am enjoying it thoroughly'. A month later Laurens wrote again to say 'I met and made friends with Jung and have been very deeply stirred by him . . .' Laurens had discovered that Jung had spent four months in Kenya in 1925 and 1926 in the Mount Elgon district on the Uganda border. This African journey had been very important to him and he evidently responded to Laurens's descriptions of his own travels on that continent. Laurens, gratified, later claimed that there had been a synchronicity in their both being in East Africa at the same time – ignoring the fact that his own youthful visit, with Captain Mori, had lasted only a couple of days and took place six months after Jung had left.[3]

How truly close was Laurens to Jung? As the years went by, after Jung's death in June 1961, Laurens increasingly laid claim to an intimate friendship. This claim lay at the heart of his biography, *Jung and the Story of Our Time*, an extremely successful book which introduced many people to Jung's thinking. This book is full of references to the close friendship between the two men. Was this friendship exaggerated, or even, to a degree, wishful thinking?

Certainly Jung and Laurens knew each other, and got on well. They met from time to time, though not, as Laurens asserted, whenever he flew from Africa to Europe. Laurens did not visit Jung at his Kusnacht home 'repeatedly', as he said in the biography, and he did not attend Emma Jung's lectures 'regularly'. There is no doubt that Laurens gave to Jung a respect, admiration and affection which he gave to no-one else. In various books he liked to remember that he achieved an instant rapport with Jung and that on their first meeting they talked for five hours, but his correspondence, and Jung's formal replies, suggest a slower and less close relationship.[4]

So what was Laurens to Jung? Jung was a gregarious, sociable, great-hearted man who was surrounded by a host of loving followers and admirers. His welcome to Laurens would have been generous, but it was scarcely unique. Laurens was instantly disposed to admire, and follow, and Jung easily encouraged such a response. All psychotherapists understand that the analysand is prone to wish, and conclude, that he or she is particularly favoured by the therapist. Laurens was not in analysis, but he was metaphorically on Jung's couch, and he might have been tempted to misread generosity for intimacy.

Laurens always explained that, although deeply interested in the world of dreams, he never underwent an analysis. 'I am not a psychologist. I was never a patient either of Jung, or any of his distinguished collaborators, or for that matter of any other psychiatrist.' This is a little disingenuous: for many years Laurens would visit his friend Dr Alan McGlashan, in what can only be described as an analytical arrangement, though it was irregular and did not conform to the professional rules which specify a more formal, regular and impersonal relationship.[5] Laurens used to say that he once asked Jung whether he should have an analysis, to which Jung replied that Laurens was the best-adjusted man he had ever met and there would be absolutely no point.* Many professional Jungian analysts find it hard to believe that Jung would ever have made that remark; though other analysts disagree. If Jung had discouraged an analysis for Laurens, it would more likely have been on the grounds that, as another Jungian analyst friend of Laurens put it after his death, 'Laurens had an extremely fluent ego-structure and Jung had the sense that it wouldn't change.'[7]

Laurens had access to Jung, even to his tower on the lakeside at Bollingen. In 1955 he and Ingaret recorded a long interview in Jung's home for BBC Radio. Years later, in 1971, long after Jung's death, Laurens made a substantial three-part film about Jung for the BBC. It included the first sighting of the 'Red Book', Jung's private and secret journal, which has still not been released by the family in its entirety. Laurens had secured the family's co-operation for the film but he afterwards complained that thirteen hours of film had been reduced to three half-hour programmes, and that the Jung Foundation had reneged on its promise to release the rest of the footage; there were rumours that the family had objected to the inclusion of the Red Book. The television version, filmed by Jonathan Stedall amid mist-shrouded snowy peaks and a Wagnerian sound-track, is evocative and seductive, and will have intro-

---

*Laurens later remembered: 'There were many people who were just not fit subjects for analysis. He [Jung] told me, for instance, that the people he found most difficult and often incapable of benefiting from analysis were "habitual liars and intellectuals".'[6]

duced many people to Jung. It contains interviews with Dr Fredy Meier and Aniela Jaffe, both of whom became good friends, and there are scenes in the lakeside tower at Bollingen as well as Jung's house in Kusnacht, and an extended glimpse of the pictures in the Red Book.[8] Most of the film's content was later re-used in Laurens's biography.

In sum, Laurens became a 'Jungian' in the early 1950s, and would soon travel the world with his version of a Jungian interpretation of the Bushmen and their folk-tales. His precise personal relationship with the elderly Jung will probably remain obscure. The correspondence that survives is brief and mutually courteous (e.g. 'Dear Colonel . . .', and signed 'C. G. Jung'). It amounts to a few rather formal letters from Jung thanking Laurens for sending him his books, and offering his greetings to Ingaret. The letters from Jung which Laurens would refer to in his books and talks cannot be found in Zurich or London. Laurens would surely not have thrown them away. Did they exist? Jung was in correspondence with scores of people, but it was Laurens who travelled the world for thirty-five years after Jung's death enlarging on the sage's teaching, claiming that he had been one of Jung's most intimate friends – the only one, he sometimes added, to whom Jung said he could relate as an equal.[9]

After his Kalahari expedition, Laurens sent Jung a Bushman 'cupid's bow'. He was on warm terms with various members of Jung's Zurich circle, with Marie-Louise von Franz and particularly with Aniela Jaffe, his secretary, who helped Jung write his autobiography, *Memories, Dreams, Reflections*, and also with Dr Fredy Meier, Jung's principal successor. Laurens later arranged for the publication of Meier's books in English. Laurens many times wrote, and told audiences, of how at the moment of Jung's death he had a vision. It was June 1961 and Laurens was returning to London by sea from South Africa: 'Suddenly, at the far end of the valley on one Matterhorn peak of my vision, still caught in the light of the sun, Jung appeared. He stood there briefly, as I had seen him some weeks before at the gate, at the end of the garden of his house, then waved his hand at me and called out, "I'll be seeing you."' A great white albatross glided past Laurens's porthole and gazed at him; the steward brought the ship's news sheet, and Laurens saw that Jung had died. 'It was clear that my dream, or vision, had come to me at the moment of his death.'[10] There could hardly be a more striking instance of Laurens's sense of his intimacy, or equality, with the great man.

Aniela Jaffe, who became secretary of the C. G. Jung Institute and was also a friend of Laurens, recalled a 'deep friendship' between Jung and Laurens, although admittedly she was writing forty years later, in the context of a *Festschrift*, which is not the place for caution or precision. In

Laurens, she said, he had encountered 'a friend capable of understanding the significance of his stories, for he had gone through similar inner and outer experiences of his own'. She added that Jung read Laurens's books 'with passion'.[11] Then again, in *Jung and the Story of Our Time*, Laurens – who throughout the book is concerned to emphasise the closeness of the friendship – recalls that some months after the death of Emma Jung, 'He wrote to me that the silence had been broken by a dream. He dreamt that he entered a vast and darkened theatre ... There in the centre of the stage, more beautiful and free of care than he had ever seen her, was his wife.' Jung does indeed refer to this dream, without any of the details which Laurens lists, in *Memories, Dreams, Reflections*.[12] But there is no evidence that this letter ever existed. It cannot be found either in Zurich or in Laurens's own archives. It is, for Jung's followers, an important dream which they all remember. The mystery may be solved in the talk which Laurens delivered to the Analytical Psychology Club of New York as far back as October 1961, in which he described how, shortly before his death, Jung had *told* him of his vision.[13] That is to say, *there was no letter*.

There is a similar mystery concerning a letter which Laurens said he received from Jung just before his death in which the psychologist discusses, for Laurens's benefit, the meaning of God. According to Laurens, Jung wrote, 'I cannot define for you what God is ... I can only say that my work has proved empirically that the pattern of God exists in every man, and that this pattern has at its disposal the greatest of all energies for transformation and transfiguration of his natural being.'[14] Where is this letter? There is no sign of it either in Jung's archive or in Laurens's. The phrase about the 'pattern of God' is not one Jung ever used – he preferred the more precise term 'God-image' – whereas 'pattern' was one of *Laurens's* favourite words. One has to ask, what is going on here?

The television film, and its success, eventually led Laurens to write *Jung and the Story of Our Time*. He claimed that he had been asked to write the official biography, though there is no evidence of such a proposal. Instead, Laurens decided, in 1973, to attempt a more personal quest under the provisional title 'A Kind of Dreaming', which eventually appeared in 1976. The problem with *Jung and the Story of Our Time*, as many Jungians have complained, is that it is first and foremost a book about *Laurens*. In fact he devotes his first sixty pages to talking about himself before he arrives at the words, 'Jung was born on July 26th, 1875'. Laurens positions himself in the early chapters at the heart of the story and describes Jung constantly with reference to himself. He underestimates the passion of scholars and diminishes the sophistication and subtlety of Jung's immense scholarship. He does not understand the mysteries of the analytical process because he was never willing fully to undergo it.

Laurens tells us that his family nicknamed him 'Joseph the Dreamer'. In the POW camp he re-read the Classics, 'all in various languages' (interestingly he had no Greek or Latin). Rejecting conventional legend and its churches and dogmas, he came to realise that 'some new language of the spirit, some new truly contemporary way of looking at the reality of our desperate day was essential . . .' When, finally, he met Jung at a party in Zurich, Laurens immediately impressed him by emphasising the true meaning of fire – the precious gift stolen from the Gods. Jung gave his great and well-known peasant laugh, and Laurens was 'in'. 'The feeling of isolation and loneliness in a vital area of myself which had haunted me all those years vanished. I was no longer alone. I had company of a noble order. For the first time in my life I had a neighbour in the inmost part of myself.' Laurens here implies his equality with Jung, the pioneer who was 'the very first great explorer in the twentieth century way'.

Jung and the Story of Our Time is scattered with references to their personal and private meetings, yet it is never clear how often they met, or when; judging by Laurens's previous record, he is indulging in what Jung in many books called 'inflation'. 'I had dropped in at Zurich on my way back to England from Africa as had become almost a matter of routine since our first meeting': in fact Laurens's visits to Switzerland were at least as likely to be arranged to meet his private banker in Geneva as to visit Jung.[15] An alarming episode is reported by E. A. Bennett in his book *Meetings With Jung*. On 16 January 1961 Jung and Bennett were joined at lunch by Laurens: 'He . . . recalled as a boy seeing his mother in a Dutch Reformed Church receiving the Holy Communion from a black clergy-man, and in that Church they hand the cup from one to another. She received it from a coloured person on her left and, having partaken herself, handed it on to another coloured person on her right. But now all that has gone.'[16] To anyone familiar with the Free State in the early twentieth century that story is unbelievable, doubly so in view of Lammie's own racial attitudes. Laurens seems here to be spinning a story, designed to cast liberal credit on his family, and therefore on himself, for his revered and innocent Jung.

Jung and the Story of Our Time is not so much a biography as a paean of praise to a man whom Laurens came close to worship, yet with whom at pivotal points he implied an equality, such that in lauding Jung he was implicitly lauding himself. To Laurens, Jung was 'a Moses who can lead millions to a new land of promise'. His work was 'a turning point in the art of human communications'. The women who famously surrounded Jung were 'one of the most remarkable groups of gifted women ever assembled round a single man, however great'. His exploration of a new world within the human spirit was 'greater . . . [and] far more significant for life on earth than the world Columbus discovered in the world without'. After Jung's famous breakdown in 1913, 'he made one of the bravest decisions, I believe, ever recorded in the history of the human spirit.'

For Laurens's readers who had not previously encountered Jung, this book was revelatory. To those already initiated, it was regrettable how little credit was given to Jung's own autobiography, *Memories, Dreams, Reflections*, published in 1963. Laurens eschews all scholarly traditions; at one point he actually declares that he has made no attempt at research, read no books about his subject, consulted none of Jung's friends or colleagues, and looked at the texts only to confirm what he remembers. The record, he himself admits, is therefore fallible.

There is no doubt that Laurens felt an affinity with Jung. They shared, as he points out, a puritanical Christian background, a remote father, a remarkable and feminine mother. They were both dreamers from childhood. In middle age (though he does not say this) they both defied conventional morality and had long-term relationships with 'mistresses', to use an old-fashioned word. Laurens paid far more attention to Toni Wolff's role than previous commentators.[17]

There is much exposition of Laurens's thoughts on Faust, Dante, Homer, Hamlet, Dostoyevsky, and his favourite classics. He is interesting on Jung's attraction to gnosticism and alchemy, and he handles convincingly the charge of Jung's alleged anti-Semitism. There are striking images: 'Dreams, symbols, spontaneous imagery and fantasy were permanent features of his real and natural world and, just like a guide I knew in the bush and desert of Africa who would not fail to recognise a tree, incline or dune that had marked a journey done only once some forty years before as a boy [that must be Johnnie Marnewick], Jung would never forget the smallest detail of significance in the dreams and fantasies and other features of his movement through this inscape of his remotest past.'

Such is his confidence by now in his own powers of analysis and interpretation, that Laurens allows himself to take over from his master, describing for example Jung's own detailed explanation of his famous dream figures of Siegfried and Salome. Not content with leaving it casually as Jung does in *Memories, Dreams, Reflections*, Laurens offers his own *explication* of the story of Jung's two women, his wife Emma and his colleague Toni Wolff. The reader becomes aware of a hidden reference to Laurens's own life. Referring to Toni Wolff, who, as he points out, is not mentioned in *Memories, Dreams, Reflections*, Laurens notes: 'Jung's gift inflicted a special form of loneliness in him that was a part of an over-whelming compulsion to serve a cause of universal meaning. The cause always had to come before men or women. Yet from what I know of such people, both in my own life and history, I find it remarkable that ... Jung ... gave so freely and generously of himself.'

Laurens tells us that Jung burned his correspondence with Toni Wolff because 'he could not bear the thought of strange, impersonal eyes of future generations prying into what had been of such intimate, immedi-ate, desperate and secret concern to him ... All that happened took place in an area of the personality where the secret must be kept forever ...'[18] He might have been writing of himself and Frances Baruch. Incidentally, Laurens does not mention that Jung's wife was rich, which greatly helped his career: there is another parallel here. But the great difference between the two situations is that Jung told his wife Emma about Toni, and the knowledge was shared with their friends, whereas Laurens never told Ingaret about Frances, although his friends knew.

Laurens may have realised that he was in danger of aligning himself too closely with Jung. In a letter dated 31 October 1972 to Hogarth's publicity department, after the television programmes, he asked them to stop describing him as a 'Jungian': 'I am nothing of the sort. My relation-ship with Jung was entirely non-psychological, due to the fact that I loved him and he became in his old age a great friend of mine. I do think he is one of the greatest, if not the greatest, figures Europe has produced for centuries, but that does not mean that he was the great formative influ-ence in my life ... Jung was to me a very great and good neighbour.'[19] Laurens's point is that he is not a *follower* of Jung so much as a friend who wishes to pay generous tribute. It was shortly after this letter that he set out to write *Jung and the Story of Our Time*.

The idea for the Jung biography came from André Schiffrin of the American publishing house Pantheon, who suggested a book based on the text of the TV series. Laurens said no, but softened as Pantheon con-tinued to press him, worried only that he would appear to be deserting his New York publisher – though he told Norah Smallwood that William Morrow in the past had persuaded him to turn down lucrative proposals from elsewhere. In the end William Morrow generously made no objec-tion; everyone agreed that Pantheon, as the American publisher of *Memories, Dreams, Reflections*, was a better vehicle for another Jung book. Pantheon offered a tempting advance of $10,000, and the deal was done in October 1973, in the month, as it happened, that Laurens had deli-vered *A Far-Off Place* to the Hogarth Press and to William Morrow.

Over the next two years, as Laurens was writing, the publishing arrangements became extremely complicated, partly because the Hogarth Press were not this time collaborating with their old friends at William Morrow, and partly because Pantheon was anxious to publish the book in Jung's centenary year of 1975. A further complication was that *Reader's Digest* was sitting on a 35,000-word article on Jung which Laurens had written some time before and which, if published in 1975, would appal Pantheon, whose print-run would be large, 20,000 copies. As usual, Laurens lagged behind his deadline. He promised Schiffrin a manuscript at the end of January, but warned him that it would be unedited, overlong, and would contain repetitions: 'As a rule,' he said, 'my manuscripts are edited by my wife, but on this occasion owing to the pressure of time we have not been able to do this.'[20]

John Charlton at Hogarth in February began to discuss a separate editing and a later publication date for the British edition; he did not think it essential to coincide with the centenary. Pantheon was finding it hard to keep to its 'rush schedule': Schiffrin wrote to John Charlton on 23 May, 'Between ourselves, I'm afraid that the manuscript does represent a great deal of work on our part. I have in fact never cut a manuscript so drastically . . .' No-one knew whether Laurens would agree to the American editing, and it was now mid-June. His eventual letter to Schiffrin on 22 June was courteous, before passing on to his reservations that 'the omissions are too large to be capable of correction by manipulation' of the proofs. Interestingly, he asked Pantheon not to describe him as Jung's 'closest' friend since that would arouse 'the ever volcanic jealousies and envies of Jungians the world over'. In his separate letter to the Hogarth Press, Laurens declared that the Pantheon version 'won't do for us'.

The American and British editions of *Jung and the Story of Our Time* are therefore different. Pantheon published in November and soon planned to reprint. Vintage Books quickly offered $20,000 for American paperback rights. The Hogarth Press edition, which Laurens always insisted was the authorised version, came out as late as June 1976, with the paperback already sold to Penguin for £2,750. This version was used for foreign rights in Germany, Latin America, Japan and Holland. This Anglo-American publishing collaboration, always difficult, ended badly with a squabble when Pantheon disputed payment of the second $5,000 instalment of the US paperback contract. Hogarth, in its capacity as Laurens's agent, stood firm. Laurens would thereafter return to William Morrow.[21]

*

The critical reception in Britain to *Jung and the Story of Our Time* was sparser than Laurens expected, and very mixed. He was wounded by reviews in two of the serious Sunday papers whose approval was important. Phillip Toynbee mocked Laurens's 'eulogy' of his 'friend' which, he said, seemed to be arguing that Jung was a new saviour; was he really suggesting that Jung's terminology be incorporated into Christian worship? The psychologist Anthony Storr in *The Sunday Times* made a similar point, that Laurens was attributing messianic qualities to 'a remarkable and interesting man who made valuable contributions to psychiatry and to the art of psychotherapy'; what was still needed was a proper critical biography, warts and all, which would rescue Jung from idolatry. *The Times* admitted that readers attracted by Laurens's reputation might find 'a new and stimulating voyage of philosophical discovery.' *New Society* was much kinder, though it described the prose as 'breathless, flowery'. Norah Smallwood and Laurens tried to reassure one another. Laurens protested that it was the most important book he had ever written and urged her to take out advertisements, however expensive: Norah promised that 'good books sooner or later sell', but she agreed to advertise.[22]

In America the critics had been kinder, as the comparative early sales figures show. *Time* magazine described the book as 'an impassioned missionary effort to portray Jung as an angelic messenger from the gods'. The *Atlantic Monthly* said that it was 'intelligent, truthful, subtle, persuasive, wordy, and relentless in his praise'. The *Nation* added to the adjectives – 'eloquent, learned and most impressive'. The *New Republic* was less impressed, accusing Laurens of 'devotional hagiography and messianic proclamation', and the *New York Times* spotted that 'Van der Post's memoir suffers from uncritical effusiveness and long paraphrases of events that are more powerfully and completely described in *Memories, Dreams, Reflections*.'[23]

Although the book would remain in print, and popular in Britain for many years, its success in America was greater, perhaps for the reason that Jung was a more familiar figure there. This is one reason why Laurens, over the next twenty years, became a frequent and lauded visitor to the US, a familiar figure at Jungian, or in due course New Age, gatherings from New York to California, Houston to Chicago, Philadelphia to Buffalo.

The three television films which had preceded his book in America had been enthusiastically received, especially on university campuses – inviting the *New Republic* critic's mischievous comment that 'The film, I believe, is regularly shown to small gatherings of the devout (accompanied, I have always imagined, by a small collation, but nothing lavish –

perhaps no more than a wafer and a sip of wine) . . . In both film and book van der Post is preaching to the converted, or more precisely he is reciting to them the gospel narrative of Jung's life.'[24]

What did Jung really make of Laurens? This question was once put to Ruth Bailey, who had been Jung's housekeeper and companion during the last years of his life. She replied, 'Oh, he liked him well enough at first, and then he decided that he was a pea who had grown too big for its pod.'[25]

The Secret Diplomat

IN THE INTERVALS between his books Laurens was a frequent broad-caster and interviewee on radio, and in the years after the success of his *Lost World of Kalahari* series, he fronted a number of well-received television programmes: *A Region of Shadow*, directed by Stephen Cross in 1971, *The Story of Carl Gustav Jung*, by Jonathan Stedall in 1971, *All Africa Within Us* in 1975, also with Stedall, a programme about *The Tempest* (1980) which he insisted be filmed in his favourite prewar island of Porquerolles, and Jane Taylor's *Testament to the Bushmen* in 1981–84. He would later be the subject of Stedall's *Laurens van der Post at Eighty*, a later 'obituary' by Stedall called *Voice from the Bundu* (1997), and in 1996 the American Mickey Lemle's *Hasten Slowly: the Journey of Laurens van der Post.*[1]*

The mid-1970s seem to have ushered in a new period in his life story. He became close to both the Prince of Wales and Mrs Thatcher (who in 1975 became leader of the Conservative Party, then in opposition), grand acquaintanceships which, according to some of his friends, led to various changes in his character. The year ahead would see a fast-growing over-confidence leading to arrogance, when he would write to world figures on the assumption that they were, if not his equals, at least accessible to him. This was also the time of the Soweto riots, which announced the eventual end of white domination in South Africa. Laurens's world was about to shift.

In the mid-1970s, able to concentrate on the politics of Southern Africa, he embarked upon an intense lobbying campaign from London, never questioning his qualifications to do so, or doubting his understanding of the forces sweeping the sub-continent. He used Mrs Thatcher's name to open doors into the Labour Government, particu-

---

*'Hasten Slowly' was always Laurens's version of *'Hamba Gahle'*, one of his favourite catch-phrases; but rather than suggesting a Zulu equivalent of the Latin 'Festina Lente', it is actually nearer to the universal greeting 'Go Well!'.

larly into the Foreign Office. In South Africa, he always claimed an old and intimate acquaintance with many members of the Government in Pretoria: in fact his only close friendship was with Dr Piet Koornhof, to whom he had been introduced by their mutual friend T. C. Robertson around 1960. Laurens and Piet Koornhof did become close confidants, as Koornhof, an intelligent and eccentric figure who did not mind that he had become a figure of fun to journalists and to the electorate, successively headed various departments of Education, Sport, Mines, Irrigation and Bantu Administration, and then became Chairman of the President's Council.

Piet Koornhof saw himself as a 'liberal' reforming figure within the National Party cabinet, one who had gone into government in order to transform and even overturn apartheid from within the system. This must sound rich coming from the man who was for six years Minister of Cooperation and Development – the department whose role it was to enforce apartheid – but his correspondence with Laurens does reveal a perplexed and sincere man who, privately, was prepared to try to soften the system. When he was ousted from office in 1987 he was sent to be Ambassador in Washington, where he would attempt to represent the acceptable face of apartheid, and on his retirement he left his Afrikaner wife, Lulu, to marry, and have children by, a young 'Coloured' woman – to the mocking delight, and perhaps the secret admiration, of his former enemies.[2] For Laurens he was not just a real friend, to visit in South Africa and to entertain in London, but a conduit into the South African Cabinet to be employed vigorously.

Laurens discreetly used this connection in ways which might surprise some of his critics. In January 1974, for example, he pleaded with Koornhof to use his influence to secure the release from Pretoria's Central Prison of Bram Fischer, who was serving a life sentence and dying of cancer. Bram, who came from the heart of the Afrikaner establishment, had been a schoolboy friend of Laurens in Grey College. Laurens was aware that he had always been a radical, and Bram indeed became not only a very distinguished lawyer but also, under cover, the head of the banned South African Communist Party. First arrested in 1964, he was on the run for a dramatic period, before being recaptured, and sentenced in 1966.

'Please, Piet, in God's name, get Bram released as soon as possible,' Laurens wrote; he and many old Grey boys could not sleep well at nights because they pictured Bram dying in prison. To release him to die at home would also impress world opinion as an act of charitable statesmanship. Laurens enclosed a personal letter to Bram which he asked Piet to attempt to pass on; in this he protested his affection to Bram, explained that he had tried to visit him but had been refused, and went on, 'I myself was in prison long enough and endured enough solitary confinement to know that prison in some strange way can be a form of liberation . . . May God bless you.'

Bram was indeed released very near the end, to stay with his son, where he died in 1975. The circumstances behind his release are disputed: his daughters believe it was mainly the result of their agitation. But on 26 July 1975, Ian Player, a friend of both Koornhof and Laurens, told Laurens that he had been with Piet who 'mentioned particularly and in confidence that a letter of yours about a now departed friend had been the instrument with which he had been able to move the Cabinet'.[3]*

Laurens also wrote to Koornhof about the fiercely disputed visit of a British Lions rugby team to South Africa in 1974, in defiance of the international sports boycott. He claimed this was a collaboration with his nephew, the Springbok rugby player, Tommy Bedford, who played in those matches, though Tom has since said that he was unaware of Laurens's lobbying. Popular demonstrations against sporting visits to or from South Africa had been growing since the late 1960s, and rugby, as the white South Africans' favourite pastime, was the obvious target. Laurens told Koornhof how the struggle to defeat the popular campaign to stop the Lions' tour had been touch-and-go, and asked him to do all he could to welcome and acknowledge the 'incredible individual and moral courage' of the young rugby players who had defied public criticism to travel to South Africa. It was a good example of Laurens's passionate, and active, hostility to the international sanctions then being developed by the anti-apartheid movement. He discovered a personal angle to the criticism which his cause attracted: Tommy Bedford, he explained, had come in for press criticism because he was Laurens's nephew.[5]

But the most important example of the link between Laurens and Koornhof was the Rhodesian crisis. Ian Smith and his Rhodesian Front Government had made their Unilateral Declaration of Independence (UDI) on 11 November 1965. Successive negotiations had failed to persuade them to return to allegiance to Britain, as Britain felt unable to send troops. The Rhodesians were sustained by South African support, although the South African Government was deeply uneasy. By the mid-

*Many years later Laurens got into a newspaper argument about the fate of Bram's corpse, insisting that the Fischer daughters were wrong in stating that their father's ashes had been buried on prison ground so that the grave would not become a site of political pilgrimage.[4]

1970s, Ian Smith was still defiant but a guerrilla war was developing fast, launched from safe enclaves in Mozambique and Zambia. Laurens, who had frequently visited Rhodesia in the 1950s, felt inspired to intervene, through his friendships with Piet Koornhof, Mrs Thatcher and the Rhodesian cabinet minister David Smith.

For five years he bombarded the participants with letters and phone calls, arguing that there was a chance for a non-violent solution to the Rhodesian impasse. As so often, Laurens's political antennae seem, with hindsight, to have been ill-tuned. In December 1976, for example, he urged that British troops be sent (an option ruled out by Harold Wilson eleven years earlier, partly because his government wasn't sure that British officers would fight white Rhodesians); he declared that the black Rhodesian middle class and peasantry abhorred the guerrillas (an assessment not borne out by later developments); he regretted that he could get no response from Anthony Crosland (then Foreign Secretary – his name always misspelled by Laurens), and said he had been forced to settle for an hour with Sir Antony Duff, the senior British diplomat. Duff patiently pointed out that the British Government would not send troops and that a settlement could only be achieved with the agreement of the neighbouring states in the region. Laurens complained to his old friend Charles Janson, a publisher of the influential *Africa Confidential* newsletter, that he seemed to have no influence. Janson sensibly replied that he must accept that he was not a political animal and did not have the tactical sense which was the art of politics.[6]

Laurens then managed to meet Dr David Owen, the new Foreign Secretary following Crosland's death, and was not impressed. Owen was a 'bad listener'. He now saw no hope in London until there was a change of government, so he focussed on the United States (where, he told Piet Koornhof absurdly, he had frequently stayed with Martin Luther King in Harlem). He began to target his American contacts, such as the *Washington Post*: 'I cannot unfortunately write for you about my recent journey to South Africa because, in confidence, I did it for a special purpose for the British Foreign Office' – not true either. He was also despondent about South Africa, where he saw men 'who have an unconscious devil at work within them' at the heart of Afrikanerdom.

Laurens then came up with the idea that he spend an afternoon with President Jimmy Carter when he was next in Washington – the usual fifteen minutes would not do – and he wrote to his friend Katharine Graham, owner of the *Washington Post*, to ask her to fix it. There was, he told her, an immense catastrophe building up in Africa, and the US was the only country which could prevent it. He explained to her that he was 'the only person alive who has this sort of information and the world experience to interpret it with reasonable accuracy in terms of its implications for the future'. All she managed for him, in June 1977, was a few sentences of conversation with the President at a social gathering, and various talks at the State Department.[7]

So Laurens was cast back on his Anglo-South African connections. He proposed to Koornhof a discreet London dinner party with Mrs Thatcher, Leader of the Opposition, at his home in Chelsea, warning him that this was his last effort to help and that he was going to say goodbye to the political dimension of life and return to his books (he was evidently bluffing). As a lobbyist, Laurens's influence was chiefly limited to the Conservative Party. He reported to Koornhof on 4 May 1977 that he had seen Mrs Thatcher and her shadow foreign secretary, Lord Carrington, the night before and was about to set off for Washington. His meeting with David Owen on 20 May was not a success; he immediately sent Owen a six-page letter to clarify his argument, adding, perhaps wisely, that he did not expect a reply. Which didn't stop him writing again at length to Owen on 18 June from America to tell him that he had just had 'the most remarkable meeting with the most powerful man in South Africa' – without disclosing who this might have been – and warning that 'the failure of Britain and America to act in time [on Rhodesia], is eroding the few unforgiving seconds left to you all so fast, that any day now you will have destroyed the standing of those who have been negotiating with you to such an extent that there is nobody representative left – black or white – to negotiate with'. His concern, he added significantly, was 'to isolate the South African issue' from events elsewhere in Africa. Again, he added that he did not hope for a reply. In his memoirs David Owen wrote of 1977, 'I was going to come under severe attack from the Conservative Right on Rhodesia, in particular since Margaret Thatcher sympathised with their views. She knew very little then about Africa and her main advisor seemed to be Laurens van der Post . . . She unwisely committed herself to Bishop Muzorewa and gave a pre-election commitment to support the internal settlement which undoubtedly hindered our diplomacy. When she won the election she found it was the first promise she was unable to fulfil.'[8]

Reporting back to Koornhof after his Washington visit, Laurens made the valid point that there was no hope of acquiring friends for South Africa abroad 'unless we set about the creation of a just society with the utmost dispatch and even then we may have left it too late'. He suggested that a new constitution would have to contain a common voters' roll and full citizenship for all South Africans on the basis of high education qualifications, an idea which clearly harked back to Capricorn ('this voters' roll need not be on a one-man-one-vote basis for that obviously would be disastrous'). There must be an immediate proclamation that apartheid was dead.

This was June 1977, in the aftermath of the Soweto uprising, and Laurens was, at any rate, in advance of many white South Africans. In a later letter, he confessed to Piet Koornhof that he had 'never in fact felt so depressed about our country and its singularly uninformed, introvert and bigoted leaders'. He applauded what he saw as his friend's lone battle in Cabinet. (This interpretation of Koornhof's role would have surprised South Africa's political journalists.) At the same period Laurens was writing to General Hendrik van den Bergh, head of the Bureau for State Security, BOSS, and a terrifying figure in South Africa, who was known to be close to Prime Minister Vorster. (He may not have understood that van den Bergh's influence was waning.) Laurens traded on their long meeting earlier in the year to tell him directly that the Prime Minister was leading the country to disaster. He quoted a Hungarian parable: 'If one man calls you a mule, laugh at him. If two men call you a mule, consider the fact. If three men call you a mule, go and buy yourself a saddle.' Shouldn't your policy makers – Laurens suggested bravely – 'go and buy themselves saddles?' He urged van den Bergh to persuade the Prime Minister to call a National Convention and he added a specific request concerning the death of Steve Biko (the young black activist who had been killed by the police in September 1977): hold a public inquest, said Laurens, and announce an enquiry into the role of the doctors, 'and above all the behaviour of your own Secret Police'.[9] There is no record of any reply from the General. In October the Government had clamped down on the Black Consciousness groups with which Biko had been associated.

But by this time Laurens was more preoccupied with the situation in Rhodesia, where the military advance of the nationalist guerrilla forces and, at last, the strangulation of international sanctions, coupled with South Africa's disinclination to support Ian Smith's regime indefinitely, brought the various parties to the conference table in London, at Lancaster House in 1979. According to his friends, Laurens had been indefatigably involved throughout the previous twelve months, continually on the telephone, and travelling to Southern Africa or America half a dozen times. He spread the word, then and later, that he had been centrally involved in the negotiations which eventually, after difficult weeks, led to a settlement and to the granting of independence to majority-rule Zimbabwe in April 1980. The emergence of his friend Mrs Thatcher as

Prime Minister, after the Tories' election victory in May 1979, would no doubt have contributed to this impression. His knighthood, on 1 January 1981, was seen by him as an acknowledgement not only of his literary achievements but also of his behind-the-scenes contribution to the Rhodesian Settlement.[10]

On 31 December 1979 Laurens wrote to his friend T. C. Robertson to thank him for introducing him twenty years before to Piet Koornhof. After a mysterious reference to TC getting Koornhof off the golf course (following a telephone call from Laurens, made from film star Robert Redford's house in California, which allegedly prevented the collapse of the Lancaster House talks), Laurens added, 'If it had not been for the two of us I doubt whether an agreement would have been reached in London ... In fact everything creative and decisive at this Conference was accomplished, not by politicians, but by friendships struck right across the lines of division.' He said that he had incurred colossal long-distance telephone bills – more than £1,000! – but he had insisted on doing what he did anonymously, and not as a paid or political instrument.[11]

The next day he wrote again to Koornhof to describe how he had just attended the Prime Minister's party at Chequers where Piet's name 'was in the forefront of our minds. They all came up to me and wanted to know more about you and I was happy to tell them about what you have done already and the direction in which I know you will want to lead South Africa as fast as is humanly possible.'[12]

Laurens was invited by Prince Charles to attend the Independence celebrations with him in Salisbury, renamed Harare, in April 1980. Incognito in the rear of the plane was the Prince's friend, Camilla Parker Bowles. The ADC to Sir Christopher Soames, the Governor, who greeted them on their arrival, was her husband, Andrew Parker Bowles.[13]

What, in reality, was Laurens's contribution to the Rhodesian Settlement? Certainly he exerted himself mightily, with scores of letters and telephone calls and numerous hints that he was the secret intermediary between the British Government and the South African Cabinet which eventually provided inescapable pressure on Ian Smith to agree to a return to legality. He interleaved his arguments with references to his latest meetings with Thatcher and Carrington. But was he truly so crucial? Journalists and commentators who followed Lancaster House closely never saw the faintest shadow of Laurens in the backstage manoeuvres.

The British diplomats who eventually achieved the Settlement were a powerful team. Lord Carrington, then Foreign Secretary, has told the present writer that he has no memory of any particular contribution by Laurens, although he remembers that he came down to the Independence celebrations. Robin Renwick, head of the Rhodesia Department, who was the professional diplomat principally involved, and later Ambassador to South Africa, also remembers no role for Laurens, except that he might have spoken to him on the phone every couple of months. Charles Powell, then 'Special Counsellor for the Rhodesian negotiation' at the Foreign Office, agrees that Laurens played no significant role, as does Ewen Fergusson, who was then the Assistant Under-Secretary of State. Piet Koornhof, speaking from his retirement outside Cape Town, is effusive in his affection for Laurens but cannot specify any particular contribution – Koornhof would not have been directly involved in the negotiations, his role was limited to conveying Laurens's views or messages to the Pretoria Cabinet. Pik Botha, the South African Foreign Secretary, who would have been most directly responsible, adds that Laurens played a valuable role in carrying messages between himself and Mrs Thatcher – though one wonders why Pik needed to use an amateur when the diplomatic channels were functioning smoothly, and also whether this version enhances in retrospect Pik's own role at a time when his rivals in the South African Department of Information were intruding on the Department of Foreign Affairs's responsibilities.[14] Once again, Laurens was greatly exaggerating his involvement at a lofty level in international politics.*

After the Lancaster House settlement, Laurens continued to take a close and, with hindsight, misguided view. In January 1980 he wrote to Rowan Cronje, a junior but influential minister in the interim Government, to suggest that after Bishop Muzorewa's electoral victory, Prince Charles be appointed Governor-General to head a period of reconciliation; he added, unrealistically, 'I would see that this appointment takes place.'

A few months later, writing to Piet Koornhof, Laurens was ready to change his mind and also to put Rhodesia behind him – 'Rhodesia RIP', as he put it. He seems to have adjusted his thinking to the (to him) unexpected victory of Mugabe. He admits that, having seen Bishop Muzorewa again, he realises how incapable he would have been of hand-

---

*In March 1992 he told Britain's Charity Commissioners that 'There were moments . . . when I stood alone but effectively between mandatory sanctions and South Africa when even the Prime Minister and her husband felt like giving up and going with the rest of the world . . . At Lancaster House I was able to help prevent South Africa in the last stage of the [Rhodesian] internal war from getting militarily openly involved.'[15]

ling a government, not to speak of an inevitable civil war. He suggests to South Africa that 'the risk of supporting the Mugabe regime unobtrusively, is far less than the risk we run of not supporting them.'[16]

From Zimbabwe, all attention switched to South Africa, where a far greater crisis was developing throughout the 1980s. As Laurens wrote to Piet Koornhof on 2 September 1980: 'I saw the Prime Minister again last night and we talked, among other things, a great deal about South Africa. She and, indeed, Lord Carrington, are very worried about South Africa ... the Prime Minister and Carrington have immense goodwill for South Africa and, as always, they want to help, but the extent and power with which they can help really depends on what South Africa does within its own frontiers to transform and give its society the contemporary character which it lacks.' Koornhof replied that nothing could stop the process of reform. He was wrong, and he would lose his Cabinet job in consequence.[17]

Nelson Mandela had been in jail, mainly on Robben Island, since 1964 and only a tiny number of people knew that in 1985 he had begun discussions with the apartheid Government of President P. W. Botha. Afrikanerdom was approaching a period of re-assessment of the fundamentals of apartheid, led, interestingly enough, by new leaders of their normally hard-line secret society, the Broederbond. In 1983 P. W. Botha had introduced his most radical offering, a Tricameral Constitution for the Whites, Coloureds and Indians. It was a flop. The United Democratic Front – a cover for the banned ANC – was formed in 1983, and mass resistance to the Government grew steadily in the mid-1980s. In August 1985 Botha delivered his famous 'Rubicon' speech which signalled his refusal to proceed down the path of reform. That same winter the international banks began to stop rolling over their loans to the country, a sanction which was to prove more effective than any other.[18]

The years 1985–1994 have been correctly described as the Decade of Negotiation, which essentially and miraculously set South Africa on the path to majority rule and its escape from revolution. F. W. de Klerk took over from P. W. Botha in early 1989 and on 2 February 1990 delivered his historic speech to Parliament in which he legalised the ANC, and from 11 February, released Mandela. After many difficulties, democratic elections were held in April 1994 and on 10 May 1994 President Mandela was inaugurated. Throughout these tempestuous (and crudely summarised) years the elderly Laurens constantly attempted, from London and with frequent visits to South Africa, to play a part.

32

The Prime Minister

THE RHODESIAN BUSINESS was only one aspect of Laurens's growing relationship with Margaret Thatcher after she came to power in May 1979. He had first met her in the mid-1970s, introduced by Airey Neave, the Opposition spokesman on Northern Ireland and Mrs Thatcher's campaign chief during her 1975 leadership battle, and quickly developed a relationship in which he became both a personal friend and an unofficial adviser. He first set out his store, so to speak, when in February 1976 he sent her an enormous 7,500-word letter which he described as the 'briefest of summaries' of his manifesto for modern Conservatism. The 'letter' was addressed to Airey Neave.* Laurens explained that Mrs Thatcher had requested this document, in which Laurens came clean about his own Conservative Party allegiance when he referred to her as 'our leader'.

Laurens's arguments were wordy and imprecise. He wrote about the loss of the will to work in British society, about irrational strikes, the estrangement of the young, the West's failure of belief in its own values, the resurgence of the tyranny of government, the vicious intellectual attack on the concept of individual freedom, the danger to traditional institutions, the absence of a sense of history – the sort of thing which would go down well in any suburban golf club and which proved such an effective Conservative platform. Laurens concluded, bizarrely, that Labour was 'the party of privilege and power . . . Conservatives the party of the increasingly dispossessed'. He urged that Mrs Thatcher stand firm on the continuing threat from Russia which, not content with its vast empire in Europe and Asia, was now planning to move into Africa just as the West was dismantling its own African empires. As a result of Moscow's propagandist education programme, there must be by now, he said, at least 100,000 'carefully conditioned, brain-washed African agents of Soviet policies' (recalling *Flamingo Feather*).

---

*Neave would be assassinated by the IRA in March 1979.

This brought him to Rhodesia on which, as we have seen, he believed himself well informed. Nothing, he said, not even the UDI which we all deplored, could justify a terrorist war, and Mr Wilson's Labour Government ought never to have taken the issue to the United Nations when the greater issue was that the whole of Africa was under threat of being swallowed up by the Soviet Empire. Laurens called on Mrs Thatcher to 'make it clear that they have had enough of appeasement in international as well as internal affairs'. Angola, he obscurely added, had been 'the gravest international act of appeasement since Munich'. The Labour Party now in power was not the natural party of Britain, as the Prime Minister proclaimed, but, 'the least natural to us, the most "foreign" ideological intrusion ever into our political affairs'. Laurens ended by apologising for his lengthiness and suggested that it might be possible to extract several themes, each of which could be turned into a major policy speech.[1]

This was the first of a sequence of memoranda which Laurens would prepare for Mrs Thatcher over the next fifteen years, though he would in future send them directly to the lady herself as their friendship developed. Initially, he told his friends, he found her 'moderately impressive', and he particularly appreciated what he saw as her real interest in Africa, which was possibly strengthened by Denis Thatcher's knowledge of, and prejudices about, South Africa; but any reservations were soon dispelled as he wrote to her of his 'warmest regards, respect and gratitude'. She replied in similarly warm terms, and Laurens was able to invite the Thatchers to Chelsea dinner parties which might include Prince Charles, Charles Douglas-Home, Editor of *The Times*, and, later, Chief Mangosuthu Buthelezi. When Mrs Thatcher became Prime Minister in May 1979 she made a point of writing to ask him to keep in close touch – which he was delighted to do.[2]

His first contribution, in late July 1979, sent in the first instance to Airey Neave to brief Mrs Thatcher on her visit to the Commonwealth Conference in Lusaka, was two long memoranda about Rhodesia, which he based on his own time governing a rebellious situation when he was 'Military Governor in Java'. At the same time Laurens wrote to Ian Smith urging him to hold on and wait for 'truly creative political action' from Mrs Thatcher once Lusaka was over; Laurens said he was now more hopeful after 'these past terrible years under Labour'. Once again, he emphasised that Rhodesia was a *domestic* British concern, nothing to do with the United Nations. Britain had for fifteen years been blackmailed – he notes the pun – by the new African countries which had projected (in the psychologists' sense) their own errors and shortcomings on the earlier authority: 'They have failed to improve on the system they inherited from us, starting already with an inferiority complex which detribalisation and rule by foreigners – however well-disposed and superb – imposed on them. The discovery that they are in reality proving inferior has driven them slightly mad, and is making them madder by the day.' Laurens warned Mrs Thatcher that in the Lusaka Conference she would be faced with 'a most dangerous and inflammable psychological situation', compounded by the Australians' and New Zealanders' guilt for exterminating their own Aborigines, and Canada with its own neuroses. Regard Lusaka as a clinical situation, Laurens counselled: listen but do not appease; stand fast in your own sanity; draw on your own vision and intuition so as to save Africa from itself. And by all means, let the Queen go to Lusaka: 'the world can only be saved by adding long-neglected feminine values to stagnant masculine power . . . Africa [longs] to be saved from its corrupted new self.'[3]

If the Foreign Office diplomats had known that this document was sitting in the Prime Minister's red box, they might well have grown pale. In the event, Mrs Thatcher did take a firm line at the Lusaka gathering. As she wrote in her memoirs, 'Our strategy was to take full responsibility ourselves for reaching a [Rhodesian] settlement.' In a hostile atmosphere she stuck to her guns and, she considered afterwards, won back enough goodwill to call the Lancaster House Conference in London which led to a cease-fire, elections, and to the surprise of both herself and Laurens, Robert Mugabe's victory. Zimbabwe's Independence followed on 18 April 1980. The Prime Minister in these memoirs noted that Laurens had been 'very helpful when we were negotiating independence for Zimbabwe', which must be a reference to his advice to her personally rather than any assistance to the Foreign Office.[4] After Lancaster House, Laurens's credentials, and his access to the leader of his adopted country, had been established. He was in his vigorous seventies and now had a political position. He was happy to be out of step with the new African orthodoxy.

Laurens used this Downing Street access discreetly over the next years. He occasionally arranged for Mrs Thatcher to see his friends – Charles Janson, for instance, to discuss Eastern Europe, or, twice, Dr van Zyl Slabbert, the South African liberal politician, when the South African opposition was struggling to get international attention. He sometimes tried to lobby her support for friends in need. She invited him to the Trooping of the Colour and he used his privileged position to persuade Central Television to let him film a television interview of her inside Number 10. The filming in Number 10 exasperated the producer,

Peter Bevan, because Laurens insisted on asking the most servile questions of the Prime Minister, while behind the camera Bevan was urging him to behave more like a TV interviewer. Laurens was widely ridiculed in the press for his excessively respectful manner. His knighthood had been announced in the New Year's Honours of 1 January 1981. Some people thought it was recognition for his services to literature; others, on the inside track, were encouraged to think that it was acknowledgement for his contribution to the Rhodesian settlement; but there is no great mystery – Laurens was by now an intimate of both the Prince of Wales and of the Prime Minister and, with hindsight, it would have been surprising if he had *not* been offered an honour; he had fantasised about such an elevation from his youth, when he read about the Court of King Arthur. He wrote in unctuous terms to thank Mrs Thatcher: 'I believe it will enable me to serve you and what you represent with a semblance of greater authority in the eyes of a world obsessed with appearances.' His family were given to understand that when the Queen knighted him she said that she had been looking forward to doing this for some time.[5]

It was a matter of wonder, and often concern, to senior officials, particularly in the Foreign Office across the road from Downing Street, that Laurens had such ready access to the Prime Minister. As several of their most senior number now agree, they would thrash out with her a policy on some delicate aspect concerning Southern Africa, and then Laurens would arrive and tell her a string of stories about the Zulus, 'to which she would listen with delight, her jaw agape', in the words of one mandarin – after which British policy would have changed again![6] Such anecdotes may have been embroidered over the years, but Laurens was always a brilliant storyteller and could mesmerise his most sophisticated audiences with his tales.

Laurens undoubtedly was close to the Prime Minister, one of her trusted advisers and friends.* They were near-neighbours off the King's Road, Chelsea, when she was in Opposition, and used to meet socially, usually at small and informal supper parties in Laurens's apartment on a Sunday evening. Lady Thatcher, as she had become, emphasised his qualities in an interview four years after his death: 'He was not only a wise man but also a great idealist,' she told the present writer. 'No evil thought

---

*Laurens was sometimes irritated that his letters and memoranda did not always get through to the Prime Minister. He blamed Charles Powell, her Private Secretary, and on one occasion protested that the policemen at the door of 10 Downing Street had been intercepting his letters. Lord Powell today replies that it was his job to filter the Prime Minister's In-tray.[7]

ever entered his mind!' 'Of all the unique people I know, Laurens was by far the most unique . . . He was very wise and very modest.' More than that, he was 'the most practical idealist I've ever known.' She felt that he was a charmer without being aware of his charm. She had particularly looked to him for guidance over Southern African affairs, where he gave her 'more than wisdom, an integral human sympathy'.*

Lady Thatcher was happy to confirm that 'Laurens influenced me very much because of his wisdom'; she also remembered that he had introduced her to Chief Buthelezi, whom she said she would afterwards meet quite often. Was it true that, after she had left office, when visiting South Africa she had once declared 'I am a Zulu!'? Lady Thatcher replied, 'I'm on the side of the Zulus, so it's quite possible.'[9] Here was Laurens's charm still at work.

Laurens's influence on Government was likely to diminish as the Thatcherite years went by and the Prime Minister grew in confidence and authority. But he was at the height of this influence – always private, never admitted except in his personal circle – when Mrs Thatcher encountered her greatest challenge: the Falklands War of 1982.

It has frequently been written that his role was to 'stiffen' Mrs Thatcher's resolve to take the firmest principled line on the Argentine invasion. Though it might be questioned whether Mrs Thatcher ever needed any stiffening, there is some truth in this. After she had appeared on television on 7 April, for instance, Laurens wrote to applaud her and also to urge her to make it clear that the British position on the Falklands surpassed even the issue of sovereignty because it was based on the fundamental principle of the Western Alliance – that naked aggression would never, anywhere, be permitted: there could be no compromise, and no diplomacy, until this was accepted. He added, 'with my experience of war', that the Opposition talk of a bloodbath was nonsense, because on islands with so vast a coastline there would be no need to start by attacking Port Stanley. Lady Thatcher specifically refers in her memoirs to 'a wonderful letter – one of a number over the years – from Laurens van der Post'.

On 15 May, he drew the Prime Minister's attention to a leader in *The Times* which, he said, 'was written in the course of a long dialogue I have been having with Charles Douglas-Home [a friend of his]'. Stand fast, he

---

*This relationship with Laurens was part of her style of government: she had a group of unofficial advisers and friends outside the system, which included people like David Hart and Woodrow Wyatt as well as Laurens, whose private opinions and information she would employ in her arguments with her civil servants.[8]

urged her, we are not merely dealing with the fate of 1,800 people, because these 1,800 are 'the proxies of the future fate of perhaps 38 million as in the last War'. He reminded her of Britain's failure in the late 1920s to join with France and the US to suppress the Japanese sally into Manchuria. Since the war the British people had been languishing because they had not been asked to give of their best: all their best values 'have been daily fudged out of their consciousness by Parliament, by Trade Unions, by intellectuals and by a general *trahison des clercs*.' This would be their first real challenge. If you fudge this issue, he warned the Prime Minister, 'you will have lost the next General Election and also lost Britain the chance of recovering its true historical self for which it is so desperately searching . . . There has been far too much talk . . . In the name of God and the future, put a stop to it as soon as possible and act.'[10]

Mrs Thatcher did indeed act, and the Argentines would surrender on 14 June.

With Mrs Thatcher's re-election to power in May 1983, Laurens continued a warm social as well as political relationship, which now focussed increasingly on the fast-deteriorating situation in South Africa. He was becoming attracted by a vision of a federal solution to South African problems, and therefore interested in the possible role of the Zulu leader, Chief Mangosuthu Buthelezi. He arranged for Buthelezi to dine with him and the Thatchers one Sunday evening in July 1985. More urgently, he was committing himself to a battle against the imposition of international sanctions on his homeland – a policy which Laurens passionately rejected. In this battle he proposed to employ his strongest weapon, that is to say, Margaret Thatcher. In October 1985 he sent her a memorandum which encapsulated the views he would preach for the rest of the decade.

He started by reminding her of their shared abhorrence of apartheid. What, then, of the growing clamour around the world to join in these economic sanctions against South Africa? He reminded her of Abraham's anguish over the impending destruction of Sodom and Gomorrah, which the angels said could be spared if only ten good people could be found. 'Is there not a moral for this in all sanctioneers who would harm innocents not in tens but in millions?' The confrontation was with a special form of government in Pretoria, not with the people and the country. What of the thousands of white opponents of apartheid who protested that sanctions would be harmful? (In fact considerable numbers of people opposed to apartheid inside South Africa called for sanctions as their best hope of release.) South Africa's history, he went on, was that of a growing sense of psychological isolation, an isolation which must be overcome, not intensified. 'One cannot achieve the right by the wrong means.' Consider – he told the Prime Minister – the experience of sanctions elsewhere, as in Rhodesia, where they had failed (a debatable conclusion). 'More than ninety per cent of [South Africans] reject [sanctions] passionately' (he cites no source). To cut off trading contact with South Africa would remove a major instrument for change, greatly increase black unemployment, and incidentally add hundreds of thousands to Britain's unemployed queues by damaging an important export market. Sanctions would reduce South Africa to 'a state of extreme economic and social misery, full of hungry rank and tatter millions confronted with a task of taking their scorched earth over . . . Sanctions are wrong, not only wrong and evil but will defeat the purpose which sanctions propose to uphold.'[11]

It was an eloquent exposition of the anti-sanctions argument, though it made no attempt to understand the contrary (and, it may be argued, eventually victorious) position. Mrs Thatcher appears to have found it persuasive. She cannot have been hard to convince. 'I no more shared the established Foreign Office view of Africa than I did of the Middle East,' she later wrote in her memoirs. Yes, fundamental changes must be made in the South African political system, but 'the worst approach was to isolate South Africa further. Indeed, the isolation had already gone too far.' Here is the unmistakable voice of Laurens, and also no doubt of her husband Denis's famous 'saloon-bar' views about the country which he knew well. 'Tribal loyalties were of great importance,' Lady Thatcher went on: 'For example, the Zulus are a proud and self-conscious nation with a distinct sense of identity . . . It was South Africa's isolation which was an obstacle to reform . . . Capitalism itself was probably the greatest force for reform and political liberalisation . . .'

For the time being, Laurens had evidently won the argument with the Foreign Office, even as the Prime Minister took a personal decision to send Robin Renwick as British Ambassador to Pretoria. He was a diplomat, blooded in Rhodesia, who would do as much as anyone to warn London of the inevitable future, and as Ambassador he would soon enjoy Laurens's public friendship and private abuse.

Mrs Thatcher came under growing pressure for her South African views, especially from the Commonwealth, and some of her most difficult moments came at a sequence of Commonwealth meetings during the second half of her Premiership. After one unpleasant confrontation she remembers, in her memoirs, 'It was a relief to dine that evening with my good friend Laurens van der Post who talks good sense about South Africa.' This 'good sense' continued to work on her even as she admitted that in 1990 'the movement which I had hoped and worked for' began. She confessed to being initially disappointed with the released Nelson Mandela ('very outdated in his attitudes, stuck in a kind of socialist time-warp'), but she was glad that due regard was being paid to Chief Buthelezi. When she met Mandela she made a point of urging him to meet Buthelezi personally to try to end the violence between their supporters.[12] All of this carries the echo of Laurens's backstage voice.

South Africa was by no means the only area in which Laurens offered his views to the Prime Minister. He tackled her, for instance, on his fears for the future of the ethnic minorities of the Kalahari – to which she replied, forgivably, that she did not really see what she could do – and held forth at length about the latest developments in Russia and Germany, in a memorandum which managed to bring in Herman Hesse, Dostoyevsky, Bismarck, Helmut Köhl, Gibraltar, Edward VIII, much popular history, and the recommendation that 'the Latins must be divorced somehow from this dubious flirtation with . . . the excitable, hysterical and unstable German soul.' On 4 September 1980 he wrote to her at length about how she should tackle a forthcoming summit with the French President Giscard d'Estaing: 'Speaking as someone whose grandmother was French . . .'[13]

Though his influence on Margaret Thatcher personally seems clear enough, it is difficult to assess his impact on her government after her re-election in 1987. Over the remaining years of his life Laurens would respond to South Africa's breakneck transition to democratic majority rule with a combination of bitter disappointment, an ungenerous and undisguised hostility to the emerging leaders, and a dangerous support for something approaching tribal secession by the Zulus.

33

The Films

Laurens enjoyed the cinema but he was in no way a *cinéaste*. He sometimes told friends that he had once been a film critic, but there is no evidence of it. From the beginning, however, he had a keen sense, as many authors did, of the financial rewards that might follow if his books could be turned into films. Over more than forty years he sought out potential producers – and collected a steady flow of option fees. In the end the result was disappointing, at least in artistic terms. Only two films were made: *Merry Christmas Mr Lawrence* in 1983, and *A Far Off Place* in 1994, a Hollywood extraction from his two Bushman novels, which after tortuous delays took wild liberties with his books and was a commercial failure.

From the moment of the sensational success of *Venture to the Interior* in 1952, Laurens was approached by agents and producers, although it is hard to see how that particular book could have been considered filmable. John Huston, for example, was asking to see the book as early as February 1952, and the Jaffa Agency in Los Angeles in July 1951 thought that there would be a market for it after the great success of *King Solomon's Mines*.[1] Nothing came of this interest until publication of *Flamingo Feather* in 1955 – 'the best adventure story I have read since Buchan,' wrote the MGM 'scout' in London. Of the studios which showed interest, Paramount Pictures eventually emerged the winner, offering $75,000 for an option which they quickly exercised. Laurens was assured that the film would be directed by Alfred Hitchcock, who had just had a success with an international thriller set in North Africa, *The Man Who Knew Too Much*. The mistake he and the Hogarth Press made, in their innocence, was to sell the film rights in perpetuity. The project – as so often in the world of cinema – did not go ahead. Hitchcock travelled to Southern Africa to prepare to shoot the film in spring 1956 and was alarmed by the logistical obstacles; he returned to Hollywood where he had another proposal which he preferred and which eventually became the classic *Vertigo*.[2]

Laurens's book sat on the Paramount shelves for no less than forty-five years. Although they had no intention of making the film, they insisted that they would only release the rights for $75,000 and refused any reversion without payment. Laurens was indignant about this for the rest of his life: 'The rights I sold . . . were the rights to make a film, not the rights to "not make a film",' he wrote to Paramount on 14 May 1990. His close friend, the London-based film producer Eva Monley, tried for years to buy the rights to *Flamingo Feather*, although she realised the plot would have to be largely rewritten. Only on his death-bed did Laurens permit her to attempt a financial offer to Paramount: 'Make this film just for me,' he said to her. She eventually did a deal with Paramount, for a yearly option of $10,000, in 1999.[3]

Laurens pressed on with other proposals. In August 1956, he wrote directly to Walt Disney in person to propose a documentary film about Africa – a subject 'of immense human appeal', though he declined to give any detail.[4] There is no sign of a reply from Mr Disney. It would be another thirty-five years before Laurens's approach to Disney came good in another form. Laurens was at this time also interested in, and distracted by, his television work. There was talk in New York, and also in London, of a film of *The Seed and the Sower*, but nothing would come of that either for some years.

Laurens's hopes for a film revived after he published his Kalahari novels, *A Story Like the Wind* and *A Far-Off Place*. He was approached in mid-1976 by a wealthy young man called Grahame Amey, who bred horses in the Welsh borders near Crickhowell. Although an amateur in the world of cinema, Amey was determined to make a film of the two novels, and set up a company called Quaternio in which his fellow directors were Laurens, Dennis Hill, a psychotherapist, and Alan Stratford-Johns, at that time playing 'Inspector Barlow' on television. Laurens was greatly taken with this project and told the Hogarth Press to grant an option for a nominal £1. Larry Boulting, son of the well-known producer Roy Boulting, was to prepare the script. Laurens expected to get between £10,000 and £25,000 for the film rights in addition to his profits as a principal shareholder in Quaternio. There was talk of beginning shooting in mid-1977.[5]

Nothing was to be so easy. There were tensions within the team: Christopher Miles, who had a good track record after making *The Virgin and the Gipsy*, was appointed director, and Larry Boulting later withdrew. Laurens told people – without justification – that the actors who had agreed to appear included John Mills, Janet Suzman, Peter O'Toole, even Jason Robards. Paramount, according to Laurens, had declared that

Larry Boulting's screenplay was 'the finest film script they had seen for the past few years'. Laurens, trying to help raise funds towards the £1.5 million budget, pulled out the stops: he wrote to a South African contact seeking funding, 'It is a film subject which will let the humanities of South Africa speak to what is left of humanity in the wide world beyond our frontiers.'[6]

In July 1977 Laurens was in correspondence with G. W. G. Browne, Secretary for Finance at the South African Treasury. He reminded Browne that during his recent visit to Cape Town he had discussed with his Minister an investment of Rand 3 million in a film which would be 'the first truly anti-terrorist document that will come out of South Africa'; these funds would make possible worldwide distribution which would 'allow its anti-terrorist message to reach the widest possible public'. Laurens, the anti-apartheid campaigner, was at the same time seeking funds from the Pretoria Goverment to finance a film of his novels.[7]

But the project eventually stalled. Laurens, weary of the frustrations of trying to launch a major film from an amateur British base, realised that he and Amey were playing out of their league, so they decided to set their sights on Hollywood. He afterwards said that he had lost £10,000 in the project and Grahame Amey £50,000.[8]

One reason why Laurens's thoughts turned to Hollywood was that he had met the actor and director Robert Redford a couple of years earlier: they got on well, and talked about travelling together one day in the South African bush. Laurens, encouraged by a brisk and affectionate correspondence with Redford's assistant, Barbara Maltbee, between 1977 and 1982, hatched a scheme to persuade Redford to star either as Mopani, the wise white hunter in *A Story Like the Wind*, or in a film based on *The Seed and the Sower*. Redford's agreement would of course have made it easy to raise Hollywood funds.[9]*

Another reason why Laurens turned his attention to Hollywood was that in 1980 Eva Monley turned up in his Chelsea penthouse with a proposal. Eva Monley, brought up in Kenya, had worked closely with Otto Preminger, and also on the film of *Lawrence of Arabia*. She and Laurens rapidly became good friends, a relationship which lasted until his death. Eva was determined to make a film of *A Story Like the Wind* and optimistically reckoned she could do it in two years. In fact it took eleven years to the day between Eva's first meeting with Laurens and the first day of shooting.

---

*Redford eventually made *Out of Africa* in 1985, a totally different project.

These eleven years were taken up with a bewildering sequence of negotiations and manoeuvres. Eva started off by taking an option for a film; she was joined by a formidable American intermediary called Kathy Kennedy, a colleague of Steven Spielberg, who put up $45,000 for an option which, when eventually exercised, brought Laurens the balance of $300,000. The first deal was with Warner Brothers (who eventually dropped it), then Spielberg; in the end, Disney made the film in association with Spielberg. Laurens was deeply involved in every twist and turn. His impatience was perhaps soothed by the fact that Kennedy continued extending the option at $15,000 a year until in April 1992 her company bought the film rights for the full $300,000. The film was shot in South Africa, Botswana and Namibia in 1992 and 1993.[10]

After so many years, and so many rewrites, it is hardly surprising that the film, at last called *A Far Off Place*, was a near-travesty of the books. Laurens had by now learned to be stoical about the way in which his tales were changed. Understandably, as he realised, it was necessary to amend the plot-line: the villains could no longer be African nationalists officered by the Chinese, so they became mere poachers. Maybe it was necessary to delete the character of the Bushman wife who is one of the foursome who cross the Kalahari Desert. But Laurens was devastated when Kathy Kennedy took it upon herself, as shooting was starting, to switch the roles of the teenage boy and girl, thus altering the whole balance and structure of Laurens's tale. This dislodging of a young male hero figure was for all sorts of reasons unacceptable to him. Visually, the finished film was stunning, set in the desert landscapes which had been reconnoitred with his and Tom Bedford's help. Steven Spielberg did the final cut but, as Eva Monley later observed wryly, 'he achieved no miracles'.

Disney chose to release *A Far Off Place* in the same week as their blockbuster *Jurassic Park*. It never recovered from this, and it didn't help that the reviews were mixed. The film was, in effect, withdrawn from full-scale marketing and distribution because the company decided that it did not have adequate 'playability'. The film never made any money: indeed, the Hollywood accountants at one stage demonstrated by their weird methods that it had lost $40 million.[11]

While this drama was dragging on, there was happier news of another of Laurens's books. In April 1979, his friend and translator in Japan, Professor Kimiyoshi Yura, wrote to say that Nagisa Oshima had been moved by *The Seed and the Sower*, and wanted to make a film drawing on the three stories. Oshima was the leading Japanese film director, successor to Kurosawa in international esteem, and Laurens – like Norah Smallwood – was enthusiastic: 'It is one of the nicest things that has ever happened to me personally; to have the Japanese find sufficient validity in my portrayal of their national characteristics in war and peace and make a film about it,' he wrote.

While Oshima was working on his own screenplay, Laurens busied himself in letters to Tokyo urging his own interpretation of the three linked stories while also stressing that he understood that a film and a book were very different things. He suggested various actors – including Robert Redford: 'I have an intuition that you will find him a person after your own heart and my own.' In February 1980 Laurens visited Japan for a week as Oshima's guest and in March Oshima met Redford in New York.[12]

This part of the plan broke down. Redford and his assistant Barbara Maltbee thoroughly disliked Oshima's screenplay, deciding that he had 'missed the book's heart and soul' and come up with a version suffering from serious structural problems. Laurens accepted that there would now be no chance of using Redford, but tried to explain to Redford and Barbara why he had so liked and respected Oshima when he met him. 'At the core of his vision . . .' he wrote, 'is an unmistakable dislike of Japanese traditionalism . . . He is an incurable, radical romantic determined to make the Japanese face up to what is false and dishonourable both in their past and their present.'

Laurens then had the tricky task of telling Oshima what he thought of his screenplay. It was, he said (contradicting what he had just written to Barbara Maltbee), 'a far-reaching, imaginative and gripping interpretation of *The Seed and the Sower* . . .' In a long letter, he queried Oshima's suggested title of 'Merry Christmas Mr Lawrence' but pressed on with his more serious objection, which was Oshima's introduction (in his first draft) of a specifically homosexual episode in the first scene. Laurens insisted that in his POW years there had been only one slight incident of homosexuality, surprising though that may seem. He also warned Oshima that a graphic homosexual scene would get the film banned in England and America. He suggested that Oshima pay for him to come out to Japan again to concentrate on a rewrite, and Oshima agreed. Laurens at this time was sending Oshima detailed briefings on conditions in the camps.

He continued to worry about Oshima's emphasis on a homosexual subtext: 'I have asked myself repeatedly why, since the introduction of this homosexual element in your first version of the book, it should have acquired so great a hold on your imagination that it is enlarged and penetrates more deeply and further into the heart of the second screenplay version . . . It seems to me that there is just a shade of implication that

Yonoi's obsession with Celliers might be an unconscious homosexual one. This, of course, could not be more remote from the truth of the original story . . . Yonoi's "fascination" with "beautiful" Celliers is that he too recognised him as a man of the same kind as himself, but one of whom his intuitive self tells him has broken out of the trap and redeemed his betrayal. The individual betrayal which in the sum of the lives of all of us leads to its collective betrayal in the form of war.' The 'implication' of a homosexual theme, he said, would cause bewilderment and incomprehension in the West.[13]

Different versions of the script went to and fro in 1980, and in the end Laurens's protests did not count for much. The film continued to imply, to most viewers, that the extremely handsome Captain Yonoi was attracted physically to Celliers, played as a New Zealander, not a South African, by the also handsome rock musician David Bowie. Laurens had nothing to do with the imaginative casting of Bowie, and was overruled in his wish that the book's important scene in Palestine be retained. It is hard to see why Laurens should have been surprised by the way things were moving. David Bowie was notorious as the first rock star who had declared his bisexuality (Captain Yonoi was also to be played by a rock star). Oshima's films – did Laurens know of them? – were highly controversial: *Ai No Corrida* was so sexually explicit that it was banned in Britain for many years. It took all of 1981 to set up joint Anglo-Japanese financing *Merry Christmas Mr Lawrence* while Paul Mayersberg was hired to do the final rewrite, with Jeremy Thomas as producer and a budget of $4 million. Shooting at last began – in New Zealand and the Cook Islands, after other possibilities such as the Philippines and Indonesia had been discarded – in August 1982. The film was premiered in Tokyo on 12 April 1983 with Laurens in attendance, at the Cannes Festival in May, and at the Edinburgh Festival in August. Laurens arranged a private showing for Prince Charles and Princess Diana and reported to Oshima that they thought the film 'marvellous and deeply moving'.[14]

The film of *Merry Christmas Mr Lawrence* did adequately well and continues to be shown on television from time to time. It remains a curious blend of the three stories which make up *The Seed and the Sower*. From *A Bar of Shadow* it takes the detail of the Soekaboemi camp, a death sentence (to which it adds a mock execution), a vicious Warrant-Officer Hara, and John Lawrence's farewell to Hara in his prison cell – 'Merry Christmas, Mr Lawrence!' From *The Seed and the Sower* it takes Celliers, whom it makes the main character of the film, a few (non-South African) scenes of 'betrayal' of his young brother, in the village and at school, and the crucial episode when Celliers embraces the Japanese Commandant in order to save his fellow officer, an act which must ensure his own death. From *The Sword and the Doll*, it takes only John Lawrence's recollection of a brief encounter, this time chaste, with an (unseen) Dutch woman.

Oshima added to this stew his own ingredients: a lot of violence on the part of the Japanese guards, two graphic examples of harakiri, a portrait of the English CO (the Nichols figure) as stupid, John Lawrence talking fluent Japanese and, to Laurens's protests, the homosexual subtext, starting off with the execution of a guard for sodomising a prisoner. This theme is picked up in a scriptwriter's line which Laurens must have hated: 'Jack,' says John Lawrence to Celliers of Yonoi, 'I think he's taken a bit of a shine to you!'[15]

Because Oshima largely left out the events in *The Sword and the Doll*, Laurens was always keen to encourage other film producers who showed an interest. The history of these negotiations is confused by the additional prospect of filming *The Night of the New Moon*, his 1970 non-fiction description of the Java camp during the final days of the war. Over the years these two projects were sometimes combined, and Laurens seemed to see no gulf between his fictional and factual record of that period.

Peter Bevan (an Englishman working out of Hollywood)* first took an option on *The Night of the New Moon* in May 1981 for $5,000. Laurens was delighted. Bevan went to Java to research the project, aided by Laurens's letters of introduction, but it was soon clear that the Indonesians would not co-operate, or would have to be heavily bribed to do so. Once again Redford was mentioned. But the option expired in 1988 and the idea passed, for a nominal sum, to Eva Monley and Lesli Lia Glatter, under the title 'Full Moon in Java': if the option were exercised (and it was extended for $2,000), the purchase price for film rights would be $125,000.[16]

Laurens was by now an old man, and he was struggling to bring his own personal memories of the events of Java in 1942, in the days before the capitulation to the Japanese, together with versions he had made of these memories in *The Sword and the Doll* in 1963. That novella tells of a one-night affair between a British officer and an unnamed Dutch woman. After the war, the officer searches for the woman, and the child whom he thinks may have been conceived: he fails to find them. Laurens, as the years passed, began to regret what he saw as the 'ambivalence' of that story, and one of the reasons he hoped that *The Sword and the Doll*

---

*Bevan's partner, Jane Brewster, would later come to London to become Laurens's secretary and assistant, and in due course marry his nephew, Tom Bedford.

might be filmed was that he saw it as an opportunity to change the ending. He thought the film might end with the officer this time tracking down the woman and their daughter in Holland.[17]

The film people were delighted, since they believed it would make for a more congenial film, complete with happy ending, but *The Sword and the Doll* was never made, and the commercial failure of *A Far Off Place* did nothing to help the prospects of another van der Post film.

The most unlikely of Laurens's affairs with cinema lasted for five years and involved two American women in Hollywood, Candice van Runkle and Claire Townsend, who approached him in January 1989 with the proposal that they make a film of *A Mantis Carol.* They offered an annual option fee of $5,000 with a proposed purchase price of $150,000. Laurens, advised by Eva Monley, accepted. The two 'beloved girls', as Laurens was soon addressing them, came to London to meet him and Eva in June 1989, and Laurens was captivated by them, as they were by him.

One problem was that the two women had to make a living and were unable to give their full attention to the project, which could therefore only limp along, fuelled by professions of mutual admiration. This should have been the clue to the more fundamental impediment, which was that Candice and Claire were probably out of their depth. They had the enthusiasm but they did not have the experience to produce an adequate screenplay, in Laurens and Eva's eyes, and they did not have the contacts or the funding. Laurens let the project run on until July 1994, when they admitted that they had failed to achieve their dreams.[18] *A Mantis Carol,* a strange book, will never be filmed.

Some would argue that Laurens's books were essentially unfilmable because their quality lies in their unvisual elements. Some of his friends and professional contacts were always aware of this problem, but thought that a genius-director might find a way. Oshima probably went as far as was possible.

34

Fiction as Autobiography

YET BEING SOMEONE OTHER, published in 1982 and therefore written by Laurens in his mid-seventies, purports to be an autobiography. Widely accepted as such, it should rather be described as a fiction, or, better, a romance. Whether Laurens was entirely aware that he was writing a long and sustained fantasy cannot be known; maybe he should be given the benefit of the doubt. Why did no-one say so, however? There were still plenty of people alive who could have pointed out that he had lost touch with the reality they had shared. Were they inhibited by friendship, or loyalty, like Weary Dunlop? Had Laurens become so famous and distinguished, so close to the English Establishment, that he seemed immune to correction? Or perhaps they shook their heads ruefully and smiled among themselves about Laurens's notorious imagination . . .

The literary critics may perhaps be excused: how were they to know that they were reviewing fiction? Even the canny foreign correspondent James Cameron, writing in the *Evening Standard*, was respectfully trusting of the tale, though he balked at the verbosity: 'It must be said, with affectionate respect and praise, that Laurens van der Post is the most gentle and persuasive of bores.' Auberon Waugh, no respecter of persons, declared, 'It is impossible to put down . . . Sir Laurens retains an honesty and an innocence which somehow add weight to his conclusions . . . I have the feeling he is a very nice, very good man.' *The Listener* said that Laurens's gift for autobiography was special. Julian Symons, in *The Sunday Times*, had the wit to notice that Laurens's description of the voyage to Japan differed from William Plomer's but absolved him as a Jungian yearning for spiritual truths. In *The Times*, Christopher Booker, who was close to Laurens, faithfully reported his stories without question.[1] To the *New York Times*, which protested only that Laurens's prose was both exquisite and plodding, he was 'a hero of chastening humility and dignity'. To the *Los Angeles Times*, it was 'an astonishing, luminous story of a soul's journey'.[2] And none of them pointed out that it was in fact largely a work of his imagination!*

Laurens first planned *Yet Being Someone Other* in mid-1977, when he secured an invitation to sail first-class to Cape Town on the final voyage of the Union Castle line to South Africa before their weekly liner service to South Africa was withdrawn. He was allowed to take Frances, whom he does not mention in his book. They travelled on the *Windsor Castle* in August, after he had arranged a three-part series for the *Sunday Telegraph* who paid him £1,250 for each article, and another piece for *The Times*. He explained to Norah Smallwood that his first effort overran to 35,000 words and suggested he make a book out of the material. As late as March 1981 Laurens was using the title 'The Time Has Come', and suggested to his publisher that it be promoted as 'an autobiographical account of a journey through time and . . . an account of two long significant journeys undertaken, one in whalers and the other in a Japanese tramp ship'. Both would be adventures, he said, 'in the contemporary mind and spirit of man'. Laurens then suggested a different title, 'A Pattern of Timeless Moments', but they settled in the end for another T. S. Eliot quotation, 'Yet Being Someone Other', which Laurens said his friends preferred. John Charlton at Hogarth continued to wrestle with the problem of finding something better, but came up with nothing more acceptable before publication in 1982.[4]

Charlton understandably found the blurb difficult to write: Laurens helpfully suggested that he concentrate on 'the essence of what has made my life what it is today . . . It must be one of the most diverse and extraordinary for a writer of our time – perhaps there would be no harm if the blurb incorporated that with a certain amount of enthusiasm and confidence!' The Hogarth Press offered a £5,000 advance. The manuscript was even more untidy than usual and Norah Smallwood diplomatically decided to wait for a proof copy to send to William Morrow in New York, which was to pay a $6,000 advance. Everyone was pleased with a flattering new picture of Laurens, in meditative profile, in his Aldeburgh tower. Laurens asked Chatto/Hogarth never to mention his knighthood in any connection with his writing. Penguin paid another £5,000 advance on paperback rights and it was taken by the book clubs. The Japanese

*The present writer, in the *London Review of Books* on 3 February 1983, went out on what was then a slender limb and declared that he did not believe a word of this 'flabby and embarrassing stuff'.[3]

came in with $3,000, then the Germans.[5] Various people noted, too late, that Laurens's quotations from T. S. Eliot were inaccurate.

The title seems appropriate in the light of what we now know of Laurens's life. It comes from Eliot's *Little Gidding*: 'So I assumed a double part . . . I was still the same, – knowing myself and yet being someone other –'. Laurens always said he had been a friend of Eliot; in fact the two men did not meet before 1959, when Laurens wrote to 'Mr Elliott' (*sic*), who had suggested they meet.[6] The poet died in 1965. His widow, Valerie Eliot, became a friend.

As autobiography, the story is swaddled, as in a suffocating shawl, in the history and the meaning to South Africa of the Union Castle line (the origin of the book). The details of Laurens's childhood and family history often repeat the family myths of Laurens's earlier books. The inventions come thick and fast: the Dutch and French Huguenot ancestors in almost equal proportions; his family estates of 500,000 acres; his father heading one of the largest legal practices in the country; his childhood sense of kinship with the Zulus; his family's part in the 'battle' of Congella; the Bushman nanny Klara, now called Koba.

One can only speculate to what extent Laurens, in his mid-seventies, understood that his compulsion to make his experiences glisten with the ideal patterns of myth had taken over the story of his life. He would touch on the subject in the opening page of his next book, *About Blady*: 'Fiction has its own truth . . . the storyteller has all sorts of advantages which the reporter of the truth, with which I am concerned, does not possess . . . [The storyteller] can marry outer eventfulness with the inner eventfulness of a story that imagination bound to the here and now cannot do, because the truth of life will only yield to the truth attained in a pattern that has been lived.'[7]

His stories and careful presentation of himself, always outrageous, grew more extreme. He used to claim that he was dubbed 'Lawrence of Abyssinia' after his adventures in 1941. John Wells, the actor and satirist, remembered how as a teacher in Bavaria he had encountered Laurens as early as 1958: '[He] seemed to me to be more expensively dressed than anyone I had ever seen . . . He said his first language had been Zulu, his second Afrikaans . . . At the age of nineteen he had captained the South African hockey team, and soon afterwards set sail for England and learned to speak English for the first time.' A South African acquaintance remembers how she boarded a Union Castle ship to find that the list of passengers for deck tennis included a mysteriously discreet 'A. N. Other' and his partner: it turned out to be her old journalist colleague Laurens, who felt that his distinction required this device.[8]

Is it possible that he felt that the bald facts about himself were simply inadequate? Did he want to compel from others an admiration which the literal truth could not justify? Laurens had such magnetism, so much comfort he could offer if he chose, such an ability to bind spells with words, that he could achieve what he wanted. He *seemed to need* to be a figure on a mythic scale; nothing less would do. He was not slow to realise that, to a surprising extent, people will accept brilliantly presented stories as truth, or at very least will collude in a myth; it is rewarding to be associated with fame and distinction. He also must have realised that, once embarked on such a course, there was no going back. Once he had managed to gain acceptance for his image of himself, he would have become not only addicted to its effect on others but also obliged to go along with others' expectations of him. He had to maintain, burnish, develop this image, and he became increasingly skilful at it. He built up such willing credit that even when, as an old man, he went over the top with *Yet Being Someone Other*, most people still admired the emperor's clothes. It may be argued that Laurens was, above all else, a superb entertainer.

Throughout his life Laurens consciously understood that he was not interested in the literal truth. Put more bluntly, he was a compulsive liar. He expressed this, as we have seen, in his 1928 journal when he wrote about his visit to Roy Campbell: 'I have no moral objection to lies but they must be well done and contain imaginative qualities. Roy's were merely stupid.' On 8 March 1930 a curious little 'second leader' appeared in the *Cape Times*, unsigned but written in a week when we know that Laurens was writing leaders, and the style seems to be his; it certainly sums up his future position: 'There is an undeniable charm in the company of wholehearted liars . . . People who tell extravagant lies with obvious relish may be ridiculed, but they are seldom disliked: for their lies are not so much a calculated attempt to deceive their hearers, as an effort to escape from themselves. They are perverted fictionists, their lies being the product of a seething imagination which cannot find scope in ordinary affairs; and in that respect they are as worthy of attention as the poets who were responsible for the romantic and marvellous elements in Greek and Irish mythology.'[9]

Near the end of his life he returned to his poet friend Roy Campbell, in an unpublished manuscript recalling the *Voorslag* days, in a manner which suggests a personal recognition: 'Roy Campbell . . . very often allowed his fantasy to get the better of the literal truth and factual eventuality. People accused him of lying about himself. I do not think it could be called lying. I think he was so deeply absorbed in the images that kept on pouring into him from his own dreaming unconscious, his own need of a personal mythology so kept him on the path of poetic meaning which was a constant hunger in him, that he could not help it.'

Does this sound familiar? The point becomes more interesting if we take it beyond the inventions with which Laurens embellished his daily life; the literal truth was never of much interest to him because he preferred the truth of the imagination. This was not merely a version which was delivered to the outside world, it was allowed to invade his private life: for instance, as early as 1941 he sent his beloved Ingaret a long fictitious description of his wartime exploits in Abyssinia over six silent months when he had in fact been in the Middle East.[10]

Sometimes Laurens would resort to bluff. In 1964 an American Professor, Frederic Carpenter, set out to write a biography in which Laurens co-operated: he exchanged letters, he gave several interviews, and he asked friends like Plomer to meet Carpenter. On 21 May 1964 Laurens wrote to the unfortunate professor: 'The biographical information in all my non-fiction books can be taken as fact. I draw in my novels obviously on my own experience of life, but the lead of day-to-day reality there has gone through the alchemical process we call fiction and, therefore, cannot be dealt with as two-dimensional fact.' This letter goes on to state, falsely, that before the war he had 'published numerous short stories and literary essays in all sorts of periodicals', all of which had been lost in the Blitz. After the book came out – it was complimentary and did not question any of the public record – Laurens always denied his participation and claimed that he was so indignant about the attempt that he had never opened the finished product. Yet Laurens wrote later to Carpenter in December 1977, 'I always remember with immense gratitude and warmth the way in which you gave public recognition to my work and supported what I have tried to do in life.'[11]

He felt bound to fictionalise the truth, even in the most trivial ways. On 5 September 1991, for instance, he wrote a business letter to his publisher and good friend, John Charlton, in which he described the 'strict Calvinist world' of his childhood, his own family being at odds with the village, his father being 'the equivalent of a Prime Minister', his sister as the first woman in the free state to go to a South African university, his father's feuds with both 'the parson and the magistrate', and so on. It can be shown that not a single word of this is true.[12]*

---

*Laurens was increasingly addicted to writing *curricula vitae* on any excuse and these became more and more fanciful, so that by his last years they had completely lost touch with the truth. He obsessively re-told, in his lectures as in his writing, the African (or Sufi) story of the man who dies in his pursuit of the 'feather of truth'. There may be

The question arises why an Afrikaner, brought up in a moralistic culture, should feel so tempted by the freedom of fantasy. Evidently the inclination was there from his youth when, isolated in a small community, inspired by his father's excellent European library, under-acknowledged, one imagines, in so large a crowd of siblings, he dreamed of the Quest for the Grail, of Odysseus, of the Knights of the Round Table. It is not so surprising that novelists, whose gifts lie in their imagination, are particularly prone to recreate their own lives. Very recently, for example, Patrick O'Brian, the masterly author of a long series of sea dramas, has been revealed as inventing his entire autobiography, and Jeffrey Archer's *curriculum vitae* has been described as 'a life of lies'. Bruce Chatwin invented his life and death, as did Richard Llewellyn and Laurie Lee. The film actor Trevor Howard made up a story of heroism during the war. In the wise words of Jan Morris: in the end O'Brian's books do not succeed because 'in O'Brian . . . I am reading the word of an artificer, a contriver of genius, and, well, a liar.' But neither O'Brian nor Archer, Chatwin nor Lee, ever proposed themselves as teachers of the highest moral and spiritual values, as did Laurens. The writer Martha Gellhorn, once married to Ernest Hemingway, has analysed what she scathingly described as Hemingway's 'mythomania' – 'Anything uncomfortable he off-loaded with a lie. He lied about everything . . . Having lived with a mythomaniac, I know they believe everything they say, they are not conscious liars, they invent to increase everything about themselves and their lives and *believe* it.'[14]

But Laurens, however mythomaniacal he may have become, surely could not believe 'everything'. At some degree of depth he would have known that he had been evacuated from Abyssinia in April 1941. He knew that he had not enlisted in September 1939. He must have been aware that he had not co-founded Capricorn. The point is that Laurens, disposed from his early years to embroider and invent, discovered at the decisive period of his life that, thanks to his charm, his eloquence and his apparent confidence, he could *get away with* embroidery and invention. This gave him the fatal – no, the successful and profitable – encouragement to embrace the un-truth as the pattern of his life. *A Mantis Carol,*

a clue somewhere in Laurens's tantalising admission of a dichotomy in his own character. 'Laurens Jan' named his own son 'Jan Lawrence'. As described above, his *alter ego* in the prison camp was 'John Lawrence', who not only featured in *The Seed and the Sower* but was first seen in a short story in camp newspaper, 'Mark Time'.[13] And Laurens titled his own autobiography 'Yet Being Someone Other', a phrase taken from Eliot's lines on that theme.

he explained, was 'a true story . . . since the truth is always more than literal or statistical fact'. For Laurens the literal fact was always less important than, and inferior to, the 'truth' of the imagination – and miraculously, this *truer* truth turns out invariably to be an endorsement of Laurens himself, a confirmation of his heroic quality. Leonard Woolf added a gloss to this, back in August 1957: 'You are quite wrong about Laurens van der Post,' he wrote to a friend. 'He is not bogus, he is one of the sincerest of men. Some of what he writes is very good and some of it, in my opinion, unmitigated nonsense. But he believes it just as Christ and Freud did theirs.'

Occasionally, Laurens admitted the point. In one of his last books, *A Walk with a White Bushman*, he replies to his interviewer: 'This is one of the problems for me: stories in a way are more completely real to me than life in the here and now. A really true story has a transcendent reality for me which is greater than the reality of life. It incorporates life but it goes beyond it.'[15] That may be the best gloss that can be put on the problematic questions posed by many of his books.

Habitual lying, or a compulsion to exaggerate, is sometimes said to derive from a lack of confidence in your own achievements. Anthony Storr has pointed out in his study of gurus that delusional systems 'make sense of a chaos within, and also preserve the subject's self-esteem. They are a creative solution to the subject's problems . . .'[16]* At the least, such delusions or illusions, or just plain lies, involve an inflated sense of importance.

The best illustration of the problem – for problem it is in any biography of Laurens – is found in the correspondence of March 1976 between Laurens and his friend, the South African writer, editor and critic, Jack Cope. Perhaps indiscreetly, Cope wrote to Laurens in London to report a conversation with their mutual friend, the writer Uys Krige. 'You know –' (Uys says as reported by Cope) '– I've often said Laurens has a range of experience any writer would give both hands to have. And old Laurens with this marvellous sensitivity and insight and his command of language – think what he could do with it if he wrote out of that actual experience . . . I would far sooner read this in straight realist form than when he fantasises . . .'

*In *Feet of Clay*, Anthony Storr has traced the word 'Guru' to its Sanskrit meaning, 'one who brings light out of darkness'. He explains that most gurus claim to possess a spiritual insight based on personal revelation, and adds that they can become unscrupulous wielders of power, unworthy of veneration: they include 'false prophets, madmen, confidence tricksters or unscrupulous psychopaths'. Their followers often find it difficult to distinguish between the saints and the crooks.[17]

'Fantasises?' Cope queries.

Uys replies, 'That's perhaps the wrong word. I mean, it's not the real thing he's been through but drawn out of the imagination and psychology and so on. And that's our loss.'

Laurens was stung by this report. He replied hotly, 'The implication is clear that what is drawn out of the imagination and psychology is somehow not the "real thing" . . . Art is never straight realism. It is what the human being has experienced, the base material of his life put through the crucible of the imagination and alchemically transformed into the poem, the story, the drama, the novel . . . One of the main reasons I do not do the "real thing", as Uys suggests, is precisely because it brings me back to the "I" – the ego and inevitably the egotistical, and draws away the attention from the fact that I have merely been an instrument of the "thou" in life . . .'[18]

At which some readers will detect the ironic point that *all* of Laurens's stories are about his ego and inspired by his ego. And we are not just talking of 'the poem, the story' emerging from the crucible of the imagination: the lies have little to do with Art, more to do with Vanity.

His friends became all too familiar with it, and because they were friends they put up with it – the wiser among them may have smiled, but many even believed him. As the woman who looked after him for the last four years of his life afterwards put it: 'He was such an astonishing liar. It seemed as automatic and necessary to him as breathing, from some flim-flam to do with socks to the engorged fabrication of his deeds. Consequently I found it impossible to see him as anything but his own invention.'[19]

That invention reached its apotheosis in *Yet Being Someone Other*.

35

Wilderness

IN THE 1980s, Laurens's literary output declined in volume as well as quality.* This is hardly surprising, as he was approaching his own eightieth year and his health was beginning to falter. After *Yet Being Someone Other* in 1982 he did not publish a substantial work for nearly ten years (*About Blady* in 1991), but his publishers cleverly concealed this by bringing out Jane Taylor's *Testament to the Bushmen* in 1984, containing a long postscript by Laurens called 'The Great Memory'. In 1988 they produced an elegant illustrated edition of *The Lost World of the Kalahari*, with fine photographs by David Coulson and a long new essay by Laurens which he titled 'The Great and Little Memory'. There was also, in 1986, *A Walk with a White Bushman*, a transcription of lengthy conversations with Jean-Marc Pottiez, whose admiration is demonstrated by the slow lobs of his questions. There should also have been a *Festschrift*, traditionally a volume which celebrates a life, for his eightieth birthday, a collection of essays by friends, organised by the Swiss-based Jungian therapist and publisher, Bob Hinshaw. This fell behind schedule and was in effect hijacked by Laurens, who re-commissioned contributions as he thought desirable, including no fewer than eleven contributions by himself. This is not normally allowed in a *Festschrift*! It eventually appeared for his ninetieth birthday under the title *The Rock Rabbit and the Rainbow*.[2] It was a good example of the way Laurens sought to control everything that was written about him.

He led a busy and grand life. To take a couple of years at random from the 1980s, in the summer of 1981 his diary records more than a dozen meetings with Prince Charles and three with the Prime Minister; in

---

*Laurens's prose deteriorated markedly, a reminder of Ingaret's importance, now lost, as his editor. Leonard Woolf in his diary for November 1952 had noted that Laurens 'leaves all the cutting to her. She took I don't know how many 1000s of words out of the novel and he wouldn't even look at what she had done.'[1]

autumn 1982, after various journeys including one to the Kalahari, he was with the Prince or the Premier at least half-a-dozen times; in 1983 he met the Prince more than a dozen times and held innumerable telephone conversations; in 1984, he met the Prince more than a dozen times and also visited Downing Street. This pattern continued, while his overseas travels were as frequent as ever. Laurens was undoubtedly an intimate of both the Prince of Wales and the Prime Minister. He was greatly gratified by this. He had also come to take for granted that he would be visited by the famous – Solzhenitsyn, for example, with whose prison experiences Laurens compared his own, or the 'cellist Yo Yo Ma, who travelled to the Kalahari to play music to and with the Bushmen for a TV film after he had been inspired by Laurens. The other side of this coin was that Laurens could be generous: for instance, he befriended and gave financial help to the aged, struggling Bengali writer, Nirad Chaudhuri.[3]

His retreat from the publishers' lists did not mean that he was contemplating retirement. On the contrary, his energy seemed undiminished, but now he directed it into various quasi-political areas. His attempt to intervene in the Rhodesian crisis had ended at the Independence ceremony in Salisbury (Harare) in April 1980 when Rhodesia became Zimbabwe. He continued to engage himself in the affairs of his own South Africa, using his London contacts, most notably the Prime Minister, and his sustained correspondence with his friend Piet Koornhof; on his frequent visits to South Africa he did not hesitate to make speeches and give outspoken interviews. As the country at last ventured on the negotiations which would lead to majority rule, he became increasingly and dangerously attracted to the Zulu cause of Chief Buthelezi in Kwazulu-Natal. But during these years he portrayed himself above all as a conservationist, an environmentalist, and a prophet of 'Wilderness'. Thanks to his international fame, and also in consequence of his energetic lobbying skills, he became quite simply the world's best-known figurehead, if not leader, of the fast-growing Wilderness movement. His closest and most effective ally was another South African, Ian Player.

Ian Player had joined the Natal Parks Board in 1952. A forceful, dedicated, sometimes controversial figure, he rose over twenty years to be Chief Conservator of all of Natal's game reserves. His brother, the golfer Gary Player, may have been more famous, but Ian became internationally celebrated in environmental circles because he was responsible for saving the White Rhino* from extinction. He protected them,

---

*This species is not 'white', but has a '*wyd*' – a 'wide' – jaw.

bred them and eventually exported them to many African, European and American game parks.

Player had been transfixed by *Venture to the Interior* when he read it, in the bush, in the mid-1950s. He became a friend of T. C. Robertson, Laurens's colleague from the *Cape Times*, who had become director of the National Veld Trust and who gave him an introduction to Laurens in Chelsea. Player and Laurens first met in 1969 and immediately became close friends. At the beginning, they needed each other – Laurens at that time wanted access to a park to make a film, and Player was developing various environmental plans for which he needed international endorsement.[4]

After the White Rhino project, Player had the second of his visionary ideas. He had moved to Umfolozi, 200 miles north-east of Durban, and had dreamed up a Wilderness Leadership School which would take groups of young people into the bush. First he developed Wilderness Trails, the participants on foot and unarmed, sleeping under the stars, which he started at Lake St Lucia in 1957 and then at Umfolozi in 1959. Player's right-hand man – his mentor, his teacher, his friend – was a remarkable and very old Zulu called Magqubu Ntombela. Laurens responded eagerly to this new thinking about Game Reserves, and on various occasions took his family, or camera crews, to go out into the bush with Player and Magqubu.

The second connection between the two men was that Player read Laurens's biography of Jung and became a passionate Jungian, which he would always say had changed his life. He was in due course to be instrumental in the founding of a Jungian centre in South Africa, in close association with Laurens. But before then, following the success of his Wilderness Trails, he had set up an International Wilderness Foundation in 1974, followed by the first International Wilderness Conference, which was held in Johannesburg in 1977. The Foundation, always strongly supported by Laurens and on occasion financially by Ian's brother Gary, had a difficult beginning, but eventually spawned the Wild Foundation USA, the Wilderness Trust UK, and a similar organisation in Australia. In all this, Player's principle was that wilderness areas could become a fount of spiritual inspiration and a source of nurturing for future generations; he used to point out that over the ages the great prophets have gone out into the wilderness. This was a theme with which Laurens could wholeheartedly engage.[5]

This concept of Wilderness, which rapidly made ground from the 1970s, needs definition. It went back to the mid-nineteenth century America of Henry David Thoreau, and in the stressful, polluted world of the late twentieth century it became a text for the environmental and ecological movements. Laurens became an eloquent prophet of Wilderness, and for the last fifteen years of his life was in constant demand around the world to lecture or write on the subject. He had again alighted on an issue of new and seemingly universal fascination, one increasingly demanded by the needs of the time.

Thoreau had written, 'In wildness lies the preservation of mankind'. Laurens, after half a lifetime proselytising the role of the primitive man in desert or landscape, was well placed to expand on this. 'The vision of wilderness is not very complicated,' he wrote. 'We try to give it elaborate definitions, but we all know what wilderness really is, because we have it inside ourselves. We know it is a world in which every bit of nature counts and is important to us, and we know when it isn't there.' He became bolder: 'Wilderness is the original cathedral, the original temple, the original church of life in which they have been converted and healed, and from which they have emerged transformed in a positive manner.' He would quote Jung, and also the Dead Sea Scrolls. 'Follow the birds, the beasts and the fish and they will lead you in [to the Kingdom of Heaven].' 'Wilderness is an instrument for enabling us to recover our lost capacity for religious experience.' 'The original "wilderness man" . . . exists in us. He is the foundation in spirit or psyche on which we build, and we are not complete until we have recovered him.'[6]

He was sometimes asked why there should be yet another movement in addition to existing bodies like the World Wide Fund for Nature and Friends of the Earth. His answer was that the Wilderness Leadership Foundation started from a new point of departure: 'the belief that we need the life of nature far more than it needs us, particularly nature in the shape of wilderness . . . At the moment indeed there is not a plant, insect, animal, bird, fish or patch of earth that will not breathe a sigh of relief if man were to vanish from the earth. Yet, wherever we have preserved and recreated a natural life in this wilderness idiom, we have discovered that we have given the earth back a kind of aboriginal sanctity, and new readiness to respond again, and that these areas are once more, in a profound sense, shrines, way-side chapels, churches and temples of the spirit of creation itself, more so even in my own experience than any conventional religious institutions.'

Laurens found an enthusiastic audience for these ideas. In both articles and talks he easily found much to illustrate them in his own life. He could return again and again to his tales of Bushmen or Zulus, he could reach back to the Abbé Breuil (the paleontologist whom he had met in Cape Town in 1930), who described the concept of the *participation mystique*. He could reminisce about Klara, and about Ian Player's beloved (and very real) Magqubu. He could repeat once more his Bushman story of the pursuit of the Feather of Truth. The exaggerations need not matter too much, because Laurens in old age threw himself vigorously into the practicalities of an effective movement for the world-wide protection of Wilderness.

He started off by endorsing, without hesitation or reservation, Ian Player's initiative in using Wilderness Trails in Natal to bring enlightenment (the word will do) not just to youngsters but also to teachers, politicians, businessmen, therapists, anyone who was able to walk into the bush for a few days, where they would sleep around the fire, protected only by Magqubu's ancient gun, and where in the morning they would be invited to describe their dreams. These Wilderness Trails became (and remain) extremely successful. Although each Trail has to be limited to eight people, by 2001 it was estimated that 100,000 people had participated in these and similar projects throughout the country. There were various plans to extend them to Kenya, the US, or to the north of Scotland, but nothing came of these in Laurens's lifetime.[7]

Ian Player's next project, for a World Wilderness Congress in Johannesburg in 1977, was in some ways an extraordinary idea because South Africa was sinking into international pariah status, visitors were likely to refuse to come, and there were no funds. Laurens became Player's strongest ally, importuning his minister friend Piet Koornhof with demands for state assistance. The 1977 Congress, held outside Johannesburg, was a surprising success. Laurens gave two keynote speeches. Ian Player was therefore encouraged to plan a second Wilderness Congress, in Cairns, Australia, in 1980. Again, the South African connection was a problem, until Laurens wrote to his old POW friend, Sir 'Weary' Dunlop, who persuaded the Prime Minister, Malcolm Fraser, to open the Congress, where he announced protection measures for the Great Barrier Reef.

The next Congress, driven ahead by the unresting Player, was at Findhorn and Inverness in Scotland in 1983. This was also tricky because of the Findhorn community's radical reputation, and Laurens, using all his lobbying skills to persuade the grandees of Inverness to co-operate, had to admit that Mrs Thatcher and Prince Charles were unavailable; he made good (through Mrs Thatcher's instruction) with the Secretary of State for Scotland, George Younger. This Congress was another success, even though one of the keynote addresses by Laurens's close friend and Jung's oldest colleague, Dr Fredy Meier, on the 'Wilderness Within . . .', was brilliant but incomprehensible to many of the delegates. There followed another Wilderness Congress in Denver, USA, and another in

Norway in 1987, neither of which Laurens was able to attend. He was feted as a patron at all of them. In 1998 a Congress was held in Bangalore, India, attended by 750 delegates. The great value of these gatherings was that environmentalists from around the world were able to meet and mingle and network.[8]

During these years Laurens gave his name and support to a host of other environmental organisations, such as Robin Page's Countryside Restoration Trust in England, Ed Posey and Liz Hosken's Gaia Foundation (which with Laurens's backing organised such causes as the defence of the Forest People of the Amazon), and the group of people who fought a long and finally victorious campaign to stop the mining by international corporations of the mineral sands of the St Lucia wetland in South Africa.

He was flattered to be asked to help, though occasionally his availability created problems. In 1992, for example, he casually told a group called Planet in Change that they might use his name when they set up a South African symposium. His endorsement was used heavily in brochures; too late, it was discovered that the speakers included a hypnotherapist whose mentor was the Archangel Gabriel, an 'immortalist' who would speak about the sacred foundations of the Planetary New Jerusalem, and a lady who was in touch with a group of aliens from the Pleiades. He tried to disengage, pleading that he had not given them his authority, but was met with copies of his own letter showing that he had.[9] Laurens may have learned a lesson from the lengthy exchanges which ensued. Planet in Change mattered only because it threatened the reputation of Laurens's foundation in South Africa – at that time called the Laurens van der Post Foundation for the Environment.

Laurens made one last venture into the extreme wilderness when in 1982 he was persuaded by Jane Taylor to go back to the Kalahari to front a BBC television film, *Testament to the Bushmen*. He was flown in twice to the rugged terrain surrounding the Tsodilo Hills and, at the age of seventy-five, managed to limp to the top of the mountain and speak to camera with his usual eloquence. The BBC did not broadcast the programmes until 1984, when they were accompanied by Jane Taylor's illustrated book, *Testament to the Bushmen*, which was published by Viking and Penguin to positive notices. Laurens added a forty-five-page essay, 'Witness to a Last Will of Man', in which he evoked the Bushman as 'a first man ... dynamic in the underworld of the spirit'; he said he knew this because the story of the Bushman, as he had told it, 'has been translated into all languages except Chinese, travelled the world and been taken into the hearts of millions as if it were food in a universal famine of spirit'. In this essay Laurens repeated and developed many of his earlier thoughts about the Bushmen, together with his increasingly tall tales of his childhood.[10]

These fantasies were rehearsed again in 1988 – shortly after Laurens had paid his final visit to the Kalahari, in the company of Prince Charles – when he wrote a new Epilogue to *The Lost World of the Kalahari*, which was re-issued, thirty years after its first publication, in a coffee-table edition with superb photographs by David Coulson. He described as well how, at the summit of the Tsodilo Hills in the 1950s, he had found 'the pool of everlasting water'. When he returned in 1982, the pool had dried up, and he here describes how his guide, Samutchau, explained, 'All gone, gone, gone! All gone with the spirits back into the earth where they come from.' Jane Taylor remembers how Samutchau had said nothing of the sort; she has the scene on film in which the bewildered guide points out that it hasn't rained in six months.

But the main interest of this last excursion into the desert is his sad discovery, and admission, that the Bushmen were doomed, 'and that my own effort to prevent the doom had utterly failed.' Moreover, for the first time he is persuaded that for his own safety he must sleep in a tent, not under the stars: 'The change in the mood of animals and birds expressed a degree of the alienation of man even greater and more alarming than the total suppression of stone-age culture and rejection of the Bushman.' He ends with a very muted optimism for the future.[11]

A Walk With a White Bushman, which eventually appeared in 1986, was not a publishing success, selling only modestly, but it is interesting because it records, without comment, Laurens's thinking, attitudes and prejudices as he approached his eighties. It is a transcription of a series of interviews he gave to a French journalist, Jean-Marc Pottiez, between 1982 and 1985. Laurens responded happily and candidly to the respectful questions of a charmed admirer; Pottiez evidently believed that every word Laurens uttered was the gospel truth. This misapprehension allowed Laurens to hold forth with unusual freedom about everything under the sun.

The interviews are riddled with Laurens's accustomed reconstructions, unchallenged by Pottiez, plus a few new ones: 'I have had to shoot a few [elephants] but always with great regret and sadness afterwards.' (When? Where? On the sheep farms of the Karoo?) He declares with a straight face, 'I never travelled from Britain to southern Africa without stopping at Addis Ababa to be with [the Emperor Haile Selassie].' Sometimes Pottiez allows him to enlarge into absurdity: for example, on a face-to-face encounter with a rhinoceros: 'I had the oddest of feelings that there was something in him that wanted a meeting too.' Occasionally, there are helpful insights into Laurens's life. Of his Bushman stories, he says, 'We had lost the meaning of the stories. So I decoded them, and they immediately began making sense all over the world' (there is some truth in this). A great deal of Laurens's philosophising to Pottiez is diluted and popularised Jung, usually unaccredited, and missing the subtleties and irony of the Swiss psychologist. His way of interpreting Bushman tales, for instance, or his discussion of Job, come via Jung.[12]

But *A Walk with a White Bushman* is most revealing when Pottiez leads him into his views of contemporary affairs. Laurens is dismissive of the new black leadership in Africa, and does not disguise his criticisms of the European powers for handing over independence too soon – not just in Africa but also in India: 'What is called "the emancipation of colonial territories" led to massacre, loss of freedom and greater tyrannies than those that preceded them.'*

Laurens admitted to Pottiez his constant homesickness for Africa and his solitude, which he saw as necessary for his writing. He said that the most important part of working was not the three or four hours a day when he was actually writing but the incubation hours in between. He explained that when he gave a public talk he had no notes and did not know how he would begin, so 'I sort of beat about the bush inside myself until a phrase like a bird comes up, an immense feeling of relief comes over me, and I just follow the flight of the bird.' This phenomenon has been noted by friends: they describe it as an almost psychic, certainly not an intellectual, acknowledgement of his audience. It is true that Laurens never spoke from notes or from a text, and he was quite capable of going on for several hours without in the least wearying his audience, who were usually captivated.

He remembered for Pottiez the Bloomsbury group of the 1930s more caustically than he had previously allowed himself. He exempted Leonard Woolf and Arthur Waley, but otherwise remembered 'a world of aberration ... Everybody was inaccurate in what they were ... It was

---

*There is a contradiction in Laurens's thinking. In Java, from 1945, he fiercely criticised the Dutch for obstructing Indonesian independence. He quotes himself telling the Dutch Governor General, 'There comes a moment in colonisation, no matter how good it is, when it is no longer good from the point of view of the colonised.' Laurens was content to be demonised by the Dutch for his support of Javanese independence. Why did he never apply this same criterion to Africa – and, for that matter, to his own homeland?[13]

as if they were playing a game with themselves rather than living . . . I was on a different course and using a different map.'

The book also illustrates Laurens's passionate support of Mrs Thatcher in all her works: 'For the first time since the War, I, personally, feel that Britain is being governed again . . .' The Thatcher Government is going to bring about the end of the Labour Party. 'The so-called Liberal Socialist elements in modern society are profoundly decadent.' Socialism, a creation of the nineteenth century, 'has long since been out of date and been like a rotting corpse whose smell in our midst has tainted the political atmosphere far too long . . . The Conservative Party has become the party of reform and change, and the others are trying to conserve, trying to anchor us to outmoded and discredited patterns of society.'

In pages like these Laurens was allowed by his respectful interviewer not just to preach but to rant. Today's pop music was 'as archaic as tribal music without the innocence of tribal music in its non-tribal context: it is . . . as impregnated with warning and somnambulism as Wagner at his worst.' As for Women's Liberation, 'the rejected, the suppressed feminine in the woman and its valid aspiration to be recognised and active, has been perverted into a form of Amazonian gang warfare.'[14] Perhaps these were the thoughts and opinions that Laurens was at this time disseminating, with his usual mesmeric eloquence, to Prince Charles, Mrs Thatcher and their charmed circles.

A Walk With a White Bushman came out in 1986, in America in 1987, and received only modest attention. *Private Eye* commented cruelly that it was 'the product of a mind which has sunk from literary pretension to outright dottiness', and called Pottiez an 'excitable sycophant'. Auberon Waugh in *The Independent* declared that 'the chief impression is of a vain self-indulgent old booby who is quite simply showing off.' He added, more seriously: 'He may well have fallen in love with his Bushperson nanny . . . I do not doubt that these Bushpeople had qualities in their natural state which have now been lost. But the truth remains that their lives were nasty, brutish and short; it is a waste of time for modern, urban man to mourn, or seek to reproduce, these qualities.' *The Times Literary Supplement* review focussed on a central question: Alan Barnard wrote, 'During my own wanderings in the Kalahari, I have always thought [Laurens] was living in a fantasy world – a world which, for better or worse, bears only passing reference to the mundane world of science and scholarship, or of real Bushmen making their living from the desert. *A Walk With a White Bushman* confirms it. Van der Post's Africa is no specific part of Africa; even the Bushmen he describes are not any specific one of the many diverse Bushman groups. They are the Bushmen of his imagination.'[15]

PART SIX

'Perhaps one of the saddest things in life is the recurrent illusion of human beings that they can improve on the truth.'

Laurens van der Post, *Yet Being Someone Other*, 1982

'I no longer know where my life ends and the story begins.'

Laurens van der Post to Richard Osler, December 1991

'It is amazing how, ultimately, truth gets out. The most wonderful thing about truth is that it never expects us to know the whole of it.'

Laurens van der Post, letter to Anna Jonker, 13 April 1982

36

Old Age

BY THE 1980s Laurens was no longer a best-selling author. His recent books had failed to bring in money on the scale of the earlier ones. But he was still far from forgotten, and he continued to enjoy a substantial revenue. In June 1991 Penguin renewed its 'licences' for seven of his books in paperback for £40,000. His flagging German sales were transformed in July 1994 when he switched from Henssel to Diogenes. English-language sales of some of his books – for example, *The Lost World of the Kalahari*, the Jung biography, the Bushman novels – continued to hold up. There was an occasional bonus from a film project too. He was in frequent demand for talks and signings and story-telling sessions. But as the years went by Laurens worried increasingly about money. He lived well and was too old to change his ways: he expected to travel first class and he stayed at five-star hotels; he had for years been accustomed to spend several months every winter skiing and working in Gstaad or Valbella. He did not have expensive vices, but he never doubted that he deserved the best of everything, from private health care to decent restaurants. His financial worries may seem absurd given that he and Ingaret owned a penthouse in one of London's most fashionable districts which would be worth £1 million; but that did not help his cash flow. He spent a lot of time arranging free flights and complimentary hotels and courtesy cars, and he was careful never to pay over the odds for secretaries or nurses. He also never lost his habit of recording his petty expenses in his pocket diary. He held substantial funds in a Swiss bank, and risked a posthumous family crisis when it was found that he had secretly transferred certain assets, held in 'rubrics' under his name in the same bank, into his own account.[1]*

He travelled wherever and whenever possible, at others' expense. In

---

*A rubric is a subsidiary bank account which, for administrative convenience, is attached to a main account.

October 1983, for instance, he went to South Africa to open a luxury game lodge, and in August 1984 he was in Johannesburg to open a new branch of Exclusive Books. He was frequently asked to lecture at American universities – for instance, in San Francisco in December 1979; in July 1983 at Kusnacht (Jung's old home) for the University of California; in Houston in October 1986 at the C. G. Jung Educational Centre; in October 1986 at Saledo, Texas. He was careful always to negotiate the highest possible fee and to explain that, for reasons of health, he had to have first-class tickets for two. In March 1993 P&O invited him to sail to South Africa with Frances on one of their container ships, a trip which Laurens particularly appreciated because he missed the old Union Castle voyages.[2] For a man of his age who suffered from painful mobility problems he travelled abroad astonishingly often, and he continued to do so at every opportunity, even after the mid-1980s when Ingaret was suffering from Alzheimer's Disease, or a similar condition.

He was troubled with various afflictions of old age. But he would suffer stoically: in late 1990 he insisted on flying to South Africa to fulfil an important engagement at Stellenbosch University, although he was in great pain. His doctors there discovered that he had a broken femur and tried to forbid him from speaking, but he insisted on doing so, balancing on two sticks, and then immediately went into a Cape Town hospital to have a hip operation.

Understandably, Laurens attached great sentimental importance to this invitation to speak at Stellenbosch, the 'Oxford' of the Afrikaners, where his parents had spent their exile and where he had been conceived. He told American friends that he saw it as 'an act of reconciliation, almost an apology for nearly two generations of rejection, and a confession that they [the Afrikaner people] had been deeply in the wrong. The invitation said that everything I stood for in the past and had predicted, had proved right . . . The great university graduate hall was packed, and the dean told me three times that number were listening on the address system outside. They said afterwards it was perhaps the most historic occasion ever sponsored by the University.' There was in fact nothing unusual in the content of Laurens's address, but he was justifiably gratified that he had been asked to deliver his message at Stellenbosch. He had to convalesce for several months in his favourite Mount Nelson Hotel in Cape Town, accompanied by Frances.[3]

On various occasions in these last years he retreated into King Edward VII Hospital in London for rest and recuperation from the stress and strain of his daily life. He now rarely went out, increasingly relying on the telephone to conduct his affairs. A small number of friends would visit him regularly, and he continued always to be available to visitors, who were often journalists. Prince Charles telephoned frequently, as did overseas friends like Ian Player. He was closer to his own family in Britain than he had been before; he built relationships for the first time with his grandchildren, and spoke with Lucia every day. His large daily correspondence was dealt with by a succession of secretaries who also played important roles in his life: Kate Littman, Jane Brewster, Tobina Johnson, Louise Stein. Indeed, he was surrounded by caring women. Mrs Pearce, Ingaret's cook and friend, who had worked with her in the munitions factory in the war, had died, to be succeeded by Margaret Czock, and then Janet Campbell, who stayed from 1993 until Ingaret's death in 1997, plus the nurses, none more appreciated than Nina Panahmand. A few of Ingaret's oldest friends continued to call on her during her illness, but one suspects that Laurens was lonely, in the way of very old men. He had lost, in effect, Ingaret's companionship, and also his dearest friends from different points in his life – William Plomer, Uys Krige, Jack Cope, Roy Campbell, Norah Smallwood, David Stirling. Most of his siblings in South Africa were gone. He and Ingaret, finding that they could no longer go to Aldeburgh, sold Turnstones in late 1992, and Laurens only revisited the town very occasionally. John and Tessa had sold Half-Crown Cottage.[4]

Laurens managed to make a few new friends: Bill Atkinson, a retired oil executive, for example, and Ronald Cohen, a South African businessman who had moved to London and who would talk with him several times a day. Another new friend was John Aspinall, the casino operator and wildlife enthusiast. Often his newer friends were women. There was Sister Maria Basini, at the closed Carmelite order in Quidenham in East Anglia, whom he visited and with whom he exchanged frequent letters; Helen Luke at her Jungian community in Apple Farm in Michigan, in whom he discovered an intense intellectual friendship, as he had a decade earlier with Winifred Rushforth, the psychologist who founded the Davidson Clinics in Scotland; and Kathleen Raine in London, the poet and creator of Temenos, an academy of spiritual exploration. (He introduced Prince Charles to Winifred and Kathleen.) He corresponded with old prisoner-of-war companions: Weary Dunlop and Ray Parkin in Australia, John Denman in Sussex, and Alex Jardine in Canada; when in London they would visit him and reminisce cheerfully about what Jardine described as 'that remarkably nasty time in Java'. Laurens was very close to Tom Bedford and his new wife Jane Brewster. There was also, of course, a wide and cosmopolitan range of less intimate friends who kept in touch by letter, telephone or the occasional visit: Harry Oppenheimer, Lady Thatcher, Piet Koornhof, Professor Johan Degenaar from Stellenbosch, and Sarel Marais (an old friend from Grey College days). To these he added the American members of his 'Company of Seven'.

An odd and interesting aspect of Laurens's friendships which has already been remarked on is that, as many of his friends discovered, he used to keep his wide range of acquaintances in carefully segregated 'boxes' – Politics, Literature, Jung, Environment, East Anglia, Wartime and so on. Sometimes you were allowed to jump into another box. Player, for example, was firmly in the 'Wilderness' box until he found Jung, when a new world of Laurens's friendships was made available to him. Tom had been 'Family', until he also became 'Politics'. Eva Monley was 'Film' until she became 'Friend'. The effect of this unusual strategy is, first, to control and manipulate, second, to defend one's privacy, third, to protect one's mystery and reputation. Laurens usually presented himself as a sociable and congenial man, but in these 'boxes' we can see that he was really a loner. He had close friends, but they could never be certain how close they truly were. Ronald Cohen, who advised him on his business affairs, was never allowed to know the detail of his various bank accounts; Charles Janson lost touch with him for a number of years, as did T. C. Robertson and Sarel Marais; Eva Monley believed that he had once been a film critic; Ian Player originally knew nothing of the Jungian connection; Tom was not told of the girlfriends; and of course, Ingaret – and Frances – knew nothing of his wider life.[5]

One side aspect of this is that Laurens prided himself on running what he called his 'whispering campaigns', when he was lobbying for one of his causes, telephoning his contacts, weaving a web of conspiracy. Another aspect is that Laurens, in his later years, would sow discord; he would belittle someone behind his or her back, and then would denigrate the recipients of his confidences to others. The secretaries (and even his own daughter) suffered this in particular, and sometimes became aware of it. It was yet another form of control, which he sustained and enjoyed until he was ninety.

Laurens's principal area of interest during these last years – the subject of the 'whispering campaigns' which he so relished – was his beloved homeland, South Africa, where he set himself to fight against the emergence to power of the African National Congress. He took up the cause of federalism in South Africa, and in particular he became the champion of one of South Africa's provinces, Kwazulu-Natal, already on the brink of civil war. He embraced Chief Mangosuthu Buthelezi and his Inkatha

Party, and the cause of the Zulus. In so doing, he ventured into deep and dangerous waters.

About Blady, which Laurens wrote in 1990, and which was first published in 1992 for an advance of £15,000, is his most peculiar book. It is a ramble, occasionally a rant, about cancer and horses – Blady is a horse – and the connections between them, laced with his reminiscences of a long life. The reminiscences were the usual ones, further embellished; his discussion of cancer, 'the great uprooter', is new. He describes four cases: his son John, who died in 1984, his friend Charles Douglas-Home, editor of *The Times*, who died in 1985, Edward, son of his friends in Madeira, the Blandys of wine fame, who died in 1984, and the National Hunt jockey Bob Champion, who overcame the disease and won the Grand National.

Laurens notes that, as the years went by, cancer seemed to replace tuberculosis as the great scourge: more and more of his friends were struck down. Then his son John came to him, to tell him of a terrifying dream of a black elephant; Laurens sent him to talk with his psycho-therapist friend Alan McGlashan. It may have been the beginning of the cancer which would kill John six years later, after he had dreamed another dream, of the sun coming up over the Cape of Good Hope 'on the wrong side'. Laurens found a message in this: the inadequacy of the conventional medical approach to something so mysterious as cancer. 'Even if doctors did . . . use dreams and their decoding as an essential part of their diagnostic equipment and perhaps could confront cancer at the point of entry, how are they to turn it aside, unless they are humble enough to keep their instruments in their cases and look for some new form of navigation over an uncharted sea of the human spirit?' And then he was told that Charles Douglas-Home was dying; Laurens describes his battle vividly and at length.

There is an awkward balance in these tragedies. Jessica Douglas-Home, who was herself close to Laurens, has said that she was always uneasy that Laurens devoted more attention in this book to the death of her husband than to that of his own son. There may of course have been private reasons why Laurens did not feel able to dwell on his son's death (they became close only in the last years), and he was involved in Douglas-Home's illness for longer. Edward Blandy had been particularly favoured by Ingaret. The three of them died bravely, and the jockey came through. In all of this, Laurens is as always at the centre of the tale: at times he seems to compare himself with Job.[6]

Laurens finds his surprising theme in the horse. At Douglas-Home's memorial service in St Paul's Cathedral, Laurens had a vision of a horse and its bareback rider. It was Champion's love of the horse, he argues, which gave the jockey the energy to conquer cancer, a thought which came to him after Fredy Meier, from Zurich, reminded him that the centaur, the horseman Chiron, was the great healer of antiquity who tutored Asclepius, the legendary Greek physician.

This eventually leads Laurens to a memory of his own childhood pony, Diamond, and his Griqua servant 'Bird of the Wind', who used to dose the farm horses on *dagga* (marijuana). Laurens (who was seven at this time) and Diamond, he says, witnessed the falling of a meteorite a few miles from where they were standing – though the meteor may well have passed overhead, it landed, according to another witness and story-teller, Roy Campbell, a hundred and fifty miles away in Basutoland.[7]

Laurens delves into his Greek classics. Chiron had taken over the Promethean role, he argues, and was an image of the horse joined to the man, instinct to intuition. The horse had a crucial role to play in the evolution from Gods and Titans to the lone individual man; there is no mythology where horses play such a distinct role as in the Greek. Which leads him back to a favourite theme, which he drew above all from his reading of *The Odyssey*, of the need for 'man' to rediscover the 'feminine' (the 'Penelope') in himself. (Laurens never talks about the 'woman' rediscovering the 'masculine' in herself.) 'I was coming to a track where the horse, all unseen, was entering the life of the world of today in the service uniquely of the feminine.'

At this point Laurens comes back to earth and tells the story of his meeting with Rosemary de Llorens. He does not name her, except in his Dedication to the book, and does not make it clear that the event in question took place forty years earlier. The owner and rider of Blady was Rosemary, an Argentine-Scot who had gone to live in Spain just before the outbreak of war in 1939. Laurens did not know her personally at that time though he afterwards claimed that he had used his Foreign Office contacts to help her with her papers. More probably they were introduced in Zurich in 1951, when Laurens accompanied Ingaret and where Rosemary was training to be a Jungian analyst with Toni Wolff and Fredy Meier.[8]

Laurens and Ingaret visited Spain in February 1953 for a month, staying with Rosemary and her husband, Professor Julio de Llorens, and the upshot was that Julio became the Spanish-language translator of Laurens's books, published by Ediciones Destino. Laurens wanted Julio to have one-half of his Spanish royalties, which irritated Norah

Smallwood at the Hogarth Press. Ingaret and Laurens went back to Barcelona for a couple of weeks in March 1954. When Laurens afterwards said that the two couples met frequently, he exaggerated, but it was probably on the second visit that Laurens, travelling from France, as he described in *About Blady*, joined Rosemary and Julio in Nîmes.

In Laurens's jumbled narrative, he talks of his growing concern about the cancer of his friends, which must have been many years later, yet he then writes of the Blady episode as 'following' the cancer. On the drive to Spain, the four of them spotted a horse drawing a plough – it was Blady. Rosemary recognised his quality, bought him on the spot from the farmer, and turned him into a great champion showjumper. Four years later, Laurens and Ingaret were invited to attend the Fiesta in Castellona at which Blady and Rosemary took on the champions. There follow, in welcome contrast to the portentous profundities of the previous chapter, eighty pages of vivid description of the Fiesta and of Blady's triumph. It seems to Laurens that the trail had started with Diamond in South Africa. He notices how the victory has brought Rosemary and her partner even closer, and he remembers how his own prewar friend, Lilian Bowes Lyon, had also loved horses and written a poem about his own Cotswold horse.

As usual, Laurens's description of these events in Spain forty years earlier should not be relied on. His verbatim account of the speeches at the final Fiesta dinner seems particularly suspect, as does the conversation between Rosemary and Julio, which Laurens admits to eavesdropping: 'Ultimately it was you, and all I felt with you, that led me to Blady. It was my love of you that precipitated, in my general love of horses, the coming of Blady.' (Laurens could never write dialogue!) Rosemary continues: 'One thing I promise you. I will never again make you feel you have to use a whip on anything . . . I shall learn to hasten slowly and so contain ourselves always for always within our own ration and measure of time . . .' This was, Laurens notes, an 'Odyssean moment', and he must have been surprised to hear his friends employ his own Zulu tag-line, '*Hamba Gahle*' ('hasten slowly'). He concludes with a perorating sentence of 250 words.[9]

The reviews of *About Blady* were not enthusiastic. *The Times* found it 'preachy' and 'often implausible'. The *Financial Times* commented that many passages 'do little to help the author's cause against those critics who suggest he is peddling merely middle-brow proverbial wisdom. Part of the problem is that the quality of our author's prose is simply not up to the enormity of the life-and-death issues he undertakes to discuss.' In America, the *New York Times* Book Review said it was 'a rather precious autobiographical indulgence', but granted that 'though Sir Laurens is prone to episodes of philosophical meandering and paeans to myth, his writing can also be keen.'[10] Not surprisingly, *About Blady* did not sell well.

The two couples drifted apart, but in the 1980s, following Julio's death and the onset of Ingaret's illness, Laurens and Rosemary resumed correspondence; Rosemary had become the senior Jungian analyst in Spain. They reminisced about Blady, shared their concern for the ageing Meier household in Zurich, which they both visited from time to time, and Rosemary told him of her problems with her children and grandchildren. To Laurens's evident relief, Rosemary was happy with *About Blady*: she told him of the horse's subsequent triumphs in the 1950s, and added a description of his eventual burial; Laurens asked for a photograph of Blady's grave to add to his picture of himself leading the horse along a beach forty years before. They had a brisk and affectionate correspondence in 1992 – Laurens assured her that Prince Charles had loved Blady's story.[11]

In his later years, Laurens was often described as 'a mystic'. There are two dictionary definitions against which this may be scrutinised. The first, 'A person who seeks by contemplation and self-surrender to obtain union with God', seems a little strong for Laurens. The second, 'One who believes in the possibility of the spiritual apprehension of knowledge inaccessible to the intellect', is much closer, and indeed could also perhaps be applied to Jung himself. A third possibility is that Laurens in his later books was so impenetrable that many of his admirers, unable to unravel their precise meaning, saw them as the work of a mystic.

Sister Maria Basini, a friend with whom he discussed such matters, suggests that 'Laurens's inability to commit himself to any particular creed was because he felt that in so doing he would be committing himself to something less than the infinitely limitless being we call God.'[12] Laurens cannot be described as a Christian, though he revered the person of Christ. In *A Mantis Carol* he writes, 'How tragic but how true that there had only been one modern man, and he had been killed two thousand years ago for the love that made him for ever immediate.' He adds, 'I had an emotion of knowing beyond doubt how, long before we were thought of or conceived and the dancing stars made, already all was loved, . . . and all would be reborn and remade into a greater expression of the love that is our origin and destination.'

Is that mysticism? Mysticism is a bewildering word (derived from the Greek for 'closure' – the refusal to disclose, the *closing* of a person from distraction). It is traditionally used of a person who is in touch with the spiritual sources of his or her being: a person who tries to reach for the invisible source, to get beyond the senses to that source, a person without ego and self-interest. Was Laurens a mystic in this sense? It is one thing to reach for truths that are beyond the senses and ordinary understanding, it is another to live up to that search. All mystical traditions agree that you must embody the truth you want to know, which is to say, with the Sufi poet Kabir, that if you have not lived through something, then it is not true.[13] One assumes that a mystic is, almost by definition, a good person. But to preach and know goodness, you have to become good; to propose truth, you have to live a truthful life. You may *seem* to be good, but *saying* it doesn't make you good. There are plenty of examples of mystics whose mysticism turns out to be sham — the test must be the *quality* of the mystic's life. In *A Mantis Carol* Laurens held forth about such elevated things at the crucial moment of the winter solstice, yet he faked the date; the suppressed synchronicity was arranged. His admirers revered him as the epitome of integrity, without realising that he did not live by the standards he proposed; it was a violation of the reader's trust.

Laurens was not well educated, he was not, he admitted, a scholar, and he was not in fact particularly well read, though he could talk convincingly about most subjects. He concealed this by referring repeatedly to the same basic texts: Homer, Dante, Malory, Yeats, Hopkins, Eliot and, always, Shakespeare's *Hamlet, The Tempest, Lear*. He sometimes did offer original insights into these texts. Above all, he always remembered the impression that the stories of *The Iliad* and *The Odyssey* made upon him in his childhood, and he could never resist a reference to the 'Homeric' dimension of his own experiences. Because of what he described as his childhood fascination with Homer, and his lack of a classical grounding, he was vulnerable to Homeric speculation, against which he had no scholar's defence.

The Voice of the Thunder is the second of his 'old man' books, written when he was eighty-six and published in 1993. The volume of that name brings together his two late essays on the fate of the Bushmen, 'The Little Memory' (published in 1988 as a new introduction to an illustrated edition of *The Lost World of the Kalahari*), and 'The Great Memory', in 1984, written to accompany Jane Taylor's *Testament to the Bushmen*, and here called 'Witness to a Last Will of Man'. These essays have already been described. Laurens added, for *The Voice of the Thunder* in 1993, a new long meditation on the matter of *The Odyssey*, which he called 'The Other Journey'.[14]

In this essay, which Laurens worked hard at for months, he took up a theme on which his friend Helen Luke had published a chapter in 1987 in her book *Old Age*. Helen Luke was a greatly respected English-born psychologist and feminist, a Jungian analyst trained briefly in Zurich who had transferred to California and then to Michigan, where she led a community at Apple Farm, outside Three Rivers. She had become a friend and devotee of Laurens, initially by correspondence, when he told her how he admired her book on Dante, and she in turn became a great admirer of his work. They corresponded frequently between 1977 and her death in 1995, and their letters are full of affection and fellow-feeling. They shared an interest and a similar approach to great literature and frequently exchanged ideas. Laurens, after Plomer's death, probably confided the detail of his life more fully to Helen Luke than to any other friend outside London. He sent people to her for counselling, and for refreshment in her community.

Helen Luke had taken up the theory that when Odysseus eventually returned to Penelope on Ithaca it was not the end of his travels. She seized on the two brief references in *The Odyssey* to Teiresias's prophecy, the first, halfway through the saga, when Odysseus meets him on the brink of Hades, and the second, immediately after Odysseus's return to Penelope and their olive-tree bed, when he tells her what has been foretold. He will have to set off again to the mainland: 'Take a well-cut oar', Teiresias had told him, 'and go on till you reach a people who know nothing of the sea and never use salt with their food . . . When you fall in with some other traveller who refers to the object you are carrying on your shoulder as a "winnowing fan", then the time will have come for you to plant your shapely oar in the earth and offer Lord Poseidon the rich sacrifice of a ram, a bull and a breeding boar . . .' Only then will Odysseus return home, where death will eventually take him, after an easy old age.

It has always been a puzzle that Homer ends his story with no reference to any achievement of Teiresias's prophecy of this next and final journey. Helen Luke in 1985 published what she described as her own version of it. Academic classical scholars have shown little interest in the question of why Homer did not continue the tale until Odysseus's happy death. It would not be hard to offer further theories as to the truth of Teiresias's prophecy. Did Odysseus's journey inland signal a transfer from a hunting/seafaring culture to pastoralism? Had the return to Penelope after nineteen years signified a reconciliation of sun and moon, after which a new journey begins? Was Odysseus making amends to Poseidon for the insults which ten years before had brought him such disasters, after which he could be permitted a peaceful old age? Has

Odysseus to go to a place where he is not recognised, where his particular trade is unknown, where he can bury his image of himself?[15]

Laurens took over Helen Luke's theory almost verbatim in *The Other Journey* as the opening section of his own book, *The Voice of the Thunder*.* 'I found myself at this point over and over again returning to Homer's *Odyssey* and in particular to the reunion at Ithaca . . . There, I was shocked into remembering, the story is not ended; the journey is not over.' In a letter on 12 July 1988 he writes, 'I continue to re-read *Old Age* . . . because it coincides completely and almost literally with a re-reading and reappraisal of the *Odyssey* which has been going on in my mind . . . The continuation of the Odyssean journey is so contemporary and immediate in my own movement, as it were, at the moment that I feel at times it was specially written for me, and your fulfilment of the Teiresian extension of the *Odyssey* is sheer fulfilment for me as well.'[16]

After this, the letters exchanged between Laurens and Helen Luke are deeply intimate. Laurens tells her how Prince Charles loved her essays (which, not surprisingly, pleases her). They both protest, like young lovers, how they want to meet soon. They debate the biblical myth of the clash between the brothers Esau, the hunter, and Jacob, the pastoralist. They discover that they both know Fredy Meier in Zurich. They exchange writers' gossip about publishers. They admire each other's books extravagantly. Interestingly, Helen Luke was one of the few people whom Laurens permitted to counsel him. On 8 March 1989, she wrote, when Laurens had confessed to her that the image of Esau had become too strong and was interfering with his writing, 'The impact of Odysseus's planting of his oar *could* mean that it is time to let go of some of your lifetime concerns because you have so splendidly planted them where they will grow into a nourishing tree of life for those whom I imagined in my story as the new generation – those who in our time *must* pass through the Jacob experience of the opposites, must find the meaning of great dreams. (They were, you will remember, those who had never seen the sea, Teiresias said . . .)'

Laurens was happy that some of his closest friends, such as Alan McGlashan and Fredy Meier, were also admirers of Helen Luke's work. He kept her in touch with the old Jungian generation in Zurich, which was now dying out. He introduced her to his Carmelite friend Sister Maria Basini in her Norfolk closed order. He told her of his visit to Bollingen, Jung's lakeside tower, with Prince Charles. He mentioned a

*One wonders why Laurens, the constant wanderer, was attracted by the idea that Odysseus returns to Penelope/Ingaret only temporarily before he sets sail again.

conversation he claimed he once had with Ernest Hemingway (there is
in fact no record of a meeting of these two incompatible writers). She
told Laurens about the people who visited Apple Farm. He sent her
copies of his Christmas sermons at the Cathedral of St John the Divine
in New York. He admitted to her that Ingaret was ill.[17]

They met only twice, in March 1982 and in June 1993, when Laurens
flew to Kalamazoo Airport to visit Apple Farm in the course of the frequent American tours which he maintained until his death (he asked
Helen Luke to pay his domestic fares). After these meetings, the relationship became almost ecstatic: 'Ever since you left I have been daily thanking the Great Spirit for the wonderful gift of your coming here,' Helen
wrote. In January 1995 she died, peacefully and serenely among her
friends and students, at the age of ninety. Laurens wrote an obituary for
the *Daily Telegraph* which was too long, too emotional and too full of
factual errors to be used, which Laurens said was 'scandalous'. He wrote
to her son, 'There is no woman of our generation I honoured and
respected and loved more.'[18]

This was the background to 'The Other Journey'. He wrote it
throughout 1992 with great difficulty. It would be his last published statement of his more spiritual beliefs, the ideas he was expanding in his
eighties in addresses, interviews and symposia, and which earned him the
reputation of a mystic; his final book, *The Admiral's Baby*, would be an
historical memoir, deliberately lacking in this spiritual dimension.

'The Other Journey' is not an easy read. It is prolix, repetitive, sometimes incomprehensible and often illiterate. For instance, he declares that
Aristotle never wrote any books, speaks of a great Theban empire and
claims that Christ was known to have been a great scholar. He focusses
on Zeus's decision, in the final pages of *The Odyssey*, to bring the fighting
and the story to an end by despatching a blazing thunderbolt of thunder
and lightning, as evidence of divine intervention, and he offers modestly,
'My own pattern seems in some sort related in a lesser way to the overall
Odyssean pattern which I believe is, known or unknown, in the unconscious of every human being.' (This is a theme developed by C. G. Jung.)
Laurens remembers a scene from his early childhood, with his Bushman
nanny Klara, when a storm struck and he heard a 'Hottentot' calling out
to his god, Heitse-Eibib, 'Listen! The Old Master speaks!' On this image
Laurens builds an extended sermon, illustrated with other memories of
his childhood.

He himself, he says, has tried to follow through the Odyssean pattern
in 'a journey of exploration of a vast new universe within myself'. He
returns to his memories of the Bushman and Bantu societies which he

claims to have known as a boy, whose sense of the living world was even more primitive than that of pre-Homeric Greece. There is, he believes, a mysterious bond between the invisible and the objective worlds: 'Life and creation in itself is the synchronicity, all paradox and polarity transcended in a great acausal moment with which creation as we know it began and moves on . . . [I] am compelled to say it . . . because it is as much as I can do.'

From this Laurens proceeds to his fear, which preoccupied him in old age, for the environmental danger to the very future of life on earth – 'the wounding of our great Mother Earth almost to death'. He sees in Teiresias's prophetic end of *The Odyssey* a hope for the future. He remembers how, under sentence of imminent death in Java in 1942, he looked out of his cell on the afternoon storm of thunder and rain and remembered that the thunder was the voice of God.[19]

This was not a book for the best-seller lists, and it was granted very little critical attention. In *Resurgence* magazine Laurens's friend, the poet Kathleen Raine, one of few reviewers, hailed him as 'a light-bearer of wisdom in our dark world'; *The Voice of the Thunder* was written, she suggested, 'not to inform but to transform'.[20]

When Laurens first warned John Charlton at Chatto in September 1992 he had nearly completed his opening section for *The Voice of the Thunder* (written 'with circumstances very much against me'), he suggested it would be a good curtain-raiser for a forthcoming anthology from his books, put together by Jean-Marc Pottiez and Jane Bedford, which was eventually called *Feather Fall*. He wondered whether might be simultaneous publication with *The Voice of the Thunder*, but Chatto refused, partly because the two books would compete with each other, and partly because Charlton was not happy with the anthology, which was far too long. *The Voice of the Thunder* appeared in late 1993; *Feather Fall* was published, after heavy cutting, in May the next year.[21]

His principal and long-term contact at the Hogarth Press, John Charlton, retired from a part-time role in June 1993, although he kept in touch with Laurens. Laurens and the head of Chatto, the dynamic Carmen Callil, were never going to be great friends. Chatto, with the Hogarth Press, was absorbed into the Random House conglomerate in 1993, with Carmen Callil as Publisher at Large. Laurens soon began to feel unappreciated. Having been cosseted by the Hogarth Press for many years, he was now just one of a large stable of writers. A new generation of editors seemed largely ignorant of his past distinction. He tried to remind them that the

Hogarth Press had guaranteed that none of its authors' books would be allowed to go out of print in their lifetime, which Leonard Woolf may have promised, though no publisher today could keep such a promise and survive. His new editor at Chatto, Alison Samuel, explained that the 'cruel truth' of today's world was that this luxury was no longer possible, at least in hardback, though they would try to keep his list in print in paperback.

Because of the decline in Laurens's sales, plans for new editions of his earlier books had to be put on hold. *Feather Fall* sold fewer than 2,500 copies; *The Voice of the Thunder*, which had a £10,000 advance, just over 3,500. Things had changed, Alison Samuel warned Laurens, and one consequence was that plans to re-issue *Jung and the Story of Our Time* would have to be dropped, as had a previous idea for an illustrated edition of *Venture to the Interior*. In mid-1995, when Chatto showed no interest in re-issuing *The Night of the New Moon* for the fiftieth anniversary of the victory over Japan, Laurens was thoroughly fed up. He was not impressed to be told by Chatto that Penguin would keep him in print, because Penguin, he thought, was already far too big and impersonal. Neither the Chatto switchboard nor the Penguin publicity department seemed to have heard of him.[22] He wrote to his old friend Charlton on 21 August 1995 that he was getting a 'rotten deal' from Chatto, which had made no adequate effort with his last two books. Now he had a new manuscript, *The Admiral's Baby*, which he thought 'a very great and very moving story of an individual person . . . a story like Conrad's *Lord Jim*, with the extraordinary thing that it was lived in every way in terms of flesh and blood, while Conrad's – which resembles it – was formed in fiction'. In Java in 1945, 'powerless and without authority, I managed to meet the future for some two years and to impose my powerless authority upon it.' Without his presence, there would have been a war of the most destructive kind. Believing this of himself, it is not surprising that he did not want to stay with Chatto, who apparently did not agree with this opinion of his new book. Charlton privately, and sadly, suggested he approach a smaller and independent publishing house such as John Murray. On 16 September Laurens announced to Alison Samuel that he was quitting Random House/Chatto. 'I do not think that Random House will enable you to give me the kind of relationship with which I want to finish my writing career . . . I am really not leaving Chatto's. Chatto's, by and large, have left me.'[23]

There was bound to be a certain amount of squabbling over the divorce. Chatto had to explain that the contracts, both domestic and foreign, on Laurens's many books could not be cancelled at a stroke.

Laurens claimed that he had never taken advances from Chatto, which was of course untrue (£15,000 for *About Blady* was a recent example). He explained that he had never before felt the need to concern himself with his financial relationship with his publisher. Laurens went to his lawyers about his rights to his paperbacks, and to the Society of Authors, which was happy to advise but discovered that he had resigned some years before on a point of principle. There was a separate argument about the fate of a proposed *Reader's Digest* version of *The Lost World of the Kalahari*.[24] Laurens's confusion, exasperation and distress were compounded because he had no agent to guide him, having refused all his life to take a literary agent to manage his complicated affairs.

So in the end Laurens went off to John Murray, where he had known the earlier head of the firm, Jock Murray, who had published him in *The Cornhill Magazine*. With him he took the manuscript of what would be his last book, *The Admiral's Baby*, the account of his service in Java between 1945 and 1947, based upon the official report which he had written at the time and whose manuscript had been sitting in his Aldeburgh house. He had been working on it for several years, complaining to friends that it was turning out to be the longest book he had ever written. The publishing process turned out to be difficult, because Laurens in old age was not accustomed to rigorous editing. John Murray eventually persuaded him to agree to substantial cuts (though John Charlton had believed that impossible) by promising that the deleted material would be carefully deposited in his archive. It was to be his last book, and was published, to sympathetic and interested reviews, in 1996.

The Admiral's Baby is a surprisingly fluent read, considering the obscurity of the subject nearly fifty years after the event. As always, Laurens sets himself at the centre although he was only one British officer out of many. In a novel, a writer may evoke a war or a battle through the thoughts and actions of a single person, as Tolstoy does in *War and Peace*, and Evelyn Waugh in his *Sword of Honour* trilogy. But *The Admiral's Baby* pretends to more. Laurens in old age insists that he was at the very heart of the action and the argument; yet Lt.-Col. van der Post is completely absent from the records and archives of both the Prime Minister, Clement Attlee, and the Supremo in Asia, Lord Mountbatten. Certainly he did a brave and valuable job; his colleagues confirm that he built up a good relationship with the Indonesian nationalists and that he was detested by the Dutch for this. Fifty years later, however, his focus has shifted solely to himself.[25]

Laurens's American publisher launched *The Admiral's Baby* as 'A True Account of One Man's Great Courage and Dedication Far Beyond the

Call of Duty', which certainly catches Laurens's tone of voice. *The Times Literary Supplement* said 'it reads like something out of one of Buchan's more portentous political thrillers, but then van der Post was nothing if not a Buchanesque hero'. *The Sunday Times* reviewer was sympathetic but added that 'there is certainly enough self-absorption . . . to bring a faint blush to the cheeks of Narcissus'. For the *Literary Review*, this was 'an important book for those who are interested in South-east Asia' — though it added that some readers would have preferred less 'portentous "philosophising"'. *The Spectator*'s critic was 'deeply impressed by the courage and fortitude of the author as well as by the political sagacity of his advice . . . A handsome book which tells a good story'.[26]

37

'My Prince'

THE PRINCE OF Wales met Laurens in the early 1970s at the Suffolk home of their mutual friends Robin and Lilias Sheepshanks, land-owners who lived outside the village of Eyke, a dozen miles from Aldeburgh. Robin and Lilias had been introduced to Laurens and Ingaret some years before by Benjamin Britten, and had quickly become close friends. The meeting of Prince Charles and Laurens had profound con-sequences for both men. Charles perhaps found in Laurens, in succes-sion to his uncle Lord Mountbatten, a father-figure who would also become a mentor and a spiritual adviser, at a time when he seemed to need all three. Laurens found in the Prince not only a gratifying disciple but a young friend he admired and loved.

It has often been assumed that Laurens was introduced to Prince Charles by Mountbatten. But Laurens and Mountbatten were never close; after serving under him in Java in 1945–47, Laurens subsequently exaggerated his role as 'Personal Representative'. They had a brief contact when Mountbatten was writing his memoirs, before he was assassinated by the IRA in 1979.[1] But Laurens's introduction to Charles came about not through Mountbatten, nor as a result of his affair in the 1930s with the Prince's great-aunt, Lilian Bowes Lyon, but through East Anglian high society in the 1970s.

Before long Laurens thought of taking the Prince on a seven-week journey into the Kalahari Desert, to explore the wilderness, together with a television camera team. As Charles's best biographer Jonathan Dimbleby observes, 'Someone of a more cynical cast of mind than the Prince might have concluded from the grandiloquent generalities and the high-flown prose [of Laurens's proposal] that van der Post was a flat-terer and a self-publicist. The Prince had no such suspicions, recognis-ing that in his esoteric fashion van der Post was entirely sincere.' The Prince was keen but the Foreign Office pointed out that Botswana's proximity to Rhodesia, then suffering civil war, was a security problem.

Laurens instead took Charles to Kenya for a five-day expedition to the Aberdare Mountains in March 1977.[2]

But the Kalahari trip was not forgotten and eventually, in March 1987, the Prince concluded an official visit to Kenya, Malawi and Swaziland by joining Laurens briefly in the Botswana desert. Laurens took great pains to ensure the success of this trip, enlisting the help of his friend the mining magnate Harry Oppenheimer (whose Anglo American Corporation provided back-up helicopters and other services) and his nephew Judge Chris Plewman, who knew the Kalahari far better than Laurens.

They managed not seven weeks but a mere four days, travelling by Land Rover and shielded from the press. They did not have time to go anywhere particularly adventurous and anyway London would not have permitted it. (Special radio masts were set up so that the Prince would be in touch with the Palace every night.) Prince Charles painted, Laurens talked and the Prince experienced the African wilderness. Dimbleby quotes from the Prince's diary: 'On first contact the desert is pretty harsh and unforgiving and I wondered what on earth I had let myself in for! But after four days, which was similar to an SAS selection test, it began to grow on you! So did the dirt, dust, and hair, and I have never been so filthy before. I hardly ate anything and only felt like liquid. It was just the place to be during Lent, but the sunsets were out of this world. It was worth going for these alone and there was something very special about lying under the stars on the last night in the bush.' The Prince did not meet any Bushmen.[3]

The friendship between Laurens and Prince Charles became extraordinarily intense.* Both of them detested the tabloids' phrase 'the Prince's Guru', which was coined almost at once and has persisted until this day, but it made a valid point. From the mid-1970s Laurens and Prince Charles were in intimate and frequent contact. There were many phone calls (and a code: a phone bell broken off and then repeated, to which Laurens would respond with a reverential '*Sir!* . . .'). There were small dinner parties in London, and Laurens would visit Highgrove, the Prince's estate in Gloucestershire, or Sandringham, the royal residence in East Anglia. There were annual visits to Balmoral in Scotland. 'I have just had five days at Balmoral with Prince Charles, at first with some old friends but then a day or two alone with him and lovely walks with him in what is left of the great Caledonian forests in a lovely valley,' he wrote. 'Oh, those trees, I wish you could see them. They are the most eloquent

*The Prince has declined to discuss it for this book.[4]

trees I know and we had a number of lovely picnics in a log cabin on the banks of a river which cuts through the Prince's land.' In these later years Laurens would protest that he was unable to undertake the lengthy walks which the Prince favoured; he asked that he be allowed to sit quietly and watch the Prince paint his watercolours.[5]

There is no doubt that Laurens loved his Prince dearly, and one suspects that the Prince loved Laurens. For twenty years they had most intimate conversations and correspondence, in which the Prince made Laurens privy to his dreams. Laurens took Charles with him to the most important venues in his own life – to the Kalahari, for example, to Jung's tower at Bollingen on Lake Geneva. He tutored Charles, seeking to educate a Prince to become a King, which may not have helped a young man in need of finding his own adulthood. When in 1982 Charles asked Laurens to become a godfather to Prince William, the future King, one might observe that Laurens, at seventy-five, was far too old to be able to fulfil a godfather's moral role to a child – but of course Charles was declaring that Laurens was *his* godfather.

Laurens had not at first realised that the public discovery that he was the Prince's 'guru' would affect his image and reputation, and not entirely for the better. Over the next twenty years he seems to have been utterly discreet about his friendship with Charles and would never discuss it, yet somehow the word got out – his framing of royal Christmas cards on the walls of his study, always mentioned by interviewers, perhaps gave the game away.* These were the years when he became famous as what was described as a mystic and spiritual guide to the Heir to the Throne, probably flaky and arguably a suspect influence on the future King. He would soon be regularly mocked in the satirical journal, *Private Eye*, as 'Van der Pump, the South African Seer'.[7]

Throughout the 1980s *Private Eye* delighted in a formula in which the luckless Prince Charles was counselled and consoled by his 'friend and mentor' in cod apothegms in the Laurensian style: 'At the centre of each life there is a great rock, which we must climb if we are to see beyond the horizon'; 'If a man dreams that he is a butterfly, then he may wake up to discover that he is only a caterpillar'; 'When the sun meets the moon, it is neither day nor night'; 'The old oak passes on its wisdom to the acorn'; 'Only in the sea of silence can we find the fish of peace', and

---

*His guard slipped occasionally. On 29 November 1995, for instance, he told the *Daily Mail*, 'He has been a great Prince of Wales and will become a great king.' As for the failed marriage, 'It's ludicrous that people expect royalty to stay in an unhappy marriage. Even princes are human beings . . .'[6]

so on. To these brilliantly wicked parodies of Laurens at his worst, usually written by Craig Brown, 'the Prince' invariably replied, 'How very true!' *Private Eye* even pursued Laurens as far as Aldeburgh, which Brown knew well: 'The two continued to walk back to "The Lighthouse", the guru's coastal retreat. Suddenly the white-haired figure bent down and picked up two pebbles, one large and one small. "We are like these stones", he explained in his familiar reassuring tones. "In life we must be both, the big and the small stones." Charles saw at once the brilliance of the metaphor.' Only after his death did *Private Eye* start referring to Laurens as 'mystic and paedophile'.[8]

One early result of the meeting in Suffolk was that Prince Charles entered into some sort of psychoanalytic relationship with Ingaret and he would visit her, discreetly, in Chelsea. Ingaret was not a fully trained analyst although she was said to be a gifted interpreter of dreams. The Prince's friendship with Laurens developed during this period and in the early 1980s Charles transferred from Ingaret to Laurens's psycho-therapist friend, Dr Alan McGlashan. Some of Ingaret's friends remember that she was not happy about this, as she herself had had an analytic as well as a personal relationship with McGlashan.*

As the years went by, this psychoanalytic connection became peri-lously complex, because Laurens was himself in a quasi-analytical rela-tionship with McGlashan, however informal, visiting him occasionally to discuss his dreams. Charles had been seeing Ingaret; Laurens advised Charles. It had the makings of an unorthodox blurring of the traditional psychoanalytical boundaries. Then Charles married Diana Spencer in June 1981, and later she, too, saw McGlashan. Their unhappy marriage, as has been reported so often, began badly when on the honeymoon cruise on the *Britannia* Charles bewildered his bride by spending his time reading Laurens's books (this should not imply that Laurens's books were responsible for the problems!). Diana, finding herself wretched in her new position – and, it seems, slowly realising that her husband was in love with someone else – understandably became saddened and deeply unhappy. Much later she spoke of depression, bulimia, and attempts to injure herself.[10]

'The Young Man' (TYM was the code by which Laurens and his friends referred to the Prince – they pronounced it 'Tim') summoned Laurens to Balmoral. In the light of their own close relationship Charles could probably not have chosen anyone less likely to be able to help

---

*Charles always maintained his affection for Ingaret, and delighted her friends by turning up, unannounced, for her funeral in 1997.[9]

Diana and indeed Laurens failed to get anywhere. Laurens then recommended that Diana should start seeing McGlashan in London – another problematic suggestion, for the same reason that he was McGlashan's close friend. Diana began to do so, twice a week. McGlashan reported back to Laurens just once (Sasha McGlashan, his widow, suggests this was rather as a consultant does to a referring GP), writing that the Princess was surrounded by a bevy of frightened doctors who seemed to think that they were confronting not just a serious illness but also a dynastic crisis, and had been tackling it with all sorts of pills and antidepressants and 'Behaviourist' techniques. This, it may be noted, was the start of a rumour which, during and after the royal divorce, would be fanned by spin doctors in both palaces – that Diana was mentally unstable. This innuendo persists even today, and surfaces again and again in the press and on television, years after her tragic death. But McGlashan after his initial session would have none of this. He assured Laurens that he found Diana to be a normal, though very unhappy, young woman, trying bravely to cope with her situation. He thought that he would be able to help her with her emotional problems so long as she realised that the analytic process took time.[11] In the event, she saw him only seven or eight times before deciding to seek help and advice elsewhere. Long after he had ceased seeing her, the Princess's condition appeared to alter, as did McGlashan's opinion.

Afterwards, McGlashan would see Charles for many years, while he, Laurens and Ingaret were very close, but Sasha McGlashan is adamant that Laurens and her husband never discussed The Young Man. She explains, 'On the few occasions they met privately over these years their talks centered around Laurens's writing, and the difficulties of writing amidst the home conditions revolving around Ingaret. Any suggestion of an ethical problem is entirely at odds both with Alan's deep-rooted integration of the Hippocratic Oath and with Laurens's respect for Alan.' She adds that the nature of her husband's relationship with Charles (who visited him frequently) was 'not analytical but a supportive friendship.'

Laurens had by now achieved an intense friendship with Charles, speaking with him constantly and meeting him often. In the light of Laurens's own marital history, where he apparently saw nothing wrong in deceiving his wife while revealing his second relationship to his friends and even inviting their complicity, one is bound to wonder what advice he gave to Charles as the royal marriage became a façade in the mid-1980s, and the Prince debated with his friend and adviser what to do about Diana and his resumed relationship with Camilla Parker Bowles.

This dangerous collaboration, however carefully restrained, continued for years. In late 1995, for instance, McGlashan – who was then 97! – complained to Laurens that the Prince had abruptly ended their arrangement; he simply did not understand why. Could Laurens, from his position of close friendship with both of them, seek out an explanation?

To that plaintive protest from a therapist in his late nineties, Laurens replied three days later: 'I have never initiated a discussion with him about your special relationship, and he has never discussed it with me, except from time to time to mention how much he valued knowing you, and how what had been a professional relationship had given him a companionship of heart and mind that he had never met before. You, I am certain better than any of us, know how misunderstood and starved he has been of really spontaneous, natural affection – and, indeed, the respect his own natural spirit deserves. I do not really think that you can think of it as you would with normal people because his life in the last few years has meant that he has terrifyingly less and less time for his "being", as he calls it, than he has ever had, and his being is something precious to which you are very important . . . Please, please, do not let that be a source of unease. There is nobody he respects more than you, and he would be terribly upset if he felt that he had hurt you . . .'[12]

A psychotherapist does not discuss his analysands with *anyone* else, let alone with someone whom the analysand knows. The fact that the subject was the Prince is beside the point.

Over twenty years Laurens was not just a spiritual adviser to the Prince, allegedly behind his controversial declaration that he intended to be 'Defender of Faith' rather than 'Defender of the Faith', the confessor-figure to whom he confided his dreams. He also provided him with a steady flow of reassurance and encouragement, political and diplomatic advice, memoranda, draft speeches and guidance for his reading.[13]

The Afrikaner whose family had fought against the British Crown in the Anglo-Boer War had become a passionate Royalist, and also something of a snob. As early as 1971, in notes he prepared to help Ingaret give a talk, he wrote: 'Nothing expresses the psychology valid to the English political evolution better than the place of the crown in British institutions . . . The first thing about a crown, of course, is that it is round and that roundness has always been the expression of wholeness, the opposite of that which is angled, slanted and incomplete.' It was why the Zulus awarded a metal headband to their wise old men; it was why the Greeks garlanded Olympic athletes with a crown of laurels. The crown is 'the chief symbol of state in Great Britain, because it is the master symbol of a society striving to achieve a rounded nature'. He reminded Ingaret of the power of the legend of Arthur's Round Table in the British imagination, 'because it is the great myth of man's striving towards wholeness. This is why, despite the fact that it is awarded also to men who have manufactured sock suspenders, margarine and plastics, the title of Knight still survives in this land and still carries some of its original meaning.'[14]

It was in this context that Laurens had been so keen to take Charles to Africa in the 1970s. He told him, 'Our Royal Family already has done an enormous amount to make the monarch more contemporary but if my intuition is right, the burden of transforming it into a dynamic and as yet unimagined role to suit the future shape of a fundamentally re-appraised and renewed modern society will fall on you.' One aspect of this must be to help restore respect for nature, 'to draw closer to the original blueprint and plan of life as we find it alas today only in the great wildernesses . . . The battle for our renewal can be most naturally led by what is still one of the few great living symbols accessible to us – the symbol of the crown.'

When the Foreign Office rebuffed his plan to film in Africa with Prince Charles, Laurens broadened his range. On 1 November 1978, he sent him a nine-page letter to help him prepare for a speech at Harvard, in which he covered spiritual insecurity, world unrest, the crisis of meaning, the loss of faith, the concept of the individual, the importance of small as opposed to great, the absence of true leadership and much else, illustrated with references to Blake, Dorothy Sayers, Alfred the Great, O. Henry, Pirandello and Jesus Christ. Ingaret scrawled on his draft that it was 'quite brilliant'.[15]

Before his marriage, Charles acquired his new home at Highgrove House, in Gloucestershire. By what they both probably saw as a Jungian synchronicity, it happened to be only a mile from Colley Farm, where Laurens had lived in the mid-1930s. Laurens would frequently go to Highgrove in the years ahead, and sometimes asked the Prince for permission to bring his friends (particularly his wealthy Americans) to see the gardens. He regularly visited Balmoral at Easter and in late summer, and had other semi-royal connections: for example, he would speak at St George's House, the private discussion venue based at Windsor Castle and patronised by the Royal Family – though his relationship was specifically with the Prince rather than with the Queen or the Duke of Edinburgh.

Throughout the 1980s, Laurens continued what he must have seen as the Education of a Monarch. As the relationship became public knowledge, there was a certain amount of protest from conventional quarters, along the lines that the future King had been hijacked by mystical Greens, protests which re-emerged when Charles made his controversial speeches, particularly when he spoke about the environment. However, the fact that Laurens was also known by now to be an intimate of Mrs Thatcher must have helped defend him. Just as with the Prime Minister, he offered briefings on subjects where he was less than expert. He wrote to Charles at length about a forthcoming visit to Nigeria, which he scarcely knew, in a document full of misspellings of names; he lectured him on the role of a university, of which he had no experience; he offered advice on Romania, on which he knew next to nothing; and he fulminated against the alleged 'Franco-German domination'. More convincingly, he briefed him for a visit to Indonesia, mentioning that he had never gone back after 1947, although he had wished to do so, 'to try and bury the dead I left behind'.[16]

A detailed study of the Prince's speeches over these years would reveal Laurens's important role. To quote just one example, Charles sent Laurens a transcript of a speech he had made on 6 March 1989 at the British Museum in which he had ad-libbed: 'Now is the time actually to start learning and listening to developing countries. To listen and learn from those traditional societies who I think have an enormous amount to teach us. I believe we should abandon the idea . . . that we in the developed world . . . have the monopoly of civilised values and attainments. Just because we are superior technologically does not mean we are superior in a civilised or even a spiritual sense . . .' This is Charles's own voice, but his tutor is Laurens, who constantly urges him to pursue his 'great crusade – this journey of individuation and re-discovery of the self . . . the search to which you are naturally deeply committed and which . . . implies defeats of those great priesthoods of science, particularly applied science, technology and economic realism which are the main instruments of devastation of the natural world.'

Laurens's letters were always intensely complimentary. When the Prince broadcast a BBC 'Thought for the Day' in May 1995 Laurens sent fulsome praise, comparing him with Prince Albert, mentioning the Divine Right of Kings, and suggesting that he travel to New York to deliver (like Laurens himself) an Advent Sermon at the Cathedral of St John the Divine. He added the 'cunning' thought (the word is his) that the congregation might raise funds for both his and the Prince's Foundations: 'Three Christmases ago one of them dropped a cheque for four million dollars into the plate . . .' The Prince declined and Laurens again blamed the Foreign Office.[17]

Sometimes Laurens's letters must have been helpful, for example when he drafted speeches for Charles's visit to Japan in 1990 and helped arrange for a friend from Cambridge, the Japanese authority Dr Carmen Blacker, to travel with him. Later, he was to ask the Prince to lobby Botswana for the preservation of the Bushmen of the Kalahari. Sometimes the correspondence drifted into surreal areas; for example, Charles wanted to discuss 'bringing back the world of Plato'. He introduced the Zulu leader Chief Buthelezi to Charles, took him to visit Highgrove, and assured Charles that 'like you, he is a great Prince'.[18]

In some areas – the personal, the emotional, the sexual, the political – it would be easy to suggest that Laurens's influence on the future King was probably unfortunate, but against this he was responsible for introducing to Charles, or at least sharing with him, a whole world of wider spiritual and philosophical, even religious, dimensions which the Prince might otherwise never have encountered. Laurens's philosophy, whatever one may think of it, did help people who were going through difficult times. No-one else played a similar role in the Prince's life, and the character of the Prince's activities in his maturity, in the years since Laurens died, surely owes a great deal to his influence in those formative years. It is also worth noting that while the Prince had a reputation for taking up people and later dropping them, his relationship with Laurens was long and unbroken.

Laurens never spoke about his friendship with the Prince, except when he left an interview for posthumous publication in which he said that he hoped that Charles would never be king since this would imprison him; it was more important that he should continue to be a great prince. 'He's been brought up in a terrible way . . . He's a natural Renaissance man. A man who believes in the wholeness and totality of life . . . Why should it be that if you try to contemplate your natural self that you should be thought to be peculiar?'

Laurens was always money-conscious, most of all in his last years, when he was incurring very heavy expenses for Ingaret's support, and he may have implicated the Prince in his concerns. In April 1996, for example, he wrote to Arianna Huffington, the Greek-born socialite and author whom he had first known in England and who had married an American millionaire, taking it on himself to explain the Prince's finances and suggesting that she and her husband might attend the Prince's forthcoming visit to North Carolina raising funds for his various charities. He concluded his appeal with a powerful story: a fashionable Austrian doctor in New York and his friends 'had all recognised me as one of the Knights of the Round Table . . . one of them claimed we had died together in defence of Constantinople . . . He said a call had gone out that the Knights of the Round Table must reassemble because the human spirit was in greater danger than it had ever been before . . . At Berkeley where I lectured I had a similar experience from another ex-Knight of the Round Table who was a Professor of Physics, and there were several other occasions on that journey when people recognised me as having been with them in previous campaigns for the human spirit. So I am sometimes almost inclined to think that perhaps I am serving a kind of Holy Grail and a Round Table summons with people like Prince Charles to rally in defense of the spirit of man.'[19]

One can only wonder what Charles made of this. On the other hand, another undated memorandum, also from the last years, conveys the flavour of Laurens's storytelling, with which he must have bewitched his Prince as he did almost everyone who encountered it. It is part of a sober briefing on Indonesia in which he reminisces about his time in Java immediately after the end of the war:

> I remember cutting again and again a footpath through the jungle under-growth with our parangs and coming back three days later and having to do all the cutting all over again, and the scars we had made already regrown and out of sight. Bamboo forests had tracks so narrow that one morning, led by an animist (and I had only a prospector's axe on one hip and a pistol on the other) we met a tiger coming towards us and neither of us could turn about. I stood still in horror with my hand on the futile pistol, but the Badoeis quickly sank on his knees and prayed to his Lord Tiger: and the tiger sud-denly stopped swishing his tail, his stare relaxed and his face went benign and slowly he did what I thought was impossible and, with unbelievable sup-pleness, turned around and walked away.[20]

He never told this story before or since. Even as fantasy, it has the authentic van der Post power.

38

The Company of Seven

THROUGHOUT THE LAST ten years of his life Laurens attracted, and energetically cultivated, the friendship of a small group of wealthy Americans. He took great pains to secure, develop, and then, it has to be said, to exploit these relationships. They were to be a source of very substantial funds over these years. Initially their charity was directed to the financing of the Jungian Centre in Cape Town. After this had been established, their contributions were paid into 'The Laurens van der Post Foundation for the Advancement of the Humanities', a newly-established charity with vague though ostensibly noble ends. In practice, as the Americans must have understood, their money was used to allow Laurens to continue his activities around the world in a period when his own earnings were faltering and his domestic costs escalating. The Foundation's real purpose was to pay for the running costs of the second apartment in the Chelsea towerblock (the Foundation's 'office'), the wages of a second secretary and also of a full-time housekeeper (to look after Ingaret), to bring various of Laurens's guests to London, and to finance his expenses as he travelled first class to South Africa or America to make speeches and address conferences. It was linked with similar Foundations in Switzerland and South Africa.

The supervision and co-ordination of these Foundations demanded a great deal of Laurens's time and energy for the last fifteen years of his life. Their function – their justification – was to employ Laurens's name to raise funds for causes he held dear: in effect, the Wilderness campaign, and the promotion of Jungian training, particularly in South Africa. Laurens in these years presided over a nexus which brought together Wilderness, the Cape Town Jungian Centre, and in due course right-wing support of Zulu federalism.

There was an interesting exchange with Britain's Charity Commissioners when Laurens and his friends in March 1992 applied to register the UK Foundation as a charity, with the tax benefits that would bring. This application included a long *curriculum vitae* in which Laurens added the previously unknown point that he had once been canvassed to be Governor-General of Kenya. But the application made the fundamental point about his Foundation, that he had reached an age when he was sought out by people from all over the world and that he needed help to pass on his ideas and experience not only through his books but through the spoken word. This, he pointed out, was what Plato, Socrates and Christ had done.

The Charity Commissioners were surprisingly helpful, suggesting a re-definition of the Foundation's proposed aims so that its educational objects should be more precisely limited to promoting 'the mental and moral improvement of man', which was to include the advancement of human knowledge and the conduct of research into the human condition (both still rather imprecise). Any private benefits accruing to Sir Laurens, the Commissioners added, were, 'given his international standing and reputation, purely incidental to the objects of the Foundation'. He could not be a Council Member, but could settle, they suggested, for the role of Honorary President. On this happy basis the Foundation was officially set up in January 1993, with Neil Crichton-Miller, Laurens's son-in-law, as Secretary.[1]

Laurens used to explain that this idea of a Foundation had come to him after his major operation in 1990 for a broken hip. Since then, he wrote, 'I've been rather haunted about the things that I have left undone in my life . . . In meeting and talking to the people who just came to me out of their own accord, I could pass on so much more than I could in the laborious process of writing.' The Foundation had arisen out of an informal group of Laurens's sponsors, largely American, whom he organised in the late 1980s and dubbed 'The Company of Seven'. The original members – they never reached seven – were Bob Schwarz, a New York media entrepreneur, Doug Greene, a thriving publisher and businessman, Arman Simone, another rich businessman of Armenian origin, and Christer Salen, a Scandinavian shipping magnate. Bill Pilder, yet another businessman who was one of Helen Luke's circle, fell out early on. The group was eventually joined by an expatriate South African, Ronald Cohen, and Jane Bedford.

Arman Simone, whose immigrant family had made a fortune out of faucets and who then in middle age determined to seek out more spiritual values – his estate, south of Washington, is called Peace Love and Joy Farm – first encountered Laurens when he asked his friend Bob Schwarz to tell him who was the most impressive person he had ever met. Schwarz replied, 'Sir Laurens van der Post', and explained that when he met him Laurens had said, 'If I had $150,000, I could save the world.' To which Simone replied, 'Then let's fly to London and give him $150,000!' Which, with Doug Greene, they did. It was this money which set up the Cape Town Jungian Centre. Out of this beginning Laurens developed his 'Company of Seven' which would support him until his death. Arman Simone remained a founder-member. He never concerned himself with the detail of what happened to his money; his only concern, he says, was to make Laurens financially secure so that he could continue his work.[2] The Company of Seven held various meetings in London, and some of them visited South Africa, where they were welcomed by Ian Player and taken on a Wilderness Trail in Natal as well as shown the Cape Town Centre where Julian David, followed by Patrick Tummon, had arrived as analysts-in-residence. Laurens spent an exhausting amount of time arranging the logistics of his Company of Seven as well as the funding and administration of the Cape Town Centre. He was helped by his newly-close friend Ronald Cohen, who personally contributed substantial sums to the Centre, in particular to its library.

In the meantime, and to complicate the situation, a separate 'Laurens van der Post Foundation for Africa' had been set up in Switzerland in mid-1991 by Theo Abt, Bob Hinshaw and Peter Ammann. While the London Foundation was phased out after Laurens's death,* the more modestly funded Swiss Foundation decided to carry on, and in 2001 published a new edition of Dr Bleek's long-out-of-print study of Bushman folklore.[4]

Throughout the last ten years of his life, Laurens was actively canvassing other friends, particularly in the US, for funds. Money came in from several independent foundations and private individuals, but the great bulk of his support would continue to be provided by the Seven, whom Laurens flatteringly addressed as modern-day Arthurian Knights seeking the Holy Grail. He gratified them with discreet references to the Prince of Wales and to Mrs Thatcher, hinting that he might be able to arrange meetings and even visits to Highgrove. When cheques arrived there were extravagant letters of thanks and promises that he would introduce them to Chief Buthelezi. He offered them confidential insights into Southern African affairs, and warned them to doubt the integrity of some South African politicians, even – incomprehensibly – his friend Piet Koornhof. Sometimes he misled them, as when he assured Arman Simone that

---

*The remaining funds were used to establish a 'Laurens van der Post Centre', set in a Memorial Garden in Philippolis, Laurens's birthplace.[3]

Winnie Mandela was Chief Buthelezi's sister! He offered each of them a sense of private intimacy: for instance, to Arman Simone he suggested a parallel between his own 'Huguenot' blood and the Armenians. Consequently, Laurens and his staff benefited from all sorts of gifts, in addition to the annual contributions pledged by the Americans.

Laurens planned that his nephew, Tom Bedford, would give up his architectural practice and mobilise a wider group of people, but for that more funds would be needed, and neither Laurens nor Tom had private money, so they would need the help of their American friends. Arman Simone appeared enthusiastic, and suggested that Tom front a world-wide campaign. Tom realised that the scheme was unrealistic, and held back.[5]

Once the Cape Town Jungian Centre was established, and recognised by the International Association of Analytical Psychologists, Laurens switched his fundraising and the contributions of the Seven to his new Foundation. He wrote to his friends that he was seeking support (and money) from people 'who may be concerned about what we regard as the increasingly urgent matter of rescuing governments and establishments from the bankruptcy of spirit into which they have sunk and which threatens not only our Western way of life but the destruction of our planet'. We might all be in favour of that. There were references to more precise projects also, such as the publication of Aniela Jaffe's unused notes from the time when she put together Jung's memoir, *Memories, Dreams, Reflections* – an interesting idea which has not yet seen the light of day. But it was always clear that the meat of the Foundation's role was to do with Laurens's personal activities, now that he was in his eighties, and in particular his promised role in rescuing South Africa from 'the disintegration by violence which threatens it in a way which the world does not realise'.[6] He may have hated the word, but he was setting himself up as a 'guru' to the world.

From four of the Company of Seven he extracted a promise of $60,000 a year – $15,000 each – for at least four years and in return sent them a steady stream of letters. There would be awkward moments ahead when Bob Schwarz seemed to vanish and Ronald Cohen decided to raise the annual subvention for the remaining three to $20,000 each, at which Arman Simone protested hotly, requiring Laurens's most emollient intervention. Laurens wanted more – he had dreamed of a $1,000,000 budget – and he continued to canvass other American friends from his address book. He approached, for example, the McMillans in Corpus Christi in Texas (who were already heavily involved in the Cape Town project); Carolyn Fay in Houston (who ran the C. G. Jung Institute and had entertained Laurens several times); George Wagner in California (who had successfully asked Laurens to lobby for his wind-farm company in Britain); Larry Hughes (Laurens's longstanding US publisher); Merrill Ford in Aspen (to whom he offered the chance of meeting 'my Prince . . . a truly inspired Renaissance Prince'); Sam Francis, the Los Angeles painter, by then seriously ill; Arianna Huffington, née Stassinopoulos (whose husband had political ambitions and, Laurens had noted, had put $1,000,000 – or was it $4,000,000, as he told Prince Charles? – into the plate at the Cathedral of St John the Divine). He also considered approaching people he did not know personally, like Steven Spielberg and the rock musician Sting.

To these people Laurens found himself spinning all manner of yarns. He frequently mentioned a deeply confidential relationship with Prince Charles; he repeated all the tales of his childhood; he revealed that the British diplomat Robin Renwick 'was my right hand at the Lancaster House negotiations without whom we could not have succeeded in bringing the negotiations to a successful conclusion . . .' (a description which will cause Lord Renwick to splutter); he explained that his Foreword to a reprint of General Smuts's address book had been 'a turning point in the political spirit of South Africa'; and so on.[7] Much of this seems to have been accepted at face value.

He also had various South African friends in mind, none more so than Harry Oppenheimer, the liberally-minded mining magnate, the master, now deceased, of the Anglo American Corporation and De Beers. Ronald Cohen was deputed to call on 'HFO' and suggest that, as a contribution to the Foundation, he might buy from Laurens the second apartment in the Chelsea tower block. Mr Oppenheimer listened, in his usual courteous manner, replied that he did not wish to enter the London property market – and wrote a cheque for £50,000. Laurens, thanking him ecstatically, assured his benefactor that he had decided that 'there is no ego in accepting so gladly and with such joy this great gift'. During this period Laurens also sent Oppenheimer, for the Africana archive at his Brenthurst Library in Johannesburg, a number of his letters from William Plomer and Roy Campbell.[8]

Frank McMillan III was a friend and admirer of Laurens who stood to one side of the Company of Seven, and is a good example of the devotion Laurens could inspire. His father, Frank N. McMillan Jnr, had made a fortune in the oil industry in the 1960s, and had been so influenced by his encounter with Jung's writings that, when he became rich, he funded at the Texas A&M University the first professorship in Jungian psychology in America.

Laurens, who became a close friend of the McMillan family, used to say that he first met the father in the mid-1950s when he gave a talk to a Jungian group in Houston; Frank had told him of his dreams, the two of them had talked for several days, and the eventual result was that Frank McMillan endowed the faculty of psychology. Laurens's memory played him false: he never went to Texas at that time, and only the last statement is true. Frank McMillan set the record straight when he wrote to Laurens for the first time on 26 March 1985 to remind him that they had met just once, not in the 1950s but twenty-five years later in April 1979, when they had lunch together in a meeting which had a great influence on McMillan's life: 'For you, sir, are the only man I have ever met whom I felt to have a full appreciation of Dr Jung and his vision . . . I picture myself as a man alone rowing like hell in a dinghy and constantly finding my course to be in the wake of a dreadnought – in this case, two dread-noughts.'

In the same letter he told Laurens of an important dream he had had when he was just seven, which he had never forgotten and which had shaped his life.* Thirty years ago, he said, he had discovered Jung's writings while he was an oil-field hand in Bay City, Texas. 'And then, in 1979, I discovered you in Houston. Both discoveries have been of immense importance to me as an individual.' Laurens replied: 'Your letter was received by me as a Bushman receives rain in the midst of the dry season.' Laurens probably did not know that McMillan was seriously ill, and near-blind, as he hailed him as a fellow-soul and suggested that McMillan might be interested in helping in 'bringing Jung to Africa' as he had long planned. 'Please let me know how and to whom or what contributions may be made,' replied McMillan on 12 September 1985: 'Your letters are manna to me . . .'[10] This was the beginning of a long involvement of the McMillan family with Laurens's projects in South Africa.

Laurens started by suggesting that the McMillan family visit Africa and join a Wilderness Trail with Ian Player and himself in Natal, with digressions to the Kalahari, the Cape and Namibia, but McMillan died in March 1988. His widow and son determined to commemorate his contact with Laurens. There followed an eight-year friendship between them to which Laurens contributed many a long and effusive letter. The

---

*'Standing in the open door was a gigantic African lion – at least twice the size of an ordinary lion. He looked directly at me with large eyes and I was forced to look at him. I was absolutely terrified. I could not move or make a sound. The great lion walked slowly towards me, extended his great tongue, and caressed my face.'[9]

relationship was undoubtedly warm, but it is difficult to resist the impression, from the tone of the correspondence, that Laurens was aware that major funds were available.

The young Frank McMillan was evidently in thrall to Laurens, who became godfather to Frank IV and visited their Corpus Christi home; he arranged Frank's visit to South Africa in 1990, and he welcomed him and his young family to London. By 1989 the family was wondering whether it could help fund Laurens's project in Cape Town, and at the same time it discussed expanding its commitment to Texas A&M University where Carolyn Fay had just endowed a series of Jungian lectures (separate from the professorship) which Laurens was invited to initiate. In February 1989 Laurens agreed to accept help from the McMillans in Cape Town to the tune of $40–$60,000: 'You best know where we might be of help,' wrote Frank III on 29 March 1989, 'and I will continue to rely on your sage counsel to guide our course . . . I am grateful for the opportunity.'

He sent Laurens his dreams and sought his help in preparing a biography of his father. Laurens assured him that his father was the clearest example he knew of what Jung hoped for; it was, said Laurens, a life which was important to 'the evolution of the cosmos', and he was planning to dedicate a book to him as well as thinking of a series of lectures based on his life story. Frank III confirmed an annual contribution of $12,000 for at least four years to help the Jungian Foundation in the Cape.[11]

It is hard to evade the suspicion that, however true the friendship, Laurens was 'playing' the McMillan family, as he did other wealthy fans and sponsors. He frequently postponed the trips to South Africa to which they looked forward so much. He held out the possibility of his own presence, knowing he was in no condition to go into the bush.* He offered them the idea that their beloved father was not dead but might live on in the Library which they were about to fund in Cape Town.

The correspondence between Laurens and the McMillan family was intense and emotional over the last six years of Laurens's life. They always said how grateful they were to be allowed to contribute to the cause. Frank would remain one of Laurens's most devoted admirers: 'What Jung gives back with science, you, Sir Laurens, give back through the dream, which is what your stories are to me,' he wrote. Laurens

---

*Frank McMillan's trip to South Africa, to the Natal Wilderness trail and to the Cape Town Centre, was postponed in 1989 because Laurens said the political situation made it unwise, but he made it in 1990, in the company of Ian Player, though without Laurens.[12]

replied, 'You are a member of our family,' and there was something true about that. Over the next years there were visits between London, New York and, in May 1994, Texas, plus frequent correspondence and phone calls. The journals of Frank N. McMillan were edited for publication by Professor David Rosen at Texas A&M: Laurens wrote a Foreword in which he could not resist his fantastical memories of his invitation to Houston and his talks with Frank McMillan about his recurring lion dreams. This biography, 'Quest for the Lion and the Eagle', has not yet found a publisher.[13]

The McMillans were not alone in their response to Laurens's charm. For example, a Canadian friend, Richard Osler, wrote to Laurens a few months before his death, 'You proclaim the truth of the mystery that so many of us in our Baboon-like states ignore or, worse still, deny and deride. That is why you continue to touch so many people and help reawaken parts of their awareness that have been put to sleep.'[14] That sentiment was shared by many others, whether or not they were in a position to send Laurens their cheques.

Thanks to the McMillans, one of Laurens's achievements during his last years was an important new library in Cape Town, connected to the Jungian Centre. This was for Laurens a labour of love and conviction, and he devoted much energy to it in the early 1990s. He did sincerely try to put his dreams into practice, even if other people had to pay for them. He raised $50,000 from the McMillans to stock the library with books relevant to the study of Jungian psychology, which he defined very broadly. He wanted more than the technical and professional volumes; he insisted on 'the in-depth illumination of the spirit . . . the sacred books of India . . . the great Greek tragedies, and the mythological stories, and the same for every country in the world'. There should be fiction as well, including contemporary novels like *The Chymical Wedding* by Lindsay Clarke, which explored ideas that could also be found in Jung.

The 'Frank N. McMillan Jnr Library' project started in mid-1991, and Laurens immediately made it clear that he would be in charge from London. Specialist booksellers in California, South Africa and London were recruited to track down the thousands of volumes required, but Laurens controlled the purse, and payments went through a tortuous process via various Foundations and Trusts in America and Switzerland. The people in Cape Town were given only a small discretionary budget. Julian David, the resident analyst, used to think that it would be so much easier if the American donations could be paid directly to Cape Town, but Laurens insisted that he was in charge, and many faxes were exchanged in discussion of the books that should be bought, after which the bills were sent to Laurens and authorised by his friend Ronald Cohen.[15]

One result was that Laurens was able to veto authors of whom he disapproved. He emphasised the world's classics and early African history, and promoted his own friends and favourites, like Fredy Meier and Helen Luke, while blocking from the shelves some of the most distinguished and successful Jungian writers. For instance, Joseph Campbell, the famous best-selling American mythologist, was dismissed as 'superficial . . . just blatant pot-boilers'. James Hillman, an equally respected figure, was ruled out because after 1979 he apparently had 'a plausible but deeply flawed sensibility . . . the worst sort of influence to whom to expose newcomers to the world we try to serve.' The author of *Women who Run with the Wolves*, Clarissa Pinkola Estes, was rejected as 'a kind of psychological Lady Macbeth, typical of the new kind of feminine hubris parading as serving the "feminine" as understood by Jung'. Andrew Samuels, one of the foremost interpreters of Jung for the contemporary mind, was ruled out as a 'terrible creature . . . who pops up all over the place trying to assassinate his father in the shape of Jung'. (Samuels had been appointed to the Chair of Analytical Psychology at the University of Essex: 'All I can say is, God help Essex University!' Laurens wrote.) He told Cape Town not to buy a new book by Renos Papadopoulos (the other Professor at Essex), who had been involved in setting up the Cape Town Centre and must have thought he was a friend, because it was 'hurried and superficial'.

What Laurens wanted, he explained in his letters to Cape Town, was to 'provide the Library with the underlying basic sources of all the diversities of literature and philosophy'. But Laurens, with no knowledge of universities and their libraries, did not subscribe, perhaps, to the ideal of impartiality and objectivity which offers students a choice. Clearly he wanted to set his individual stamp on the new institution. Not all of the funds dispatched from Texas to Switzerland actually landed up in the Cape Town Library, probably because the many bank accounts which Laurens held, either in his own name or those of his Foundations, in Zurich, Geneva, Durban and London, sometimes got into a muddle.[16]

Nevertheless, the result has been a happy one. The Frank McMillan Jnr Library operates successfully, and is attractively laid out, thanks to a donation by Ronald Cohen, in a house below the campus of the University of Cape Town. By the time of his death in 1996 Laurens had achieved a library which was his own contribution to the world of scholarship with which he had had such an uneasy relationship.

Notwithstanding the regular arrival of substantial dollars in his London Foundation, all of which were in practice under his control, Laurens continued in his old age to worry about money. This was the background to the strange episode of his bid for the Nobel Prize.

A measure of Laurens's vanity during these last years – and also, perhaps, a clue to his financial preoccupations – is that he seriously considered that he was a contender for the Prize. He was aware that in 1984 his American and British publishers had discussed among themselves, not too seriously, how they might put forward his name for the Literature award. The idea was dropped. Twelve years before, he had suggested to his American publisher that he be put up for the Nobel Prize. The letter was signed by Ingaret but the style is unmistakably that of Laurens, and he slipped up when referring to 'myself' and to 'my book, *The Seed and the Sower*'. This letter made claims for Laurens which were extraordinarily inflated – it compared him, to his advantage, with Solzhenitsyn, claimed that *In A Province* had inspired the whole anti-apartheid movement, and, intriguingly at so early a date, offered possible referees in the British Royal Family. This may well mark the moment when Laurens's opinion of himself abandoned proportion. Now, in 1993, he took the initiative on his own behalf, recruited the support of his friends and lobbied energetically. His dilemma, as he saw it, was whether he should aim for the Nobel Literature Prize, or for 'the so-called Peace Prize'. Perhaps, he wrote to his friend Ronald Cohen, 'the Peace Prize may suggest itself as an alternative to the Nobel selectors in case they waiver on Literature.' He was encouraged by his Company of Seven and by his several Foundations, and he hoped that his new Norwegian friend Christiaan Sommerfelt would have influence.

In all his letters on the matter Laurens took pains to emphasise that he was embarrassed by the idea and had never thought of himself in connection with prizes like this. Nevertheless, he drafted long letters and memoranda in 1993–94, which were signed by Ronald Cohen as Chairman of his London Foundation. He also wrote to his publishers and to the Principal of the University of St Andrew's, which had given him an honorary degree years before, to ask them to nominate him. He was at least aware of the delicacy of the situation: 'Much as my travel-stained old ego might rejoice in promoting myself,' he wrote in a round-robin letter to his Company of Seven in February 1993, '. . . there is something not right about me working as I have done like the prover-bial beaver at telling the Nobel people what a wonderful literary phe-nomenon I am. If the selection committee knew of it, they would instantly disqualify me.' In the same letter he confessed that he did not know whether he could cite support from an appropriate academic insti-tution: he wondered whether he could depend on Kathleen Raine, 'perhaps the finest poet in the whole cavalcade of women poets in English literature'.[17]

Laurens's friends warned him that it might be wiser to concentrate on an application for the Literature Award, and in August 1993 Ronald Cohen signed a lengthy memorandum to the Nobel Foundation, sent from Laurens's Chelsea address and drafted by him. This memo is lit-tered with the usual biographical extravagances: it quotes ecstatic reviews of each and every one of the books, describes him as a 'full Colonel' and a 'KT' (which should mean Knight of the Thistle, one of Britain's highest Orders), and adds that Jung had said he had valued his friendship as the most important among all the men he had known. It also threw in a gratuitous crack at his South African friend Nadine Gordimer, recently awarded the Nobel Literature Prize in 1991: 'We our-selves have been brought to take this step of appealing to you with a keen sense of guilt aroused in us when we saw the citation which . . . com-mended the recipient . . . for the way in which her work had changed the attitude of white South Africans towards the black and coloured peoples of her native country. We in no way want to diminish the achievements of the writer, whom we all admire, but it is nonetheless important for the objectivity these matters demand from us all, that if helping to change the attitudes of a vicious apartheid system in Southern Africa is under consideration . . . there is no-one in our view, not only in South Africa but in the world, who has done more to bring this about than Laurens van der Post.'

Laurens was passed over in 1993, when the Peace Prize went to his fellow South Africans Nelson Mandela and F. W. de Klerk (an award which Laurens described as 'bizarre'), and the Literature Prize to the black American writer Toni Morrison. Ronald Cohen wrote to Professor Arnott, Principal of St Andrew's University, that Laurens's Foundation was 'disappointed and rather shocked'. Another attempt the next year had a similar fate.[18]

During this period, Laurens also tried to develop a relationship with the Dalai Lama. He met him in April 1993 and decided that the exiled Tibetan leader should go to Africa, preferably on a Wilderness Trail, and possibly in his company. He hastened to tell Prince Charles about this plan, and suggested that he arrange a meeting between the two of them; he explained that the Dalai Lama had long wanted to meet the Prince because he felt himself much in sympathy with what Charles was trying to do. Nothing came of this, although the Dalai Lama expressed interest in a South African trip. It was Laurens who in April 1994 put a dampener on the idea: 'The country has been in such a state of disorder, so much killing, so much insecurity, that I could not responsibly ask you to come.' Various television companies, said Laurens, had suggested that they film a dialogue between the Dalai Lama and himself. Laurens had refused: 'I feel very deeply that in these matters your voice should not be diminished by the voices of others . . . You speak of things which are beyond dialogue and discussion.'[19]

Ronald Cohen, as Chairman, was able to summarise the Foundation's work in a letter to a supporter in October 1996. It had, he explained, pursued a crusade to protect the last Bushmen; it was involved with Kathleen Raine's 'Temenos Academy for the Rediscovery of the Sacred Sources of Knowledge'; it had helped bring about the end of apartheid in South Africa and was trying to promote a proper democratic constitution in that country; it was supporting a project to bring out a sequel to Jung's *Memories, Dreams, Reflections*; it was supporting the South African Association of Jungian Analysts; it had enabled Laurens to lecture to many bodies, including Prince Charles's Institute of Architecture and the Royal College of Defence Studies; it had made it possible for Laurens, in his Chelsea home, to welcome his many visitors – 'he regards this as perhaps the most important task of all'. The Number 9 apartment was also made available to various visitors from overseas.

Laurens tried to arrange for his donors to gather in London at least once a year, when he promised theatres and dinner parties. He continued to offer 'confidential' insights into South Africa and international affairs. He told them of his meetings with F. W. de Klerk, with Harry Oppenheimer and with the Afrikaner magnate Anton Rupert. He wanted to raise more money so that the Foundation could publish his speeches and videos from the past forty years. Now his letters became increasingly taken up with his detestation of Nelson Mandela. 'The world has created a dangerous myth out of Mandela. They have made him into a God, much as they made Hitler and Stalin into Gods.' True, Mandela was not a Hitler or a Stalin, he was a singularly brave man, but he was not a leader and 'he is intellectually not very bright'. He was changing South African foreign policy in a way that should alarm every democracy in the world, while his ANC 'continue with their campaign of communist political killings'.[20]

In his last months, these letters to his American supporters, behind the politics and the pontificating, always carried a cry for help: less than a month before his death, for instance, he wrote to Arman Simone, who had been his principal supporter for nearly ten years, admitting that his problem was that Ingaret, at ninety-five, was far from well: 'Whereas I used to struggle along with one helper in the house I now need three, and ideally should really have four, because Ingaret cannot be left alone and I cannot give more than I have done and do if I am to go on with my work.' A few days before Laurens died, Simone wrote to promise another $15,000 for 1997.[21]

39

The Zulus

THERE SEEMS NO obvious reason why Laurens should have associated himself so fervently with the Zulus. He had been brought up in tribal Tswana and Sotho areas many miles from the Zulu heartland of Natal. He had worked in Durban for only a few years as a young man and again, briefly, in 1948. He did not speak Zulu, as was sometimes claimed.

Chief Mangosuthu Buthelezi, often called 'Gatsha' by his intimates, played a pivotal and controversial role in South African affairs from the mid-1970s, when he founded a Zulu 'cultural movement' called Inkatha – the name was taken from the round head-coil of a Zulu chief – and became Chief Minister of the Zulu Territorial Authority which had been set up in 1970 when the apartheid Government planned the 'separate development' of South Africa's tribal regions. Buthelezi was of royal Zulu blood, and had a privileged rural upbringing. His great importance in the 1970s was that he bravely refused to accept for his seven million Zulus the 'independence' which Pretoria was thrusting on the other Bantustans and which was readily accepted by his counterparts in the Transkei, Ciskei and Bophuthatswana. Buthelezi's refusal to play the apartheid game did as much as anything to frustrate the fuller development of a South African system of tribal client 'states' subservient to white control. The ANC initially applauded Buthelezi's stand and appreciated his frequent public demands for the release of Nelson Mandela. Buthelezi was even originally a member of the ANC Youth League, but the ANC and Inkatha would eventually fall out, with tragic consequences.*

---

*The Zulus and the Xhosas are the two predominant ethnic groups in South Africa, and are sometimes misleadingly described as traditional enemies. The ANC leaders Nelson Mandela and his successor as South Africa's president, Thabo Mbeki, are both Xhosas, though notably cosmopolitan.

Apartheid created a fertile ground for the growth of ethnic feeling among the Zulus, and this was skilfully exploited by Chief Buthelezi who at the same time projected himself as the new moderate national black leader, acceptable both to the whites and to the outside world. His appeal extended, or so he believed, beyond the borders of Zululand. Inkatha, of course, became, as Buthelezi's ambitions were revealed, anathema, a challenge, to the ANC, which was a genuinely pan-ethnic, largely urban, national (and banned) organisation. The ANC could hardly be expected to defer to Buthelezi, even in his own homeland. As hostilities became serious, the logical outcome – 'My enemy's enemy is my friend' – suggested that Buthelezi and the white Government would eventually collaborate.[1]

Laurens was first introduced to Buthelezi in 1977 by Ian Player, who, thanks to his long involvement in Natal's game parks, knew him well. Laurens and the Chief immediately took to each other, and the relationship developed into a firm friendship which lasted until Laurens's death. They met frequently, either in London or in South Africa, and their correspondence over these years became considerable. It also became conspiratorial.

Chief Buthelezi was never an easy man to deal with, as fellow-politicians and journalists could confirm. He was ambitious, touchy, verbose, mercurial, and his relationship with the ANC, such as it was, soon collapsed. He was obsessive about his Zulu nation. Even while bravely defying the pressures of the Nationalist Government, he came to believe that the ANC, whose leaders were in exile, were quasi-communists who were planning to drag his KwaZulu into a unitary, Xhosa-dominated South Africa.

He became a respectful and even extravagant admirer of Laurens, who responded with affection as well as gratification. Here Laurens had found a black South African leader who abhorred communism, who had broken with the ANC, who opposed the 'armed struggle', who endorsed capitalism, who rejected sanctions, and who seemed happy to agree a gradualist progress towards a more democratic system in South Africa on a federal model. He also represented the traditional Zulu cultural values which, in the Natal hills if not in South Africa's industrial townships, were as close as Laurens could get to his dream of the 'primitive man' in Africa today.

Why, one might ask, would a fiercely ambitious South African politician and tribal leader like Chief Buthelezi pay court to an elderly expatriate writer? The answer, confirmed by the Chief's closest advisers, is that Laurens had been identified as the gatekeeper not just to the British

Prime Minister but also, perhaps even more important, to the Prince of Wales, future King of England and one of the most famous men in the world. If Prince Charles could be enlisted to the Zulu cause, and could be persuaded to use his influence on behalf of that cause, who knows what might be achieved? But the Chief needed the introduction. Laurens was only too happy to help. The details of his involvement with Chief Buthelezi in his late old age may cast a little more light on the murky and dangerous years preceding the majority-rule elections of April 1994, the most extraordinary and important event in South Africa's history.

Laurens first met Buthelezi at the first World Wilderness Congress in Johannesburg in October 1977. Not long afterwards the Chief was made aware of the danger of being seen as a 'stooge' of apartheid when in March 1978 he was stoned by the Soweto crowd at the funeral of the Pan-Africanist leader Robert Sobukwe.[2] Laurens immediately understood the Chief's dilemmas and hastened to reassure him. 'I feel you are the only statesman of stature to stand for a future of the totality of all South Africans, and will happily do all I can to help you in so cruel and hard a task,' he wrote from London on 15 May 1978. 'Violence will not go on being fashionable indefinitely and the kind of non-violence that you represent [will] become the end and purpose of all once again. It is just a matter of standing fast.' Buthelezi replied by assuring Laurens that they were brothers and fellow-countrymen and colour did not divide them.[3]

They agreed at once on the need for a National Convention of all races, which would bury the past and plan for the future, but they did not meet again for six years and their friendship did not develop until 1984, when Buthelezi sent condolences on the death of Laurens's son John. Laurens was moved, and offered to put him up in his apartment when he was ever in London – he added that he could serve him mealie meal, which was, one hopes, a joke. Soon after this, Laurens began to plan to introduce Buthelezi to Mrs Thatcher, just as he had recently arranged a meeting between the Prime Minister and Dr van Zyl Slabbert, the South African Opposition leader. He thought that dinner at his home would be preferable and also discreet, and it eventually took place in August 1985.

This meeting, Laurens assured the Prime Minister's diary secretary, would be 'extremely . . . important not only for Britain and South Africa but the world': Gatsha, he went on, would be the key element in the South African situation, so long as he was not assassinated by the ANC. 'This could be one of the most important meetings ever held between a British Prime Minister and the leader of the biggest nation in South

Africa.' In this same month Laurens was able also to introduce Buthelezi to Prince Charles, Charles Powell and the Foreign Secretary, Sir Geoffrey Howe. Throughout the next twelve months Laurens had various meetings with the Prime Minister, as well as frequent contact with the Prince of Wales.[4]

By this time Laurens's nephew, Tom Bedford, had become his trusted liaison with Buthelezi. Tom, still living in Durban, was able to warn Laurens that the situation inside South Africa was deteriorating fast, and Laurens in turn could explain that he had just seen Geoffrey Howe, and had urged him to try to promote a meeting between 'our friend' (Buthelezi) and 'the man in clink' (Mandela). He added, 'It is quite clear that the man in clink is twice a prisoner: both of the state, and of the bosses of his party in the world outside.' Laurens did not dream that in November 1985 the first highly secret contact had been established between Mandela and the South African Justice Minister, Kobie Coetsee, a contact which would eventually bring the ANC to power after a long negotiation in which Buthelezi had no role.[5]

Laurens continued to hold the line between Buthelezi and the Tory Government. In July 1988, for instance, he arranged another meeting for the Chief with Mrs Thatcher and then with Prince Charles, and again in October 1989. He and Buthelezi made a point of meeting whenever they visited each other's territory. Buthelezi – although now in his early sixties, older than his appearance – seemed to defer to the Afrikaner: on 1 June 1988 he confessed to Laurens that he was in a state of spiritual and political siege. Laurens told Charles Powell that he had instructed Gatsha to prepare meticulously for his next meeting with the Prime Minister, because the Zulu leader 'really has no substitute'. He wrote to Buthelezi to assure him that 'our Lady and our beloved Young Man – who follows your fortunes so closely – are well informed'.[6]

This was a period when Buthelezi had extended the authoritarian grip of Inkatha across the whole of his province so that it had become a compulsory mass movement of the Zulu people. Assured of the financial backing of Pretoria, Inkatha could in effect enforce party membership upon almost all public servants and teachers. At the same time the United Democratic Front (UDF), which was a cover for the banned ANC, was trying to build its position in KwaZulu, and was doing so successfully in the urban areas. The two parties' mutual hostility was focussed in the UDF/ANC antagonism towards Buthelezi in person. Here were the seeds of civil war. Years later, evidence emerged of what had been scarcely believable at the time, that the South African Defence Force was beginning to arm the Zulus and encourage them to attack

ANC supporters, and that in 1986 Buthelezi had sent several hundred Inkatha soldiers for secret training by the Defence Force. We may assume that Laurens did not know this.

Mrs Thatcher and Geoffrey Howe, thanks in part to Laurens's activities, had become Buthelezi's most committed supporters overseas, even more so than President Reagan or Helmut Kohl. In August 1986 the US Senate voted for sanctions against South Africa on investment and oil: with hindsight that vote may be seen as the beginning of the end for apartheid. Mrs Thatcher, advised by Laurens, was deeply opposed to sanctions, although she did have to accept some limited EEC sanctions. She also pressed for Mandela's release from prison. But at Commonwealth meetings in 1986 and 1987 Mrs Thatcher continued to insist that the ANC was a terrorist organisation, and she refused to recognise it. This was the period when Britain's Foreign Office diplomats, famously unrespected by their Prime Minister, would work on her to shift her South African policy, and then watch with horror as Laurens arrived in Downing Street to spend the afternoon telling her Zulu stories.[7]

In February 1989 Laurens was visited in London by a small ANC delegation (led by Thabo Mbeki, the future President), which was lobbying British opinion. Laurens told them his 'parable of the cup of coffee', the well-honed story of the Japanese journalists in Pretoria in 1926, which had led to his trip to Japan and so the saving of his life in Java in 1942. The ANC men didn't understand what he was talking about. Laurens, reporting this meeting to Buthelezi, said he continued to feel that the ANC politicians really did not want to go home from their comfortable exile, that they had no vision of a new and greater South Africa (as 'we' did), and that it would be wrong to build up their 'self-importance'. Buthelezi wrote back to agree: he said he feared that Mrs Thatcher had not been given the whole truth [by the British Ambassador, Robin Renwick]. Laurens was at this time sending effusive letters to Renwick, reminding him that '[Gatsha] is a truly noble person, the only person in the political dimension whose vision is truly beyond politics and I only wish that we had him as leader of our country.' Laurens was also using Sir Ian Gow, who had once been Mrs Thatcher's Parliamentary Private Secretary and a junior Tory minister,* as a conduit into Downing Street: 'Gatsha . . . is far more important to the future in the heat and the dust than Nelson can ever be.' Buthelezi was back in Britain in October 1989 and Laurens arranged his schedule, including a meeting with the American donors from his Company of Seven, who were of course flat-

---

*Gow had been Laurens's solicitor. He was killed by the IRA in 1990.

tered to meet so famous a figure; Buthelezi took them sufficiently seriously to prepare a six-page speech for the meeting.[8]

On 2 February 1990 President F. W. de Klerk made his momentous speech to Parliament in Cape Town in which he announced the legalisation of the ANC and the South African Communist Party, and the release of political prisoners, including Mandela. Mrs Thatcher hailed this dramatic *volte face* and in a gesture of political realism she promptly invited both Mandela and de Klerk to London. Laurens indignantly sent a long memorandum to Ian Gow, deploring the failure to give credit to the other black leaders (by whom he meant Buthelezi) who had fought apartheid at home while Mandela was in jail and his ANC colleagues safely in exile.

At this point Laurens's critical attitude to Mandela became uncontrolled and irrational, and would remain so for the rest of his life. He and his friends, he said, 'have fought the battle of apartheid . . . for many more years than Mandela'. He urged on the Prime Minister a re-awakening of her intuition: she had been badly advised by the Foreign Office; it was necessary to detach the myth of Mandela from the man, whose years in prison had evidently failed to give him an apolitical integrity. Rather than welcome de Klerk's bombshell announcement, Laurens was evidently terrified that the future of South Africa would now be negotiated between Mandela and de Klerk. Of course, this is precisely what did happen over the next four years.[9]

Laurens never set aside his detestation of Mandela, or his uncritical endorsement of Chief Buthelezi. He spoke out wildly against Mandela, culminating in a widely reported outburst during a speech at the Cape Town Press Club on 29 November 1990. There he declared that Mandela had brought no vision of the future to South Africa, only tired and well-worn clichés. He announced that he had searched Mandela's speech on his release from prison and had found no vision: 'All I heard was slogans . . . the moth-eaten fourth hand clothes of the spirit.' He and Mandela had both been through 'the greatest school that a human being can have in life', where his own 'best' jail experience had been worse than Mandela's worst. He later repeated his criticisms of Mandela for a 'dreary little political speech', and added that Chief Buthelezi was 'a man of vision . . . better prepared than any leader in South Africa that I know to lead the way ahead'.[10]

The bewildering detail of the subsequent two-and-a-half years of negotiation, against a background of escalating violence, does not affect the broader story of Laurens's efforts to influence South African history at its crucial moment. On 26 September 1992, the National Party and the ANC signed a Record of Understanding which, it was afterwards clear, marked a critical step on the rocky road to majority rule. Chief Buthelezi was left out, and was furious. He must have known that his strategy of teaming up with the National Party – to make an alliance between Afrikaners and Zulus in order to resist the ANC – was threatened with failure. From that time on he would not understand that he was not, as he always believed, indispensable to the negotiation process. Encouraged always by Laurens, he would continue to huff and to puff, to storm out of meetings, to threaten to boycott the election.[11] How much time, and how many lives, would be wasted?

As early as September 1992, it may be said, the game was up. There would be many problems ahead, and many people would die, but Mandela and de Klerk were going to achieve their historic settlement. At this point, Laurens became involved with the far Right in South Africa and also the maverick Right in Britain. In November 1992 he was introduced to John Aspinall, the eccentric and wealthy casino operator, zoo-keeper and 'honorary White Zulu'. Aspinall and Laurens immediately fell for each other, having in common a passionate commitment to both the African environment and the cause of the traditional Zulu nation. Through Aspinall, Laurens met other friends of his, who included Sir James Goldsmith, the tycoon, and Kerry Packer, the Australian media billionaire. Laurens liked Aspinall in particular, inviting him to his storytelling sessions. Ian Player in Natal was another important link between Laurens, Aspinall and Buthelezi; and Aspinall and his friends were to be a valuable source of funds to the chronically impoverished Inkatha Party.[12]* Buthelezi, always desperate for funds, played up to his millionaire patrons' fantasies of a primitive Zulu nation: for example, Aspinall and Goldsmith sometimes flew down to Natal by private jet for a weekend. Buthelezi attended their parties and provided tribal dancers in skins and spears: in effect, he was willing to play the traditional Zulu for them. But Aspinall was potentially more dangerous than this sounds. He once explained, 'I stumbled across the Zulus when I read Rider Haggard . . . I took on board his heroic vision of that people. I like to keep it, but urbanisation has . . . deracinated and decultured them.' He apparently saw no need for restraint, even while thousands of people were dying in the killing fields of KwaZulu-Natal in the

---

*Before the April 1994 election Aspinall and Goldsmith put up Rand 4,000,000, about £1,000,000.[13]

early 1990s. He publicly recommended the sabotage of the power lines which supply Durban, for instance, and Charles Powell, formerly the Prime Minister's private secretary, remembers an Inkatha party rally in Ulundi when Aspinall seized the microphone and urged his plump and affluent middle-aged audience to sharpen their spears and fall on the Xhosas, their traditional enemy.*

Lord Powell afterwards confessed that he could never take this sort of white right-wing passion for the Zulu cause too seriously, but he added that, in the context of Mrs Thatcher's hostile attitude to the Foreign Office and its policies (she regarded the Foreign Office as 'the enemy' on South African matters), Laurens's most important role was to arrange access for Buthelezi to the Prime Minister, to get a fair hearing for the Zulu point of view, and to give her some perspective on South Africa's history and culture.[15] Laurens would not have favoured anything like Aspinall's war-mongering, but his friendship with his wilder friends inflamed them, and in the meantime he energetically encouraged Buthelezi to stand firm against Mandela's ANC and to demand a 'federal democracy and . . . genuine self-determining federal autonomy'. In effect Laurens was urging on Buthelezi the loosest possible federal system for the new South Africa in which KwaZulu-Natal would be granted a maximum degree of self-rule, with the clear aim of holding the ANC and its allegedly 'communist' policies at bay.[16] The ANC was committed to a unitary state with power held at the centre. The temptation, and the danger, in the highly-charged atmosphere of these years, was that a demand for federation, if denied, might turn into a break-out for secession. This is what Laurens, Aspinall and their friends were flirting with.†

In this delicate and perilous situation Laurens sought to involve the Prince of Wales. South Africa was threatened with 'Balkanisation', Laurens assured the Prince in a long memorandum dated 5 September 1993: '[Gatsha] may be driven to going it alone, as the Afrikaners threaten to do at the moment . . . A great effort must now be made to stop the drift into chaos which is threatening the country. We have got to go all out to prevent an election before we have a proper Constitution

---

*The distinguished British journalist Peregrine Worsthorne confessed in his newspaper column in March 1994 that at an Aspinall dinner Laurens's 'passionate and moving championship of [the Zulu] cause stirred even my thin blood into wanting to take up an assegai on their behalf'.[14]

†The interest in Natal of Laurens's right-wing friends was not entirely cultural. Goldsmith, Aspinall and Packer formed a consortium to bid to develop the Durban Point waterfront. They were unsuccessful.[17]

which will provide a proper framework of values and law and order and protection of minorities . . . I wonder if you could possibly feel what sort of initiative we might launch from this country to send an invitation to leaders to meet and talk together, in confidence, under the guidance of some immensely respected person as Chairman . . . The Foreign Office has no idea of the cataclysmic consequences of letting this drift in South Africa go unchecked.'

This is surely an invitation to the Prince to volunteer to be the chairman of a meeting which might discuss the dismemberment of South Africa. It was, as one of Chief Buthelezi's most senior advisers afterwards confirmed, a long-term Zulu plan – 'The Prince coming out for the Inkatha Freedom Party'. Prince Charles had met Buthelezi several times through Laurens, most recently on 1 May 1993, when he invited him to visit his Highgrove home privately.[18] The consequences of support from the heir to the British Throne for the Zulu leader before the multi-racial elections scarcely six months away would have been disastrous, for the Prince as well as for British policy, and also for ANC-Zulu relations. The Foreign Office, should they have known any of this, would have been frantic. However, Charles, with or without his advisers, had the wisdom to hold back, whatever his personal sympathies and whatever his respect for Laurens's guidance.

At this most inflammable moment in the resistance of the Zulu leadership to the march towards a unitary South Africa, while thousands of lives were at risk, Laurens could have used his influence on Buthelezi to urge compromise and reconciliation. On the contrary, on 21 December 1993 he sent a message to the Chief: 'You may feel more kindly disposed towards your allies in the North [by which he meant the white Right-wingers in the Transvaal] when you know all the detail of what they've done . . . You must prepare, as I'm certain you've already started to prepare, for the period in which you have to go alone and take what you can of Natal with you.' Laurens added that he was about to speak to the 'Chairman of Foreign Affairs' (it's not clear who this might be) 'who is honourable and a friend of my boss [i.e. the Prince], and see what I can prepare for a support of what I believe is moral and even legally a case that this so-called constitution breaks the contract of union under which Natal and the Zulus were dragged into the Union of South Africa.'

Buthelezi was entitled, Laurens assured him, 'to reclaim at the very least your pre-1910 status within the British Commonwealth.' Buthelezi replied that Laurens was really a gift from God to the Chief and to their fatherland. On 28 December Laurens told him, 'I am so glad you stood fast in the historic and ethical right the Zulu nation possesses not to have a 1910 repeat of being swept blindly, by sheer numbers, into an ill-defined, limitless and unenforceable pattern of sheer political power. I believe deep down you have a right not only to help from Britain but to active protection against such a disregard of obligations to you and your people. I am exploring at the highest level an opportunity of a better hearing for you from the British people.'[19]*

This comes very close to incitement to secession, which would have led to a catastrophic civil war, and, if Prince Charles had spoken publicly, a constitutional crisis in Britain.

Buthelezi continued to send Laurens long memoranda ventilating his anger and rehearsing the reasons why he would definitely refuse to co-operate with the rest of the constitutional process. Back on 7 October 1993, when Laurens was in South Africa to collect an honorary degree from the University of the Orange Free State, Buthelezi had pointed out in a letter to him that white right-wingers were preparing for war and argued that it might be wise to accommodate their demand for a white '*Volkstaat*', which might be possible under a federal system. He refused to allow Inkatha to be marginalised: he told Laurens in October 1993 that he had called on his supporters to set up self-protection units in which all young men in KwaZulu would undergo six weeks of training. This was an extremely dangerous development, promising an escalation of the violence which was already killing thousands. The 'Self-Protection Units' were going to be in the thick of the intensified fighting which followed.[21] Laurens did nothing to recommend caution or restraint.

A critically important figure in these last months of white South Africa was General Constand Viljoen, retired Commander of the South African Defence Force, who in May 1993 formed the Afrikaner Volksfront. It was intended to operate as an umbrella grouping but Viljoen's relations with his allies, the Conservative Party and the paramilitary and supremacist Afrikaner Weerstandsbeweging (the AWB), led by Eugene Terre Blanche, were always tricky. Viljoen's unrealistic ambition was to try to secure ANC agreement to a 'Volkstaat', a sort of whites-only homeland for those Afrikaners who wished to opt out of a multi-racial South Africa. Its intended location was never clear, though presumed to be in the Northern Cape. The Volksfront developed into the 'Freedom Alliance', adding the homeland governments of Ciskei and Bophuthatswana – plus Inkatha.

General Viljoen, who continued to command the personal loyalty of

---

*This is historically wrong: the South Africa Act of 1909, which unified South Africa in 1910, gave no undertaking to the Zulus, and was endorsed in a Natal referendum.[20]

many members of the Defence Force, had been introduced to Laurens by Harry Oppenheimer at a Brenthurst dinner party. Laurens had wanted to reassure himself about the future and the circumstances of the Bushmen who had been recruited into the Army in the late 1970s to help the war for South-west Africa (now Namibia).* Laurens and the General became friends – the General stayed in his Chelsea apartment – but they did not agree about South Africa's future. 'Laurens could never understand why I could negotiate with the ANC,' Viljoen said in an interview. 'His position was always that you can't negotiate with the Devil himself.' Laurens's commitment to the role of Buthelezi was always clear. The General added, 'I have no doubt that the value of Laurens van der Post to Buthelezi at that stage, apart from his intellectual capabilities, was his contacts with the British Royal Family.'

Laurens took it upon himself to start sending General Viljoen long letters of advice which sometimes read like lectures. He warned him against going to war, however prepared he might be: a federal system, he said, was the only solution in South Africa's particular situation; don't allow the Alliance to split up; support Chief Buthelezi rather than the young Zulu King, Goodwill Zwelithini (whose relationship with Buthelezi was frequently problematic). Viljoen replied, sensibly, that the domestic situation was very difficult, that the Government 'is really gunning for Chief Minister Buthelezi', and that mediation from outside might be the only way out, though the idea might be completely unacceptable to the ANC.[23]†

Laurens meanwhile was impressing on Buthelezi the importance of the Freedom Alliance standing fast: 'I still believe that the Afrikaners and the Zulus can form a combination for the future which will ultimately save

---

*Most of these Bushmen came from Angola. When South Africa withdrew from Namibia these soldiers insisted that they be evacuated, so the '31 Battalion' was relocated in 1990 to a remote area of the Northern Cape, near the Vaal river at Schmidtsdrif; some Defence Force generals saw them, fancifully, as the local equivalent of the British Army's Gurkhas. Laurens's concern was that they would lose their traditional bushcraft, while General Viljoen was willing to grant that these developments were bringing the social problems which have since so gravely damaged the remnants of Bushman society. They were certainly a traumatised people, and in 1994 the battalion was disbanded. In the years ahead, the Kalahari Bushmen were steadily dispossessed.[22]

†The idea of 'mediation' was that the warring parties call in international and impartial advice to help them resolve their differences; it became Laurens's best hope.

South Africa.' Nothing, he admitted, could now stop the coming April election, although it was 'flawed and amoral and an attempt at achieving power under a spurious cloak of a dubious democracy . . . you must not touch it with a barge pole . . . I am very hard at work in reinforcing your particular Zulu claim on English fairness and the English relationship with you since the days of Chaka.' He urged the Chief to keep in close touch with the General.[24]

The situation was desperately dangerous. General Viljoen had made his plans: 'As a matter of fact I had all the war machine ready, prepared . . . The final decision not to go for war was taken just after 23 April 1994.' He reckoned that he could bring at least half the South African Defence Force with him; then they would mark out a Volkstaat and defy the world. But he changed his mind after a disastrous episode in the homeland state of Bophuthatswana on 11 March 1994. General Viljoen had sent his men to defend his Freedom Alliance ally, the local President, Lucas Mangope, but he was pre-empted by the arrival of the undisciplined racists of the AWB, who so provoked the local army that they were chased out and the shooting of three whites was screened on prime-time TV. It was a cathartic climax to the short, unhappy life of the Homelands. 'The AWB buggered up the whole thing,' General Viljoen recalled. He had a rethink, re-assessed the economic problems in going it alone, and decided to join the electoral process. It was a decision which effectively defused the threat of a right-wing white rebellion. Buthelezi – and Laurens – were on their own.

Still, it is worth noting how close the country was to a civil uprising in these weeks in 1994. To secure his followers General Viljoen needed the 'Volkstaat Agreement', a vague commitment by the Government to reconsider, after the election, the case for a white enclave. In mid-April he despaired of persuading the ANC to deliver it: 'I said to my wife, "I have to let the dogs loose, the ANC is playing difficult".' But he remembered a promise that he telephone his friend the American Ambassador, Princeton Lyman, to warn him of any dramatic developments. The Ambassador asked him to give him just half-an-hour; twenty minutes later Lyman called back and promised the General that the Agreement would be signed before the end of the week, which it was. The General went into the election, won nine seats with two per cent of the vote, and sat on the Opposition benches in Parliament for seven years. He was invited by Mandela to visit him at his home, and was asked for his help in conveying the thinking and the wishes of the Afrikaner people.[25] The two men always respected each other. Laurens never condescended to respect Mandela.

As the April election approached, Laurens faced a dilemma. 'It is a phoney illegitimate election, and therefore entitles you to do what you think necessary for a democratic federal assertion of Zulu rights,' he wrote to Buthelezi on 7 February 1994, endorsing the Zulu leader's apparent inclination to maintain the violence which had swept across his province. But in the same letter Laurens urged him to hold back Viljoen from the 'some fighting' which he was reportedly contemplating. 'It may be that fighting could break out, at the very latest after the election but possibly even before it. But it must never, never be started as a policy by any of our people.' Meanwhile John Aspinall was giving hysterical interviews in Britain: 'What will happen eventually is absolutely clear . . . South Africa is bound to break up . . . Then it will be a loose confederacy like Switzerland . . . All these idealistic idiots think the ANC has enough power to superimpose a unitary state, but it hasn't. Chaos is going to ensue and tens of thousands will face unnecessary death.'

Laurens wrote alarmist and ill-informed letters to his Norwegian friend, Christiaan Sommerfelt, an elderly industrialist with excellent government contacts in Oslo, whom he had met in 1993. He spoke of a 'drift into chaos . . . [a] virus of potential anarchy . . . I doubt if the election could, ultimately, be held in April at all . . . de Klerk is now reduced to such a state of impotence . . . a very highly organised and determined attempt in the last few days to assassinate General Viljoen.' On 4 April he was telling Sommerfelt that the emergency in Bophuthatswana was the result of an illegal act prepared by the ANC, that Mandela was countermanding de Klerk's orders, that the 'Shell House' episode in Johannesburg on 28 March (a confrontation outside the ANC headquarters when fifty-three people were killed) was 'one of the most sinister things that ever happened in South African history', that the move had started towards 'a ruthless police state', and that he was still working with Gatsha 'to try and preserve a core of the best of South Africa'. He ended with a plea that the Nobel Peace Prize Committee issue an unconventional statement in a bid to halt 'Mandela and his Communists'.[26]

The fact that Laurens was not of course in South Africa during this period may well have influenced his apocalyptic and unbalanced outlook. True, the situation was dangerous and explosive – thanks largely to the murderous activities of the extreme-right white extremists – but the country pulled through. Buthelezi at the very last moment agreed that Inkatha contest the nationwide election, and South Africans of all races went to the polls on 27 and 28 April of that year amid scenes of great emotion. The result was that the ANC, as expected, secured a massive majority, just short of the two-thirds which would have given their MPs the right to change the new and long-argued Constitution. Buthelezi's Inkatha Freedom Party won a majority of 51 per cent in KwaZulu-Natal, but only a tiny vote elsewhere. That disposed of his claim that it was a nationwide party.

To Laurens's dismay and consternation, Buthelezi thereupon agreed to join the Government of National Unity as Minister for Home Affairs. It is possible to see this as a courageous, indeed statesmanlike decision, which greatly helped the prospect of peace. On 25 May 1994 Laurens sent him a long memorandum which illustrates that the eighty-seven-year-old sage's political judgement had now become little more than a frantic and dogmatic justification of his own eccentric vision. The Zulus, he said, had 'a wholeness, a sense of the importance of mind and of honour which did not exist elsewhere in Africa'. These qualities had now become more important than ever. He therefore called upon Buthelezi to pull out of national politics and come home to Natal where he could create 'a model of a new world, a model of a Zulu – and ultimately Afrikaner – renaissance into the spirit of a new South Africa'. He could begin by making Ulundi (a remote bush town) into 'a small, renaissance capital'; he could build there 'a model school on public school lines'; he would have a sports stadium where the Zulus would take up rugby, rather than 'the inferior game of soccer' (never mind that soccer is black Africa's passion); then the Zulus could have a wonderful cricket team, following the West Indies' example; there would be a theatre and a small concert hall and Ulundi would have lovely parks, with lawns and indigenous trees and buck wandering around . . . Finally, Laurens suggested the ideal person to be First Minister – none other than his own nephew, Tom Bedford! For all of this Laurens would be happy to raise a financial endowment from his friends like John Aspinall, Jimmy Goldsmith and the rest.[27]

Buthelezi did not respond to these proposals for a Utopia in Zululand. As the months went by, Laurens became despondent, not just about his lurid impressions of the situation in South Africa under its Government of National Unity, but because the various opposition parties seemed so reluctant to join together to oppose 'a kind of Stalinist centrally-controlled state'. He and his friends continued to urge Buthelezi to return to Natal. Buthelezi for his part was bitter that the Government reneged on its promise to submit the argument about the powers of the provinces to international mediation, and he withdrew Inkatha from the Constituent Assembly and demanded virtual autonomy for KwaZulu-Natal. The ANC seemed to become even more enraged with him than they had ever been with de Klerk. But, in the end, for whatever reason –

ambition? realism? a knowledge that his presence in a national government was essential if civil war was to be averted? – Buthelezi stayed on board, and, miraculously, the political killings ceased.[28]

Throughout these months Aspinall, Goldsmith and their friends were active: for example, sending money to pay for Inkatha to transport Zulu peasants to Buthelezi's rallies. Aspinall approached the King, Goodwill Zwelithini, in March 1995, in his self-appointed capacity as a 'white Zulu' and as an 'honorary *induna*' (chief), to offer to give a feast in Durban to help the reconciliation between the King and his Chief Minister: 'I am growing old and the grave beckons,' Aspinall wrote. 'Before I join the spirits I would like to see with my bare eyes, uncle and nephew – Prime Minister and King – joined together in an embrace which will bring joy to the people – a reunion that could save the nation.'[29]

Laurens continued to imply that he had the Prince of Wales up his sleeve. He assured Buthelezi that he always shared his information with 'your host at tea in Gloucester . . . He asks me especially to send his warmest regards and greetings to you and particularly says that what you experience by way of not being understood and appreciated is in a sense also his lot . . . [He] sends you not only his faith and admiration but also condolences.' More seriously he claimed, in a letter to Buthelezi on 12 March 1996, that Prince Charles was active on his behalf: 'Your host in the country . . . is doing quite a remarkable intervention with people in the right places who might help your cause in this country. Both he and I feel there is really no help in this country: how can it help others when it is incapable of helping itself? . . . His regard for you is higher than ever and he has a deep fellow feeling that in some way his life is bonded with yours and that you both have to soldier on and the light will shine upon you both again.'[30] (There is no reason to suppose that Laurens, a master of embellishment, was reporting the Prince's deeds and feelings accurately.)

Laurens never got over his disappointment that Buthelezi, the second of his beloved princes, decided to do a deal with Mandela and the 'Communists' of the ANC. Buthelezi soon showed that he had no intention of abdicating from national government. When F. W. de Klerk and his National Party withdrew from the Coalition Government in May 1996, de Klerk asked Buthelezi when he was going to follow suit. Buthelezi sat tight, and even became Acting President when Mandela and Mbeki were both out of the country. Nonetheless, in August 1996 Laurens told Aspinall he still hoped that the Chief would retreat from 'this horrible political mess'. Buthelezi represented 'the inevitability of the reality of the emerging people from their wonderful world of instincts and their own spirituality and having to make a positive peace with that "now" of themselves'. One wonders what Buthelezi might have made of that paternalistic and even racist exchange between two white men. But though he had shown himself a political realist, Buthelezi did not forget that he was a friend: in June he flew to London especially to attend Aspinall's seventieth birthday party; when he came again, for Aspinall's memorial service in November 2000, he brought with him a Zulu troupe who danced for Aspinall at the church with their skins and knobkerries.[31]

Both before and after the 1994 election Laurens directed his main energies towards a vain attempt to secure international 'mediation' to settle the differences over the future Constitution. He thought of the Canadians, then focused on the Norwegians, who had had a recent success in the Middle East. Laurens's point of contact with 'the land of ice and snow' – his code-name for Norway in letters and faxes to South Africa – was not the Norwegian Government but Christiaan Sommerfelt. Laurens deluged him with briefings, invariably critical of Mandela. He suggested that Norway and Sweden might sponsor, on neutral ground, 'a non-political Conference of South African leaders to decide on the basic values of a modern democratic federal Constitution for South Africa'.*

In late November, before the majority-rule election, Laurens had been able to relay to Sommerfelt a personal message from Buthelezi appealing to Norway to launch an eleventh-hour mediation to stop the new draft Constitution. Sommerfelt involved the Norwegian Secretary of State, who said that his government would be happy to help, though there would have to be a formal request from South Africa. Sommerfelt visited Laurens, and Tom and Jane Bedford, in London in December. Laurens showed him an exchange of letters between Buthelezi and the British Prime Minister, John Major, which apparently touched on the possibility of KwaZulu's secession. He promised

---

*He also asked Sommerfelt to become a Trustee of the Laurens van der Post Foundation for the Advancement of the Humanities: 'All that you represent and what you've told me suggests so much that you are one of what I hope to call "us".' Laurens had earlier believed that Sommerfelt might be able to influence the Nobel Prize Committee on his behalf.[32]

Sommerfelt that 'we are almost the only people in the outside world at the moment who get an accurate, balanced and total view of the situation in South Africa.'[33]

Mediation became a lively topic in early March 1994 on the eve of the election, when Mandela made a magnanimous gesture and went to Durban to see Buthelezi. He offered, to his own colleagues' mixed feelings, to submit the dispute between the ANC and Inkatha to international mediation. In retrospect this was the move which eventually brought Inkatha into the election. A different sort of mediation was attempted in the dangerous weeks of April when Lord Carrington and Henry Kissinger arrived, and left shortly afterwards without success. It was not the Norwegians but a Kenyan called Washington Okumu, an old friend of Buthelezi, who persuaded him to participate in the election. Laurens was not involved.

The election came and went and neither Mandela nor de Klerk showed much interest in taking up Norway's offer of mediation. Laurens was even more indignant than Buthelezi that an apparent promise of mediation had been forgotten, and urged him again to resign from the Government. At the end of June he held meetings in London with 'the men of ice and snow', who explained to him, again, that they could only help if they were officially invited. Laurens suggested a protracted consultation and discussion by a distinguished international Chairman who would then put his proposals to the people of South Africa – it was all terribly vague, and the professional diplomats would have realised that the mediation issue was fading from view, particularly now that Mandela had cleverly co-opted Buthelezi into government. The Norwegian Prime Minister, Mrs Gro Brundtland, visited South Africa and, to Laurens's disgust, 'failed to carry out her brief . . . [and] did not live up to the opportunity'. That is to say, she must have decided that there was no need to take the matter of Norwegian mediation any further. Buthelezi agreed that her visit had been a dismal failure, and said that she had made it clear that the only person that she was prepared to listen to was Mandela.[34]

By this time Laurens had lost all contact with the realities of diplomacy. He wrote at impassioned length to Sommerfelt on 15 March 1995 insisting that he and his friends would not give up on mediation, and asked Norway to stand by what he called its pledge: he spoke of 'this monster of a common market Europe', the 'unholy alliance . . . between Germany and France', his fear that the socialists – 'a creeping form ultimately of totalitarianism' – might win the next British election, and his fury that the Norwegian Prime Minister, Mrs Brundtland, had failed to be 'immune to the attractions of a very attractive man like Mandela (Dear God, if ever there has been a god with clay feet, he is one)', while ignoring the violence, the horrendous killing and the corruption which had gone on since his release from prison. 'The most awful thing' was the failure of the British Foreign Office: 'We had a disastrous series of Ambassadors in South Africa who from the word go were pledged to the ANC and to Mandela.'

Sommerfelt continued to send affectionate letters, but reported that there was little to be done without a direct invitation from the South African Government.[35] After that Laurens had nothing left to say.

The background to this chapter, which features only rarely in Laurens's correspondence, was that a low-level but bloody civil war was in progress between the Zulus in Natal, spilling over into the townships of the Transvaal. The contestants were the Zulu members of the ANC and Inkatha. Elements in the national Defence Force were helping Inkatha covertly in various ways, thereby making a dangerous situation even worse. Laurens invariably laid all the blame on the ANC. He never admitted the possibility – perhaps he did not want to believe it – that his friend Buthelezi might be involved. The 'Findings and Conclusions of the Truth and Reconciliation Commission', set up in February 1996, which issued an Interim Report in October 1998, take a different view.

The Commission declared that Inkatha (which it defined as interchangeable with the KwaZulu government) had begun paramilitary training as early as 1982, and that as a result violence had became institutionalised in KwaZulu. Inkatha supporters in other regions turned to violence after July 1990. Inkatha, the Commission concluded, was responsible for 3.5 killings for every one killing attributed to the ANC. 'At a time when it portrayed itself nationally and abroad as a liberation movement, the IFP [Inkatha Freedom Party] . . . was receiving direct financial and logistical assistance from the highest echelons of the apartheid state's security apparatus . . . Inkatha's opposition to the South African government's policies had changed to covert collaboration by the latter half of the 1980s, and the two had united against a common enemy, the UDF/ANC and their affiliates . . . Speeches by the IFP President . . . had the effect of inciting supporters of the organisation to commit acts of violence . . . Chief M. G. Buthelezi . . . is held by this Commission to be accountable in his representative capacity.' Buthelezi, the Commission found, was among those responsible for paramilitary 'hit squads' organised in collaboration with the South

African Defence Force and leading to gross violation of human rights, including killings.

Buthelezi complained furiously about this and demanded, through the courts, that the Truth and Reconciliation Commission produce the documents on which it based its finding. An out-of-court settlement was announced in November 2000 just before the dispute reached the Constitutional Court. The argument continues, and the Final Report on the Commission will probably be a political compromise.

The best estimate is that 20,000 people died in KwaZulu and the Transvaal between 1986 and 1994. The South African miracle is that there were not many more deaths, not only there but throughout the country.[36]

In May 2000, Lady Thatcher sent a message to Chief Buthelezi, to be read out at a Soweto rally marking the twenty-fifth anniversary of the Inkatha Freedom Party: 'Under your strong and skilful leadership, Inkatha became a crucially important force for progress, and without your wise counsel the transition to full democracy in South Africa could not have been successful.'[37]

Laurens would have been proud of her.

Laurens in high old age refused to admit that Nelson Mandela's emergence in 1994 as President of a multi-racial majority-rule South Africa might possibly be a positive and heartening development. He had spent his life protesting against apartheid. Could he really have believed that Mandela was a Communist? Perhaps he disliked Mandela's being a Xhosa and not one of his favourite Zulus. Perhaps he was jealous, at some deep level, that Mandela so evidently possessed an aura of kingship and had constantly demonstrated in all kinds of practical ways that he had truly forgiven his enemies; and that Mandela so manifestly embodied the Jungian archetype of 'Hero/Saviour', in comparison with which his own worldly distinction was insignificant. For the rest of his life he continued to reject the advice of friends that he re-assess his opinion of Mandela and consider that the new President represented South Africa's best possible future. In taking this negative position, Laurens knew very little about Mandela. They never met.

Laurens's analysis of southern African affairs over forty years, from Capricorn to majority rule, was almost always wrong-headed. He deplored and detested apartheid, and spoke out against it frequently, publicly and courageously. But his hopes for the future of his native land remained paternalistic. He retreated from the imminence of majority black rule, with its inevitable threat to the supremacy and prosperity of the whites, into a fantastical dream of a Zulu renaissance; the Zulu came to represent the primitive African he lauded and mythologised in his books. He never admitted, never knew, that most urbanised blacks had no interest in his dreams.

Mandela had the last word. To Laurens's memorial service in Chelsea in March 1997, the President sent a magnanimous message, which was delivered, in a splendid irony, by Chief Buthelezi: 'Laurens van der Post could, by virtue of his birth, have embraced a life of privilege in our divided country . . . Instead, he was driven by a larger vision to affirm the common humanity of all who share our land . . . Such spirits, treading a lonely path ahead of their time, helped lay the foundations of our Rainbow Nation.'[38]

40

Die Sterre

Laurens lived his last years in what was, for a man so old, a frenzy of activity. While orchestrating a campaign to change South Africa's draft constitution, he continued to involve himself in matters of environment and wilderness, and although he had stepped back from the running of the Jungian Centre in Cape Town he continued to keep an eye on it, not least by controlling its overseas funding. He was constantly available to make a speech (always unscripted), to give an interview, to write a foreword, to make an introduction, to address a conference, to tell his African stories to audiences large or small. It was this generosity which won him so many followers and admirers during these last years, when his books had lost their earlier impact. People who visited him in Chelsea almost invariably left with feelings of affection and respect.

With the overthrow of Mrs Thatcher, Laurens lost his inner voice in the Tory Party; he saw less of Lady Thatcher, and had no access to John Major, though he kept up his social contacts even as he increasingly withdrew into his Chelsea penthouse.

During these last years, Laurens demonstrated astonishing stamina and courage. He was near-crippled and in great pain from osteoporosis, but never complained. His sight and his hearing both deteriorated: he was unable to read his proofs, he did not watch television (or read the newspapers in detail), and he had increasing difficulty in following conversations which were not specifically directed to him.

In his eighties his health declined as his body began to fail him. For a time he had to walk with two sticks. This did not stop him travelling overseas in a style and to a degree inconceivable to most octogenarians. He continued, for example, to visit Switzerland. Laurens had always loved that country and had a permit to buy property there, obtained before the Swiss made this extremely difficult. But it had to be renewed every year, so he made a visit each June, which he used to combine with a holiday with Frances and a call on his Geneva banker. He had friends looking out for a suitable house, and the original idea seems to have been to move there with Frances, leaving Ingaret behind, or perhaps assuming that Ingaret would pre-decease him. But he later changed his mind, decided he would have to take Ingaret with him, and suggested that Frances bring her elderly mother and take a house nearby. This disposed of the idea for good. Laurens blamed the decision on Swiss bureaucracy.[1]

The care of Ingaret was his most alarming and expensive problem, and there seemed no end in sight. Her life changed rapidly after the mid-1980s. As early as 1983 Laurens had consulted a neurologist, and in 1984 had written to Fredy Meier in Zurich, asking for guidance about Ingaret's 'increasing forgetfulness. It is something that she feels very deeply. Being Ingaret she knows precisely what is happening and has faced up to the problem very bravely.' Was there any medical development which could help her?

Ingaret took her own decision to stop playing bridge, when she realised that her brain was failing her. Friends realised that they could no longer invite her out to lunch because she had become disruptive. She could no longer, of course, attempt to write her books and plays, or edit publishers' manuscripts. Her memoirs, *The Way Things Happen*, were published by Chatto in 1989, and it was scarcely a secret that the final chapters were written not by Ingaret – this was now beyond her – but by Laurens. He denied it, but he would have appreciated the chance to put into Ingaret's memoir his own version of her meeting with him on the *Watussi* in 1936. Chatto published it because Laurens insisted; as a book it has a certain prewar charm, but it is riddled with the factual errors of a deteriorating memory, and was never expected to sell. Laurens contributed to the publishing costs and paid for a copy editor.[2]

By the late 1980s, Laurens had at last begun to admit to a few friends that Ingaret was 'slowly withdrawing her attention from this world of appearances'. Some of her oldest friends found that their regular visits, to a woman who had been so smart and intelligent, became too distressing. Additional staff were brought in from several nursing agencies. On one occasion Laurens, whose anti-racism was never straightforward or complete (despite the Bushman nanny), reprimanded an agency for sending a black temporary nurse, insisting that only whites were acceptable.

Friends admired Laurens for his loyalty and devotion to the sick Ingaret, but they never satisfied a simple, perhaps unworthy if understandable curiosity which they used to discuss among themselves. Laurens had been openly 'with' Frances since 1966: was it possible that

Ingaret really did not know? Laurens had not kept Frances a secret. He enjoyed introducing her to his friends, he travelled with her, explaining that he could no longer travel alone because of his physical afflictions. Frances never met Ingaret.

Ingaret's story may seem an unhappy one. She adored Laurens from the moment she met him, and she was cared for by him until his death. But he was away so often, and all her friends confirm that she felt his absences terribly. She would sit at home every evening waiting for his phone call. Did she know of Frances, let alone the others? Some of her friends were certain that her powerful intuition had given her warning. Some insist that she knew and chose to accept. The better answer only came to light after her death. On 24 June 1980, she wrote a letter to a psychotherapist friend of them both which is both poignant and eloquent of her feelings for Laurens and also of her enslavement to him:

> I have felt for some years that L. has got another woman in his life . . . I do not *feel* jealous. I sense that a great man (and I judge L. to be that) almost certainly needs more than one woman in his life . . . It is, in a sense, both fortunate and unfortunate that I met L. when he was rock-bottom in despair: and I was the only person at that period who stood by him (pre-war). Consequently he feels 'indebted' to me; he also knows the depth of my love for him. Hence his secrecy . . . which couples (possibly?) with guilt. Yet I grudge him nothing . . . If he has 'deceived' me it will only have been not to hurt me . . . I think on the whole I should say nothing. But if anything did happen to me I would like him to know that I *knew, understood,* and remained, as *always,* with him . . .[3]

This is a sad and moving letter. Was Laurens truly a great man, and if he weren't, would that have changed Ingaret's views? If he were, would it matter? Was she content that, from the independent writer and training analyst of the 1940s, she had been turned into Laurens's helpmeet?

At Ingaret's funeral in 1997, some months after Laurens's own death, one of the friends who knew her best, Dorothea Wallis, gave the address: 'I remember her saying that to love someone sometimes means having to withhold love, which is something few people are either aware of or have the strength to do. You may have to resist showing your love to allow the other to go his or her own way. It must have been hard for her to do this because she was naturally demonstrative. But she practised what she preached, letting Laurens go away, with her support, on long expeditions, after the long war-time separation, and when she passionately wanted him with her.'

For more than ten years, at the end of his life, Laurens lived with a wife who had ceased to be the person he knew. Some of his friends thought he should, or might have wanted to, marry Frances. Ingaret's illness, his love and gratitude to her, may have made that impossible. He knew that Ingaret, fifty years before, had been his salvation.

None of the friends is happy to settle on a date when her illness became clear. It must have been some time in the mid-1980s, though small personality changes were becoming evident before then. She was drifting into a form of senile dementia (possibly Alzheimer's), bringing the tragic and well-known sequence of memory loss, bewilderment, fear, unstable behaviour, disruption, anger, aggression, incontinence, and eventually a sort of serenity. A few friends advised him that Ingaret needed to be hospitalised, for which they incurred his furious displeasure. In public Laurens's reaction to Ingaret's dementia was to deny it: he would merely admit that 'little Ingaret' was rather absent-minded these days, perhaps a little deaf, or some such phrase, and would adamantly deny obvious evidence that she was severely disruptive of his life, including his work, since she would interrupt him, throw away pages of his manuscript, talk gibberish to his visitors, flee the building and have to be rescued, half-clothed, in the street. Afterwards, as the years went by, some questioned whether Ingaret's illness had in some way been her own way of retreating from her intuitive realisation that she had lost Laurens's true love.[4]

Laurens could not cope with the practicalities of tending for a wife in the advanced stages of senile dementia. In 1992 he had come up with the idea that his first wife, Marjorie, move from Cape Town to Chelsea where she would help look after Ingaret; Marjorie declined. Conditions in the penthouse in fashionable Chelsea deteriorated. Eventually, in 1993, Laurens and Ingaret were rescued by the arrival of a new housekeeper, a formidable woman of Scottish and South African background, Janet Campbell. She discovered a slum, with Ingaret unwashed and unkempt and the mattresses and carpets soaked in urine. Laurens seemed scarcely aware of this, and actually explained that 'the Bushmen never wash'. Mrs Campbell imposed order on chaos, with the help of a day and a night nurse, and though she was never a real friend because she refused to become another acolyte, Laurens must have realised that he and Ingaret depended on her. She stayed with them until his death, and observed his final request that she remain with Ingaret until she, too, died. He was insistent that Ingaret should not be removed from the apartment if she survived him.

Ingaret quietened a little, although she was never easy, and a simple routine was established. She and Laurens would breakfast together, he would retreat to work, at lunchtime he would leave to visit Frances, he and Ingaret would meet again in the late afternoon, sometimes at their favourite Kensington hotel, and she would be early to bed. Although he was always happy to receive visitors, on many days he was not disturbed. Lucia and Neil would usually arrive for supper on Sunday, Eva Monley, Kate Bertaut (née Littman) and Tom Bedford would visit regularly, Neil would come in to sit with Ingaret. A secretary was there every day. The telephone had become Laurens's main contact with the world. Ronald Cohen spoke to him daily, as did Lucia.[5] The near-daily exchanges with South Africa had eased, now that Chief Buthelezi and the Zulus had made their accommodation.

During these years Laurens extended his Jungian message to South African businessmen: Paul Semark of Escom, for example, and Jeremy Ractliffe of Murray and Roberts, both senior executives in major corporations, were attracted and enlisted, and assisted Laurens in various ways.

There had been a visit to Highgrove when Laurens gave Prince Charles a Bible allegedly inherited from King Charles I in the seventeenth century, which had been in the possession of the Giffard family since then and willed to the Prince by Ingaret, under Laurens's influence, years before. 'I so wished that Ingaret could have been with me to experience the immense emotions aroused by her very generous gift to my Prince,' wrote Laurens. Ingaret could not possibly have understood or agreed to this donation, and her family were furious: the Earl of Halsbury arrived in Chelsea Towers to protest that 'this writer chappie' had no right to give away a family heirloom.* On the same visit to Highgrove, Laurens declined Prince Charles's suggestion that they drive over to neighbouring Colley Farm, where Laurens had lived in the 1930s: 'I simply could not get myself to go back, but just feel happy that it is now within his own keeping and part of the Highgrove Estate.'[7]

Laurens continued to travel. Ingaret hated his absences, as she always had, but this did not persuade him to stop travelling. Her friends knew how her state of mind deteriorated when he was away. He visited America in December 1994, Canada in May 1995, America again in December 1995 and in September and October 1996. After his first wife Marjorie died in Cape Town in January 1995 Laurens felt unable to travel to the funeral, just as he had not attended the large van der Post family reunion in March 1994. In fact, he did not visit South Africa again after the coming of Majority Rule in April 1994.

---

*After Laurens's death the Halsbury family asked the Prince to return the Bible; the Prince's office refused.[6]

In May 1995 he went to Canada, to Calgary, on a visit arranged by his admirer Richard Osler, where he spoke on a number of occasions, including a Convocation address at the university to accept an honorary degree. It was a great success, he reported afterwards, writing to a friend that he had a standing ovation before nearly 1,000 people, and that his hosts declared that they knew of no similar event at other universities: 'It is good to be applauded in that way by so many young people, but I am glad I do not do it often because I think it could become seductive, and one's old unsleeping ego would be wide awake and asking for more and more. I was very glad to be back here with my little Ingaret and to listen with her into what comes through in silence and has no words.' He had not lost his ability to charm: Osler remembers him in Calgary at at the age of eighty-eight bewitching an attractive young woman with the line, 'May I call you Daughter of the Morning Star?'[8]

His visits to New York in December had become a great delight for him, with his sermons in the Cathedral of St John the Divine on the last Sunday in Advent. Laurens arranged for Frances to sculpt a series of eight reliefs which were bought by the Cathedral for $16,000 and dedicated at the Advent service, attended by both Laurens and Frances, in December 1995. Laurens asked the Cathedral to pay his fare.

He continued to write. In the last year of his life he found the energy to write *The Secret River*, a children's version of an African folk tale he had used many times. He tried to preface it with a long autobiographical essay, clearly of interest only to adults; his publishers, Barefoot Books, spiked the Introduction and published an illustrated version of what became his last book.[9]

To the end, he was still in demand all over the world. In October 1996 he flew to Boulder, Colorado, where Doug Greene had arranged a five-day celebration of his life and work. Laurens's American friends flew in to support him, but there was no doubt of his wider popularity, and the conference was a triumphant and crowded success for him. Despite being frail and old, in pain and not sleeping properly, he managed to give talk after talk during the course of the week on his usual subjects: the Bushmen, Jung, literary life in prewar London, the Japanese, and so on, a great achievement for a man in his ninetieth year. Some of his friends later thought that the effort killed him.

In November he insisted on giving Lucia a large birthday dinner party in his favourite Chinese restaurant. Exhausted, he then flew to Zurich to accept an award from the Marie-Louise von Franz Foundation, the money to go to his Foundation. Marie-Louise, one of the most distinguished of Jung's circle, was too old and ill to attend. Laurens struggled to introduce a film, give a talk, attend a conference and dinner; he had a fall, and a doctor was called. Back in London he went into hospital.[10]

Approaching ninety on 13 December, Laurens busied himself with instructions for his Estate, and in particular for Ingaret's future care. His family, and also Prince Charles, planned celebrations for his birthday. He was able to attend a gathering at his daughter Lucia's home on Wednesday 11 December, when he was at last presented with Bob Hinshaw's delayed *Festchrift*. He made a great effort, demanding cup after cup of his favourite white coffee, while greeting his friends from a chair as they literally knelt before him. The next day his health declined dramatically. He was forced to cancel a party which the Prince of Wales had arranged at Highgrove.[11]

By Sunday the 15th, Laurens's condition was grave. Family and close friends gathered around him. He slipped into occasional coma, attended at the end by Lucia and Neil, Frances, Tom and Jane, Emma, Janet, Nina and his doctor; Rupert, Louise Stein, Ronald Cohen, Bob Hinshaw, Eva Monley, came in and out. Several times he spoke in Afrikaans, and Tom Bedford came to his bedside to translate and to respond: Laurens was talking of '*die Sterre*', the stars, remembering how he had looked out on the southern heavens. He lapsed again into coma, and was not conscious when Prince Charles arrived, too late. The Prince, distressed, was introduced to Frances, whom he had never met. Laurens died in the early hours of the morning of Monday, 16 December, 1996.

The funeral service was held at Christchurch, Chelsea, on 20 December 1996, followed by cremation. It was attended by Prince Charles and the Address was given by his American publisher, Larry Hughes. A crowded memorial service was held in the Chapel of the Royal Hospital, Chelsea, on 18 March 1997. Lady Thatcher and Lucia read the lessons, Chief Buthelezi, representing Nelson Mandela, flew in from South Africa to give an address, Ian Player delivered the Eulogy, Tom Bedford and Ian McCallum read poems in Afrikaans and English. There was another memorial gathering in Djakarta of Laurens's Indonesian friends of fifty years ago. Laurens's ashes were buried in South Africa on 4 April 1998 in a newly-created Memorial Garden in Philippolis, and also beneath a tree in the garden of the house of his childhood.[12]

Ingaret had not understood. Perhaps she thought that Laurens had gone on his travels again; after sixty years she was accustomed to his absences. She sat in her room, unaware of any change. Laurens had left complex instructions and guarantees designed to ensure that she would be able to stay in her own home until her death. The staff remained as before. The only difference was that the family cancelled her private doctor of many years and called in the National Health Service.

Some weeks later a friend decided that she should know the truth, and told her. Ingaret thereupon faded away, and she died on 5 May 1997. Her funeral service was held in her own Chelsea church, and attended by Prince Charles, who had read of her death in *The Times*. Ingaret's ashes were later buried, in November 1998, in her Devon homeland, on top of the Brentor on Dartmoor. There was no suggestion that she and Laurens be buried together.[13] Like CWH and Lammie, they lie in separate graves.

41

The Fantasist

To RETURN TO THE central question: how did Laurens van der Post manage to achieve such eminence and fame from so obscure a beginning? What was the secret of his success?

A part of the answer must lie in his ambition. He dreamed from his youth of a life in Britain at the heart of Empire, a career as a famous writer, and even a knighthood. Until middle age, this dream seemed absurd. The war, when he discovered in himself qualities of courage, leadership and great ingenuity, offered a new start. After the war, with good fortune and the support of a devoted second wife, he began to write books which were good, and some of them were immensely successful. This gave him confidence.

A second answer, which should not be underestimated, is that Laurens had immense charm and he never ceased to employ it. Early reports speak of his intelligence as well as good looks. He used these gifts to conceal his limited education and the modesty of his youthful achievements. He networked, and cultivated and valued his friendships as well as his image. He was bold and energetic, and after the low times of the 1930s he could project himself as a successful man of letters and of affairs. For the rest of his life he ceaselessly made propaganda of his war record, his 'explorations', his diplomatic initiatives and his political achievements.

His admiration for Carl Gustav Jung, whose thinking pervades most of his books, offers another clue. All his work, fiction and non-fiction alike, suggests that Laurens longed to be seen as the 'archetype' of the 'Hero/Saviour'. Perhaps in the same Jungian language he was equally, or rather, the classic archetypal Hermes figure, the 'Trickster', the charmer and scoundrel of all ages, the Loki of Nordic myth. Like all Tricksters, Laurens lived off half-truths and fictional facts, and sometimes he must surely have wondered how he could maintain the whole web of fabrications which he had created, or whether one day he might be exposed. After he died, a doctor who knew him well, when asked the cause of death, replied that he had become 'weary of sustaining so many lies . . .'[1]

These elements explain, or instead arise out of, his obsessive need to fantasise. He created himself as a figure far removed from the farms of South Africa's barren Karoo; he invented a family history to fit and illustrate his aspirations. He had the wit, and the literary skills, together with this same charm and energy, to persuade the world that his inventions were real. The family background is of great importance. Laurens was an Afrikaner born soon after the Boer War, and he never escaped that legacy, for all the years he spent with monocle and Savile Row suits in a Chelsea penthouse. There were racial prejudices buried deep down, a cultural insecurity which came from the parochialism of the Orange Free State, and a family history which, if truth be told, included treachery, dishonesty, intrigue, greed, insecurity.

The war was the making of Laurens. He went into it reluctantly in his mid-thirties when his life must have seemed a confusion and, in dark moments, a failure. After the critical success of his first novel, he had been unable to write a second book. His journalism was undistinguished, and barely paid his bills; his marriage had failed; he had had to sell his Gloucestershire farm; he was drinking heavily. His experiences and his sufferings during the war seem to have given him an authority and a maturity which he had not previously known of himself. He faced danger and death, and discovered that he could be brave. He chose to exercise command, and found that his leadership was accepted by both colleagues and men. He understood that the random experiences of his youth at last added up to an investment which now paid dividends. He was able to confirm that he was a teacher, and, more significantly for the future, that he had a gift for telling stories to an audience. And he began to see that he might be able to inspire other people. Few of these qualities had been evident in 1939.

But in these same wartime years, exaggeration and fantasy became his daily recourse. These protected him throughout this dangerous and decisive period, and they would bring him international fame and profit for the rest of his long life. He began to develop a style of storytelling – about his family, his childhood, his early career, his military experiences. Thereafter he would similarly weave stories about almost everything. He became a masterly storyteller, both in his books and, especially, in the ancient craft of 'telling tales' to a live audience. After many years of inventing aspects of his life, it is not so surprising that he might eventually have come to believe the fictions, whether because he could no longer remember that he had made them up, or because he thought that no-one would find him out, or because he did not care whether they were true or not.

Laurens's fantasies were never without a distant base in reality. His skill was to develop, and exaggerate, a true experience. His tales of travels in Africa after the war were greatly expanded from the original events. He had met and talked with Jung, but that didn't make him his best friend. He visited Japan for just two weeks in 1926 but that doesn't mean he had a deep knowledge of and familiarity with Japan and the Japanese. He took an interest in the Rhodesian drama of 1965–1980 and afterwards spoke as if he had been personally responsible for the settlement. He was a member of several British expeditions to the Kalahari and in future years fostered the impression that he had been the leader and that he had explored unknown regions. (He told the Royal Geographical Society in a 1990 lecture that he had explored regions of the Kalahari where no man had been before.)

Laurens went to great pains to camouflage, conceal and re-create the story of his life. This book is an attempt to discover the simpler truth. The trouble is that he told so many stories about himself, and often he is the only source. Sometimes we may hope, and even assume, that he was telling the truth. The biographer's problem is that he is forced, again and again, to rely on Laurens's version of the truth, although he has learned to be very wary of it; his is the old dilemma of meeting with the Cretan who says 'all Cretans are liars' (so is *he* telling the truth?). Throughout these pages the reader will have learned to bear this point in mind.

When I began to write this book I was not, I think, biassed either towards or against Laurens. I knew him a little and I knew his books and, like most of his readers, assumed that his non-fiction was true and his fiction somewhat autobiographical. Over several years of research I was startled to discover how much of Laurens's own autobiography, whether in his books, his speeches, his articles or even his conversation, was 'unreliable'. It occurred to me that many of Laurens's admirers, friends as well as disciples, would be distressed by what I would have to write. This gave me no pleasure: on the contrary.

At this stage I was greatly encouraged by the advice of Sister Maria Basini of the Carmelite Monastery at Quidenham in Norfolk, who had been a dear friend of Laurens in his last years. Although she was dismayed by some of what I told her, she insisted that I must not hesitate to report the truth of Laurens, to focus on the Man rather than the Myth. It would be a great disservice to Laurens, she assured me, to allow the eulogies of his admirers to go unchallenged. In a phrase which would make sense to both Jungians and Christians, she urged me to write of the 'Shadow' as well as the 'Light' in order to arrive at a true portrait.[2] I have greatly appreciated that advice.

When a biographer discovers that his subject has so frequently replaced the literal truth with fantasy, he cannot agree that his subject's preference for the 'truth of the imagination' is acceptable. Laurens's peculiar and lifelong attitude to 'truth' can be spotted throughout the years in the countless examples of events which either did not happen or else happened very differently. This habit of storytelling is not a question of exaggeration, which we all indulge in, or of a shaky memory years after the event, or even of a human inclination to spin a yarn. Laurens told stories – inventions – lies – *constantly* throughout his long life. Some extravagances he inherited from his formidable and devious mother in the form of family legends. But the events of his own adult life are surely a different matter.

The search for the Shadow and the Light, the discovery of the truth, or even a portion of the truth, in Laurens's long and full and complicated life, has had to develop into a sequence of investigations: the biographer had to become detective, rather than the literary critic or the simple historian which he would have preferred to be. Laurens had a genius for reshaping his past. Once his initial inventions had been accepted, he built upon them, repeating his elaborations again and again like one of his Homeric bards, confident that he could create an ever higher artifice in which he would, of course, always remain the central, and by definition the ever loftier, Hero figure. His lies were not careless or unconsidered; as the years went by he returned time and again to his earlier adventures and experiences, adjusting them so as to reconstruct himself and, it should be noted, increasingly denigrating others. His later books are breathtaking in their exaggeration, or distortion, of earlier versions of events; the trapeze artist climbs higher and higher, the prestidigitateur grows ever more inventive, and no-one seems to spot the tricks, no-one falls down.

How did he get away with all the fabrications upon which he constructed the myth of his life? Why did no-one blow the whistle? Why was it that his fellow prisoners-of-war did not protest at his fictions? Why did the real experts on the Bushmen not speak out sooner? Why did the professional analysts let him interpret Jung as though he was an authority? Why did the diplomats not tell him to stop meddling in their business? Why didn't the British security services alert the Prime Minister and the Heir to the Throne that their confidant and adviser was not all that he seemed?

We may now begin to see other explanations for the success of his life-long self-promotion. It was premeditated, deliberate, even ruthless, never missing a trick. He possessed colossal vanity. There must have been a certain coldness in him, for if we lie to others we use them for our own purposes in which they cannot share. He put his version of the truth on the record, many times and in many modes, immensely helped by his gift for storytelling. Midway through his career, he began to benefit from the insulation which came from his newly-perceived membership of the English Establishment. He gained authenticity from the celebrity culture – he was an internationally-famous figure, and it became an important part of his spell, until the spell began to wear off during the last years. Then he was bewildered to encounter criticism, even mockery and dis-regard. (He tried to turn this to his advantage, saying that it was the result of his friendship with Prince Charles – that, in his words, he was caught in the Prince's collective 'shadow'.) In old age Laurens discovered that, while his social, political, environmental and Jungian reputations per-sisted, his distinction as a writer – which was always what he had prized most, the great ambition from his youth – was increasingly denied.

He became more sensitive about his reputation. For instance, in a 1993 interview with the publisher and businessman Naim Attallah, he (unusu-ally) lost his temper. Said Attallah, rather bold: 'There are those who regard you as less of a sage and more of a charlatan . . . Do you perhaps mix fantasy and truth sometimes?' Laurens: 'This is quite absurd – these are idiots talking . . . I have done certain things quite well in life. For example, I won a prize for best-run small farm in Gloucestershire in the Three Counties Show. Or is that being a charlatan and a romancer? And my record in the war – is that also romancing? I shouldn't even have to respond to these remarks; they're obviously made by singularly stupid people.'[3]

Perhaps his many readers and followers did not want to know the truth. Laurens, it seems, personified some of our own ambitions: he fought and survived an heroic war, he explored the wilds of Africa, he befriended primitive and romantic peoples, he wrote best-selling books, he became an intimate friend of The Great – while at the same time appearing to be a good and kind and charming man. He was undeniably generous with his time and with his talents. His greatest achievement was that he introduced countless people to ideas, possibilities, dimensions, values, concepts, together with the language in which to think about them, which they might otherwise never have encountered. That is why so many will continue to be grateful to him, whatever has been revealed in this book. Laurens was responsible for many acts of special kindness, of consideration, of unselfishness. He bravely refused to co-operate in the Japanese war trials and for the rest of his life urged forgiveness. He could be spontaneously sympathetic, whether in gifts to his family or in supporting organisations, or individuals, who came to him for help. He tirelessly took care of his friends when they were in need, offering them financial assistance as well as the devotion of his indefatigable energy on their behalf. When John Hardbattle, half-Bushman, fell ill with stomach cancer, Laurens contributed considerably to his medical expenses in Germany, and also asked help from Prince Charles, whom he had sent Hardbattle to visit in Balmoral.[4]

It is also important that he was an *exotic* figure, tinged with the mysteries of places which we do not know. He was a stranger, he was the man who came from far away, he was *different*, which gave him a special licence. An Afrikaner, he stood out even in South Africa, as in his first job in Durban when he was the back-veld boy in an English-speaking world. In prewar London he was a handsome and intriguing stranger. In the British Army he may or may not have been Lieutenant-Colonel but he was always rather unlike the other Colonels. He understood this and underlined it in his books, his films and his interviews; he knew that most of us are unfamiliar with the African bush, its wildlife and its remote peoples, which meant that he could get away with all sorts of embellishment and even invention – there are always lions roaring and thunder crashing in his books, happily accepted by his international audience, though at home in South Africa giving rise to occasional protest, and even, on occasion, stifled mirth.

Even when he was accepted at the heart of the British Establishment, Laurens was never really 'one of us'. Both insider and outsider, he had the best of both worlds, wielding the power which came of his exotic difference from those around him. This made it easier for him to impress his own version of the truth on his friends, his associates, and especially his readers. More importantly for many, he articulated and gave voice to our shy aspirations for moral consciousness, for goodness, for spirituality, for a vague sort of modern-day religion – for 'Faith' – unencumbered by tired churches and creeds.

His followers did not guess that he did not feel obliged to live his own life by the high moral and spiritual values which he preached. Even close friends who did know him chose to keep quiet. Why? Out of love for him, because he was a man who always attracted love. Four years after his death Prince Charles opened St James's Palace to host the first in a series of annual lectures in Laurens's memory.[5] None of the guests, many of them distinguished in their own right, was unaware of at least some of Laurens's failings. But they had all loved him.

Notes

In order to reduce the number of notes in this book, these have been compacted. Each note number in the text refers not only to the immediate fact or quotation but also to the material in the previous lines or paragraphs since the last end-note. Laurens van der Post is hereafter referred to as 'LvdP'.

The following abbreviations have been used:

LvdP Archive, c/o The LvdP Estate – LvdPA
Public Records Office, London – PRO
Imperial War Museum Library, London – IWML
Nederduitse Gereformeerde Kerk Archives, Bloemfontein – NGK
Free State Archive, Bloemfontein – FSA
Cape Archive, Cape Town – CA
Pretoria Archive, Pretoria – PA
Supreme Court Records, Bloemfontein – SCRB
National Afrikaans Literary Museum, Bloemfontein – NALM
Alan Paton Centre, University of Natal, Pietermaritzburg – APC
Durham University Library, Durham – DUL
Brenthurst Library, Johannesburg – BL
Cullen Library, University of the Witwatersrand, Johannesburg – CL
Colonial Development Corporation Archive, London – CDC
Chatto & Windus Archive, Reading University – C&W
Leonard Woolf Archive, University of Sussex, Brighton – LW
William Morrow Archive, New York – WM
BBC Written Archive, Caversham – BBC
The Britten-Pears Library, Aldeburgh – BPL
National English Literary Museum, Grahamstown – NELM

Dates of interviews are provided, unless multiple interviews were conducted; all of the latter were conducted between 1998 and 2001. Although LvdP's books are listed with original publisher and date of publication in the bibliography, page references in the notes refer to the Penguin editions of his books.

The LvdP Estate can be contacted at 32 Gordon Place, London, W8 4JE.

Introduction
1. Janet Campbell, letter to author, 3 Feb. 1999.
2. LvdP, The Royal Geographical Society Television Lecture of the Year, 1990: 'Exploration', LvdPA.

Part One
I
1. LvdP, *Yet Being Someone Other*, pp. 298 & 311; Ingaret Giffard, *The Way Things Happen*, p. 326.
2. LvdP, *Jung And The Story Of Our Time*, pp. 22–23; Certificate for First Class Cadets, Grey College, LvdPA.
3. Janet Campbell, letter to author, 22 Jan. 1999; Lucia van der Post, letter to author, May 2001; *Yet Being*, p. 298; Ministry of Defence Records (A. K. Ghana, letter to James Sanders, 28 Apr. 1999); LvdP, letter to Ingaret Giffard-Young, 10 & 13 Oct. 1939, LvdPA.
4. M. M. van der Post, letters to LvdP, 25 Feb. & 3 Apr. 1940, LvdPA.
5. Ministry of Defence Records; *Yet Being*, p. 311.

6. *The Way Things*, pp. 287–88, 329–331 & 337; LvdP, letter to Ingaret Giffard-Young, 12 Feb. 1941, LvdPA; Joan Brind, interview with author, 19 Jan. 1998.
7. Ministry of Information, *The Abyssinian Campaigns: The Official Story of the Conquest of Italian East Africa*, pp. 9–14, 22 & 67; W. E. D. Allen, *Guerrilla War In Abyssinia*, p. 126; General Sir Archibald P. Wavell, 'Operations in East Africa, November 1940-July 1941', *Supplement to the London Gazette*, 10 July 1946, pp. 3527–3530.
8. Wilfred Thesiger, *The Life of My Choice*, p. 433; LvdP, *First Catch Your Eland*, p. 34.
9. Ministry of Information, op. cit., pp. 56–64; Thesiger, op. cit., pp. 313–21; see also Trevor Royle, *Orde Wingate: Irregular Soldier.*
10. Carel Birkby, *It's A Long Way To Addis*, pp. 265–66; Horace Flather, *The Way of an Editor*, p. 40.
11. *Yet Being*, p. 305–6; *The Guardian*, 27 Oct. 2000.
12. Allen, op. cit., pp. 48, 51 & 60; *Yet Being*, pp. 306–7; Lucia van der Post, interview with author.
13. LvdP, letter to Ingaret Giffard, 6 May 1941, LvdPA.
14. Allen, op. cit., pp. 54–56, 63–65, 82; *Yet Being*, pp. 307 & 311; *Eland*, pp. 36–37.
15. *Yet Being*, pp. 302–3, 307–10; *Eland*, pp. 21–22.
16. LvdP, letters to Ingaret Giffard, 12 Feb., 1 & 6 May 1941, LvdPA; *Eland*, p. 33.
17. Allen, op. cit., pp. 84 & 87–88, 91–92; *Eland*, pp. 22–29.
18. Hugh Boustead, *The Wind of Morning: The autobiography of Hugh Boustead*; Thesiger, op. cit.; Allen, op. cit.
19. Birkby, op. cit., p. 268; Desmond Young, *Try Anything Twice*, p. 277; George Rodger, *Desert Journey*, pp. 85–86.
20. Ministry of Defence Records; LvdP, telegram and letters to Ingaret Giffard-Young, 29 Oct., 1, 5 Nov. 1941 & undated, LvdPA.
21. Ministry of Defence Records; LvdP, *The Seed and the Sower*, pp. 108–9; Rodger, op. cit., p. 86. See also Joe Bryant, letter to LvdP, 12 July 1957, LvdPA; Michael Asher, *Thesiger*, p. 211; Thesiger, op. cit., pp. 363–65; *Eland*, op. cit.; LvdP in conversation with Jean-Marc Pottiez, *A Walk With a White Bushman*, p. 306.
22. [Natal] *Daily News*, 5 July 1941; Birkby, op. cit., pp. 265–66; *Seed*, p. 116.
23. LvdP, letter to Ingaret Giffard-Young, 12 Jan. 1942, LvdPA.

2
1. *Yet Being*, pp. 314–16.
2. The basis of the following research was conducted in the 1980s by Ian Sayer for *World War II Investigator* magazine.
3. Ian Sayer, 'When An Inner Voice Spoke', *World War II Investigator*, Dec. 1988; LvdP, 'The Story of No. 43 Special Mission', Mar. 1948 (WO106 5035); Field (SW Pacific Command), signal to War Office, 24 Feb. 1942 (WO 193/609), PRO; Afrikaners of LvdP's age were educated in 'High Dutch', an archaic form of modern Dutch.
4. Jane Flower, interview with author, 20 Nov. 2000; see also Richard Gough, *Special Operations Singapore, 1941–1942*, pp. 152–160.
5. Field Marshall Wavell's Report: Evacuation from Singapore and Sumatra, Feb-Mar. 1942 (WO 141/100), PRO.
6. '43 Special Mission', PRO; John Denman, interview with author; *World War II Investigator*, Dec. 1988.
7. LvdP, *The Admiral's Baby*, pp. 29–30.
8. D. W. N. Kriek, letter to LvdP, 10 Oct. 1979, LvdPA; Paul Vogt, letter to author, 12 Nov. 2000; '43 Special Mission', PRO; *World War II Investigator*, Dec. 1988.
9. '43 Special Mission', PRO; *World War II Investigator*, Dec. 1988.
10. '43 Special Mission', PRO.
11. D. W. N. Kriek, letters to LvdP, 20 Aug. 1979, 20 Oct. 1979 & 10 Dec. 1979, LvdPA.
12. LvdP, letter to C. F. Gresswell, 23 Oct. 1979; LvdP, letters to P. P. Groat, 1 Jan., 26 Mar., 23 May, 1 & 5 June 1980; C. F. Gresswell, letter to LvdP, 18 Oct. 1979; P. P. Groat, letters to LvdP, 10 Dec. 1979, 28, 29 May & 4 June 1980; LvdP, letter to C. T. Walker, 6 May 1947; C. T. Walker, letter to D. W. N. Kriek, 9 May 1947, LvdPA.
13. D. W. N. Kriek, letter to LvdP, 20 Aug. 1979; LvdP, letter to D. W. N. Kriek, 1 Jan. 1980; LvdP, letter To Whom It May Concern, 1 Jan. 1980, LvdPA.
14. D. W. N. Kriek, letter to LvdP, 5 Feb. 1980, LvdPA; David W. N. Kriek, *Speciale Missie Nr. 43 in Bantam (Java)*; D. W. N. Kriek & Phillip Clarke, '43 Special Mission' (internet).
15. Paul Vogt, letter to author, 12 Nov. 2000.
16. Ministry of Defence Records; *World War II Investigator*, Dec. 1988; Field (SW Pacific Command), signal to War Office, 24 Feb. 1942 (WO 193/609), PRO; Brigadier L. F. Field, letter to Ingaret Giffard-Young, 1 Aug. 1942, LvdPA.
17. Sir Robin Black, letter to author, 3 Aug. 1998.
18. Jane Flower, interview with author, 20 Nov. 2000; Field (SW Pacific Command), signal to War Office, 24 Feb. 1942 (WO 193/609), PRO.

19. Colonel Sir LvdP, 'Foreword', E. E. Dunlop, *The War Diaries of Weary Dunlop: Java and the Burma-Thailand Railway, 1942–1945*, p. x; *Yet Being*, p. 309; *Admiral's Baby*, p. 155.
20. *The King's Regulations For The Army and the Royal Army Reserve*; Ministry of Defence Records; *Quarterly Army List*.
21. Japanese Prisoner-of-War Records (WO 345/53), PRO.

3
1. LvdP, *Venture To The Interior*, p. 8; *Yet Being*, p. 316; LvdP, *About Blady: A Pattern Out of Time*, p. 47.
2. LvdP, speech to the Cape Town Press Club, 29 Nov. 1990.
3. LvdP, 'The Desired Earth', LvdPA; *Seed*, op. cit.
4. 'World of Books', BBC Radio, 11 Feb. 1963, BBC; *Venture*, pp. 209–10; Colin Wilson, *The Outsider*, p. 169; Fyodor Dostoyevsky, *The Idiot*.
5. LvdP, Obituary: W. T. H. Nichols, *The Times*, 10 May 1986 & draft version.
6. *Venture*, pp. 207–211.
7. John Denman, 'An Honourable Moment'; LvdP, *The Night of the New Moon*, p. 144.
8. Ron Bryer, *White Ghosts of Nagasaki*, pp. 39, 41, 50, 53 & 56.
9. Frank Foster, *Comrades In Bondage*, pp. 13 & 44–46.
10. Leslie J. Robertson, letter to LvdP, 9 Aug. 1977, LvdPA.
11. Foster, op. cit., p. 50–52.
12. Dunlop, op. cit., pp. ix-xi, 43–44 & 51; LvdP, draft extract of 'The Night of the New Moon', LvdPA.
13. E. E. Dunlop, letter to Ian Sayer, 12 Apr. 1992.
14. Graeme Allen, letter to author, 13 Nov. 1998; Colin Castle, *Lucky Alex: The Career of Group Captain A. M. Jardine AFC, CD, Seaman and Airman*, p. 190.
15. John Denman, interview with author.
16. John Denman, interview with author; Harold Goulding, *Yasme: Some Recollections of a Former FEPOW*; *New Moon*, p. 9.
17. Dunlop, op. cit., pp. 5, 52–55, 57, 62, 87 & 128–129; John Denman, interview with author; Sue Ebury, *Weary: The Life of Sir Edward Dunlop*, p. 341.
18. Dunlop, op. cit., pp. 197–98.
19. Dunlop, op. cit., p. ix; Goulding, op. cit.
20. See for example Dunlop, op. cit., pp. 67 & 90; Castle, op. cit., pp. 193 & 196.
21. *New Moon*, p. 11; Dunlop, op. cit., pp. xi-xii, 13 & 67; Penry Rees, interview with author, 6 July 1998; John Denman, 'Notes on Prison Journal', 1999; *New Moon*, pp. 10–11; Ebury, op. cit., pp. 365–66.
22. *New Moon*, pp. 15–18; the Imperial War Museum possesses a collection of copies of *Mark Time*, some of which were donated by LvdP (*Daily Telegraph*, 7 Sept. 1988), IWML. See also Ray Parkin, *Out of the Smoke: The Story of a Sail, Into The Smother: A Journal of the Burma-Siam Railway* & *The Sword and the Blossom*; LvdP, 'Prison Journal, 1943', unpublished, LvdPA.
23. *New Moon*, pp. 132–33; 'Prison Journal, 1943', LvdPA; *The Times*, 18 July 1962.
24. Denman, 'Notes'; 'New Moon', draft version, LvdPA; Dunlop, op. cit., p. 68.
25. 'Far East Interlude', LvdPA.
26. LvdP, 'Pigs, Japanese and the Moon', *The Countryman*, Summer 1948; 'Countrymen in Gaol: How some British Prisoners of War in Japanese hands cultivated slight and desperate land', draft version, LvdPA; Dunlop, op. cit., p. 88; *New Moon*, p. 86.
27. *New Moon*, pp. 38–39; W. T. H. Nichols, letter to Peter Bevan, 29 Dec. 1981; Denman, 'Notes'.
28. John Denman, interview with author; LvdP, letter to Mr and Mrs Rae Smith, 24 Nov. 1945; LvdP, letter to John Denman, 24 Apr. 1946; W. T. H. Nichols, letter to LvdP, 21 Mar. 1947, LvdPA.
29. *New Moon*, pp. 32 & 53–54; A. H. Ireson, letter to LvdP, 1 Mar. 1948, LvdPA; Jonathan Stedall, 'Laurens van der Post at 80', BBC 2, 13 Dec. 1986.
30. Dunlop, op. cit., pp. 109–12, 114–17 & 119; Ebury, op. cit., pp. 349–50; Sue Ebury, interview with author, 14 Feb. 2001.

4
1. 'Prison Journal, 1943', LvdPA; *New Moon*, p. 17–21.
2. *New Moon*, pp. 12–13, 48, 54, 82–83 & 96; Denman, 'An Honourable Moment'.
3. *New Moon*, pp. 83–89 & 96–102; Robert Leeson, 'The Wartime Experiences of A. W. H. Phillips', LvdPA.
4. Dunlop, op. cit., pp. 69 & 76; *New Moon*, p. 68; Denman, 'Honourable Moment'; John Denman, interview with author.
5. *New Moon*, pp. 33–35; LvdP, postcards to Ingaret Giffard-Young, 3.11. 2603 (Japanese calendar) & 20 July 1945, LvdPA; 'Secret Weekly Intelligence Summary "A": No. 122, Royal Netherlands Headquarters S-SEA', 14 May 1945 (WO 32/11128); 'Allied P. W. in Jap Hands', 21 Sept. 1944 (WO 32/11128), PRO; John Denham, interview with author; Jane Flower, interview with James Sanders, 3 June 2001.

6. George Cooper, interview with author, 13 Aug. 1989.
7. 'Far East Interlude', LvdPA; *New Moon*, pp. 72–77.
8. Ed Stern, 'Memoir', IWML; John Denman, interview with author; Alex Jardine, interview with author, 3 Feb. 2001; David Wyllie, letter to LvdP, 2 May 1983, LvdPA; Castle, op. cit., p. 208.
9. John Denman, interview with author; *New Moon*, pp. 49–50 & 61; W. T. H. Nichols, letter to Peter Bevan, 29 Dec. 1981.
10. *New Moon*, pp. 47–49, 56–59, 69–71, 103, 105 & 115–117. Don Wall, *Kill the Prisoners*; see also *New Yorker*, 31 July 1995.

5
1. *New Moon*, pp. 109–10 & 112; *Admiral's Baby*, p. 7.
2. John Denman, interview with author; *Admiral's Baby*, pp. 25–26.
3. Major R. B. Houston, 'What Happened in Java in 1945–46', *The Army Quarterly*, Jan. 1948; Major-General S. Woodburn Kirby, *The War Against Japan, Vol. V: The Surrender of Japan*, pp. 307–308, 310–312 & 316.
4. *Admiral's Baby*, pp. 7, 9, 20 & 146; *New Moon*, pp. 112 & 120; *Yet Being*, pp. 322 & 324; *Venture*, p. 7.
5. W. T. H. Nichols, letters to LvdP, 12 June 1946, LvdPA; *Admiral's Baby*, pp. 14–17.
6. LvdP, letter to Lammie van der Post, 13 Dec. 1945, LvdPA; *Admiral's Baby*, p. 146; W. T. H. Nichols, letters to LvdP, 12 June 1946 & 24 Aug. 1947, LvdPA; John Denman, interview with author; LvdP, postcards to Ingaret Giffard-Young, 3.11.2063 (Japanese calendar) & 20 July 1945, LvdPA.
7. *Admiral's Baby*, p. 66.
8. Kirby, op. cit., p. 312; *Admiral's Baby*, p. 15; *Yet Being*, pp. 321–22.
9. LvdP, 'Political and Economic Survey of Events in Netherlands East Indies during the period of occupation by British Imperial forces from September 29th 1945 to November 30th 1946', Jan. 1947, LvdPA; LvdP, 'Report on Conditions in Republican Java', 5 May 1947 (FO 480/1), PRO; *Admiral's Baby*, op. cit.; LvdP, letter to John Charlton & John Murray, 21 Aug. 1995; see also LvdP, letter to Jean-Marc Pottiez, 26 Aug. 1995: 'The report is, as I say, self-contained, and Gilbert MacKereth told me over and over again he thought it one of the most remarkable, if not the greatest dispatch ever written for the Foreign Office.', LvdPA.
10. *Admiral's Baby*, pp. 44, 64 & 180; *White Bushman*, p. 249; *Yet Being*, p. 323; LvdP, Memorandum on Rhodesia I (for Margaret Thatcher), 25 July 1979, LvdPA; *Who's Who, 1979*; *Who's Who, 1981*.
11. *Admiral's Baby*, pp. 15–17, 19–22, 25–26, 44 & 137; British Consulate General, report to the Secretary of State for Foreign Affairs, Jan. 1947, LvdPA.
12. *Yet Being*, p. 324; *Admiral's Baby*, pp. 20 & 121; Lawrie Pendred, letter to LvdP, 10 Jan. 1947, LvdPA.
13. *Admiral's Baby*, pp. 76–83, 146 & 178–80. There are only three examples of correspondence between LvdP and Mountbatten in the LvdP archive: Mountbatten of Burma, letters to LvdP, 12 Jan. 1948 & 17 May 1974; LvdP, letter to Lord Mountbatten, 31 May 1974, LvdPA.
14. *Admiral's Baby*, pp. 22–26; Kirby, op. cit., pp. 244–247 & 316.
15. *Admiral's Baby*, pp. 28, 56, 59 & 137–138.
16. Kirby, op. cit., pp. 247–248; *Admiral's Baby*, pp. 34–37 & 71; LvdP, letter to Admiral Patterson, 23 Jan. 1947, LvdPA.
17. Admiral Patterson, letter to friends, 7 Oct. 1947, LvdPA.
18. *Admiral's Baby*, p. 74.
19. Admiral Patterson, letter to friends, 7 Oct. 1947, LvdPA; *Admiral's Baby*, pp. 51–52, 56–58, 60–63, 67 & 216.
20. *Admiral's Baby*, pp. 77–80, 83–84 & 89–90; LvdP, letter to General Christison, Nov. 1980, LvdPA.
21. *Admiral's Baby*, pp. 97–99 & 103–5; *White Bushman*, p. 56; David Lean, *Lawrence of Arabia*, feature film, 1962; LvdP, letter to Frederic Carpenter, 11 May 1964, LvdPA; see also *Trek*, June 1952; LvdP, letter to Larry Hughes, 7 Nov. 1992, LvdPA.
22. Ministry of Defence Records; *Admiral's Baby*, p. 101.
23. LvdP, Passport (D4104), LvdPA.
24. *Admiral's Baby*, pp. 102–7; see also P. F. R. B., note to P. J. Dixon, 20 Oct. 1945; LvdP, 'Dictated Statement on the Present Situation in Java', Oct. 1945 (PREM 8/70), PRO.
25. *Admiral's Baby*, pp. 111 & 114–15; Anonymous [LvdP], 'The Java Crisis', BBC Home Service, 1 Nov. 1945; A British Officer [LvdP], 'The Japanese Legacy in Java', *The Listener*, 8 Nov. 1945.
26. LvdP, letters to Ingaret Giffard-Young, 8, 10, 20 Nov., 4 & 12 Dec. 1945, LvdPA.

6
1. Kirby, op. cit., pp. 322–32; *Admiral's Baby*, p. 113; Tilman Remme, *Britain and Regional Cooperation in South-East Asia, 1945–49*, p. 30.
2. Dirk Bogarde, *A Gentle Occupation*; Dirk Bogarde, verbal message to author, July 1998; LvdP, letter to Ingaret Giffard-Young, 2 Dec. 1945, LvdPA.
3. Bryan Ibotson Hunt, 'Java and Sumatra, 1945–46 Diary', IWML; Bogarde, op. cit.

4. Kirby, op. cit., p. 327; *Admiral's Baby*, pp. 132–33.
5. LvdP, letter to M. M. van der Post, 13 Dec. 1945, LvdPA; *Admiral's Baby*, pp. 145–47.
6. *Admiral's Baby*, pp. 172–73, 175–77 & 279; *White Bushman*, pp. 248–49; John Tucker, 'My General – Some Views', IWML.
7. *Admiral's Baby*, pp. 152, 156 & 207–8; Kirby, op. cit., pp. 250–51; LvdP, 'Political and Economic Survey', Jan. 1947, LvdPA.
8. *Admiral's Baby*, pp. 157 & 181; Lanham Titchener, letters to LvdP, 17 Nov. 1946 & 10 Jan. 1947; Sri, letter to LvdP, 28 Nov. 1946, LvdPA.
9. LvdP, letters to Ingaret Giffard-Young, 4 Mar., 26 May, 23 June & 5 Aug. 1946; Ingaret Giffard-Young, letters to LvdP, 23 Mar., 9, 30 Apr., 1, 10, 26 May, 25 July & 21 Aug. 1946, LvdPA; *Daily Mail*, 31 July 1946.
10. George Cooper, interview with author, 13 Aug. 1999; Guy Innes, letter to LvdP, 4 Jan. 1952; LvdP, letter to George Fisher, 18 June 1981; LvdP, letter to Ingaret Giffard-Young, 3 Oct. 1946, LvdPA; *Supplement to the London Gazette*, 1 Aug. 1946.
11. LvdP, letter to Ingaret Giffard-Young, 21 Dec. 1946; Ingaret Giffard-Young, letters to LvdP, 5 Sept. 1946 & 30 Apr. 1947, LvdPA.
12. Bill Drower, interview with author, 20 Oct. 2000.
13. *Admiral's Baby*, pp. 285–86, 288 & 291.
14. Colin MacLaren, interview with author, 30 Sept. 2000; Lanham Titchener, letter to Colin MacLaren, 16 Dec. 1947; Gilbert MacKereth, letter to Colin MacLaren, 12 Dec. 1947; *Supplement to the London Gazette*, 25 Sept. 1947.
15. *Admiral's Baby*, pp. 296 & 298–99.
16. 'Illegible' Lt-Colonel, letter to Force Paymaster, 20 Mar. 1946; Officers' Accounts Branch, letter to British Army Pay Office, 10 Apr. 1946; Lt-General Robinson, letter to Under Secretary of State for War, 3 May 1946; HQ Allied Forces, NEI, signal to HQ ALFSEA 2nd Echelon Jhansi, 13 May 1946; HQ ALFSEA, signal to British Army Pay Office, Meerut, 21 May 1946, LvdPA; *Admiral's Baby*, p. 101.
17. Brigadier Field, letter to LvdP, 12 Mar. 1948; Brigadier Field, letter to Ingaret Giffard-Young, 1 Aug. 1942, LvdPA.
18. Air Vice Marshal Sir Paul Maltby, letter to W. T. H. Nichols, 26 Mar. 1948; Air Vice Marshal Sir Paul Maltby, letter to F. G. Brockman, 28 Mar. 1948; F. G. Brockman, letter to W. T. H. Nichols, 5 Apr. 1948; W. T. H. Nichols, letter to Group Captain F. G. Brockman, 8 Apr. 1948; 'Illegible' Colonel, letter to LvdP, 12 June 1948, LvdPA.
19. *Admiral's Baby*, pp. 286, 301–2, 304, 306–7, 309 & 311; Robin Jeffrey (ed.), *Asia – The Winning of Independence*, pp. 140–155; M. C. Ricklefs, *A History of Modern Indonesia since c. 1300*, pp. 224–34.
20. Sybil Bauer, postcard to LvdP, 13 Dec. 1973, LvdPA.

Part Two

7

1. *Venture*, pp. 13, 22 & 30.
2. Ibid., pp. 13–15, 23 & 24–26; LvdP, *The Voice of the Thunder*, pp. 152–55.
3. Detailed family tree commissioned by author; C. C. de Villiers (Revis.), C. Pama, *Genealogies of Old South African Families, Vol. I*, p. xliii; P. Coertzen, *The Huguenots of South Africa, 1688–1988*, pp. 143–52; J. E. Malherbe, 'Jacques Mouton', *Huguenot Society of South Africa Bulletin*, 1990–91, pp. 34–36; *Venture*, p. 23.
4. *White Bushman*, pp. 281–82.
5. Pippa Skotnes (ed.), *Miscast: Negotiating the Presence of the Bushmen*; Shula Marks, 'Khoisan Resistance to the Dutch in the Seventeenth and Eighteenth Centuries', *Journal of African History*, 1972.
6. V. C. Malherbe, *Krotoa, Called Eva: A Woman Between*; S. Nuttall & C. Coetzee (eds.), *Negotiating the Past: The Making of Memory in South Africa*, pp. 112–119; Harriet Deacon (ed.), *The Island: A History of Robben Island, 1488–1990*, p. 19.
7. G. S. Preller, 'Trekkers en Trekboere' in 'Historikus', *Spore Van Die Kakebeenwa*, pp. 32–48; George McCall Theal, *History of the Boers in South Africa*, p. 75; Maria Magdalena 'Lammie' van der Post, 'Memoir', unpublished fragments, 1931–1954, LvdPA; *Sarie Marais*, 21 May 1952; LvdP, 'Lost World of Kalahari', BBC Television, 15 June–20 July 1956; *Venture*, p. 13.
8. S. J. Halford, *The Griquas of Griqualand*, pp. 95–108; R. Ross, *Adam Koks Griquas: A Study in the Development of Stratification in South Africa*, pp. 94–103; Martin Legassick, 'The Griqua, the Sotho-Tswana, and the missionaries, 1780–1840: the politics of a frontier zone', PhD thesis, 1969.
9. *Sarie Marais*, 21 May 1952; M. M. van der Post, 'Memoir', LvdPA.
10. R. M. Britz, *Die Geskiedenis Van Die Nederduitse Gereformeerde Kerk Fauresmith, 1848–1998*, pp. 5 & 8; the town of Fauresmith has a 'Lubbe Street'; *N Kort Oorsig Van Die Geskiedenis Van Fauresmith, 1848–1948*, p. 13, NGK.
11. *Venture*, p. 15; M. M. van der Post, 'Memoir', LvdPA; J. F. Midgley, 'The Orange River Sovereignty (1848–1854)', *Archives Year Book for South African History, Vol. II*, pp. 123–56.
12. Elisabeth Louisa Lubbe, née Liebenberg, Will (L518), FSA.

8

1. *Venture*, p. 24; *Sarie Marais*, 21 May 1952; The Grey Collection, FSA; C. W. H. & Johanna van der Post, C. W. H. & M. M. 'Lammie' van der Post Wedding Certificates, NGK; Hendrik van der Post Birth Certificate & Johanna van der Post Death Certificate (L319), FSA.
2. J. Ploeger & G. de Kock, *Nederlandse Emigrasie Na SA, 1800–1900*; *Venture*, p. 23; William Plomer, *Double Lives: An Autobiography*, p. 167.
3. Family tree; LvdP, letter to Fred van der Post, 23 Nov. 1995, LvdPA; C. L. Heesakkers, *Album Amicorum van Janus Dousa*; Ella Bedford (van der Post), speech at Van der Post family reunion, 25–27 Mar. 1994. See also Lucia van der Post, *Financial Times*, 23 Apr. 1994.
4. For Hendrik Pieter van der Post's employment as a bank teller & bankruptcy, see Ref: TAB496871558 & TAB49610329, CA; *Venture*, p. 24; *Braby's Orange River Colony Directory, 1910*, p. 881; Marietjie Cilliers, interview with Mark Ingle, 12 Sept. 1999; D. C. McGill, *A History of Koffiefontein Mine and Town*, p. 90.
5. C. W. H. van der Post, letter to Lourens Hermanus Fourie, 7 Oct. 1889 (Accession A272), FSA; LvdP, interview with Lucia van der Post, undated tape recording, LvdPA; LvdP, *The Face Beside The Fire*.
6. C. W. H. & M. M. 'Lammie' van der Post Wedding Certificate, NGK; see also various correspondence (Accession A272), FSA.
7. Anna van der Post, preface, C. W. H. van der Post, *Ignas Prinsloo of Volharding Bekroond*; C. J. P. le Roux, *CWH van der Post*; *Weekend Argus*, 28/29 Nov. 1992; J. Haasbroek, *Die Rol van Cornelis Hermanus Wessels in die Oranje-Vrystaat, 1885–1924*, pp. 75, 85–87, 113, 133–36, 138, 154, 156–57, 159 & 276; A. M. Grundlingh, *Die 'Hensoppers' en 'Joiners'*, p. 16; *Venture*, pp. 24–25 & 30; *Sarie Marais*, 21 May 1952.
8. A. A. Cooper, *The Freemasons of South Africa*, pp. 157 & 178; O. H. Bate, *The Lodge de Goede Hoop*; Japie van Rensburg, conversation with Mark Ingle, 1 Feb. 1999; LvdP, letter to John Charlton, 5 Sept. 1991, C&W.
9. Thomas Pakenham, *The Boer War*.
10. Grundlingh, op. cit.; F. Pretorius, *The Anglo-Boer War, 1899–1902*, pp. 67–73; M. M. van der Post, 'Memoir', LvdPA; C. W. H. van der Post, letter To Whom It May Concern, 1 May 1911; C. W. H. van der Post, letter to A. P. Lubbe, 30 Jan. 1900 (Accession A272), FSA; H. ver Loren van Themaat, *Twee Jaren in Den Boerenoorlog*, pp. 30–49.
11. M. M. van der Post, 'Memoir', LvdPA; Cooper, op. cit., p. 75.
12. A. P. Lubbe, Compensation claim, 23 June & 20 July 1903 (CO 5158/03), FSA.
13. C. W. H. van der Post, letters to A. P. Lubbe, 30 Jan. & 6 Feb. 1900 (Accession A272), FSA; Sarah Raal, *The Lady Who Fought: A Young Woman's Account of the Anglo-Boer War*; Leslie Jacobson, interview with James Sanders and Mark Ingle, 10 Dec. 2000; Documents on A. P. Lubbe's second wife (CO1354/04), FSA.
14. *Venture*, p. 25.
15. M. M. van der Post, 'Memoir', LvdPA; Military memorandum, 23 Jan. 1901; memorandum, undated; C. W. H. van der Post, affidavit, undated (A956), PA.
16. C. W. H. van der Post, 'Outline for a Memoir', undated (Accession A272), FSA; memorandum, undated (A956), PA.
17. M. M. van der Post, 'Memoir', LvdPA.

9

1. C. W. H. van der Post, *Piet Uijs of Lijden en Strijd der Voortrekkers in Natal*; *Ignas Prinsloo*; *Venture*, p. 25; LvdP, Biographical note, unpublished, 1991, LvdPA; Le Roux, op. cit., p. 6; M. M. van der Post, 'Memoir', LvdPA.
2. *Face*, pp. 8 & 46–47; *Yet Being*, p. 155; *Thunder*, pp. 184–85.
3. M. M. van der Post, 'Memoir', LvdPA.
4. *Venture*, p. 28; C. W. H. van der Post, letter to Dr Mac Rae, 23 Jan. 1911 (Accession A272), FSA; *Yet Being*, p. 32; *Thunder*, pp. 92–97; *Eland*, pp. 135 & 200.
5. *Yet Being*, pp. 11–13, 15 & 17; *About Blady*, p. 31; *Weekend Argus*, 28/29 Nov. 1992.
6. LvdP, interview with Lucia van der Post, LvdPA; *Eland*, pp. 1, 187–88 & 191–92; *About Blady*, pp. 28 & 92–126; *Thunder*, p. 181; *Yet Being*, p. 155; *Face*, p. 46; Tibby Steytler, interview with author, 12 Feb. 1998.
7. *Men Of The Times*, directory, 1906; Philippolis Town Council minutes, 1907–14, FSA; Le Roux, op. cit., p. 7; C. W. H. van der Post, letter to Dr Mac Rae, 23 Jan. 1911 (Accession A272), FSA.
8. LvdP, letter to John McArdle, 19 Feb. 1989, LvdPA; C. W. H. van der Post, Documents (Accession A272), FSA; *Thunder*, pp. 92–97; *Face*, p. 38; LvdP, interview with Lucia van der Post, LvdPA; *Venture*, p. 29; Chris Schmidt, interview with author, 9 July 2000; Philippolis Town Council minutes, 1907–14, FSA.
9. *Face*, p. 9; LvdP, *The Lost World of the Kalahari*, pp. 11–12; *Thunder*, p. 9; *White Bushman*, p. 3; LvdP, *A Story Like the Wind*, p. 9.
10. Ella Bedford (van der Post), interview with author, 11 Sept. 2000; C. W. H. van der Post & Daniel Liebenberg, letter to Secretary of the School Committee, 20 Feb. 1907 (Accession A272), FSA; M. M. van der Post, 'Memoir', LvdPA.

11. *Lost World*, pp. 57–58; *Eland*, pp. 1–3.
12. *About Blady*, pp. 103 & 111; *Thunder*, p. 158; *Eland*, pp. 1–3; Naim Attallah, *Asking Questions*, pp. 500–1, originally published in *Sunday Telegraph*, 12 Sept. 1993.
13. *Yet Being*, p. 294; D'Arbez, *Kort Geskiedenis van die Hugenote*, pp. 1–4; *Voor Land en Volk*; *De Grensbewoners*; *De Familie van de Zieketrooster*, Isabel Hofmeyr, 'Building a nation from words: Afrikaans language, literature and ethnic identity, 1902–1924' in Shula Marks & Stanley Trapido (eds.), *The Politics of Race, Class & Nationalism in Twentieth Century South Africa*, Longman Group, Harlow, 1987.
14. C. W. H. van der Post, Ledger-Journal, 26 Oct. 1910 & 30 Dec. 1913 (Accession A272), FSA; Petronella van Heerden, *Kerssnuitsels*, pp. 151–52; 'Verslag van het Derde Kongress van de Oranje Vrouwen Vereniging Gehouden te Winburg op 18, 19, 20 en 21 November 1913', FSA; *Yet Being*, pp. 11 & 32–33; *Thunder*, p. 23; LvdP, *African Cooking*, p. 17; LvdP, interview with Lucia van der Post, LvdPA.
15. *About Blady*, p. 108; Tom Bedford, interview with author; C. W. H. (Pooi) van der Post, 'Memoir Fragments', unpublished, undated, LvdPA.
16. C. W. H. van der Post, Estate documents (P2606), FSA; Tom Bedford, interview with author; Ella Bedford (van der Post), interview with author, 11 Sept. 2000.
17. C. W. H. van der Post, Estate documents (P2606), FSA; M. M. van der Post, Estate documents (1258/54), SCRB; Herman van der Post, Estate documents (26833), FSA; Papers related to Succession Duty (TAB496876241), CA.
18. C. W. H. van der Post, Estate documents (P2606), FSA.
19. *Thunder*, p. 183; H. Oost, *Wie is Die Skuldiges?*; *Sarie Marais*, 21 May 1952; Andries van der Post, letter to Jack Holloway, 12 July 1915, NALM.
20. Margaret (Tiny) van der Post, interview with author, 18 July 2000; *Seed*, pp. 55–56; Andries van der Post, letter to Jack Holloway, 14 Apr. 1912, NALM.
21. Andries van der Post, letters to Jack Holloway, 30 Jan., 10 Feb. 1911, 5, 12 Mar. 1912, 21 Aug. 1913 & 18 Oct. 1914, NALM; C. W. H. van der Post ('Cincinnatus'), poems, undated; C. W. H. van der Post, letter to Joey Marais, 30 Nov. 1910 (Accession A272), FSA.
22. Margaret (Tiny) van der Post, interview with author, 18 July 2000; Tom Bedford, interview with author; Ella Bedford (van der Post), interview with author, 11 Sept. 2000; Chris Plewman, interview with author, 9 Feb. 1998; C. W. H. (Pooi) van der Post, 'Memoir Fragments', LvdPA; *Grey College*, A South African School Centenary Publication, p. 51; [Johannesburg] *Star*, 18 Oct. 1955; LvdP, letter to Johan Volsteedt, 28 Feb. 1996, LvdPA; *Seed*, pp. 69–83; LvdP, Matriculation certificate, Feb. 1925, LvdPA.
23. *Sarie Marais*, 21 May 1952; Leslie Jacobson, interview with author, 2 Feb. 1998; *Southern African Jewish Times*, 4 Mar. 1966; LvdP, letter to John McArdle, 19 Feb. 1989.
24. Ella Bedford (van der Post), interview with author, 11 Sept. 2000; Margaret (Tiny) van der Post, interview with author, 18 July 2000; Tom Bedford, interview with author.

10

1. LvdP, 'The "Turbott Wolfe" Affair' in William Plomer, *Turbott Wolfe*, p. 16; *Yet Being*, p. 34; *Natal Advertiser*, 21 Feb. 1925.
2. 'Affair', *Turbott Wolfe*, op. cit., pp. 16–17; *Yet Being*, p. 35; Flather, op. cit., pp. 70–71.
3. *Yet Being*, pp. 35–36; *Natal Advertiser*, 5, 10 Mar., 3, 7 June 1925 & 30 Jan. 1926; LvdP's cuttings book, LvdPA.
4. See Irving Hexham (ed.), *The Scriptures of the AmaNazaretha of EKuphaKameni – Selected Writings of the Zulu Prophets Isaiah and Londa Shembe*; LvdP, *The Heart of the Hunter*, pp. 130 & 205.
5. *Yet Being*, pp. 141–42; LvdP, 'Shembe: Zulu Witchdoctor & Prophet – Note of Visit & Conversation at Inanda in 1926', LvdPA; *Jung*, p. 49.
6. *Natal Advertiser*, 24 Apr. 1926; *Yet Being*, pp. 36 & 57–59.
7. *Natal Advertiser*, 14 Aug. 1926; Roy Campbell, *Light on a Dark Horse: An Autobiography: 1901–1935*, pp. 65 & 174; Peter Alexander, *Roy Campbell: A Critical Biography*, pp. 46 & 69; Leif Egeland, interview with Peter Alexander, 2 Feb. 1990, APC; Leif Egeland, *Bridges of Understanding*.
8. *Yet Being*, pp. 67, 72–73 & 80–86; Janet Campbell, letter to author, 3 Feb. 1999; LvdP, *The Hunter and The Whale*.
9. *Natal Advertiser*, 5 May, 17, 19 & 27 June 1925; *Yet Being*, p. 107; *The Oldie*, Sept. 1997.
10. *Natal Advertiser*, 3, 4 & 7 Aug. 1926; *Yet Being*, pp. 107–109; LvdP, Passport: D8140 (issued 30 Aug. 1926), LvdPA.
11. William Plomer, *The Autobiography of William Plomer*, p. 211; *Natal Advertiser*, 18 Jan. 1928.
12. *Yet Being*, p. 109; Roy Campbell, *The Flaming Terrapin*; Plomer, *Turbott Wolfe*, op. cit.; Alexander, *Campbell*, pp. 45 & 48; William Plomer, '*Voorslag* Days', *London Magazine*, July 1959; *About Blady*, p. 37; Peter F. Alexander, *William Plomer*, p. 8; Plomer, *Double Lives*, p. 9.
13. Plomer, *Double Lives*, p. 166; *Voorslag*, No. 1, June 1926.
14. 'Affair', *Turbott Wolfe*, op. cit., pp. 18–20 & 24–25; *Natal Advertiser*, 19 Mar. 1926; Peter F. Alexander, *William Plomer*, pp. 26–27; LvdP, 'Campbell, Plomer, Paton & Myself', unpublished essay, 1996, LvdPA; Roy

Campbell, William Plomer & LvdP, *Voorslag: A Magazine of South African Life & Art*, Facsimile reprint of Numbers 1, 2 and 3 (1926), p. 4; Tom Bedford, interview with author.

15. LvdP, 'Kuns Ontwikkeling in Afrikaans', *Voorslag*, No. 2, July 1926; C. W. H. van der Post, *'n Een-Jaar Afrikaanse Kursus – A One-Year Afrikaans Course*.

16. LvdP, 'Nimrods van die See', *Voorslag*, No. 3, August 1926; unsigned, 'There She Blows', *Natal Advertiser*, 14 Aug. 1926; Campbell, *Dark Horse*, pp. 6, 65 & 164–65.

17. Alexander, *Campbell*, pp. vii & 217.

18. Ibid., pp. 54–55, 67; Roy Campbell, letter to William Plomer, 7 June 1927; Mary Campbell, letter to William Plomer, 7 May 1927, DUL.

19. 'Campbell, Plomer, Paton & Myself', LvdPA.

11

1. *Yet Being*, p. 111.

2. Ibid., p. 248; *Natal Advertiser*, 15 Jan. 1927; Flather, op. cit., p. 71.

3. *Yet Being*, pp. 116–19, 121, 126–28, 130 & 132–33.

4. Ibid., pp. 136–37, 142–43, 147–48, 152, 154, 159–60, 163–64, 169–71 & 178.

5. Ibid., pp. 182, 199–200 & 205–7; Alexander, *Plomer*, p. 177.

6. *Yet Being*, pp. 211–12, 214–15, 220–28, 248–50 & 336.

7. Plomer, *Double Lives*, pp. 171, 174–75, 177 & 179; Plomer, *The Autobiography*, pp. 184–85.

8. *Natal Advertiser*, 18, 31 Dec. 1926 & 8 Jan. 1927.

9. *Natal Advertiser*, 8, 15, 22, 29 Jan., 5, 12 & 19 Feb. 1927.

10. 'Campbell, Plomer, Paton & Myself', LvdPA.

11. Robert Hinshaw (ed), *The Rock Rabbit and the Rainbow: Laurens van der Post among Friends*, pp. 81–82.

12

1. *Yet Being*, pp. 261–62.

2. *Natal Advertiser*, 7, 28 May, 16 July & 6 Aug. 1927.

3. Lucia van der Post, letter to author, May 2001; Flather, op. cit., p. 40; Marjorie van der Post, *Theo Wendt: A Biography: The musical world of his days, including the first decade of the Cape orchestra, 1914–1924*; see also *Dictionary of South African Biography, Vol. IV*, pp. 769–70.

4. LvdP, 'Journal, 1928–1931', LvdPA.

5. LvdP, *In A Province*, p. 9; *Feather*, p. 32.

6. 'Journal, 1928–1931', LvdPA; Alexander, *Campbell*, pp. 85–86.

7. 'Journal, 1928–1931', LvdPA; LvdP, 'A remarkable team and a remarkable period', *Cape Times*, 27 Mar. 1976; LvdP, letter to Peter Alexander, 10 Dec. 1977, LvdPA; Alexander, *Campbell*, pp. 84–86.

8. Lucia van der Post, interview with author; LvdP, Enslin du Plessis: Obituary, undated, LvdPA; Virginia Woolf, *The Diary of Virginia Woolf, Vol. IV: 1931–1935*, p. 85 (18 Mar. 1932); Alexander, *Plomer*, pp. 153–54; *Yet Being*, p. 265; Gerald Heard, letter to LvdP, 19 Apr. 1929, LvdPA; William Plomer, *At Home*, p. 60.

9. William Plomer, letter to LvdP, 25 Feb. 1927, BL; Alexander, *Plomer*, p. 165; Keith Millar-Jones, letter to LvdP, 19 Oct. 1929, LvdPA; William Plomer, letter to Enslin du Plessis, 5 Nov. 1929, DUL; *Yet Being*, p. 283; see *Cape Times*, 18 Jan. & 20 Mar. 1930.

10. Enslin du Plessis, letter to LvdP, 7 Mar. 1930; *Cape Times*, 27 Mar. 1976; LvdP, 'South Africa in the Melting Pot', *The Realist*, Nov. 1929.

11. T. C. Robertson, letter to Julian Rollnick, 24 July 1967, CL; *Cape Times*, 27 Mar. 1976; *Yet Being*, pp. 266–67.

12. See for example *Cape Times*, 10 Jan., 19 Feb., 10 Mar. & 11 Apr. 1930; Alexander, *Plomer*, op. cit.

13. LvdP, Passport: D8140, LvdPA; William Plomer, letters to LvdP, 6 Mar. & 18 June 1930, BL; Alexander, *Plomer*, p. 199.

14. *Yet Being*, p. 283; Gerald Shaw, *The Cape Times: An Informal History*, pp. 39–40 & 140; Leonard Barnes, *Caliban in Africa*; *Cape Times*, 27 Mar. 1976.

15. *Cape Times*, 28 Feb., 5 Mar. 1930 & 27 Mar. 1976; *Yet Being*, pp. 284–85; *White Bushman*, pp. 177–78; Janet Byrne, *A Genius for Living: A Biography of Frieda Lawrence*, pp. 297 & 322.

16. Duncan Fallowell, 'Memoir', in draft, Mar. 2001.

17. *Cape Times*, 2, 15, 31 July, 14 Sept., 1 Oct. 1929, 22 Feb., 5, 27 Mar., 5, 8 Apr., 2 May 1930 & 27 Mar. 1976; Shaw, op. cit., pp. 41–49; T. C. Robertson, in conversation with Ian Player, undated tape recording.

18. *Cape Times*, 19, 23 July, 12, 15 Oct. 1929, 20 Feb., 1 Apr., 30 May, 18 June, 23, 29 July, 17, 20 Nov. 1930 & 27 Mar. 1976; T. C. Robertson, conversation with Ian Player; *Thunder*, pp. 98–112 & 177–79; W. L. Maree, *Uit Duisternis Geroep*, p. 208; Petronella van Heerden, *Die 16de Koppie*, pp. 131–32; *White Bushman*, p. 260; LvdP, letter to Dorothy Pope, 8 Feb. 1957, LvdPA.

19. *Cape Times*, 27 Mar. 1976; T. C. Robertson, conversation with Ian Player; Flather, op. cit., p. 39.

20. Mary Royds (Cloete), interview with author, 19 Aug. 1998.

21. Nadine Gordimer, interview with author, 20 July 2000.

13

1. *Yet Being*, pp. 285–89.
2. LvdP, letter to T. C. Robertson, 7 June 1931, CL; 'Journal, 1928–1931', LvdPA.
3. Chris Schmidt, interview with author, 9 July 2000; R. M. Barrington Ward, letter to LvdP, 3 June 1929; 'Journal, 1928–1931', LvdPA.
4. LvdP, letter to T. C. Robertson, undated, CL; 'Journal, 1928–1931', LvdPA; 'Introductory Note', T. C. Robertson archive, CL; LvdP, T. C. Robertson: Obituary, draft version, 18 Jan. 1989, LvdPA; T. C. Robertson, conversation with Ian Player.
5. William Plomer, letter to LvdP, 4 Sept. 1930, BL; Roy Campbell, letter to LvdP, undated, LvdPA.
6. William Plomer, letter to LvdP, 4 Sept. 1930, BL; *About Blady*, p. 156; David Wilson, 'Shakespeare in Perspective: The Tempest', BBC 2, 22 Feb. 1980.
7. M. M. van der Post, letter to Laurens and Marjorie van der Post, 27 Apr. 1932; Keith Millar-Jones, letter to LvdP, 19 Oct. 1929; William Plomer, letter to LvdP, 7 Sept. 1929, LvdPA; René Janin, letter to William Plomer, 3 Dec. 1932 & undated, SCRB; *Province*, p. 5.
8. William Plomer to LvdP, undated & 3 Jan. 1933, BL.
9. Lilian Bowes Lyon, letter to LvdP, 18 July 1933; William Plomer, letter to LvdP, 18 Dec. 1929; Lilian Bowes Lyon, letter to William Plomer, 1932, LvdPA; Alexander, *Plomer*, p. 189; Lilian Bowes Lyon, *Bright Feather Fading*, p. 27 ('If Still The Casual Sun'); Rosamond Lehmann, letter to LvdP, 27 Aug. 1949, LvdPA.
10. Donald Zec, *The Queen Mother*; Lilian Bowes Lyon, *The Buried Stream*; D. J. Cotman, *Spreading Tree*; Alexander, *Plomer*, p. 189; William Plomer, letters to LvdP, undated, BL.
11. Janet Campbell, letter to author, 22 Jan. 1999; René Janin, letter to William Plomer, 21 Jan. 1934; William Plomer to Enslin du Plessis, undated, SCRB.
12. Leonard Woolf, letter to LvdP, 7 Sept. 1933, LvdPA.
13. William Plomer, letter to LvdP, undated, LvdPA; Alan Paton, *Cry The Beloved Country*; *Province*, pp. 5, 14, 61, 73–74, 108–9, 127–29, 133–34, 140–41 & 162.
14. *Province*, pp. 194, 221–24, 237, 243, 246, 251–52 & 254.
15. Mary Benson, *South Africa: The Struggle for a Birthright*, pp. 45–54; H. & R. Simons, *Class and Colour in South Africa, 1850–1950*, p. 416; on William Ballinger, see *Dictionary of South African Biography, Vol. 5*, pp. 25–26; *Cape Times*, 26 Feb., 8 Mar. & 28 Apr. 1930.

14

1. *The Spectator*, 2 Mar. 1934; *Daily Mail*, 15 Mar. 1934.
2. Stephen Spender, *The Destructive Element: A Study of Modern Writers and Beliefs*, pp. 237 & 247.
3. *New York Times* Book Review, 3 Feb. 1935.
4. *Yet Being*, pp. 294 & 299; *White Bushman*, pp. 228–30; LvdP, *The Dark Eye in Africa*.
5. See reviews in *Daily Worker*, 17 Sept. 1953; *Truth*, 20 Nov. 1953.
6. Lucia Harris, interview with author, 4 May 2000; Attallah, op. cit., p. 518; *Smith's Trade News*, 11 Jan. 1964; Patrick Downes, interview with James Sanders, 23 Aug. 1998. See also [Johannesburg] *Star*, 1 Jan. 1936: 'Recently Mr van der Post's dairy farm was awarded the second prize in a "best kept" competition embracing the whole of Gloucestershire.'; LvdP, letter to Pat Lancaster, 16 Nov. 1981, LvdPA.
7. Lilian Bowes Lyon, letter to LvdP, 17 June 1936 & 4 Jan. 1937, LvdPA.
8. Lincoln Kirstein, *Mosaic Memoirs*, pp. 239 & 255–56.
9. *White Bushman*, pp. 226 & 294–95; *Yet Being*, p. 272; Kirstein, op. cit., p. 238; LvdP, letter to Lincoln Kirstein, 21 Dec. 1933, LvdPA; Lucia van der Post, interview with author.
10. LvdP, interviews with Jean-Marc Pottiez for *White Bushman*; *White Bushman*, pp. 225–26; *Venture*, pp. 9–10; *Admiral's Baby*, pp. 180–181; LvdP, letter to Ingaret Giffard-Young, 9 Mar. & 15 Apr 1947; 'Prison Journal, 1943', LvdPA.
11. LvdP, Passport: D8140, LvdPA; *Yet Being*, pp. 290–94.
12. *The Way Things*, op. cit., pp. 282 & 284; Ingaret Giffard, *Sigh No More, Ladies*; 'Because We Must', performed at the Wyndham Theatre, London, 1937, LvdPA; *The Times*, 19 Jan. 1937. See also Hugo Vickers, *Vivien Leigh*, pp. 74–75; Joan Brind, interview with author, 19 Jan. 1998.
13. *Yet Being*, pp. 291 & 293; *Face*, p. 255.
14. *The Way Things*, pp. 289–90.
15. LvdP, letter to Ingaret Giffard-Young, 5 Aug. 1937, LvdPA; Jimmy Young, interview with author, 28 June 1998; Ingaret Giffard-Young, letter to LvdP, undated, LvdPA.
16. LvdP, Passport: D4104[A], LvdPA; *Yet Being*, p. 297; Madeleine Masson, interview with author, 10 Mar. 1999.
17. *Yet Being*, p. 298; Lucia van der Post, interview with author.
18. LvdP, letters to Ingaret Giffard-Young, 2 Aug. 1936 & undated, LvdPA.
19. Jimmy Young, interview with author, 28 June 1998; *The Way Things*, pp. 296 & 298.
20. *The Way Things*, pp. 298–99; LvdP, letters to Ingaret Giffard-Young, 5 Aug., 11 Oct., 1 Nov. 1937, 20 Mar., 7 June 1938 & undated, LvdPA.

21. Ingaret Giffard-Young, letters to LvdP, undated; LvdP, letter to Ingaret Giffard-Young, 13 Oct. 1938, LvdPA.
22. LvdP, letters to Ingaret Giffard-Young, 10 & 13 Oct. 1939, LvdPA.

Part Three

15

1. LvdP, letter to Ingaret Giffard-Young, 26 May 1946, LvdPA; *White Bushman*, pp. 224–26 & 229; *Yet Being*, p. 299; *About Blady*, pp. 38–39.
2. 'The Desired Earth', LvdPA; *Seed*, op. cit.; *Face*, op. cit.; *New Moon*, p. 75; *Yet Being*, op. cit.
3. *Admiral's Baby*, pp. 316–17; *About Blady*, pp. 3–4; LvdP, Preface, *Wilderness and the Human Spirit: An Anthology*, p. 12. See also [Johannesburg] *Star*, 5 Feb. 1952.
4. [Johannesburg] *Star*, 14 June 1947; Mickey Lemle, 'Hasten Slowly: The Journey of Sir Laurens van der Post', film, 1996; Chris Plewman, interview with author, 9 Feb. 1998; Lucia van der Post, interview with author; Chris Schmidt, interview with author, 9 July 2000.
5. Bonny Kohler-Baker, interview with James Sanders, 24 Nov. 1999; Fleur Mostert, interview with James Sanders, 20 Apr. 2000 & with author, 2 May 2001.
6. Ingaret Giffard-Young, letter to LvdP, 1 Aug. 1946, LvdPA; *New Moon*, p. 120; Eileen Sinfield, letter to LvdP, Jan. 1956, LvdPA; Ministry of Defence Records.
7. Queen Mother via John Bowes Lyon, message to author, 1 Feb. 2000; Zec, op. cit.
8. Lilian Bowes Lyon, *Collected Poems*; Lilian Bowes Lyon, letter to William Plomer, 28 Oct. 1946, DUL; *White Bushman*, p. 237; Dr John Murray, 'Lilian Helen Bowes Lyon: 1895–1949', *The Poetry Review*, Feb.-Mar. 1949; James Wentworth Day, *The Queen Mother's Family Story*, pp. 120–26.
9. William Plomer, letters to LvdP, 12 Sept. 1947 & 9 Feb. 1948, LvdPA; LvdP, letter to William Plomer, 15 Sept. 1947, DUL.
10. LvdP, 'A Bar of Shadow', *The Cornhill*, Spring 1952; *Seed*, op. cit.
11. Editor of [Natal] *Daily News*, letter to LvdP, 28 Oct. 1948, LvdPA; LvdP, letter to William Plomer, 23 Sept. 1948, DUL.
12. LvdP, letters and telegrams to Ingaret Giffard, 22, 23 Feb., 7 & 12 Mar. 1948; Ingaret Giffard, letters to LvdP, undated, LvdPA.
13. *About Blady*, p. 68; R. F. Blandy, letter to author, 26 June 2000.
14. LvdP, letters and telegrams to Ingaret Giffard, 22, 23 Feb., 3, 5, 7 & 9 Mar. 1948, LvdPA.
15. C. W. H. (Pooi) van der Post, letters to LvdP, 15 Jan. & 18 Aug. 1946; John van der Post, letter to LvdP, 2 Apr. 1949, LvdPA; Lucia van der Post, interview with author; LvdP, letters to Ingaret Giffard, 31 Mar., 9, 20 & 27 Apr. 1948, LvdPA.
16. Dan O'Meara, *Forty Lost Years: The apartheid state and the politics of the National Party, 1948–1994*, pp. 19–37; Frederic I. Carpenter, *Laurens van der Post*, p. 35; LvdP, letters to Ingaret Giffard, 29 Mar. & 20 Apr. 1947; Editor of [Natal] *Daily News*, letter to LvdP, 28 Oct. 1948, LvdPA.
17. [Natal] *Daily News*, 22, 27 May, 7 July, 7, 12, 16 Aug., 4 Sept., 18–20, 22 Oct., 25 Nov., 18 & 20 Dec. 1948.
18. Madeleine Masson, interview with author, 10 Mar. 1999; [Natal] *Daily News*, 15 Oct. 1948; *The Way Things*, p. 362; Peter Alexander, 'The Enigma of Laurens van der Post', *English Academy Review*, 1996; LvdP, letters to Ingaret Giffard, 15 Oct. 1966 & undated, LvdPA.
19. LvdP, Passport: L6257, LvdPA; *About Blady*, p. 26; LvdP, letter to A. R. Rendall, 10 Apr. 1949, LvdPA.
20. Lilian Bowes Lyon, letter to LvdP, 4 Feb. 1949 & undated, LvdPA; Lilian Bowes Lyon, letter to William Plomer, Apr. 1949, DUL.
21. Rosamond Lehmann, letter to LvdP, 27 Aug. 1949, LvdPA; *White Bushman*, pp. 238–39; Lilian Bowes Lyon, Last Will and Testament, 25 Jan. 1949.
22. Ingaret Giffard to LvdP, 3 Mar. 1950; LvdP, letter to Barclays Bank, 22 May 1957, LvdPA.
23. Sir E. Wood, letter to LvdP, 10 Sept. 1948, LvdPA; Michael Hubbard, *Agricultural Exports and Economic Growth: A Study of the Botswana Beef Industry*, p. 122, citing Secretary of State for the Colonies, circular letter, 15 June 1947; LvdP, letter to H. Weskob, 15 May 1950, CDC; *Lost World*, p. 63; LvdP later wrote 'I, myself was always grateful to [Sir Evelyn] Baring for being my introduction to the ICS . . .' (*The Sunday Times*, 20 Aug. 1978).
24. Treasury official, letters to LvdP, 5 Jan. & 30 Sept. 1948; LvdP, Diary, LvdPA.

16

1. Treasury official, letter to LvdP, 2 Jan. 1948; Sir E. Wood, letter to LvdP, 30 Sept. 1948; LvdP, 'Survey of the Mlanje and Nyika areas of Nyasaland', Report for the CDC, July 1950, LvdPA.
2. Patrick Mullins, *Retreat From Africa*, pp. 29–30.
3. LvdP, Diary (1951); 'Nyasaland Journal, 1951', unpublished, LvdPA.
4. *Venture*, pp. 143–61; LvdP, 'The Art of Travel', BBC Radio 4, 14 Aug. 1992.
5. 'Nyasaland Journal, 1951', LvdPA.

6. *Venture*, p. 257; 'Survey of the Mlanje and Nyika areas of Nyasaland', LvdPA.

7. CDC Annual Reports, 1952–56, extracts, CDC; John McCracken, letter to author, 7 Jan. 2000.

8. J. C. Cater, letter to C. S. Hubbard, 20 Jan. 1951; C. S. Hubbard, letter to Divisional Manager, Forestry, CDC, 23 Apr. 1951; LvdP, letter to Lord Reith, 28 Oct. 1951, CDC.

9. LvdP, letter to Leonard Woolf, 11 Dec. 1949, C&W.

10. Leonard Woolf, letter to LvdP, 13 Dec. 1949; LvdP, letter to Leonard Woolf, 31 Dec. 1949; unsigned to Ingaret Giffard, 14 Mar. 1950. Ingaret van der Post, letters to Leonard Woolf, 3 Oct. 1950, C&W, & 10 Mar. 1951, LW.

11. *Venture*, pp. 8–10.

12. *Venture*, pp. 13, 61, 66, 68, 72–73 & 86; Ernest Hemingway, *The Green Hills of Africa*, p. 157.

13. *Venture*, pp. 84–85, 90 & 106; John McCracken, letter to author, 6 Oct. 1999.

14. *Venture*, pp. 98, 101, 105, 108–110, 112, 115 & 117.

15. Ibid., pp. 121, 126, 136, 144–46, 149–50 & 155–57.

16. Ibid., pp. 162–64, 187–88, 205, 207–11 & 215.

17. Ibid., pp. 226–28, 232 & 238–39; C. G. Jung, *Collected Works, Vol. VIII: The Structure and Dynamics of the Psyche*, pp. 208–9.

18. 'The Art of Travel', BBC Radio 4, 1992; Jennifer Cardin, letter to LvdP, 20 July 1992, LvdPA; Mary E. Hartshorne, *From Hackney to Hill Farm: A Tapestry Three Score Years and Ten*; LvdP, letter to Jennifer Cardin, 5 Aug. 1992, LvdPA.

19. Mary Hartshorne, letter to author, 22 Jan. 1998; Jean Renoir, *My Life and My Films*; Jean Renoir, *Renoir on Renoir: Interviews, Essays and Remarks*; Jean Renoir, *Letters*.

20. *Venture*, first edition, p. 54; Marvyn J. E. Morgan, letter to the Hogarth Press, 22 Mar. 1952; Stanley & Co., letter to Mervyn J. E. Morgan, 9 Apr. 1952; Mervyn J. E. Morgan, letter to Messrs. Stanley & Co., 16 Apr. 1952; Mervyn J. E. Morgan, letter to Stanley & Co., 28 Jan. 1953; John V. Allen, letter to Harold Raymond, 30 June 1953. Eventually the Hogarth Press agreed to pay Madame Perigueux £600 to include Solicitor's costs. LvdP contributed £150, C&W.

21. Mullins, op. cit., pp. 29–30.

22. Jimmy Skinner, interview with author, 19 Jan. 2000.

23. John McCracken, letter to author, 7 Jan. 2000.

24. *Venture*, p. 6; Cecil Day Lewis, minuted notes to Ian Parsons, 11 Aug. 1950; Ingaret Giffard, letters to Leonard Woolf, 3 Oct. 1950 & 10 Mar. 1951; William Morrow, cable to the Hogarth Press, 23 Apr. 1951, C&W.

25. Daniel George, letter to Ian Parsons, 20 Apr. 1951; Frances Phillips, letter to Ian Parsons, 23 Apr. 1951; Ian Parsons, letter to Daniel George, 24 Apr. 1951, C&W.

26. *New York Times*, 24 Oct. 1951; *Chicago Sunday Tribune*, 25 Nov. 1951; *New York Times* Book Review, 4 Nov. 1951; *New Yorker*, 8 Dec. 1951.

27. LvdP, letter to Norah Smallwood, 4 July 1951; LvdP, letter to Ian Parsons, 22 May 1951; Ian Parsons, letter to LvdP, 31 May 1951, C&W.

28. *Daily Telegraph*, 25 Jan. 1952; *Daily Mail*, 2 Feb. 1952; *Evening Standard*, 28 Jan. 1952; *The Listener*, 24 Jan. 1952; *New Statesman*, 26.1.52; *The Spectator*, 22 Feb. 1952; *Daily Worker*, 31 Jan. & 12 Feb. 1958.

29. *Cape Argus*, 2 Feb. 1952; [Johannesburg] *Star*, 10 Feb. 1952; *Natal Witness*, 18 Feb. 1952.

30. Norah Smallwood, letter to LvdP, 3 July 1951; S. Grieggran, letter to Norah Smallwood, 25 Sept. 1951; William Morrow, letter to the Hogarth Press, 9 Jan. 1952; the Hogarth Press, letter to LvdP, 23 June 1952; LvdP, letter to Ian Parsons, 29 July 1952; Ralph Sloane, letters to LvdP, 23 & 25 Sept. 1952; Ian Parsons, letter to Penguin, 30 Mar. 1954; Norah Smallwood, letter to H. Hagerup's Forlag, 23 June 1954; Eunice E. Frost, letter to Norah Smallwood, 6 Apr. 1955, C&W; Joyce Grenfell, letter to LvdP, undated, LvdPA.

31. LvdP, letter to Miss Burch, 7 May 1951, C&W.

17

1. LvdP, 'Pigs, Japanese and the Moon', *The Countryman*, Summer 1948; 'Travellers & Mountaineers', *The Countryman*, Spring 1951; Ingaret Giffard, 'From Coral Reef to Mountain Top', *The Countryman*, Autumn 1952.

2. LvdP, 'The Witch Doctor's Come Back', *The Countryman*, Spring 1952; 'The Real Kalahari and its People', *The Countryman*, Winter 1950; 'A Bar of Shadow', *The Cornhill*, Spring 1952.

3. R. E. Brook, letter to Sir Evelyn Baring, 2 Jan. 1950, CDC; *Thunder*, pp. 113 & 133; Professor Edwin Wilmsen, letter to author, 17 Aug. 1999; Frank Debenham, *Kalahari Sand*; LvdP, Passport: L6257. See also Frank Debenham, 'Report on the Water Resources of the Bechuanaland Protectorate, Northern Rhodesia, The Nyasaland Protectorate, Tanganyika Territory, Kenya and the Uganda Protectorate' (Colonial Office); A. Gaitskell, C. U. Pickrell, B. Curry, Tshekedi Khama, Bathoen II & LvdP, 'Report of a Mission to the Bechuanaland Protectorate to investigate the possibilities of economic development in the Western Kalahari, 1952' (Commonwealth Relations Office), LvdPA.

4. Ingaret Giffard, letter to Leonard Woolf, 9 Nov. 1950; LvdP, letter to Leonard Woolf, 8 May 1951; LvdP, letter to Leonard Woolf, 27 Mar. 1952, LW.

5. Jeremy Lewis, *Kindred Spirits: Adrift in Literary London*, pp. 164–67 & 176–77.

6. LvdP, 'Address for the Memorial Service of Norah Smallwood, OBE, Dec. 1984, LvdPA.

7. Ian Parsons, letter to Frances Phillips, 13 May 1952; Frances Phillips, letters to Ian Parsons, 8 Aug. 1952, 22 May 1953, C&W, & 3 Sept. 1954, WM; Thayer Hobson, letters to Ian Parsons, 10 Mar. & 15 Sept. 1952, C&W; Ian Parsons, letters to Thayer Hobson, 12 & 22 Sept. 1952, WM.

8. *Face*, pp. 3, 9 & 46–48.

9. Ibid., pp. 49, 59, 63–65, 72–73, 91, 113, 125–33, 148, 155–56, 158, 162, 184 & 225–26.

10. Ibid., pp. 206, 229, 243–51, 255, 261, 273–83, 285, 287, 293–94 & 311.

11. *The Times Literary Supplement*, 24 May 1953; *The Sunday Times*, 12 Apr. 1953; *The Spectator*, 10 Apr. 1953; *Daily Express*, 9 Apr. 1953.

12. Rosemary de Llorens, letter to LvdP, 22 Apr. 1953; LvdP, Passport: L6257, LvdPA; *About Blady*, p. vii.

13. Fleur Mostert, interview with James Sanders, 20 Apr. 2000 & with author, 2 May 2001; Bonny Kohler-Baker, interview with James Sanders, 24 Nov. 1999 & with author, 23 Apr. 2001; Cari and Mauritz Mostert, interview with author, 3 May 2001; *Mail on Sunday*, 22 Dec. 1996. See also LvdP, letter to Mr Mackenzie, 21 May 1975, in which LvdP complains that he cannot claim tax relief on the Baker 'covenant': 'It may not be possible for me to have any claims of benefit incurred on the Inland Revenue . . . but surely it is a double injury to tax me now . . . All I can say at the moment is that the charge is against all concepts of natural justice as I see it.'

18

1. LvdP, Passport: L6257; Diary (1953), LvdPA; Norah Smallwood, letter to LvdP, 10 Nov. 1953; Norah Smallwood, letter to Maxwell Arnot, 10 Feb. 1954, C&W; *The Way Things*, p. 362.

2. *The Guardian*, 12 Nov. 1954; *Daily Telegraph*, 8 Oct. 1954; *The Sunday Times*, 26 Sept. 1954; *The Times Literary Supplement*, 29 Oct. 1954; *The Tatler*, 20 Oct. 1954.

3. 'Prison Journal, 1943', LvdPA; Frances Phillips, letter to Norah Smallwood, 19 Feb. 1954; LvdP, promotional material, undated, C&W.

4. Leonard Woolf, letter to LvdP, 24 Feb. 1954; Ian Parsons, letter to LvdP, 11 Mar. 1954; Helga A. Wittgrele, letter to Ian Parsons, 26 Mar. 1954; Ragnar Svanstrom, letters to Norah Smallwood, 11 & 28 Apr. 1954; John Willey, letter to Norah Smallwood, 25 May 1954, C&W.

5. Norah Smallwood, letter to LvdP, 31 May 1954; Norah Smallwood, letter to Ragnar Svanstrom, 1 June 1954; Ragnar Svanstrom, letters to Norah Smallwood, 3 June & 16 Oct. 1954; E. Maxwell Arnot, letter to Norah Smallwood, 3 June 1954, C&W.

6. Norah Smallwood, letter to LvdP, 6 Sept. 1954; Kathleen Hale, letter to Norah Smallwood, 1 Nov. 1954; unsigned, letter to R. G. Emm, 26 Jan. 1955; K. J. Gummerus Osakeyhtio, letter to the Hogarth Press, 1 Mar. 1955, C&W; Nancy Stern (The Selznick Studio), letter to the Hogarth Press, 18 Feb. 1955; Kathleen Selby (Paramount British Productions), letter to Norah Smallwood, 7 Mar. 1955, C&W.

7. *Feather*, pp. 10, 13–14, 23, 25, 27, 30–31 & 35–39; J. B. Peires, *The Dead Will Arise: Nongqawuse and the Great Xhosa Cattle-Killing Movement of 1856–57*.

8. *Feather*, pp. 9–20, 41–43, 51–52, 64–65, 98–99, 102–14, 137 & 142–43, 204–5; John Buchan, *The Courts of the Morning*.

9. *Feather*, pp. 205, 211, 215–216, 222, 232–37, 252–54, 266–80, 283–84, 286, 293 & 302; H. Hagerup's Forlag, letter to the Hogarth Press, 19 Jan. 1955, C&W; John Buchan, *Prester John*.

10. *The Spectator*, 25 Mar. 1955; *The Times Literary Supplement*, 29 Apr. 1955; *The Sunday Times*, 13 Mar. 1955; *Encounter*, June 1955; *Daily Worker*, 8 June 1955; *Time and Tide*, 9 Apr. 1955.

11. *Pretoria News*, 2 May 1955; [Johannesburg] *Star*, 28 May 1955; *Cape Times*, 25 May 1955.

12. *New York Times*, 21 Feb. 1955; *Christian Science Monitor*, 17 Feb. 1955; *New York Times* Book Review, 20 Feb. 1955.

19

1. Hubbard, op. cit., p. 122, citing Secretary of State for the Colonies, circular letter, 15 June 1947; LvdP, letter to H. Weskob, 15 May 1950, CDC.

2. Hubbard, op. cit., pp. 125–26.

3. R. F. Brook, letter to Sir Evelyn Baring, 2 Jan. 1950, CDC; LvdP, letter to Barbara Debenham, 10 Feb. 1996, LvdPA; *Thunder*, pp. 117–18.

4. 'Real Kalahari', *The Countryman*, Winter 1950; *About Blady*, p. 8; Professor Edwin Wilmsen, interview with author.

5. Debenham, *Kalahari Sand*, p. 42.

6. LvdP, CDC Diary (1950), LvdPA; 'Real Kalahari', *The Countryman*, Winter 1950.

7. LvdP, 'Return to the Kalahari', BBC Home Service, 3 Oct. 1951, BBC.
8. LvdP, Radio Log, 1950, LvdPA.
9. 'Cattle Ranching in Bechuanaland', unsigned, undated document; A. B. Fowler, letter to Dr A. E. Romyn, 23 May 1950; R. L Robinson, letter to Dr. A. B. Fowler, 13 Sept. 1950, CDC; LvdP, Passport: L6257, LvdPA.
10. R. L. Robinson, letter to Dr A. B. Fowler, 1 Feb. 1951; T. A. Rees, letter to Dr A. B. Fowler, 30 Mar. 1950; A. B. Fowler, letter to Lord Reith, 24 July 1951; A. B. Fowler, letter to R. L. Robinson, 26 Oct. 1950; LvdP, letter to Lord Reith, 21 May 1952, CDC.
11. LvdP, letter to L. P. Yates, undated; Minutes of Final Meeting held at Panda-ma-Tenga, 25 May 1952, CDC.
12. H. Hagerup, letter to the Hogarth Press, 20 Oct. 1952, C&W; Mr Foster, letter to LvdP, 22 Aug. 1952; LvdP, letter to Mr Foster, 28 Aug. 1952; Notes of Points for Discussion with Colonel van der Post, undated; LvdP, letters to W. A. W. Clark, 31 Aug. & 1 Sept. 1952 (DO 35/4393), PRO.
13. Mr Foster, letter to LvdP, 22 Aug. 1952; LvdP, letter to Mr Foster, 11 Nov. 1952; Notes on Meeting between His Excellency and Members of the Kalahari Mission, 9 Dec. 1952 (DO 35/4393), PRO.
14. LvdP, 'The Story of a Mission', BBC Home Service, 19 July 1954, BBC.

20

1. Robert Bogdan, *Freak Show: Presenting Human Oddities for Amusement and Profit*, pp. 187–92; Elizabeth Dell, '". . . Gulliver's travels are no longer a fable." Exhibiting the "Savage" in 19th Century Britain; Live South Africans on Show', Societies of Southern Africa, Institute of Commonwealth Studies, symposium paper, 10 Dec. 1993; Edwin N. Wilmsen, 'Primitive Politics in Sanctified Landscapes: The Ethnographic Fictions of Laurens van der Post', *Journal of Southern African Studies*, June 1995.
2. Edwin N. Wilmsen, 'Knowledge as the Source of Progress: The Marshall family Testament to the "Bushmen"', *Visual Anthropology*, 1999, p. 248; Phillip Tobias, Foreword, in A. Clement (ed.), *The Kalahari and Its Lost City*.
3. John Marshall, *The Hunters*, film, 1957; Elizabeth Marshall Thomas, *The Harmless People*; Wilmsen, 'Primitive Politics', *JSAS*, June 1995, p. 203; Wilmsen, 'Knowledge', *Visual Anthropology*, 1999.
4. Professor Phillip Tobias, interview with author, 23 May 2001.
5. Alan Barnard, 'Laurens van der Post and the Kalahari Debate' in Skotnes, op. cit., pp. 243–49; Alan Barnard, 'The Lost World of Laurens van der Post?', *Current Anthropology*, Feb. 1989; Shula Marks, 'Khoisan Resistance to the Dutch in the Seventeenth and Eighteenth Centuries', *Journal of African History*, 1972; *Lost World*, pp. 13–14 & 30.
6. *Lost World*, pp. 26, 33–34 & 41; *Thunder*, p. 154; Wilmsen, 'Primitive Politics', *JSAS*, p. 204; 'The Lost World of Kalahari', BBC, 1956; G. W. Stow, *The Native Races of South Africa*, p. 230.
7. *Lost World*, p. 61; Conrad, op. cit.; *About Blady*, p. 16.
8. *Lost World*, pp. 5 & 57–58; *Heart*, p. 148; T. C. Robertson, conversation with Ian Player; see for example, LvdP, CDC Diary (1950), LvdPA.
9. *Lost World*, p. 67.
10. Donald Boyd, letter to C. T. (Home Sound), 27 Jan. 1954; LvdP, letter to Donald Boyd, 14 Sept. 1954; Hugh C. Greene, Memorandum, 28 June 1954, BBC.
11. 'Lost World of Kalahari', BBC, 1956.
12. LvdP, 'Boer Farmer of the High Veldt', BBC Home Service, 19 Jan. 1939 & 'My Sheep Farm in the High-Veldt', BBC Home Service 21 Nov. 1941, BBC; Anonymous [LvdP], 'The Java Crisis', BBC Home Service, 1 Nov. 1945; LvdP, letter to Mr Rendall, 10 Apr. 1949, LvdPA; LvdP, 'Hunters' Road', BBC Home Service, 12 Aug. 1951; 'Return to the Kalahari', 3 Oct. 1951; 'The Story of a Mission', 19 July 1954, BBC.
13. 'Opinion on Central Africa', Chronique de l'Empire, BBC French-language service, 9 May 1952; LvdP, 'The Afrikaans language', BBC Third Programme, 24 Aug. 1954; LvdP, letter to Prudence Smith, 1 Nov. 1951; Prudence Smith, letter to LvdP, 10 Dec. 1953, BBC; J. C. Steyn, *Van Wyk Louw: 'n Lewensverhaal Deel I & II*, p. 738.
14. Donald Boyd, letter to Chief Assistant, Talks (Home Sound), 17 June 1954; Donald Boyd, letter to C. T. (Home Sound), 27 Jan. 1954; John Morris, letter to Donald Boyd, 23 Feb. 1954; LvdP, letter to Donald Boyd, 14 Sept. 1954, BBC; M. M. van der Post, Last Testament, 8 Feb. 1954, SCRB; Chris Plewman, interview with author, 9 Feb. 1998.
15. LvdP, letter to Mary Adams, 18 Apr. 1955; G. del Strother, letter to LvdP, 11 May 1955; LvdP, letter to Brian E. Church, 4 May 1955; LvdP, letter to J. H. Baldwin, 25 Aug. 1955; LvdP, 'The Kalahari Expedition' (summary), undated, LvdPA; *About Blady*, p. 23; LvdP, letter to Urs Schwarz, 31 Mar. & 13 Apr. 1955; Urs Schwarz, letter to LvdP, 4 Apr. & 25 Apr. 1955; LvdP, letter to Piet Meiring, 4 Apr. 1955, LvdPA.
16. *Lost World*, pp. 79–80; Anthony Sampson, conversation with James Sanders, 3 June 2001.
17. LvdP, letter to Arthur Dodds-Parker, 4 May 1955; R. W. D. Fowler, letter to LvdP, 5 May 1955; J. C. Martin, letter to M. C. Wray, 23 May 1955; Tom Scrivener, letter to R. W. D. Fowler, 12 Aug. 1955; Tom Scrivener, Secret Inward Telegram to CRO, 16 July 1955 (DO 35/4445), PRO; Anthony Sampson, *Mandela: The Authorised Biography*, p. 110.

18. LvdP, letter to Margaret Thayer, 14 June 1955; G. del Strother, letter to LvdP, 11 May 1955; Urs Schwarz, letter to LvdP, 25 Apr. 1955; Charles Parker, letter to LvdP, 4 Aug. 1955; Richard L. Field, letter to LvdP, 13 May 1955; LvdP, letter to Enrico Pratt, 7 July 1955, LvdPA; *Lost World*, pp. 82, 84–85 & 87; LvdP, letter to J. H. Baldwin, 25 Aug. 1955, LvdPA; For LvdP's reports, see *The Times*, 12 Sept., 5, 22 Oct., 14, 22 & 23 Dec. 1955.
19. *Lost World*, pp. 93, 96, 113, 116–19, 121 & 152; Professor Phillip Tobias, interview with author, 23 May 2001; Anthony Sampson, Diary, unpublished, 12 Nov. 1955.
20. *Lost World*, pp. 127–31, 139, 141–42, 149–51, 158–59, 165–67, 170–81, 185–88 & 192–97.
21. François Balson, *Capricorn Road*, pp. 121, 139–40, 151 & 161–63; *Thunder*, pp. 131–38; 'Lost World of Kalahari', BBC, 1956.
22. Professor Phillip Tobias, interview with author, 23 May 2001.
23. *Lost World*, pp. 201–5, 213–15 & 243–45.

21

1. 'Lost World of Kalahari', BBC, 1956; the films were re-broadcast during July 1957 (Daphne Meier, letter to LvdP, 28 June 1957), LvdPA; Professor Edwin Wilmsen, interview with author; A. Millar-Jones, letter to LvdP, 20 July 1956, LvdPA; *The Spectator*, 22 Dec. 1984.
2. LvdP, letter to Frances Phillips, 26 May 1956, WM; LvdP, letters to Norah Smallwood, 7 Oct. 1957, 17 & 26 July 1958; Norah Smallwood, letter to LvdP, 26 Feb. 1958; Norah Smallwood, letter to Leonard Woolf, 27 Feb. 1958, C&W; Leonard Woolf, letter to LvdP, 5 Mar. 1958, LW; Norah Smallwood, letter to John Willey, 5 June 1958, C&W; Adele Dogan, cable to Norah Smallwood, 7 Mar. & 15 Apr. 1958; Frances Phillips, letter to Norah Smallwood, 20 Mar. 1958; Norah Smallwood, letter to Adele Dogan, 21 Apr. 1958; LvdP, letter to Adele Dogan, 25 Apr. 1958; Norah Smallwood, letter to John Willey, 7 May 1958, WM.
3. LvdP, letters to Norah Smallwood, 17 & 26 July 1958; Norah Smallwood, letter to LvdP, 24 July 1958, C&W.
4. Cliftons Solicitors, letter to LvdP, 25 Nov. 1955; M. Thursby, letter to Clara Urquhart, 4 Jan. 1956; Clara Urquhart, letter to M. Thursby, 7 Jan. 1956, LvdPA; Sampson, Diary, 12 Nov. 1955; Cliftons Solicitors, letter to Walters & Hart, 17 Feb. 1956; LvdP, letter to J. H. Max-Muller, 27 Feb. 1956, LvdPA.
5. Michael Rubenstein, letter to Ian Parsons, 24 Apr. 1958; J. H. Max-Muller, letter to Michael Rubenstein, 5 May 1958; LvdP, letter to Ian Parsons, 1 May 1958; Antony Gibbs & Sons, letter to the Hogarth Press, 16 July 1958, LvdPA; LvdP, letters to Norah Smallwood, 26 July & undated; Norah Smallwood, letter to Adele Dogan, 15 Aug. 1958; H. W. Grigsby, letter to Norah Smallwood, 29 Oct. 1958; Penguin Books, letter to Norah Smallwood, 18 Nov. 1958; Norah Smallwood, letter to LvdP, 7 Aug. 1958; 'LvdP: British Empire Sales', 1962, C&W.
6. *The Sunday Times*, 9 Nov. 1958; *The Economist*, 15 Nov. 1958; *The Times Literary Supplement*, 25 Nov. 1958; *New Statesman*, 15 Nov. 1958; *The Spectator*, 21 Nov. 1958.
7. *New York Times* Book Review, 9 Nov. 1958; *New York Herald Tribune*, 9 Nov. 1958.
8. D. W. Lloyd, 'Transformations of the Colonial Narrative: Laurens van der Post's *The Lost World of the Kalahari*', *English Academy Review*, 1993.
9. *Heart*, p. 100; Wilmsen, 'Primitive Politics', *JSAS*, pp. 203–4.
10. Alan Barnard, 'Laurens van der Post and the Kalahari Debate', in Skotnes, op. cit., pp. 243–47. See also Barnard, 'Lost World', *Current Anthropology*, Feb. 1989; Marks, 'Khoisan Resistance', *JAH*; *Thunder*, pp. 137–43; *New York Times*, 13 Nov. 1997.
11. *Heart*, p. 117; *Lost World*, pp. 67–68; *Thunder*, pp. 89, 97–100, 134, 169 & 171; Professor Edwin Wilmsen, interview with author.
12. *Heart*, pp. 43, 116 & 136.
13. *Lost World*, pp. 33 & 58; Stow, op. cit.; W. H. I. Bleek, *Specimens of Bushman Folklore*, p. 291, to be republished in 2001 by Daimon Verlag, Einsiedeln, Switzerland; Janette Deacon, 'A Tale of Two Families: Wilhelm Bleek, Lucy Lloyd and the /Xam San of the Northern Cape' & Michael Godby, 'Images of //Kabbo' in Skotnes, op. cit., pp. 93–127; The Grey Collection, FSA.
14. *Heart*, p. 14; Professor Edwin Wilmsen, interview with author.
15. Bleek, *Specimens*; W. H. I. Bleek, *Second Report concerning Bushman Researches, with a Short Account of Bushman Folklore*; L. C. Lloyd, *A Short Account of Further Bushman Material Collected*; D. F. Bleek, *The Mantis and his Friends*; Stow, op. cit; *Heart*, pp. 13–14 & 166.
16. *Heart*, pp. 126, 128 & 135.
17. Wilmsen, 'Primitive Politics', *JSAS*, p. 218.
18. *Heart*, pp. 43, 157, 165–66, 171–73, 179–84, 191–96, 200, 208–9 & 222–25; Bleek, *Specimens*, pp. 3–37, 57–65, 73–79, 81–83, 85–98, 175–91, 333 & 389–97.
19. *Heart*, p. 156: 'I must first sit a little, cooling my arms, that the tiredness may go out of them . . . watching for a story I want to hear . . . while I sit waiting that it may float into my ear.'; Bleek, *Specimen*, p. 303.
20. *Heart*, pp. 139 & 173; *Feather*, p. 3.

21. *Heart*, pp. 166–68; Doris Lessing, introduction to Olive Schreiner, *The Story of an African Farm*, pp. xiii & 138–49.
22. *Heart*, pp. 176–77 & 183.
23. Ibid., pp. 187–88, 207 & 232–33; D. F. Bleek, op. cit., p. 9. For reviews of *Heart* see *The Times*, 26 Oct. 1961; *The Sunday Times*, 29 Oct. 1961; *New Statesman*, 27 Oct. 1961; *New York Times* Book Review, 26 Nov. 1961.
24. Wilmsen, 'Primitive Politics', *JSAS*, pp. 218–22; *Heart*, p. 117; A. F. Comfort, letter to M. J. Fairlie, 13 Jan. 1958; T. G. Hunt, letter to M. J. Fairlie for 21 Jan. 1958; M. J. Fairlie, notes to T. G. Hunt, 18 Feb. & 14 Apr. 1958; E. L. Sykes, Note for the Record: Bushmen, 31 May 1960; I. Glyn Thomas, letter to Prof C. H. Philips, 3 Aug. 1960 (DO 35/7167), PRO.
25. Resident Commissioner, Mafeking, letter to The High Commissioner, Pretoria, 27 Sept. 1960 (DO 35/7167), PRO.

Part Four

22

1. LvdP, Diary (1955–57); Passports: L6257 & L2122, LvdPA; LvdP, letters to Benjamin Britten, 2 Jan. 1951 & 5 Jan. 1959, BPL; LvdP, letter to Stephen Solomon, 30 Apr. 1969, LvdPA.
2. *The Way Things*, pp. 282–83; Kate Bertaud, interview with author; *The Times*, 13 Sept. 1967; Robin & Lilias Sheepshanks, interview with author, 29 Sept. 2000.
3. *Yet Being*, p. 337; *White Bushman*, p. 210; Alexander, *Plomer*, pp. 269–79, 304–6 & 315–16.
4. Private Information.
5. M. M. van der Post, letters to LvdP, 25 Feb. & 3 Apr. 1940, LvdPA; *Venture*, pp. 17–21; Margaret (Tiny) van der Post, interview with author, 18 July 2000; Chris Schmidt, interview with author, 9 July 2000; Tom Bedford, interview with author; Lucia van der Post, interview with author.
6. M. M. van der Post, 'Memoir'; LvdP, letter to P. J. du Toit, 21 Mar. 1957; LvdP, letter to Betys du Toit, 25 Apr. 1957, LvdPA; Margaret (Tiny) van der Post, interview with author, 18 July 2000; *Thunder*, p. 155; Norah Smallwood, letter to Ragnar Svanstrom, 4 Oct. 1954, C&W; Frances Baruch, interview with author.
7. LvdP, letter to K. van der Post, 24 Nov. 1955; LvdP, letter to Pauline Schmidt, 21 Mar. 1957; LvdP, letter to Ella Bedford (van der Post), 6 Dec. 1984, LvdPA; Margaret (Tiny) van der Post, interview with author, 18 July 2000; Chris Schmidt, interview with author, 9 July 2000; LvdP, letter to George Aschman, 23 May 1975, LvdPA.
8. LvdP, Notebook (1950), LvdPA; Mignonne van der Post-Bryant, letter to author, 7 Sept. 2000; LvdP, letter to John Max-Muller, 25 May 1959; LvdP, letter to Tom Bedford, 12 Dec. 1984, LvdPA; Anton van der Post, interview with author, 14 July 2000; Margaret (Tiny) van der Post, interview with author, 18 July 2000.
9. Kate Bertaud, interview with author; C. W. H. (Pooi) van der Post, letters to LvdP, 15 Jan. & 8 Aug. 1946, LvdPA; Lucia van der Post, interview with author; J. Andrews Christie, letter to LvdP, 2 Mar. 1991, LvdPA; *The Times*, 20 Mar. 1984; William Plomer, letter to LvdP, 31 July 1962, LvdPA; *About Blady*, pp. 43–44.
10. Lucia van der Post, letter to author, May 2001; Rupert van der Post, interview with author, 8 Dec. 1999; David Crichton-Miller, interview with author, 13 Dec. 2000; Marjorie van der Post, op. cit.

23

1. Richard Hughes, 'Capricorn: David Stirling's African Campaign'.
2. *White Bushman*, p. 113; 'Sir LvdP – brief outline of his interests and achievements' (Charity Commission application, 6 Mar. 1992), LvdPA; Alan Hoe, *David Stirling*, p. 292.
3. Hughes, op. cit., citing David Stirling & N. H. Wilson, 'A Native Policy for Africa', Salisbury, Apr. 1950 & File 68, University of York Archive.
4. Ibid., citing The Salisbury Declarations, Apr. 1952; Hoe, op. cit., pp. 292 & 303–4.
5. David Stirling, memorandum on the Capricorn Africa Society, Sept. 1953; John W. Russell, letter to A. Campbell, 18 Dec. 1953; Ian Maclennan, letter to Herbert Baxter, 6 Feb. 1954; G. H. Baxter, letter to Ian Maclennan, 29 Jan. 1954 (DO 35/4705), PRO; *East Africa and Rhodesia*, 18 Feb. 1954.
6. Hughes, op. cit.; Susan Wood, *A Fly in Amber*, pp. 157–64.
7. LvdP, 'The Africa I Know', *African Affairs*, July 1952, pp. 219–220.
8. The Capricorn Africa Society, 'Newsletter', Sept. 1956, LvdPA; Wood, op. cit., pp. 90–95 & 100–5; Hughes, op. cit.; *The Times*, 18 June 1956.
9. LvdP, letter to Alan Hoe, 29 Sept. 1991; LvdP, letter to Peter Mackay, 23 May 1956; LvdP, letter to David Stirling, 29 May 1956, LvdPA.
10. *Rhodesia Herald*, 9 & 10 Apr. 1956; *Umtali Post*, 11 Apr. 1956; LvdP, letter to David Stirling, 29 Feb. 1956, LvdPA. *Nyasaland Times*, 10, 13 & 17 Apr. 1956; Peter Mackay, letter to LvdP, 10 May 1956, LvdPA; Jeannine Scott/Bartosik, interview with author, 17 Oct. 1999.
11. Hughes, op. cit.; LvdP, letter to Dr J. H. Oldham, 3 Apr. 1956, LvdPA; Dr J. H. Oldham, *New Hope in Africa*; Jeannine Scott/Bartosik, interview with author, 17 Oct. 1999.
12. LvdP, letter to Canon John Collins, 5 Apr. 1957; Canon John Collins, letter to LvdP, 14 Apr. 1957, LvdPA.

13. David Stirling, letters to LvdP, 5 Nov. 1956 & 2 Sept. 1957; LvdP, letter to Roger Lyons, 8 Mar. 1957; Roger Lyons, letter to LvdP, 26 Mar. 1957, LvdPA; *Thunder*, p. 130; Sampson, *Mandela*, p. 128.
14. Hoe, op. cit.; Stephen Dorril & Robin Ramsay, *Smear! Wilson and the Secret State*, pp. 222–23; Adam Curtis, 'The Mayfair Set', BBC 2, May 1999; LvdP, letter to Jeanine Bartosik, 14 Jan. 1991, LvdPA.
15. Jonathan Lewis, 'Confidential Report to General Council on Visit to Society's Branches in Africa', Sept. 1960, in Hughes, op. cit., appendix; LvdP, 'Dissenting Report', Jan. 1961; LvdP, letter to Charles Marsh, 7 Dec. 1960, LvdPA.
16. The Zebra Trust, promotional leaflet (undated); LvdP, letter to Lady Susan Wood, 24 May 1994, LvdPA.
17. *White Bushman*, p. 228; *Yet Being*, p. 299.
18. *Dark Eye*, pp. 5, 14–15, 19, 40–41, 46, 54–56, 59, 60 & 62; Wolfram Von Eschenbach, *Parzival*, p. 372.
19. *Dark Eye*, pp. 63–64, 69, 75–76, 82, 99, 104, 113–14 & 118; Norah Smallwood, letter to Thayer Hobson, 30 Aug. 1955, C&W.
20. *Dark Eye*, pp. 125, 137–39, 141–43, 145 & 149–50.
21. Ian Parsons, letter to Miss Burch, 4 Mar. 1955; William Morrow, letter to Norah Smallwood, 5 Apr. 1955; Norah Smallwood, letter to Kurt Wolff, 6 May 1955; Norah Smallwood, letters to LvdP, 16 Feb. & 30 Mar. 1955; Norah Smallwood, letter to Thayer Hobson, 12 & 30 Aug. 1955; Thayer Hobson, letter to Norah Smallwood, 26 Aug. 1955, C&W.
22. *Daily Telegraph*, 21 Oct. 1955; *Evening Standard*, 18 Oct. 1955; *The Spectator*, 16 Dec. 1955; *Time and Tide*, 22 Oct. 1955; *The Times*, 1 Dec. 1955; *The Observer*, 23 Oct. 1955.
23. *The Times Literary Supplement*, 11 Nov. 1955; *New Statesman*, 15 Nov. 1955; *The Economist*, 12 Nov. 1955; *Saturday Review*, 17 Dec. 1955; *New York Herald Tribune*, 30 Oct. 1955; *New Yorker*, 12 Nov. 1955.

24
1. *Rand Daily Mail*, 30 Mar. 1968 & 8 May 1973; *The Observer*, 6 Apr. 1969; Paton, op. cit.; Trevor Huddleston, *Naught for Your Comfort*.
2. LvdP, letter to the Hon. Mr J. Sisson, 25 May 1956, LvdPA.
3. LvdP, letter to Canon John Collins, 25 Feb. 1957; LvdP, letter to Alan Paton, 29 Jan. 1957; Alan Paton, letter to LvdP, 22 Feb. 1965, LvdPA.
4. Denis Herbstein, 'IDAF: The History'.
5. Ibid.; Alan Paton, letters to LvdP, 22 Feb., 19 Aug. 1965 & 23 June 1970; LvdP, letter to Alan Paton, 29 Jan. 1957, LvdPA.
6. LvdP, letter to Alan Paton, 6 June 1970; Alan Paton, letter to LvdP, 23 June 1970; LvdP attributed many of the problems in England to 'coloured immigrants'. He believed that the British government should refuse to accept responsibility for East African Asians (6 June 1970), APC.
7. Herbstein, op. cit.; LvdP, letters to Alan Paton, 17 May & 13 July 1977; Alan Paton, letters to LvdP, 8 Aug. 1977, LvdPA, & 27 Dec. 1977, APC; Gordon Winter, *Inside BOSS: South Africa's Secret Police*, pp. 350–55; *The Observer*, 6 Jan. 1980; LvdP also blamed left-wing groups for the disappearance of his letters: 'There are cells of all sorts of anti-South African bodies from communists to SWAPO-ites in sorting offices everywhere . . .' (13 July 1977), LvdPA.
8. LvdP, letter to Jack Cope, 9 Dec. 1975, NELM.
9. Ingrid Jonker, 'The Child' in *Selected Poems*, p. 27; *Cape Times*, 25 May 1994; [Johannesburg] *Sunday Times*, 29 Sept. 1994.
10. Anna Jonker, letter to LvdP, 30 Mar. 1996; LvdP, letter to Prof. & Mrs J. Degenaar, 15 Apr. 1996, LvdPA.
11. LvdP, letters to William Plomer, 2 July 1964 & 3 Aug. 1965, DUL; William Plomer, 'The Taste of Fruit', *The Times Literary Supplement*, 16 Sept. 1965.
12. Alexander, *Plomer*, p. 227, 245, 247 & 292–96; Francis Kilvert, *Kilvert's Diary*.
13. Plomer, *Autobiography*, p. 412; Plomer, *Double Lives*; Bowes Lyon, *Collected Poems*; LvdP, letters to William Plomer, 15 Sept. 1947, 18 July 1949 & 7 Feb. 1951; William Plomer, letter to LvdP, 24 Apr. 1951, DUL.
14. LvdP, letters to William Plomer, 9 Apr. 1952, 23 Apr., 13 June 1953, 1 Feb. 1955, 25 June 1956 & 5 Nov. 1957, DUL.

25
1. LvdP, 'Africa', *Holiday*, Mar. 1954; Jacques Chambrun, letter to LvdP, 4 May 1955; Richard L. Field, letter to LvdP, 14 Apr. 1955, C&W; LvdP, 'Tracking the First African', *Holiday*, Oct. 1956.
2. LvdP, 'Introduction to Africa', *Holiday*, Apr. 1959; The Curtis Publishing Company, letter to LvdP, 28 Mar. 1956; LvdP, letter to Harry Sion, 2 July, 7 Oct., 18 Nov. 1957, 13 Apr. 1959; Albert Farnsworth, letter to LvdP, 24 Aug. 1961, LvdPA; LvdP, 'Japan: Journey Through A Floating World', *Holiday*, Oct. 1961; LvdP, 'Memorial Address in Honor of Dr. Jung', *Analytical Psychology Club Supplement*, Jan. 1962.

3. LvdP, 'A View Of All The Russias', *Holiday*, Oct. 1963; LvdP, *Journey Into Russia*.

4. *Russia*, pp. 11, 45–47, 313–15 & 318; Jung, *Collected Works, Vol. VI: Psychological Types*, pp. 87–88, *Vol. VII: Two Essays on Analytical Psychology*, pp. 33–34.

5. *Russia*, pp. 15, 37, 113, 205–6,233, 272, 294 & 314.

6. *The Times*, 23 Jan. 1964; *The Times Literary Supplement*, 23 Jan. 1964; *The Sunday Times*, 26 Jan. 1964; *Glasgow Herald*, 25 Jan. 1964; *Tribune*, 3 Apr. 1964.

7. *Saturday Review*, 2 May 1964; *Newsweek*, 4 May 1964; *New York Times*, 27 May 1964.

8. *Sunday Telegraph*, 5–19 Jan. 1964; Norah Smallwood, letter to Ian Parsons, 22 Oct. 1963; Norah Smallwood, letter to LvdP, 17 Mar. 1964; Norah Smallwood, letter to Tony Godwin, 8 Apr. 1964, C&W; LvdP, *A View of All the Russias*.

9. 'Japan', *Holiday*, Oct. 1961; LvdP, *A Portrait of Japan*, pp. 12, 34, 59 & 73.

10. LvdP, letters to Captain Mori, 14 June 1956 & 5 Apr. 1957; Captain Mori, letter to Hilda Young, 11 Feb. 1957, LvdPA; 'Japan, *Holiday*, Oct. 1961; *Japan*, pp. 73–5 & 136–39; LvdP, letter to William Plomer, undated, DUL.

11. John T. Lawrence, letter to LvdP, 1 Oct. 1965; Lawrence Hughes, letter to Frances Phillips, 15 Sept. 1967; Norah Smallwood, letter to John Willey, 3 Mar. 1969; John Willey, letter to Norah Smallwood, 3 Mar. 1969; Larry Hughes, letter to Norah Smallwood, 22 Nov. 1967, C&W; *Japan*, op. cit.

12. *Socialist Commentary*, Feb. 1968; *New Statesman*, 25 Oct. 1968.

13. Harry Sions, letters to LvdP, 30 May 1959, 22 June 1961 & 21 Aug. 1963; Don A. Schanche, letter to LvdP, 20 Jan. 1965 & telegram, 29 Dec. 1966, LvdPA; *New York Times*, 12 Oct. 1964; Norah Smallwood, letter to Sam Lawrence, 8 Jan. 1965, C&W.

14. LvdP, 'The Ageless Mosaic of India', *Holiday*, Oct. 1967; 'The Vivid Variety of India, Sikkim', *Holiday*, Nov. 1967; 'Nepal', *Holiday*, Sept./Oct. 1970.

15. Richard L. William, letter to LvdP, 2 Aug. 1968, C&W; *Eland*, p. 5; *African Cooking*, p. 18; LvdP, Passports: 953849 (UK) & L531705 (SA), LvdPA.

16. LvdP, letters to Norah Smallwood, 18 & 24 July 1973; unsigned, Study of 'A Jar of Pickle', Nov. 1976; Norah Smallwood, letter to John Willis, 3 Oct. 1977, C&W; LvdP, letters to J. Korn, 16 Nov. 1976, 14 Feb. & 4 May 1977; Jerry Korn, letters to LvdP, 3 Feb. & 7 July 1977; Norah Smallwood, letter to LvdP, 17 Oct. 1977, LvdPA.

17. *Eland*, pp. 1–5, 28, 51, 53, 55, 69, 85 & 87; *Wind*, p. 326; Douglas Wheeler & René Pelissier, *Angola*, pp. 178–91; see also John A. Marcum, *The Angolan Revolution, Vol. II: Exile Politics and Guerrilla Warfare (1962–1976)*.

18. *Eland*, pp. 123, 135, 144, 151, 172 & 209; Marjorie van der Post, letter to LvdP, 1 July 1969; Christine Sandford, letter to LvdP, 2 Mar. 1969; LvdP, Desk Diaries (1968 & 1969), LvdPA.

19. Jane Flower, interview with author.

20. *The Observer*, 11 Dec. 1977; *The Guardian*, 24 Nov. 1977; *Encounter*, Jan. 1978; *New York Times* Book Review, 6 Aug. 1978; LvdP, interviews with Jean-Marc Pottiez for *White Bushman*.

26

1. 'A Bar of Shadow', *The Cornhill*, Spring 1952; LvdP, letter to William Plomer, 1 Dec. 1951, DUL; Norstedt, letter to Chatto & Windus, 28 May 1954; LvdP, letter to Norah Smallwood, 1 June 1954; Norah Smallwood, letter to Karin Marcus, 9 June 1954; William Plomer, letter to Ian Parsons, 3 Aug. 1954; Norah Smallwood, letters to Ragnar Svanstrom, 16 Aug. 1954 & 21 Apr. 1958; Norah Smallwood, letters to LvdP, 6 Apr. 1956, 27 Nov. 1957 & 25 Oct. 1962; Peter Calvocoressi, letter to LvdP, 24 May 1957; Subsidiary Rights Dept., letter to Y. Katahira, 3 Aug. 1962, C&W; Leonard Woolf, letter to LvdP, 4 Apr. 1962; Ingaret van der Post, letter to Leonard Woolf, 5 Apr. 1962, LW.

2. *Seed*, pp. 13–15 & 35–38; *Admiral's Baby*, p. 20.

3. *Seed*, pp. 41–46, 48–52, 55, 62–68, 77–83, 87–94, 110–16, 118–20, 123, 153 & 156–59; original manuscript of *The Seed and the Sower*, LvdPA.

4. Nagisa Oshima, *Merry Christmas Mr Lawrence*, feature film, 1983; Captain Mori, letter to Hilda Young, 11 Feb. 1957, LvdPA; *Seed*, p. 199–204, 210–18 & 221–223.

5. *Seed*, pp. 12–15, 22–24, 136–37 & 146; *New Moon*, pp. 41–43; 'The Desired Earth'.

6. *Seed*, pp. 14, 17, 26, 112–13, 119, 124, 127–29, 131, 136 & 144–45; *New Moon*, p. 76.

7. *Seed*, pp. 48, 50, 163, 171, 176, 185, 188–195, 197, 208, 213 & 220.

8. *New Moon*, pp. 5, 23, 30 & 38–39; Primo Levi, *If This Is A Man*.

9. *New Moon*, pp. 103, 113, 119–20 & 123–25.

10. *Yet Being*, pp. 71 & 81; *Whale*, pp. 9, 11, 24, 29, 52, 81–82, 86, 98–99, 116–21, 128, 131–32 & 182.

11. *Whale*, pp. 102, 140–41, 147, 151, 154, 199, 203–4, 211, 230, 233, 258, 283, 294, 299, 301, 305 & 317; Herman Melville, *Moby Dick*.

12. *The Sunday Times*, 15 Oct. 1967; *Sunday Telegraph*, 15 Oct. 1967; *The Observer*, 15 Oct. 1967; *New York Times* Book Review, 6 Oct. 1967.

13. Leonard Woolf, letter to LvdP, 1 Jan. 1967, LW; Norah Smallwood, letter to LvdP, 2 Jan. 1968, C&W; Lettres

et Arts, BBC French Service, 10 Oct. 1967, BBC; promotional material for Odhams Book Club edition, 15 June 1968, C&W.

14. *Yet Being*, pp. 64–69, 71, 74, 78–79, 86, 89, 94, 97–98 & 105–6; *Cape Times*, 28 Nov. 1929.

27

1. Janet Campbell, letter to author, 22 Jan. 1999; LvdP, letter to P. J. Duthie, 27 Mar. 1980, LvdPA.
2. Louise Stein, interview with author; John Charlton, interview with author, 29 May 1998.
3. Rupert van der Post, interview with author, 8 Dec. 1999; David Crichton-Miller, interview with author, 13 Dec. 2000; LvdP, letters to Marjorie van der Post, 24 May 1988 & 27 Jan. 1989, LvdPA; Tom Bedford, interview with author; Lucia van der Post, letter to author, May 2001.
4. See for example LvdP, introduction, Eliot Elisofon, *The Nile*; Anne Baring & Jules Cashford, *The Myth of the Goddess: Evolution of an Image*.
5. LvdP, letter to William Plomer, 20 June 1961, DUL.
6. *The Times*, 18 July 1962; SACSEA, signal to AFNEI, & AFNEI, signal to SACSEA, Feb. 1946, LvdPA; LvdP, letters to William Plomer, 4 July 1962, DUL; Ian Horobin, letter to LvdP, 18 June 1972, LvdPA.
7. William Plomer, letters to LvdP, 12 Dec. 1962, LvdPA & 12 Oct. 1970, DUL; Ian Horobin, *Collected Poems*.
8. LvdP, letters to William Plomer, 27 July & 24 Nov. 1962, DUL; William Plomer, letters to LvdP, 31 July 1962, 7 Feb. 1963 & 16 Jan. 1965, LvdPA; G. L. Lewin, letter to William Plomer, 1 Dec. 1962, DUL.
9. LvdP, letters to William Plomer, 19 Feb., 27 Apr., 12 May 1964, 24 & 28 May 1965, DUL; William Plomer, letters to LvdP, 8 June 1964 & 29 May 1965, LvdPA; Leonard Woolf, letter to William Plomer, 21 Oct. 1964, DUL.
10. 'Affair', *Turbott Wolfe*, op. cit. pp. 13, 44–45 & 52.
11. LvdP, letters to William Plomer, 10 July, 3 Aug. 1965, 14, 21 May 1968, 14 July 1969, 18 Jan. & 12 Feb. 1970, DUL; William Plomer, letters to LvdP, 3 Oct. 1967, LvdPA, 13, 20 May, DUL, & 7 Sept. 1968, LvdPA; Carpenter, op. cit.; *Thunder*, pp. 3–4.
12. Lucia van der Post, interview with author; Alexander, op. cit., p. 329; see also LvdP, 'William Plomer: Classical Anger at Race Prejudice', *The Times*, 28 Sept. 1973.
13. *Yet Being*, pp. 117–19, 121–22, 126–28, 146, 154, 182, 207, 211, 217, 238, 250 & 253–54; Plomer, *The Autobiography*, pp. 179–190; Plomer, *Double Lives*, pp. 169–182.
14. 'Campbell, Plomer, Paton & Myself', LvdPA; see also *White Bushman*, pp. 196–98, 207–8 & 210; Plomer, *Double Lives*, p. 167.
15. Janet Campbell, interview with author, 18 Oct. 2000; Private Information; LvdP, letters to Ingaret van der Post, 13 Oct. 1966, 31 Aug. 1977 & undated.
16. Victoria Dixon, interview with author, 18 Mar. 1998; Fleur Mostert, interview with James Sanders, 20 Apr. 2000; Janet Campbell, interview with author, 18 Oct. 2000; Private Information; Lucia van der Post, letter to author, May 2001.
17. F. G. Butler, letter to LvdP, 22 June 1977, LvdPA; *Rand Daily Mail*, 8 May 1973; *The Guardian*, 22 Jan. 1964; A. White, letter to LvdP, 6 June 1980, LvdPA.
18. LvdP, letter to Keith Millar-Jones, 6 Nov. 1957; LvdP, letter to Elaine van der Post, 1 Nov. 1960; LvdP, letter to Professor Schmidt, 24 Apr. 1975; LvdP, letter to Stuart de Kok, 24 Apr. 1975; LvdP, Affidavit, 31 Aug. 1977, LvdPA; *Who's Who, 1970 & 1974*.
19. LvdP, letter to Mr Mackenzie, 21 May 1975; LvdP, letter to Chief Inspector of Taxes, 24 Aug. 1975. Despite the fact that Wolwekop was sold in 1982, LvdP continued to claim that he was domiciled in South Africa (T. D. Sewell, letter to LvdP, 19 Dec. 1994), LvdPA; Lucia van der Post, interview with author.
20. LvdP, letter to Pauline Schmidt, 4 July 1959; LvdP, letters to Breytenbach & Van Der Merwe, 9 Apr. 1980, 19 May 1981 & 7 June 1982; LvdP, letters to Tom Bedford, 26 Aug. 1981, 19 May 1982 & 29 Apr. 1983; John van der Post, letter to Tom Bedford, 29 Apr. 1983; LvdP, letter to W. E. Sutton, 9 June 1983, LvdPA; Tom Bedford, interview with author; LvdP, letter to Marjorie van der Post, 29 Apr. 1983, LvdPA; Leslie Jacobson, interview with Mark Ingle and James Sanders, 10 Dec. 2000; Lucia van der Post, letter to author, May 2001.

Part Five

28

1. Skotnes, op. cit., pp. 93–127; LvdP, *A Far-Off Place*, pp. 9–10, 12, 16–17.
2. LvdP, letter to Helen Luke, 8 Sept. 1987, LvdPA.
3. *Place*, p. 402; *Wind*, pp. 8–12; Bleek, *Specimen*, pp. 299–305.
4. *Wind*, pp. 13, 22, 27, 39, 41, 53–57, 60, 64, 89–90, 124, 151–52, 158, 273 & 307.
5. Ibid., pp. 186–90, 230–48, 279, 346, 399, 427–32, 436, 439, 452–55, 459–60, 466–68 & 472–74.
6. *Place*, pp. 35, 46, 53–55, 164, 228–29, 271–74, 280, 285, 317, 355, 367, 370, 373–76, 379–80, 387–90, 397, 401–10 & 413.

7. LvdP, letter to Norah Smallwood, 28 Sept. 1970; Norah Smallwood, memorandum on 'A Story Like The Wind', 16 Nov. 1971; LvdP, letter to Gill Coleridge, 26 June 1972; Norah Smallwood, letter to LvdP, 19 Oct. 1971., C&W.

8. *The Times Literary Supplement*, 9 June, 17, 28 July & 18 Aug. 1972; LvdP, letter to Gill Coleridge, 20 June 1972; LvdP, letter to Hugo Brunner, 26 June 1972; LvdP, letter to the Editor, *The Times Literary Supplement*, 30 June 1972, C&W.

9. LvdP, letters to Norah Smallwood, 9 Nov. 1972 & 3 Aug. 1973; John Willey, letter to Norah Smallwood, 6 Dec. 1973; Norah Smallwood, letter to John Willey, 3 Jan. 1974; Penguin Books, letter to Chatto & Windus, 8 Aug. 1974, C&W; LvdP, letter to author, 13 Oct. 1996.

10. *The Sunday Times*, 8 Sept. 1974; *The Observer*, 15 Sept. 1974; *The Spectator*, 21 Sept. 1974.

11. *New Statesman*, 6 Sept. 1974; *Evening Standard*, 24 Sept. 1974; *The Listener*, 17 Sept. 1974; *Washington Post*, 1 Oct. 1974; *Anti-Apartheid News*, Nov. 1974.

12. James Vance Marshall, *The Children*; Nicolas Roeg, *Walkabout*, feature film, 1971.

29

1. LvdP, *A Mantis Carol*, pp. 1–2; LvdP, letter to Norah Smallwood, 7, 31 Aug. 1974 & 8 Apr. 1975; Norah Smallwood, letter to LvdP, 31 Aug. 1974, C&W.

2. Elizabeth Dell, '". . . Gulliver's Travels are no longer a Fable." Exhibiting the "Savage" in 19th Century Britain: Live South Africans on Show', seminar paper, Institute of Commonwealth Studies, University of London, 1993; Stephen S. Bloomer, letter to LvdP, 6 June 1979, LvdPA.

3. *Mantis Carol*, p. 2; Neil Parsons, '"Clicko" or Franz Taaibosch: South African Bushman Entertainer in Britain, France, Jamaica and the USA: His Life from 1908–1940', seminar paper, African Studies Association, Seattle, Nov. 1992; Q. N. Parsons, 'Frantz or Klikko, The Wild Dancing Bushman: A Case Study in Khoisan Stereotyping', *Botswana Notes & Records*, 1988.

4. *Mantis Carol*, pp. 33–36, 41 & 50.

5. Evelyn Cook, letter to LvdP, 16 May 1978 & 29 Nov. 1989, LvdPA; *Mantis Carol*, pp. 142–52.

6. Evelyn Cook, letter to LvdP, 7 Jan. 1990; LvdP, letter to Evelyn Cook, 22 Jan. 1990; Barbara de Romain, letter to LvdP, 25 Feb. 1993; Barbara de Romain, letter to Neil Parsons, 28 Jan. 1993, LvdPA.

7. *Mantis Carol*, pp. 8, 10, 21 & 24–27; Carey Jones, letter to LvdP, 2 Feb. 1956; Martha Jaeger, letter to LvdP, 19 Oct. 1956; LvdP, letter to Martha Jaeger, 2 Nov. 1956; Dr. E. Bertine, letter to LvdP, 13 Nov. 1956; LvdP, letter to Sonia Robinson, 8 Jan. 1957, LvdPA.

8. Alex Jardine, interview with author, 3 Feb. 2001.

9. *Mantis Carol*, pp. 74–81 & 114–15. Evelyn Cook, letter to LvdP, 26 Oct. 1978, LvdPA.

10. *Mantis Carol*, pp. 120, 142, 148 & 157.

11. Ibid., pp. 126, 133 & 164–65; LvdP, letter to Martha Jaeger, 28 Dec. 1956; LvdP, Passport: L2122; Evelyn Cook, letter to LvdP, 16 May 1978, LvdPA.

12. LvdP, letter to Norah Smallwood, 16 Sept. 1974; LvdP, letter to John Charlton, 14 Aug. 1975; *Reader's Digest*, letter to Norah Smallwood, 9 May 1976; John Willey, letter to Norah Smallwood, 19 June 1975; Norah Smallwood, letter to John Willey, 1 Mar. 1976, C&W; LvdP, 'A Mantis Carol', BBC Radio 4, 21 Mar. 1976.

13. *The Sunday Times*, 2 Nov. 1975; *The Listener*, 18 Dec. 1975; *Sunday Telegraph*, 21 Dec. 1975; *Christian Science Monitor*, 4 Nov. 1980; *Atlantic Monthly*, June 1976.

14. *Daily Telegraph*, 23 Dec. 1991; LvdP, letter to Christian Sommerfelt, 22 Dec. 1994, LvdPA.

30

1. C. G. Jung, letter to John d'Oyly, 21 June 1934; Dr Godwyn Baines, letter to John d'Oyly, 11 Oct. 1935, LvdPA; *The Way Things*, pp. 217–20, 339–46, 352–56 & 361; *Jung*, p. 43.

2. *Yet Being*, p. 298; *Jung*, p. ix; LvdP, letter to Mr Radley, 20 Jan. 1951; LvdP, letter to Donald Boyd, 6 Mar. 1954, BBC.

3. LvdP, letters to William Plomer, 3 Nov. & 1 Dec. 1951, DUL; *Jung*, pp. 49–55; *White Bushman*, p. 33; C. G. Jung, *Memories, Dreams, Reflections*, pp. 282–304.

4. *Jung*, pp. 49–55, 225 & 249; *White Bushman*, pp. xiii–xv & 37, *Yet Being*, p. 330.

5. *Jung*, p. ix; Private Information.

6. *White Bushman*, p. 313; *Jung*, p. 133.

7. *White Bushman*, p. 311; LvdP, interview with author; Private Information.

8. Jonathan Stedall, 'The Story of Carl Gustav Jung', BBC 1, 28 Nov.–12 Dec. 1971; Laurens & Ingaret van der Post, 'Portrait of Jung', BBC Home Service, 10 May 1955, BBC; *Jung*, p. 267; Jonathan Stedall, interview with author, 6 Apr. 2001.

9. C. G. Jung, letters to LvdP, 16 Dec. 1954, 28 Feb., Sept. 1956, Apr. 1957 & 1 Oct. 1958, LvdPA; *Jung*, p. 55; Private Information.

10. C. G. Jung, letter to LvdP, 28 Feb. 1956; Aniela Jaffe, letter to LvdP, 14 Jan. 1976, LvdPA; Jung, *Memories*;

LvdP, letter to Norah Smallwood, 16 May 1974, C&W; LvdP, letter to Katherine Kidde, 15 Aug. 1980; LvdP, letters to Professor Fredy Meier, 27 June 1975, 6 May 1977, 11 Sept. 1981 & 14 May 1993, LvdPA; *Jung*, pp. 263–64.

11. Aniela Jaffe, 'A Last Look at a First Encounter' in *Rock Rabbit*, pp. 217–18.

12. *Jung*, pp. 254–55; Jung, *Memories*, p. 327.

13. 'Memorial Address in Honor of Dr. Jung: 20 October 1961', *Analytical Psychology Club Supplement*, Jan. 1962.

14. *Jung*, p. 216; C. G. Jung, *C. G. Jung: Letters*, p. 293; Jung, *Collected Works, Vol. IX*, Part 1: 'The Archetype and the Collective Unconscious', pp. 4–5, 78. Jung described an archetype as like 'the pattern of behaviour in biology' (p. 5).

15. LvdP, letters to Norah Smallwood, 26 July & 4 Sept. 1973, C&W; *Jung*, pp. 3, 30, 40–41, 47–48, 55, 63–64 & 124; Jung, *Memories*, p. 414: 'Expansion of the personality beyond its proper limits by identification with the persona ... or with an archetype ... or in pathological cases with a historical or religious figure. It produces an exaggerated sense of one's self-importance and is usually compensated by feelings of inferiority.'

16. E. A. Bennett, *Meetings With Jung*, 16 Jan. 1961.

17. *Jung*, pp. x, 77–82, 155–56, 171–78, 191, 239 & 273.

18. Ibid., pp. 86–89, 100–1, 109–10, 156–58, 161–173, 195–99, 201 & 206–7; Jung, *Memories*, pp. 204–6.

19. LvdP, letter to Gill Coleridge, 31 Oct. 1972, C&W.

20. André Schiffrin, letter to LvdP, 14 Mar. 1973; LvdP, letters to Norah Smallwood, 18, 26 July & 4 Sept. 1973; Pantheon Books to Chatto & Windus, 23 Oct. 1973; LvdP, letter to John Charlton, 16 Sept. 1974; LvdP, letter to André Schiffrin, 12 Jan. 1975, C&W.

21. John Charlton, letters to André Schiffrin, 7 Feb. 1975, 17 Feb., 21 Mar. & 13 Apr. 1977; André Schiffrin, letters to John Charlton, 7 Mar., 23 May, 24 Nov. 1975, 1 Feb., 10 Mar. & 21 Apr. 1977; LvdP, letter to André Schiffrin, 22 June 1975; LvdP, letter to John Charlton, 22 June 1975; André Schiffrin, letter to LvdP, 12 Feb. 1976; John Charlton, letter to LvdP, 17 June 1976; Penguin Books, letter to Chatto & Windus, 15 Jan. 1976, C&W.

22. *The Observer*, 20 June 1976; *The Sunday Times*, 15 Aug. 1976; *The Times*, 1 July 1976; *New Society*, 24 June 1976; LvdP, letter to Norah Smallwood, 22 June 1976; Norah Smallwood, letter to LvdP, 25 June 1976, C&W.

23. *Time*, 1 Dec. 1975; *Atlantic Monthly*, Dec. 1975; *Nation*, 15 Nov. 1975; *New Republic*, 6 Dec. 1975; *New York Times* Book Review, 27 June 1976.

24. *New Republic*, 6 Dec. 1975.

25. Ruth Bailey, conversation with Jackie Stedall, date unknown.

31

1. Stedall, 'Story of Carl Gustav Jung', BBC 1, 1971; Stephen Cross, 'A Region of Shadow', BBC 2, 10 July 1971; Stedall, 'The World About Us: All Africa Within Us', BBC 1, 1975; Wilson, 'Shakespeare in Perspective: The Tempest', BBC 2, 1980; Jane Taylor & Paul Bellinger, 'Testament to the Bushmen', BBC 2, 1984; Stedall, 'Laurens van der Post at 80', BBC 2, 1986; Lemle, 'Hasten Slowly: The Journey of Sir Laurens van der Post', film, 1996; Stedall, 'Voice from the Bundu', BBC 2, Dec. 1997; see also Jonathan Stedall, 'On Laurens and Film-Making' in *Rock Rabbit*, pp. 170–72; Paul Bellinger, 'Filming with Laurens van der Post' in *Rock Rabbit*, pp. 173–75.

2. LvdP, letter to T. C. Robertson, 31 Dec. 1979, CL; Piet Koornhof, interview with James Sanders, 1 Dec. 2000.

3. LvdP, letter to Piet Koornhof, 7 Jan. 1974; LvdP, letter to Bram Fischer, 7 Jan. 1974, LvdPA; Stephen Clingman, *Bram Fischer: Afrikaner Revolutionary*, pp. 39, 76, 115 & 450; Ruth Rice, conversation with author; Ian Player, letter to LvdP, 26 July 1975, LvdPA.

4. Anthony Sampson, *The Independent*, 24 Mar. & 14 Apr. 1990; LvdP, *The Independent*, 14 Apr. 1990.

5. LvdP, letter to Piet Koornhof, 8 May 1974; LvdP, letter to George Aschman, 23 May 1974, LvdPA.

6. LvdP, letter to Lord Home, 9 Dec. 1976; Antony Duff, letter to LvdP, 31 Jan. 1977; Charles Janson, letter to LvdP, 22 Jan. 1977, LvdPA.

7. LvdP, letter to Mrs Thatcher, 18 May 1977; LvdP, letter to Piet Koornhof, 2 Mar. & 29 June 1977; LvdP, letter to Mr Koven, 9 Nov. 1976; LvdP, letter to Charles Douglas-Home, 3 Apr. 1977; LvdP, letter to Katharine Graham, 12 Apr. 1977, LvdPA.

8. LvdP, letters to Piet Koornhof, 15 Apr. & 4 May 1977; LvdP, letters to David Owen, 23 May & 18 June 1977, LvdPA; David Owen, *Time to Declare*, p. 270; see also LvdP, letter to the Editor, *The Times*, 2 Aug. 1978, in which LvdP states that his meeting with Dr Owen had 'depressed me as much as the press conference called at the Foreign Office after Munich.'

9. LvdP, letters to Piet Koornhof, 25 June & 14 Dec. 1977; LvdP, letter to Hendrik van den Bergh, 14 Dec. 1977, LvdPA.

10. Charles Janson, letter to LvdP, 23 July 1980, LvdPA; Lucia van der Post, interview with author; LvdP encouraged this impression: 'Some public recognition of the world of these activities are perhaps to be seen in my ... knighthood "for public services" – I believe the only instance of a knighthood being awarded for services in the plural' (Charity Commission application, 6 Mar. 1992), LvdPA. The actual citation was

'The Queen Has been graciously pleased to signify her intention of conferring the Honour of Knighthood upon the undermentioned: Laurens Jan van der Post, CBE, For Public Service.'

11. LvdP, letter to T. C. Robertson, 31 Dec. 1979, CL; LvdP, letter to Barbara Maltbee, 22 Apr. 1980, LvdPA.
12. LvdP, letter to Piet Koornhof, 1 Jan. 1980, LvdPA; M. Tamarkin, *The Making of Zimbabwe: Decolonization in Regional and International Politics*; Stephen John Stedman, *Peacemaking in Civil War: International Mediation in Zimbabwe, 1974–1980*.
13. 'Zimbabwe Independence Celebrations 17–19 Apr. 1980' documents, LvdPA; Michael Shea, interview with author, 21 Apr. 1999; John Bridcutt, 'Rebellion!', BBC 2, 1999.
14. Lord Carrington, letter to author, 13 Oct. 1998; Robin Renwick, interview with author, 14 Mar. 1999; Charles Powell, interview with author, 3 Aug. 2000; Ewen Fergusson, interview with author; Piet Koornhof, interview with author, 14 Feb. 1998; Pik Botha, interview with James Sanders, 11 Dec. 2000.
15. LvdP, Charity Commission application, 6 Mar. 1992, LvdPA.
16. LvdP, letter to Rowan Cronje, 12 Jan. 1980; LvdP, letter to Piet Koornhof, 25 Apr. 1980, LvdPA.
17. LvdP, letter to Piet Koornhof, 2 Sept. 1980; Piet Koornhof, letter to LvdP, 3 Oct. 1980, LvdPA.
18. Sampson, *Mandela*, pp. 331–2, 338–9, 352 & 362.

32
1. *Mail on Sunday*, 14 Dec. 1986; LvdP, letter to Airey Neave, including memorandum on Conservatism (Feb. 1976), LvdPA.
2. LvdP, letter to Charles Janson, 9 Aug. 1977; LvdP, letter to Margaret Thatcher, 18 May 1977; Margaret Thatcher, letters to LvdP, 23 Aug. 1977, 24 July 1978 & 24 May 1979, LvdPA.
3. LvdP, letter to Airey Neave, 28 July 1979; LvdP, letter to Ian Smith, 30 July 1979; memorandum on Rhodesia I, 25 July 1979, & II, 28 July 1979, LvdPA.
4. Margaret Thatcher, *The Downing Street Years*, pp. 74–78 & 521.
5. Charles Janson, letter to LvdP, 30 May 1981; LvdP, letter to F. Van Zyl Slabbert, 2 Sept. 1980; LvdP, letter to Doris Langley, 4 June 1981; LvdP, letter to the BBC, 20 Nov. 1981, LvdPA; Peter Bevan, 'The Woman at Number Ten', Central Television, 29 Mar. 1983; Peter Bevan, interview with author, 27 Sept. 2000; see for example, *The Sunday Times*, 3 Apr. 1983; *The Observer*, 3 Apr. 1983: '[Mrs Thatcher] was interviewed by Sir Laurens van der Post (the thinking Royal's Terry Wogan), who grovelled dutifully in return for his knighthood. Not that he seemed to have done much homework'; LvdP, letter to Margaret Thatcher, 17 Nov. 1980, LvdPA; Janet Campbell, interview with author.
6. Charles Powell, interview with author, 3 Aug. 2000.
7. LvdP, letter to Ian Gow, 6 Feb. 1990; LvdP, letters to Charles Powell, 15 & 19 Feb. 1990; Charles Powell, letter to LvdP, 16 Feb. 1990, LvdPA; Charles Powell, interview with author, 3 Aug. 2000.
8. Seumas Milne, *The Enemy Within: The Secret War Against The Miners*, pp. 364–75; Woodrow Wyatt, *The Journals of Woodrow Wyatt, Vol. I*.
9. Margaret Thatcher, interview with author, 26 Sept. 2000; Walter Felgate, interview with James Sanders, 18 June 1999.
10. *Sunday Telegraph*, 24 Oct. 1982; Thatcher, op. cit., p. 186; LvdP, memorandum on the Falklands War I, 7 Apr. 1982; memorandum on the Falklands War II, 15 May 1982, LvdPA; *The Times*, 14 May 1982.
11. Margaret Thatcher, letter to LvdP, 7 Feb. 1985, in which Mangosuthu Gatsha Buthelezi's name is spelled 'Gatsba Butheleze'; LvdP, memorandum on South Africa, Oct. 1985, in which Buthelezi's name is spelled 'Gatsba Butlalezi', LvdPA.
12. Thatcher, op. cit., pp. 512–14, 521 & 531–33; Sampson, *Mandela*, p. 321.
13. LvdP, memorandum on Ethnic Minorities of Namibia (27 Oct. 1989); Margaret Thatcher, letter to LvdP, 17 Nov. 1989; LvdP, memorandum: 'The Hour of the Karamazovs', 29 Nov. 1989; Charles Powell, letter to LvdP, 3 Dec. 1989; LvdP, letter to Michael Alexander, 4 Sept. 1980, LvdPA.

33
1. Eva Monley, interview with author; John Huston, letter to LvdP, 29 Feb. 1952; R. L. Goldfarb, letter to Leonard Woolf, 3 July 1951, C&W.
2. Kathleen Bourne, letter to the Hogarth Press, 5 July 1954; David J. Grimes, letter to LvdP, 2 May 1955; Norah Smallwood, letter to LvdP, 11 May 1955; Norah Smallwood, letter to Harold Grieg, 11 May 1955; Jay Shanker, letter to John Charlton, 7 Feb. 1983; Norah Smallwood, letter to LvdP, 12 July 1977, C&W; Dan Auiler, *Vertigo: The Making of a Hitchcock Classic*, pp. 2–3, 5–6 & 33; Francois Truffaut, *Hitchcock*, pp. 248–49; Donald Spoto, *The Dark Side of Genius: The Life of Alfred Hitchcock*, pp. 410–11; see also [Salisbury] *Sunday Mail*, 21 Aug. 1955.
3. Jay Shanker, letter to John Charlton, 7 Feb. 1983, C&W; LvdP, letter to Vice President, Legal Affairs, Paramount, 14 May 1990, LvdPA; Eva Monley, interview with author.
4. LvdP, letter to Walt Disney, 20 Aug. 1956, LvdPA.

5. Grahame Amey, interview with author, 10 Aug. 2000; Grahame Amey, letter to Alan Stratford Johns, 17 Aug. 1976, LvdPA; memorandum on LvdP's Film Rights (28 Jan. 1977), C&W; Grahame Amey, letter to LvdP, 27 July 1976, LvdPA; Richard Thomas, letter to Norah Smallwood, 25 Jan. 1977, C&W; LvdP, letter to Alex Noble, 4 May 1977, LvdPA; see also *The Sunday Times*, 8 May 1977.

6. Richard Thomas to Dolores Heeb, 4 July 1977; LvdP, letter to Grahame Amey, 24 June 1977; Richard Bell, letter to Sue Turner, 13 Oct. 1977; LvdP, letter to Professor T. Satoh, 3 Oct. 1978; Grahame Amey, letter to G. Arnold, 8 June 1979; 'Xhabbo: An Introduction', unsigned, undated memorandum; LvdP, letter to Bill, 13 Apr. 1977, LvdPA.

7. LvdP, letter to G. W. G. Brown, 1 July 1977. Within sixteen months the South African Department of Information was engulfed in what became known as the Information Scandal or 'Muldergate'. A minor aspect of this scandal was the funding of 'friendly' feature films, see Mervyn Rees & Chris Day, *Muldergate: The Story of the Info Scandal*, pp. 93–94; see also O'Meara, op. cit., pp. 229–49; James Sanders, *South Africa and the International Media, 1972–1979: A Struggle for Representation*, pp. 54–81.

8. Grahame Amey, interview with author, 10 Aug. 2000.

9. LvdP, letter to G. W. G. Brown, 1 July 1977; LvdP, letters to Barbara Maltbee, 19 Nov. 1979 & 22 Apr. 1980; Barbara Maltbee, letter to LvdP, 18 Oct. 1979, LvdPA.

10. Eva Monley, interview with author; LvdP, letter to Albie Venter, 21 May 1980; LvdP, letter to Grahame Amey, 15 Aug. 1992, LvdPA.

11. Mikael Salomen, *A Far Off Place*, feature film, 1993; LvdP, letter to Hazel Adair, 17 Aug. 1993; LvdP, letter to Randall J. Dicks, 25 May 1993; LvdP, letter to Grahame Amey, 25 May 1993; Eva Monley, interview with author; Jeffrey Katzenberg, letter to LvdP, 22 Dec. 1993; Walt Disney Pictures Participation Statement Period Ended: Dec. 31, 1996; LvdP claimed '. . . very much in confidence, a showing to members of the Prince of Wales's family and establishment was a huge success' (LvdP, letter to Jeffrey Katzenberg, 28 Oct. 1993), LvdPA.

12. Kimiyoshi Yuba, letter to LvdP, 26 Apr. 1979; LvdP, letter to Nick, 30 July 1979; LvdP, letters to Nagisa Oshima, 11 Oct. & 6 Dec. 1979; Nagisa Oshima, letters to LvdP, 18 Feb. & 22 Mar. 1980, LvdPA.

13. Barbara Maltbee, letter to LvdP, 13 Mar. 1980; LvdP, letter to Barbara Maltbee, 27 Mar. 1980; LvdP, letters to Nagisa Oshima, 18 Feb., 22 Mar., 8, 14 Apr. & 19 May 1980, LvdPA.

14. LvdP, letters to Nagisa Oshima, 15 Aug. 1980 & 12 Jan. 1984; Nagisa Oshima, letters to LvdP, 9 July, 19 Nov. 1981, 7 June & 28 July 1982; Glinwood Films Limited, memorandum on Budget, 3 Nov. 1981; Kuniko Usui, letter to LvdP, 10 June 1983; Paul Webster, letter to LvdP, 17 June 1983, LvdPA; *Melody Maker*, 22 Jan. 1972, republished in Hanif Kureishi & Jon Savage (eds.), *The Faber Book of Pop*, pp. 391–96; Audie Bock, *Japanese Film Directors*, pp. 311–330; Christopher Lyon (ed.), *The International Dictionary of Films and Filmmakers, Vol. I: Films*, pp. 16–17.

15. Oshima, *Merry Christmas Mr Lawrence*, feature film, 1983.

16. Agreement between LvdP & Peter David Bevan, 30 May 1981; Peter Bevan, letter to LvdP, 26 Aug. 1981 & 23 June 1982; Lesli Lia Glatter & Eva Monley Agreement with LvdP, 23 Sept. 1988, LvdPA; see also Peter Bevan, *Night of the New Moon*, BBC Radio 4, 15 Sept. 1988.

17. 'The Sword and the Doll': transcript of meeting with LvdP, Sonia Herman Dolz and Eva Monley, London, 13–15 July 1996; Eva Monley, interview with author.

18. Candice van Runkle, letter to LvdP, 12 Jan. 1989; Claire Townsend & Candice van Runkle, letter to LvdP, 28 Feb. 1989; LvdP, letters to Claire Townsend & Candice van Runkle, 12 Mar. & 2 Dec. 1989; LvdP, letter to Claire Townsend, 30 Aug. 1990; Claire Townsend, letter to LvdP, 17 July 1994; Candice van Runkle, letter to LvdP, 20 July 1994; Eva Monley, interview with author.

34

1. *Evening Standard*, 1 Dec. 1982; *Sunday Telegraph*, 17 Oct. 1982; *The Listener*, 18 Nov. 1982; *The Sunday Times*, 24 Oct. 1982; *The Times*, 21 Oct. 1982.

2. *New York Times* Book Review, 1 May 1983; *Los Angeles Times*, 20 May 1983.

3. J. D. F. Jones, *London Review of Books*, 3 Feb. 1983.

4. *Sunday Telegraph*, 7 & 14 Aug. 1977; *The Times*, 24 Sept. & 21 Nov. 1977; *Sunday Telegraph*, letter to the Hogarth Press, 5 Aug. 1977, C&W; Frances Baruch, interview with author; LvdP, letters to Norah Smallwood, 31 July 1977, 17 Mar. 1981, 13 & 15 Jan. 1982; John Charlton, memorandum, 17 Feb. 1982, C&W.

5. LvdP, letter to Norah Smallwood, 11 Feb. 1982; Norah Smallwood, letter to LvdP, 19 Feb. 1982, C&W; Larry Hughes, letter to the Hogarth Press, 18 June 1982, WM; LvdP, letter to the Hogarth Press, undated; unsigned memorandum, 17 Sept. 1982; John Charlton, letter to LvdP, 28 Oct. 1983; Jill Rose, letter to LvdP, 14 June 1983, C&W.

6. *Yet Being*, pp. 212 & 228: 'Midnight shakes memory, like a madman a dead geranium' was corrected in later editions to 'Midnight shakes memory, as a madman shakes a dead geranium.' 'Webster was much obsessed with death he saw the skull beneath the skin, eyes that dull and a lipless grin' was corrected to 'Webster was

much possessed by death and saw the skull beneath the skin; and breastless creatures underground leaned backward with a lipless grin.'; T. S. Eliot, *Little Gidding*, 1942 in T. S. Eliot, *The Complete Poems and Plays*, pp. 193–94; LvdP, letter to Mr Elliott, 11 May 1959, LvdPA.

7. *Yet Being*, pp. 21, 31, 38, 45 & 319; *About Blady*, p. 1.
8. LvdP, letter to Frederic Carpenter, 11 May 1964; *The Oldie*, Sept. 1997; Margaret Legum, interview with author, 27 May 2001.
9. 'Journal, 1928–1931', LvdPA; *Cape Times*, 8 Mar. 1930.
10. 'Campbell, Plomer, Paton & Myself'; LvdP, letter to Ingaret Giffard-Young, 1 Nov. 1941, LvdPA.
11. Carpenter, op. cit.; LvdP, letter to John Charlton, 25 July 1988; LvdP, letters to William Plomer, 10 July & 3 Aug. 1965, DUL; LvdP, letters to Frederic Carpenter, 21 May 1964 & 8 Dec. 1977, LvdPA.
12. LvdP, letter to John Charlton, 5 Sept. 1991.
13. LvdP, 'Notes for E. Huxley for *Times* Obit.', Jan. 1965, C&W; Lvdp, letter to Frances Phillips, 13 Aug. 1972, WM; LvdP, biographical note, 1991; LvdP, Charity Commission application, 6 Mar. 1992, LvdPA; *Heart*, p. 167; *Thunder*, p. 222; Mark Time, No. 5, 1942, LvdPA.
14. Dean King, *Patrick O'Brian: A Life Revealed*; Nicholas Shakespeare, *Bruce Chatwin*; Michael Crick, *Jeffrey Archer: Stranger Than Fiction*; 'Panorama: Jeffrey Archer – a Life of Lies', BBC 1, July 2001; Valerie Grove, *Laurie Lee: The Well-Loved Stranger, Sight & Sound*, May 2000; *The Observer*, 5 Dec. 1999 & 3 Sept. 2000, *Sunday Telegraph*, 5 Sept. 1999; *Daily Telegraph*, 15 Apr. 2000; *Independent on Sunday*, 28 June 1998.
15. *Mantis Carol*, p. 1; Leonard Woolf, *The Letters of Leonard Woolf*, p. 360, Leonard Woolf, letter to Lyn Irvine Newman, 1 Aug. 1957; *White Bushman*, p. 172.
16. *The Times*, 9 Sept. 1999, citing Anthony Storr, *Feet of Clay: A Study of Gurus*.
17. Storr, op. cit., pp. xi–xii.
18. Jack Cope, letter to LvdP, 11 Mar. 1976; LvdP, letter to Jack Cope, 17 Mar. 1976, NELM.
19. Janet Campbell, letter to author, 22 Jan. 1999.

35
1. Leonard Woolf & Trekkie Ritchie Parsons, *Love Letters (1941–1968)*, p. 183, 12 Nov. 1952.
2. LvdP & Jane Taylor, *Testament to the Bushmen*; LvdP; *The Lost World of the Kalahari*, ill. ed.; *White Bushman*, op. cit.; *Rock Rabbit*, op. cit.; Robert Hinshaw, letter to T. C. Robertson, 13 Dec. 1986, LvdPA.
3. LvdP, Desk Diary (1981–1984); LvdP, letter to Mrs Solzhenitsyn, 28 June 1983, LvdPA; LvdP, letter to Frances Phillips, 13 Aug. 1972: '[I have] fought as bravely and much longer and with as great personal agony as Solyetznitzen [*sic*] against the social tyranny in his country', WM; Sheila Milne, letter to LvdP, 4 June 1989, LvdPA; 'Yo-Yo Ma: Distant Memories', Channel 4, 1993; Nirad C. Chaudhuri, letters to LvdP, 12 Nov. 1968 & 22 June 1974, LvdPA.
4. Ian Player, 'My Friend Nkunzimalanga' in *Rock Rabbit*, pp. 64, 66 & 71–72; Ian Player, 'Trail to the Future' in *Wilderness*, pp. 16–19; LvdP, letters to T. C. Robertson, 20 Dec. 1969, 5, 25 Oct. 1973 & 17 Feb. 1974, CL; LvdP, 'Wisdom from the Wilderness', *The Sunday Times*, 22 July 1973; *White Bushman*, p. 139; Ian Player, letter to LvdP, 1 Nov. 1979, LvdPA; Stedall, 'All Africa Within Us', BBC 1, 1975.
5. Player, 'Nkunzimalanga' in *Rock Rabbit*, pp. 73 & 76, 'Trail to the Future' in *Wilderness*, pp. 16–19 & 'A Portrait in Black and White', typescript; LvdP, letter to Ian Player, 20 Dec. 1983, LvdPA; Ian Player, interview with author; Vance G. Martin, letter to LvdP, 31 July 1996; Sir David Checketts, letter to LvdP, 1 Nov. 1991, LvdPA.
6. Player, 'Trail to the Future' in *Wilderness*, p. 22; Robert D. Richardson Jr., *Henry Thoreau: A Life of the Mind*; Player, Introduction to *Wilderness*, p. 7; LvdP, Preface to *Wilderness*, pp. 9–12; LvdP, 'Wilderness: A Way of Truth' in *Wilderness*, p. 43; *White Bushman*, p. 141.
7. Player, 'Nkunzimalanga' in *Rock Rabbit*, pp. 74–77; LvdP, paper on Wilderness, undated, LvdPA; 'Wilderness: A Way of Truth' in *Wilderness*, pp. 40–42; LvdP, 'Wilderness and Jung' in *Wilderness*, p. 109; LvdP, 'Man as redeemer or destroyer' in *Wilderness*, p. 14; Ian Player, interview with author.
8. Ian Player, letters to LvdP, 7 July & 13 Oct. 1977; LvdP, letter to Piet Koornhof, 19 July 1980; LvdP, letters to Ian Player, 24 June 1980 & 30 Dec. 1981; LvdP, letter to Alan Lennon, 22 Apr. 1980; LvdP, letters to E. E. Dunlop, 3 Apr & 6 May 1980; E. E. Dunlop, letter to LvdP, 30 Apr. 1980; LvdP, letter to Wally O'Grady, 8 May 1980; LvdP, letter to Malcolm Fraser, 19 June 1980; LvdP, letter to Alan Sellar, 15 Apr. 1982; LvdP, letter to Vance G. Martin, 15 Apr. 1982; LvdP, letter to Margaret Thatcher, 26 Apr. 1983; LvdP, letter to George Younger, 17 June 1983, LvdPA; Ian Player, interview with author.
9. *Daily Telegraph*, 12 Aug. 1995 & 11 July 1998; Robin Page, 'The Lark Ascending' in *Rock Rabbit*, pp. 295–300; Ed Posey, conversation with author; LvdP, letter to Ian Player, 25 Oct. 1993; Nic Slabbert, letters to LvdP, 28 July & 1 Aug. 1992; LvdP, letters to Nic Slabbert, 30 July & 1 Aug. 1992; Anna Holmes, letter to LvdP, 23 Mar. 1992; LvdP, letter to Anna Holmes, 7 Apr. 1992; Planet In Change, International Symposium, brochure, LvdPA.
10. Taylor & Bellinger, 'Testament to the Bushmen', BBC 2, 1984; *Testament*, p. 123; *Thunder*, p. 148.

11. *Lost World*, ill. ed., pp. 256–57 & 260–61; *Thunder*, pp. 135, 138 & 141–43; Jane Taylor, interview with author, 12 Sept. 2000.
12. *White Bushman*, pp. 3, 7, 17, 20, 79–83 & 306; Jung, *Collected Works, Vol. IX*, Part 1, 'The Archetype and the Collective Unconscious', pp. 207–254 and *Vol. XI: Psychology and Religion*, pp. 355–470.
13. Ibid., pp. 134–6.
14. Ibid., pp. 87–88, 90, 93, 99–100, 113, 149, 157, 221, 225–26 & 273; Guy Butler, 'Sir Laurens van der Post: A Reminiscence', *English Academy Review*, 1996.
15. *Private Eye*, 31 Oct. 1986; *The Times Literary Supplement*, 23 Jan. 1987; *The Independent*, 15 Nov. 1986.

Part Six
36
1. Jenny Chapman, letter to LvdP, 25 June 1991; LvdP, letter to Jenny Chapman, 1 July 1994, C&W; Private Information.
2. LvdP, letter to Professor Needleman, 15 Oct. 1979; Carolyn Grant Fay, letter to LvdP, 14 Jan. 1985; Patty Barron, letter to LvdP, 16 May 1983; Harry A. Wilmer, letters to LvdP, 20 Dec. 1983 & 24 Feb. 1985; LvdP, letter to R. B. Woods, 25 Sept. 1992; Jane Bedford, letter to Alison, 2 Dec. 1992, LvdP; Jeremy Gordin, telex to Mike Allen, 23 July 1984, C&W; LvdP, Desk Diary (1983), LvdPA.
3. Dr Ian McCallum, interview with author, 6 July 2000; LvdP, letter to Generous Threesome, 9 Jan. 1991; Jill Wannop (BUPA), letter to LvdP, 23 Apr. 1991, LvdPA.
4. A collective source: 'Friends' is used in various places in Part Six. 'Friends' consists of Lucia van der Post, Neil Crichton-Miller, Emma Crichton-Miller, Janet Campbell, Frances Baruch, Louise Stein, Bill Atkinson, Eva Monley, Ronald Cohen, Tom Bedford, Jane Bedford & Kate Bertaud; LvdP, letter to W. Gray, 27 Oct. 1992; LvdP, letter to Doris Langley, 30 Aug. 1994, LvdPA.
5. Winifred Rushforth, 1885–1983, unsigned obituary notice; LvdP, letter to Winifred Rushforth, 16 May 1983, LvdPA; [Johannesburg] *Sunday Times*, 2 Aug. 1987; LvdP, letter to Kathleen Raine, 6 June 1992, LvdPA; Alex Jardine, interview with author, 3 Feb. 2001; Ian Player, interview with author; Tom Bedford, interview with author.
6. Alison Samuel, letter to LvdP, 13 Jan. 1985, C&W; *About Blady*, pp. 42, 44, 47–50 & 75–79; *The Times*, 31 Oct. 1985; Jessica Douglas-Home, interview with author, 19 Oct. 1999.
7. *About Blady*, pp. 64, 90, 98, 101, 104–8, 115–16 & 129; Campbell, *Dark Horse*, p. 47.
8. *About Blady*, pp. vii, 137–40, 142–45 & 148; Rosemary de Llorens, letter to LvdP, 22 Apr. 1953, LvdPA.
9. LvdP, Passport: L6257 & L2122; LvdP, letter to Rosemary de Llorens, 22 Oct. 1956, LvdPA; LvdP, letter to Norah Smallwood, 30 Apr. 1953; Norah Smallwood, letter to LvdP, C&W; *About Blady*, pp. 160, 168, 228–32 & 251–54.
10. *The Times*, 16 Nov. 1991; *Financial Times*, 16 Nov. 1991; *New York Times* Book Review, 2 Aug. 1992.
11. Rosemary de Llorens, letters to LvdP, 24 Jan. 1979, 4 Dec. 1987, 10 Mar. 1991, 23, 28 Mar., 2 July & 7 Oct. 1992; LvdP, letters to Rosemary de Llorens, 28 Feb., 15 Sept., 3 Oct. 1991 & 26 May 1992, LvdPA.
12. Sister Maria Basini, letter to author, 1 Oct. 2000.
13. *Mantis Carol*, pp. 158 & 165; Kabir, *The Bijak*.
14. *Thunder*, op. cit.; *Lost World*, ill. ed., op. cit.; *Testament*, op. cit.
15. Helen Luke, *Old Age*, pp. 1–24; LvdP, letters to Helen Luke, 14 Feb. 1977 & 15 May 1992; Helen Luke, letter to LvdP, 2 Mar. 1977, LvdPA; Homer, *The Odyssey*, p. 163.
16. *Thunder*, p. 11; LvdP, letter to Helen Luke, 12 July 1988, LvdPA.
17. LvdP, letters to Helen Luke, 12 July, Autumn 1988, 19 Feb., 27 May 1989, 15 May 1992, 5 June 1994 & undated; Helen Luke, letters to LvdP, 7 Dec. 1988, 8 Mar., 25 Apr. 1989 & 22 July 1992, LvdPA.
18. Helen Luke, letters to LvdP, 3 Dec. 1981 & 15 July 1993; LvdP, letter to Helen Luke, 30 Dec. 1981; Robert Luke, letters to LvdP, 14 & 23 Jan. 1995; LvdP, Helen Luke: obituary, unpublished, 9 Jan. 1995; LvdP, letter to Robert Luke, 26 Jan. 1995, LvdPA.
19. *Thunder*, pp. 3–4, 20–21, 49, 53–55, 57, 63–64, 72–73 & 77–78; Jung, *Collected Works, Vol. V: Symbols of Transformation*, p. 205.
20. *Resurgence*, No. 162, Jan./Feb. 1994.
21. LvdP, letters to John Charlton, 26 Sept., 29 Oct. & 4 Nov. 1992; LvdP, *Feather Fall*.
22. LvdP, letters to Alison Samuel, 4 Aug. 1993, 4 Apr., 7 Sept. 1994 & 27 May 1995; Alison Samuel, letters to LvdP, 11 Aug. 1993, 13 Jan. & 7 July 1995; LvdP, letter to Jenny Chapman, 9 Aug. 1994; Jane Bedford, letter to Alison Samuel, 2 June 1995; LvdP, letter to John Charlton, 21 Aug. 1995, LvdPA.
23. LvdP, letter to John Charlton, 21 Aug. 1995; John Charlton, letter to LvdP, 8 Aug. 1995; LvdP, letter to Jean-Marc Pottiez, 26 Aug. 1995; LvdP, letter to Alison Samuel, 16 Sept. 1995, LvdPA.
24. LvdP, letters to Alison Samuel, 18 Jan. & 27 Apr. 1996; Dibb, Lupton & Bloomhead, letter to LvdP, 12 June 1996; John R. Murray, letter to LvdP, 21 May 1996; LvdP, letter to The Chairman, The Society of Authors, 10 May 1978: 'I was very sad . . . to find that the Society of Authors had decided to become a trade union. I would have thought that evidence of the harm trade unionism has done . . . and in particular the extent

to which they have diminished the freedom of the individual and respect for individual conscience, would have been enough to deter a body which represents the artist.'

25. Carmen Callil, letter to LvdP, 28 Apr. 1993; LvdP, letter to Jean-Marc Pottiez, 26 Aug. 1995; LvdP, letter to Jessica Douglas-Home, 3 Sept. 1996; LvdP, letter to author, 4 Sept. 1996, LvdPA; John Murray, conversation with author.

26. *Admiral's Baby*, US book jacket; *The Times Literary Supplement*, 31 Jan. 1997; *The Sunday Times*, 6 Oct. 1996; *Literary Review*, Oct. 1996; *The Spectator*, 19 Oct. 1996.

37

1. Private Information; *Sunday Express*, 9 Nov. 1989; Mountbatten of Burma, letter to LvdP, 17 May 1974; LvdP, letter to Lord Mountbatten, 31 May 1974, LvdPA.

2. David Checketts, letter to LvdP, 15 July 1976; LvdP, letters to Alistair Milne, 23 July & 23 Dec. 1976, LvdPA; Jonathan Dimbleby, *The Prince of Wales: A Biography*, pp. 302–4, citing FCO, letter to David Checketts, 9 Dec. 1976 [RA/POW/EA/76].

3. LvdP, letter to The Prince of Wales, undated; Chris Plewman, letter to LvdP, 28 Sept. 1983, LvdPA; Dimbleby, op. cit., pp. 495–96, citing The Prince of Wales, Foreign Diaries, 2 Apr. 1987; *The Times*, 8 Apr. 1987.

4. Stephen Lamport, letter to author, 13 Mar 2000.

5. Janet Campbell, letter to author, 22 Jan. 1999; Janet Campbell, interview with author, 18 Oct. 2000; LvdP, letter to Helen Luke, 18 Aug. 1992; LvdP, letter to The Prince of Wales, 1 Apr. 1991, LvdPA.

6. *Daily Mail*, 29 Nov. 1995.

7. LvdP, letter to Dr Carmen Blacker, 14 Mar. 1994; Janet Campbell, letter to author, 22 Jan. 1999; *Private Eye*, 22 Apr. 1983.

8. *Private Eye*, 19 Feb., 1 Apr., 13 May, 8, 22 July, 5 Aug., 30 Sept. 1988 & 18 Apr. 1997.

9. Janet Campbell, letter to author, 22 Jan. 1999.

10. Private Information; LvdP, letter to Lady Esher, 1 Apr. 1994, LvdPA; Dimbleby, op. cit., p. 355; Andrew Morton, *Diana: Her True Story – In Her Own Words*, pp. 43, 127, 131 & 140.

11. Morton, op. cit., p. 140; Alan McGlashan, letter to LvdP, 5 Feb. 1983 [Private Source]; *Sunday Mirror*, 10 Dec. 1995; *Daily Mail*, 11 Dec. 1995 & 20 June 2001; *Mail on Sunday*, 9 June 2001.

12. Morton, op. cit., p. 140; Alan McGlashan, letter to LvdP, 4 Nov. 1995 [Private Source]; LvdP, letter to Alan McGlashan, 7 Nov. 1995, LvdPA.

13. *The Times*, 10 Sept. 1996; Humphrey Carpenter, *Robert Runcie*, pp. 221, 253.

14. LvdP, Notes for Ingaret, 3 Dec. 1971, LvdPA.

15. LvdP, letters to The Prince of Wales, undated & 1 Nov. 1978, LvdPA; Dimbleby, op. cit., p. 304, citing FCO, letter to David Checketts, 9 Dec. 1976 [RA/POW/EA/76].

16. LvdP, letter to The Prince of Wales, 29 Apr. 1995; LvdP, letter to Janet Campbell, 10 Apr. 1995; Tom Batho, letter to LvdP, 11 Jan. 1985; LvdP, memorandum on Nigeria, 1988; memorandum on the Role of the University, 1987; memorandum on Romania, 9 Mar. 1989; memorandum on Indonesia, Sept. 1989, LvdPA.

17. Speech made by The Prince of Wales at a Dinner for Heads of Delegation attending the World Conference 'Saving the Ozone Layer' at the British Museum, London, 6 Mar. 1989; LvdP, letters to The Prince of Wales, 8 Jan. 1990 & 4 Aug. 1995; LvdP, letters to the Very Revd. James Park Morton, 4 June & 28 Aug. 1995, LvdPA.

18. Dr Carmen Blacker, letter to LvdP, 17 Nov. 1990; LvdP, letters to The Prince of Wales, 25 May 1992, 8 May 1993 & 21 Aug. 1996; LvdP, memorandum on Botswana, 30 Apr. 1996; Stephen Lamport, letter to LvdP, 19 Apr. 1996; The Prince of Wales, letter to Dr Q. K. J. Masire, 28 May 1996; The Prince of Wales, letter to Malcolm Rifkind, 28 May 1996, LvdPA.

19. Private Information; *Daily Mail*, 18 Dec. 1996; LvdP, letter to Arianna Huffington, 23 Apr. 1996, LvdPA.

20. LvdP, memorandum on Indonesia, Sept. 1989, LvdPA.

38

1. LvdP, letter to Olivier Bernier, 16 Jan. 1989; LvdP, letter to Andrea Nachtigall, 26 July 1993; T. J. Bennett, letter to Ronald Cohen, 6 Mar. 1992; T. J. Bennett, letter to Charity Commissioners, 6 Mar. 1992, including LvdP, Charity Commission application; Miss D. F. Taylor, letter to T. J. Bennett, 3 Dec. 1992; LvdP, letter to Neil Crichton-Miller, 28 Jan. 1993, LvdPA; Ronald Cohen, interview with author.

2. LvdP, letters to Harry Oppenheimer, 11 Oct 1988 & 20 May 1993; LvdP, 'A Thought for the Future' for the Company of Seven, undated, LvdPA; Arman Simone, interview with author, 21 Apr. 2001.

3. Lucia van der Post, interview with author.

4. LvdP, letters to Arman Simone, 4 Feb. 1988, 18 Apr., 1 Aug. 1989; 18 & 30 Apr. 1990; Ronald Cohen, letter to LvdP, 9 Aug. 1990; LvdP, letter to Julian David, 11 Aug. 1990; LvdP, letter to Theo Abt, 6 May 1991; LvdP, letter to Patrick Tummon, 2 July 1990, LvdPA; Bleek, *Specimens of Bushman Folklore*, to be republished in 2001.

5. LvdP also referred to the Company of Seven as being a re-creation of Lord Milner's 'Kindergarten', a group of young men who had assisted in the reconstruction of South Africa after the Boer War and, following their return to London, had operated as a 'think-tank' and founded the journal, *The Round Table*.

LvdP wrote: 'I am certain that a new "Round Table" around Tom [Bedford], started by our little Company of Seven, will form the future of South Africa.' (LvdP, letter to Arman Simone, 23 Nov. 1988); LvdP, letters to Arman Simone, 7 Oct., 8 Dec. 1988, 2 May, 20 July, 9 Sept 1989 & 23 Jan. 1993; LvdP, letter to Bill Pilder, 15 Mar. 1988; LvdP, letter to Doug Greene, 27 Jan. 1993; Arman Simone, letter to LvdP, 2 Feb. 1989, LvdPA; Tom Bedford, interview with author; during 1995 Arman & Fera Simone visited the Highgrove gardens, see LvdP, letter to The Prince of Wales, 29 Apr. 1995; Arman Simone, letter to LvdP, 31 Oct. 1995, LvdPA.

6. LvdP, letter to Arman Simone, 28 Dec. 1992; LvdP, letter to Carolyn Fay, 21 Oct. 1992; LvdP, letter to Dr Gerwin David, 23 July 1991; LvdP, letter to Robert Hinshaw, 22 Feb. 1996; Ronald Cohen, letter to F. E. C. Brown, 29 Oct. 1996, LvdPA.

7. Arman Simone, letter to LvdP, 6 Aug. 1996; LvdP, letters to Arman Simone, 3 June 1991, 2, 23 Nov. 1992, 20, 23 Jan., 6, 26 Feb., 17 Mar. 1993 & 26 July 1996; Doug Greene, letter to LvdP, 26 Jan. 1994; LvdP, letter to Caroline Fay, 21 Oct. 1992; LvdP, letter to Mabel McMillan, 26 May 1993; LvdP, letter to George Wagner, 23 July 1991; George Wagner, letters to LvdP, 30 Mar. 1990 & 18 Nov. 1991; LvdP, letter to Ian Gow, 11 Apr. 1990; LvdP, letter to Sam Francis, 25 Jan. 1993; LvdP, letter to Andrea Nachtigall, 26 July 1993; LvdP, letter to Dielle Fleischman, 24 July 1993; LvdP, letters to Larry Hughes, 8 Feb. & 2 Mar. 1992; LvdP, letter to Merrill Ford, 6 Mar. 1993, LvdPA; LvdP, 'Some Leaves of Grass' in *The Personal Address Book of Jan Christian Smuts*; Ronald Cohen, interview with author.

8. LvdP, letter to Harry Oppenheimer, 20 May 1993; LvdP, letter to Christiaan Sommerfelt, 21 July 1993, LvdPA; Ronald Cohen, interview with author.

9. Frank N. McMillan Jr., letter to LvdP, 26 Mar. 1985, LvdPA.

10. Frank N. McMillan III, 'A Biography of Frank N. McMillan, Jr.', Jan. 1989; LvdP, letter to Molly Tuby, 19 Apr. 1985; LvdP, letter to Carolyn Fay, 3 July 1991; Frank N. McMillan Jr., letters to LvdP, 26 Mar., 12 Aug. & 12 Sept. 1985; LvdP, letter to Frank N. McMillan Jr., 23 Sept. 1985, LvdPA.

11. LvdP, letter to Frank N. McMillan Jr., 23 Sept. 1985; David Rosen, letter to LvdP, 14 Apr. 1988; Frank N. McMillan III, letters to LvdP, 29 Mar. & 22 May 1989 & 7 June 1994; LvdP, letter to Frank N. McMillan III, 14 Feb. 1989, LvdPA.

12. Frank N. McMillan III, letter to LvdP, 22 May 1989; LvdP, letter to Frank N. McMillan III, 16 Mar. 1990, LvdPA.

13. Mabel McMillan, letter to LvdP, 9 Oct. 1989; LvdP, letters to Frank N. McMillan III, 27 July 1989, 29 Jan., 16 Mar., 6 Oct. 1990 & 14 Jan. 1991; Frank N. McMillan III, letters to LvdP, 17 Sept. 1989 & 28 Mar. 1990, LvdPA; LvdP, Foreword to David H. Rosen, 'Quest for the Lion and the Eagle: The Journals of Frank Ney McMillan Jr.'; David Rosen, letter to LvdP, 10 Jan. 1994, LvdPA.

14. Richard Osler, letter to LvdP, 19 Oct. 1996, LvdPA.

15. LvdP, letter to Lore Zeller, 3 Oct. 1992; LvdP, letter to Ronald Cohen, 3 June 1995, LvdPA; Lindsay Clarke, *The Chymical Wedding: A Romance*; Dr Gerwin Davis, letter to LvdP, 3 June 1991; LvdP, letter to Theo Abt, 21 Aug. 1992; LvdP, letter to Frank N. McMillan III, 14 Feb. 1989; LvdP, letter to Arman Simone, 10 Feb. 1989, LvdPA.

16. LvdP, letter to John Costello, 4 July 1991; LvdP, letters to Ronald Cohen, 8 July 1992 & 3 June 1995; LvdP, letter to Dr Gerwin Davis, 11 Mar. 1993; LvdP, letter to Charles Cameron, 20 Apr. 1994; 'Books brought from LvdP fund as of 30 June 1995'; LvdP, letter to Jean Albert, 9 Aug. 1995, LvdPA; Clarissa Pinkola Estes, *Women Who Run With The Wolves*; Ronald Cohen, interview with author, Julian David, interview with author, 12 May 2000.

17. Lawrence Hughes, letter to John Charlton, 17 Oct. 1984, C&W; LvdP, letter to Frances Phillips, 13 Aug. 1972, WM; LvdP, letter to Ronald Cohen, 18 Feb. 1993; LvdP, letter to Arman Simone, 18 Feb. 1993; LvdP, letter to Christer Salen, 19 Feb. 1993; LvdP, letter to the Company of Seven, 24 Feb. 1993; Christiaan Sommerfelt, letter to LvdP, 28 May 1993; Ronald Cohen, letter to Professor Struther Arnott, 24 Aug. 1993, LvdPA.

18. [Johannesburg] *Sunday Times*, 17 Oct. 1993; Ronald Cohen, letter to The Nobel Foundation, 10 Aug. 1993, LvdPA; Ronald Cohen, interview with author; Ronald Cohen to Prof. Struth Arnott, 24 Oct. 1994, LvdPA.

19. LvdP, letter to the Prince of Wales, 8 May 1993; LvdP, letters to the Dalai Lama, 11 Aug. 1993 & 25 Apr. 1994, LvdPA.

20. Ronald Cohen, letter to F. E. C. Brown, 29 Oct. 1996; LvdP, letter to the Company of Seven, 4 June 1996; LvdP, letter to Arman Simone, 3 Jan. 1995, LvdPA.

21. LvdP, letter to Arman Simone, 11 Nov. 1996; Arman Simone, letter to LvdP, 5 Dec. 1996, LvdPA.

39

1. Tom Lodge, *Black Politics in South Africa since 1945*, pp. 350–52; Sampson, *Mandela*, p. 314; see also Gerhard Mare & Georgina Hamilton, *An Appetite for Power: Buthelezi's Inkatha and the Politics of 'Loyal Resistance'*.

2. Walter Felgate, interview with James Sanders, 18 June 1999; Ian Player, interview with author; *Observer Foreign News Service*, 21 Mar. 1978.

3. LvdP, letter to Mangosuthu Buthelezi, 15 May 1978; Mangosuthu Buthelezi, letter to LvdP, 9 June 1978, LvdPA. The correspondence between Buthelezi and LvdP was normally addressed to 'Gatsha' and

'Oubaas' (old master). Tom Bedford was referred to as 'Kleinbaas' (little master).

4. LvdP, letters to Mangosuthu Buthelezi, 21 June 1984 & 17 May 1985; LvdP, letter to Tom Bedford, 19 Nov. 1984; LvdP, letter to Carolyne [Margaret Thatcher's Diary Secretary], June 1985, LvdPA; LvdP, Desk Diary (1985 & 1986), LvdPA.

5. Tom Bedford, letter to LvdP, 29 May 1986; LvdP, letter to Tom Bedford, 8 July 1986, LvdPA; Sampson, *Mandela*, pp. 343–44 & 363–65; Allister Sparks, *Tomorrow is Another Country: The Inside Story of South Africa's Negotiated Revolution*, pp. 24–36.

6. LvdP, Desk Diary (1988 & 1989), LvdPA; Mangosuthu Buthelezi, letter to LvdP, 1 June 1988; LvdP, letter to Charles Powell, 30 June 1988; LvdP, letter to Mangosuthu Buthelezi, 24 Apr. 1989, LvdPA.

7. Shula Marks, 'The dog that did not bark, or why Natal did not take off, ethnicity and democracy in South Africa: the case of KwaZulu-Natal', seminar paper, 2000; Sampson, *Mandela*, pp. 321 & 356–57; *Truth and Reconciliation Commission of South Africa Report, Vol. I*, p. 416; Thatcher, op. cit., pp. 520–24; *Africa Confidential*, 3 Mar. 1989.

8. Tom Bedford, interview with author; LvdP, letters to Mangosuthu Buthelezi, 24 Apr. & 3 Oct. 1989; LvdP, letter to Ian Gow, 29 July 1989; Mangosuthu Buthelezi, letter to LvdP, 29 May 1989; LvdP, letter to Robin Renwick, undated; Jane Brewster, letter to Christer Salen, 28 Sept. 1989; Mangosuthu Buthelezi, 'Memorandum presented at a meeting with the American Friends of Sir Laurens van der Post', London, Oct. 1989, LvdPA.

9. Thatcher, op. cit., pp. 531–32; F. W. de Klerk, *The Last Trek – A New Beginning: The Autobiography*, pp. 159–72 & 184; Sampson, *Mandela*, pp. 402–3 & 414; LvdP, memorandum on South Africa for Ian Gow and Margaret Thatcher, 13 Feb. 1990.

10. [Johannesburg] *Sunday Times*, 30 Dec. 1990; LvdP, speech to the Cape Town Press Club, 29 Nov. 1990.

11. Sampson, *Mandela*, pp. 456–66; see also Sparks, op. cit.; Patti Waldmeir, *Anatomy of a Miracle: The End of Apartheid and the Birth of the New South Africa*.

12. LvdP, letter to John Aspinall, 29 Nov. 1992, LvdPA; Charles Powell, interview with author, 3 Aug. 2000; John Aspinall, letter to Tom & Jane Bedford, 8 Dec. 1992, LvdPA; Walter Felgate, interview with James Sanders, 18 June 1999; Ian Player, interview with author.

13. Walter Felgate, interview with James Sanders, 18 June 1999.

14. *Sunday Telegraph*, 20 Mar. 1994.

15. Walter Felgate, interview with James Sanders, 18 June 1999; *Sunday Telegraph*, 13 Feb. 2000; John Aspinall, interview with author, 30 Sept. 1999; General Constand Viljoen, interview with author, 20 July 2000; Charles Powell, interview with author, 3 Aug. 2000.

16. LvdP, letter to Mangosuthu Buthelezi, 21 Feb. 1993, LvdPA.

17. *Africa Confidential*, 5 July 1996.

18. LvdP, memorandum on South Africa for The Prince of Wales, 5 Sept. 1993, LvdPA; Walter Felgate, interview with James Sanders, 18 June 1999; *The Independent*, 24 June 1993.

19. LvdP, letters to Mangosuthu Buthelezi, 21 Dec. & 28 Dec. 1993; Mangosuthu Buthelezi, letter to LvdP, 20 Dec. 1993, LvdPA.

20. E. Brookes & C. Webb, *A History of Natal*, pp. 238–43; P. S. Thompson, *Natalians First*, p. 1.

21. Mangosuthu Buthelezi, memorandum for LvdP, 7 Oct. 1993, LvdPA; Walter Felgate, interview with James Sanders, 18 June 1999; Waldmeir, op. cit., pp. 244–45.

22. Ian Uys, *Bushman Soldiers: Their Alpha and Omega*, pp. 257–59; General Constand Viljoen, interview with author, 20 July 2000; *The Observer*, 9 Mar. 1997.

23. General Constand Viljoen, interview with author, 20 July 2000; LvdP, letter to General Constand Viljoen, 30 Oct. 1993; General Constand Viljoen, letter to LvdP, 15 Dec. 1993, LvdPA.

24. LvdP, letter to Mangosuthu Buthelezi, 20 Jan. 1994, LvdPA.

25. General Constand Viljoen, interview with author, 20 July 2000; [Johannesburg] *Sunday Independent*, 25 Mar. 2001; Sampson, *Mandela*, pp. 481–85.

26. LvdP, letter to Mangosuthu Buthelezi, 7 Feb. 1994, LvdPA; *The Sunday Times*, 20 Feb. 1994; LvdP, letters to Christiaan Sommerfelt, 9 Mar. & 4 Apr. 1994, LvdPA.

27. Sampson, *Mandela*, pp. 485–94; LvdP, memorandum on the future of KwaZulu-Natal for Mangosuthu Buthelezi, 25 May 1994, LvdPA.

28. LvdP, letter to Christiaan Sommerfelt, 6 Apr. 1995, LvdPA; on the issue of political killings, see Marks, 'The dog that did not bark': 'It should be noted that not all violence in KwaZulu-Natal has died down: a good deal of what used to be called old-fashioned "faction fighting" which long preceded the 1980s continues.'

29. John Aspinall, letter to King Zwelithini ka Bhekuzulu, 7 May 1995, LvdPA.

30. LvdP, letters to Mangosuthu Buthelezi, 16 Aug. 1995 & 12 Mar. 1996, LvdPA.

31. Sampson, *Mandela*, pp. 534–36; de Klerk, op. cit., pp. 356–68; LvdP, letter to John Aspinall, 9 Aug. 1996; John Aspinall, letter to LvdP, 26 June 1996, LvdPA; *Daily Telegraph*, 16 Nov. 2000.

32. LvdP, letters to Christiaan Sommerfelt, 16 Aug. 1993 & 8 Mar. 1995; Christiaan Sommerfelt, letter to LvdP, 4 Aug. 1993, LvdPA.

33. LvdP, letters to Christiaan Sommerfelt, 3, 24, 30 Nov., 3 & 17 Dec. 1993, 'Notes on telephone conversation with Mr Sommerfelt', 29 Nov. 1993; LvdP, letter to Tom Vraalsen, 16 Mar. 1994; Mangosuthu Buthelezi, 'Message for the Oubaas' to Tom Bedford, 30 Nov. 1993; LvdP, letter to Chief Mangusothu Buthelezi, 9 June 1994, LvdPA.
34. Sampson, *Mandela*, pp. 486–87; LvdP, letters to Mangosuthu Buthelezi, 9 June, 6 July 1994 & 12 Mar. 1996; Mangosuthu Buthelezi, letter to Tom Bedford, 20 Feb. 1996, LvdPA.
35. LvdP, letter to Christiaan Sommerfelt, 15 Mar. 1996; Christiaan Sommerfelt letters to LvdP, 13 June, 17 Oct. & 19 Dec. 1994; see also LvdP, memorandum on South Africa II for The Prince of Wales, 21 Aug. 1996: 'I cannot understand why nobody in this country will accept what a horror story South Africa has become, when daily the curtain is lifted on the total inadequacy and, I believe corruption . . . of Mandela . . . I feel deeply worried about what the Foreign Office may plan for you, should you decide to go to South Africa next year. I think even your going could not fail to diminish the true picture the world outside should have of South Africa, and I wish in that regard it could be postponed', LvdPA.
36. *TRC Report, Vol. V*, pp. 230, 232–35; *Mail & Guardian*, 3 Nov. 2000; Professor Shula Marks, conversation with James Sanders.
37. *Mail & Guardian*, 26 May 2000.
38. Nelson Mandela, 'Last Words' in *Rock Rabbit*, p. 357.

40

1. LvdP, letter to Jean Albert, 12 Oct. 1995, LvdPA; Neil Crichton-Miller, letter to author, 23 Apr. 2001; LvdP, memorandum to the Company of Seven, 19 July 1991, LvdPA.
2. Lucia van der Post, letter to author, May 2001; LvdP, letter to Fredy Meier, 21 Nov. 1994, LvdPA; Friends, interviews with author; *The Way Things*, op. cit.; John Charlton, memorandum, 2 Nov. 1986; John Charlton, letter to Robin Baillie, 10 Mar. 1988, C&W; LvdP, letter to John Charlton, 2 Dec. 1988, LvdPA.
3. LvdP, letter to Cathie, 16 Nov. 1988; LvdP, letter to Dorothea Wallis, 14 Dec. 1988; LvdP, letter to Carolyn Fay, 23 Sept. 1988, LvdPA; Janet Campbell, letter to author, 22 Jan. 1999; Friends, interviews with author; Ingaret van der Post, letter to psychotherapist friend, 24 June 1980 [Private Source].
4. Dorothea Wallis, Address at Ingaret van der Post's Funeral, 8 May 1997; Friends, interviews with author.
5. Lucia van der Post, interview with author; Janet Campbell, letter to author, 22 Jan. 1999; Janet Campbell, interview with author, 18 Oct. 2000; Friends, interviews with author.
6. Neil Crichton-Miller, letter to author, 23 Apr. 2001.
7. Paul Semark, letter to LvdP, 23 June 1993, LvdPA; Jeremy Ractliffe, interview with author, 11 Feb. 1998; Paul Semark, interview with author, 11 Feb. 1998; LvdP, letter to Janet Campbell, 10 Apr. 1995; Janet Campbell, letter to author, 22 Jan. 1999; LvdP, letter to Winifred Rushforth, 2 Nov. 1978; LvdP, letter to The Prince of Wales, 14 Apr. 1995; Ingaret van der Post, letter to the Earl of Halsbury, 13 July 1981; the Earl of Halsbury, letter to Ingaret van der Post, 17 July 1981, LvdPA.
8. Friends, interviews with author; LvdP, Passport: 876109 F; LvdP, Desk Diary (1995 & 1996), LvdPA; *The Argus*, 18 Jan. 1995; 'Marjorie van der Post: Obituary', *The Times*, 27 Jan. 1995; LvdP, letter to Janet Campbell, Aug. 1995, LvdPA; Richard Osler, interview with author, 15 Dec. 2000.
9. LvdP, 'A Child of the Stars', Cathedral of St. John the Divine, New York, 22 Dec. 1991; LvdP, 'Let in the Wind', Cathedral of St. John the Divine, New York, Dec. 1992; LvdP, Sermon, Cathedral of St. John the Divine, New York, 17 Dec. 1995; LvdP, letters to Very Rev. James Parks Morton, 4 Aug. 1995 & 9 Dec. 1996; LvdP, *The Secret River: An African Myth*; Tessa Strickland, conversation with author.
10. Laurens van der Post Festival: 25–28 September, Boulder, Colorado, promotional leaflet; Dr Theo Abt, interview with author, 14 Feb. 2001; Lucia van der Post, interview with author.
11. *Rock Rabbit*, op. cit.; Stedall, 'Voice from the Bundu', BBC 2, Dec. 1997; *Evening Standard*, 16 Dec. 1996.
12. Friends, interviews with author; Lucia van der Post, *Cape Argus*, 8 Oct. 1999; Lawrence Hughes, 'Address for Laurens van der Post, London, December 20, 1996', in *Rock Rabbit*, pp. 347–51; *The Times*, 21 Dec. 1996; 'A Service of Thanksgiving to Celebrate the Life and Work of Sir Laurens van der Post CBE', 18 Mar. 1997; Ian Player, 'On A Free State Hill: Eulogy to Col. Sir Laurens van der Post CBE' in *We will lose something deep within ourselves if we allow wilderness to be destroyed*, Apr. 2000; '"Selamat Jalan" to Sir Laurens van der Post', 24 Jan. 1997; Mark Ingle, conversation with author.
13. Janet Campbell, letter to author, 22 Jan. 1999; Friends, interviews with author.

41

1. Plomer, *Double Lives*, p. 167; Janet Campbell, letter to author, 3 Feb. 1999.
2. Sister Maria Basini, letter to author, 1 Oct. 2000.
3. Attallah, op. cit., pp. 518–19.
4. LvdP, letter to Rebecca Adamson, 17 July 1996; LvdP, letter to Elspeth (the Office of The Prince of Wales), 8 Aug. 1996; Commander Richard Aylard, letter to LvdP, 4 Nov. 1996, LvdPA.
5. Lilias Sheepshanks, invitation to author, 5 Jan. 2001.

Select bibliography

Books by Laurens van der Post
In A Province, Hogarth Press, London, 1934
Venture To The Interior, Hogarth Press, London, 1952
The Face Beside The Fire, Hogarth Press, London, 1953
A Bar of Shadow, Hogarth Press, London, 1954
Flamingo Feather, Hogarth Press, London, 1955
The Dark Eye in Africa, Hogarth Press, London, 1955
The Lost World of the Kalahari, Hogarth Press, London, 1958
The Heart of the Hunter, Hogarth Press, London, 1961
The Seed and the Sower, Hogarth Press, London, 1963
Journey Into Russia, Hogarth Press, London, 1964, U. S. title: *A View of All the Russias*
A View of All the Russias, Illustrated ed., William Morrow, New York, 1967
The Hunter & The Whale, Hogarth Press, London, 1967
A Portrait of Japan, Hogarth Press, London, 1968
The Night of the New Moon, Hogarth Press, London, 1970, U. S. title: *The Prisoner and the Bomb*
African Cooking, Time-Life Books, New York, 1970
A Story Like the Wind, Hogarth Press, London, 1972
A Far-Off Place, Hogarth Press, London, 1974
A Mantis Carol, Hogarth Press, London, 1975
Jung And The Story Of Our Time, Hogarth Press, London, 1976
First Catch Your Eland, Hogarth Press, London, 1977
Yet Being Someone Other, Hogarth Press, London, 1982
Testament to the Bushmen, Viking, London, 1984, with Jane Taylor
A Walk With a White Bushman, Chatto & Windus, London, 1986, in conversation with Jean-Marc Pottiez
The Lost World of the Kalahari, Illustrated ed., Chatto & Windus, London, 1988
About Blady: A Pattern Out of Time, Chatto & Windus, London, 1991
The Voice of the Thunder, Chatto & Windus, London, 1993
Feather Fall, Chatto & Windus, London, 1994, edited by Jean-Marc Pottiez
The Admiral's Baby, John Murray, London, 1996
The Secret River: An African Myth, Barefoot Books, Bath, 1996

Essays, introductions and published lectures by Laurens van der Post
Roy Campbell, William Plomer & LvdP, *Voorslag: A Magazine of South African Life & Art*, Facsimile reprint of
    Numbers 1, 2 and 3 (1926), Killie Campbell Africana Library, Durban, 1985
'South Africa in the Melting Pot', *The Realist*, Nov. 1929
A British Officer, 'The Japanese Legacy in Java', *The Listener*, 8 Nov. 1945
'Pigs, Japanese and the Moon', *The Countryman*, Vol. XXXVII, No. 2, Summer 1948
'The Real Kalahari and its People', *The Countryman*, Vol. XLII, No. 2, Winter 1950
'Travellers & Mountaineers', *The Countryman*, Vol. XLIII, No. 1, Spring 1951
'The Witch Doctor's Come Back', *The Countryman*, Vol. XLV, No. 1, Spring 1952
'A Bar of Shadow', *The Cornhill*, No. 991, Spring 1952
'The Africa I Know', *African Affairs*, Vol. 51, No. 204, July 1952
'Africa', *Holiday*, Vol. 15, No. 3, March 1954
'Report of a Mission to the Bechuanaland Protectorate to investigate the possibilities of economic develop-

ment in the Western Kalahari, 1952', His Majesty's Stationery Office, London, 1954 (Commonwealth Relations Office), with A. Gaitskell, C. U. Pickrell, B. Curry, Tshekedi Khama & Bathoen II & LvdP

'Tracking the First African', *Holiday*, Vol. 20, No. 3, Oct. 1956

'The Spirit of Africa', *Optima*, Dec. 1956

'The Creative Pattern in Primitive Africa', Eranos Lecture No. 5, 1957

'Introduction to Africa', *Holiday*, Vol. 25, No. 4, April 1959

Introduction, Ray Parkin, *Out of the Smoke: The Story of a Sail*, Hogarth Press, London, 1960

'Japan: Journey Through A Floating World', *Holiday*, Vol. 30, No. 4, Oct. 1961

'Memorial Address in Honor of Dr. Jung: 20 October 1961', *Analytical Psychology Club Supplement*, Vol. 24, No. 1, Jan. 1962

'A View Of All The Russias', *Holiday*, Vol. 34, No. 4, Oct. 1963

Introduction, Eliot Elisofon, *The Nile*, Viking Press, New York, 1964

'The "Turbott Wolfe" Affair', William Plomer, *Turbott Wolfe*, Hogarth Press, London, 1965, originally published 1925

'The Ageless Mosaic of India', *Holiday*, Vol. 42, No. 4, Oct. 1967

'The Vivid Variety of India, Sikkim', *Holiday*, Vol. 42, No. 5, Nov. 1967

'Nepal', *Holiday*, Vol. 48, No. 2, Sept./Oct. 1970

'Christianity and Apartheid', *New York Times*, 15 Jan. 1971

'A Region of Shadow', *The Listener*, 5 August 1971

'Man and the Shadow', 53rd Conway Memorial Lecture, 1 Nov. 1971

Introduction, Ian Horobin, *Collected Poems*, The Jameson Press, London, 1973

'Wisdom From the Wilderness', *The Sunday Times*, 22 July 1973

'William Plomer: Classical Anger at Race Prejudice', *The Times*, 28 Sept. 1973

'A Remarkable Team and a Remarkable Period', *Cape Times* centenary supplement, 27 Mar. 1976

Foreword, E. E. Dunlop, *The War Diaries of Weary Dunlop: Java and the Burma-Thailand Railway, 1942–1945*, Penguin Books, Harmondsworth, 1990, originally published in 1986 in Australia

'Obituary: W. T. H. Nichols', *The Times*, 10 May 1986

Ingaret Giffard, *The Way Things Happen*, Chatto & Windus, London, 1989

'Some Leaves of Grass' in *The Personal Address Book of Jan Christian Smuts*, South African Institute of International Affairs, Johannesburg, 1989

Introduction, Anne Baring & Jules Cashford, *The Myth of the Goddess: Evolution of an Image*, Viking, London, 1991

Preface, *Wilderness and the Human Spirit: An Anthology*, compiled by Ian Player, Wilderness Foundation, Cape Town, 1996

Robert Hinshaw (ed), *The Rock Rabbit and the Rainbow: Laurens van der Post among Friends*, Daimon Verlag, Einsiedeln, 1998

Films, Television and Radio Broadcasts by Laurens van der Post

'Boer Farmer of the High Veldt', BBC Home Service, 19 Jan. 1939 & 'My Sheep Farm in the High-Veldt', BBC Home Service 21 Nov. 1941

Anonymous, 'The Java Crisis', BBC Home Service, 1 Nov. 1945

'Hunters' Road', BBC Home Service, 12 Aug. 1951

'Return to the Kalahari', BBC Home Service, 3 Oct. 1951

'The Story of a Mission', BBC Home Service, 19 July 1954

'The Afrikaans Language', BBC Third Programme, 24 Aug. 1954

'Portrait of Jung', BBC Home Service, 10 May 1955, with Ingaret van der Post

'Lost World of Kalahari', BBC 1, 15 June–20 July 1956

'World of Books', BBC Radio, 11 Feb. 1963

'Lettres et Arts', BBC French Service, 10 Oct. 1967

Stephen Cross, 'A Region of Shadow', BBC 2, 10 July 1971

Jonathan Stedall, 'The Story of Carl Gustav Jung', BBC 1, 28 Nov.–12 Dec. 1971

Jonathan Stedall, 'The World About Us: All Africa Within Us', BBC 1, 1975

'A Mantis Carol', BBC Radio 4, 21 Mar. 1976

The World About Us: 'Zulu Wilderness – Black Unfolozi Rediscovered', BBC 1, 1979

David Wilson, 'Shakespeare in Perspective: The Tempest', BBC 2, 22 Feb. 1980

Nagisa Oshima, *Merry Christmas Mr Lawrence*, feature film, 1983

Peter Bevan, 'The Woman at Number Ten', Central Television, 29 Mar. 1983

Jane Taylor & Paul Bellinger, 'Testament to the Bushmen', BBC 2, 1984

Jonathan Stedall, 'Laurens van der Post at 80', BBC 2, 13 Dec. 1986

Peter Bevan, 'Night of the New Moon', BBC Radio 4, 15 Sept. 1988

'The Art of Travel', BBC Radio 4, 14 Aug. 1992

'Yo-Yo Ma: Distant Memories', Channel 4, 1993
Mikael Salomen, *A Far Off Place*, feature film, 1993
Mickey Lemle, 'Hasten Slowly: The Journey of Sir Laurens van der Post', film, 1996
Jonathan Stedall, 'Voice from the Bundu', BBC 2, Dec. 1997

Unpublished work by Laurens van der Post
'Journal, 1928–1931'
'Mark Time', 1942–1943, various articles
'Prison Journal, 1943'
'Dictated Statement on the Present Situation in Java', Oct. 1945
'Political and Economic Survey of Events in Netherlands East Indies during the period of occupation by British Imperial forces from September 29th 1945 to November 30th 1946', Jan. 1947
'Report on Conditions in Republican Java', 5 May 1947
'The Story of No. 43 Special Mission', Mar. 1948 (WO106 5035)
'Survey of the Mlanje and Nyika areas of Nyasaland', Report for the CDC, July 1950
CDC Diary (1950)
'Nyasaland Journal: 1951'
'Shembe: Zulu Witchdoctor & Prophet – Note of Visit & Conversation at Inanda in 1926', 1960 Memorandum on Conservatism (Feb. 1976) for Margaret Thatcher
Memorandum on Rhodesia I (25 July 1979) for Margaret Thatcher
Memorandum on Rhodesia II (28 July 1979) for Margaret Thatcher
Memorandum on the Falklands War I (7 Apr. 1982) for Margaret Thatcher
Memorandum on the Falklands War II (15 May 1982) for Margaret Thatcher
Memorandum on South Africa (5 Sept. 1993) for The Prince of Wales,
Memorandum on South Africa (Oct. 1985) for Margaret Thatcher
Memorandum on the Role of the University (1987) for The Prince of Wales
Memorandum on Nigeria (1988) for The Prince of Wales
Memorandum on Romania (9 Mar. 1989) for The Prince of Wales
Memorandum on Indonesia (Sept. 1989) for The Prince of Wales
Memorandum on Ethnic Minorities of Namibia (27 Oct. 1989) for Margaret Thatcher
Memorandum: 'The Hour of the Karamazovs' (29 Nov. 1989) for Margaret Thatcher
Memorandum on South Africa (13 Feb. 1990) for Ian Gow & Margaret Thatcher
'A Child of the Stars', Cathedral of St. John the Divine, New York, 22 Dec. 1991
'Let in the Wind', Cathedral of St. John the Divine, New York, Dec. 1992
Memorandum on the Future of KwaZulu-Natal (25 May 1994) for Mangosuthu Buthelezi
Foreword to David H. Rosen, 'Quest for the Lion and the Eagle: The Journals of Frank Ney McMillan Jr.', 1994
Sermon, Cathedral of St. John the Divine, New York, 17 Dec. 1995
'Campbell, Plomer, Paton & Myself', 1996
Memorandum on Botswana (30 Apr. 1996) for Margaret Thatcher
'The Sword and the Doll': Transcript of Meeting with LvdP, Sonia Herman Dolz and Eva Monley, London, 13–15 July 1996
Memorandum on South Africa II (21 Aug. 1996) for The Prince of Wales
'The Desired Earth', undated manuscript
LvdP, interview with Lucia van der Post, undated tape recording

Other sources
Peter Alexander, *Roy Campbell: A Critical Biography*, David Philip, 1982
Peter F. Alexander, *William Plomer: A Biography*, Oxford University Press, Oxford, 1989
Peter F. Alexander. *Alan Paton: A Biography*, Oxford University Press, Oxford, 1994
Peter Alexander, 'The Enigma of Laurens van der Post', *English Academy Review*, No. 13, 1996
W. E. D. Allen, *Guerrilla War In Abyssinia*, Penguin Books, London, 1943
Michael Asher, *Thesiger*, Viking, London, 1984
Naim Attallah, *Asking Questions*, Quartet Books, London, 1996
Dan Auiler, *Vertigo: The Making of a Hitchcock Classic*, Titan, London, 1999
Francois Balson, *Capricorn Road*, Arco Publications Limited, London, 1954
Alan Barnard, 'The Lost World of Laurens van der Post?', *Current Anthropology*, Vol. 30, No. 1, Feb. 1989
Leonard Barnes, *Caliban in Africa*, Victor Gollancz, London, 1930
O. H. Bate, *The Lodge de Goede Hoop*, privately published, Cape Town, 1972
E. A. Bennett, *Meetings With Jung*, Daimon Verlag, Einsiedeln, 1985
Mary Benson, *South Africa: The Struggle for a Birthright*, International Defence & Aid Fund, London, 1985

Megan Biesele, *Women Like Meat: The Folklore and Foraging Ideology of the Kalahari Ju/'hoan*, Witwatersrand University Press, Johannesburg, 1993

Carel Birkby, *Thirstland Treks*, Faber & Faber, London, 1936

Carel Birkby, *Zulu Journey*, Frederick Muller, London, 1937

Carel Birkby, *Limpopo Journey*, Frederick Muller, London, 1939

Carel Birkby, *It's A Long Way To Addis*, Frederick Muller, London, 1942

Carel Birkby, *In The Sun I'm Rich*, Howard Timmins, Cape Town, 1953

D. F. Bleek, *The Mantis and his Friends*, T. Maskew Miller, Cape Town, 1923

W. H. I. Bleek, *Second Report concerning Bushman Researches, with a Short Account of Bushman Folk-lore*, Saul Solomon & Co., Cape Town, 1875

W. H. I. Bleek, *Specimens of Bushman Folklore*, George Allen & Company, London, 1911

Audie Bock, *Japanese Film Directors*, Kodansha International Ltd., Tokyo, 1978

Dirk Bogarde, *A Gentle Occupation*, Chatto & Windus, London, 1980

Robert Bogden, *Freak Show: Presenting Human Oddities for Amusement and Profit*, University of Chicago Press, Chicago, 1988

Hugh Boustead, *The Wind of Morning: The autobiography of Hugh Boustead*, Chatto & Windus, London, 1971

Lilian Bowes Lyon, *Bright Feather Fading*, Jonathan Cape, London, 1936

Lilian Bowes Lyon, *Collected Poems*, Jonathan Cape, London, 1948

Lilian Bowes Lyon, *The Buried Stream*, Jonathan Cape, London, 1929

Braby's Orange River Colony Directory, 1910, A. C. Braby, Bloemfontein, 1910

John Bridcutt, 'Rebellion!', BBC 2, 1999

R. M. Britz, *Die Geskiedenis Van Die Nederduitse Gereformeerde Kerk Fauresmith, 1848–1998*, NG Kerk, Fauresmith, 1998

E. Brookes & C. Webb, *A History of Natal*, University of Natal Press, Durban, 1965

John Brown, *The Thirsty Land*, Travel Book Club, London, 1954

The Rev. A. T. Bryant, *Olden Times in Zululand and Natal*, Longman, Green & Co., London, 1929

Ron Bryer, *White Ghosts of Nagasaki*, privately published, London, 1997

John Buchan, *Prester John*, Thomas Nelson, London, 1910

John Buchan, *The Courts of the Morning*, Hodder & Stoughton, London, 1929

Mangosuthu Buthelezi, Memorandum presented at a meeting with the American Friends of Sir Laurens van der Post', London, Oct. 1989

Mangosuthu Buthelezi, Memorandum (7 Oct. 1993), for LvdP

Guy Butler, 'Sir Laurens van der Post: A Reminiscence', *English Academy Review*, No. 13, 1996

Janet Byrne, *A Genius for Living: A Biography of Frieda Lawrence*, Bloomsbury, London, 1995

John Campbell, *Margaret Thatcher, Vol. I: The Grocer's Daughter*, Jonathan Cape, London, 2000

Roy Campbell, *The Flaming Terrapin*, Jonathan Cape, London, 1924

Roy Campbell, *Light on a Dark Horse: An Autobiography: 1901–1935*, Hollis & Carter, London, 1951

Frederic I. Carpenter, *Laurens van der Post*, Twayne Publishers Inc., New York, 1969

Humphrey Carpenter, *Robert Runcie*, Hodder & Stoughton, London, 1999

Colin Castle, *Lucky Alex: The Career of Group Captain A. M. Jardine AFC, CD, Seaman and Airman*, Fighting Fit Publishers, Victoria, 2000

Lindsay Clarke, *The Chymical Wedding: A Romance*, Jonathan Cape, London, 1989

Stephen Clingman, *Bram Fischer: Afrikaner Revolutionary*, David Philip, Cape Town, 1998

P. Coertzen, *The Huguenots of South Africa, 1688–1988*, Tafelberg, Cape Town, 1988

Joseph Conrad, *Heart of Darkness*, originally published 1902

A. A. Cooper, *The Freemasons of South Africa*, Human & Rousseau, Cape Town, 1986

D. J. Cotman, *The Spreading Tree*, Jonathan Cape, London, 1931

Michael Crick, *Jeffrey Archer: Stranger Than Fiction*, Hamish Hamilton, London, 1995

Adam Curtis, 'The Mayfair Set', BBC2, May 1999

D'Arbez, *De Familie van de Zieketrooster*, J. H. de Bussy, Pretoria, 1917

D'Arbez, *Voor Land en Volk*, J. H. de Bussy, Pretoria, 1920

D'Arbez, *De Grensbewoners*, J. H. de Bussy, Pretoria, 1920

D'Arbez, *Kort Geskiedenis van die Hugenote*, J. H. de Bussy, Pretoria, 1927

James Wentworth Day, *The Queen Mother's Family Story*, Robert Hale, London, 1967

Harriet Deacon (ed.), *The Island: A History of Robben Island, 1488–1990*, Mayibuye Books & David Philip, Cape Town, 1996

Frank Debenham, 'Report on the Water Resources of the Bechuanaland Protectorate, Northern Rhodesia, The Nyasaland Protectorate, Tanganyika Territory, Kenya and the Uganda Protectorate', His Majesty's Stationery Office, London, 1948 (Colonial Office)

Frank Debenham, *Kalahari Sand*, G. Bell & Sons, London, 1953

Elizabeth Dell, '". . . Gulliver's travels are no longer a fable." Exhibiting the "Savage" in 19th Century Britain;

Live South Africans on Show', Societies of Southern Africa, Institute of Commonwealth Studies, symposium paper, 10 Dec. 1993

F. W. de Klerk, *The Last Trek – A New Beginning: The Autobiography*, Macmillan, London, 1998

John Denman, 'An Honourable Moment', unpublished, undated manuscript

John Denman, 'Notes on Prison Journal', unpublished, 1999

C. C. de Villiers (Revis.), C. Pama, *Genealogies of Old South African Families, Vol. I*, Balkema, Cape Town, 1981

Dictionary of South African Biography, Vols. IV & V, Human Sciences Research Council, Pretoria, 1987

Jonathan Dimbleby, *The Prince of Wales: A Biography*, Warner Books, London, 1995

Stephen Dorril & Robin Ramsay, *Smear! Wilson and the Secret State*, Fourth Estate, London, 1991

Fyodor Dostoyevsky, *The Idiot*, originally published 1869

E. E. Dunlop, *The War Diaries of Weary Dunlop: Java and the Burma-Thailand Railway, 1942–1945*, Penguin Books, Harmondsworth, 1990, originally published 1986 in Australia

Sue Ebury, *Weary: The Life of Sir Edward Dunlop*, Viking, Australia, 1994

Leif Egeland, *Bridges of Understanding*, Human & Rousseau, Cape Town, 1977

Leif Egeland, interview with Peter Alexander, 2 Feb. 1990

T. S. Eliot, *The Complete Poems and Plays*, Faber & Faber, London, 1969

Clarissa Pinkola Estes, *Women Who Run With The Wolves*, Rider, London, 1992

Duncan Fallowell, 'Memoir', in draft, Mar. 2001

Horace Flather, *The Way of an Editor*, Purnell, Cape Town, 1977

Frank Foster, *Comrades In Bondage*, Skeffington & Son, London, 1948

Perceval Gibbon, *Margaret Harding*, Methuen, London, 1911

Ingaret Giffard, *Sigh No More Ladies*, Jarrolds, Norwich, 1931

Ingaret Giffard, 'Because We Must', performed at the Wyndham Theatre, London, 1937

Ingaret Giffard, 'From Coral Reef to Mountain Top', *The Countryman*, Vol. XLVI, No. 1, Autumn 1952

Richard Gough, *Special Operations Singapore, 1941–1942*, Heinemann Asia, Singapore, 1985

Harold Goulding, *Yasme: Some Recollections of a Former FEPOW*, People's Publications, London, 1988

Grey College, A South African School Centenary Publication, Juta, Cape Town, 1955

Valerie Grove, *Laurie Lee: The Well-Loved Stranger*, Viking, London, 1999

A. M. Grundlingh, *Die 'Hensoppers' en 'Joiners'*, Protea Boekhuis, Pretoria, 1999, originally published 1979

J. Haasbroek, *Die Rol van Cornelis Hermanus Wessels in die Oranje-Vrystaat, 1885–1924*, J. Haasbroek: Nasionale Museum, Bloemfontein, 1987

S. J. Halford, *The Griquas of Griqualand*, Juta & Co., Cape Town, 1949

Geoffrey Haresnape, 'The Writings of Roy Campbell, William Plomer and Laurens van der Post, with special reference to their collaboration in *Voorslag* ('Whiplash') Magazine in 1926', PhD thesis, University of Sheffield, 1982

Mary E. Hartshorne, *From Hackney to Hill Farm: A Tapestry Three Score Years and Ten*, Country Books, Bakewell, 1997

C. L. Heesakkers, *Album Amicorum van Janus Dousa*, Lustrum, Leiden, 2000

Ernest Hemingway, *The Green Hills of Africa*, Jonathan Cape, London, 1936

Denis Herbstein, 'IDAF: The History', unpublished manuscript, 1998

Irving Hexham (ed.), *The Scriptures of the AmaNazaretha of EKuphaKameni – Selected Writings of the Zulu Prophets Isaiah and Londa Shembe*, University of Calgary Press, Calgary, 1994

Alan Hoe, *David Stirling*, Little, Brown & Co., London, 1992

Isabel Hofmeyr, 'Building a nation from words: Afrikaans language, literature and ethnic identity, 1902–1924' in Shula Marks & Stanley Trapido (eds.), *The Politics of Race, Class & Nationalism in Twentieth Century South Africa*, Longman Group, Harlow, 1987

Homer, *The Odyssey*, Penguin, Harmondsworth, 1991

Ian Horobin, *Collected Poems*, Jameson Press, London, 1973

Major R. B. Houston, 'What Happened in Java in 1945–46', *The Army Quarterly*, Vol. LV, No. 2, Jan. 1948

Michael Hubbard, *Agricultural Exports and Economic Growth: A Study of the Botswana Beef Industry*, KPI Limited, London, 1986

Trevor Huddleston, *Naught for Your Comfort*, Collins, London, 1956

Richard Hughes, 'Capricorn: David Stirling's African Campaign', unpublished manuscript, 1999

Bryan Ibbotson Hunt, 'Java and Sumatra, 1945–46 Diary', unpublished

Henry James, *The Aspern Papers*, originally published 1888

Robin Jeffrey (ed.), *Asia – The Winning of Independence*, St. Martin's Press, New York, 1981

Ingrid Jonker, *Selected Poems*, Jonathan Cape, London, 1968, transl. by Jack Cope & William Plomer

C. G. Jung, *Memories, Dreams, Reflections*, recorded & ed. Aniela Jaffe, Fontana Paperbacks, London, 1977, originally published in German, 1962

C. G. Jung, *Collected Works*, ed. Michael Fordham & Gerhard Adler, Routledge Kegan Paul, London 1973

C. G. Jung, *C. G. Jung: Letters*, selected & ed. Gerhard Adler in collaboration with Aniela Jaffe, Routledge Kegan Paul, London 1976

Kabir, *The Bijak*, transl. by Linda Hess & Shukden Singh, Norton Point Press, San Francisco, 1983

Philip Kerr (ed.), *The Penguin Book of Lies*, Viking, London, 1990

Francis Kilvert, *Kilvert's Diary*, 3 vols, Jonathan Cape, London, 1938–40, ed. William Plomer

Dean King, *Patrick O'Brian: A Life Revealed*, Hodder & Stoughton, London, 2000

The King's Regulations For The Army and the Royal Army Reserve, His Majesty's Stationery Office, London, 1940

Major-General S. Woodburn Kirby, *The War Against Japan: Vol. V: The Surrender of Japan*, Her Majesty's Stationery Office, London, 1969

Lincoln Kirstein, *By With To & From: A Lincoln Kirstein Reader*, ed. Nicholas Jenkins, Farrar, Strauss & Giroux, New York, 1991

Lincoln Kirstein, *Mosaic Memoirs*, Farrar, Strauss & Giroux, New York, 1994

David W. N. Kriek, *Speciale Missie Nr. 43 in Bantam (Java)*, privately published, Amsterdam, 1985

D. W. N. Kriek & Phillip Clarke, '43 Special Mission' (http://www.icon.co.za/"pjclarke/missoo.html)

Hanif Kureishi & Jon Savage (eds.), *The Faber Book of Pop*, Faber & Faber, London, 1995

David Lean, *Lawrence of Arabia*, feature film, 1962

Robert Leeson, 'The Wartime Experiences of A. W. H. Phillips', essay, Murdoch University, Australia, Feb. 1993

Martin Legassick, 'The Griqua, the Sotho-Tswana, and the missionaries; 1780–1840: the politics of a frontier zone', PhD thesis, UCLA, 1969

C. J. P. le Roux, *CWH van der Post*, Transgariep Museum Series No. 4, Free State Museum Service, 1979

Doris Lessing, introduction to Olive Schreiner, *The Story of an African Farm*, Century Hutchinson, London, 1968

Primo Levi, *If This Is A Man*, Vintage, London, 1996, originally published in Italian, 1960

Jeremy Lewis, *Kindred Spirits: Adrift in Literary London*, HarperCollins, London, 1995

D. W. Lloyd, 'Transformations of the Colonial Narrative: Laurens van der Post's *The Lost World of the Kalahari*', *English Academy Review*, No. 10, 1993

L. C. Lloyd, *A Short Account of Further Bushman Material Collected*, David Nutt, London, 1889

Tom Lodge, *Black Politics in South Africa since 1945*, Longman Group, London, 1983

Helen Luke, *Old Age*, Parabola Books, New York, 1987

Christopher Lyon (ed.), *The International Dictionary of Films and Filmmakers, Vol. I: Films*, Firethorn Press, London, 1984

J. E. Malherbe, 'Jacques Mouton', *Huguenot Society of South Africa Bulletin*, No. 28, 1990–91

V. C. Malherbe, *Krotoa, Called Eva: A Woman Between*, UCT Centre for African Studies, Cape Town, 1990

John A. Marcum, *The Angolan Revolution, Vol. II: Exile Politics and Guerrilla Warfare (1962–1976)*, MIT Press, Cambridge, 1978

Gerhard Mare & Georgina Hamilton, *An Appetite for Power: Buthelezi's Inkatha and the Politics of 'Loyal Resistance'*, Ravan Press, Johannesburg, 1987

W. L. Maree, *Uit Duisternis Geroep*, NGK, Johannesburg, 1966

Shula Marks, 'Khoisan Resistance to the Dutch in the Seventeenth and Eighteenth Centuries', *Journal of African History*, Vol. XIII, No. 1, 1972

Shula Marks & Stanley Trapido (eds), *The Politics of Race, Class and Nationalism in Twentieth-Century South Africa*, Longman Group, London, 1987

Shula Marks, 'The dog that did not bark, or why Natal did not take off, ethnicity and democracy in South Africa: the case of KwaZulu-Natal', seminar paper, 2000

James Vance Marshall, *The Children*, Joseph, London, 1959, later re-titled *Walkabout*

John Marshall, *The Hunters*, film, 1957

D. C. McGill, *A History of Koffiefontein Mine and Town*, De Beers Consolidated Mining, Kimberley, 1911

Herman Melville, *Moby Dick*, originally published in 1851

Men Of The Times, directory, 1906

J. F. Midgley, 'The Orange River Sovereignty (1848–1854)', *Archives Year Book for South African History, Vol. II*, Government Printer, Cape Town, 1949

Seumas Milne, *The Enemy Within: The Secret War Against The Miners*, Pan Books, London, 1995

Ministry of Information, *The Abyssinian Campaigns: The Official Story of the Conquest of Italian East Africa*, His Majesty's Stationery Office, London, 1942

Andrew Morton, *Diana: Her True Story – In Her Own Words*, revised ed., Michael O'Mara Books, London, 1997

E. E. Mossop, *Old Cape Highways*, Maskew Miller, Cape Town, 1927

Patrick Mullins, *Retreat From Africa*, Pentland Press, Edinburgh, 1992

Dr John Murray, 'Lilian Helen Bowes Lyon: 1895–1949', *Poetry Review*, Vol. XL, No. 1, Feb.-Mar. 1949

V. S. Naipaul, *Beyond Belief*, Little Brown & Co., New York, 1998

N Kort Oorsig Van Die Geskiedenis Van Fauresmith, 1848–1948, booklet

S. Nuttall & C. Coetzee (eds.), *Negotiating the Past: The Making of Memory in South Africa*, Oxford University Press, Cape Town, 1998

Dr J. H. Oldham, *New Hope in Africa*, Longman Green & Co., London, 1955

Dan O'Meara, *Forty Lost Years: The apartheid state and the politics of the National Party, 1948–1994*, Ravan Press, Randburg, 1996

H. Oost, *Wie is Die Skuldiges?*, Afrikaanse Pers, Johannesburg, 1956

David Owen, *Time to Declare*, Michael Joseph, London, 1991

Thomas Pakenham, *The Boer War*, Weidenfeld & Nicolson, London, 1979

'Panorama: Jeffrey Archer – A Life of Lies', BBC 1, July 2001

Ray Parkin, *Out of the Smoke: The Story of a Sail*, Hogarth Press, London, 1960

Ray Parkin, *Into The Smother: A Journal of the Burma-Siam Railway*, Hogarth Press, London, 1963

Ray Parkin, *The Sword and the Blossom*, Hogarth Press, London, 1968

Neil Parsons, '"Clicko" or Franz Taaibosch: South African Bushman Entertainer in Britain, France, Jamaica and the USA: His Life from 1908–1940', seminar paper, African Studies Association, Seattle, Nov. 1992

Q. N. Parsons, 'Frantz or Klikko, The Wild Dancing Bushman: A Case Study in Khoisan Stereotyping', *Botswana Notes & Records*, Vol. 20, 1988

Alan Paton, *Cry The Beloved Country*, Jonathan Cape, London, 1948

J. B. Peires, *The Dead Will Arise: Nongqawuse and the Great Xhosa Cattle-Killing Movement of 1856–57*, Ravan Press, Johannesburg, 1989

Ian Player, 'On A Free State Hill: Eulogy to Col. Sir Laurens van der Post CBE' in *We will lose something deep within ourselves if we allow wilderness to be destroyed*, Apr. 2000

J. Ploeger & G. de Kock, *Nederlandse Emigrasie Na SA, 1800–1900*, University of Port Elizabeth, Port Elizabeth, 1989

William Plomer, *Double Lives: An Autobiography*, Jonathan Cape, London, 1943 & 1949

William Plomer, *At Home*, Jonathan Cape, London, 1958

William Plomer, '*Voorslag* Days', *London Magazine*, Vol. VI, No. 7, July 1959

William Plomer, *Turbott Wolfe*, Hogarth Press, London, 1965, originally published 1925

William Plomer, 'The Taste of Fruit', *The Times Literary Supplement*, 16 Sept. 1965

William Plomer, *The Autobiography of William Plomer*, Jonathan Cape, London, 1975

G. S. Preller, 'Trekkers en Trekboere', in 'Historikus', *Spore Van Die Kakebeenwa*, Afrikaanse Pers Boekhandel, Johannesburg, 1949

F. Pretorius, *The Anglo-Boer War, 1899–1902*, Struik, Cape Town, 1998

Quarterly Army List, His Majesty's Stationery Office, London, 1940–1947

Sarah Raal, *The Lady Who Fought: A Young Woman's Account of the Anglo-Boer war*, Stormberg Publishers, South Africa, 2000, originally published as *Met Die Boere In Die Veld* in 1936

Mervyn Rees & Chris Day, *Muldergate: The Story of the Info Scandal*, Macmillan South Africa, Johannesburg, 1980

Tilman Remme, *Britain and Regional Cooperation in South-East Asia, 1945–49*, Routledge, London, 1995

Jean Renoir, *My Life and My Films*, Collins, London, 1974

Jean Renoir, *Renoir on Renoir: Interviews, Essays and Remarks*, Cambridge University Press, Cambridge, 1989

Jean Renoir, *Letters*, ed. David Thompson & Lorraine LoBianco, Faber & Faber, London, 1994

Robert D. Richardson Jr., *Henry Thoreau: A Life of the Mind*, University of California Press, Berkeley, 1986

M. C. Ricklefs, *A History of Modern Indonesia since c. 1300*, Macmillan, Basingstoke, 1993

T. C. Robertson, in conversation with Ian Player, undated tape recording

George Rodger, *Desert Journey*, Cresset Press, London, 1944

Nicolas Roeg, *Walkabout*, feature film, 1971

R. Ross, *Adam Koks Griquas: A Study in the Development of Stratification in South Africa*, Cambridge University Press, London, 1976

Trevor Royle, *Orde Wingate: Irregular Soldier*, Weidenfeld & Nicolson, London, 1995

Anthony Sampson, Diary, unpublished

Anthony Sampson, *Mandela: The Authorised Biography*, HarperCollins, London, 1999

James Sanders, *South Africa and the International Media, 1972–1979: A Struggle for Representation*, Frank Cass, London, 2000

Ian Sayer, 'When An Inner Voice Spoke', *World War II Investigator*, Dec. 1988

Olive Schreiner, *The Story of an African Farm*, Century Hutchinson, London, 1968, originally published 1883

Nicholas Shakespeare, *Bruce Chatwin*, Harvill, London, 1999

Gerald Shaw, *The Cape Times: An Informal History*, David Philip Publishers, Cape Town, 1999

H. J. & R. E. Simons, *Class and Colour in South Africa, 1850–1950*, Penguin, Harmondsworth, 1969

Pippa Skotnes (ed.), *Miscast: Negotiating the Presence of the Bushmen*, University of Cape Town Press, Cape Town, 1996

Allister Sparks, *Tomorrow is Another Country: The Inside Story of South Africa's Negotiated Revolution*, Heinemann, London, 1985

Stephen Spender, *The Destructive Element: A Study of Modern Writers and Beliefs*, Jonathan Cape, London, 1935

Donald Spoto, *The Dark Side of Genius: The Life of Alfred Hitchcock*, Ballentine Books, New York, 1984

Stephen John Stedman, *Peacemaking in Civil War: International Mediation in Zimbabwe, 1974–1980*, Lynne Rienner, Boulder, 1991

Ed Stearn, 'Memoir', unpublished and undated

J. C. Steyn, *Van Wyk Louw: 'n Lewensverhaal Deel I & II*, Tafelberg, Cape Town, 1998

Anthony Storr, *Feet of Clay: A Study of Gurus*, HarperCollins, London, 1996

G. W. Stow, *The Native Races of South Africa*, Swan, London, 1905

M. Tamarkin, *The Making of Zimbabwe: Decolonization in Regional and International Politics*, Frank Cass, London, 1990

Margaret Thatcher, *The Downing Street Years*, HarperCollins, London, 1993

George McCall Theal, *History of the Boers in South Africa*, Struik Reprint Series: Africana Collectanea Vol. XLV, Cape Town, 1973, originally published 1887

Wilfred Thesiger, *The Life of My Choice*, Collins, London, 1987

Elizabeth Marshall Thomas, *The Harmless People*, Alfred Knopf, New York, 1959

Leonard Thompson & Monica Wilson (eds.), *The Oxford History of South Africa*, 2 vols, Oxford University Press, Oxford, 1971

P. S. Thompson, *Natalians First*, Southern, Johannesburg, 1990

Phillip Tobias, Foreword, in A. Clement (ed.), *The Kalahari and Its Lost City*, Longmans, London, 1967

Phillip V. Tobias, *Images of Humanity: The Selected Writings of Phillip V. Tobias*, Ashanti Publishing, Rivonia, 1991

Francois Truffaut, *Hitchcock*, Revised ed., Simon & Schuster Inc., New York, 1985

Truth and Reconciliation Commission of South Africa Report, Vols II & V, TRC, Cape Town, 1998

John Tucker, 'My General – Some Views', unpublished & undated

Ian Uys, *Bushman Soldiers: Their Alpha and Omega*, Fortress Publishers, Germiston, 1993

C. W. H. van der Post, *Piet Uys of Lijden en Strijd der Voortrekkers in Natal*, Amsterdam Boekhandel, Pretoria, originally published 1897

C. W. H. van der Post, *Ignas Prinsloo of Volharding Bekroond*, J. H. de Bussy, Pretoria, 1920, originally published 1899

C. W. H. 'Pooi' van der Post, *'n Een-Jaar Afrikaanse Kursus – A One-Year Afrikaans Course*, Die Natalse Pers, Pietermaritzburg, 1928

C. W. H. 'Pooi' van der Post, 'Memoir Fragments', unpublished, undated

Maria Magdalena 'Lammie' van der Post, 'Memoir', unpublished fragments, 1931–1954

Marjorie van der Post, *Theo Wendt: A Biography: The musical world of his days, including the first decade of the Cape orchestra, 1914–1924*, Tefelberg, Cape Town, 1974

Petronella van Heerden, *Kerssnuitsels*, Tafelberg, Cape Town, 1969

Petronella van Heerden, *Die 16de Koppie*, Tafelberg, Cape Times, 1965

H. ver Loren van Themaat, *Twee Jaren in Den Boerenoorlog*, H. D. Tjenk Willinck & Zoon, Haarlem, 1903

Hugo Vickers, *Vivien Leigh*, Hamish Hamilton, London, 1988

Voltaire, *Première Lettre sur Oedipe*, originally published 1780

Wolfram Von Eschenbach, *Parzival*, transl. by A. T. Hatto, Penguin, Harmondsworth, 1980

Patti Waldmeir, *Anatomy of a Miracle: The End of Apartheid and the Birth of the New South Africa*, Viking, London, 1997

Don Wall, *Kill the Prisoners*, privately published, Mona Vale, New South Wales, 1996

General Sir Archibald P. Wavell, 'Operations in East Africa, November 1940-July 1941', *Supplement to the London Gazette*, 10 July 1946

Douglas Wheeler & René Pelissier, *Angola*, Pall Mall, London, 1971

Who's Who, 1970, 1974, 1979, 1981, Adam & Charles Black, London, 1970, 1974, 1979 & 1981

Edwin N. Wilmsen, *Land Filled with Flies: A Political Economy of the Kalahari*, University of Chicago Press, Chicago, 1989

Edwin N. Wilmsen, 'Primitive Politics in Sanctified Landscapes: The Ethnographic Fictions of Laurens van der Post', *Journal of Southern African Studies, Vol. XXI*, No. 2, June 1995

Edwin N. Wilmsen, 'Knowledge as the Source of Progress: The Marshall family Testament to the "Bushmen"', *Visual Anthropology, Vol. XII*, 1999

Edwin N. Wilmsen, *Journeys with Flies*, University of Chicago Press, Chicago, 1999

Colin Wilson, *The Outsider*, Pan Books, London, 1978, originally published 1956

Gordon Winter, *Inside BOSS: South Africa's Secret Police*, Penguin, Middlesex, 1981

Susan Wood, *A Fly in Amber*, Collins-Harvill, London, 1964

Leonard Woolf, *The Letters of Leonard Woolf*, ed. Frederic Spotts, Weidenfeld & Nicolson, London, 1990

Leonard Woolf & Trekkie Ritchie Parsons, *Love Letters (1941–1968)*, ed. Judith Adamson, Chatto & Windus, London, 2001

Virginia Woolf, *The Diary of Virginia Woolf, Vol. IV: 1931–1935*, ed. Anne Olivier Bell, Hogarth Press, London, 1983

Woodrow Wyatt, *The Journals of Woodrow Wyatt: Vol. I*, ed. Sarah Curtis, Macmillan, London, 1998

Desmond Young, *Try Anything Twice*, Hamish Hamilton, London, 1963, p. 277, originally published as *All The Best Years*, Harper and Row, New York, 1961

Sgt. Kevin Young, interview with Ian Sayer, 8 Sept. 1987

Donald Zec, *The Queen Mother*, Sidgwick & Jackson, London, 1990

Philip Ziegler, *Mountbatten: The Official Biography*, William Collins Sons & Co., London, 1985

Acknowledgements

In addition to my three researchers, mentioned in my Foreword, I must thank first and foremost Laurens's immediate family – Lucia and Neil Crichton-Miller, who, with family and friends, took the difficult decision to authorise this biography and grant me exclusive access to the archive. They have helped me immensely, as have Tom and Jane Bedford, Emma and David Crichton-Miller and Rupert van der Post in Britain. In South Africa I had similar co-operation from the family, notably the late Ella Bedford, Anton, Margaret, Alec, Hugh and Chris van der Post, Chris Schmidt, Chris Plewman and Marietjie Cilliers.

I owe particular debts to Ian Sayer, Professor Ed Wilmsen and Richard Hughes for generously sharing with me their expertise and their research.

Among many other people who were uniformly helpful and candid, I want to acknowledge with my thanks: Dr Theo Abt, Graeme Allen, Mario Ambrosini, Grahame Amey, Dr Peter Ammann, Mrs R. H. Arden, the late John Aspinall, Bill Atkinson, Dr Doreen Atkinson, Anne Baring, Pam Barnes, Admiral and Mrs Jeannine Bartosik, Frances Baruch, Sister Maria Basini, Paul Bellinger, Steve and Gerlind Bayliss, Kate Bertaut, Peter Bevan, the late Robin Black, Carmen Blacker, Richard Blandy, the late Dirk Bogarde, Christopher Booker, Anne Boston, Pik Botha, Mike Bott, Douglas Botting, John Bowes Lyon, the late Joan Brind, Mignonne Bryant, Ron Bryer, Janet Campbell, the late John Charlton, Danie Cilliers, Ronald Cohen, the late Captain George Cooper, Jean Coulter, Mrs Paddy Crampton, Pauline Cunningham, Julian David, John Denman, Noel de Villiers, Victoria Dickson (Nichols), Jessica Douglas-Home, Patrick Downes, Bill Drower, Dawie du Plessis, Lady Sue Ebury, Stephen Ellis, Duncan Fallowell, Walter Felgate, Ewen Fergusson, Jane Flower, Nadine Gordimer, Belinda Gordon, Dom. Bertie Haasbroek, Janie Hampton, Mrs Lucia Harris, Rupert Hart-Davies, Mary Hartshorne, Selina Hastings, Joe Henderson, Denis Herbstein, James Hillman, Bob Hinshaw, Michael Holman, Diane Hood, Dr Trevor Hudson, Lawrence Hughes, Jonathan Hyslop, Elizabeth Inglis, Major and Mrs Paul Ingram, Richard Ingrams, Leslie and Benjamin Jacobson, Charles Janson, Alex Jardine, Barbara Jones, Jim and Frances Jones, Chris Josiffe, Denis Kiley, Bonny Kohler-Baker, Piet Koornhof, the Kriek family, Stephen Lamport, Colin and Margaret Legum, Mrs Ross Llewellyn, Hansie Lubbe, Rupert Lucas, Tobina Mackenzie, Colin MacLaren, Sean Magee, Sarel Marais, Prof. Shula Marks, Madeleine Masson, John McArdle, Dr Ian McCallum, Prof. John McCracken, Sasha McGlashan, David McLennan, Innes Meek, Frances Miller, Eva Monley, Cari and Mauritz Mostert, Fleur Mostert, the late H. F. Oppenheimer, Richard Osler, Ian Player, Ed Posey, Charles Powell, Jeremy Ractliffe, Kathleen Raine, Mervyn Rees, Penry Rees, Robin Renwick, Ruth Rice, Helen Risdon, D. G. Roome, Claudia Roth-Pierpont, Mary Royds, Anthony Sampson, Paul Semark, David Sexton, Gerald Shaw, Michael Shea, Robin and Lilias Sheepshanks, Yola Sigerson, Arman Simone, Jimmy Skinner, Mungo Soggot, Lady Spender, Jonathan Stedall, J. D. H. and Tibby Steytler, the late Dr Anthony Storr, J. A. Tasseron, Jane Taylor, Lady Thatcher, Ralph Tittley, Prof. Phillip Tobias, Prof. Tony Traill, Molly Tuby, Patrick Tummon, Stanley Uys, Japie van Rensburg, Gen. Constand Viljoen, Paul Vogt, Dorothea Wallis, Martin Welz, Dr Harry Wilmer, Lady Susan Wood, the late Jimmy Young, Philip Ziegler.

I am also indebted to the staff of the following libraries, archives and research facilities:
The Library, University of Reading; the Manuscript Collections, University of Sussex; the Library of the University of Durham; the Britten-Pears Library, Aldeburgh; the Library of the School of Oriental and African Studies, London; the Royal Institute of International Affairs, London; the London Library; the British Film Institute Library, London; the Army Records Centre, Ministry of Defence, London; the Hartley Library, University of Southampton; the Institute of Commonwealth Studies Library, London; the Library of Congress, Washington, D.C.; The Royal College of Physicians, London; the University of London Library; the British Library, London; Colindale Newspaper Library, London; the Royal Military Academy, Camberley; the Imperial War Museum, London; the Lamont Library, Harvard University; the New York Public Library. In South Africa, the *Star* Cuttings Library, Johannesburg; the Institute for Contemporary History, University of

the Orange Free State, Bloemfontein; the Cullen Library, University of the Witwatersrand, Johannesburg; the National English Literary Museum, Rhodes University, Grahamstown; the Free State National Archive, Bloemfontein; the NG Kerk Archive, Bloemfontein; the War Museum, Bloemfontein; Grey College, Bloemfontein; the National Library of South Africa (Cape Town and Pretoria); Johannesburg Municipal Library; the Cape National Archive, Cape Town; the National Afrikaans Literary Museum, Bloemfontein; the Pretoria National Archive; the Don Africana Library, Durban; the Alan Paton Centre, Pietermaritzburg; the Bloemfontein Municipal Library; the Kemper Museum, Colesberg; the Brenthurst Library, Johannesburg. And of course the Laurens van der Post Archive, generously opened to me by the Estate.

James Sanders also undertook the Footnotes, Bibliography and Index with enthusiasm and scholarly rigour. My agent, Christopher Sinclair-Stevenson, and my editor, Grant McIntyre, have been wonderful representatives of the older, now-threatened tradition of British publishing.

The author and his researchers have done their best to deliver a definitive record of Laurens's life. If readers have any further information – or corrections – to offer, it would be greatly appreciated if they would write, care of the publisher.

Index

Index